GABRIELE
D'ANNUNZIO

D'Annunzio—a portrait painted in 1910 by his lover, Romaine Brooks

GABRIELE D'ANNUNZIO

Poet, Seducer, and Preacher of War

LUCY HUGHES-HALLETT

ALFRED A. KNOPF   NEW YORK   2013

THIS IS A BORZOI BOOK
PUBLISHED BY ALFRED A. KNOPF

Copyright ©2013 by Lucy Hughes-Hallett

Library of Congress Cataloging-in-Publication Data
Hughes-Hallett, Lucy.
Gabriele d'Annunzio : poet, seducer, and preacher of war / by Lucy Hughes-Hallett.—First edition.
pages   cm
Published simultaneously in Canada.
"A Borzoi book"—Title page verso.
Includes bibliographical references and index.
ISBN 978-0-307-26393-3
1. D'Annunzio, Gabriele, 1863–1938. 2. D'Annunzio, Gabriele, 1863–1938—Political and
social views. 3. Nationalists—Italy—Biography. 4. Poets, Italian—20th century—
Biography. 5. Fascism—Italy—History—20th century. 6. Militarism—Italy—History—
20th century. 7. Italy—Politics and government—1914–1945. 8. Politics and
literature—Italy—1914–1918—Territorial questions—Croatia—Rijeka. I. Title.
DG575.A6H84 2013
858'.809—dc23
[B]   2012033943

Front-of-jacket photograph of Gabriele d'Annunzio, 1917
© Alinari/The Image Works
Jacket design by Carol Devine Carson

Map copyright © John Gilkes

Manufactured in the United States of America
First United States Edition

For Lettice and Mary, with love

CONTENTS

· I ·

ECCE HOMO

The Pike

IN SEPTEMBER 1919, Gabriele d'Annunzio—poet, aviator, nationalist demagogue, war hero—assumed the leadership of 186 mutineers from the Italian army. Driving in a bright red Fiat so full of flowers that one observer mistook it for a hearse (d'Annunzio adored flowers), he led them in a march on the harbour city of Fiume in Croatia, part of the defunct Austro-Hungarian Empire over whose dismemberment the victorious Allied leaders were deliberating in Paris. An army representing the Allies lay across the route. Its orders from the Allied high command were clear: to stop d'Annunzio, if necessary by shooting him dead. That army, though, was Italian, and a high proportion of its members sympathised with what d'Annunzio was doing. One after another its officers disregarded instructions. It was, d'Annunzio told a journalist later, almost comical the way the regular troops gave way, or deserted to follow in his train.

By the time he reached Fiume his following was some 2,000 strong. He was welcomed into the city by rapturous crowds who had been up all night waiting for him. An officer passing through the main square in the early hours of that morning saw it filled with women wearing evening dress and carrying guns, an image that nicely encapsulates the nature of the place—at once a phantasmagorical party and a battleground—during the fifteen months that d'Annunzio would hold Fiume as its *Duce* and dictator, in defiance of all the Allied powers.

Gabriele d'Annunzio was a man of vehement, but incoherent, political views. As the greatest Italian poet, in his own (and many others') estimation, since Dante, he was *il Vate*, the national bard. He was a spokesman for the irredentist movement, whose enthusiasts wished to regain all those territories which had once been, or so they claimed, Italian, and which had been left *irredenti* (unredeemed) when Italians liberated themselves from foreign rulers in the previous century. His overt aim in coming to Fiume had been to make the place, which had a large Italian population, a part of Italy. Within days of his arrival it became evident this aim was unrealistic. Rather than admitting defeat, d'Annunzio enlarged his vision of what his little fiefdom might be. It was not just a patch of disputed territory. He announced that he was creating there a model city-state, one so politically innovative and so culturally brilliant that the whole drab, war-exhausted world would be dazzled by it. He called his Fiume a "searchlight radiant in the midst of an ocean of abjection." It was a sacred fire whose sparks, flying on the wind, would set the world alight. It was the "City of the Holocaust."

The place became a political laboratory. Socialists, anarchists, syndicalists, and some of those who had begun, earlier that year, to call themselves fascists, congregated there. Representatives of Sinn Féin and of nationalist groups from India and Egypt arrived, discreetly followed by British agents. Then there were the groups whose homeland was not of this earth: the Union of Free Spirits Tending Towards Perfection who met under a fig tree in the old town to talk about free love and the abolition of money, and YOGA, a kind of political-club-cum-street-gang described by one of its members as "an Island of the Blest in the infinite sea of history."

D'Annunzian Fiume was a Land of Cockaigne, an extra-legitimate space where normal rules didn't apply. It was also a land of cocaine (fashionably carried in a little gold box in the waistcoat pocket). Deserters and adrenalin-starved war veterans alike sought a refuge there from the dreariness of economic depression and the tedium of peace. Drug dealers and prostitutes followed them into the city: one visitor reported he had never known sex so cheap. So did aristocratic dilettantes, runaway teenagers, poets and poetry lovers from all over the Western world. Fiume in 1919 was as magnetic to an international confraternity of discontented idealists as San Francisco's Haight-Ashbury would be in 1968; but, unlike the hippies, d'Annunzio's followers intended to make war as well as love. They formed a combustible mix. Every foreign office in Europe posted agents in Fiume, anxiously watching what d'Annunzio was up to. Journalists crammed the hotels.

D'Annunzio was already a bestselling novelist, a revered poet, and a dramatist whose premieres were attended by royalty and triggered riots. Now he boasted that in Fiume he was making an artwork whose materials were human lives. Fiume's public life was a non-stop street-theatre performance. One observer likened life in the city to an endless fourteenth of July: "Songs, dances, rockets, fireworks, speeches. Eloquence! Eloquence! Eloquence!"

By the time his occupation of Fiume came to an end, d'Annunzio's dream of an ideal society had deteriorated into a nightmare of ethnic conflict and ritualised violence. For over a year it suited none of the great powers to bestir themselves to eject him, but when, eventually, an Italian warship arrived in the harbour and bombarded his headquarters, he capitulated after a five-day fight. But for the duration of his command, Fiume was—precisely as he had intended it should be—the stage for an extraordinary real-life drama with a cast of thousands and a worldwide audience, one in which some of the darkest themes of the next half-century's history were announced.

D'Annunzio believed he was working to create a new and better world order, a "politics of poetry." So did observers from every point on the political spectrum, from the conservative nationalists who eagerly volunteered to join his Legion, to Vladimir Ilyich Lenin, who sent him a pot of caviar and called him the "only revolutionary in Europe." His followers saw Fiume as a place where life could begin afresh—rinsed clean of all impurities, freer and more beautiful than ever before. But the culture created there rapidly took on a character which, seen in retrospect, is hideous. Black uniforms decorated with lightning flashes which made malign supermen of their wearers; military spectacles staged as though they were sacred rites; a cult of youth which degenerated into licensed delinquency; the bullying of ethnic minorities; the never-ending sequence of processions and festivals designed to glorify an adored leader: all of these phenomena are now recognisable as typical of the politics, not of poetry but of brute power. Later, Benito Mussolini encouraged the writing of a biography of d'Annunzio entitled *The John the Baptist of Fascism*. D'Annunzio, who saw the fascist leader as a vulgar imitator of himself, was not happy with the suggestion that he was a mere harbinger, preparing the way for Mussolini's Messiah. But though d'Annunzio was not a fascist, fascism was d'Annunzian. The black shirts, the straight-armed salute, the songs and war cries, the glorification of virility and youth and *patria* and blood sacrifice, were all present in Fiume three years before Mussolini's March on Rome.

A great deal has been written about the economic, political and military circumstances in which fascism and its associated political creeds flourished. D'Annunzio's story provides a lens through which to examine those movements from another angle, to identify their cultural antecedents, and the psychological and emotional needs to which they pandered. To watch d'Annunzio's trajectory from neo-Romantic young poet to instigator of a radical right-wing revolt against democratic authority is to recognise that fascism was not the freakish product of an exceptional historical moment, but something which grew organically out of long-established trends in European intellectual and social life.

Some of those trends were apparently unexceptionable. D'Annunzio was a man of broad and deep culture, thoughtful, widely read in the classics and in modern literature. He spoke for Beauty, for Life, for Love, for the Imagination (his capitals)—all of which sound like good things. Yet he helped to drag Italy into an unnecessary war, not because he believed it would bring any advantage but because he craved cataclysmic violence. His adventure in Fiume fatally destabilised Italy's democracy, and opened the way for all the bombast and thuggery of fascism. He prided himself on his gift for "attention," for fully experiencing and celebrating life's abundance. "I am like the fisherman who walks barefoot over a beach uncovered at ebb tide, and who stoops, again and again, to identify and gather up whatever he feels moving under the soles of his feet." He posed as a new St. Francis, lover of all living things. Yet his wartime rants are, in every sense, hateful. Italy's enemies are filthy. He ascribes grotesque crimes to them. He calls out for their blood.

'His gift for pleasing is diabolical," wrote Filippo Tommaso Marinetti. Even people who heartily disapproved of d'Annunzio found him irresistible. Similarly, reprehensible though the Europe-wide fascist movements were (and are), history demonstrates the potency of their glamour. To guard against their recurrence we need not just to be aware of their viciousness, but also to understand their power to seduce. D'Annunzio was never as supportive of fascism as Mussolini liked to make out. He jeered at the future *Duce* as a cowardly windbag. He despised Hitler too. But it is certainly true that his occupation of Fiume drastically undermined the authority of Italy's democratic government, and so indirectly enabled Mussolini's seizure of power three years later; that both Mussolini and Hitler learned a great deal from d'Annunzio; and that an account of d'Annunzio's life and thought amounts to a history of the cultural elements that eventually came together, in the two decades following d'Annunzio's annexation of his City of the Holocaust, to ignite a greater and more terrible holocaust than any he had ever envisaged.

The poet was fifty-six years old when he set out for Fiume, as notorious for his debts and duels and scandalous love affairs as he was celebrated for his wartime exploits and his literary gifts. A plane crash had left him blind in one eye, and, as he embarked on his great adventure, he was so weakened by an alarmingly high temperature that he could barely stand (something not to be taken lightly during a period when some fifty million people died of Spanish flu).

Small, bald, with narrow sloping shoulders and, according to his devoted secretary, "terrible teeth," he was unimpressive to look at, but the long tally of his lovers included the ethereally lovely Eleonora Duse, one of the two greatest actresses in Europe (Sarah Bernhardt was her only rival), and he could manipulate a crowd as easily as he could entice a woman.

Poets nowadays are of interest only to a minority. But d'Annunzio was a poet, novelist and playwright at a time when a writer could attract a mass following, and deploy significant political influence. On the opening night of his play *Più Che l'Amore* (More Than Love) there were calls for his arrest. After the premiere of *La Nave* (The Ship) the audience spilled out of the theatre and processed through the streets of Rome intoning a line from the play, a call to arms. When he gave readings, agents of foreign powers attended, fearful of his influence. When he wrote polemical poems, Italy's leading newspaper cleared the front page and published them in full.

Italy was a new nation. Its southern half (the Bourbon Kingdom of the Two Sicilies) was annexed to the northern kingdom of Piedmont two and a half years before d'Annunzio's birth. He was seven years old in 1870 when the French withdrew from Rome and the new country was complete. The heroes of the Risorgimento had made Italy. Now someone had to "make Italians" (the phrase recurs in the political rhetoric of the period). D'Annunzio, after spending much of his twenties writing erotic lyrics in archaic verse-forms and Frenchified fiction, accepted the task. Goethe in Germany and Pushkin in Russia had been celebrated, not just as authors of fine literature, but as the creators of a new national culture. So would d'Annunzio be. "The voice of my race speaks through me," he claimed.

He was much admired by his peers. In his twenties he was one of the acknowledged leaders of the aesthetes. As he matured he wrote works which won admiration not only from his own generation, but also from his younger contemporaries. James Joyce called d'Annunzio the only European writer after Flaubert (and before Joyce himself) to carry the novel into new territory, and ranked him with Kipling and Tolstoy as the three "most naturally talented writers" to appear in the nineteenth century. Proust declared himself *"ravi"* by one of his novels. Henry James praised the "extraordinary range and fineness" of his artistic intelligence.

But though he was an author first and foremost, d'Annunzio was never solely a man of letters. He wanted his words to spark uprisings and set nations ablaze. His most famous wartime exploits were those occasions when he flew over Trieste or Vienna, dropping not bombs (although he dropped those too), but pamphlets. For d'Annunzio, writing was a martial art.

He was a brilliant self-publicist. He associated himself with Garibaldi, the romantic hero of the Risorgimento, whose image—poncho, red shirt, the dash of the guerrilla fighter combined with the integrity of a secular saint—was as important to the cause of Italian unity as his military prowess. D'Annunzio borrowed the lustre of figures from the past: he also identified himself with the dynamism of the future. He had himself photographed alongside torpedo boats and aeroplanes and motor cars—sleek, trim and modern from his gleaming bald pate to the toes of his patent-leather boots. Looking back, in his years of retirement, he saw exactly what had been his greatest strength as a politician. "I knew how to give my action the lasting power of the symbol." The hero of his first novel learns that: "One must *make* one's life as one makes a work of art." D'Annunzio himself worked ceaselessly on the marvellous artefact that was his own existence.

He made canny use of the brand new mass media. As a young man he was a prolific hack, pouring out reviews and gossip and fashion notes and quasi-autobiographical sketches. His more earnest-minded friends thought he was debasing himself, but he wrote that the seed of an idea, sown in a journal, would germinate and bear fruit in the public consciousness more quickly and surely than one planted in a book. He describes one of his fictional alter egos as being drawn to his public as a predator is drawn to its prey.

Reaching a mass audience, d'Annunzio became a new kind of public figure. The first television broadcasts were made only in the last years of his life, but his influence was akin to that of a modern mass-media pundit. Instead of looking up the social scale and the political hierarchy, seeking endorsement from the ruling class, he looked to the people, turning popularity into power. As the historian Emilio Gentile has put it, what fascism took from Fiume was not a political creed but "a way of doing politics." That way has since become almost universal.

In December 1919, d'Annunzio called for a referendum in Fiume. The people were to decide whether he was to stay and rule them, or to be expelled from the city. He waited for the result of the vote sitting in a dimly lit restaurant, sipping cherry brandy with his supporters. He told them about a life-size wax effigy of himself that, so he claimed, was in a Parisian museum. Once his present adventure was concluded, he said, he would ask to be given the figure and seat it by the window of his house in Venice, so that gondoliers could point it out to tourists. He was aware that someone like himself had two existences, one as a private person, the other as a public image. He knew that his celebrity could be used—to amuse trippers, to make himself some cash, to boost an army's morale, perhaps even to overthrow a government.

D'Annunzio's story is worth telling for reasons beyond his great talent and his life's drama, lurid and eventful though it is. It illustrates a strand of cultural history which has its apparently innocuous origins in the classical past, passes through the marvels of the Renaissance and the idealism of early nineteenth-century Romanticism, but which leads eventually to the jackboot and the *manganello*, the fascist club.

D'Annunzio read voraciously in several languages. He was adept at reviving neglected ideas whose time had come round again and he could spot a developing trend at the very moment of its formation. It is hard to find a cultural fad of the late nineteenth or early twentieth century which was not explored in his work. His flair for sensing what was new and influential moved Romain Rolland (a friend who became an

enemy) to liken him to a pike, a predator lurking "afloat and still, waiting for ideas." He was repeatedly accused of plagiarism, with some justice. He was a brilliant *pasticheur*, adopting and adapting the techniques
of each new writer whose work impressed him. He wrote like Verga,
he wrote like Flaubert, he wrote like Dostoevsky. But more intelligent
critics noticed that he didn't imitate so much as appropriate. When he
saw something that could nourish his intellect drifting by on the current, he would snap at it, pike-like, and swallow it, and send it forth
again better expressed.

He borrowed, but he also anticipated. Before Freud, he was fully
aware of the nature of the excitement he derived from sleek machinery:
the prow of a metal warship, he wrote, is "a monstrous phallic elon-
gation." Reading Nietzsche in the 1890s he recognised ideas already
implicit in his own work. He had been modelling his verse on that of
pre-Renaissance poets for a quarter of a century by the time Ezra Pound
began to imitate the troubadours. He was writing about priapic fauns
and pre-pagan ceremonies three decades before Nijinsky and Stravinsky sparked off a riot with *The Rite of Spring*. In 1888, a full two decades
before Marinetti proclaimed a ruthless new machine-age aesthetic in
the "Futurist Manifesto," d'Annunzio wrote an ode to a torpedo. He
loved motor cars and telephones and aeroplanes and machine guns.
Marinetti's manifesto is full of unacknowledged d'Annunzian sentiments, including the notion that civil society was so foul that only war
could cleanse it.

His politics were as eclectic as his cultural tastes. He was not a party
man, having far too lively a sense of his unique importance to sub-
scribe to a programme imposed by others. Besides, the period when he
was most active politically was a time when groups which would, only
months after he marched on Fiume, separate out into mutually hostile phalanxes, made common cause, the extremes meeting to oppose
the centre. Nationalism (now identified with the right) and syndicalism
(leftist) were, according to one of d'Annunzio's contemporaries, alike
"doctrines of energy and the will." Both preferred violence to negotiation; both understood the political process in terms, not of reason, but
of myth. In a "venal and materialist society" of democratic "stockbrokers and chemists," they were heroic: the "only two aristocratic tendencies." What mattered to d'Annunzio, and to the fascists after him, was
not a theoretical programme, so much as style, vitality, vigour.

In Fiume, d'Annunzio drew up a constitution for his little state. "The

Charter of Carnaro," as he called it, is in many ways a remarkably liberal document. It promised universal adult suffrage and absolute legal equality of the sexes. Socialists applauded it. But in the 1920s it was hailed as "a blueprint of the fascist state."

There is an acceptable d'Annunzio, who writes lyrically about nature and myth, and there is an appalling d'Annunzio, the warmonger who calls upon his fellow Italians to saturate the earth with blood, and whose advocacy of the dangerous ideals of patriotism and glory opened the way for institutionalised thuggery. Those who admire the former have often tried to ignore, or even deny, the existence of the latter. After the fall of Mussolini it became conventional to suggest either that d'Annunzio could not really have had any sympathy for fascism, because he wrote such beautiful poetry, or—conversely—that because his politics were deplorable, his poetry cannot really be any good. I contest both arguments. The two d'Annunzios are one and the same.

D'Annunzio knew exactly how ghastly conflict could be. As a young man he visited hospitals out of curiosity. He was an attentive nurse to his mistresses when they fell ill, loving them the most, he told them, when they were suffering or near death. In wartime he spent weeks at the front, witnessing the slaughter, smelling the unburied corpses. He made careful notes about wounds, and the effects of decomposition on the bodies of his dead friends. In his wartime oratory he used the word "sacrifice" over and over again in knowing reference to religious fables (pagan and Christian) where young men were killed that the wider community might benefit. When two fighter pilots of whom he was fond went missing in 1917 he wrote in his private diary that he devoutly hoped they were dead.

He was one of the cleverest of men, but also one of the least empathetic. He was as ruthless and selfish as a baby. "He is a child," wrote the French novelist, René Boylesve, "he gives himself away with a thousand lies and tricks." Child-like, he saw others only in relation to himself. In love, he was adoring, but once he had tired of a woman he ceased to think about her. He was an excellent employer (though far from punctilious about paying salaries). He was moved by the sweetness of small children. He was very kind to his dogs. But the woman who brought in his meals, he once wrote, was no more to him than a piece of furniture, a cupboard on feet.

One of his most famous poems is about the Abruzzese shepherds who could be seen at summer's end traipsing along the beaches, robed and bearded like biblical patriarchs, their woolly charges churning around them like warm surf. It is a lovely lyric, tender and grand; but to those who know d'Annunzio it cannot be read as harmless pastoral. He wrote often about the sheep herded before dawn through the sleeping streets of nineteenth-century cities, their wool eerily silvered by the moonlight—a commonplace sight which few other writers notice. To him the animals weren't pretty reminders of the countryside. They were hosts of creatures on their way to be slaughtered. So were armies. The thought didn't appal him. In 1914, three years before his British contemporary Wilfred Owen made the same comparison, d'Annunzio was likening the herds of bullocks who churned up the roads of northern France, driven to the front to feed the army, to the trainloads of soldiers going the same way. Like Owen, d'Annunzio knew that in war men died as cattle. Unlike Owen, he considered their death not only *dulce et decorum*, sweet and fitting, but sublime.

One evening in Rome in May 1915, d'Annunzio was chatting lightly in his hotel room with a couple of acquaintances. One was the sculptor Vincenzo Gemito, the other was the Marchese Casati (with whose wife—"the only woman who could astonish me".—d'Annunzio had a long *amitié amoureuse*). Then, this agreeable interlude over, he stepped out onto his balcony to deliver one of his most incendiary speeches, urging the crowds beneath his window to transform themselves into a lynch mob. "If it is considered a crime to incite citizens to violence then I boast of committing that crime." Three paces and a window pane separated the sphere in which he was an urbane socialite and man of letters from that in which he was a frenzied demagogue calling upon his countrymen to murder their elected representatives and to drench the soil of Europe with blood. Both personae are genuine. In writing about him I have tried to find a form which does justice to them both.

D'Annunzio's must be one of the most thoroughly documented lives ever lived. He had a notebook in his pocket at all times. Those notebooks were his precious raw material. Their contents reappeared in his poems, his letters, his novels. When he flew (or rather was flown—he never learned to pilot himself) he took a specially bought fountain pen with him so that he could jot down his impressions even while dodging anti-aircraft fire. He noted the clothes and sex appeal of the women he met so immediately that it seems he must have been reaching for his book even before they turned away. Eating alone at home, he wrote down a description of the maid as she served him his lunch. A discriminating eater, he also made notes on the asparagus.

His works are full of descriptions of sex so candid they still startle. In his morning-after letters he would describe back to a lover the pleasures they had enjoyed, an intimate kind of pornography which was also an aide-mémoire for himself and, often, the first draft for a fictional scene. We know in enormous detail what d'Annunzio did in bed, or on the rug before a well-banked-up fire (he felt the cold dreadfully), or in woods and secluded gardens on summer nights. We know he liked occasionally to play at being a woman, pushing his penis out of the way between his thighs. We know how much he enjoyed cunnilingus, and that he therefore preferred a woman to be at least five foot six inches tall, or, failing that, to wear high-heeled shoes, so that when he knelt before her his mouth comfortably met her genitals. We have his descriptions not only of his lovers' outward appearances but of the secret crannies of their bodies, of the roofs of their mouths, of the inner whorls of their ears, of the little hairs on the back of a neck, of the scent of their armpits and their cunts.

The notebooks, d'Annunzio's enormous literary output, and his even larger correspondence, have allowed me to show the man's inside: his thoughts, tastes, emotions and physical sensations; how moved he was by the pathos of a pile of dead soldiers' boots; how he relished the slithery warmth of a greyhound's coat under his hand. And because he was a public figure for over half a century, I have been able to draw on dozens of others' accounts of him and his doings to show his outside as well. This book has many viewpoints. And because d'Annunzio's life, like any other, was complex, they sometimes contradict each other. An acquaintance, seeing him in Florence, leaning on the stone parapet over the River Arno one grey November day, noticed the elegance of his raincoat (he was always dapper) and tactfully refrained from greeting him, supposing him to be absorbed in the composition of a poem. From his own account, though, we know he could think of nothing but of whether his mistress would shortly appear, and what he would do with her once he had got her back to the room he kept for their assignations, where he had already stowed scented handkerchiefs behind cushions and strewn the bed with flowers.

I have made nothing up, but I have freely made use of techniques commoner in fiction-writing than in biography. I have not always observed chronological order; the beginning is seldom the best place to start. Time's pace varies. I have raced through decades and slowed right down, on occasion, to record in great detail a week, a night, a conversation. To borrow terms from music (and one of the themes of d'Annunzio's life to which I have not had space to do full justice is his musical connoisseurship) I have alternated *legato* narrative with *staccato* glimpses of the man and fragments of his thought.

I have tried to avoid the falsification inevitable when a life—made up, as most lives are, of contiguous but unconnected strands—is blended to fit into a homogeneous narrative. In Venice in 1908 for the premiere of *The Ship*, d'Annunzio attended banquets and civic ceremonies in his honour, delivering convoluted speeches full of noble sentiments and incitements to war. He records, though, that "between one acclamation and another" he spent a great deal of time hunting for the perfect present for his mistress. An antique emerald ring—which he could certainly not afford (he was at this period unable to go home for fear of his creditors)—satisfied him, but there was still the question of a box to put it in. He visited half a dozen places before finding the very thing—a pretty little casket in green leather (to match her eyes) in the shape of a miniature doge's hat. I aim to do justice both to the man pontificating at the banquet, and the man fossicking through curio shops.

Two images help to describe my method. The first dates from 1896, when d'Annunzio was thirty-three, and staying in Venice to be near Eleonora Duse. There he came to know Giorgio Franchetti, who had recently bought the Ca' d'Oro, the most fantastical and ornate of all the palaces along the Grand Canal, and was restoring it to its fifteenth-century Venetian-Moorish splendour. Franchetti was working himself on the installation of a mosaic pavement, crawling, covered with sweat and stone dust, over the varicoloured expanse of rare stones with slippers strapped to his knees. There d'Annunzio would join him, laying tiny squares of porphyry and serpentine in the fresh cement. Placing comments and anecdotes alongside each other like the tesserae in a pavement, my aim has been to create an account which acknowledges the disjunctions and complexities of my subject, while gradually revealing its grand design.

Another image comes from Tom Antongini, who knew and served d'Annunzio well for thirty years as his secretary, agent, personal shopper, and, in the sexual sphere, Leporello to his Don Giovanni. Antongini described the hectic months d'Annunzio spent in Paris in 1910 as "kaleidoscopic." In an old-fashioned kaleidoscope, fragments of jewel-bright glass are rearranged as the cardboard tube is twirled—the same parts, a changing pattern. Images and ideas recur in d'Annunzio's life and thought, moving from reality to fiction and back again: martyrdom and human sacrifice, amputated hands, the scent of lilac, Icarus and aeroplanes, the sweet vulnerability of babies, the superman who is half-beast, half-god. I have laid out the pieces: I have shown how they shift.

D'Annunzio has been much disliked. His contemporary, the philosopher and historian Benedetto Croce, said he was "steeped in sensuality and sadism and cold-blooded dilettantism." Tom Antongini, who was fond of him, wrote that he "has been accused of polygamy, adultery, theft, incest, secret vices, simony, murder, and cannibalism . . . in short, Heliogabalus is his master in no particular." When, on his death in 1938, there was discussion in the British Foreign Office as to whether it would be in order to offer official condolences, the proposal was vehemently opposed by Lord Vansittart, who called him "a first-class cad." This hostility persists. Mark Thompson, the outstanding historian of Italy's part in the Great War, writes with judicious moderation about General Cadorna, the Italian commander-in-chief who sent hundreds of thousands of soldiers to a certain death. Thompson's tone, in describing Mussolini and the beginnings of fascism, is temperate. But these are the words he uses of d'Annunzio: "odious," "vicious," "psychotic."

I have been sparing of such language. I am a woman writing about a self-styled "poet of virility" and a pacifist writing about a warmonger, but disapproval is not an interesting response. D'Annunzio cannot be dismissed as being singularly hateful or crazy. He helped to talk his country into an unnecessary war, and the views he expressed, then and throughout his life, are frequently abhorrent. But to suggest that his thinking was aberrant is to deny the magnitude of the problem he presents. Over and over again throughout the Great War, d'Annunzio called upon teenage conscripts, very few of whom had any idea what Italy's war aims were, to die because the blood of those who had already died called out to them from the earth to emulate their "sacrifice." At the time of writing a very similar thought—less floridly expressed—is regularly advanced to justify the continuation of the war in Afghanistan. Many have died. To admit that the fighting is futile, and put a stop to it, would be to betray them. So more must die. This reasoning may be odious (I consider it so). But if to be "psychotic" is to think in a way few healthy people think, then it is not psychotic. It is all too normal.

In 1928, Margherita Sarfatti published a biography of her lover, Mussolini. In it she praised d'Annunzio for having "prophesied, preached and fought the war" (preaching war being, in fascist opinion, a laudable practice) and hailed the poet as having given expression to "an arrogant, knightly, derisive, fascinating and cruel spirit that belongs to the immortal youth of fascism." Later Sarfatti, who was Jewish, would have to leave Italy hastily in order to escape that "fascinating and cruel spirit," but for the time being she adored it, and admired d'Annunzio, whose work seemed to her to be as full of "daring, hope, greatness and limitless faith" as the sound of the blackshirts belting out popular songs as they converged on Rome in October 1922.

In the first winter of the Great War, d'Annunzio was living in France, and made several trips to the front as a privileged observer. There he saw—or pretended to have seen—dead soldiers bound upright, to stakes, in groups of ten. At the time, Mussolini had only recently left the Italian Socialist Party and had yet to find a new following. But already d'Annunzio had found an image all too hideously symbolic of the militarism which he himself so enthusiastically approved, and of the political creed which would shortly grow out of it. Those bloody clumps of upstanding corpses reminded him of an emblem frequently shown on Roman coins, one which would soon, once again, be omnipresent in Italy, that of a bundle (a *fascio*) of rods tied around an axe. The axe signified the law's power over life and death. The bundled rods represented the gathering of powerless individuals into a single powerful entity, a "fascist" state.

Sightings

Rome, 1881. Here is Gabriele d'Annunzio, seventeen years old, just out of school, the precocious author of two highly praised volumes of verse. Observing him is Edoardo Scarfoglio, himself only twenty-one, another ambitious young man making his way in the ancient capital of the eleven-year-old Italian nation. Scarfoglio is in the office of the weekly paper of which he is editor. The room is full of chattering people. Scarfoglio is lounging on a bench, yawning, when in comes the juvenile poet. "At the first glimpse of this little fellow with his curly head and sweetly feminine eyes . . . I started and sprang up, extraordinarily struck . . . Gabriele was the object of a craze, of an incredible cult, for all of us. He was so friendly and modest, and he carried the weight of his newborn glory with such grace that everyone ran to him, spontaneously drawn by feelings of friendship and affection."

The curls will soon be gone (by the age of thirty d'Annunzio will be almost completely bald) and the modesty may never have existed outside of Scarfoglio's imagination. Already the young poet is an adroit self-publicist. A few months before his arrival in Rome, he anonymously informed newspaper editors of his own untimely death in a fall from his horse. The pathetic story of the brilliantly gifted youth, cut off at the outset of what would surely have been a dazzling career, was widely reported and lamented over. The second volume of poems by the tragic boy, published later that month, sold well. By the time the "mistake" was discovered, d'Annunzio was considerably more famous than mere merit, however substantial, could have made him.

Scarfoglio will lament that, only a few months after that first meeting, the androgynous innocent is on his way to becoming a smart young man about the booming capital. "I will never forget how stupefied I was, the first time I saw Gabriele all spruced up and perfumed for

a party." At the age of twenty, d'Annunzio (seen by Scarfoglio as being like a "timid, wild girl") will demonstrate his worldly ambition and his virility by impregnating and eloping with a duke's daughter. At the age of twenty-six, already the author of four volumes of poetry and two of short stories, as well as of reams of knowing, gossipy journalism, he will publish the first of his novels.

1893. D'Annunzio, now aged thirty, is living in Naples. He left Rome to escape from his creditors, and before the end of the year he will have to scarper from Naples for the same reason. He has written three novels and dozens of stories which are beginning to make money, but never enough to pay off his exorbitant debts. He has abandoned his wife and three sons, and left Elvira Fraternali, whom he loved passionately for eight years. Now he is living with the Sicilian princess Maria Gravina, together with whom he faces a jail sentence for adultery (a general amnesty will spare them). His writing—as scandalous as it is brilliant—and his flamboyant lifestyle, his debts, his duels and his love affairs, have made him, by this time, an international celebrity.

During this period of his life, in personal terms so harum-scarum, the groundwork of d'Annunzio's political thinking is being laid. He has been reading Nietzsche and finding in the philosopher's work confirmation of his own elitism. Acting the pike again, he makes provocatively Nietzschean declarations. "Man will be divided into two races," he writes. "To the superior race, which shall have risen by the pure energy of its will, all shall be permitted; to the lower, nothing or very little." D'Annunzio never doubts his own membership of the former class.

Now he is enthralled by Richard Wagner. D'Annunzio adores music, but he is not himself a musician. To hear it he must seek out those who are. He goes repeatedly to call on the composer Niccolò van Westerhout and prevails upon him to play entire operas on the piano, while he follows the libretto, going through *Tristan and Isolde* at least ten times. He is learning to hear the patterning of reprise and variation, to feel the great surges of emotion released by the music and to understand how they are controlled. He keeps van Westerhout at the piano for hours and hours. "*Tristan* filled his spirit with a kind of morbid obsession." He insists on hearing certain passages over and over again. He is transfixed by the "sufferings that begin with the love potion."

At home he is in desperate straits. The bailiffs are encamped outside the door of his borrowed lodgings. Maria Gravina's sanity is precarious. But d'Annunzio has the knack of closing himself off from all emotional and practical demands. The musical sessions with van Westerhout pass straight into his influential essay on Wagner and into his suicide-haunted novel *Il Trionfo della Morte* (The Triumph of Death), in which the lovers spend days on end playing and singing *Tristan and Isolde* together, before the hero drags his mistress over a cliff in an involuntary *liebestod* (love-death).

Later that year Maria Gravina will try to kill herself. His wife has already attempted suicide.

AUGUST 1895. D'Annunzio is sunbathing stark naked on the deck of a yacht bound for Greece. He has recently received his largest payment to date, for the French edition of his first novel, *Il Piacere* (Pleasure). Among his fellow guests on the cruise is his French translator, Georges Hérelle.

Hérelle is disappointed. He has been looking forward to earnest literary discussions interspersed with serious sightseeing, but d'Annunzio seems only to want to bask in the sun while swapping smutty jokes with the other young Italians on board, and fretting about the difficulty of getting his shirts properly ironed ready for dinner engagements in port. When they go ashore at Eleusis, Hérelle notes that d'Annunzio "hardly looks, chatting all the time of things which have nothing to do with our excursion; about amorous adventures, about society people." On train journeys he doesn't feast his eyes on the passing landscape, he puts a silk handkerchief over his face and dozes. In Patras and again in Piraeus he goes off, almost as soon as they've landed, to find a prostitute. "Truly," notes Hérelle in his journal, "there is something puerile about Gabriele d'Annunzio."

What Hérelle doesn't grasp is that d'Annunzio's mind works so fast he doesn't need to gaze at length in order to receive impressions, or to preserve a solemn silence in order to reflect upon what he sees. Within days of returning from the cruise he will start planning his first play, *La Città Morta* (The Dead City), inspired by the party's visit to Mycenae. Eight years later he will write his modern epic, *Maia*. The visit to a Patras brothel which Hérelle found so sordid ("These awful women . . . these sailor's women . . . I cannot understand how in Greece one can waste time so foolishly"), will appear transmuted into a half comic, half profoundly sorrowful episode in which Helen of Troy, terribly aged, symbolises the transience of the pleasures and beauties of the flesh.

DECEMBER 1895. The Caffè Gambrinus, Florence. André Gide, who is in the café with him, is watching d'Annunzio carefully. "He is greedily eating little vanilla ice creams served in cardboard cones. He talks with charming good manners without, I think, making much effort . . . Nothing about him suggests literature or genius. He has a little, pointed, pale-blond beard, and he speaks with a clear voice, rather icy but soft and wheedling. His glance is quite cold: perhaps he is cruel, or perhaps it is his refined sensuality that makes him seem so to me. On his head he wears a plain black bowler hat."

Since returning from Greece, d'Annunzio has begun his relationship with Eleonora Duse. He tells Gide: "I have read Sophocles under the crumbling gates of Mycenae." This reading must have been brief—d'Annunzio's visit to Mycenae was over in time for lunch—but the claim fits with his sense of himself as heir to the great classical tradition, and with the project he and Duse are cherishing. They want to build an amphitheatre in the Alban Hills and run it as an al fresco national theatre where d'Annunzio's plays will be performed in tandem with those of the Greek tragedians.

The talk turns to contemporary European literature. D'Annunzio tells Gide that he dislikes Maeterlinck's "banality" and Ibsen's "lack of beauty." He knows all the French authors' work.

"With a smile I say to him: 'But you've read everything!'

'What can you expect?' he says, as though to excuse himself, 'I am Latin.'"

Being "Latin" is very important to d'Annunzio's sense of self. Later it will become the dominant theme of his politics. He calls all Anglo-Saxon or Germanic people "barbarians."

"I'm a terrible one for work," he tells Gide. "For nine or ten months of the year, non-stop, I work twelve hours a day. I've already written a score of books." This is only a slight exaggeration. D'Annunzio's love life is so scandalous that the public thinks of him as a dilettante, but the majority of his time is passed in near solitude and intensely concentrated effort. "When I write," he says, "a sort of magnetical force takes hold of me, like an epileptic. I wrote *L'Innocente* (his second novel) in three and a half weeks in an Abruzzese convent. If anyone had disturbed me, I would have shot him."

"All of these things," records Gide, "he said without any boastfulness, with gentle sweetness."

The ability to conjure that same lulling sweetness which entranced Scarfoglio was a gift which never deserted d'Annunzio. Even those who know him well enough to perceive the indifference it masks, find it irresistible. "His face lights up in greeting you," writes one of his aides years later. "And you succumb! You have to succumb! In reality, he doesn't give a damn!"

JANUARY 1901. Turin. In the five years since his encounter with Gide, d'Annunzio has written several plays and his most celebrated novel, and he has embarked on the exquisite sequence of lyric poems, *Alcyone* (Halcyon). He and Duse are living in adjacent houses in Settignano, in the hills above Florence, their every outing reported by the gossip columns, their incongruous appearance as a couple (Duse is nearly five years older and several inches taller than her lover) repeatedly caricatured.

D'Annunzio's literary career is at its apogee, and he has begun his transition from poet to politician. In 1897 he contested and won an election in his native Abruzzi. In his electoral campaign he hymned the "politics of poetry." Voted out of office after barely two years, he has been writing the poetry of politics, composing odes in an aggressive and nationalist vein. He is in Turin to give a public reading of the latest of them, a thousand-line tribute to Giuseppe Garibaldi.

Filippo Tommaso Marinetti is in Turin as a contributor to the Parisian journal *Gil Blas*. Marinetti, who will soon become better known as the impresario and spokesman of the futurist movement, is a prolific journalist. Quizzically, Marinetti observes d'Annunzio in his new role as public speaker. *Il Vate*, the bard, as he now likes to be styled, is thirty-eight, but he could be any age, or ageless. Tightly buttoned into his dark suit he looks like "a little ebony idol with a head of ivory." His eyes "sharpened and electrified by the expectation of triumph" are "strangely resplendent." His face is "pale, dried, as though burnt by the fire of Ambition." This is not an objective description. Marinetti is jealous of d'Annunzio, whom he sees as "corsetted by ambition and pride." He sneers that "at all times and in all places Gabriele is dreaming of turning the world upside down with a well-turned phrase." This is something Marinetti also dreams of doing, and so far d'Annunzio is proving better at it.

D'Annunzio takes his place on the platform, and begins his performance with, thinks Marinetti, the smugness of a cordon bleu chef lifting a lid to display a steaming dish of lentils. He reads very slowly, softly beating time with his fist on the table. His lips are preternaturally red: several contemporaries report that he uses make-up.

The recitation over (it takes an hour and a half) the crowd noisily acclaims him. He half rises to acknowledge the applause, bowing his head. Marinetti notices how the new-fangled electric light is brilliantly reflected off d'Annunzio's shiny bald pate: a thoroughly modern nimbus for a machine-age hero.

1904, SETTIGNANO. Here is another view of d'Annunzio, this one by an anonymous lady whom he takes to bed one afternoon.

He is compulsively promiscuous. Within the last three years he has completed his immense poem-cycle, *Laudi*. His eight-year-long affair with Eleonora Duse is over and he is spending money more prodigally than ever before. His new lover, an aristocratic young widow, the Marchesa Alessandra di Rudinì, is dangerously ill. It is probably during one of Alessandra's sojourns in hospital that the unknown lady arrives in response to an invitation with the pointed postscript, "I shall expect you alone."

She is shown into a small sitting room crammed with roses. "They were everywhere—in vases, in amphorae, in bowls—and their petals were strewn on the carpets." D'Annunzio takes great care over dressing the set for his seductions. Outside the long windows a pergola covered with wisteria casts a mauve veil over the sunlight. The room is suffocatingly overheated, and the atmosphere is further laden with *Acqua Nuntia*, the scent d'Annunzio has concocted himself from a formula which he claims to have found in a fourteenth-century manuscript. He has had quantities of it made up by a chemist in Florence. It is bottled in Murano glass bottles (also made to the poet's orders) and labelled (a lot of thought goes into the design of the labels).

The host appears, dressed in a dark blue kimono bordered with black. It is d'Annunzio's habit to dress in this conveniently removable garment for an assignation and he always provides a kimono for his female visitor's use. On a small ebony table a large silver tray has been set, bearing a samovar, two cups, and marrons glacés on silver plates. D'Annunzio pours the tea (Chinese, very fragrant), then seats himself crosslegged on the rug by the lady's chair, takes both her hands in his and embarks upon his seduction. "From his gestures, from his voice, there came an invincible wave of desire which engulfed my whole being in an irresistible atmosphere of love." There are a number of descriptions of this process: d'Annunzio was a highly persuasive wooer. The anonymous lady feels herself swept "into mysterious spheres where there are no laws nor conventions." Thus conveniently "drugged by the delicious poison of the Poet's musical words," she somehow swoons her way, without compromising herself by explicitly consenting to sex, into his bedroom.

Their transports ended, d'Annunzio leaves her. "A quarter of an hour later I found him in the library, turning the pages of a book." Without a word he escorts her to her carriage. She is driven away, feeling "the horrid sensation of being discarded like a toy." On d'Annunzio's orders, her carriage has been filled, "like a rich coffin," with roses.

SUMMER 1906. D'Annunzio is in a palatial rented villa, a former home of the dukes of Tuscany, at the seaside near Pisa. His play *La Figlia di Jorio* (Jorio's Daughter) has made him not just a literary star but also the voice of his people. *"Evviva* the poet of Italy!" shouted the audience at its first night.

Alessandra is here, but she is addicted to morphine now and d'Annunzio is already writing daily to his new love, a Florentine countess. For the first time in nearly twenty years he has all three of his sons with him. In the mornings they box in an improvised ring on the beach. D'Annunzio gallops his horse through the pine woods, or swims, or paddles his brand new canoe—throwing himself into each activity with energy which astonishes the younger men. For lunch, served formally by some of the fifteen servants, he changes into a white linen suit, one of the hundred or so he has brought with him. He writes late into the night.

An aspiring poet, Umberto Saba, guest of d'Annunzio's son Gabriellino, is our witness at this gathering. D'Annunzio, still physically trim at forty-three, greets Saba with exquisite courtesy. Flatteringly, he draws him away from the assembled company and out into the garden, where they sit down together on a stone bench. "He asked me, if I was not too tired from my journey, and if it would not be too much of a nuisance for me, to recite some of my poetry?" This is the acme of Saba's hopes. He can hardly believe his good fortune. He obliges. D'Annunzio is all compliments. He asks if he may recommend Saba's work to his editor? Saba, overwhelmed by the great man's generosity, is close to tears. Everything about the marvellous moment stays with him. Years later it will be as though he can still hear the pine needles creaking beneath their feet.

The conversation continues. There have only been three great poets in Italy, d'Annunzio says—Dante, Petrarch and Leopardi—before, that is, (and he repeats this twice) himself. Saba notices that the poet's sons are not allowed to call him "Papa." He requires them to address him as "Maestro."

Afterwards Saba posts his precious manuscript. He gets no response. D'Annunzio does not pass his poems on to anyone. He doesn't even send them back.

SEPTEMBER 1909. The Brescia air show: for most of the 50,000 people present their first sight of the amazing spectacle of a man aloft in a flying machine. It is only six years since Wilbur and Orville Wright made their first powered flight, thirteen months since Wilbur first demonstrated their *Flyer I* in Europe, barely six weeks since Louis Blériot (who is here at Brescia) flew across the English Channel, crash-landing in a vertical fall of sixty-five feet to arrive, with a smashed undercarriage but himself unharmed, in a meadow near Dover Castle. D'Annunzio is ecstatic. Humanity's conquest of the air, he proclaims, presages, "A new civilisation, a new life, new skies!" A poet is called for, "capable of singing this epic." That poet must be himself. He stages a poetry-reading-cum-press-conference-cum-photo-opportunity at Brescia, reciting verses for the assembled journalists and photographers. The poem, about Icarus, was first published ten years previously: d'Annunzio has been dreaming of flight since he was a schoolboy.

He is at Brescia to gather material for his next novel. He is also planning, courageously (already several aviators have died), to cadge a ride. Now he is being observed by Franz Kafka and his friend Max Brod. The two are holidaying together on Lake Garda. Kafka is depressed: his inspiration has deserted him; his stomach feels to him like a person on the brink of tears. To get him writing again Brod suggests they compose competing accounts of the air show.

The two young men are in the immense crowd on the parched airfield. They both notice d'Annunzio among the "sparkling ladies" and gentlemen on the stands. Brod is struck by d'Annunzio's "feminine charm," and finds him "marvellous through and through." Kafka is less impressed. By his account d'Annunzio is "short," which is the simple truth, but also "weak" (which may be another way of saying "feminine"). Kafka notes that d'Annunzio is "skipping" among the ladies and "shyly" trotting around after Count Oldofredi (one of the show's organisers).

D'Annunzio isn't shy, but his body language can be deferential, his posture placatory and insinuating. (Photographs show him with his head dipped slightly to one side, leaning in towards a companion.) Oldofredi is his host for the day, whose consent he must have before he can fly, but he is no ordinary supplicant. To Brod it seems that at Brescia the bigwigs are treating him "like a second King of Italy."

Later that day he makes two short flights, as passenger to the American aviator Glenn Curtiss and the Italian Mario Calderara. He poses for the cameras in a leather flying helmet. Immediately upon landing he gives an interview to the reporter for the *Corriere della Sera* (his flair for self-promotion never leaves him). Flying, he says, is divine; so divine that even he, the *divo* of words, is for the moment at a loss as to how to describe it. It is as ineffable as sex.

Increasingly bellicose and nationalist in his politics, d'Annunzio sees—years before the military establishment begins to invest in aviation—the strategic potential of the new flying machines. In the following year he will repeatedly deliver (for handsome fees) a lecture on the need for Italy to achieve Great Nation status by seizing control of the skies.

1910. The bailiffs are in d'Annunzio's house in Settignano. Pursued by his creditors, himself in pursuit of a long-legged Russian countess with a lovely singing voice and a complaisant husband, announcing to the world that he needs to visit a French dentist, d'Annunzio has decamped to Paris. There his arrival causes quite a stir: he has been a bestselling author in France for two decades. At once he begins to circulate in society, and those he meets are recording their impressions.

He is forty-eight now. To Gide he seems "pinched, wrinkled, smaller than ever." Certainly he needs a good dentist. He has "funny little crenellated unhealthy teeth," notes a French actress on whom he tries his charm. "He is the only man I have ever seen with teeth of three colours, white, yellow and black." As he has aged his aura of sexual ambiguity has become more marked, intriguing to women, repulsive to most men. Several of his new acquaintances remark on his narrow, feminine shoulders and wide womanly hips, his little beringed white hands, his fussy fluttering gestures, his extravagant compliments. "An unprepossessing figure," notes René Boylesve. "He enters like a character from an Italian comedy; one could easily imagine him with a hump."

For all that, for some he is irresistible. Isadora Duncan testifies that the woman courted by him, "feels that her very soul and being are lifted as into an ethereal region where she walks in company with the Divine Beatrice." The young English diplomat Harold Nicolson, discussing d'Annunzio with two equally snobbish European noblemen, decides that the petit-bourgeois poet is "a chap one couldn't know," but, having heard him declaim his verses in an aristocratic drawing room, the bisexual Nicolson is instantly besotted. Nicolson leaves the party abruptly and walks along the quays, "still fervent with excitement," d'Annunzio's voice ringing in his ears "like a silver bell."

There are Parisians who see beyond the bewitching surface. D'Annunzio accepts advances for books he will never write. He decamps from hotels leaving bills unpaid. Maurice Barrès, the French nationalist writer whose work d'Annunzio has correctly been accused

of plagiarising, plainly sees the self-serving, exploitative side of the poet. "He is like a bird which scratches about for seed with its hard beak . . . this hard little soldier, this grasping conqueror, pecking and hurting the palm of my hand." Others sense his weariness. His greatest loves are past; his best poetry is written; in leaving Italy he has lost his role as national figurehead. The flamboyant homosexual Count Robert de Montesquiou has taken him up, and is introducing him to Parisian high society, but notices that occasionally his mask drops. Then one sees "something withered . . . the nostrils become deformed like those of a face on a shield that has been dented in combat, and the corners of the mouth express unutterable horror."

Diaghilev's Ballets Russes are in Paris, performing *Cleopatra*, choreographed by Fokine with designs by Léon Bakst. The title role is mimed by Ida Rubinstein—a bisexual Russian beauty. She comes on in an immense blue wig and drifts of diaphanous, gem-scattered gauze, most of which she sheds before the evening is out. D'Annunzio is in the audience with de Montesquiou. After the performance they go backstage, where Rubinstein is holding court still clad only in massive "barbaric" jewellery and an exiguous amount of chiffon. Barrès is there, and Edmond Rostand, and other literary luminaries, all in evening dress. D'Annunzio takes up the story. "Seeing at close quarters those marvellous naked legs, with my usual boldness I threw myself to the ground and—quite oblivious of my swallow-tail coat—kissed the feet, rose, still kissing, from the ankle to the knee, and up along the thigh to the crotch, kissing with lips as swift and supple as a flautist's scurrying over the stops of a double flute. *Tableau! Scandale!*" The bystanders are embarrassed. Rubinstein is amused. D'Annunzio lifts his eyes (even when standing upright he is a good six inches shorter than she) and sees, beneath the great tangled blue cloud of false hair, that she is smiling, and that she has a "dazzling" mouth.

Soon they will be having some sort of a sexual relationship (in their private encounters, as well as this public one, it is mostly a matter of d'Annunzio's mouth and Rubinstein's nether parts) and she will be playing the title role in his *The Martyrdom of St. Sebastian*. The saint has long featured in d'Annunzio's sexual fantasies. Now he converts them into a long, lush piece of music drama, with a score by his new friend Claude Debussy and designs—again—by Bakst. The Bishop of Paris forbids his flock to attend it. It is placed on the Papal Index of books no good Catholic may read.

MARCH 1915. Since the outbreak of war, d'Annunzio, who believes only "a great conflict of the races" can purge society of its decadence, has been calling from Paris for Italy to enter the war on the side of Britain and France (its "Latin Sister"). He is planning to return to Italy, but as he awaits his moment he accompanies the Italian journalist, Ugo Ojetti, to Reims, to see the venerable cathedral which went up in flames while under German occupation the previous September. Ojetti has obtained a pass, and a motor car. He stops off at the seventeenth-century *hôtel particulier* in the western Marais, where d'Annunzio has an apartment cluttered with oriental artefacts—a visitor has dubbed it "the House of the Hundred Buddhas." A servant comes out first with several suitcases (d'Annunzio never travels light) and hampers full of food. Then d'Annunzio appears, "elegant and glossy as ever," in an outfit which (unlike Ojetti's suit and trilby) has a vaguely military air: his civilian status shames him. He is wearing a motoring cap, riding breeches with grey puttees, and a rich brown overcoat lined with curly yellow fox fur.

They drive through the "lunar landscape" of the battlefields to Reims. Everywhere there are dead horses, their bellies inflated, their legs in the air. The great Gothic cathedral is roofless, its windows empty, its stones blackened. Guns are audible: they are not far from the front. D'Annunzio is silent and attentive. He picks up a shard of stained glass, a twisted strip of lead, a carved stone flower fallen from one of the pinnacles (all three will be on his desk at the time of his death twenty-three years later). He scrambles over sandbags to view the statues which he knows are there; he has been studying the guidebooks assiduously. He is making notes: "Pigeons fly up as though the wing of an angel had suddenly opened."

This is his first visit to Reims but he has already written an account of the fire, each paragraph introduced with the lie "I saw . . . ." He knows what a potent image of German "vandalism" the blackened ruin of the cathedral makes, and he understands how his own celebrity endorses it. His pseudo-eyewitness account was useful propaganda: it didn't need to be true.

On the return journey—still, in that deathly landscape, the aesthete and poet—d'Annunzio notes how the road curves like the *banderoles* in mediaeval depictions of saints.

17 MAY 1915. ROME. The Capitol. D'Annunzio has returned after five years in France, re-energised. He is past fifty, but the most exciting period of his life is only just beginning. Europe is at war and he has found a new medium—the spoken word; a new persona—that of national hero; and a new mission—that of urging his compatriots to be great. Italy is still neutral. Ever since d'Annunzio arrived in the country twelve days ago he has been delivering oration after oration, each one more virulent in its contempt for the peace party, each one more bellicose.

Now he is speaking at the heart of ancient Rome to an already volatile crowd. D'Annunzio himself recalls the scene months later as he lies wounded: "Faces, faces, faces without number run past my bandaged eyes, like hot sand pouring through a fist. Is it not the Roman crowd, of that May evening on the Capitol? Enormous, rippling, howling?"

Fastidious to the point of neurosis, d'Annunzio has always been shudderingly preoccupied with dirt. Now he translates that private anxiety into political rage. In a virtuoso display of his immense vocabulary, he loads his speeches with synonyms for filth. The old order reeks and must be utterly destroyed. Cautious politicians are to be disposed of like rotten meat. "Sweep away all the filth! Into the sewer with all that is vile!" Italy, its government, its entire political system, is dirty, foul, filthy, polluted, besmirched, sullied, soiled, stinking, fetid, contaminated, shitty, rancid, infected, diseased, putrid, rotten, corrupt, festering and defiled. He calls for a cauterisation by fire, a holocaust (a word he uses often), a great outpouring of blood to purge the stench of corruption.

He is beside himself. "I feel my own pale face burn like a white flame. There is nothing of me in me. I am as the demon of the tumult . . . Each of my words resounds beneath my cranium like the reverberation of curved metal."

As his tirade reaches its climax he produces a prop, a sword which once belonged to Nino Bixio, the most aggressive of Garibaldi's lieutenants.

"I take it and draw it . . . I press my lips to the naked blade . . . I abandon my soul to delirium."

The crowd weeps and howls. D'Annunzio thunders on. He is urging his listeners to ensure, by any means, up to and including murder, that the appeasers should not be allowed to take their seats in parliament again. "Make out lists. Proscribe them. Be pitiless. You have the right."

His speech triggers a riot. Hundreds of people are arrested. One of them is Marinetti, who has declared in his "Futurist Manifesto" that he would celebrate "the multicoloured, polyphonic tides of revolution in the modern capital." Another is a magazine editor named Benito Mussolini.

One week later Prime Minister Salandra declares that Italy is at war.

AUGUST 1917. War. As a roving "liaison officer" d'Annunzio has been on night manoeuvres on board warships in the Adriatic, and has been down in a submarine. He has been repeatedly under fire in the terrible battles in the mountains and along the River Timavo, and he has flown repeatedly. He has survived a plane crash after which he had to lie motionless in a darkened room for months, and which has left him blind in one eye. Even Ernest Hemingway, who can't stand his highfalutin rhetoric, grants that he has been "divinely brave."

This is d'Annunzio's account of a mission flown in pursuit of Austrian troops in the Slovenian mountains. He is now in command of a squadron of fighter planes. The letter is to his latest lover, mistress of one of Venice's great palaces, whom he calls Venturina because her gold-flecked, tawny eyes remind him of one of the colours used by the Murano glass-makers (he is a discriminating collector of glass): "I think Venturina will be pleased with her friend. It was an inferno of fire. I went down to 150 metres over the enemy infantry in order to machine-gun them. I could make out their uniforms, and the flap of canvas they wear hanging down the back of their necks to keep off the sun . . . Miracle! A bullet heading for my head hit the bar at the back of the cockpit, and rebounded. I heard the clear *ping* it made, and turned round. The steel bar was dented. Another bullet passed through the canvas between my legs. Innumerable others have made holes in the wings, splintered the propellers, snapped the cords. And we are unharmed!"

Twelve days earlier, d'Annunzio, ever attentive to the ritual of warfare, has taught his squadron a new battle cry. Instead of the *"Ip, Ip, Ip,
Urrah!"* which he finds crude and barbarous, he has ordered them to
shout the Greek: *"Eia, Eia, Eia, Alalà!"* It is, he claims, the battle yell of
Achilles. He has found it in Aeschylus and Pindar. He has used it in his
plays. Now he is demanding that the men under his command give the
shout standing upright in the cockpits of their flimsy little wood and
canvas planes.

The aircraft circle round, flying beneath the enemy troops on the
high mountain passes and then climbing again "up the sides of Mount
Hermada like a cart crawling up a slope." They return to base to load
up with more bombs, and fly back into battle over the Austrians' big
guns. "We saw shells passing the prow and the stern like ugly big rats
tunnelling through the air." This is the fiercest fire d'Annunzio has
ever yet endured. It is "a marvellous hour, which I would not exchange
for any other I have lived."

APRIL 1919. The war is over. The peace-makers are still conferring at
Versailles, carving up the remains of the defunct Austro-Hungarian
Empire. Ever since the war ended d'Annunzio has been crying out that
Italy is being cheated of its fair share, that its victory has been "muti-
lated." Now he is in Venice, speaking in the Piazza San Marco, call-
ing upon Italians to take up arms again and lay claim to the territory
(Istria, Croatia and the Dalmatian coast) which the newborn state of
Yugoslavia is claiming, but which he calls "Italy's left lung." The Irish
Italophile Walter Starkie is there and, at first, is horribly disappointed
by d'Annunzio's appearance. "A dwarf of a man, goggle-eyed and thick-
lipped—truly sinister in his grotesqueness, like a tragic gargoyle." Starkie, like many others, wonders incredulously: "Is this the man that
Duse loved?"

D'Annunzio begins to speak; at once Starkie is "fascinated."
D'Annunzio plays on the crowd "as a supreme violinist does upon a
Stradivarius." He pretends to be reluctant to speak. "The time for words
has passed." But he has come prepared, bringing with him an enormous Italian flag, which he employs as a prop in a brilliantly manipulative, quasi-liturgical performance. His bearing is priestly, his delivery
carefully measured. "Never a hurried, jerky gesture: occasionally one
arm raised slowly as though wielding an imaginary wand." The effect
is mesmerising. "The tones rose and fell in an unending stream, like

the song of a minstrel, and they spread over the vast audience like olive oil on the surface of the sea."

This oil is designed not to calm troubled waters but to set them surging. Very, very gradually, his voice rising in a patiently extended crescendo, d'Annunzio strings his public's emotions ever tighter. He incites the crowd to call out in reply to him, involving them in their own bewitchment. His own record of the speech notes their responses. "All the people cry out 'We want it'"; "the whole piazza resounds to unanimous acclamation"; "frenetic cheering"; "the people cry 'Yes'"; "the people cry 'Yes!' again, more loudly"; "the people repeat the shout and brandish their flags." As he reaches his thundering climax, writes Starkie, "the eyes of the thousands [are] fixed upon him as though hypnotised by his power."

SEPTEMBER 1919. D'Annunzio has taken action. He has marched into Fiume and made himself ruler of the tiny but now world-famous city-state. Among his new acolytes is Giovanni Comisso, another poet (some thirty years younger than d'Annunzio), who was serving with the Allied garrison when d'Annunzio marched into the city, and who promptly deserted to join him.

Comisso is there when d'Annunzio arrives at the Governor's Palace amid a din of bands playing and crowds singing. Stepping out of the car he looks small and, feverish as he is, "very, very weak." Comisso joins the throng who jostle along behind d'Annunzio up the marble staircase to the wide balcony from which he is to address the people massed below. To Comisso's wonder the frail invalid begins to speak "with incredible force," declaring that Fiume is the only brightness in a mad, vile world. The assembled crowd weep and laugh and howl out their enthusiasm. "This man convinced me," writes Comisso "as though he was one of the prophets of olden times."

A few days later Comisso is shaving when he hears a hubbub outside his window and leans out, his shirt open, his face covered with soap, to see what's causing the commotion. Down in the street soldiers are milling around a very small man wearing the jaunty-brimmed felt hat of the Alpine troops. "He seemed like a boy, agile and restless. He kept taking one of the others by the arm and having himself photographed." It is d'Annunzio, turning some of his prodigious energy to the job he does so well—making a spectacle of himself. When he arrived in the outskirts of Fiume he paused to allow a camera crew to catch up. One of his first measures on taking power in Fiume is to establish his press office. During the next fifteen months d'Annunzio's image, carefully groomed by himself, will appear in newspapers all over the Western world.

NOVEMBER 1920. The aristocratic English man of letters Osbert Sitwell has come to Fiume, curious to see what "the man who has done more for the Italian language than any writer since Dante" has made of his city-state. Sitwell finds the streets full of colourful desperadoes: "Every man seemed to wear a uniform designed by himself; some wore beards and had shaven heads like the commander, others cultivated huge tufts of hair, half a foot long, waving out from their foreheads, and a black fez at the back of the head. Cloaks, feathers and flowing black ties were universal, and all carried the Roman dagger."

Sitwell succeeds in securing an audience. He passes through a pillared hall, full of palm trees in "pseudo-Byzantine flower pots . . . where soldiers lounged and typists rushed furiously in and out." In an inner room "almost entirely covered with banners," he finds two more-than-lifesize, carved and gilded saints from Florence, a huge fifteenth-century bronze bell, and the Commandant (as d'Annunzio now likes to be called) in military grey-green, his chest striped with the ribbons of his many medals. He seems nervous and tired. But, bald and one-eyed as he is, "at the end of a few seconds one felt the influence of that extraordinary charm which has enabled him to change howling mobs into furious partisans."

Since Sitwell arrived in Fiume the great conductor, Arturo Toscanini, has brought his orchestra to the town. To celebrate Toscanini's visit, d'Annunzio lays on a mock battle which is as lethal as an ancient Roman circus: 4,000 men take part, attacking each other with real grenades. The orchestra, which initially provides a musical accompaniment (Beethoven's Fifth Symphony), becomes involved in the fighting. Over a hundred men are injured, including five musicians.

Now d'Annunzio, discussing the event with Sitwell, explains that his legionaries are "weary of waiting for battle. They must fight one another." But he doesn't really want to talk about the mayhem around him. Sitwell's visit, he says, is welcome as an alleviation of his "great loneliness." Soldiers are all very well, but he misses the fellowship, not of equals (he does not, in his opinion, have any equals) but of well-informed admirers. He quizzes Sitwell about the new English poets (one of the best of whom is Sitwell's sister, Edith). They talk about Shelley, and about English greyhounds.

JANUARY 1921. The Italian government, on whose behalf d'Annunzio claims to have annexed Fiume, but for whom his escapade has been embarrassing abroad and destabilising at home, has sent troops and a warship to dislodge him. For years d'Annunzio has been leading crowds in chants of "Fiume or Death!" but he hadn't expected his opponent to be his own people. After five days of fighting he agrees to withdraw. The Italian populace of Fiume, some 12,000 people, turn out to see him leave. "Under a deluge of flowers," according to a supporter, "he forces his way through a city in tears." Later that day he arrives by car, alone but for his driver, at a landing stage on the Venetian lagoon. His long-serving aide, Tom Antongini, and an officer of his Legion, have brought a motor launch to meet him. The light is failing. Land and water are both shrouded in mist. D'Annunzio is enveloped in a grey cape and fur motoring cap. To Antongini he seems "suddenly aged" and barely conscious. He embraces the two men and goes silently aboard the launch.

They make the short journey to the Palazzo Barbarigo. D'Annunzio has a rented apartment there, but it is less a home than a furniture depository, being crammed with the contents of the house in France that he left six years previously. Nine lorries were required to bring the mass of his possessions to Venice—the thousands of books, the hundreds of Buddhas, the scores of reproductions of paintings of St. Sebastian. Now they are stacked up, higgledy-piggledy, in the lofty rooms. Documents spill from boxes. Dusty carpets are heaped in a corner. D'Annunzio's housekeeper has sought to please her master by heating the place to his preferred inordinate temperature. As they enter, Antongini and the officer begin to sweat.

The next day d'Annunzio summons six of his acolytes. He is tetchy, exasperated by the mess surrounding him. He orders them off to search northern Italy for a new home for him. He needs a grand piano, a bathroom, a laundry, plenty of wood and coal, an enclosed garden. "If within eight days," he says "none of you has found a suitable house for me, I shall throw myself into the canal."

JANUARY 1925. D'Annunzio is in the house on the mountain slopes above Lake Garda, where he will spend the rest of his life and which he will gradually transform into a bizarre piece of installation art: part display case for his vast and eclectic range of possessions; part externalisation of his own multi-faceted personality; part war memorial, part garden of earthly delights; part mausoleum. He calls it the Vittoriale.

Benito Mussolini has taken his political place, bullying his way to the premiership by marching on Rome in October 1922. It suits Mussolini that the Italian public should believe that d'Annunzio is wholeheartedly behind the new regime, but in truth they are suspicious of each other. The poet is a maverick, and still dangerously influential: he has to be kept on side. His insatiable need for money presents a point of leverage. "When a decayed tooth cannot be pulled out it is capped with gold," says Mussolini. He acts accordingly.

Mussolini greatly increases the strangeness of the Vittoriale by contributing to the jumble of objects it contains some Brobdingnagian souvenirs. First comes the plane in which d'Annunzio once overflew Vienna (d'Annunzio will build a rotunda especially to house it). Next is the motor boat in which d'Annunzio made a daring raid on the Austrian fleet: d'Annunzio roars up and down the lake in it (and catches a bad cold). Next, dismantled and transported on over twenty flat-bed railway trucks, comes the forward half of a battleship, the *Puglia*. Offloaded at the railway station in Desenzano and laboriously transported piecemeal along the lake shore and up the mountainside to d'Annunzio's fastness, it is there reassembled. Set in concrete, its missing rear recreated in stone, it juts out from the side of the cypress-covered slope above d'Annunzio's rose garden as though breaking through a petrified wave. The gift comes complete with a set of real live sailors, whom d'Annunzio drills on deck.

And now we can see d'Annunzio with our own eyes. On YouTube we can watch a Fox Movietone newsreel showing a little party he gives on the *Puglia*'s deck soon after its installation. Proceedings open with the tolling of a great bell. Then comes a six-gun salute, smoke from the ship's cannon cloaking the hillside. The host appears on deck, in military uniform with a chest full of decorations, smilingly escorting some ladies in cloche hats. A string quartet plays: d'Annunzio listens attentively (the camera politely staying on the side of his good eye). He is stouter now, and slightly stooped. He plays a few notes on a clarinet. Cut. Now d'Annunzio is cackling merrily, revealing that he is almost toothless. People are often surprised—given the total humourlessness of his writing—to find how playful he can be. He has been invited to recite some verse for the film crew. He waves his hands and gabbles, amidst more laughter, the opening lines of Dante's *Inferno*, before turning back to his female friends.

Only three years before his own accession to power, Mussolini wrote to d'Annunzio suggesting the overthrow of the Italian monarchy and the establishment of a "Directory" with d'Annunzio as president. It was d'Annunzio who was the *Duce* then, while Mussolini was content to act as his enforcer. Now d'Annunzio is a lost leader. Throughout the 1920s there will be people looking to him to exploit his immense public following and give them a lead: fascists dismayed by the compromises Mussolini makes on his way to consolidating his power; anti-fascists who believe the poet could become the figurehead of a less brutal regime. They look in vain.

SEPTEMBER 1937. The railway station in Verona. Mussolini is on his way back to Rome after visiting his new ally, Adolf Hitler, and showing himself to the German people. D'Annunzio—vehemently anti-German all his life—has described Hitler to Mussolini as "a ferocious clown." All the same, although he seldom leaves the Vittoriale now, he travels from Garda to pay his respects. He is seventy-four, and although he is still goatishly proud of his sexual prowess, he is dreadfully aged, by

time, but also by syphilis and by the quantity of cocaine he has been taking.

A newsreel, here described by d'Annunzio's French biographer Philippe Jullian, records the occasion: "D'Annunzio, on the arm of the architect Maroni, shuffles along the red carpet up to the carriage window, through which the *Duce* is leaning. With the smile of an ogre, Mussolini takes the poet's hand in his." Mussolini, descending from the train, makes his way towards a balcony from which he is to address the assembled crowd. "The little old man toddles after him, chattering away and waving his withered hands in the air; Mussolini, without slowing down, smiles down at him from time to time, but the ovations of the crowd prevent him from hearing a word of what d'Annunzio is saying." Eventually the *Duce* pushes brusquely ahead, pointedly not inviting d'Annunzio to join him, leaving the poet to struggle back to his car through the oblivious crowd.

According to Mussolini's spy at the Vittoriale, what d'Annunzio claims to have been trying to say to the *Duce* was: "I admire you more than ever for what you are doing." But Maroni, whom d'Annunzio trusts, reports that he returns to the Vittoriale in a state of acute depression, murmuring: "This is the end." Five months later he will be dead.

Six Months

JUST AFTER DAWN on Good Friday 1915, Fly, Gabriele d'Annunzio's
favourite among his several dozen greyhounds, died in a veterinary
clinic in Paris. The poet had stayed up most of the night while Fly
leaned trembling against him, one of her legs so swollen she couldn't lie
down. Eventually the vet declared that he must "liberate" her. While
he did so d'Annunzio walked the streets. It was a public holiday, the
most doleful festival in the Christian calendar, and Paris was anyway
three-quarters empty: most of the city's well-to-do inhabitants had fled
when the government decamped to Bordeaux the previous autumn.
What few people d'Annunzio passed were all men in uniform, and
wounded. He stopped at the window of a musical instrument shop to
admire some violins (as a connoisseur of music and of fine workmanship he was very interested in the luthier's craft). Their delicate lines,
their gilded darkness, reminded him of his dear dog.

Back at the surgery, the attendant uncovered Fly's body for him. Her
eyes, always before so adoringly fixed on him, were "blackened slots."
He had the corpse wrapped in cotton wool, then in a linen sheet, then
in red damask, and finally laid in a white lacquered casket. As the work-
man nailed down the lid he remembered how much Fly had feared
being alone in the dark. With the coffin in the back of his car he drove
very slowly out to the farm near Versailles where his more-or-less-
discarded mistress, Nathalie Goloubeff, cared for his dwindling pack of
hounds. Since France had gone to war many of them had had to be put
down for lack of food.

The grave was dug. Nathalie laid a basket of forget-me-nots and ivy
at Fly's head. D'Annunzio's notebook entry for that day is listlessly
bleak: the crackle of machine-gun fire (they were very near the front);
a cock crowing; smoke drifting. "The mole hills, pale-coloured like

dried-out clay . . . this terrible life . . . the throbbing of the aeroplanes, Fly's poor eyes already putrefying . . . a sadness beyond words." Afterwards d'Annunzio ate breakfast with Nathalie, whom he had followed to France five years earlier, and with whom he still sometimes passed delicious nights. They were quiet. D'Annunzio was watching the dogs, Fly's children and grandchildren, and thinking of the hound's svelte body beginning to rot underground.

D'Annunzio writes about his dogs with a tenderness he seldom displays in writing about his women. Within days he would part from Nathalie, never to see her again; his references to her in his subsequent writings are more irritable than elegiac. That day of muted private emotion fell in the middle of a month of whirling excitement in his public life. As he buried Fly in a spoiled field he was in the midst of burying a phase of his life of which he was tired, and impatient for the beginning of a new one.

Since the outbreak of war the previous summer he had been stalled, stuck in the wrong place, unsure of his role, feeling his age (he was fifty-two). But on 7 March 1915 he finally got around to looking at a letter he had received days before (recipient of enormous quantities of fanmail, he often left his post unopened for weeks, or for ever). The letter contained a photograph of a monument to be erected at the harbour town of Quarto, near Genoa, from which Giuseppe Garibaldi and his followers had embarked for Sicily. The Sicilian expedition was, and is, the most thrilling episode in modern Italy's myth of origin. In 1860, without the sanction of any government, at the head of a troop of just over a thousand ill-equipped volunteers, Garibaldi landed in Sicily. Over the next few months he drove the armies of the Bourbon King of Naples out of southern Italy, beginning the process which would lead to the creation of a free and united Italy.

Garibaldi was as famously beautiful as d'Annunzio was notoriously odd-looking. Garibaldi was renowned for his asceticism and his absolute integrity: after making himself dictator of half of Italy he took nothing for himself but a sack of seed corn. D'Annunzio was an inveterate breaker of contracts and non-payer of debts who bought suits by the dozen and shirts by the hundred. But the two men had some important things in common, among them prodigious sexual energy and a detestation of the Austrians (for centuries overlords of much of Italy).

In Paris in 1915, d'Annunzio was in contact with Peppino Garibaldi, the great man's grandson, who was commanding a legion of Italian volunteers fighting alongside the French. D'Annunzio had been waiting for the right occasion for his return to Italy. The letter, which so narrowly escaped the waste-paper basket, gave him his opportunity. The monument was to be unveiled on 5 May, the fifty-fifth anniversary of Garibaldi's setting out. Would d'Annunzio, the organisers wondered, consider returning to his home country to speak on the occasion? "I opened the letter. I read it, and lo! Everything turned bright!"

When the war began, the previous year, Italy remained neutral. Prime Minister Antonio Salandra and Foreign Minister Sidney Sonnino, aware that their armed forces were ill-prepared for conflict, announced that they would observe the terms of the 1882 Triple Alliance, whereby Italy had agreed with Austria and Germany to refrain from making war on each other. To d'Annunzio that neutrality seemed shameful. Italy should fight, not for advantage but as a matter of pride. Too many people around the world thought of the country as "a museum, an inn, a holiday destination, a horizon touched up with Prussian blue for international honeymoons." They must be shown otherwise. Throughout the winter of 1914/15, d'Annunzio had been calling on the Italian government, through the pages of journals both French and Italian, to intervene on the side of France (Britain and Russia's part in the war was of no interest to him) against the Teutonic "horde." "This war is not a simple conflict of interests, which might be transient, sporadic or illusory," he wrote, "it is a struggle of races, a confrontation of irreconcilable powers, a trial of blood."

The French government was naturally eager to encourage d'Annunzio to bring his compatriots into battle on their side. The evening before he read the letter from Genoa, a French official, Jean Finot, came to see him. D'Annunzio didn't like him much. "A little hunched man, held upright by a kind of dried-out vanity." Nor was he impressed by the plan Finot had come to discuss. Peppino Garibaldi's volunteer legion had been fighting heroically: a quarter of the men, including two of Garibaldi's other grandsons, had been killed. Now the survivors were to be sent home to rouse their fellow Italians to action. Madame Paquin, the couturier, had promised 2,000 red shirts of the kind that the great Garibaldi's own men had worn half a century before, but made of silk this time. The venture was something like a coup d'état, something like a piece of political theatre. As the former it seemed incompetent: as the latter it felt muzzily ill-directed. D'Annunzio was anxious. After Finot left he applied a mustard plaster to his chest—he had a bad cough—and went to bed, but lay for a long time restless. All his life his moods oscillated between prodigious energy and depression. On this night he was very low. He waited for sleep, "as for death."

When he read the letter from Genoa the following morning he was instantly high again. "I will go. I will lead the *Garibaldini* Legion, the red wave," he told his notebook. "To reach Quarto . . . to cross the Tyrrhenian Sea with a ship loaded with blood eager to be spilled!" An "Apollonian providence" had come to his aid.

Peppino Garibaldi came to see him in the afternoon. The two men paced around the room, both of them too excited to sit down. D'Annunzio small, neatly groomed as always; Garibaldi tall, with his deeply lined face and brilliant eyes, in the blue tunic and red breeches of a colonel in the French army. D'Annunzio expounded his vision: "Two thousand young men in arms . . . encircling the solemn monument ready to set out from there to conquer and to die." He himself as creator, director and star of this martial show. "It is impossible that Italy, however blind or deaf, does not see the sign, does not hear the appeal, rising up from the rock of Quarto." Garibaldi was equally moved. It will be a flame, he said, or a poem. D'Annunzio, who had woken that morning feeling seedy, with a touch of "the humiliating little complaint" (either piles or a recurrence of the venereal disease which he had contracted the previous year), ended the day enraptured, swept away on "a torrent of interior music."

Just over three weeks later came the sad day of Fly's death, and a mournful Easter spent with Nathalie, followed by the melancholy process of packing up. "Life flows from the house as though from an open vein," wrote d'Annunzio, watching the removal men dismantle his Parisian home. He gave away some of his best greyhounds—two of them to Pétain, the future Marshal. D'Annunzio was, as usual, badly in need of money. To finance his journey he pawned some splendid emeralds which Eleonora Duse had given him. With another month to go before he was due in Quarto, he set out for his villa on the Atlantic coast at Arcachon. There he poured his energies into writing two furiously bellicose articles and the speech for Quarto, and into his last love affair on French soil, with a surgeon's daughter, a fine horsewoman (d'Annunzio admired "Amazons") to whose presence in the neighbourhood his housekeeper-cum-concubine-cum-procuress Amélie Mazower (whom he called "Aélis") had alerted him.

Back in Paris, assiduous as ever in self-promotion, he gave a press conference. The *Revue de Paris* correspondent was positively shocked by the splendour of his wardrobe. His secretary had been busy chasing up the suits he had on order from his tailor, and his accounts for that month reveal he had also bought a prodigious number of new cravats. He delivered the text of his speech to Salandra, the Italian premier, and to newspaper editors in Paris and Milan, with strict instructions that it was to be embargoed until the morning of 5 May. He told the editor of *Le Figaro*, "the die is about to be cast." The verbal flourish reveals that he saw himself as a second Julius Caesar, imposing a heroically martial destiny on an unwilling Rome.

He was given a grand send-off at the Gare de Lyon. "Women rushed to the station," he wrote. "Almost all of them were acquainted with my bed." Nathalie was not on the platform. D'Annunzio, who had begun referring to her as "the nuisance," had sent her back to the farm. But the Amazon from Arcachon was in the crowd gathered to see him off, and so, probably, were several of his other lovers. The lesbian novelist Sibilla Aleramo, like him a member of the sexually ambiguous coterie who met at Nathalie Barney's salon, and a friend of the painter Romaine Brooks, whose only male lover he was, alleges he had been carrying on affairs with "four, five or six" women simultaneously during the previous year.

On 4 May 1915, just over five years after he had left Italy bankrupt and with ignominious haste, he recrossed the border. While he had dallied in Paris through the first months of the war, ordering haute-couture outfits for his dogs (red and blue, made by the couturier Charles Worth), teaching himself glass-blowing and twiddling at the recipe for his patent perfume, d'Annunzio had become, in his compatriots' collective imagination, the man who could save their national honour. He had left the country as a celebrity whose escapades, however amusing, were becoming undignified. He returned as a nationalist messiah.

Giosuè Carducci, the great poet of the previous generation, had heralded the advent of such a man. "Prepare the way for the master who is to come, for the spirit of Italy, grand and great, for the genius, the beatings of whose approaching wings we already hear." So had d'Annunzio himself, writing enigmatically that "He will come from the silence, defeating death,/The necessary Hero." During his absence in France he had, for Italians of a nationalist and militarist persuasion, acquired the status and glamour of such a messianic hero. In Milan, his supporters organised a series of readings of his poems to celebrate his advent. "Rapt in his sublime visions, he seemed to have forgotten his beautiful fatherland," wrote an admirer. "But no! As soon as the new dawn appeared in the skies, he arose proudly and with a shudder of love he ran to the breast of the great mother."

As d'Annunzio's train approached the great mother's border, he bound his eyes, lest, as he explained, the first sight of his homeland prove too emotionally overwhelming. Once he was on Italian territory, he was met at every stop by enthusiastic crowds. Young women climbed on the train's running board, kissing the glass of his compartment's windows and handing him flowers. In Turin, according to the following day's *Corriere della Sera*, "thousands of hands reached out to him," while d'Annunzio, with a catch in his throat, addressed them from the window of the train. As he approached Genoa, a professor at the university cancelled a lecture, urging his students not to learn history but to go meet d'Annunzio at the station and "live history" instead.

With difficulty d'Annunzio was got into a motor car and driven through the press of people. Safely arrived at his hotel, he came out onto a balcony and spoke to the excited crowd. "Five long years of absence and sadness lie behind me, abolished!" There had, in fact, been nothing but his own inclination to prevent him returning to Italy earlier, but he referred to his absence as an "exile." "Now I live, I wish only to live, a new life."

The next day he spoke on the waterfront. Having read the text of his oration, King Victor Emmanuel had decided he had better stay away. So did all the government ministers. Italy was still neutral. D'Annunzio's rhetoric was too aggressive to receive the sanction of a royal or ministerial audience. He was not, however, asked to tone it down.

The quayside was thronged. Some hundred survivors of Garibaldi's "Thousand," living mementoes of Italy's heroic foundation, were there, as well as the new *Garibaldini* in their Paquin-tailored tunics. News photographs show the monument engulfed in a sea of straw boaters. Men (there are few women visible) scramble out on the rocks for a better view, or take to their boats to avoid the crush on land. The mayor, who opened proceedings, addressed himself to the dignitaries assembled on the platform. Neatly demonstrating his understanding of the modern political process by turning the other way, d'Annunzio spoke out to the crowd.

Without any kind of amplification, he could make himself heard by thousands. The German caricaturist, Trier, depicted him later that year as a ranter, his face contorted, his mouth gaping wide. But the image is misleading. Even when inciting his hearers to make war, his strategy was not to harangue but to fascinate and seduce. His language was violent, his manner dulcet. His oration at Quarto was a magnificent piece of word-music. In it d'Annunzio paid tribute to the heroism of "The Thousand," thus appropriating their glory for himself. He quoted Garibaldi's most famous line: "Here we make Italy, or we die!" He spoke of the noble aspirations of Rome's ancient heroes. He flattered his audience and challenged them, daring them to be worthy of their great antecedents. He wrapped his provocative politics in the lulling grandeur of liturgical rhythms. He ended with a series of beatitudes:

> Blessed are the young who hunger and thirst for glory,
>   for they shall be satisfied ...
> Blessed are the merciful, for they shall be called upon
>   to staunch a splendid flow of blood, and dress a
>   wonderful wound ...
> Blessed are they that have most, because they can give
>   most, dare most ...
> Blessed are they who return with victories, for they shall
>   see the new face of Rome.

It was incantatory. It was enthralling. It was blasphemy. "This man!" wrote Romain Rolland, outraged. "This man, who is the incarnation of literary falsehood, dares to pose as Jesus!" Rolland had once enjoyed d'Annunzio's company, but they were now diametrically opposed in their attitudes to war. Rolland was a pacifist, while d'Annunzio had recreated "the Sermon on the Mount to incite Italy to violate her treaties and make war on her allies."

There were those who thought d'Annunzio's showmanship too contrived and his speech preposterously over-erudite. But d'Annunzio knew what he was doing. He was aware that politics was a performance art. Later in the year he noted how dull and patronising was a priest who spoke over-simply to uneducated solders, "believing that humble hearts don't know how to understand high and noble eloquence." That was not a mistake he ever made. He offered intoxicating rhythms, clanging declarations, the invocation of grand abstractions and resonant myth. Whether or not his audience followed the meaning of everything he said, they responded fervently to the hypnotic way he said it. At Quarto the crowd surged forward, sang the *Marseillaise* in sign of their support for their "Latin sister" France, and shouted out for war.

The city was full of fervent nationalists. Again and again d'Annunzio was called upon to address them. In four days he spoke seven times. His speeches were reported all over Europe. Italian government ministers were nervous: they were engaged in secret negotiations of the utmost delicacy and d'Annunzio was a dangerously loose cannon. Sonnino called his appearance at Quarto "clowning." Minister Marini dismissed

it as "stupid." But French reporters were full of admiration and gratitude. His enemies were respectful too: a German cartoon, showing
him ranting and frenzied, was captioned "all would go well if we had
cannon of the calibre of his big mouth."

What seemed to be taking place in Genoa was the transfiguration of
d'Annunzio from dandy-poet into national redeemer. But when he
stepped back into the privacy of his hotel room he was still the incorrigible spendthrift and libertine. Ugo Ojetti, who had arrived in Genoa
with him, wrote to their mutual editor and friend Luigi Albertini that
week, imploring Albertini to use his influence on the poet, who was
in danger of compromising his own reputation and the interventionist cause. "He's only interested in snouting around under the most
disreputable skirts." A hostile deputy was soon asking a parliamentary question expecting the answer "yes"—whether it was true that
Signor d'Annunzio had left Genoa's Hotel Eden Palace without paying
the startlingly large bill run up by himself and the two unidentified
women who were accompanying him there?

It wasn't only d'Annunzio's personal renaissance that was less simple
than it seemed. So too was his part in the political drama in which
he claimed such a stellar role. He had come to urge his compatriots
to repudiate the Triple Alliance and to agree to go to war alongside
France, Britain and Russia, the nations subscribing to the Entente. Over
the next two weeks he was repeatedly, and in increasingly virulent language, to denounce the government ministers who apparently hung
back from doing so. But without his knowledge they had already done
precisely that which he was urging them to do.

Throughout the winter, Prime Minister Salandra and his Foreign
Minister Sonnino had been negotiating with both sides, and concluded
that the terms offered by the Entente were the more attractive. On 26
April, while d'Annunzio was still in Paris, Italy's rulers had secretly
signed the Treaty of London with Britain and France, agreeing to enter
the war on their side. On 1 May, Sonnino asked the cabinet to repudiate the Triple Alliance, so that he could reach an agreement with the
Entente (an agreement that had in fact already been reached). On 3
May, the day before d'Annunzio took the train south, Salandra's government formally (but still secretly) severed Italy's ties with Germany
and Austria-Hungary.

Later, d'Annunzio was to claim to have been privy to the government's secrets all along, but he was lying. During the last few weeks of his time in France, he was gleaning information from the secondhand gossip of the press corps and peripheral politicians. He had no secret collusion with the authorities he was shortly to be subjecting to such furious verbal abuse. He didn't know it, but in calling for intervention he was banging, noisily and with big gestures, on an already open door.

The morning after he spoke at Quarto, the city of Genoa presented d'Annunzio with an 800 kilo plaster cast of a fourteenth-century stone lion. He accepted the lion (emblem of St. Mark and of the Venetian Empire he was intent on reviving) by delivering his first oration of the day. Homeless as he was, he was always pleased with titanic bric-a-brac. At noon he was speaking again, this time to Garibaldi's veterans. That evening he was presented with a bronze shield by the mayor, and responded with more speechifying. With each oration he became more incendiary. He told the university students: "Go! You are the flying sparks of the sacred blaze. Go start the fire!"

After five days' rest and recreation with his two female friends, he moved on to Rome. Salandra's administration, secretly committed to military intervention, was at an impasse. The majority of Italians, including the King, the Pope and a large proportion of military leaders, still favoured neutrality, and so did parliament. The peace party was headed by Giovanni Giolitti, the liberal statesman whose canny pragmatism had already made him a hate figure for d'Annunzio. Giolitti had been premier four times. He was out of office in 1915 but he still dominated parliament, as he had done for nearly two decades. There he repeatedly argued against intervention in a war from which, in his view, Italy would gain next to nothing (he was to be proved correct). He had many supporters. Over 300 deputies left their visiting cards on him that month as a sign of solidarity.

Giolitti's opponents, though, were more vociferous. All over Italy pro-war demonstrations were taking place. British visitor and aspiring politician Hugh Dalton reported there were "hundreds and thousands of good people of all classes walking slowly through the streets of Rome and other Italian cities, intoning with a slow and interminable repetition, 'Death to Giolitti, Death to Giolitti'." In Rome the British ambassador Sir Renell Rodd estimated that the crowd assembled in the

Piazza del Popolo to demonstrate in favour of intervention was 200,000 strong. "They were not the type which ordinarily furnishes demonstrations, but an orderly and disciplined throng which seemed to include the best of the bourgeoisie."

These British witnesses were naturally inclined to think well of Italians eager to fight alongside their own country: their description of the demonstrators as being "the best" people reflects their bias. The ambassador's wife threw flowers over the embassy balcony to the pro-war demonstrators, even though Rodd himself—the secret of the Treaty of London not yet being out—had to keep mum. In truth not all of the interventionists were so "disciplined" and "orderly." In Rome neutralist politicians were beaten up in the street. The then magazine editor Benito Mussolini called upon his readers to, "Shoot, I say shoot, a dozen [neutralist] deputies in the back." But though, as Rodd put it, "the people had come down into the piazza" and "manifested their will," Salandra couldn't mobilise the armed forces without parliament's consent, and Giolitti commanded the majority in the house. Something, or perhaps someone, was needed to break the deadlock.

D'Annunzio arrived in Rome on 12 May. The reporter from the *Corriere della Sera* estimated that 100,000 turned out to meet his train. There were tumultuous scenes at the railway station. D'Annunzio narrowly escaped being trampled to death by his admirers before he was hustled into a car. Photographs show the Via Veneto crammed from end to end, a dark river of hats. Arriving at the Hotel Regina, he made it to safety through the kitchen door. Shortly thereafter he reappeared on a balcony, declaring his devotion to the King and the Queen Mother (who was known to favour intervention) and calling upon his listeners to turn on cowards and appeasers, the "enemies within."

Repeatedly, over the next few days, he addressed the increasingly volatile crowds. Jean Carrère, correspondent with *Le Temps*, describes him: "Never have I seen an orator advance before the public with such composure. Standing on his improvised tribune he was magnificently alone, of a marble pallor, with two eyes of flame." He glittered. Another observer wrote of "the light gleaming off his bald pate and flashing off his spectacles" (actually a monocle, which he called his "caramel").

Over and over again, with a terrible, measured fury, he denounced the government of his country. He once wrote musingly about how, to one inflamed by desire, a woman's mouth might seem like a flower, like paradise, like the luscious epitome of all delight, while days or hours later (with lust appeased) it could seem repellent—slimy, disgustingly warm, alarmingly muscular. Now the revulsion with which, in the past, he had recoiled from lovers and pleasures he had tired of, was turned on the social mores and political institutions of peacetime Italy. Rome was a sewer; its rulers were drivelling, stale-smelling old men; civilian life was a foul morass.

He was voicing sentiments that would have found their echoes all over Europe. Marinetti had called war "the hygiene of Europe." In the political rhetoric and the poetry of the period, civilian existence is grey, dim, morally compromised and physically grubby. The battlefield by contrast is bright, aglitter with weapons and flashing with joy. Above all it is clean. When Britain declared war Rupert Brooke proclaimed his gladness to "Leave the sick hearts that honour could not move/And half-men, and their dirty songs and dreary." Like d'Annunzio, Brooke saw the war as a saving freshness into which he could plunge "as swimmers into cleanness leaping." In Germany, Thomas Mann welcomed the conflict as "a purging and a liberation." "Let the storm come," cried the Hungarian Dezsö Kosztolányi, "and sweep out our salons."

The morning after he arrived in Rome, d'Annunzio visited the minister Ferdinando Martini, who, as editor of the journal the *Fanfulla della Domenica* in the 1870s, had known him as a precocious schoolboy contributor. There is no record of their conversation. Contemporaries speculated that Martini must have spoken of the repudiation of the Triple Alliance and the Treaty of London. He probably did, even though he didn't trust d'Annunzio. A few days earlier, advising that the King should stay away from Quarto, he had written: "D'Annunzio thinks only of himself and his own success . . . He has no political sense whatsoever, sometimes even, despite his marvellous genius, not even any common sense . . . he could easily compromise us." But the decision to go to war could not be implemented until parliament and people had been swayed in its favour. D'Annunzio could help.

That evening, speaking from his hotel balcony, d'Annunzio launched into his most furious oratory to date. He may by now have been speaking with the tacit approval of the government, but his language was dangerously seditious, the actions he sought to instigate were criminal.

He attacked the advocates of peace in vitriolic terms. The very air of Rome stank of their treachery. Those who still hung back from war were traitors, "assassins" of the *patria*, Italy's executioners. Giolitti was strangling the nation with a Prussian rope.

D'Annunzio was openly advocating violent attacks on the people's elected representatives. He called upon the Roman mob to take the law into their own hands. He urged his listeners to attack the appeasers who "lick the boots on sweaty Prussian feet." He called for "stonings and arson." His rhetoric was becoming ever more frenzied. "I tell you, there is treason here, in Rome! We are being sold like a herd of diseased cattle." He urged the people to hunt down anti-war deputies. "Form squads!" (*"squadro"* was one of the many words the fascists would pick up from him). "Lie in wait. Seize them. Capture them!" An observer reports that the applause when he paused was like a storm. When he resumed to denounce Giolitti in ever more vituperative terms ("that diabolical old blubber-lipped hangman"), the storm "was transformed into a cyclone."

D'Annunzio was high on his own eloquence, on the frenzy of the crowds he flattered and inflamed and on the prospect of blood. Fifty-two years old, he extolled the "ruthless purity" of youth. A poet whose life's work had been the threading together of obscure and beautiful words, he inveighed against verbiage and called for action, swift, cruel if need be, and unambiguous. "It is not the time for speaking but for doing." He ended by leading the crowd in the Risorgimento anthem, beating time with his little white hands while the people beneath bellowed out the refrain: "Let us join the cohort, / We are ready to die! / Italy has called!" Tom Antongini reports that the Queen Mother, listening from behind the shutters of her palace window, was moved to tears.

That night Salandra sought a more secure mandate by offering to resign. The following day, 14 May, Rome was in uproar. The painter Giacomo Balla, in his hectic, swirling canvases, *Forms Cry Long Live Italy* and *Patriotic Demonstration* (both inspired by the turmoil of which d'Annunzio was part) conveys the violence and elation in the air. The Austrian embassy was cordoned off by infantry with bayonets fixed for fear of the mob. A crowd burst into the parliament building, the Palazzo Montecitorio, smashing furniture and terrifying the deputies. In the afternoon the King summoned Giolitti and asked him to form a government. Giolitti declined. His life was in danger. But it was not fear, but principle, that made it impossible for him to assume power.

The King had signed the Treaty of London; his new premier would be obliged to implement it. Giolitti could not lead the country into a war to which he was so publicly and vehemently opposed. The King and Salandra had manoeuvred him into an impossible position. Declining the chance to govern, he lost his power to oppose.

That evening, d'Annunzio spoke at the Press Association and then moved on to Rome's grand opera house, the Teatro Costanzi. Interrupting the scheduled performance, he stepped out onto the stage at the end of the first act. There he took it upon himself to make public the news that Italy would fight. His delivery was peremptory, dramatic (as a demagogue he had come a long way in the few days since he had delivered his piece of elaborate prose-poetry at Quarto). "Hear me!" he began "Hear me! I have momentous things to tell you, things you don't know. Keep silent. Listen to me. Then leap to your feet, all of you!" Again he raved against Giolitti, "an icy lie armed with flexile cunning, as the horrible sac of an octopus is equipped with twining tentacles" who "betrays the King, betrays the fatherland." D'Annunzio urged "good citizens" to take their vengeance. His speech was an incitement to murder. "If blood flows, such blood will be as blessed as that shed in the trenches." Afterwards some of his supporters hijacked a fire engine and used its ladders in an attempt to break into Giolitti's house: they were driven off by the military guard.

The King invited Salandra to form a new government. Giolitti conceded defeat and left the city. The war party had carried out what historian Mark Thompson calls a "coup d'état in all but name." The socialist leader Filippo Turati expressed his despair with the percipient words: "Let the bourgeoisie have its war. There will be no winners; everyone will lose." The road to war was open. But still d'Annunzio talked. The task he had set himself was greater than a simple change in government policy. He was assisting at the birth of a new, greater Italy. "The crowd howls like a woman in labour. The crowd writhes in giving life to its own destiny . . . Everything is ardour and clamour, creation and intoxication, peril and victory, beneath the murky sky of battle where the swallows flash and cry."

Those hectic days in Genoa and Rome were to enter d'Annunzio's personal mythology as "radiant May," a period haloed in glory during which he created a masterpiece in a hitherto unknown art form. In

1906 he had watched his friend, the sculptor Clemente Origo, casting a bronze statue inspired by one of his own poems, a large and complex piece showing a centaur wrestling with a mighty stag. The scene in the workshop—the fierce heat, the courage of the foundry workers, the combination of artistry and danger—had haunted him. He used it in a novel. Now he repeatedly evoked it as an image of what he was doing to the Italian people. He was breaking up the decadent old forms of Italian society in order to make the nation anew, as a smith might smash up scrap metal ready for use in a new compound. He was cleansing his human material of its impurities. He was melting it down in the white heat of his eloquence. On 17 May he spoke on the Capitol Hill, and in his account of the occasion he likens his words to the blows with which the foundry man strikes out a plug to let the liquefied metal flow into the mould. "The tumult" seems to him like a furnace's fiery breath. The crowd is an incandescent mass of molten bronze ready to be shaped by his will. "All the mouths of the mould are open. A gigantic statue is being cast."

There were swallows on the Capitol that day, a numerous flock of them squabbling noisily as they swooped around the green-bronze equestrian statue of Marcus Aurelius. We know it, because d'Annunzio made a note about them. Surrounded by an ecstatic crowd whose excitement he himself was orchestrating, he was yet sufficiently detached to observe birds and flowers (the masses of red carnations in the Teatro Costanzi on the night he spoke there) or the feel of a horse's rump under his hand.

He was fast developing a brilliantly manipulative oratorical technique. He allowed his public no break in his contrivance of their hysteria. He played on them with rhetorical tricks borrowed from religious liturgy or from classical drama. "Hear me!" he cried "Listen to me!" "Understand me!" The crowd was urged to join him, howling out responses to his insistent "*Evvivas!*" These were not speeches to be rationally appraised but acts of collective self-hypnosis. D'Annunzio's works as a dramatist had frequently been grandiose in conception, spectacular in their staging and appalling for the violence of their sentiments, but never before had he produced anything like the shows he put on during that "radiant May."

He had found his métier. Romain Rolland, recoiling, likened him to Marat. He had become the figurehead of a mass movement. When he drove away from the Capitol, "dishevelled boys, their faces crazy, dripping with sweat as though after a fight," threw themselves at the car, nearly lifting it off the ground. "The battle is won. The great bell has sounded. The whole sky is on fire. I am drunk with the joy of war."

Quite how much political effect this extraordinary sequence of public demonstrations had is a matter of dispute. The Treaty of London had been ratified already, before d'Annunzio returned from France, but it is conceivable that without his intervention Salandra and his cabinet might have failed to carry the electorate (the majority of whom dreaded war) with them. But, whatever the extent of his actual influence, it certainly appeared to the public that d'Annunzio—a private individual without any constitutional authority—had imposed his will on the elected government, and that he was the man who had taken them to war. He had done it by directing a stream of virulent abuse against representatives of Italy's democratic institutions, and by urging the crowds that gathered around him to begin what might have amounted to a civil war. If anyone in Rome in those frenzied days was an enemy of the state it was surely not Giolitti, but d'Annunzio himself.

Nietzsche defined the state as "a remorseless machine of oppression," a "herd of blond beasts of prey." D'Annunzio—who fancied himself (in some moods) to be a Nietzschean *Übermensch* (superman), unshackled by social conscience or civic duty—had no respect for the electorate, and no compunction about undermining the authority of democratic institutions. A decade later Mussolini would refer to the events of May 1915 as a "revolution" and boast that in that glorious month the Italian people, incited by d'Annunzio "the first *Duce*," had risen up against their corrupt and lily-livered rulers, clamouring for the right to prove their honour and gain glory, and that those rulers had ignominiously surrendered. The truth is otherwise. But the spectacle of a government apparently harangued into action by a demagogue with no respect for the rule of law was ominous for constitutional democracy.

Immediately after the fierce excitement of his appearance on the Capitol, d'Annunzio withdrew and walked, alone and quiet, on the Aventine Hill. The lovers in his novel *Pleasure* had ridden the same way, "with ever before their eyes the great vision of the imperial palaces set alight by the sunset, flame-red between the blackening cypresses, and through it drifting a golden dust." So had d'Annunzio himself with Elvira Fraternali, the great love of his Roman years. He thought about her that evening (although he was to leave the letter she wrote him that month unanswered: he did not like to see what age did to women he had once doted on). He brooded over the five years of his "exile" in France. To return to the city where he had made his name, and married, and several times fallen in love, and been young (he wrote that year that he would give anything, even *Halcyon*, his finest poem-sequence, to be twenty-seven years old again) moved him deeply. By the gate of the Priorato of Malta, with its famous view through a keyhole of the dome of St. Peter's, he saw what looked like a tiny star hovering at the level of his eyebrows. It was a glow-worm, the first he had seen since he left Italy in 1910.

In his notebook, in his letters, in his memoir *Notturno*, the glow-worm is accorded almost as much space as the preceding oration. D'Annunzio's case has always puzzled those simple-minded enough to believe that artistic talent and refined sensibility are incompatible with political extremism and an appetite for violence. Only hours after he had been raving against his political opponents and urging a mob on to murder, he was strolling—pensive and nostalgic—through the jasmine-scented Roman night, his appreciation of Rome's multi-layered beauty that of a man of deep erudition; his response to a minuscule natural wonder that of a poet.

On the day Italy declared war on Austria-Hungary, d'Annunzio dined with some of his supporters. Very late, as dawn was breaking, he spoke to them. This address makes a quiet, gravely ominous coda to the stridency of the public speeches. He looked forward to the ensuing carnage without compunction for his part in involving his country in it. He referred blasphemously to his days of non-stop oratory as "the Passion Week." This was his night in the Garden of Gethsemane, the moment when he allowed himself and his hearers to feel the horror of what was to come. "All those people who yesterday were tumultuous in the streets and squares, who yesterday with a great voice demanded war, are full of veins, are full of blood." He had exulted in the idea of arriving at Quarto with a legion of sacrificial victims, "young blood to be spilt." Now he looked forward to making the oblation of countless others' lives to his "tenth muse, Energy," who "loves not measured words but abundant blood" and who was about to get her fill of it. He concluded with a muted prayer: "God grant that we find each other again, living or dead, in a place of light."

Show over, d'Annunzio relaxed. In the summer of 1915, between his prodigious feats of oratory in May and his setting out for the front in July, he sank, according to his secretary Tom Antongini, into "the most abject state of frivolity." He summoned Aélis from Paris to join him (Nathalie was pointedly not invited) and went, so Antongini tells us, "from a reception to a dinner and from an intimate tea to an even more intimate night." As the forger of Italy's new martial destiny he was the man of the hour: women found him less resistible than ever. D'Annunzio's son Mario reports that a rich Argentinian lady took a room in the hotel expressly to be near him. (He accepted the flowers with which she presented him, but rejected their donor—"too thin," he said.) Isadora Duncan was there too, and perhaps more fortunate. His philandering did nothing to decrease his popularity with the public. His militancy added to his sexual allure; his sexual conquests enhanced his virile, iron-clad image.

He was not writing. Now he was a hero he was more marketable than ever, and the people he had hurried into war looked to him to compose their battle hymns. But no words came. "I have a horror of sedentary work," he wrote that summer. "Of the pen, of the ink, of paper, of all those things now become so futile. A feverish desire for action devours me."

He had not, as a young man, shown much enthusiasm for the soldier's life. He had been a resourceful evader of national service and, when he found himself unable to defer the evil day any longer, he served his country with extreme ill grace. "It is certain death for me," he wrote to his lover. "Ariel a corporal!" (Like Shelley, one of the models for his own persona, he named himself after Shakespeare's androgynous spirit.) "The delicate Ariel! Can you imagine it?" He was obliged to live in barracks and groom his own horse. He left the army with relief. Now, a quarter of a century later, he was avid to rejoin it.

As he waited in Rome for instructions as to where he was to present himself he fretted over the difficulty of getting his uniforms made. Luigi Albertini, who was expecting a *Song of War* from him for publication in the *Corriere della Sera*, received instead a letter complaining about the difficulty of finding a tailor. Soon, though, he was wearing the elegant white outfit of the Novara Lancers, and experiencing curiously mixed feelings about it. "I already feel I belong to a caste, and that I am the prisoner of rules." He was to be attached to the staff of the Duke of Aosta—the King's taller, more charismatic cousin who commanded the Third Army—and given almost unlimited licence to define his own war work. He had permission from the commander-in-chief, General Cadorna, to visit any part of the front and to participate in any manoeuvres he chose. He was to be, not a leader, but an inspirer.

His progress northward at the end of July was attended by almost as much excitement as his arrival in Italy had been. Minister Martini, who saw the pushy adolescent he remembered all too clearly in the world famous poet, wrote irritably that d'Annunzio would have done better to have gone directly and "in silence" to the military base at Udine, "but he can't live without *réclame*." He went to Pescara to pay a farewell visit to his mother, who was by this time paralysed and mute, and was lavishly fêted by his fellow Abruzzese. He stopped off in Ferrara and presented the manuscript of his play *Parisina* to the mayor in a public ceremony, declaring that he "carried the beauty of that city in [his] intrepid heart." Martini wrote that this was "all foolishness which annoys the public," but he was wrong: the public responded warmly.

As usual, d'Annunzio was spending money like there was no tomorrow—a natural response to the onset of a war perhaps, but one which was exasperating to Albertini, who was acting as his unofficial manager and saw all too clearly how close d'Annunzio was coming to another financial catastrophe. He was unable to settle his bill at the expensive Hotel Regina where he had stayed for two months; nearly three years later he was still trying to retrieve the trunks full of clothes and knick-knacks he was obliged to leave there in lieu of payment. He had to beg his book publisher, Treves, for an advance to pay for the two horses which, as a cavalry officer, he was expected to provide. Now Albertini urged him to go straight to the Duke of Aosta's headquarters: good sensible advice. "There you'll eat regular meals for four lire a day. Perhaps you won't need to pay for lodging. They'll give you 400 lire a month. See what horizons open up!" Not the kind of horizons that drew d'Annunzio. On arrival in Venice he checked into the Hotel Danieli, then, as now, one of the grandest hotels on earth.

For Italians the Great War was fought along the border with Austria, in the mountains to the north and east of Venice. The city was drastically changed. The summer of 1914 had been, according to the contemporary

Venetian historian Gino Damerini, an especially brilliant season. American, English, French, German, Hungarian and Russian visitors packed out the hotels, restaurants and beaches, "each competing with the others in luxury, nudist exhibitionism, hedonist wildness, carnivalesque fancies and pretentious elegance." The palaces along the Grand Canal, many of whose proprietors were d'Annunzio's old acquaintances, were all open, flooding the hot, still nights with light and music. Then came the assassination at Sarajevo, and "at the echo of the first cannon shot all those people . . . the illuminations, the silk, the jewels, the kaleidoscopic game of devil-may-care sophistication . . . vanished, as though sucked away by a whirlwind." By the time d'Annunzio arrived a year later, Venice had assumed the character of a military and naval base, and a city under imminent danger of attack. The larger canals were blocked. The *altane*, the rickety wooden roof terraces with which the land-starved Venetians have been consoling themselves for their lack of gardens since at least the fifteenth century, had been taken over by air-raid wardens: on the high platforms where Carpaccio painted courtesans bleaching their hair in the sun, there were now searchlights and sirens. Statues were hidden by mounds of sandbags. The palaces and churches stood stripped, their treasures removed and hidden. Hotels were hospitals. The entrance halls of grand houses sheltered refugees. At the brightest of times Venice is a place in which one easily loses oneself. Blacked out, it became a labyrinth through which its inhabitants fumbled at night as though blind.

En route north, d'Annunzio wrote in his notebook: "Sense of emptiness and distance. Life and the reasons for living elude me. Between two streams, between past and future . . . Tedium. Lukewarm water . . . Necessity for action." On arriving in Venice, finding action was, accordingly, d'Annunzio's first priority. Within two days, he was on board the leading destroyer of a naval squadron on night manoeuvres, travelling east along the coast towards Austrian-held Trieste in the hope of encountering enemy vessels.

He made notes about the moonlight, the crisscrossing lines of the ships' wakes, the sailors eating as they sat silent around their guns, all of which later found its way into his wartime writings. He was to be a witness: he was also to be an "inspiration." Two weeks before his arrival the Italian cruiser *Amalfi* had been torpedoed and sunk. Scores of Italian seamen died. D'Annunzio addressed the survivors, who were being sent back into action. "Now is not the time for words," he said, for the first of many, many times; but words were what he brought them. Throughout the remainder of the war he was to speak again and again, to men going into battle, to men returning exhausted, to men burying their dead. He spoke of blood and sacrifice, of memory and patriotism, and the duty owed by the living to those who had died for Italy. His funeral orations posthumously awarded the wretched conscripts the dignity of heroes; his pre-battle harangues presented the bloody slog of modern warfare as noble sacrifice. His gift for oratory had become an instrument of war.

To urge others on, though, was not enough to satisfy him. He sought a role appropriate to a superman. He found it in the air. D'Annunzio had always been fascinated by flight. For decades he worked and reworked the myth of Icarus in his poetry. We have already seen him making his first flight at the 1909 Brescia air show. When he moved to France he frequented the airfield at Villacoublay, and several times he flew again. Shortly after arriving in Venice in July 1915, he made his way to the island airbase at Forte Sant'Andrea, at the mouth of the lagoon. There he met the young pilot, Giuseppe Miraglia.

Well connected (his father was director general of the Banco di Napoli and a political insider) and, according to d'Annunzio, bronze-skinned, with greenish-yellowish eyes flecked with gold, Miraglia was a paragon to his fellow servicemen, known for having gone alone into enemy-occupied Pola with only a pistol for defence. He was to be the first of a series of young men who became for d'Annunzio, during the war years, at once beloved comrades and incarnations of his ideals of youthful valour and fit sacrifice. "Blessed are those who are now twenty years old," he said. He worshipped and envied their beauty and took

enormous pleasure in the opportunities the war afforded him to live alongside them as companions-in-arms. Their deaths were marvellous to him. When they were killed, as one after another they were, he took them into the pantheon he was elaborating in his writing and speeches, making them the martyrs and cult heroes of his new mythology of war.

From Miraglia, d'Annunzio learned that a bombing raid on Trieste had been proposed. Trieste, the cosmopolitan city at the head of the Adriatic, then Austria's chief port, was one of the irredentists' most yearned-after lost territories. Here was an exploit exactly to d'Annunzio's taste. He was an aviator. Venice and Trieste are barely 150 kilometres apart, a short hop for a modern plane, but in 1915 a formidable distance. As a showman d'Annunzio saw how the flight could become a piece of splendidly theatrical propaganda. He determined to claim it for himself. He and Miraglia would drop explosives on the Austrian emplacements in the harbour but—more importantly as far as d'Annunzio was concerned—they would also drop pamphlets (written, of course, by himself) over the town's main squares.

With Miraglia he began to talk of ways and means. He studied maps of the coastline they would overfly. He thought about the best design for the little sandbags to which the leaflets would be attached, and went himself to the Rialto market to buy the necessary canvas. He reflected happily that, thanks to his rigorous programme of exercise followed over many years, he was more than fit enough for the physical ordeal of the flight and confident of being able to hurl bombs or sandbags from the unstable perch of a tiny plane. He drafted a message to "the Italians of Trieste," assuring them of his devotion to the cause of their imminent liberation, and copied it out over and over again in his own hand, taking care that his signature (often an exquisite but illegible arabesque) should be unmistakably clear.

Word got out, and reached a reporter. Anything d'Annunzio did was not only a gossip column item, but a news story. A Venetian journal announced the projected flight, and that the poet was to join it. The admiral commanding the tiny air force was doubly dismayed, firstly by the breach of security—clearly it was going to be hard to keep any operation in which d'Annunzio was involved secret from the enemy—secondly, by the risk of this inconveniently famous subordinate getting himself killed. D'Annunzio alive could help to encourage the troops and, if he continued to produce the kind of furiously nationalist poetry that he had been writing over the previous decade, help maintain the civilian population's support for the war. His death, on the other hand, would have a deleterious effect on the entire nation's morale.

The admiral vetoed the flight. D'Annunzio protested. The admiral consulted his superiors. Telegrams went back and forth between Rome and Venice and the military headquarters near the front at Udine. None of the authorities wanted to sanction the flight. The order came down: d'Annunzio's life was *"preciosissimo"* and must be conserved. He was forbidden to join this or any other dangerous operation. Furious, d'Annunzio went to the top. On 29 July he wrote an impassioned letter to Prime Minister Salandra.

He flattered: "You, whose own spirit is so hard-working and so generous, must understand me." He stressed his physical competence. He was not "a man of letters of the old type, in skull cap and slippers." He was an adventurer. "My whole life has been a risky game." He boasted of his past daring. "I have exposed myself to danger a thousand times against the fences and hedges of the Roman Campagna" (he adored fox-hunting). In France he had often been out on the Atlantic in chancy weather "as the fishermen of the Landes could tell you." He had ventured repeatedly into enemy territory on the Western Front (he visited the front twice, staying on the safer side of the French lines). Most importantly, "I am an aviator . . . I have flown many times at high altitude." (This wasn't strictly true either.) And he wasn't only brave: he had knowledge and skills which could be useful. He knew Istria, he knew Trieste. He had an "observant spirit."

Having presented his credentials, he made his request, in the most insistent terms. "I pray, I beg . . . repeal this odious veto." He hinted that if he were not allowed to risk his life in his own way he would deliberately endanger it by going straight to the front. To bar one with "my past, my future" from living the heroic life would be "to cripple me, to mutilate me, to reduce me to nothing." The troops, the press, the people of Italy all saw him as "the poet of the war"—now the authorities were trying to treat him as an exhibit in a museum.

Minister Martini scoffed at the suggestion that fox-hunting and jaunts in pleasure boats provided the necessary experience for the kind of role d'Annunzio was claiming. But Salandra was impressed by d'Annunzio's earnest tone. The ban was lifted. The flight would go ahead.

Exultant, d'Annunzio went shopping again. At the haberdashers he chose ribbons (red, white and green, the colours of the Italian flag) with which to adorn his missives to the people of Trieste. He filched a sandbag from among those banked up along the façade of St. Mark's. Its contents, sanctified by contact with the ancient building, the hub of the Venetian Empire, would give his little packets historical gravity as well as physical weight. He bought himself thick woollen vests and long johns and when all was ready, all the little bags stowed away in one big one, he danced "a pyrrhic dance of joy around them."

The date of the enterprise was fixed for 7 August, which d'Annunzio considered an auspicious date. He prepared himself—as was only realistic in those early days of flying—for death. He would write a few months later about the mornings on which he set out for such missions, "the thought of returning was left in the vestibule, despised, as a vile encumbrance," and recall how he sat once with a pilot before a flight, talking easily about routes and equipment, but aware that "each of us, by noon, could be a fistful of charred flesh, a crushed skull with gold teeth glinting in the mess." He drew up a will, and entrusted it to Albertini.

On 6 August he and Miraglia made a test flight. D'Annunzio had flown before, but only rising briefly over airfields. Now he looked down on a great city, seeing Venice as only a handful of human beings had ever yet seen it. He was the first writer to record the experience. He wore, as all the aviators did, heavy leather gloves. When he took one off to help Miraglia tighten the elastic of his chinstrap he at once felt his fingers begin to freeze. All the same, belted into the forward seat, exposed to every wind in the shaky little flying machine, he persistently scribbled down his impressions. The diverging lines of a ship's wake were like "the palms in the hand of Victory." Venice's islands, divided up by canals, resembled the segments of a loaf of bread. The long railway bridge was the stem to the city's flower. The wind-ruffled water by the lagoon's outlet was iridescent as a pigeon's throat. The mainland—in August's dryness—was blonde, feminine, girdled by the pale ribbons of dykes. Avidly absorbing these new sights, fixing them with similes, d'Annunzio makes no mention of discomfort, or vertigo or fear.

On the morning of the seventh he performed his usual toilette—a vigorous massage administered by his servant followed by a bath—and thought about the possibility that the body he was tending might, by nightfall, be stripped and laid out dead. After breakfast (strong coffee) he went shopping again, for another woollen jumper: he must have felt the cold the day before. Walking back towards the Hotel Danieli he encountered the Countess Morosini, with her daughter, the Countess di Robilant. It is one of the oddities of d'Annunzio's war experience that on his way into action of the most serious kind he might find himself chatting with an acquaintance about a social engagement. Annina Morosini, known to the gossip columns as the "uncrowned Queen of Venice," was the chatelaine of the Palazzo da Mula on the Grand Canal and a generous friend to the poet. That morning he noticed how lovely her eyes were, and jotted in his notebook "still desirable" (she was fifty-one). He told her what he was about to do and asked her playfully to give him a talisman. She demurred, offering him only her blessing, but saying she would telephone that evening. He was offhand about the latter promise. "I don't know what she's calling for," he noted. Given his thoughts at bathtime, the coming evening must have seemed remote. Back in his hotel room he filled a cigarette case with cartridges, laid out his woollen flying gear and wondered: "Will it be cold up there, or <u>down there</u>?" (The underlining is his.) He was thinking of the sea bed. Remembering that he might not die but be taken prisoner, he put six of the laxative tablets he swore by, and some cash, in his pocket, then went down and took the waiting gondola to the airfield. Miraglia was ready for him. They set off on the flight which would take them further than any Italian pilot had flown before, and well within range of enemy guns.

In the notebook d'Annunzio was carrying that day, his poet's-eye observations—"the teeth of the breakwaters which gnaw at the unhappy sea"—are interspersed with dialogue. The two men couldn't speak to each other. The only complaint d'Annunzio makes about the physical circumstances of the flight are about the engine's atrocious din: he regrets not having brought wax earplugs. He and Miraglia communicate by passing book and pen back and forth, d'Annunzio having to twist awkwardly in order to do so. Their initial exchanges are pleasantly companionable: "Are we still climbing?." "You look like a bronze *bonze* [a Japanese Buddhist monk]," says d'Annunzio to Miraglia. "Do you want some coffee? It's really hot." Soon though, more urgent messages are passing between them. D'Annunzio was not just there to make notes on the landscape ("in the pallor of the lagoon the twisting canals are green as malachite"), he was also the bombardier.

They were carrying several bombs in cylinders fitted to the plane's undercarriage. It became evident that one of them was jammed. D'Annunzio struggled to free it. "It's impossible to pull it up." "Have we got any string?"

Miraglia gave him anxious directions: "You absolutely <u>must not</u> turn the screw . . . See if you can push it so it falls out, but <u>don't twist it</u>." It might explode at any moment. Even if it didn't, unless they could free it first it would almost certainly blow up when they touched down. "When we're landing I'll hold onto it with both hands," d'Annunzio told Miraglia. There have been those who sneered at d'Annunzio's war record, but the dangers he ran were real, and so was the courage with which he met them.

They came in sight of Trieste, the white stone city luminous in the August sun against the backdrop of the Carso, the rocky wilderness which would be, for the next three years and more, a battlefield. They saw puffs of smoke way beneath them, signs that they were under fire. Soon they could hear the gunfire, and feel the hits (on their return they would find a bullet embedded in the fuselage a few inches from d'Annunzio's elbow). They continued their descent. They saw the enemy submarines in the marina and dropped bombs on them. As they came in low, d'Annunzio hurled down his little bags, and watched the ribbons and pennants attached to them flutter down, some uselessly into the sea, others into Trieste's grand waterfront piazza, with its palatial banks and customs houses. His purpose in dropping his pamphlets was not just to convey a message: it was also to show that where he had sent down words, he could have sent down explosives. He was there to encourage the pro-Italian population, but also to terrorise their Austrian rulers. Like most of his wartime exploits, this first flight was an attack not so much on enemy forces, as on enemy morale.

It was as they turned back that he and Miraglia discovered the malfunctioning bomb. D'Annunzio struggled awkwardly with it in his tiny cockpit, deafened by the engine noise, careful not to make any abrupt movement for fear of unbalancing their fragile conveyance. He had often longed for an heroic death: now he was bothered by the idea that the plane—coming down only to bounce up as it exploded—would look not tragic but ridiculous. Somehow (it is a measure of his insouciance that we don't know how) he managed to deal with the problem—perhaps, as his and Miraglia's notes suggest, with the help of a rag and d'Annunzio's belt. They came safely back to earth.

From that moment onward, according to Damerini, the Venetian people engulfed d'Annunzio in "a wave of anxious affection." He had been a privileged visitor in aristocratic circles. Now he became, in Venice as he already was in Rome, the people's idol. His admirers mobbed him. They hung around outside the Danieli hoping to catch a glimpse of him. When he went out on foot crowds followed him along the Riva degli Schiavoni. When he came back by gondola or in one of the recently introduced motorboats they pressed so thickly around the landing stage he could scarcely make his way ashore.

He had embarked on his new life as national hero, and the character in which he had done so was both archaic and up to date. In preferring the weapons of propaganda to those of material destruction he was displaying a quintessentially modern sophistication. He was a newfangled PR man, but he was also a hero from the age of chivalry, one who had exchanged his charger for an aeroplane. As the British Prime Minister Lloyd George put it, "the pilots are the Knighthood of the Air, without fear and without reproach. Every aeroplane fight is a romance, every record an epic." In a war which was becoming, on its every front, more brutal and more gruesome, d'Annunzio with his beribboned leaflets, skyborn and dancing invulnerable through the enemy anti-aircraft fire, seemed gallant, joyous and debonair.

He returned to the Danieli. We do not know whether the Countess Morosini telephoned that evening as promised, but we do know that the next day she sent d'Annunzio a little silver box engraved with her name and the date of his exploit, and that he thanked her, saying that he would carry it always because the day it commemorated was more precious to him "than all my odes." After having been for decades a self-described genius and one of the most famous people in Europe, he had begun what felt like a second, and more important existence. "All the past flows together towards all the future," he wrote. "All my life I have waited for this hour."

It is time to turn back from that point, and to map some of the streams flowing through his life and mind towards it, to see how far back they rise, how variously muddy or silvery fresh their sources are, to observe how they join and braid together and diverge again before merging at last, and to trace how they eventually debouch into a sea of blood.

· II ·

STREAMS

Worship

GABRIELE D'ANNUNZIO—Gabriel of the Annunciation. Everything about his own name was delightful to the poet: the aristocratic particle, the scriptural associations, the way it marked him out as super-human. He was an archangel, bringing revelations to the wondering world. The name (so felicitous that some of his contemporaries insisted he must have made it up) was his real one, or at least a family name to which he was genuinely entitled. His father had been born Francesco Paolo Rapagnetta, but when Francesco's childless uncle d'Annunzio made him his heir he changed his surname by deed poll. His son took the prompt. On the back of the winged dining chair d'Annunzio used during his period of greatest fame and fortune were carved the words: "The Angel of the Lord is with us."

D'Annunzio was not a pious man but he revelled in the trappings of Christian worship. He surrounded himself with lecterns and prayer stools and censers and alabaster stoups originally carved to hold holy water. His addresses to his political supporters were structured, like the liturgy, as a sequence of calls and responses. To him soldiers were martyrs and battered weapons were relics. He was an arch-sensualist, but he was also an ascetic. After visiting Assisi he discovered an affinity between himself and St. Francis, and liked to dress in a friar's habit (the penitential roughness of the garment mitigated by the fact he wore it over a shift of mauve silk).

In Fiume he staged pseudo-sacred ceremonies in the cathedral of St. Vito, and encouraged a cult of his own personality so fervid that the Bishop of Fiume noted furiously that his flock were forsaking Christ for this modern Orpheus. His last years were devoted to the conversion of his house above Lake Garda into a self-glorifying shrine. He revered no one but himself, but reverence fascinated him. If a deity's defining act is that of creation, then d'Annunzio—whose creativity was so exuberant that nothing but physical exhaustion ever slowed his pen—was god-like. He thought so. The hero of his novel *Forse che sì, Forse che no* (Maybe Yes, Maybe No), crash-lands his plane on a beach in Sardinia and, alone in a wild landscape, reflects: "There is no God if it is not I."

Faith shaped the culture into which he was born: faith in the Christian God and his saints; faith in magic. As an adult, d'Annunzio would embrace modernity and all its racket, but he grew up in a world where the sounds were made by sheep and cattle, creaking carts and rustling straw. The Abruzzi was, in the 1860s, and to an extent remains, a place apart. Blocked off by the Apennines from the great cities of Italy's western seaboard, it is bounded by bald mountains, where bears and wolves still live, and in whose foothills walled towns perch on crags fluted like the underside of mushrooms. From there the terrain slopes gradually to the Adriatic, across which Abruzzese mariners have, for centuries, traded with their counterparts on the eastern, Dalmatian shore. The land is edged by low cliffs or, near Pescara, the region's capital and d'Annunzio's home town, by flat sand and pine woods (most of them now felled to make way for beachside hotels). Returning in middle age, d'Annunzio was moved to be back among the stone walls, the low hills scattered with flowering trees. "A painted cart passes along the shore, drawn by a pair of white oxen. The sandy soil sloping down to the sea is ploughed almost to where the waves break. Rows of beans. Vines contorted like arthritic old hands. A blackened stack of straw. Parsimony, diligence . . . The mountain rearing grand above."

All of this (especially the parsimony) d'Annunzio would put firmly behind him. But though he left the Abruzzi in fact, in his fiction and memoirs it was ever-present. He liked to hear its dialect. In middle age, at the height of his fame, he hired a fellow Abruzzese to be the steward of his household. He sought out its landscapes. At Marina di Pisa during his years in Tuscany with Duse, and at Arcachon on France's Atlantic coast during his "exile," he chose to live by pine-fringed beaches resembling the Adriatic coastline he had known as a boy. He wrote about the place repeatedly. And the aspect of it which charged his imagination most potently was the religious life of its inhabitants, a phenomenon he found both repugnant and fascinating.

In remote villages the church was not only a place of worship, it was the community's totem, on whose decoration much hard work and devotion and the peasants' meagre savings were lavished. Troops of pilgrims passed along the country paths "in profile as in the embroideries of our old bedspreads." During d'Annunzio's childhood an itinerant priest, known to his followers as the Messiah, wandered the region, wearing blue tunic, red cloak and wooden clogs, and calling on the people to leave their crops and herds and follow him. Hundreds did so, singing and begging their way from town to town. "A wind of fanaticism," wrote d'Annunzio later, "ran through the land from one end to the other."

In the Abruzzi, houses are modest and great churches scarce. The most remarkable monuments in the region are the high mountain hermitages—caves or crevasses in which solitary mystics lived a thousand or more years ago and around which their devotees have, over the centuries, constructed precarious shrines. In defining the kind of stock he came from d'Annunzio borrowed their image. "I come from an ancient breed," he wrote. "My ancestors were anchorites in the Maiella . . . They flagellated themselves till the blood came . . . They throttled wolves; they stripped eagles of their feathers, and they scratched their seals on giant rocks with the nail Helen took from the Cross." Lacking—to his enduring chagrin—the kind of aristocratic antecedents he gave his fictional heroes, he awarded himself membership of another kind of elite, that of the ferociously holy.

D'Annunzio's father, Francesco Paolo, was far from being an anchorite. He was a petty landowner and wine merchant. During Gabriele's childhood he was the Mayor of Pescara, a prominent man in a provincial town. In d'Annunzio's first stories, set in or around Pescara, he conjures up a place where the bustle of port and barracks and market are contrasted with the frustration of women confined to small, dark rooms, who watch the life of the street through chinked shutters or small high windows. The church bell clangs out the hours. Priests pass in the streets carrying extreme unction to the dying. Young people, strictly segregated as a rule, furtively press up against each other in the merciful darkness when the church lamps are extinguished in Holy Week to mark Christ's passion. Funerals, the bier followed by long lines of hooded mourners, their faces covered all but a slit for the eyes, or processions of girls in sacrificial white on the way to their first communion, provide the town's main spectacles.

The sacred is all-pervasive. In the bedroom Gabriele shared with his brother, the main item of furniture, other than the beds, was a prayer stool. On the wall hung lithographs of religious paintings by Titian and Raphael. In one of d'Annunzio's novels, set in the Abruzzi, a woman lightly remarks that before she and her lover can enjoy an afternoon in bed they will have to hang veils over the numerous saints' pictures on the walls. God and his representatives were all around the boy d'Annunzio, and they were not a comfort so much as a form of surveillance.

Francesco Paolo d'Annunzio was a man of the flesh—self-indulgent and corpulent. In later life d'Annunzio was repelled by him (not least because he saw his father's disorderly love life and compulsive over-spending as a horrible caricature of his own); but in childhood he yearned to please him. Francesco Paolo's extravagance could seem grand. During carnival he would stand on his balcony and, as custom demanded, toss handfuls of gold and silver coins down to the revellers in the street, deeply impressing the small son who would, in his turn, spend most of his life throwing his money away. Francesco Paolo liked a show and he liked to astonish (both attributes Gabriele inherited). He used to colour his white doves with the new-fangled aniline dyes, and released them to fly—pink, green, purple, orange—around the house's inner court.

Gabriele was his parents' darling. His father used to watch him gravely. "He never made light of me, nor ever mocked me." He had a brother (who became a musician and a swindler, before emigrating to America) and three sisters. But he was the prodigy, the little prince. He adored his mother, Luisa de Benedictis, mainly, as he tells it, because of the gratify-ing way she adored him: "Her glances made my heaven."

The house was full of women—maids, his sisters, unmarried aunts, his grandmother—and he was everyone's precious treasure. When ladies came to visit his mother he would sit on his own little stool in the middle of their circle, while they gazed at him admiringly as at "a rare beast." Sent away to boarding school at the age of eleven, he wrote nostalgic letters home in which he conjured up luminous images of his early childhood, scenes that might have been lifted from accounts of the infancy of saints. "Do you remember how when I was little I used to come first thing in the morning into your room all sparkling with joy, and I used to bring you flowers? . . . No shadow of a cloud ever troubled my happiness."

Actually, there were shadows. To live in the countryside (as the d'Annunzio family partly did—they had a second house, the Villa Fuoco, on their land outside town) was to be exposed to gory realities. Many of the stories d'Annunzio related about his childhood concern dying animals. There was the death of his little Sardinian horse, a bay with a white muzzle named Aquilino, whom he would feed with apples and sugar lumps in the peace of the nighttime stable. There was the quail the farm manager gave him in a cage made of twigs. Half a century later d'Annunzio could still recall how the tiny creature dashed itself against its makeshift bars, gashing its head until the bone showed. On killing days the howling of the stuck pigs and their blood spurting into basins so appalled him that he would hide in a corner, face to the wall, his hand over his contorted mouth. "Life scared me as though it stalked me with a pig-sticking knife in hand." After the "massacre" he sobbed all night.

Gabriele's education was begun by a pair of devout, unmarried sisters whom he was to cruelly traduce in a story of disease and sexual desperation—*The Book of the Virgins* (later reworked as *The Virgin Orsola*). The passage in which he describes the two women's lessons in reading, writing and religion sounds like actual experience recalled. "In solemn voices they spoke of sin, of the horrors of sin, of everlasting punishment, while all those wide eyes filled with amazement and all those small pink mouths opened aghast. In the vivid imaginings of the children, objects came alive . . . the Nazarene, bound with thorns and bloody drops, gazed from every side with agonised, haunting eyes, and beneath the great hood of the chimney each plume of smoke took on an atrocious form." Other children elsewhere might be terrified by the scissors man, the big bad wolf, or the fierce bad rabbit, but for d'Annunzio and his fellows, the bogeyman was one and the same with the deity.

Luisa was socially a cut above her husband. She would take her son to stay with her parents down the coast in Ortona. Their house, a rambling old structure wedged between the monastery and the fortress, was a complex of massive walls and hidden courtyards, of long corridors and cell-like rooms. As a tiny crawling child, d'Annunzio was fascinated by the floor tiles with their depictions of flowers and animals. Once upright and talking he would demand accounts of the fables illustrated on the ceramic panels let into the whitewashed walls.

The most wonderful part of his sojourns in Ortona were his visits to another relative, an abbess. She fed him with little twisted biscuits called "vipers." When she told him she would teach him "glorious mysteries" and gave him an amethyst rosary to hold, Gabriele, who was to become an insatiable collector of holy trinkets, and an inventive stager of pseudo-religious ceremonies, began to hyperventilate with excitement. Even more thrilling, she allowed him, as a favoured nephew, to pass through the visitors' parlour into the convent. There in the secrecy of her cell, he watched her practising "her arts of divination." He was nine years old, a boy in a place no male should ever have been permitted to enter, assisting at rituals forbidden by the Church. In a confused but ecstatic awareness of the multiple transgression, he watched while she threw aromatic herbs on the fire and peered at the homely ingredients of her spell, "the innards of a mullet, iridescent fish scales, sage leaves." For all her neat wimple and nun's bands, the old lady was a sorceress. He was afraid of her. She took his hands, and explained that his past and future were written on their two palms as a sacred story might be painted on a diptych. The room was full of smoke. Kneeling, arms outstretched, the sleeves of her habit hanging like sails, the Abbess seemed to go into a trance. Gabriele panicked. Beating frantically at the door he yelled until a novice appeared and released him.

Sorcery and divination had penetrated the convent walls. Outside they were ubiquitous. The people of the Abruzzi might be church-goers and observers of fasts and festivals, but Christianity coexisted in their culture with heathen magic. D'Annunzio witnessed cacophonous ceremonies when the frenzy of the "possessed" was aggravated by a din of yells and whistles. In one of his stories a woman of Pescara seeks out a witch doctor, a bearded old man who rides into town on a white mule, wearing gold triangles in his ears and with silver buttons as big as the bowls of spoons on his coat. He is said to be able to make the blind see, and calm those possessed by wicked spirits. His wife, with whom he lives in a cave outside town, is an abortionist. In other stories d'Annunzio writes about an unsuccessful fisherman who believes himself to be cursed, about a dead dog, putrid and stinking, left across the door of a hut at night to keep away vampires, about a child dying as its mother declares it has been bewitched. Some of these magical practices he filched for his fiction from his friend, the folklorist de Nino. Others he observed as a child.

The Abruzzi is sheep country. Green roads, like rivers of grass, lead from the high mountain pastures down the long, long incline to the sea. D'Annunzio's poem about the shepherds, who would bring their flocks down them annually "in the footsteps of ancient fathers," was written long after he had ceased to return home with any regularity, but when he was a child their transhumance would have been one of the great public events of the year, marking the season as clearly as the harvest or the ripening of the first cherries. Those shepherds, and the peasants who farmed the coastal plain, preserved intact a rich cache of beliefs and ceremonies. D'Annunzio describes the endlessly repetitive, mournful chant which accompanied every solemnity from birth to death: the travelling songs sung in parts by groups of men and women on the road together "like a wave continually rising and falling." He records a ritual which is still extant in the villages of the Abruzzi. "A white ox, fattened by a year of abundant grazing, caparisoned in vermilion, ridden by a little boy, processes in pomp to the church between banners and candles . . . arriving in the centre of the nave, it lets fall its droppings; in the heap of steaming matter the devout read the agricultural auspices."

D'Annunzio described the elaborate praise-singing that was customary at harvest time. Lines of women, laden with food and wine in tall, painted jars, would process out into the fields, lauding the sun and the landowner and God as they went. When the men heard them coming they would lay down their scythes, and the foreman led the prayer— "inflamed with enthusiasm, he expressed himself spontaneously in couplets" (this improvised rhyming is well documented)—and the rest of the gang roared out their responses "while the red light of sunset flashed reflected off the iron blades, and the topmost sheaf on the corn stook glittered like a flame."

The child saw, and the man remembered, how a group of people could be bound together and excited by the power of the word.

D'Annunzio felt the lure of Christian devotion. During his recurring bouts of depression he would crave the peace of religious seclusion. So too he had his private rituals and a predilection for magical thinking. At birth he narrowly escaped being choked by the caul. Those so born were believed to have the second sight, and the caul itself was a charm which could save its wearer from drowning. D'Annunzio's was preserved in a little package of silk hung on a cord which, as a child, he wore always around his neck. Recalling this as an adult, he wrote patronisingly about the "superstition" of the women—his mother, aunts and nurse—who believed in its efficacy, but, throughout the Great War, whenever he went into action, he carried an amulet or two in his pocket.

He was always a ditherer. Frequently, when faced with a decision, he resorted to primitive forms of divination. He opened books at random and searched for messages in the first phrase he read (a practice he claimed to have taken from "the ancient priests of Cybele"). He looked for omens. Emeralds brought good fortune (both magically and—as it happens—practically: Eleonora Duse gave him two enormous emeralds, the pawning of which several times saved him from financial disaster). He visited clairvoyants, he consulted astrologers. He carried a pair of ivory dice in a little jewelled box with the Caesarean inscription *"Alea jactae sunt"* ("the dice have been cast") and, when required to make a decision, would frequently allow the fall of the dice to make it for him. He abhorred the primitive religiosity of the peasants he knew as a child, but he took with him into his sophisticated adulthood many of the superstitions of the village society he had left behind.

When he was five or six years old, one of d'Annunzio's sisters beckoned him aside and, opening her childish fist, showed him her treasure, an artificial pearl. At once he was seized by a craving for something similarly rounded and lustrous. There were swallows' nests beneath the house's eaves. He would steal an egg. He ran up to a top-floor room and out onto the narrow balcony, but he was too small to reach a nest. Going back indoors he found a bench and, struggling doggedly, dragged it out. Women at a window of the opposite house called out to him. He took no notice. He scrambled up onto the bench and thence onto the wrought-iron railing three storeys above the paved street below. Clinging to the slatted shutters, he groped upwards. The women called more loudly. Down in the street passers-by stopped. Shopkeepers came out to see what was going on, craning their heads upward. The little boy could hear a growing hubbub beneath him. He struggled to haul himself up, but his arms weren't strong enough. Agitated swallows beat around his head.

Suddenly he was being gripped around the waist and dragged down. His parents were there, his mother trembling, his father pale and threatening to beat him. He was lifted back through the window and laid, faint and shaking, on a bed. In retrospect he saw them—mother, father, child—as a secular trinity. His aunts hung over him weeping, as the sorrowing Marys wept over the dead Christ. But the family's communion was interrupted. The crowd now gathered in the street, believing the child to be dead, began on the chilling ululations customary at funerals. Gabriele's father picked him up, and carried him, limp and white-faced, back out onto the balcony. The keening turned to shouts of joy.

Describing the incident in old age, d'Annunzio made of this, his first balcony appearance, a portent. He was marked out from childhood, so he asserted, for a public life. More pertinently, it demonstrates how religious imagery pervaded his imagination. One of his school reports describes him as "very unbelieving." At sixteen he was enthusiastic about *Paradise Lost* and Byron's *Cain,* both poems whose heroes defy God. He admired Darwin. He shocked his teachers (most of them priests) by "gross heresies," suggesting that if the deity existed at all he was a "villain or an imbecile" who has "created mankind to amuse himself by watching us suffer." But, for all that, it came naturally to him to see himself as Christ, and his parents as Mary and Joseph. The public life of the people among whom he spent his childhood, their faith, their songs and prayers, their spells and festivals, became part of the furnishings of his mind.

Glory

TOWARDS THE END of each afternoon, when d'Annunzio was a child in Pescara, the paranze, the Abruzzese fishing boats with their wide sails the colours of oranges, or saffron or terracotta, would appear at the mouth of the river. One day when he was nine years old, Gabriele ran down to the quay to greet them. He had a friend on one of the boats who used to bring him gifts of cockles. Having received his offering, he carried it off to a niche in the dilapidated ramparts of Pescara's fort, settled himself astride a rusty old cannon and began forcing open the shells with his pocket knife. It was hard. The knife slipped. He cut himself badly. Blood poured over his hand and down the cannon. He began to feel dizzy. His handkerchief was too small to use as a tourniquet. He cut off a sleeve of his shirt to bind up the wound. At once the bandage was soaked with blood.

The place was lonely and night was coming on. A goat's head appeared over the ancient wall above him, regarding him with its mad, devilish eyes. He remembered that the vaults of the old arsenal were infested with spiders and that the local women used their webs to staunch bleeding. Trembling now, he made his way into the dark and ruinous chambers, yelling to scare off the horrid scampering things, cut down a web with his knife, and wrapped it around his bloody hand before staggering home half-fainting.

When, in middle age, he wrote his account of this escapade, d'Annunzio placed it in a splendid setting of distant mountains and fiery-coloured clouds. He cherished the scar on his thumb as "the indelible sign of my innate difference." The essay in which he described the incident is entitled "The First Sign of a High Destiny."

. . .

The images and stories of heroes surrounded d'Annunzio as he grew up. The main salon in the d'Annunzio family's house in Pescara is decorated with a painting of Aeneas. In the background, Troy burns. Aeneas, undismayed, looks stagily outwards to the future, as he sets off to fulfil the great destiny his father Anchises has foreseen for him. So d'Annunzio was to be launched out into the world to fulfil his father's ambitions.

He was growing up in an heroic age for Italy. The Abruzzi had been a part of the Kingdom of the Two Sicilies, ruled through the middle years of the nineteenth century from Naples by a Bourbon monarchy. Three years before Gabriele's birth, Garibaldi led his thousand volunteers to Sicily and drove the Bourbon troops, who outnumbered them twenty-six to one, off the island. The King was nervous and vacillating. His officers were hopelessly demoralised. As Garibaldi swept on up through Calabria to Naples, the armies of the teetering monarchy changed sides, or stripped off their uniforms and ran for home. In one of his stories d'Annunzio recreates the scene, which he must have heard repeatedly described, of the day when the fort at Pescara was evacuated and "the troops scattered, throwing their weapons and equipment into the river."

King Victor Emmanuel of Savoy came south at the head of his army to annex the regions Garibaldi had conquered. Francesco Paolo d'Annunzio was one of the delegation who travelled to his camp at Ancona to invite him to bring his troops into Pescara. When they did so, the King himself (shortly to assume the title of King of All Italy) passed a night under the d'Annunzio family's roof. In their small way the family had assisted in the making of the Italian nation state.

It was the first age of mass reproduction. Prints of Garibaldi and Victor Emmanuel adorned the walls of houses all over the peninsula, revered much as sacred paintings were revered. In d'Annunzio's home they were juxtaposed with depictions of the exploits of classical heroes: it was as though the time for glorious deeds had come again. When Gabriele was seven years old the French withdrew their support for the Pope's temporal power, and Victor Emmanuel's troops marched into Rome. The state of Italy, independent and united, was complete. Years later d'Annunzio was to recall being wakened, after going to bed that September evening, by people parading though the streets with lighted torches, by raucous songs, fanfares of trumpets and cries of "Rome!"

When he was eleven, d'Annunzio was sent to a boarding school, the Royal College of the Cicognini at Prato, which was considered to be the finest in Italy. Francesco Paolo wanted him to be "Tuscanised." The Tuscan dialect, the language of Dante and Machiavelli and Lorenzo the Magnificent, was to be the language of the new Italy's elite.

The Cicognini is grand but grim. Behind its eighteenth-century façade lie long corridors, with vaulted ceilings and wrought-iron lanterns. There is a chapel and an elegant little theatre, but there is little to make a boy feel at home. Gabriele felt the misery of boarding-school children everywhere. In writing his recollections of his years there, he describes the college as his "prison." He recalls the gloom with which he walked back through its "sad portal" after the daily walk and the relief, on his few exeats, of escaping from its atmosphere of confinement and prohibition. He was not allowed back to Pescara, even for the long summer holidays, for four whole years.

Children obliged to fend for themselves in a loveless environment grow a shell around their hearts which can be hard to crack open later. D'Annunzio matured into an adult notably lacking in empathy, an exploitative friend, an unreliable lover and a negligent father, for whom people en masse seemed no more interesting than herds of cattle. Some at least of his emotional frigidity can probably be ascribed to his early banishment to school. At the time, though, he responded to his spartan treatment, not only dutifully, but with fervid enthusiasm and declarations of love. The mission that had been laid upon him, that of making a prodigy of himself, was one he accepted enthusiastically. In his first year he wrote to tell his "dearest Daddy" he was top of his class. "Oh how sweetly these words flash from my lips, what joy I'm feeling now I have made your wish come true."

Already, as a schoolboy, he was a passionate little patriot. He wrote, aged thirteen, that he had two missions: "To teach the people to love their country . . . and to hate the enemies of Italy to the death!" The shrillness was not peculiar to him. Italy was an unstable new amalgam of regions with widely differing histories. Its peoples, whose dialects differed so markedly as to make them in many cases unintelligible to each other, were going to need to be taught to love it. Italian nationalism was both anxious and bellicose. The late nineteenth century was, for all Europeans, a nationalist age, but for newly forged, insecurely unified nations—Germany and Italy prominent among them—it was one where a simple loyalty to the state was linked to a complex web of quasi-religious, quasi-erotic impulses, among them the yearning for heroes to worship. For d'Annunzio those vaguely defined but extreme emotions coalesced around the idea of his own "high destiny."

Francesco Paolo and Gabriele alike believed in that destiny. Aged fifteen, the son wrote to the father: "I love praise, because I know that you will enjoy praise offered to me; I love glory because I know that you exult to hear glory attached to my name."

Glory, glory, glory: the word tolls through his adolescent correspondence. "He is entirely dedicated," reads one of his school reports, "to making a great name for himself." An early photograph shows a curly-haired teenager, his expression solemn, his eyes fixed. It is inscribed, in his own hand, with "To Glory." His path there would be literary, but he prepared himself for it with the kind of self-punishing dedication that a religious novice might devote to asceticism, or a would-be soldier to physical training.

The standard curriculum was not enough. He learned to play the violin and the flute. He took singing lessons. He set himself holiday tasks—the translation of Ovid's *Metamorphoses*, the compilation of a book of "observations." When the signal was given for the end of evening study, and the rest of the boys prepared for bed, he went around collecting the others' left-over lamp oil so that he could work far into the night. He wrote to tell his father he was top of the class again, adding, "If you knew what it had cost me to reach that position!" He saw himself as a hero who bore the marks of his exploits written on his body. His left shoulder, he wrote later, was lower than the other, so many hours had he spent, as a growing boy, hunched over his desk.

When he was permitted to bypass an exam, he wrote to tell his mother how disappointed he was, "I am certain I would have taken first place." When he was sixteen he wrote six letters to his parents for Easter, one in Italian, the others in Greek, Latin, English, French and Spanish. The great book he felt certain he would write one day, was, he wrote, a "peak" he would climb.

The College of the Cicognini was run on military lines. The boys wore smart little uniforms, turquoise trousers and tunics with frogging and epaulettes. They were students, but they were also toy soldiers. They

were drawn up into two "companies," each consisting of four "squads," and well-behaved boys were honoured with officer status. In his second year d'Annunzio was made a "corporal." Three years later he was promoted to the rank of "sergeant" and in his last winter at the school he became "commandant" (the title he would give himself at Fiume). The boys' days were punctuated by drum rolls announcing the beginning and end of lessons and study periods; their exercise was drill, their excursions were route marches, their games were battles, their heroes were conquerors.

The study of the classics took up a high proportion of the students' time. So it did at schools all over the Western world, but for an Italian child Latin literature and Roman history had a potent local significance. British schoolboys might be encouraged to cultivate the stoic virtues the Roman Republic had borrowed from Sparta, and to trace the similarities between Roman stoicism and late-Victorian stiff-upper-lippery. They might identify the British Empire with the Roman one, and, reading Macaulay's *Lays*, compare the dogged courage of his Roman heroes with that of Britain's own colonial officers. For Italian children no such imaginative effort was required. In Plutarch's *Lives*, they found the stories of Italy's own native heroes. Reading Ovid and Horace they were studying the poets whose genius constituted part of their own nation's claim to greatness. Virgil's *Aeneid* described the founding of the state which—after a hiatus lasting a dozen centuries—had newly re-emerged. Livy and Caesar told how that state had fought and conquered. Tacitus (this was especially pleasing) described how the Italians/Romans had defeated the Germanic peoples to the north, the forebears of the Austrians who had, in the boys' parents' and teachers' lifetimes, ruled most of northern Italy. Towards the end of d'Annunzio's life, Mussolini was to make a public cult of *Romanità*. To a child educated as d'Annunzio was, that cult was no artificially imposed construct, but a cluster of associations which had shaped his sense of history and his notions of virtue from the very beginnings of his intellectual life.

Glory was not confined to antiquity. For nineteenth-century Europeans the great conqueror was Napoleon. In a world where, as Thomas Carlyle lamented in 1848, great men were scarce, the memory of Napoleon's rise from modest beginnings to become a Europe-bestriding superman was inspirational. Even those for whom he had been unequivocally the enemy (Englishmen like Byron, Russians like Tolstoy) were fascinated by him. For Italians it was even possible, with a little patriotic sophistry, to claim him as one of their own. One could dwell, not on the French Bonaparte's invasion of Italy at the head of a French army, but on the Corsican Buonaparte's success (however temporary) in driving out the hated Austrians. Napoleon had called upon Italians to rise up together, to unite. He had given them their tricolour flag. True, he had pillaged their art galleries and made their principalities perks for his relatives, but Italy could console itself by claiming a part in his glory.

Francesco Paolo d'Annunzio made use of his numinous memory in his efforts to make a hero of his son. Visiting Gabriele in Prato, he brought him a coin, bearing the image of Napoleon as King of Italy, and the *Mémorial de St. Hélène* by the Comte de Las Cases. The count was one of Napoleon's aides and was with the fallen emperor on his prison-island. His eight-volume memoir was a tremendous bestseller, and the essential source book for the cult of Bonapartism. Reading it, d'Annunzio became obsessed. He established the first of his many collections, a hotch-potch of rags and horseshoe nails; he called it his "reliquary." He became a worshipper, not of God, but of "Our Lord, who was called Napoleon Bonaparte."

The teachers he found in Prato did not meet with d'Annunzio's approval. He wrote to his old Abruzzese tutor complaining that "soft, plump" priests could teach him nothing. Hard working he might be, but docile he was not. His memoirs of his schooldays describe the time he climbed out onto the roof and stayed there for a day and a night, and the food-slinging battles in the refectory, in which he was one of the warring generals. He was a rebel, in approved romantic tradition; brilliant but unruly.

He was aware, though, that he needed guidance and sponsorship. Francesco Paolo did what he could, but d'Annunzio wanted more fathers, influential older men with connections in the great world of letters, who could help him on. With breathtaking self-confidence, he set about creating for himself a kind of inverted academy, one where, instead of a sage and those eager to learn from him, there was to be just one student—himself—and an illustrious team of sages.

At the age of fifteen he was at last allowed home for the summer. Stopping over in Bologna on his way back to school he bought a copy of Carducci's *Odi Barbare* (Barbarian Odes). Giosuè Carducci was Italy's acknowledged master poet. His manner was famously brusque. His views were contrarian. Attacking Christian values in general and the Catholic Church in particular, he was the most eloquent Italian advocate for a return to the holy sensuality of paganism (a theme English aesthetes, Pater and Swinburne among them, had already explored). His most celebrated work was entitled *Hymn to Satan*. D'Annunzio, the boy who jeered at God, was immediately impressed by Carducci's work, and set himself to imitate it. A few months later he wrote to the great man, using the vocabulary not of a student but of a warrior. He felt vibrating though all his fibres "the genius of battles," inflaming him with a mania for "glory and hard blows": "I want to fight at your side, O Poet!"

Carducci does not appear to have replied to this oddly belligerent fan letter. D'Annunzio had begun by imploring him not to "consider me a presumptuous boy, as empty as the peel of a squeezed lemon" who wrote to the famous just so that he could boast of their correspondence. There would have been little reason at this point why Carducci should think him anything else. Soon though, d'Annunzio would begin to prove himself.

His first poem to appear in print was an ode written in the month he turned sixteen, and addressed to King Umberto. Francesco Paolo had it printed, and he distributed copies to the people assembled to listen to the band playing in Pescara's main piazza on the King's birthday. A few months later, Gabriele's first volume of poems, *Primo Vere*—a title punning on the words for "spring" and "first verses"—was published (again at his father's expense). D'Annunzio himself described the poems as "rosy flashes of youthful life," full of "sky-blue serenity and smoky darkness." Their subject matter was so erotic, so perverse, that the teachers at the Cicognini wondered whether they ought to ban the volume from being brought into the school, or even perhaps expel d'Annunzio, brilliant student though he was. His subject matter was disgraceful: "With trembling agitation I laid you on the water lilies and kissed you with convulsed lips, crying 'You are mine!' . . . Like a viper, you writhed and groaned." But his command of syntax was perfect, his employment of classical verse-forms correct. He was allowed to stay on.

Carducci had ignored his letter, but d'Annunzio had his calling card now. Still at school, still only sixteen, he made overtures to another distinguished stranger. Enrico Nencioni was a critic and lover of English literature. D'Annunzio wrote to him from school—"my sad prison"—enclosing *Primo Vere*. Nencioni invited the boy to visit him in Florence, a conveniently short train ride from Prato. Soon the two, despite an age gap of nearly twenty-six years, were close friends.

Nencioni was lanky and nervous. He had long hands with which he gestured expansively as he recited poetry and "something tremulous about his every attitude." D'Annunzio was to liken their relationship to that of Socrates with the beautiful Alcibiades, the lordly youth with whom the philosopher was besotted. Nencioni's influence on the young poet was immense. Much later, d'Annunzio described the day they first met as a kind of religious rite of passage, his "confirmation."

Nencioni showed him prints of pre-Raphaelite paintings by Burne-Jones and Rossetti. He advised him to read Walter Pater, an Oxford don whose *Studies in the History of the Renaissance* (first published in 1873, the year before d'Annunzio went to the Cicognini) was to provide the English aesthetes, and d'Annunzio himself, with their creed. The book combined a re-evaluation of the art-historical canon (it was Pater who promoted Botticelli to the small number of the acknowledged great) with fervent declarations of faith in the value of beauty and passion. Life is short: "A counted number of pulses are given to us of a variegated, dramatic life." Nothing—certainly not convention or received morality—should hold the aesthete back from pulsating with ardour, from burning, in Pater's most famous phrase, with a "hard gem-like flame." D'Annunzio was a receptive student. All his life he would pride himself on his wide-openness to each transient pleasure, each glimpse of loveliness.

Nencioni introduced him to the works of Thomas Carlyle, whose *On Heroes, Hero-worship and the Heroic in History* would confirm d'Annunzio's veneration for great men, and reinforce his conviction that it was not economic forces, as the socialists maintained, but the actions of superb individuals that shaped human history. Under Nencioni's tutelage he read Keats, whose voluptuous way with words he was to emulate, and, with especial enthusiasm, the two English Romantics who had spent large part of their adult lives in Italy: Shelley and Byron. There are some traces of their poetry's influence in his, but it was what he learned of their personalities and their politics which seemed most significant for him. Later in life he owned a ring which he claimed had belonged to Byron, and liked to dwell on how much he and Byron had in common: their prowess at swimming; their periods of "exile" (self-inflicted in both cases); their love of Venice; their promiscuity; their prodigious fame.

Both Shelley and Byron were aristocrats who had scandalised their compatriots, defying convention and cutting themselves off from home and family. Both were passionately political. Shelley's radical egalitarianism didn't chime with d'Annunzio's veneration for imperial glory, but his impatience with the dreariness and moral corruption of everyday life, his striving after visions of transcendental glory, excited d'Annunzio immeasurably. "He fights for light," wrote d'Annunzio, against "law, faith, tyranny, superstition." He was a demi-god, "one of the greatest poets in the world."

Byron was an even more alluring model. He was remembered as the sexually irresistible libertine, an aspect of his fame intensely interesting to the teenage d'Annunzio. He was also a poet whose work had brought him large sums of money and—even more enticingly—the kind of celebrity previously only enjoyed by victorious warriors or heads of state. He was politically active. In the early 1820s, living in Venice, Byron had contacts with the Carbonari (the "charcoal burners"), the Italian nationalists whose outlawed revolutionary organisation was a precursor of the movement that, a quarter of a century later, would become the Italian Risorgimento. He had called the vision of a free and united Italy the "very *poetry* of politics." Thrillingly for d'Annunzio, his example suggested that a poet could also be a hero, that poetry and politics could merge, and lead on to glory.

Still busily promoting himself and his work, d'Annunzio obtained some kind of introduction to Cesare Fontana, a rich Milanese, a connoisseur of the arts and a prodigal spender of his own considerable fortune. D'Annunzio sent him a "psychological sketch" of himself.

He pulsates, he writes, with "the first fires of approaching young manhood." He has "an inordinate desire for knowledge and for glory, which burdens me often with a dark, tormenting melancholy." He cannot tolerate any "yoke." He despises "meanness of spirit." He is "an ardent lover of new Art and lovely women: most unusual in my tastes: most tenacious in my opinions: outspoken to the point of harshness: prodigal to the point of ruin: enthusiastic to the point of madness . . . What else? Ah! There's something I forgot: I'm a wicked poet and an intrepid chaser of dreams." Apparently so artless, with its disdain for punctuation and exclamation marks, this letter is a deft piece of self-advertisement. In it d'Annunzio fits himself to the model of the romantic hero. He lays claim to sophisticated vices (those beautiful women, those wicked poems). He slips in a gentle reminder of how very young he still is. Several times over the next two years he asked Fontana to put in a word for him with editors in Milan.

Further copies of *Primo Vere* were sent out. One went to the influential critic Guiseppe Chiarini. In approaching him, d'Annunzio wrote, he felt as bashful as a loutish peasant who, on being introduced to a distinguished person, turns red as a boiled prawn and twists his hat in his hands unable to say a single sensible thing. Having summoned up this image of sweet diffidence, the shameless self-publicist proceeded to make such a good impression on the older man that the two were soon corresponding genially about their shared love of Heine and Horace. D'Annunzio had found himself yet another first-rate master (he addresses subsequent letters to Chiarini: *"Mio carissimo Signor Professore"*) and he had also got himself some invaluable press coverage. In May 1880, Chiarini reviewed *Primo Vere* in the widely read Roman journal, the *Fanfulla della Domenica*. He hailed the now just seventeen-year-old d'Annunzio as "a new poet" with an "uncommon aptitude." Within days d'Annunzio had sent him his next volume, along with a letter asking the question that was always on his mind. If he is going to be "charming," "pleasing" and no more, he'll give up writing straight away. He can't stand "little artists . . . little poets." He'd much rather be an engineer, or a lawyer. He'd even rather be a small-town mayor (like his father). So the important question was: "Can I cover myself with glory?"

Within a year of his first book's appearance, d'Annunzio, whose collected works were eventually to run to forty-eight volumes, had brought out two more. *In Memoriam*, dedicated to his grandmother, who had recently died, was published in May 1880, followed in November by a second edition of *Primo Vere* with forty-three new poems (throughout his career d'Annunzio was to repeatedly revise, re-package and resell his work). In each case Francesco Paolo paid the printer's bills, but d'Annunzio himself was personally responsible for the books' design. He was already knowledgeable about book production and literary business. Writing from his school desk to the printer, he fussed over paper quality and font sizes. He argued vigorously over the printer's terms and negotiated a distribution deal with a local bookseller. As for the books' promotion, father and son each did their part of the work. To celebrate the appearance of *Primo Vere* (second edition), Francesco Paolo gave a banquet on the terrace of the Villa Fuoco. Gabriele found a more ingenious way of attracting attention to the work.

Reading the English Romantics, he had reflected on the ways Keats's and Shelley's early deaths had left their names enveloped in a glimmering haze of pathos. It was a few days before *Primo Vere*'s second publication that the editor of the Florentine *Gazzetta della Domenica* received a postcard from Pescara, from an unknown informant (d'Annunzio himself), advising him that the "young poet already noted in the republic of letters" had died suddenly after falling from his horse. The editor ran the story prominently. The news was picked up by papers all over Italy. In Turin the tragic death of the "last-born of the Muses" was lamented. In Ferrara tribute was paid to the marvellous boy who was "the joy of his parents, the love of his friends, the pride of his masters." The schoolboy poet had ceased to be someone spoken of only in the "republic of letters." He had become a celebrity. He might not yet have achieved glory, but he had attained fame.

Liebestod

A DAY OF TUSCAN SPRING SUNSHINE, a stream running between banks
starred with flowers; nearby the cupola of a church glinting, tall
cypresses rising above the walls of an ancient villa; in the background
blue hills. Along the path comes a dark maiden: black eyes, black hair,
black eyebrows, pale, pale face. A young man walks towards her. Days
later he writes to tell her that he is hers forever.

It could be a tableau painted by Dante Gabriel Rosetti or Burne-
Jones, prints of whose work Gabriele had seen in Nencioni's rooms. It
could be a scene from Tennyson's *Idylls of the King*, or from Swinburne's
Laus Veneris (In Praise of Venus). Gabriele had been reading both poets.
It was in fact the meeting of two flesh-and-blood teenagers as described
by one of them: d'Annunzio, in Florence for the Easter vacation before
his last term at school, falling precipitately in love with the seventeen-
year-old daughter of his favourite teacher.

It wasn't his first erotic experience, but it was the first of his romances.
In d'Annunzio's case the ambiguous word is the right one. All of his love
affairs were at once real relationships—carnal and ardent—and literary
creations. *Vivere scrivere* was one of his mottoes—"To live to write."
Sexual experience especially fuelled his creative energy. Looking back
years later on his first kiss, he wrote that it was "the very moment when
my life began to be my art and my art began to be my life." In love, he
reached for his pen.

The black-eyed girl by the stream was Giselda Zucconi. Dark-
haired and heavy-jawed (like Gabriele's mother, like several more of
the women he would love), she was unusually well-educated for a girl,
and a competent pianist. Her father, Tito Zucconi, taught modern languages at the Cicognini, and had become yet another of d'Annunzio's
mentors. Zucconi was a dashing figure, a teacher very different from

the "greasy-handed priests" about whom d'Annunzio wrote so contemptuously. He had fought alongside Garibaldi: he was himself a poet.
He befriended the brilliant student, took him for long walks on days off
and invited him to visit his family in Florence.

D'Annunzio, looking back regretfully in middle age, describes himself as he looked then: "the brow smooth beneath the dense mass of
dark hair. The eyebrows drawn in such a pure line as to give something
indefinably virginal to the melancholy of the big eyes. The beautiful
half-open mouth." Self-regarding as it is, the description matches the
photographs. Giselda was entranced. D'Annunzio had begun writing

short stories set in the Abruzzi, heavily influenced by Guy de Maupassant and Giovanni Verga. On his second visit to the house he read Giselda one of them, a morbid tale involving a dumb beggar and the frozen corpse of a little girl. When he first encountered Giselda walking by the stream he had felt "an I-don't-know-what." When he saw her eyelashes wet with tears as she listened to his story he decided it was love.

He returned to school. Back in Prato he confessed his love to Tito, who gave him permission to write to Giselda. Within days she had told him she loved him in return. In the school dormitory d'Annunzio stayed awake until dawn, kissing her photograph and writing her long letters. Sometime he expressed himself as any teenager might: "I am happy, happy, happy." Or, "I love you, I love you, I love you." Sometimes his letters show how unusual he was. "Kiss me Elda, kiss me. Thrust your little hands into my hair and hold me nailed down and quivering like a leopard enchained."

D'Annunzio's erotic career began early. As the smartly uniformed boys of the Cicognini marched around Prato he was much inclined, so one of his teachers noted, to turn and stare at passing young women. Spending his school holidays with family friends in Florence, he escorted the daughter of the house (aged seventeen to his fourteen) to the Museum of Archaeology and kissed her in the Etruscan Room, falling on her mouth (as he recalled years later) as ravenously as a famished labourer might fall on food at the end of a day's hard work and thinking—with a kind of delirious horror—about the other secret "mouth" beneath her skirts. On a school trip he slipped away from his teacher, and sold his grandfather's gold watch to pay for his initiation by a prostitute. That summer, sixteen years old and allowed home at last, he flirted with several young ladies in Pescara's polite small-town society, and—according to his own later account—raped a peasant girl who struggled and babbled and shook with terror as he hunted her down in a vineyard and knocked her to the ground.

By the time he met Giselda two years later his craving for sex had become entangled with an appetite for suffering and with fantasies of death. It was the sight of Giselda's tears that had first fired him with love. "I want to make those tears fall again," he wrote to her. He imagined she would be sobbing, frantic for a word from him. He luxuriated in the idea of her unhappiness. He even told her how much he would like to see her corpse. He loved it that she was deathly pale, like "the Blessed Damozel," the dead girl of Rossetti's famous poem and painting, but he would have preferred her even paler. He told her that he would go around all the florists in the city, fill a carriage with assorted flowers, and come to bury her beneath them. "Yes! To bury you! I want to make you die!"

He wrote to Tito Zucconi, not, as one might expect, promising to cherish and protect Tito's daughter, but announcing: "I and Elda cannot live long." Both he and Giselda were, so far as we know, in perfectly good health, yet d'Annunzio wrote: "Our cold bodies will fall to the earth to feed the flowers; and we will be swept away, unconscious atoms, in the irresistible currents of the universal force." D'Annunzio had not yet heard Wagner's *Tristan and Isolde* (on which his novel *The Triumph of Death* would be a variation) but the fantasy of *Liebestod* already possessed him. "If you were here now," he wrote to Giselda, "we would kill each other . . . Don't you feel all the tragic terror of this passion?"

Letters began to pass between the young couple almost daily. She sent him her photograph and pressed flowers (her father acting as emissary). He sent her words, thousands upon thousands of them (around 500 letters in under two years). This was a love affair all made of words on paper. D'Annunzio wrote proudly to Chiarini, only six days after he had met Giselda, that he had found his "Beatrice." So d'Annunzio was the new Dante and poor Giselda had been assigned the role of the girl whom Dante (if his poeticised account of their meetings is to be taken literally) laid eyes on only twice, who inspired his poetry and personified his ideal, but in whose actual life he played no part at all.

D'Annunzio set about remaking Giselda as an accessory suited to his own self-image. He deplored the conventional pose ("so, so common") of the photograph she had given him. He wanted her to look like a "proud and pensive queen, on the arm of her poet." He renamed her (he would give all his lovers new names). "I want to call you Elda," he wrote. The name was more caressing than the full-length Giselda, more fitting for the child he wanted her to be. "You're not a great big woman," he wrote. (He was to address many of his lovers, even when they towered over him, as "Little One"). He called her *"bimba"* (baby), and imagined nursery scenarios, in which she played a petulant child.

"It'll do you no good to stamp your little feet on the ground . . . Come Elda . . . Baby, little pretty pretty pretty one. Forgive me? . . . You're laughing, aren't you?" But if he liked to infantilise and dominate her, he also liked to be dominated. He told her that she was "bad," "wicked." He instructed her to wear black. "I detest, detest, detest pale colours on a woman." It would set off the pallor of her skin and it was appropriate to the other role he had assigned her, that of a "witch," like Keats's "La Belle Dame sans Merci" or Tennyson's Morgan le Fay.

Term ended, the young lovers could at last meet for the first time since they had declared themselves. "What happy hours we had yesterday!" d'Annunzio wrote to Giselda the next day. "Do you know that for twelve hours we were always in each other arms, always kissing with those long long kisses which made us tremble in every limb, always whispering those soft words?" Of course she knew, but for d'Annunzio an experience was insubstantial until he had written it down. During the eleven days he stayed in Florence he wrote several of the lyrics which would appear the following year in his next collection, *Canto Novo*, with its dedication to Elda, "the great the beautiful the most adored inspiration." By the time he left for Pescara he considered himself engaged to her. Tito, who knew that his daughter had caught the eye of an exceptionally talented boy, made no objection. D'Annunzio confidently told both father and daughter that his own parents doted on him. They would agree to anything that would make him happy. And so off he went to Pescara.

In his first novel, *Pleasure*, d'Annunzio describes his hero, Andrea Sperelli, anguished by his bewitching mistress's sudden and inexplicable announcement that she is leaving him. She stops her carriage. He descends. He is in despair. "What did he do, once Elena's carriage had disappeared in the direction of the Four Fountains?—Nothing, to be honest, out of the ordinary." Sperelli goes home, changes into evening dress and goes to a dinner party, not apparently to give Elena much thought until they meet again by chance two years later. Sperelli is by no means a faithful self-portrait of his creator (he is very much richer and more aristocratic), but author and fictional character have a great deal in common, and this trait is one they share. There is no reason to suppose that d'Annunzio was cynical in his treatment of Elda. He was, for a while, in love with her. He probably really thought of marrying her. And yet, once he had left Florence, he doesn't seem to have missed her very much.

Life was sweet for d'Annunzio that summer. Eighteen years old, finished with school at last, he was poised to enter the adult world where his reputation, going before him, would guarantee him a welcome. Returning to places he loved and a growing circle of entertaining friends, he enjoyed a long, delicious and productive summer by the sea. His family were gratifyingly proud of him. Francesco Paolo had had the titles of the poems in *Primo Vere* written into the frescoes on the drawing-room walls. He was working fast, writing the stories of peasant life that would be published the following year in *Terra Virgine*, and more poems for *Canto Novo*. He was also enjoying himself. He rode, he swam, he went boating by moonlight.

His letters to Elda are full of tactless hints of how full and merry his life was without her. People burst in on him while he's writing to her. "Curses! There is an absolute eruption of friends in the room . . . Forgive me if I leave off . . . They've taken all the foils and sabres out the rack and they're making the most awful din." (Then and later, d'Annunzio loved to fence.) He was doted on and fussed over. Preparing for a trip, he reported that his mother, his three sisters and his two aunts were all in the room helping him to get ready. When he wanted other female company the resort town of Castellamare, just the other side of the Pescara river, provided—by his own account of the following year—plenty of diversions. There were bathers on the long sandy beach, and on the promenade "what vaporous floating of veils around women's heads! What feline flexibility of bodies confined by the arabesques or flower patterns of an outfit *à la Pompadour*! . . . What flurries of young laughter ringing out from beneath big hats laden with flowers!" The Abruzzese journalist Carlo Magnico would describe d'Annunzio bobbing around a group of such young women "cocky as a wagtail." As dapper as a glossy little bird, preening under the attention afforded a local hero, full of energy and self-love, he enjoyed himself while Elda pined.

He had been wrong, as it turned out, to assure her that his parents would consent to their engagement. His father, especially, was far too proud of him to welcome the idea of his committing himself so young to marrying a mere schoolmaster's daughter. Somehow it was settled that, rather than enrolling at the University of Florence, where he could have continued his studies while seeing Elda as often as the two of them pleased, he would go instead to Rome. How far Gabriele resisted the decision is unrecorded. Rome, the capital, was surely the place for an ambitious young man, and d'Annunzio was very ambitious indeed. Besides, his need to be with Elda does not appear to have been all that urgent.

He wrote to her daily; he composed poems celebrating her bewitching beauty. But when she suggested that he could perhaps make a *scappata*, a "jaunt," to Florence to see her, he treated the idea as absurd. She has no idea of distances, he wrote. "You really think Pescara to Florence is a 'jaunt'?" Perhaps, he adds, he'll stop off on his way home from visiting the Exhibition of Fine Arts in Milan. (He didn't do so.) Elda might well ask why, if he was able to go to Milan, he should find it impossible to reach Florence, which was so much nearer. "If I can't kiss you again I'll die," he wrote, but still he allowed time to slip by without doing so. "Just think," he wrote, on the eve of his departure for Rome in November, "it is five months, five long, long months, since we saw each other"—a fact for which he had no one to blame but himself.

Finally, at Christmas, half a year after their last meeting, he took the train from Rome to Florence to see her again, and stayed until Twelfth Night. By the time he left Elda's mouth was sore and swollen from all their "savage kisses." There followed another six months, during which he assured her almost daily by post that he "was all yours, all yours, all yours for ever." Giselda wrote again and again imploring him to come to her; but always there was some excuse. He had deadlines to meet; he had to sign the university register on a regular basis in order to avoid being called up for national service; his parents were coming to visit. On 15 April, the anniversary of their first meeting, he wrote lamenting his inability to be with her and elaborating a happy vision of their future domestic life. He will have a lovely bright study, he writes, full of pictures and antique weapons and rare fabrics, "and I will break off in the middle of a hexameter to come and give you a kiss on the mouth." It is noticeable that he seems to have put more creative energy into picturing the room than into imagining her. It is so hard, he says, that he cannot run to her. He seems to hear her crying out to him. And yet, he says, he cannot possibly visit her. He doesn't explain why not.

Two weeks after writing that letter he went to Rome's railway station with two friends who were on their way to Sardinia. He intended only to see the others off, and then on an impulse, he went along too, declaring he couldn't pass up the opportunity of seeing the full moon rising over the sea. He was wearing a white rose in his buttonhole and carrying nothing but a cane with a lotus-flower handle. (For aesthetes of his generation, the lotus, the "sceptre of Isis," was both a phallic symbol and a kind of shorthand for all things Orientalist and exotic.)

The trip was hilarious, its planning shambolic. On the train the young men fell in with some aristocratic acquaintances in hunting gear, who were going out to the marshes to shoot quail. Much jovial talk, then, once the huntsmen had got out, the remaining three lay full-length along the seats, dangling their feet out of the window. At Civita-vecchia, where they were to embark, d'Annunzio dithered. First he said that he wasn't going any further, then he said he'd come but wandered off and ordered a vermouth in a bar, thereby nearly missing the boat. That night, at sea, he began by strolling on deck, jotting down notes for an ode on the moonlight. The weather changed. A wind got up and he abruptly turned first yellow, then green and went below, where he spent a miserable night retching and shivering in his linen suit.

The trip to Sardinia began as a boyish lark, but developed into a mind-altering experience. The friends visited the mines at Masua, and d'Annunzio wrote a powerful account of the hellish conditions in which the miners lived and worked. They went down into the lightless, foul-smelling tunnel, where "the hot viscid mass of vapour embraced us; we felt it on our faces like a soft, wet tongue; it seemed as though two hands drenched in sweat were wringing our hands." He wrote to tell Giselda about it, but she—poor girl—was struck only by the fact that he had been free to leave Rome at a moment's notice for a three-week trip, while declaring himself unable to spare even a day or two to be with her. The following month he was with her in Florence for ten days before going onto Pescara for the remains of the summer. There he named a rowing-boat *Lalla*, but the frequency of his letters to the real Giselda dwindled. In February 1883, he wrote to her for the last time.

D'Annunzio was rapidly to acquire the reputation of a Don Giovanni who seduced and deserted his women without a qualm. In fact he always found it immensely hard to take his leave. It was partly that he was chronically indecisive: his havering on the quay at Civitavecchia is characteristic of the man. And it was partly that he could say neither "no" nor "goodbye" to anyone. He never turned down commissions. He would agree to anything, and then default on his promise. Years later, when he was a great man plagued by fans or presumptuous ex-friends, he was incapable of bringing tedious conversations to a close. Instead he would mutter something enigmatic and leave the room. His visitors would wait, expecting him to return at any moment, but they would wait in vain. He found it dreadfully hard to dismiss a servant. When he was living on the French coast he once went to Paris (a day-long train journey) to avoid being present when his major-domo, on his orders, sacked his groom. Rather than give a straight "no" to unwelcome invitations he would invent preposterous excuses: he once got his chauffeur to telephone his host for a lunch with the information he had gone up in a balloon and might not be coming down to earth for some time.

There is a further reason why his love affairs had such protracted endings. The more unhappy a woman was, the more interesting to him she became. The more he tantalised Elda with promised visits which were repeatedly deferred, the more adorable her image seemed to him. "You must be sad, immensely sad, my poor angel!" he wrote. "You will be thinking of me with desperate desire." The idea of her disappointment—denied his "savage kisses"—was one he liked to dwell on. Seeing her so seldom, he was really in no position to report on how pale and wan Elda really was, but he addressed her in a rapture of sadistic pity as: "My pallid Ophelia, my poor betrayed virgin." That he himself was the betrayer he seldom directly acknowledged. Instead he responded to her reproaches by becoming, or so he tells it, frenzied with grief.

The d'Annunzio who wrote the letters was as much a fictional construct as the girl to whom they were addressed. The Sardinian escapade ended with a scene that might have been lifted from Mozart's *Don Giovanni*. D'Annunzio and his two friends, who had been overly familiar with the local women, were chased down to the ferry by a crowd of hostile male Sardinians. A comical (though probably frightening) episode, it gives us a glimpse of the real-life "wagtail" d'Annunzio—a very young man strutting and flirting on a trip out of town. One of his companions on the voyage wrote: "He would be off and then, before he'd even been missed, he'd be back like a cat with a mouse in his jaws"—the "mouse" being a young woman.

Writing to Elda he was a very different person, palpitating with love and anxiety, frequently suicidal. "I am surrounded by a terrifying abyss," he wrote after she had threatened to break off their relationship. "I am alone on a pinnacle of rock. I see no light, I have no hope, you have taken everything from me." His very last letter must have been bewildering for her to read. "We love each other always," he writes, but then, "the memories disperse inexorably like empty dreams." He dwells with repellent arrogance on the unhappiness he's caused her. The letter ends in a cruel sequence of contradictions. *"Addio,"* he writes repeatedly. He is sad, he says. To write more will only make her sad as well. *"Addio"* again, but then "I kiss your mouth with a desire beyond words." More maddening pity—"Oh my poor martyr!" Again *"Addio, addio."* And then finally, the by-now-evident-untruth twice affirmed: "Yours, always yours." He was just about to turn twenty. Four months later he was married, and not to Elda.

In 1921, after a silence of thirty-eight years, Giselda wrote to d'Annunzio asking for his permission to sell his letters. She hoped that they would fetch enough money to allow her son to marry. She was unusual among d'Annunzio's women in having kept them so long. At the end of each of his subsequent love affairs he wrote his once-beloved woman a letter full of mellifluous expressions of regret for the fading of a great passion, but ending with a brusque request for the return of his letters. He replied to Giselda by suggesting she hand the letters over to his lawyer. He did not invite her to visit him.

Homeland

THE BOISTEROUS GROUP who burst into Gabriele's room, making a distracting racket with the fencing foils, were not his only companions in the Abruzzi. A few miles south of Pescara, in Francavilla, lived the painter Francesco Paolo Michetti, who was to become the most loyal and generous of all d'Annunzio's friends. Michetti was eighteen years older than Gabriele, old enough to become one of his extra fathers, and a successful artist. During the summers he was joined in Francavilla by a creative group of comrades who called themselves— with playfully blasphemous arrogance—the *"Cenacolo"* (the word translates as dining club, or dining room, but in Italian it is most frequently used of the Symposium over which Socrates presided, or of Christ's Last Supper). The most constant guests were Francesco Paolo Tosti, the composer who would later set many of d'Annunzio's verses to music, and the sculptor Constantino Barbella.

By the summer of 1880, when Gabriele was seventeen, with another year of school ahead of him, he was already an established member of the *Cenacolo*, riding over from Pescara or moving in to stay, initially in Michetti's small house by the sea and later in the rambling deconsecrated convent which Michetti transformed into his studio and home. "Oh beautiful days of Francavilla!" he wrote later, recalling the "solitary beachside house," through all of whose rooms blew the salty sea wind: "There life bloomed." He was, by more than a decade, the youngest of the group, several of whom were men with well-established reputations. If Nencioni and his other invited mentors had been the tutors who saw him through his secondary education, the *Cenacolo* was his university. He and Michetti talked and talked, "seven hours on end," he told Elda, "and always about Art, always about Art."

It was not, primarily, a literary group. Among Michetti's friends, poets were outnumbered by artists, musicians, scholars. One of d'Annunzio's great strengths as a writer and as a cultural commentator was that he was as knowledgeable about music and the visual arts as he was about literature, and valued them as highly. He was always intensely observant of visual effects. He was an exhaustive sightseer. His plan to visit the exhibition of contemporary art in Milan was not just a ploy to put Elda off. He was really excited by the prospect. Artworks perform important functions in his novels and plays, as symbols, as points of reference, as inspiration, as aphrodisiacs. One of his heroes models himself on a portrait by Leonardo. Another propositions a woman by telling her that he can see from her hands that her naked body would be as lovely as that of Correggio's *Danae*. His poetry is full of colour. He frequently dresses his novels' heroines in grey, but not just any old grey. He specifies each shade: the grey of ashes, of pigeon feathers, of pewter or a pale sky. At Francavilla he was learning to see through his painter-friend's eyes. His early stories are full of brilliant unexpected colour: scarlet poppies luminous against a bleached background of dry rock, sky the colour of beryl or turquoise, purple mountains, a beggar's crimson jacket, a river bright green with reflected trees and—over and over again—the almost fluorescent brilliance of orange and tawny-brown sails on a silver or lead-grey sea. These were the scenes Michetti painted. D'Annunzio's task was to convert his images into words.

His ear was as discriminating as his eye. His most anthologised poem, *La Pioggia nel Pineto* (Rain in the Pine Wood), is a piece of beautifully modulated word-music which at once describes and imitates the sounds made by rain falling on leaves. He boasted that he once astounded the conductor Toscanini by detecting which instrument in an orchestra was out of tune. Throughout his life music was one of his greatest pleasures. "No one," wrote Romain Rolland, "could *hear* music better than he."

At Francavilla he could talk about composition with composers, and observe how a sculptor and a painter gave form to their visions. There he would write, so he tells us, in rooms papered with his host's sketches, with the sculptor Barbella modelling a bust beside him, with another comrade playing Schubert on a mandolin, and Tosti singing the refrain of a lullaby. "[Michetti's] villa is truly the Temple of Art and we are its priests."

It was in that temple that d'Annunzio began to see his native region as a fit subject for literary treatment. With Michetti he embarked on long rides into the region's mountainous hinterland. These outings took him into a world at once archaic and exotic. The rural people were "almost dwarfs, with snub noses and flattened lips," but dressed with a kind of "oriental" splendour. D'Annunzio described a wedding party as a riot of "silk dresses, brocade scarves, big gold earrings; toasts accompanied by the delirious-making hum of guitars . . . gunshots . . . hailstorm of confetti . . . joyful cries."

The members of the *Cenacolo* all shared an interest in the traditional culture of the Abruzzi. Tosti was collecting folk songs. Michetti's friends also included Gennaro Finamore, author of a vocabulary of the Abruzzese dialect and a transcriber of folk tales, and the ethnologist Antonio de Nino, whose *Abruzzese Customs and Costumes* ran to six volumes. The poet Bruni wrote verse in the Abruzzese dialect, which Tosti set to music for a "chorus of youths" to sing during an al fresco ceremony on Easter Monday. The subject of all Michetti's art, wrote d'Annunzio later, was the "ancient vital race of the Abruzzi, so vigorous, so thoughtful, so full of song."

For over a century European intellectuals had been searching in isolated rural communities for remnants of obsolete folk cultures. Ethnography was practised most enthusiastically in situations where nationalism needed to assert itself against an alien regime. James Macpherson, "discovering" ancient Gaelic poems (most of them, published under the name of Ossian, his own forgeries) and his admirer and successor Sir Walter Scott, collecting songs and tales in the Scottish Highlands, were intent on demonstrating that Scotland had as rich a cultural heritage as England, its politically dominant neighbour to the south. While Jacob and Wilhelm Grimm were growing up, the majority of German states were under Napoleonic rule. Their collecting of fairy tales "found among the common German peasantry" was not just conservationist, it was "imaginative state-building." The Gaelic League, set up in Ireland in 1893 for the preservation and promotion of Gaelic language and literature, aimed to provide inspiration for an independent Irish state.

So Michetti, touring the Abruzzi in search of picturesque peasant girls in embroidered bodices and home-spun red skirts, and Tosti, with his transcriptions of the songs sung by harvesters in the fields, were providing the cultural underpinnings for the new Italian nation. But

it was not easy, as many patriotic ethnographers discovered, to identify authentic relics of indigenous culture. Several of the stories the
Grimms collected to provide the new Germany with an unadulterated
German back-story were in fact imported by French Huguenots. So
d'Annunzio's Italian friends were swayed by non-Italian influences.
Their subject matter was local, but their interest in it was aroused by
foreign examples. Michetti's paintings owe much to the French realists: Corot, Courbet and Millet. Even the name of their fellowship was
a borrowing. Over half a century earlier, in Paris, Victor Hugo had
presided over a *"Cénacle."*

At Francavilla, d'Annunzio swam: he was an exceptionally strong
swimmer. "We bathed down there, like savages on the bare beach."
He galloped his horse along the sand and rowed his little boat offshore. He and his friends cooked for each other, as inexpertly as young
men accustomed to being waited on by servants or mothers have

always cooked; he was to remember with pride a gigantic omelette he managed. Michetti posed his guests for photographs on the beach: d'Annunzio looks as faunlike as he liked to imagine himself—curly hair falling forward, a slight body taut with energy. There are women in some of the pictures, incongruously overdressed by contrast with the men, in long-sleeved gowns and big hats. This was not the monastic retreat d'Annunzio suggested in writing to Elda.

In the evenings there was wine, although d'Annunzio—then and for the rest of his life—was an abstemious drinker. There was opium, which he took to with gusto ("in no time I became a passionate opium eater"). Aware that he was being "stunned" by the drug, he soon left off taking it ("but what beautiful moments I had!"). At night, sitting out among olive trees whose branches had been turned silver by the full moon (an effect d'Annunzio would use repeatedly in his fiction), they sang the choruses and lullabies that Tosti had been collecting and weaving into his newly composed "serenades." Sometimes they would hear those eerie, repetitive melodies echoed back to them by unseen workers in the countryside around.

During the summer of 1880, Michetti and d'Annunzio made two excursions which were to be particularly fruitful for both of them. One took them to the village of Tocco di Casauria at harvest time. There they witnessed a scene involving a handsome young woman and some drunken harvesters. Michetti began that winter to make studies for one of his most celebrated paintings, *La Figlia di Jorio* (Jorio's Daughter), which was finally exhibited at the first Venice Biennale fourteen years later. It shows a peasant girl, in a scarlet dress and shawl, hurrying past a group of leering men. D'Annunzio was to make something much more violent of the subject. He described the event in an interview: "Suddenly there burst into the little square a beautiful young woman, crying and dishevelled, followed by a throng of harvesters, brutalised by the sun, by wine and lust." From that one tableau he would devise a story of sexual transgression and mob violence which, nearly a quarter of a century later, became his most successful play, also called *Jorio's Daughter*.

The other memorable outing was their visit, on a suffocatingly hot summer's day, to the church of San Pantaleone at Miglianico. The church was crammed with pilgrims who had come to celebrate the saint's feast day, to expiate sins and pray for miracles. Michetti depicted the scene in his painting *The Vow*, which was exhibited in Rome in 1883 to great acclaim. He makes a grand spectacle of the gorgeous colours of the girls' embroidered costumes, the slanting light from the church's high windows and the tragic drama of the dying come to beg for grace.

To d'Annunzio, though, the scene in the church was a horror show. In his account an animal stench rises from the bodies crammed together in the dimly lit church. At the centre of the crowd a kind of furrow is left open, a narrow passage walled with humanity, along which crawl devotees. "Three, four, five lunatics came writhing with their bellies on the ground, with their tongues on the dust of the tiles, with their feet rigidly flexed to support the weight of their bodies. Reptiles." There is blood on their feet and hands. They are licking the floor before them as they inch forward, drawing crosses with their own saliva. "The red stains that one fanatic has left, are rubbed by the dry tongue of the next fanatic." The crawlers, one by one, approach the silver effigy of the saint, each one grasping him around the neck "with a supreme effort which seemed akin to hatred" and each fix a bleeding mouth to the saint's metal mouth and hang there, "with a kind of convulsion of pleasure." The watchers moan.

D'Annunzio was to return to the scene again and again. His fullest description of what he had seen at Miglianico would not be published for another fifteen years, forming part of *The Triumph of Death*, but in his early stories he repeatedly plays variations on the themes of religious solace, religious frenzy and the power of the mob.

During his last winter at school, d'Annunzio wrote several of the short stories which would be published in his first prose collection, *Terra Virgine*. Probably prompted by Tito Zucconi, he was reading Zola (in particular *The Sin of Father Mouret*), Victor Hugo's *Hunchback of Notre Dame*, and Giovanni Verga's newly published *Life in the Fields*. Soon, he discovered de Maupassant and Flaubert. Each new addition to his reading list can be detected in his own writing. He lifts a great deal from his foreign examples. He repeats phrases and reproduces syntactical construction. His plots are borrowed (one of his tragic-comic lovers is a bell ringer who pines away for love of a gypsy girl). His structures are ready made (*The Virgin Anna* follows the progression of Flaubert's *Un Cœur simple* movement by movement). More importantly, the other writers' realism had shown d'Annunzio that he could make use of the material he had found in his native province.

D'Annunzio was not a sentimentalist like Victor Hugo, nor a campaigner for social justice like Zola. When he describes the stultifying hardness of the lives of peasants or labourers, he does so not with compassion but with something closer to disgust. His stories of the Abruzzi are full of stupid violence. A beggar exhibiting his crippled child, a fisherman's love perverted by jealousy, a pathetic idiot who takes pleasure in killing lizards very, very slowly. D'Annunzio took these examples of human degradation and embroidered around each of them a piece of carefully wrought prose. Michetti and his friends had taught him to pay attention to the culture of his homeland, with its rich heritage of ritual and belief. They had not persuaded him to like it. He has one of his fictional alter egos reflect that to discover that the countryside, whose beauty he loves, is home to so much primitive fear and credulity, is like running one's fingers through a woman's scented hair only to find, hidden beneath, "a teeming mass of lice."

D'Annunzio's sense of homeland would become an important theme in his politics and his self-presentation—"I carry the soil of the Abruzzi on the soles of my feet," he wrote—but he certainly didn't want to live there. In 1914 the Pescaran authorities offered to give him a house in recognition of his status as the region's great man. He declined. He was by then bankrupt in Italy and amassing enormous debts in France too, but for him the Abruzzi was a philistine back-water and Pescara a place redolent of old age and gross, squalid sins. Despite professing the greatest affection for what he called "*my* Abruzzi," he much preferred swindling hoteliers or sponging off his admirers to being confined to his homeland.

Youth

S ING THE IMMENSE JOY . . . of being young," wrote the eighteen-year-old d'Annunzio. "Of biting the fruits of the earth/With sound, white voracious teeth." The clandestine nationalist movement which Giuseppe Mazzini had founded in the 1830s, and which eventually drove the Risorgimento, was called Young Italy, signalling that the new nation was to be, not an amalgam of the decrepit statelets it united, but a vigorous new entity. D'Annunzio would employ the same rhetoric once he began his political career, but he also prized youth for its own sake. And when he first arrived in Rome he could exult in being the youngest of his circle of friends and patrons.

That circle was ready. The night before he set out for Rome in November 1881, he wrote to Elda, pretending to complain about his precocious celebrity. "So, so many friends are waiting for me there, so many admirers. It'll be a fearful bore for the first few days!"

He was registered at the university's Faculty of Literature, he may even have attended a few lectures. But most of his energies were directed elsewhere. While he was still at school his first published stories had appeared in the *Fanfulla della Domenica*, whose editorial board included his mentor Nenciono and in whose pages Chiarini's generous review of *Primo Vere* had been published. Another useful contact was a fellow Abruzzese, Edoardo Scarfoglio, poet and editor of the weekly paper *Capitan Fracassa*—irreverent, satirical, written by and aimed at the young. It was Scarfoglio who, yawning at his desk one day, had been so electrified by d'Annunzio's first appearance in his office, and it was Scarfoglio with whom, the following summer, d'Annunzio would take off for Sardinia. With his already published volumes as calling-cards, d'Annunzio was soon a prolific freelance writer, selling poems, stories and occasional pieces to the journals springing up to feed the new market of educated middle-class readers.

Scarfoglio saw him as something from the pages of Chateaubriand or Victor Hugo, "the incarnation of the romantic ideal of the poet." Another of his new acquaintances described his "chestnut locks, slick and scented with unguents" (all his life he tended his body as carefully as any courtesan), and his "forehead as smooth and white as that of a small angel in a Church procession." Before long he met Angelo Sommaruga, a risk-taking young impresario (who would soon be facing criminal charges for bribery and extortion). Sommaruga prided himself on his readiness to take on potentially scandalous new work. Soon he had d'Annunzio contributing to his magazine, and had undertaken to publish the young author's next volume of verse, and his first collection of stories.

It was only just over a decade since the Pope had ceded his temporal power to Italy, and the Italian government, formerly based in Turin, had moved to Rome. For centuries the city had been a beautiful backwater. By 1881 it was an enormous building site. Olive groves and cow pastures and aristocratic gardens which had survived within the ancient walls for a millennium were being built over to accommodate the hordes of politicians and courtiers and civil servants and journalists and entrepreneurs who had descended on the newly booming city.

D'Annunzio lodged initially in an attic room in the heart of the city, between the Corso and the Piazza di Spagna. Close by was a brothel. When he returned home at night he would find its clients leaning against his front door or attempting to kick it in. Physically energetic, he went to the fencing schools in the mornings, and rode out into the countryside in the afternoons. He enjoyed his new friends. The *Capitan Fracassa*'s editorial office, facetiously nicknamed the "yellow drawing room," was a single room above a beer shop, whose two windows gave onto a narrow alley. Its yellow wallpaper was covered with sketches and slogans left by the writers, artists, actors and politicians who came there to deliver their contributions and to pick up gossip. It was always buzzing with conversation, and when more space was needed the regulars would move on to the pastry shop nearby, where they had euphoric dawn breakfasts after the journal had been put to bed each week. Sommaruga's *Cronaca Bizantina* had grander premises in the Palazzo Ruspoli and a more louche atmosphere. D'Annunzio described himself taking the stairs one morning "with great leaps," hopeful of finding there "a magnificent, unlettered lady" for whose favours he and some of his fellow writers were competing.

Michetti provided introductions. There were convivial evenings in the Caffè Roma or the elegant eighteenth-century Caffè Greco. The latter was a favourite meeting place for painters, several of whom would become d'Annunzio's friends and the illustrators of his books. There were evenings with Paolo Tosti "in a mysterious apartment full of dark corridors." Tosti would improvise at the piano for hours on end, while the singer Mary Tescher, in black lace and jet jewellery, sang Schubert's *Lieder* and the guests lolled on sofas or on the floor. There were gatherings at the studio of the sculptor Moïse Ezekiel inside the ruins of the Baths of Diocletian. There were evenings in a house down by the Tiber where a "pleiade" of young artists lived and worked. There were available women. D'Annunzio wrote to an Abruzzese friend boasting that he had inscribed some verses "on the white shoulders of a lascivious hetaera." The tableau evoked is literary—d'Annunzio is modelling his self-image here on the cynical Vicomte de Valmont in Laclos's *Les Liaisons Dangereuses*. But what he is describing is a visit to a brothel.

In the year and a half between his first arrival in Rome and his marriage, d'Annunzio wrote a sequence of poems in which lubriciousness alternates with a nauseous revulsion from sex. The sonnet *L'Inconsapevole* epitomises the mood. It describes luxuriant foliage fertilised by the rotting flesh of a corpse, and someone reaching out to pluck a flower like a bloody wound and finding his hand stung by a bitter poison. The poems triggered off a heated public debate about "indecency." D'Annunzio boasted that in them he described sex in impeccable prosody and with a frankness unknown since the work of the Renaissance pornographer, Pietro Aretino.

He writes about letting his tired head fall at dawn on sloping breasts, about "ascending a furrow" between feminine loins. He devotes a sonnet to the sensation, vividly described, of fellatio. He was pursuing pleasure both in bed and on paper, but he was not happy about it. "Atrocious sadness of the unclean flesh when the flame of desire is extinguished in icy disgust and no veil of love is cast around the inert nakedness." In his first novel he gives his own taste for Aretino to a wholly unsympathetic character, a debauched English milord. He told

Scarfoglio that he was craving the bracing cold of an Abruzzese winter, that he was feeling jaded and seedy. "The strength of my barbarous youth lies slain in the arms of women," he wrote in *Sed non Satiatus*. For him the female was always somehow overripe. Youth was pure, clean, strong, barbaric, male.

Nobility

ONE SUNDAY MORNING in May 1879 a troop of the Cicognini boys, preceded by the school band, marched in military order from Prato to Poggio a Caiano, some ten kilometres distant. They stopped for a picnic breakfast of bread, salami and wine in a park en route and picked between them an immense bunch of daisies. Somehow (because that was the kind of boy he was) it fell to Gabriele d'Annunzio to present the bouquet to the head teacher's wife.

With flowers in their buttonholes and their cap bands, the boys marched on into Poggio. They were met by another band from the town, and, with shouts of "Long Live the King!" they proceeded on to the Villa Medici, built by Giuliano di Sangallo for Lorenzo the Magnificent, and by this time a (seldom-used) royal residence.

D'Annunzio was enraptured. Here was a setting for the kind of life he dreamed of. "Great rooms painted with flowers and adorned with immensely valuable paintings: elegant and mysterious bedrooms; and everywhere a profusion of lamps, of mirrors, of carved chests, of marble tables, and over all something entrancingly venerable and ancient." He hung back as the other boys hurried out into the gardens. For a quarter of an hour he stayed alone in the frescoed salon that Vasari once called the most beautiful room in the world, indulging in a reverie that was part erotic fantasy, part awed contemplation of the glamour and grandeur of the Italian aristocracy. "I seemed to hear the rustle of Bianca Capello's silk dress, to hear her yielding sighs and sweet words." Bianca Capello was a sixteenth-century beauty whose portrait by Allori d'Annunzio could have seen in the Uffizi. She and her Medici lover died mysteriously on the same day in 1578, probably poisoned by his relatives. D'Annunzio was thrilling himself with a tale of murder and forbidden passion. Any moment, he told himself, he might see a knight in armour, "his eyes flaming behind his visor, his sword unsheathed."

The boys ate their lunch al fresco and went boating, but then it began to rain. An arcade runs all around the villa at ground level. The boys took shelter there, and began to dance. It was a jolly scene, but for d'Annunzio, as precocious sexually as he was intellectually, it lacked a certain something. He had been eyeing the major-domo's three daughters. He slipped into the house "for a glass of water," and asked the prettiest of the trio if she would dance with him—"Just one waltz?" She assented. They passed into the great salon. Soon some other boys joined them. "So we had a real dancing party . . . a bacchanal." He was twirling over the floor where Lorenzo the Magnificent had once trod, between walls decorated by some of the most revered artists of Italy's golden past. "I enjoyed myself," the sixteen-year-old d'Annunzio told his mother; "very much; perhaps even very, very much."

As a child in Pescara, d'Annunzio was a person of consequence, the mayor's eldest son, living in one of the best houses in town. At the Villa Fuoco, the family's country retreat, there were wide balustraded terraces, with stone pillars topped by terracotta pots in the shape of the busts of kings and queens, their crowns formed by living aloe plants. When his father's profligacy obliged the family to sell some land Gabriele watched the peasants, their dependants, crowding around his mother, as though around a queen going into exile. People brought offerings, a branch laden with apricots, a carafe of wine, a lamb. "Some of them knelt to kiss the hem of her dress. Others kissed my hands, bathing them with tears." Gabriele grew up with an expectation of deference. He would play with other children, but one of them later recalled that if anyone tried to question his leadership, "he would fire up, his face went red and three veins would swell visibly on his forehead." At home in the Abruzzi he seldom met anyone to whom he felt socially inferior.

In Rome things were different. Later he was to write that the human race was divided into those superior beings who had the leisure and the capacity to think and feel and, on the other hand, those who must work for their living. He never doubted that he belonged by nature to the first class, but circumstances, to his great chagrin, consigned him to the latter. He was a hired scribbler, a hack. He couldn't make enough by selling his poems alone. Soon, as well as reviewing books and music and exhibitions, and writing about shops and cafés and the best way to incorporate the newly fashionable Japanese knick-knacks into the décor of a European drawing room, he had become a gossip columnist, the kind of social parasite the snobbish narrator of Henry James's *Daisy Miller* (James was also living in Rome at the time) calls a "penny-a-liner."

Seven years after he arrived in Rome, d'Annunzio took himself off to Francavilla, and there, in six months, wrote his immensely successful first novel *Pleasure*. It recounts the amorous adventures of Andrea Sperelli, Count Ugenta. He loves first Elena Muti, a young widowed duchess, beautiful, wilful and depraved, who first signals her availability by asking Sperelli to buy her an enamelled death's-head, and who loops her feather boa around his neck in a closed carriage and draws him wordlessly into her dangerous embrace. Abandoned by Elena, and vulnerable after being wounded in a duel, Sperelli subsequently falls in love with Maria Ferres, equally beautiful but high-minded and purehearted, a gifted pianist who succumbs to Sperelli's seduction only after protracted hesitations and is ruined by him.

Into the novel went observations d'Annunzio had been recording as a journalist throughout those seven years. He describes a race meeting, a charity auction, a concert, the bustle around the antiquarian jewellers' shops in the Piazza di Spagna. All these were venues where a writer obliged to work for his living could stand alongside the members of the otherwise so inaccessible upper classes. The great d'Annunzio scholar Annamaria Andreoli has noted the poignancy of the fact that Elena Muti is first seen from behind and below, as she mounts the steps of the palace where she is to dine. D'Annunzio, newly arrived in Rome, was the outsider on the pavement, watching those more privileged going through doors he was not invited to enter. And even when some of those doors began to open to him, they did so, not as to a welcome guest, but to a barely tolerated reporter.

The nobility were everywhere visible in Rome, even to those who would never get to know them. D'Annunzio saw carriages driving up and down the Corso, ladies lying back in them, heavily veiled and lapped in furs. In Spillman's cake shop he listened in on a pair of princesses chatting "indolently" as they bought bonbons, and noticed their headgear: "a tiny hat of black lace"; "an aigrette of ostrich plumes and heron feathers." He went to the races and stood among the crowd, composing verses to the "goddesses" in the stands: to the "unknown blonde Diana" with the "hippopotamus husband," whose marble-white arms were loaded with gold bracelets and half concealed by flower-patterned tulle; to the Amazon in the green dress and the red-plumed hat. At the opera he sat in the stalls and gazed up at the ladies in the boxes, taking fashion notes for his column. The Princess di San Faustino, in a "dress of palest blue, shading into sea green, flowing, almost transparent . . . over her bare shoulders a blonde beaver fur, trimmed with red satin . . . a half-moon of brilliants glittering on her high-piled hair." The Countess Chigi-Londalori in white satin, "slender as the stem of a lotus." The Princess di Sciarra and the Duchess di Avigliana, both in black brocade. The Countess Antonelli in a tight dress of turquoise-striped silk. And so on and so forth. Day after day, week after week, he poured out these lists of names and jewels and textiles, caressingly itemising the physical attributes and expensive accessories of women he didn't know.

He was resentful when ladies kept their furs on in the opera house. "They don't show the moon-pale arch of their shoulders." After the publication of *Pleasure* his public would assume that Sperelli was d'Annunzio's self-portrait, but the lordly Sperelli is a very different person from the young reporter with a notebook, whose only chance of glimpsing a grand lady in evening dress is to peer up at her from the opera house's stalls hoping that she'll feel inclined to remove her stole.

On returning to Rome from the Abruzzi for his second winter in the capital, the nineteen-year-old d'Annunzio had himself measured for a suit of evening dress, and wrote to tell his father he was embarking on the *"high life"* (his English). As a "penny-a-liner" he would not have been accorded the same kind of welcome as better-entitled guests, but gradually he gained entry to the concerts, the balls, the *"pique-niques"* (indoor events which began around midnight, but which featured oriental tents and forests of hot-house plants). He was working his way in.

Scarfoglio was shocked. D'Annunzio, who had arrived in Rome with a sheaf of neo-classical poems and high-minded realist stories, had transformed himself into a frivolous sycophant to the idle rich. "For six months he has been going from one ball to another, from a morning's riding in the Campagna to a supper party at the house of some pomaded old idiot furnished with nothing more than a set of quarterings. Not one serious thought enters his head. He is a puppy dog on a silken string." One night when some of the *Cenacolo* were having an unpretentious, Abruzzese-style supper together, the two quarrelled. Scarfoglio was irritated by the way d'Annunzio cherished and protected his spotless white cuffs (laundry was expensive). D'Annunzio was seriously annoyed when Scarfoglio—probably deliberately—dropped some bread crumbs on the poet's black suit.

There was a part of d'Annunzio that agreed there was something shameful about what he was doing. The need to earn his living was abhorrent to him, as it would always remain. "What craven humiliations, Elda . . . Here men are sold like cattle." But there was nothing wrong, in his opinion, with popular journalism. He wanted readers, plenty of them. Besides, when he wrote about shops and table settings and ladies' hats, he didn't feel he was demeaned by his subject matter. To Scarfoglio these might be trivia, but d'Annunzio was observing and recording aspects of life which delighted him.

He gave a lot of thought to clothes. The heroines of his novels have wonderful dresses, minutely described. For a walk in the garden, Maria Ferres wears a Fortuny-style pleated gown. D'Annunzio devotes two full paragraphs to the cut of its sleeves, and its "strange, indefinable colour," like rust, or like the stamen of a crocus. He tells us about the sea-green ribbon around its waist, the turquoise scarab brooch with which the collar is fastened and the hat, wreathed in hyacinths, which completes the outfit. In doing so he alludes to the Italian primitives, and to two of his favourite contemporary painters, Dante Gabriel Rossetti and Lawrence Alma-Tadema. To him fashion was an extension of the visual arts. He saw no reason why the décor of a drawing room or a woman's dress should not be considered as worthy of serious attention as a landscape or a painting.

High society was not just a pleasing spectacle. The "ancient Italic nobility," wrote d'Annunzio in *Pleasure*, had "kept alive, from generation to generation, a family tradition of elite culture, of elegance and of art."

Everywhere around him he saw monuments to that tradition. Rome is a palimpsest, and d'Annunzio was an indefatigable explorer of the ruins of its multi-layered past. He clambered across the temples and fallen arches of the forum. He rode over the outlying hills past convents and basilicas, and out into the Campagna with its outcrops of titanic masonry, its aqueducts and tombs. He wandered through the immense ruins of imperial palaces. He went from church to church, listening to music, making notes on the statuary. But what moved him most was not the Rome of the Caesars, or the Rome of the Popes (the two predecessors Italian nationalists had in mind when they talked about the capital of the new nation as "the third Rome"). The Rome to which d'Annunzio responded most passionately was the Rome of the great aristocratic families.

He loved the patrician villas. He admired their façades from the outside only, but in many of their grounds he was free to wander. Topiary, fountains, cypresses and obelisks echoing each other's forms; broad, curved steps; pergolas draped with wisteria; marble benches supported by carved lions: these gardens were marvellous places. He stored them away in memory to feed his imagination for years to come. He took his women into them on summer nights, to carve their names onto mossy stone parapets, to kiss, to hear the nightingales, and on at least two occasions that we know of, to strip off all his clothes and make love.

Those gardens, like landscapes glimpsed in a dream, were under threat. "We must build Italy in Rome," declared Francesco Crispi, the nationalist statesman who was to dominate Italian political life for the next two decades. Every open space was a target for speculators. The Aventine and Gianiculum Hills were being divided up into lots for sale. The Corso Vittorio Emmanuele was being driven through the city centre, at the expense of a swathe of mediaeval and baroque alleyways. Within months of d'Annunzio's arrival in the capital, Augustus Hare, an English resident, wrote that in twelve years the new regime had "done more for the destruction of Rome, with its beauty and interest, than the invasions of the Goths and Vandals."

D'Annunzio was to become, once fame gave him influence, an energetic conservationist. It is, for instance, largely thanks to his advocacy that Lucca still has its mediaeval walls. As a young journalist though, all he could do was lament the desecration. Parks "where, last spring, the violets appeared for the last time, as numerous as blades of grass," were covered with white hillocks of plaster and piles of red bricks. In groves where nightingales had sung undisturbed for centuries "the wheels of wagons screech. The cries of artisans alternate with the hoarse yells of carters." The laurels of the Villa Sciarra, whose grounds had been sold for development, "lie felled, or stand, humiliated, in the little gardens of stockbrokers and grocers." In the gardens of the Ludovisi family's magnificent Villa Aurora, to be sacrificed to the apartment blocks of the newly widened Via Veneto, he saw ancient cypresses uprooted, their blackened roots ignominiously exposed to the sky. A wind of Barbarism was blowing over Rome, he wrote. "Even the box hedges of the Villa Albani, which appeared as immortal as the caryatids and the herms, tremble at the presentiment of the market and of death."

That wind was a metaphor for the influx of middle-class officials and tradesmen and businessmen who had followed the new Italian administration into the city. In Rome in the 1880s, d'Annunzio's fervent patriotism, which might have led logically to joy at Italy's recent liberation and devoted loyalty to the regime running the unified country, came into conflict with his artistic sensibilities. The culture that he credited the aristocracy with having kept alive was in danger of being engulfed by "today's grey democratic flood . . . which is drowning in meanness so many beautiful and rare things."

He wasn't uncritically admiring of the aristocrats he gradually began to meet. But, debauched or silly though the upper-class characters in his novels may be, they still have graces denied lesser beings. D'Annunzio's imaginary Count Andrea Sperelli, standing "on guard" at the beginning of a duel, displays in every line of his person the "*sprezzatura* of a great lord." In another novel, d'Annunzio describes a refined young man's revulsion on seeing his bourgeois mistress's bare feet. They seem to him deplorably vulgar, suggestive of squalor and meanness. Even the curve of an upper-class instep was somehow more noble than that of a plebeian.

On that school outing to Poggio, d'Annunzio had gained access to a grand house by ingratiating himself with the girls. In Rome as an adult he played the same game. In the fencing schools and stables he encountered the young men of the upper classes; he saw them striding, immaculately dressed, up the steps of their clubs; he might share a compartment on a train with them; but he was not one of them. He was a brave horseman, but it would be another twelve years before he became a member of the *Circolo della Caccia*, the exclusive fox-hunting club. Women, however, were more approachable. Scarfoglio took it for granted that d'Annunzio's enthusiasm for high society was sexually motivated. "As winter opens the doors of the great Roman houses, so he ceded to the flatteries of ladies."

The three or four streets between the Piazza di Spagna and the Corso—then full of antique shops and jewellers—were his hunting ground where, as he tells it, open-air *"flirtation"* (his English) was rife. In a teasing piece for *La Tribuna* he described the erotic opportunities shopping afforded. "Your hand can brush furtively against a lady's, in feeling an embroidered silk." Advice on the choice of a Christmas present, he explained to his readers, can have "an infinity of madrigals" as its subtext. "You can tell her you have seen an unusual object in a little-known curio shop and offer to accompany her there, and as the two of you bend over to inspect the knick-knack in question you will feel your ear tickled by her hair." And then, a little later, you can play on the memory of that intimacy. "'Do you remember Duchess . . . You were wearing a chestnut-coloured mantle trimmed with chinchilla, and you were so fair, at Janetti's shop, standing in a ray of sunlight, between a piece of marquetry and a screen of leather tooled with silver and rose-coloured chimeras . . . You were so beautiful that morning . . . And you were so kind . . . and sweet . . . etc. etc. Do you remember?' If the Duchess remembers, you've almost certainly made a conquest."

It is not hard to guess of whom he was thinking. In April 1883, a couple of months after he wrote his last letter to Elda, d'Annunzio attended a gathering of high-ranking ladies in the Palazzo dei Conservatori. The piece he wrote is his usual confection of artistic references, fashion notes and social gazette. He mentions the Duchessa di Gallese, serene in crushed velvet, and notes that she smiles frequently at her blonde daughter, Maria, who stands by a marble statue and wears a white plume. D'Annunzio ends the piece with an enigmatic reference to a pair of "living turquoises speckled with gold" beneath long eyelashes. In his scandalous poem, *Peccato di Maggio* (Sin in May) published the following month, he describes seducing a young woman with just such eyes. Shortly thereafter he and Maria di Gallese eloped.

He wrote to Nencioni: "Finally, I have given myself up entirely to love, forgetting myself and everything else." The Duchessina Maria Hardouin di Gallese (pictured with their son Mario) was a year younger

than him, described by a contemporary as "a graceful creature, fragile, an eighteenth-century pastel . . . the image of poetry."

The family bore a noble name, but neither of Maria's parents was born into the ancient aristocracy. Her father was the son of a clock-maker from Normandy, who had come to Rome as a junior officer in the French army in 1849. Billeted in the Gallese palace, or perhaps just frequenting the stable yard, he had met, wooed and won the widowed duchess, marrying her and—thanks to a special papal decree—sharing her title. When she died he married again, to a much younger woman of the bourgeoisie. But however come by, the duke's title was ancient and respected; his home, the fifteenth-century Palazzo Altemps, was imposing; his second wife, Maria's mother, was a court insider and lady-in-waiting to the Queen.

Persistent gossip suggests that it was the duchess who first became interested in d'Annunzio. She was described by her neighbour, Count

Luigi Primoli, who would become a good friend of d'Annunzio's, as "graceful, seductive, but as hysterical as the heroine of a novel." Primoli adds that she was constantly going about with poets. In her salon writers and artists met high society. This was the kind of inclusive circle into which d'Annunzio could have been invited. Or perhaps he met mother and daughter with Primoli, who also made a practice of inviting "the two aristocracies, of the mind and the blood," to meet. D'Annunzio certainly visited his house at about this time, and wrote fondly of a "mysterious corner" where a little low divan in a heavily curtained alcove, half screened by a palm tree, provided the perfect place to "converse in peace with a lady."

Whatever may have passed between d'Annunzio and the duchess, he soon transferred his interest to her daughter. Count Primoli, recounting the affair in his diary, imagines Maria finding him in a corner of the palace. "A young poet . . . as beautiful as a mediaeval page. Was he there for her mother? She took him for herself." It wasn't difficult for the young couple to meet. Later, Maria wrote nostalgically to Primoli of how she would *ooh!* and *aah!* at the lovely things in Janetti's shop window, or buy violets from the flower stall in the Piazza di Spagna (in *Pleasure* all the ladies carry little posies of violets inside their muffs). D'Annunzio was frequently there too. Soon they were meeting while out riding as well. And if *Sin in May* is to be taken as the description of an actual event, those outdoor assignations were soon deliriously pleasurable. In a wood where blackbirds sing, the poem's narrator falls to his knees before his "slim blonde companion." His hands play upon her body like a harp. She hangs over him, swaying, swooning. They lie down. Her tumbled hair forms a bed on which she stretches out: "I felt/The points of her breasts rising, at the lascivious/Approach of my fingers, like fleshy flowers . . . ." A rigor as of death freezes her, but "she revives as on a wave of pleasure./I bend entire over her mouth, as if to drink from a chalice, trembling at the conquest."

The woman in the poem is called Yella (a diminutive of Mariella, a common variant of Maria). D'Annunzio was being flagrantly indiscreet, perhaps having calculated that the only way he could win Maria was by compromising her beyond redemption. The duke might himself be an upstart who had entered the ranks of the nobility by way of the bedroom: it did not follow that he would welcome a son-in-law who followed his lead. Quite the reverse. Some time early that summer Maria became pregnant (Mario d'Annunzio was born the following January), but still her father adamantly refused to sanction her marriage to the "penny-a-liner."

On 28 June 1883, Gabriele d'Annunzio and Maria di Gallese took the train to Florence. Their flight was widely reported: d'Annunzio himself had probably tipped off the press. There was some attempt to veil the impropriety: most journalists covering the scandalous elopement alleged that the pair were met at the railway station (telegrams flying faster than trains) by the prefect of police, and sent straight back to Rome. It was a polite fiction. It was not until the following morning that the prefect found them at the Hotel Helvetia. Maria was hustled back to Rome, but by passing the night together in a public place the lovers had ensured that Maria's parents would be obliged to permit their marriage.

To permit, but not to approve or bless. The duke was so outraged at a mere writer having carried off his girl that he wouldn't attend their wedding in the chapel in the Palazzo Altemps. Worse, he refused to give Maria and her new husband any financial support, or ever to meet them. To do him justice, d'Annunzio has left no sign that he was disappointed by Maria's lack of dowry, or by the fact that as an outcast she was unable to provide him with an entrée to the aristocratic circles that fascinated him so. The couple left town to enjoy a marital idyll. Maria was d'Annunzio's pearl-pale, high-born damozel and he was her curly-headed page, and for a while they were entirely happy. He took her off to Pescara and lived there with her for over a year in his father's Villa Fuoco, revelling in his freedom to enjoy a legitimate "horizontal life" with his delicately lovely wife. When eventually he returned to Rome he took on another dependant. Maria's parents separated soon after their daughter's hasty marriage and, for a while, the duchess lived with d'Annunzio and Maria. If d'Annunzio was a fortune-hunter, he was an inept one. Instead of riches and position, he had acquired for himself two disgraced and dependent women whose upkeep he could ill afford.

Beauty

WHEN D'ANNUNZIO first went to Count Primoli's house he might have had something to say about the host, a pioneering photographer and a flamboyant dandy who took pictures of himself dressed in velvet knickerbockers. Primoli was to become another of d'Annunzio's mentors, and played the part of go-between in two of his later love affairs. But in his account of one of his first evenings at the count's, d'Annunzio ignores the human and lingers over the inanimate.

A large room painted Chinese red, a mass of flowers, glass lampshades shaped like birds or lilies, every surface cluttered with things. D'Annunzio made notes. "A dazzling shimmer: a gold-embroidered sash encircles a Hispano-Moresque platter, a length of Venetian velvet is secured by a samurai sword: a sixteenth-century globe and a mauve cope are the backdrop to a profane picture by an ultra-modern artist." This rich jumble, in which the very old and very new, the beautiful and the bizarre, are juxtaposed, was a model for the interiors d'Annunzio later created in his own homes, spaces which were both settings for the drama of their creator's life and works of installation art.

D'Annunzio wrote about his contemporaries' "bric-à-bracomania." "Every drawing room in Rome . . . was laden down with 'curiosities', every lady covered her cushions with a bishop's cope or arranged her roses in an Umbrian pharmacist's jar or a Chalcedon goblet." It was a craze he entered into with enthusiasm. He rummaged through the stalls in the Campo dei Fiori, looking for coins and prints and figurines. He frequented auction houses. In *Pleasure*, Sperelli and Elena Muti attend the sale of a dead cardinal's effects. Tiny, exquisite objects are passed round for prospective buyers' inspection—Roman cameos, illuminated missals, jewels made by the goldsmiths of the Borgia court. When Elena touches something particularly fine, her "ducal" fingers quiver a little, a *frisson* which pleases Sperelli both as boding well for her capacity for sexual ecstasy, and as evidence of the fineness of her aristocratic taste.

A shop that d'Annunzio particularly enjoyed was that run by the Beretta sisters, selling all things Japanese. He loved its clutter—"lacquers, bronzes, textiles, earthenware, all the rare and precious things are scattered about in a wonderful confusion of colours and shapes." Japanese artefacts had been gradually reaching the West since the 1850s and by the time d'Annunzio arrived in Rome they were quite the fashion. Identifying a vogue, be it for a new style of hair ornament, an innovative narrative technique or a political theory, was already one of his talents. He was devouring the writings of his French contemporaries, alive to the Parisian *dernier cri* as well as to what was being worn, read and thought in the Italian capital. He reviewed Judith Gautier's translations of Japanese poetry; he praised the Goncourt brothers for the way they promoted oriental art. The Berettas' shop, with its crimson walls and glossy black woodwork, its air scented with cedar and sandalwood, was another of the places which would shape his own style.

Rare and precious things, unfortunately, are expensive, and in the early 1880s, d'Annunzio, for all the volume of his work, was not earning nearly as much as he thought he needed. Meanwhile his responsibilities were growing. He and Maria passed the first fifteen months of their married life in Pescara, Francesco Paolo having allowed them the Villa Fuoco. There, in January 1884, their son Mario was born. D'Annunzio was not to prove a dependable father, but the birth moved him. "I went round and round the room like a beast in a cage . . . I could hear a feeble, sweet mewling . . . I don't know how to tell you what I felt." He wrote dotingly about the little pink creature with blue eyes and a tiny, tiny mouth, and made plans for him. Mario would be a painter, or perhaps a scientist. His second novel, *The Innocent*, contains lovingly detailed descriptions of a baby's tiny hands and wet gums, its wildly waving arms and unfocused eyes. The novel ends though, with the fictional father killing the infant, which is impeding its parents' love life. Less than a month after Mario was born d'Annunzio reported that he had sent his baby to stay with its grandparents. "It yelled too much."

In the Abruzzi he completed another collection of stories, heavily influenced by Flaubert, describing the sexual cravings of upper-class women. The volume was published that summer of 1884 by Somma-ruga, with a jacket design featuring three nude women. D'Annunzio protested that the image was "indecent." Author and publisher exchanged heated letters in the columns of the journals, but it has been plausibly suggested that this apparent falling out was contrived between them in order to publicise the book.

D'Annunzio was also sending articles back to the Roman journals, but he was running out of material. A piece on the brass bands which processed around Pescara on public holidays was a particularly desper-ate bit of barrel-scraping; privately d'Annunzio admitted to detesting the bands' raucous music. He was missing his friends. "No one comes to see me," he wrote to Scarfoglio. He felt out of touch. He begged to be sent the latest journals. "Nothing reaches me here and I'm desper-ate." In November 1884, still only twenty-one years old, he returned to Rome, taking his wife and baby with him, to take up a job as an editor and regular contributor to *La Tribuna*.

Over the next four years, day after day, he was to write literally hun-dreds of pieces, vignettes of Roman social and cultural life. Sometimes he played the erudite critic: he reviewed books and exhibitions. In dis-cussing Renan's *Life of Jesus* he launched into a discursive piece on Hom-er's Elysian fields. More often he was an observer of the frivolous "high life." He wrote about funerals and race meetings, about concerts and parties. He gave a lasciviously detailed account of a meal eaten after a day's hunting: hare with rosemary and thyme; goose-liver pâté with a glaze scented with truffles; champagne. He prescribed the most grace-ful way to take snuff. He laid down rules about what it was appropriate for a gentleman to wear to the opera.

He had a multiplicity of names. He wrote as Sir Charles Vere de Vere; as Lila Biscuit; as Happemouche; as Bull-Calf; as Puck or Bot-tom (in 1887 he announced that he was about to publish a translation of *A Midsummer Night's Dream*—it never appeared); as Miching-Mallecho (another Shakespearean reference); as the Japanese Shiun Sui Katsu Kava and—most frequently—as Duke Minimo. These fake personae were not just names, but fully developed characters, each with their own servants, houses and social lives. He invented peccadilloes for them and spoke through their differentiated voices. Sir Charles Vere de Vere describes his friend Donna Claribel, and then quotes at length from the diary she keeps in a notebook bound with wild ass's skin (d'Annunzio had discovered Balzac). Doubly distanced from its actual author, Donna Claribel's account of a meet of the foxhounds is an airy piece of fiction, light and funny. D'Annunzio's major works give no hint that he had any sense of humour whatsoever, but these early pieces are playful and droll. The hack-writer was not only observing settings and characters and situations which would be recreated by the novelist. He was also trying out fictional techniques.

His most-used pseudonym was a noble one, but there was a sad irony in the name Duke Minimo (least of the dukes). In one of the "Duke's" pieces he records how he and a group of friends have been refused access to a railway carriage. "We were repelled by main force, as though we were so many journalists." D'Annunzio was well aware how the person he actually was was viewed by the kind of person he aspired to be.

Andrea Sperelli, his fictional alter ego, lives in a huge, sumptuously decorated apartment in the Palazzo Zuccari, at the top of the Spanish Steps, around the corner from where d'Annunzio had rented one attic room next to a brothel. Elena Muti, d'Annunzio's imaginary duchess, has an apartment in the Palazzo Barberini, where room after room is furnished with carved chests, classical busts, bronze platters and curtains embroidered with golden unicorns. D'Annunzio and his family lived in a cramped rented apartment in a narrow street nearby. In 1886 his second son, Gabriellino, was born. Veniero followed a year later. When Andrea Sperelli returns to his tapestry-hung rooms after a lunch party, he is at leisure to stretch languidly in front of his fire and muse on beauty and art until his manservant reminds him that it is time to dress for a dinner. His creator had deadlines to meet, bills to pay and, increasingly, creditors to placate. What he called the "miserable daily grind" permitted him no respite.

Before going to a ball, Sperelli is invariably invited to dinner in one of Rome's great palaces. D'Annunzio, by contrast, eating alone once in a beer shop, dozed off and dreamt of a ballroom all hung around with camellias and cradles. In each cradle there is a baby: each baby is crying loudly. The noise is excruciating. As the ballroom fills with couples, the gentlemen each take up several babies and attempt to dance while carrying them on their shoulders or under their armpits or beneath their waistcoats. The babies scream and wriggle, and poke their fingers into the dancer's eyes, setting up such a hullabaloo that eventually the dreamer/writer awakes. It's a dream that any exhausted new parent can identify with, that of a young father living in a small apartment with (at the time this piece was written) two children under the age of two and a half, striving to lead the exquisite life he so admired and coveted, but sleep-deprived and encumbered night and day by his offspring.

D'Annunzio's need for money troubled him perhaps less than it ought to have done. Maria relates that, on receiving a fee desperately needed for the payment of household bills, he went "light and gay as a little bird" to squander it all on a jade ornament. His compulsion to spend was at best reckless, at worst pathological.

He was not unmercenary. His correspondence demonstrates how much of his energy went into wheedling or browbeating his publishers into advancing him inordinately large sums against books as yet (and in some cases always to remain) unwritten. Once his novels were being published abroad, he studied exchange rates and timed his demands for the payments of his foreign royalties accordingly. When, in his famous middle age, he heard that a hotelier had, rather than banking his cheque, kept it for the sake of his autograph, he wondered if there was any way of persuading others to do likewise. But acquisitive as he was, he was also incorrigibly extravagant. While Maria, housekeeping for the first time in her hitherto privileged life, struggled to find cash for the butcher and baker, her husband allowed Sommaruga to pay him for his contributions to the *Cronaca Bizantina* with credit at the florist's shop.

After two years at *La Tribuna* he wrote to the proprietor, Prince Maffeo Colonna di Sciarra, a letter which was in part a request for a pay rise, in part another literary self-portrait. "By temperament and by instinct I have a *need for the superfluous*." He must have beautiful things about him. "I could have lived very well in a modest house . . . taken tea in a threepenny cup, blown my nose on handkerchiefs at two lire the dozen . . . Instead, fatally, I have wanted Persian carpets, Japanese plates, bronzes, ivories, trinkets, all those useless, lovely things which I love with profound and ruinous passion." There is nothing apologetic about this self-description. An archangel cannot be expected to match his expenditure to the means available, after the manner of a penny-pinching tradesman. Nor can one of those superior beings whose role it is to "think and feel." Prodigality is an aristocratic vice, a perverted form of largesse. Besides, d'Annunzio was not simply a self-indulgent squanderer (although he was that too). He was, in the most literal meaning of the word, an aesthete, one for whom the cult of beauty took the place of morality.

Writing art reviews and journalistic essays, d'Annunzio was pleased to be following the lead given by Baudelaire in the previous generation. The author of *Les Fleurs du mal* was also an influential art critic, and his essay on the "dandy" defined a new kind of hero. "These beings have no other aim, but that of cultivating the idea of beauty in their own persons, of satisfying their passions, of feeling and thinking." Baudelaire had many followers among the French Decadents and Symbolists whom d'Annunzio was reading greedily—Théophile Gautier, Henri Régnier, Stéphane Mallarmé. In 1882, d'Annunzio's first year in Rome, Walter Pater, whom d'Annunzio had read with Nencioni, visited the city for the first time, subsequently writing *Marius the Epicurean*, a novel in which homoerotic fantasy entwines itself around philosophical musings. Meanwhile Oscar Wilde, who called Pater's essays "the holy writ of beauty," was touring the United States. There Wilde, in velvet frock coat and satin breeches, lectured on the "House Beautiful," not so much a style of interior decoration as an aspiration closely parallel to the d'Annunzian injunction that a life must be *made* in the same way as a work of art.

That beautiful life was at once ancient and modern. "All the literature of the present day is abject rubbish," wrote Giosuè Carducci. "Let us return then to true art, to the Greeks and the Latins. What ridiculous little dwarfs are these Italian realists!" D'Annunzio had been one of those dwarfs, but the poems written during the first year and a half of his marriage, which would be published under the collective titles of *La Chimera* (pseudo-classical) and *Isaotta Guttadauro* (pseudo-mediaeval), are newly written examples of centuries-old verse-forms. Their words are archaic, their imagery (lilies, pomegranates, ailing damozels) is pre-Raphaelite. Their rhyme-schemes are tight, their rhythms song-like. Jewels and flowers heavy with erotic symbolism are disposed around the figures of noble maidens and their knightly suitors. Even the spelling is pseudo-antique. Soon after the publication of *Isaotta Guttadauro* a parody appeared, entitled *Risaotto al Pomidauro* (tomato risotto—spelt in an equally faked-up olde-worlde manner).

Scarfoglio had published the parody. D'Annunzio, ostensibly deeply offended, challenged him to a duel, which took place without injury to either party. It was widely suspected that (like the spat with Sommaruga over the "obscene" jacket illustration) the parody, challenge and duel had been got up between the two friends as a way of drawing attention to the poems.

Elitism

IN SEPTEMBER 1885, d'Annunzio quarrelled with a journalist, Carlo Magnico, and challenged him to a duel. At school d'Annunzio had been a prize-winning fencer. In Rome he had kept himself in training, but Magnico, who had the advantage of being considerably taller, bested him. D'Annunzio received a wound to the head, only a shallow cut, but it rattled him. (*Pleasure*'s hero comes close to being killed in a duel.) The writer and editor Mathilde Serao was present at the fight. She relates that the doctor, alarmed by the amount of blood d'Annunzio was losing, poured iron perchlorate over the wound. The bleeding was staunched, but the chemical did irreparable damage to d'Annunzio's hair follicles—or so Serao, perhaps prompted by d'Annunzio, maintained. Soon afterwards he was bald.

The story, which has been repeated by all d'Annunzio's biographers, doesn't stand up. Photographs of d'Annunzio show no noticeable scar on his bald pate. What they do show is his hair receding gradually and along the usual lines. He goes bald just as other men go bald. But d'Annunzio did not want to be as other men. He had been proud of his "forest of curls." The beginning of the end of his life as an "ephebe" (a favourite word of his) was painful, and required transformation. The banal misfortune of losing his hair was reimagined as a battle wound. No longer an androgynous sprite, he began to construct a new persona for himself, that of the virile hero.

Many Italians were looking for such a hero, an autocratic Great Man. Italy's parliamentary democracy was (as it has remained) desperately unstable: in its first forty years it saw thirty-five different administrations. In the 1860s, the first decade of its existence, it was stained by a scandal surrounding a manifestly corrupt deal over the tobacco monopoly. By 1873 one of its members described parliament as "a sordid pigsty, where the most honest men lose all sense of decency and shame."

The aristocrats who had previously had a monopoly of power despised parliament as a talking shop for the vulgar. Politicians on the left complained that its members represented no one but the wealthy. Elections were all too obviously rigged. Even where the ballot boxes were untampered with, few votes were truly free. Initially the electorate was tiny, and successive reform bills extending the franchise only served to shore up the forces of reaction. The lower down the social scale the voter, the more likely he was to vote docilely as his priest or his landlord instructed him. In the countryside the new democracy looked much like mediaeval feudalism. British historian Christopher Duggan sums up: "Bribery of all sorts was commonplace—money, food, offers of jobs, loans—and in many parts of the south men with a reputation for violence—bandits, or *mafiosi*—were widely deployed to intimidate voters. Election days were frequently turned into carnival occasions with landowners marching their supporters, as if they were a feudal army, off to the polling stations accompanied by musicians, priests and dignitaries." Those few "new men" who attained a seat in parliament were perceived (largely correctly) as being as self-serving as their predecessors, and ill-educated to boot.

In 1882, a few months after d'Annunzio's arrival in Rome, Giuseppe Garibaldi died. Garibaldi had been extremely troublesome to Italy's government up to the end of his life but, dead, he became its totem. Francesco Crispi, who had been one of his lieutenants, announced, paraphrasing Carlyle, that "in certain periods of history . . . Providence causes an exceptional being to arise in the world . . . His marvellous exploits capture the imagination, and the masses regard him as superhuman." Garibaldi was such a being. "There was something divine in the life of this man."

In his lifetime Garibaldi had proposed that he should be made a "dictator." The word was a long-unused Latin title, which had yet to acquire the fell associations it now has, meaning one granted extraordinary powers for a limited period at a time of national crisis. On occasion, explained Garibaldi, he had wished for such powers as, in his time as a seaman, he had sometimes seized the ship's helm, knowing he was the only man on board who could steer it through a storm. In the Italy he had helped bring into being there were many who, disenchanted with the corruption and incompetence of their parliamentarians, longed for just such a "dictator." "Today Italy is like a ship in a mighty storm," wrote a political commentator in 1876. "Where is the pilot? I cannot see one."

D'Annunzio read Darwin while he was still at school, and quickly grasped the salient point that evolution was a continuing process. It followed that, in any generation, there will be some individuals who are more highly evolved than others. Men (and women) were not, in d'Annunzio's view, born equal. As *Pleasure*'s Andrea Sperelli passes from palace to palace he is depressed by the sight of workers in the streets. Some are injured or sick. Others are swaggering arm in arm, singing lewd songs. They are jarring reminders that, outside the warm, scented drawing rooms in which the god-like aristos indulge themselves, swarm the lesser kind of humans, most of them "bestial."

D'Annunzio wrote to a composer friend: "Make much of yourself, for God's sake! . . . Don't be afraid of the fight: it is Darwin's *struggle for life* [d'Annunzio's English], the inevitable, inexorable struggle. Down with him who concedes defeat. Down with the humble!" His friend should not be scandalised by these "unchristian maxims," he goes on. Altruism and humility must be laid aside. "Listen to me . . . I have much experience of fighting furiously with my elbows." He is aggressive and competitive and proud of it. D'Annunzio had yet to read Nietzsche but already he was thinking along Nietzschean lines. "The reign of the nonentity is finished. The violent ones rise up."

Martyrdom

W HEN I MARRIED MY HUSBAND," the Duchessina Maria said once, "I thought I was marrying poetry. I would have done better to buy, for three and a half lire, each of his volumes of verse."

Their idyll was short-lived. Shortly after d'Annunzio brought his wife and baby back to Rome he began an affair with a fellow journalist, Olga Ossani, who wrote for the *Capitan Fracassa* under the name of Febea. Olga had, according to her new lover, the head of Praxiteles' Hermes. D'Annunzio was pleased by her "strange bloodless face" and her prematurely white hair. She was clever and unconventional: it was by no means common for a woman to write for the press. He described her at a press ball in the month their liaison began, stretched out on a sofa, laughing and exchanging witty "little impertinences' with the gentlemen besieging her.

D'Annunzio was attracted to independent-minded women. He liked to try out his ideas on them, inserting into his love letters extended passages of prose which would reappear in his essays or novels. He wanted them to be discriminating readers, and to be capable of entertaining him. He had called Elda "child" (which, given her age when they met, was almost literally descriptive), but he didn't usually choose infantile partners. Olga Ossani, a few years older than d'Annunzio, was one of a line of mature, talented women who were to become his lovers.

They used to meet in a room rented for the purpose (a reckless extravagance for a man who could barely pay for his main home) which he decorated with Japanese screens and swathed with green silk. Or they would walk in the gardens of the sixteenth-century Villa Medici (then and now the French Academy of Rome). Henry James called the villa's mannerist gardens "the most enchanting in Rome." James loved the wooded hill which rises above the formal parterres. "The

Boschetto has an incredible, impossible charm . . . a little dusky forest of evergreen oaks. Such a dim light as of a fabled, haunted place, such a soft suffusion of tender grey-green tones." One day, after a bout of love-making during which Ossani had covered him with "the bites of a vampire," d'Annunzio left their room with his body "as spotted as a panther." The following evening they met again in the Villa Medici's "dusky forest." "Sudden fancy. The moon was shining through the holm oaks. I hid. I took off my light summer suit. I called her, leaning against an oleander, posing as though I was tied to it. The moon bathed my naked body, and all the bruises were visible."

A fashionable parlour game of the period was that of *tableaux vivants*: players dressed up (often very elaborately) and posed as historical or legendary characters. Other party guests were required to identify them. Olga guessed d'Annunzio's conundrum at once. "'Saint Sebastian!' she cried." As she embraced him, he felt, with a delicious shudder, that invisible arrows were thrust through his wounds and fixed into the tree behind.

Soon after that night, d'Annunzio wrote to Olga, signing himself "St. Sebastian," and urging her to read *Salammbô*, Flaubert's novel set in ancient Carthage, in which a physically splendid Libyan warrior allows himself to be tortured to death for love of a priestess, and in which scores of human victims are sacrificed to a pitiless god. "Your exquisite intellect will derive from this reading one of the most extended and profound of voluptuous pleasures," he told her.

The association of pain with pleasure was a commonplace of late nineteenth-century art and literature, and it often manifested itself in biblical stories or legends of the saints. Flaubert wrote about the self-inflicted tortures endured by Christian saints. "Thou hast conquered, O pale Galilean!" wrote Swinburne, "the world has grown grey from Thy breath," but Swinburne's poetry, like d'Annunzio's, is replete with religious imagery. Oscar Wilde (like Flaubert before him) would soon be writing a jewelled and sadistic version of the story of Salome and John the Baptist. Biblical themes provided both an oriental setting and an antique grandeur, combining the two exoticisms of place and time, and the cult of the martyrs added to the mix the intoxicating stench of blood.

St. Sebastian is a sexually suggestive martyr. Vasari tells us that a painting of him by Fra Bartolommeo had to be removed from its altar because it "sparked lascivious desire" in women who saw it. Nearly three centuries later, Stendhal reported that the problem hadn't gone away. Guido Reni's paintings of St. Sebastian (of which there are several) had been taken down because "pious women kept falling in love with them."

Sebastian was a Roman officer at the beginning of the fourth century, condemned to death for his Christian beliefs. *The Golden Legend*, the thirteenth-century compendium of saints' lives, relates that he was shot full of arrows and left for dead. He revived and returned to the imperial palace in the hope that his miraculous escape would convince the co-emperors, Diocletian and Maximianus, of Christ's divine power. The emperors remained obdurate. Sebastian was condemned a second time. He was beaten to death and his body thrown into the main sewer.

In early representations he is a mature, bearded man, fatherly and fully dressed as befits an officer. But by the fourteenth century it had become conventional for painters to depict him as a beautiful youth stripped bare. In the 1370s, Giovanni del Biondo showed him hoisted on a stake, nude but for a loincloth, in a pose which invites comparison with Christ's crucifixion, and so bristling with arrow shafts he looks—as an early iconographer remarked—"like a hedgehog." Subsequent depictions are more graceful, more erotic. Piero della Francesca, Antonello da Messina, Mantegna, Guido Reni and numerous others have him standing or leaning, head falling back as though in an ecstasy of pain, his beautiful nearly naked body cruelly pierced.

Arrows are associated with Cupid. To be struck by them is to be inflamed by sexual passion. When d'Annunzio and Olga had their tryst in the Villa Medici gardens, Sigmund Freud had yet to begin studying nervous disorders, but d'Annunzio would not have needed psychoanalytic theory to point out to him that the vision of a physically perfect youth helplessly exposed to penetration by his tormentors' shafts is a potent image of ravishment.

D'Annunzio shared his preoccupation with the saint with a number of his celebrated contemporaries: writers Marcel Proust, Thomas Mann, Oscar Wilde (who assumed the name Sebastian after his release from prison) and the photographer Frederick Holland Day. These men, and subsequent Sebastianophiles Yukio Mishima (whose ideas and life story in many ways reflect d'Annunzio's), film-maker Derek Jarman, and the photographers Pierre et Gilles, were all, at least to some extent, homosexual. Magnus Hirschfeld, the pioneering German sexologist and contemporary of d'Annunzio, identified pictures of St. Sebastian as being among the images in which an "invert" would take special delight. D'Annunzio's Sebastian cult raises unavoidable questions about his sexual orientation.

That d'Annunzio was an eager lover of women is a copiously documented fact. Whether he also enjoyed sex with men is unknown. Some of his schoolboy letters could be interpreted as suggesting so, but it was not unusual in d'Annunzio's lifetime for same-sex friends to write to each other as sentimentally as lovers. Here is his account of an adolescent friendship with another boy: "We smiled at each other, scarcely, scarcely glancing at each other from beneath the corners of our eyelids . . . and I have never forgotten that moment of our friendship; which glows for me with an inexplicable beauty." Writing to his elder patrons he was flirtatious and emotional. He told Cesare Fontana: "I have read and reread your lovely letter twenty times . . . What can I say in return for so many sweet, fond, expressions of affection? That I love you too? . . . Oh believe it, believe, dear friend."

If d'Annunzio did have sexual contact with any of these boys or men, it would not be surprising that he didn't publicly admit to it; few men at this time would have dared do so. But given the quantity of his private writings—letters, notebooks, jottings—to which we now have access, and given his compulsion to note everything, even the most intimate details of his love life, the absence of any recorded trace of a homosexual affair strongly suggests that he never had one. In his memoirs he explicitly distinguishes his sentimental "friendships" with other boys, from the "love" which he had yet—at the time recollected—to experience. In his late novel, *Maybe Yes, Maybe No*, he imagines a pair of male friends, comrades who undertake a sequence of masculine adventures together. Their comradeship is so strong precisely because it is "clean." Like a great many other men of his generation, he idealised male companionship as an escape from the erotic, from the clinging, energy-sapping, over-ripeness of the women whom he bedded.

Whatever his orientation, though, there was something sexually ambiguous about d'Annunzio. The adolescent whose feminine prettiness and girlish voice had so enchanted Scarfoglio, matured into a small man with wide womanly hips who took a far greater interest in clothes and flowers and table-settings than was generally considered consonant with heterosexual masculinity.

People, especially women, whose gender identity was equivocal, interested him. One of the things that pleased him about Olga Ossani was her "fine androgynous head" and his fictional Andrea Sperelli is writing a "Story of a Hermaphrodite." In his fiction d'Annunzio was repeatedly to conjure up pairs or trios of women, sisters or close friends, between whom the hero must choose, or into whose sensuously intimate sorority he must insert himself. Maria Ferres and her hostess, both in love with Sperelli, remember with delight their voluptuous pleasure in brushing each other's hair at boarding school and there are two overtly lesbian characters in *Pleasure*. One of them is a great lady with a "strong masculine voice" whose black eyes, in the course of a lunch party in a princely residence, "all too often meet and mingle with the green eyes of the Princess." The other is a demi-mondaine, heavily made-up but with her curly hair so short it looks like an astrakhan cap, and wearing a jacket and waistcoat of masculine cut, a monocle and a starched cravat. She smokes at the dinner table, and swallows oysters greedily. Sperelli is attracted by the suggestion of "vice, of depravity, of the monstrous" in her manner and appearance.

Eleonora Duse, d'Annunzio's lover for eight years, was rumoured to be bisexual. Romaine Brooks, with whom he had an affair during his years in France, was lesbian. Ida Rubinstein, the actress and mime, and the eccentric millionairess Luisa Casati—with each of whom he had great friendships and minor affairs—both played theatrical variations on their gender identities, appearing naked in public, or cross-dressing. But when, a quarter of a century after that night in the Villa Medici gardens with Olga, d'Annunzio would write a play (with music by Debussy) of *The Martyrdom of Saint Sebastian*, he wrote it expressly for Ida Rubinstein. Sebastian—victim-hero of so many gay male fantasies—would be played in d'Annunzio's version by a woman.

Probably not an active homosexual, then, but certainly a sado-masochist. Exploring Rome and its treasures, d'Annunzio was particularly moved by Michelangelo's *Pietà*. He elaborated a self-regarding fantasy in which he imagines his mother as Michelangelo's Madonna and himself as the dead Christ, thus placing himself imaginatively in another tableau vivant in which he plays a beautiful, tortured nearly nude young man.

The cult of the dying youth was one of the themes d'Annunzio had found in the English Romantics. He alluded frequently to Keats, the tragic poet "half in love with easeful death," whose last home on the Spanish Steps d'Annunzio walked past almost daily; and to Shelley, who mourned Keats so mellifluously in *Adonais*, before dying himself, aged thirty, drowned whilst out sailing. In 1883, d'Annunzio wrote his own *Adonis*, which concludes: "Thus died the youth, in a great mystery of Pain and Beauty as imagined by my Dream and Art." In *Pleasure*, Sperelli takes Maria Ferres to the English Cemetery in Rome. (Oscar Wilde, visiting Keats's grave there, mused on the resemblances between Keats and St. Sebastian, each of them "a Priest of Beauty, slain before his time.") D'Annunzio's fictional lovers are mournful: Maria takes off her black veil, wraps it around a bunch of white roses and leaves them on Shelley's grave. "He was *our* poet."

Six decades after Shelley's death, Romanticism had ripened into the late Romantic melancholy of Tennyson and Baudelaire, and then overripened into decadence. The exquisite sadness clinging to the Romantic image of doomed youth had given way to a more feverish mood and a more knowing discourse. Posing for his sexual partner as a martyred saint, d'Annunzio was titillating himself with the image of a young man tortured and killed. Later he would have plentiful opportunities to see that image made reality. In 1915 he planned his arrival at Quarto at the head of a troop of young volunteers whose "blood was ready to be spilt," human sacrifices like the slaves killed in the "holocaust" Flaubert describes in *Salammbô*. Throughout the Great War, d'Annunzio was to refer over and over again, and in increasingly exalted tones, to dead soldiers as "martyrs," whose deaths must be honoured by the sacrifice of further beautiful youths. What had begun as an erotic fantasy shaped by an aesthetic trend would become a motive for slaughter.

Sickness

ELVIRA FRATERNALI LEONI, whom d'Annunzio called Barbara or Barbarella, was a year or two older than he, golden-skinned with huge pale eyes. He made her acquaintance at a concert in April 1887, when he was just twenty-four and his wife was pregnant with his third child. By the end of the month he and Barbara were meeting almost daily, initially in the studio of one or other of d'Annunzio's artist friends, and soon in a room he rented for the purpose.

"Neither the strength of Hercules nor the beauty of Hippolytus has as much power to thrill a woman as fame does," wrote d'Annunzio. By now he enjoyed fame of a particularly seductive kind. He was the poet celebrated for his erotically transgressive verses, and the lover whose elopement had been scandalous. He was both a serious artist, acclaimed by his peers, and a known libertine. "How sweet it must be for the loving women to be able to say . . . I possess, body and soul, this mysterious being, the flight of whose chimeras makes women swoon with passion." In other words the poet was a star, and like any star he had his groupies. A male friend wrote that d'Annunzio was a "Siren. No one could resist him." By the time he met Barbara he had had at least one fleeting affair since parting from Olga. There were probably other, undocumented liaisons. But with Barbara he fell abjectly in love. When she left Rome briefly, he haunted the post office, desperate for her letters, and sat uncharacteristically silent in the Caffè Morteo, until, overcome, he left in tears.

Barbara was not one of the aristocrats about whom he wrote. Her parents were lower-middle class, devout Catholics who spoke with a pronounced regional accent. She had been married off when she was twenty to a Count Leoni, a Bolognese businessman whose title may have been spurious. Leoni treated her so brutally that she left him

within weeks and returned to live with her parents, but from time to time he would reappear, demanding his marital rights. When Andrea Sperelli's mistress tells him, after her marriage, that if he wishes to continue their affair he will have to share her sexual favours with her husband, he refuses, aghast. In real life, in this and several other instances, d'Annunzio was obliged to accept the situation. He even seems to have relished the fact that Barbara was bruised and shaken after one of Leoni's visits.

Barbara was alluring: photographs show a chic young woman, with a full-lipped, painted mouth and eyes uplifted to reveal an arc of dazzling white beneath the irises ("the most beautiful eyes in Rome," according to one of d'Annunzio's contemporary biographers). D'Annunzio, delighting as usual in gender confusion, praised her boyish figure and masculine little hats. She was well read and intelligent: it was she who recommended to her lover the newly translated works of Tolstoy and Dostoevsky. She was a skilled pianist who had studied at the Milan

Conservatory. Most fascinating of all, or so it seems from d'Annunzio's many hundreds of letters to her, she was chronically ill. She was epileptic, and she suffered from some sort of gynaecological complaint. She may have contracted a sexually transmitted disease from her husband; she may have undergone a botched abortion; or perhaps she had some congenital malformation. Either way, she was ailing and often in pain.

All of this was very exciting for d'Annunzio. As a student he had neglected the lectures and classes he should have attended, but he had sat in on the course given by the noted physiologist Jacob Moleschott. His early stories are full of images of disease and wounding, described with unflinching exactitude. He would turn to Barbara to corroborate the details of the ailments of his heroines Elena Muti (in *Pleasure*), Giuliana Hermil (*The Innocent*) and Ippolita (*The Triumph of Death*), all of whom are, like their real-life prototype, especially alluring when their illness makes them temporarily untouchable. Brows damp with sweat, pale skin, cracked lips, clouded eyes are described as though they were the signs of sexual rapture. Illness as an aphrodisiac was a commonplace of Decadent literature, but it was one to which d'Annunzio responded with particular enthusiasm. In *Pleasure* he would give an intensely erotic account of a sickbed seduction. Barbara provided that thrill in real life. "Sick and tired like this you please me," he wrote to her when she was ill in bed. "Your beauty is spiritualised by illness . . . Your face takes on a profound, superhuman pallor . . . I think that when you are dead you will reach the supreme light of beauty."

There were times, including the first few occasions they were alone together, when Barbara's complaint made penetrative sexual intercourse impossible for her. No matter: the impediment to their love-making seems only to have heightened their pleasure. D'Annunzio wrote letters full of ecstatic gratitude, reminiscing about their protracted kisses, telling all over again how he licked and sucked and bit every inch of her body. He described how they wound themselves around each other, head to tail, on and under a big armchair in their rented room. "As I write in a fever (how I tremble!) I can still feel between my lips the little soft folds of your rose, which I sucked greedily as one sucks the juice from a fruit. Do you remember?" (The rose for d'Annunzio, as for the mediaeval poets he had been reading, stood for the female genitals.) He recalls delicious hours in bed as he lay, eyes shut, wondering on which part of his body he would next feel her cool lips. And then there were the days when they no longer needed to hold back. His letters tell of a "savagely" urgent coupling in a railway carriage (he would repeat the passage almost verbatim in *The Triumph of Death*).

His relationship with Barbara gave rise to his *Roman Elegies*, the first of his mature poem-cycles. Their title is borrowed from Goethe. Their philosophical underpinning is provided by Shelley and Schopenhauer. Their insistence on the *correspondances* between the material world and human emotion is inspired by the French Symbolists whom d'Annunzio had been reading, but the dazzling achievement of the elegies is d'Annunzio's own.

By this time the poet was fully in control of his medium. He stretches his verse-form to its limits; he twists it to his emotional purpose, he exploits its rhythms to make effects now plangent, now joyful. In one of the poems Barbara is named. In all of them she is the "the one who was at my side," and she was among his first readers. In the poems describing the early stages of their affair, happiness beats through the lines. One afternoon, in the gardens of the Villa d'Este with Barbara, d'Annunzio wrote two versions of an elegy in which he claims that the fountains, the roses, the trees, every leaf and stalk of the marvellous Tivoli gardens owed their beauty and their gushing life to her. Both manuscripts survive, one dated five o'clock and one six o'clock of the same June afternoon.

He couldn't get enough of Barbara; he was racked whenever they were apart by his insatiable craving for her body. Several of his biographers have described her as the love of his life, but the word he uses most often in his letters to her is not "love," but "desire." Readers of *Pleasure* imagined the novel's author to be a nonchalant seducer like Andrea Sperelli, who makes love to his friend's mistress for no reason whatsoever, out of idleness and vanity. But d'Annunzio was not a careless Don Juan. His appetite for sex has been the occasion for much salacious merriment, in his lifetime and ever since, but it was often cruel, to others and to himself as well.

Centaurs, chimeras, satyrs and other hybrid beings recur in his imaginative work. Repeatedly, he describes himself as a faun: a feral half-human, smooth-skinned homo sapiens from the waist up, a hairy beast below. Fauns were fashionable. D'Annunzio had read Mallarmé's famous poem, but for him the image expressed a fundamental conflict. Sometimes the self-description is gleeful, the conceit of a physically self-confident young man pleased to see himself as a mischievous animal. Sometimes it hints at self-loathing and shame.

A few weeks after he met Barbara, d'Annunzio was summoned to Pescara to help deal with a family crisis. His father, Francesco Paolo, had been running through money at a disastrous rate. D'Annunzio's mother's inheritance was all but gone. There was little chance of finding dowries for his sisters. Over the next six years, d'Annunzio was to find his own financial problems greatly aggravated by his father's. He would be sending handouts to his mother for the rest of her life.

It is nearly always unwise to imagine one can deduce anything certain about a novelist's life from a reading of his fiction, but d'Annunzio's *The Triumph of Death* (begun in 1889 and published in its final form five years later) is an exceptional case. It is a novel in which the author's own love letters are quoted verbatim, and one which describes in exact detail the place in which it was first written. D'Annunzio told Romain Rolland that it was "not imaginary at all." Its hero, Giorgio Aurispa, a sophisticated young city-dweller like d'Annunzio, revisits his family in the Abruzzi. His fictional father is a portrait of d'Annunzio's real one. More painfully, it is also a kind of self-portrait: the author as seen in a hideously distorting glass.

When he went to see Francesco Paolo that summer of 1887, d'Annunzio himself was already spending way over his income. Aurispa's father, like d'Annunzio's, is plundering his wife and children's home to pay his mistress's expenses. D'Annunzio was renting a room for his meetings with Barbara with money desperately needed by his legitimate family. The fictional father is shifty, telling transparent fibs. D'Annunzio, still living with his wife but meeting Barbara nearly every day, must have been lying hour by hour. Aurispa is fastidious and physically refined. So was d'Annunzio, the neat little man who even as a schoolboy was already spending inordinate sums on laundry. Aurispa contemplates his father: "Fat, full-blooded and powerful, a hot breath of carnal vitality seemed to emanate from his whole person . . . His face bore the impress of a violent and harsh nature . . . All this inspired him [Aurispa] with a feeling akin to nausea . . . And I, I am the son of this man!" Looking at his real-life father, d'Annunzio likewise recoiled as though from a hideous caricature of himself. Like the picture in Dorian Gray's attic (Oscar Wilde's novel would be published in the same year as the first instalment of *The Triumph of Death*), Francesco Paolo d'Annunzio was the image of his son's worst faults. If the son was a faun—a pretty creature from an artificial pastoral—the father was the stinking goat that begot him.

During the summer of 1887, probably while d'Annunzio was absent in the Abruzzi seeing to his father's affairs, Maria, pregnant for the third time, read a letter to him from Barbara, one which made the nature of their relationship unmistakable. We do not know what passed between husband and wife after this discovery. It was to be another three years before they separated definitively. But d'Annunzio afterwards alluded to "violent scenes."

The Sea

D'ANNUNZIO REPEATEDLY BOASTED that that he was born at sea, on board the brigantine *Irene*, and that his "marine nativity" had made a natural-born sailor of him. He identified himself with the sea-god Glaucus. He claimed to have a "nautical daemon" and called himself a "wolf of the sea."

Most of this is fanciful nonsense. D'Annunzio's birth on dry land, in the family home in Pescara, is well documented, as is his tendency to turn queasy in high seas. But it is true that Pescara and all its neighbouring coastal towns were, in d'Annunzio's lifetime, seafaring communities. Before the arrival of the railways a landmass was a formidable obstacle; an expanse of water was a highway. Peoples were linked not by a common land but by a common sea. D'Annunzio's father's income (while he still had one) came from trading across the narrow Adriatic with the Dalmatian towns of Fiume, Zara, Sebenico, Ragusa, Spalato (now Rijeka, Zadar, Sebenik, Dubrovnik and Split), all of which then had substantial Italian populations and close ties, of trade and also frequently of kinship, with the ports of Italy's eastern coast. Several of d'Annunzio's early stories are about sailors who cross and recross the water, trading in timber and grain, wine and dried fruits. If the Abruzzi was his native land, the Adriatic was, even more emphatically, his native sea.

In old age he liked to dwell on memories of swimming far out: "My body completely naked, meeting playful dolphins, the effort to reach the fishing boats; the fishermen who dried me and wrapped me in their rags beneath the flapping of the orange and rust-coloured sail; the hot soup, cooked right there in a terracotta pot, mullet, sole, squid, all scarlet with peppers; hunger, hunger, pleasure and forgetfulness, with those sailors standing astonished around me, as though wondering at a sea creature dragged up from the deeps in the net along with the abundant fish."

In the summer of 1887, his personal life was in uproar. Barbara had been sent off by her parents to spend some weeks with her sister in Rimini. Her husband had reappeared to escort her to the station. It seems likely that parents and husband alike had got wind of, and for differing motives deplored, her relationship with a married man whose debts were already threatening to overwhelm him. Maria had discovered this latest and most serious infidelity. His recent visit to his parents had been traumatic, and practically worrying. Deliverance came in the form of an invitation to run away to sea.

In a playful sketch written early that August, "Duke Minimo" makes fun of an unnamed friend who is always coming up with hare-brained schemes. One hot night, in a bar near the Palazzo Ruspoli, this friend is one of a jolly group drinking long glasses of iced lemonade with the "Duke" beneath artificial trees of painted zinc, while a singer warbles *The Cuckoo Song*. He announces that he is going to sail around the Adriatic, setting out from a port on the Abruzzi coast, going northwards to Venice, on to Trieste, around Istria, and then south along the Dalmatian coast. There, he promises, they will find trees bearing marvellous fruit, and water glittering like diamonds. They will meet beautiful women—white-skinned, blue-eyed blonde women, fierce black-haired women. Everyone laughs, but one Adolfo de Bosis, "ardent apostle of Shelley," is alight with enthusiasm. He volunteers to come along too, declaring, "We will die like Percy," and embarking on lengthy Shelleyan quotations which the others shush or shout down. The piece ends in bathetic whimsy: the scheme's proposer turns up at Rome's railway station too late for the train to the coast and ruefully resigns himself to a summer in the city. In reality, though, it had a sequel. De Bosis existed. He was Shelley's translator and chief advocate in Italy, and a close friend of d'Annunzio. It was he who had a boat, a cutter called the *Lady Clara*. And it was d'Annunzio who impulsively accepted his suggestion that they sail in her around the Adriatic.

Leaving Maria, by now in the last month of her pregnancy, he met up with de Bosis in Pescara. Their voyage began in aesthetic style. They

took with them Persian rugs, lots of cushions and an intarsia stool. They hired two sailors, frivolously chosen by d'Annunzio for the sake of their high-sounding names, and both, as soon became obvious, incompetent.

One of the many ways in which d'Annunzio was ahead of his time was in his passion for sunbathing. He lay on deck all day, stark naked, moving only to turn his other side to the sun. He contrived to see Barbara briefly in Rimini. She was so heavily chaperoned there that he could barely steal a kiss, but at least she was able to give him a red banner she had embroidered for him to fly from the *Lady Clara*'s mast. Back at sea with de Bosis he enjoyed himself in posturingly aesthetic style. When they stopped to picnic on beaches, the two young men dressed in white linen and took ashore with them their rugs and cushions and a silver tea-set, and photographed each other, revelling in their own sophistication.

North of Rimini they strayed too far out to sea. A stiff wind got up. The boat was being driven onto the Dalmatian coast. D'Annunzio, green-faced again, was useless. The two hired crewmen were little better. De Bosis struggled with his little vessel but it was soon frighteningly out of control. Dying "like Percy" suddenly seemed all too likely, but by happy chance a squadron of Italian warships were performing a practice manoeuvre nearby. The *Lady Clara* was seen floundering and rescued by the cruiser *Agostino Barbarigo*. The little sailing boat was first taken in tow and then hoisted aboard the ironclad warship. Their lives had been saved, and d'Annunzio's had been given a new direction. He was to identify the escapade as the transition from his existence as a "mere poet" to the beginning of his life as the mouthpiece of his nation.

As the *Agostino Barbarigo* steamed towards Venice, where the two hapless literati were to be dropped off, d'Annunzio exulted in being aboard a potent steel vessel. The following year he published his ode *To a Torpedo Boat in the Adriatic*, hymning the glittering ship, "beautiful as a naked blade," throbbing with power "as though the metal encloses a terrible heart." Such a gigantic weapon, he wrote, could be wielded only by men of "cold courage." At sea there was still a place for a hero, bestriding the shuddering bridge of a colossal warship, as the knights of old had bestridden their iron-clad steeds.

The pact between Italy, Austria and Germany—the Triple Alliance against which d'Annunzio was to rail so furiously two decades later—had been agreed five years previously, in 1882. At the same time, the Italian administration, unhappy at being obliged by weakness to accept such uncongenial allies, had begun to build up Italy's army and to create a fighting fleet. Now d'Annunzio, self-styled "sea-wolf," immersed himself in the subject. Briefed by the officers on the *Agostino Barbarigo*, he wrote a series of polemical pieces, published under the collective title of *The Italian Armada*, calling for the construction of more ships on nationalist grounds. "The shouts and greetings and blessings accompanying the happy descent of a new ship into the sea reverberate from one end of the peninsula to the other."

The articles were full of practical suggestions about the financing and equipping of the fleet and the training of seamen. The languid Sir Charles Vere de Vere, the pleasure-loving Duke Minimo, the flighty Happemouche, had transformed themselves into a commentator who had read and thought carefully about engineering and naval discipline, and one moreover with a frighteningly bellicose nature. D'Annunzio predicted the future role of torpedo boats and the havoc they might cause to enemy shipping. He imagined the mood of their crews. "No human joy will equal theirs as they see the monstrous dreadnought keel over." This was his own voice. The articles, unlike his gossip and fashion pieces, were published under d'Annunzio's own name.

D'Annunzio and his companions were put ashore in Venice and the *Lady Clara* was delivered to the shipwrights of the Arsenal, where the great ships that once made Venice ruler of the eastern Mediterranean had been built. It was d'Annunzio's first sight of the city. Arriving there as he did with the theme of maritime glory on his mind, it became for him the symbol of all Italy's past greatness. Even more than imperial Rome, it was the Venetian Empire which was to shape his politics in the modern world.

Within days of his arrival in Venice, d'Annunzio received word that in his absence his third son had been born. He telegraphed back to his wife that the baby was to be named Veniero, after the great Venetian admiral and doge, commander at the battle of Lepanto.

Veniero's father was prevented from assisting at his birth by the arrival of Barbara and by his lack of money. In *The Triumph of Death*, the heroine Ippolita joins Giorgio Aurispa in Venice. Only one detail of the remembered idyll is provably untrue. In the novel, the lovers stay in grand style at the Hotel Danieli. In actuality d'Annunzio had a room in a far less glamorous hotel further along the Riva degli Schiavoni. Even that he couldn't afford. Unable to pay his bill, he was prevented from leaving until de Bosis kindly lent him the necessary cash.

Decadence

Here, from the pages of *La Tribuna*, is d'Annunzio's advice to young gentlemen invited to the newly fashionable late afternoon events known as *"garden-parties"* (his English). They should not wear evening dress, "but a simple *redingote*." Their trousers should be neither too pale nor too tight, "but loose, as fashion requires." The cravat should be light-coloured, with a large knot, "and the top hat should be white, for preference, with a black ribbon, as in half mourning."

Seriously as d'Annunzio took the subject of personal adornment, it was by this time as evident to him as it was to Scarfoglio that he was wasting his talent. Was it for this he had stolen his school fellows' lamp oil? Was it for writing such tosh that he had prepared himself by making himself conversant first with the classics and, more recently, with the latest, most innovative writing from England, France and Russia? Was this a proper way for a prodigy to employ his talents? Were such fripperies appropriate interests for one born to a high destiny? Clearly not. In July 1888, when he was twenty-five years old, he gave up his job at *La Tribuna*. He left Rome. He retreated to Michetti's convent in Francavilla and painted the word *"clausura"* ("enclosure," as in an enclosed religious order) above the door of a cell.

There he stayed, seeing neither his lover nor his wife and sons, for five months. He had become persuaded that the novel was the literary form best suited to his own era. He was resolved to make it new and at the same time to establish his own reputation as a great modern writer. By the time he returned to Rome he had finished *Pleasure*.

He dubbed Michetti *"Cenobiarca,"* an archaic word meaning the leader of a colony of monks, and acted as though he had joined his order. In his cell he worked indefatigably. Barbara wrote asking him to meet her in Turin, or imploring him to return to Rome at least for a few days. He refused. His work must not be interrupted. It was an ordeal, an heroic labour, an act of devotion.

For months he was, as far as we know, celibate (if only because, according to him, "the only women for thirty or forty miles around were infected baggages or the worn-out mothers of at least twenty sons." He was as self-punishingly dedicated as an anchorite. "Yesterday, after working for five hours in the morning, I stayed at my desk in the afternoon for *seven consecutive hours*, without ever getting up. When I stopped I was dying of exhaustion."

He was intent on creating a form of fiction as yet unknown. He had written realist stories, and poems full of dreamy pre-Raphaelite imagery. Now he would combine the two strands, creating women as dangerous as the jewelled biblical temptresses of Gustave Moreau's paintings, but ones who inhabited not the distant, exotic past but the Rome he knew; real women with pubic hair and rank-smelling armpits, whose mouths, when kissed, tasted of the newly popular Peek Frean biscuits.

As always, he was drawing on the ancient and the modern alike. D'Annunzio knew the classics, he knew early Italian literature as few others did. He was studying the writings of mediaeval churchmen, learning from their incantatory rhythms, their minute examinations of the human heart and conscience. But he was also a modernist, abreast with critical theory (he had recently been much impressed by Paul Bourget's *Essais de psychologie contemporaine*) who believed that a literature capable of representing a person's inner life and the "invisible forces" which shape it must begin with the "total abolition of literary tradition."

In the evenings Michetti climbed the stairs to his cell and d'Annunzio would read his day's new pages aloud. The steam rising from their China tea seemed to him an image of their intelligence, perfuming the tranquil atmosphere of the room as incense perfumes a church. They were hermits dedicated to the exercise of their respective arts. They were also heroes, he recorded, who broke their daily "laborious fast," as Homer's warriors did, by eating their supper beside the sounding sea.

Pleasure opens with an aerial shot of the quarter of Rome around the Piazza di Spagna. The square and surrounding streets are busy. A vague hum of passing carriages and human voices can be heard. It is an autumn afternoon and the light is golden, hazy, a touch melancholy (d'Annunzio had written poems describing just such an afternoon). The viewpoint zooms down and, as though passing through the window, into a set of rooms in Palazzo Zuccari. It pans around the interior, lingering on masses of roses arranged in gilded crystal vases. It cuts (by means of an explicit reference) to an almost subliminal glimpse of a Botticelli painting in which an identical vase is visible behind the Madonna, and then cuts back to the room across which our hero, Andrea Sperelli, is now visible.

The cinematic language suits d'Annunzio's narrative technique. Half a decade before the motion picture camera was invented, he structured his first novel as though it were a film script. *Pleasure's* narrative is a sequence of lucidly visualised scenes. It employs flashbacks and abrupt cuts, distant views and voice-over-like meditations. In Francavilla, d'Annunzio told Michetti, his novels (like the yet-to-be-invented cinema) would combine "the precision of science with the seductions of the dream."

In *Pleasure*, d'Annunzio holds out a vision of a beautiful life, only in the end to condemn it as empty and sterile. He describes people whose gait and dress sense and taste in flower arrangements all proclaim them members of an elite. He places them in settings of dreamlike loveliness—tapestry-hung apartments in Renaissance palaces, terraced gardens large enough to get lost in. He gives them gorgeous clothes and precious bibelots, all so lasciviously described that the entire fictional environment seems fetishised. But he always insisted that his book was an exposé in which, "I study, with sadness, so much corruption and so much depravity and so much deviousness and falsity and futile cruelty."

The novel's hero is a libertine who idly seduces other men's wives, without passion and without remorse, and who passes his unoccupied evenings with prostitutes he despises. Gambling, heartless seduction and brutal sexual abuse all form part of the plot, and all—so d'Annunzio implies—are endemic in this apparently exquisite world. The ladies look divine from a distance in their satin evening gowns, but when d'Annunzio sends his sound boom close enough to pick up their chatter, their pettiness and malice are manifest. They mock others' appearances. "She looks like a camel dressed up as a cardinal." They gossip spitefully about others' love affairs; they boast of their own transgressions. Young noblemen stand in the corner of a ballroom, their clothes impeccable, their conversation lewd. These people are the last specimens of an exhausted caste. In one of the novel's most evocative passages, d'Annunzio takes a gavotte by Rameau as the inspiration for a vision of ennui, sterility and despair. "The future is lugubrious, like a field of graves already dug and ready to receive the corpses." Sperelli, with his fine appreciation of beautiful things and his quasi-autistic failure to empathise with his fellow humans, is left, in the end, futilely attempting to console himself for the loss of love, by buying up his lover's furniture. *Pleasure* is a study in decadence.

"We are dying of civilisation," wrote Edmond de Goncourt, one of the French authors d'Annunzio had been reading with enthusiasm. French intellectuals identified themselves as the inheritors of a Latin culture beset by the "barbarians" who had so humiliatingly defeated them in the Franco-Prussian War of 1870. Perversely enough, given the immense creative energy palpable in the industrial and artistic life of late nineteenth-century France, they felt themselves part of a civilisation embarked on its decline and fall. They employed the word "decadence" to describe a particular sensibility they shared, a languid disdain for anything so clumsy and naïve as sincere emotion. They congratulated themselves upon it—so refined, so sophisticated—while at the same time deploring it as an enervation of the energy and the will.

This decadence was nothing new. Reading Byron at school, d'Annunzio had aspired to emulate the persona of the disenchanted poet-lord. Chateaubriand's novel *René*, ur-text of French Romanticism, presented him with the type of a superior spirit too noble to be happy in a levelled-down democratic world, but also too intelligent not to despise his degenerate peers. Andrea Sperelli, the hero of *Pleasure*, owes much to these prototypes, and something as well to Pushkin's Eugene Onegin, who flirts with an innocent young woman to relieve his ennui and then kills her fiancé in a pointless duel. He had also, though, a more contemporary model.

In 1883, Stéphane Mallarmé visited Comte Robert de Montesquiou, a key figure of the fin-de-siècle cult of decadence. In his home, dimly lit by candelabra, Mallarmé saw a sled positioned on a white bearskin, one room furnished as a monastic cell, another as the cabin of a yacht, and a third with a Louis XV pulpit, choir stalls and an altar rail. In the library there were books with jewel-coloured bindings, and the gilded shell of a tortoise who had died as a result of being so adorned. He described the visit to his friend, Joris-Karl Huysmans.

Huysmans, like d'Annunzio, had previously written realist fiction heavily influenced by Zola's, with working-class or peasant characters. Like d'Annunzio he was himself a hard-working member of the bourgeoisie (he was a civil servant). Like d'Annunzio he was fascinated by those who, unlike himself, had the prestige of an ancient name and the leisure to devote themselves to thinking and feeling in exquisitely decorated rooms which were their lives' chief work. In 1884, the year in which d'Annunzio returned to Rome with Maria and their baby, Huysmans published *À Rebours* (Against Nature) a novel which is also a kind of compendium of decadent tastes and values.

À Rebours soon reached d'Annunzio; he later acknowledged to his French translator that *Pleasure* was something like it. It was immensely congenial to him. Huysmans's literary style is as mannered as his hero's lifestyle. Its syntax is convoluted, its vocabulary archaic. Huysmans was a word collector, like d'Annunzio, who crammed his notebook with arcane phrases, and subsequently sprinkled them over his writing, he said, like "sequins," to make his sentences glitter.

Huysmans's hero, Jean des Esseintes, partitions his drawing room to form a series of niches, each one differently decorated so as to provide an appropriate setting for the reading of one of his favourite books. He drinks fine yellow tea imported from "China via Russia in special caravans for his express use." (We have seen how d'Annunzio savoured his China tea.) This "liquid perfume" des Esseintes sips from porcelain cups as translucent as eggshell and sometimes (though he has little appetite for food) he takes tiny morsels of toast served on plates of slightly worn silver-gilt. (D'Annunzio's Andrea Sperelli has silver-gilt tableware worn in just the same way.) Following de Montesquiou, des Esseintes sets off the colours of his carpet by letting loose on it a tortoise which is still alive, but gilded and studded all over with jewels.

Barbey d'Aurevilly declared of *À Rebours* that the novel expressed such world-weariness that its author would surely have to choose "between the muzzle of the pistol and the foot of the cross." Huysmans chose the latter. Eight years after his novel's publication he retreated to a Trappist monastery: he later took holy orders. In this, he and d'Annunzio differed fundamentally. D'Annunzio cluttered his own and his hero's rooms with ecclesiastical bric-a-brac, but, unbeliever as he was, when he secluded himself, he did so just for a bit, every now and then.

In *Pleasure*, Sperelli, embittered by his lover's cruel rejection, embarks on a sequence of affairs. A "taste for contamination" impels him to seduce ladies of previously impeccable reputation. His promiscuity is as damaging to himself as it is to the women. "Degradation, like leprosy," has marked him. D'Annunzio's novel glitters, but it is also intended to burn. From Francavilla he wrote to Emilio Treves, a Milanese to whom Michetti had introduced him and who would be his publisher for the next twenty-eight years. He had written, he told Treves, "the saddest and most spiritual of books," a novel full of "the highest morality."

He was protesting perhaps a tad too much. Huysmans's des Esseintes retreats permanently to the country and becomes a recluse. D'Annunzio's Andrea Sperelli once resolves to spend an evening alone in reflection, but within an hour has accepted an invitation to dine out with three other young noblemen and assorted ladies of pleasure. D'Annunzio in his twenties might need a few months' clausura, but he had no wish—even in his imagination—to permanently forswear the pleasures of the world and the flesh.

Blood

D RIVING BACK TO HIS PALATIAL APARTMENT after a concert one day, *Pleasure*'s Andrea Sperelli is annoyed to find his carriage delayed by an uproar on the streets of Rome. It is January 1887. People are marching on the parliament buildings while troops attempt to disperse them. The demonstrators are distraught and angry. Sperelli has heard the news of the massacre of Italian troops at Dogali in Ethiopia, but it is nothing to him. The dead men, he says to the woman with him, are merely "four hundred brutes, killed brutally."

Those "brutes" were part of an ill-prepared invasion force. They had been set upon by an Ethiopian army which outnumbered them ten to one, and had been slaughtered to a man. Dogali was to Italians what Rorke's Drift was to the English or Little Big Horn to the Americans, a waste of life converted by popular rhetoric into a tale of heroism and self-sacrifice. The deaths of these hundreds of white men, inflated into legend and misted over with grief, eclipsed other, more embarrassing stories, of thousands of indigenous people dispossessed, driven off their lands or killed. By the time *Pleasure* was published in the summer of 1889 the 400 dead men had become 500 glorious martyrs in the patriotic cause, commemorated with a monument in front of Rome's railway station, and a second Italian invasion of Ethiopia was in the offing.

The line in *Pleasure* provoked a chorus of indignation from those who took Sperelli to be one and the same with his creator. D'Annunzio was indignant in his turn. He protested that this passage was the point in the novel where Sperelli shows most clearly that he is a "monster." He, d'Annunzio, most certainly didn't share his character's decadent anti-militarism. Had he not written an ode in honour of those who died in the African wars?

Grievance and failure had shaped Italian patriotism from the very beginning of the new nation's history. In 1866, when d'Annunzio was three years old, the still-incomplete nation intervened, unprovoked, in a war between Austria and Prussia. The conflict between the two northern powers offered an opportunity for Italy to acquire Venice and its hinterland without any bloodshed: the Austrians would have ceded control of the region in exchange for Italy's neutrality. But bloodshed was precisely what Italy's rulers wanted. In parliament a follower of Garibaldi's announced, "We must . . . shed much Italian blood if we are to secure the place in the world that we deserve." He was echoed by Francesco Crispi. Italy must have its "baptism of blood" to prove its status as a "great nation." The writer Edmondo de Amicis records the exultant crowds filling the streets when war was declared, the atmosphere of carnival. "These are great days for Italy! A great war! . . . This is how nations are made!"

The outcome was humiliating. Within weeks Italian troops were surprised and routed at Custoza. Again the Austrians, hard pressed by Prussia on their northern front, offered to hand over the Veneto if Italy would withdraw from the war. King Victor Emmanuel and his generals refused. They wanted not territory but glory. In July came the sea battle of Lissa. A numerically inferior Austrian force defeated the Italians. The admiral in command was found guilty by the Senate of incompetence, negligence and disobedience. Giuseppe Verdi wrote: "What a wretched time we live in! What a pygmy time! Nothing great: not even great crimes!"

Italy gained the Veneto anyhow, not as the spoils of victory, but as a favour granted by the French emperor, Napoleon III. Good sense might have suggested this was something to be celebrated, but to patriots longing for a bloody baptism and a nation-building great war, it was a disappointment. Crispi wrote: "To be Italian was something we once longed for; now in the present circumstances, it is shameful." For Italians of d'Annunzio's generation that shame was a stain that had to be erased by blood.

Blood streams through the utterances of late nineteenth-century nationalists and Romantics. Blood. Blood. Blood. The word tolls in parliamentary speeches and newspaper articles. Blood must flow, the

motive or occasion for its shedding being of only secondary importance. In the realm of literary fantasy, d'Annunzio's Andrea Sperelli is
nearly killed in a duel over an insignificant insult (as numerous young
men were in fact). In the realm of real politics statesmen cast around
for a pretext for conflict.

Across Europe the same sanguinary rhetoric was in use. In England,
the poet-laureate Lord Tennyson gave the narrator-hero of "Maud" a
starry vision of "a hope for the world in the coming wars," not because
there was any rational justification for those unspecified wars but
because peace "was full of wrongs and shames,/Horrible, hateful,
monstrous, not to be told," while "the blood-red blossom of war with
a heart of fire" was "pure and true." In France, General Georges Boulanger talked of the invigorating power of bloodshed. In Germany,
canny Chancellor Bismarck might protest that Germany had no further need to fight but his realism was out-shouted by the bellicosity of
the circles around the young Prince (soon to be Kaiser) Wilhelm. By
the 1880s spokesmen of all the Italian groupings were expressing their
patriotism in calls for war—any war, anywhere. Peace was demoralis-
ing. The national character must be strengthened in the "crucible of
war." This war need have no precise strategic aims. War was great and
glorious, and good for the soul.

The unprovoked Italian invasion of Ethiopia ended only in the calamity at Dogali. Francesco Crispi, seen as a strong man who could infuse
the country with his strength, became prime minister shortly afterwards. While d'Annunzio was writing *Pleasure*, Crispi was persistently
attempting to lure France into a fight. The British chargé-d'affaires
reported that "the great ambition of Signor Crispi, and perhaps the
mainspring of his actions, is to obtain a military success for Italy, no
matter where or how." The intelligentsia supported Crispi's belliger-
ence. "Glory to you!" wrote Giuseppe Verdi, addressing the premier as
"the great patriot."

The pointless war was postponed. Crispi's emissary to Vienna
reported that the Austrians (now Italy's intended allies in a projected
war against the French) had "a kind of sentimental and philanthropic
love of peace" (which he evidently found both puzzling and deplorable) which meant that "it will be very difficult for us to provoke a war
simply for our own interests." Italy's bloodthirst was only semi-slaked
by a second invasion of Ethiopia in 1889. But the rhetoric which made it
possible for d'Annunzio and others to carry Italians into a "great war"
a quarter of a century later was already forming.

Fame

AT CONCERTS WHICH HE ATTENDED during his first years in Rome, both for the music and for the erotic opportunities they offered, d'Annunzio occasionally saw Franz Liszt. Forty years earlier all Europe had been gripped by Lisztomania. Adoring women had made bracelets out of the maestro's discarded piano strings and lockets from his smoked-out cigar butts. His performances had been said to induce trances and conjure visions. Entire audiences had fainted in instances of mass hysteria described by Heinrich Heine in 1844 as "a veritable insanity, one unheard-of in the annals of furore!" By the time d'Annunzio saw him, Liszt was in his seventies and very frail, but still had the numinous presence of a star. He would sit between two ladies in the front row and when the music ended he would process down the aisle, while his admirers stood reverently by to watch him go.

D'Annunzio was fascinated. Liszt's famous shoulder-length hair, now white, seemed to be made of solid silver. His adorers gazed at the back of his head, wrote d'Annunzio, in "a kind of religious ecstasy . . . as devotees might gaze when the priest elevates the host." Liszt would sit completely still, his head cocked to one side as he listened. D'Annunzio checked his watch: the old man could hold his pose, immobile, for half an hour at a time. "It almost seemed he was not a living man but an idol made of metal and wax."

Like Liszt, d'Annunzio was to become that oddly disjunct thing, a celebrity, and he well understood the difference between the person and the "idol," the persona fame foisted on him. In old age he was to write feelingly of the "horror of being 'Gabriele d'Annunzio.'" Horror or not though, that persona was one he himself created, showing extraordinary energy and invention in his pursuit of fame.

.   .   .

He set about promoting his novel with gusto. Emilio Treves was, in d'Annunzio's opinion, the only publisher in Italy "who knows how to *launch* a book." The two of them devised a campaign designed to overlay the figure of d'Annunzio himself—the hard-working, hard-up scribbler—with the image of his fictional hero Sperelli, son of a Byronic nobleman, "tall and slender, with that inimitable elegance which only ancient lineage can confer."

The membrane separating fact from fiction became permeable. The real artist Aristide Sartorio, a friend of d'Annunzio's, was commissioned to produce in reality a version of the fictional etching which the fictional Sperelli (who is, in an amateur, gentlemanly way, a fine poet and draughtsman) makes in the novel. Its subject matter is titillating. Elena Muti lies asleep beneath a sumptuous blue silken bedspread embroidered with all the signs of the zodiac. In Sartorio's depiction the cover, which d'Annunzio describes with loving detail in the novel, has—as is the way of drapery in such images—slipped. Elena's lovely upper body is exposed and (here's the detail which gives the image its particular *frisson*) a greyhound leans over to lick her naked breast. D'Annunzio had been at pains to insist his novel was not pornographic: he was not so fastidious when it came to publicity material. "We'll print a limited number of copies, we'll sell them with an air of mystery," he wrote to Sartorio, explaining how they would both benefit. Sartorio, entering into the spirit of the thing, signed the picture *"Andrea Sperelli calcographus."* It went on display in the front window of a picture-dealer's shop on the Corso.

D'Annunzio wanted a wide public. He never completely gave up journalism, even once he was earning prodigious sums from his fiction and poetry. "I like this quick communication with the unknown mass," he wrote. "It's good for the modern artist to immerse himself from time to time in the current, vital media." For the same reason he had chosen to write in a genre which was both up to date and popular. He had noticed that when a journal included an extract from a new novel its sales figures increased enormously. There was a demand for fiction, and, in Italy, very little supply. In d'Annunzio's opinion Manzoni (the author of *I Promessi Sposi*—*The Betrothed*—published in 1840 and generally considered to be the great Italian novel) had no worthy successors. Nor, come to that, did he much admire Manzoni.

He was writing now, not only for the educated elite, but for a mass market. Novels' readers, he ascertained, were predominantly female. The majority of them were neither rich nor upper class, but enjoyed reading about those who were. In his early stories he had written about beggars and work-worn seamen. But the audience whom he now sought to please weren't interested in the tribulations of the Abruzzese peasantry. They wanted to be lifted above "mediocre reality." Accordingly he gave them a fantasy world where no one did paid work, where life was passed in pleasures variously voluptuous or intellectually arcane.

In doing so he wasn't writing down to his public: he was following his own bent. He wanted popularity, but he made no compromises in order to achieve it. *Pleasure* is that rare thing in literary history, an uncompromisingly experimental novel which became a huge popular success. It was the occasion of much scandalised gossip and an immediate bestseller. In the words of a contemporary journalist, "thousands of young men dressed, moved, spoke, walked and smoked in the style of Andrea Sperelli. Women imitated his heroines' attitudes and the décor of their rooms." In the longer term, it became an international *succès d'estime*. Henry James praised it for d'Annunzio's "excited sensibility," his "splendid visual sense" and "his ample and exquisite style." Even Casanova's autobiography, concluded James, was "cheap loose journalism compared with the directed, finely condensed iridescent epic of Count Andrea." D'Annunzio was made.

Superman

DURING THE SIX YEARS following the publication of *Pleasure*, d'Annunzio lived in Rome, the Abruzzi, Rome again, various military barracks, Rome again, the Abruzzi again, Naples (successively in several rented or borrowed houses around the bay), Rome, Francavilla, Pescara and Rome again. A number of these moves were involuntary. In this period d'Annunzio wrote a novella and three more novels, as well as substantial quantities of poetry and journalism, and he began to earn large sums from his writing; but it was never enough to pay his debts. In public he posed successfully as the aesthete/dandy/poet, but his home life was repeatedly disrupted by the horrid rumpus of the bailiffs at the door.

His relationship with Barbara continued, increasingly shadowed by ambivalence, into its fifth year. After he separated definitively from his wife in 1888 and moved to Naples he was still receiving visits from Barbara—and assuring her how ardently he adored her—as he embarked on his next and most disastrous affair, with the Princess Maria Gravina Cruyllas di Ramacca. There were calamities, variously pathetic, sordid and deadly serious. His father died, after being declared bankrupt. His wife, Maria Hardouin di Gallese and his new mistress, Maria Gravina, each attempted suicide, their desperation at least in part the result of d'Annunzio's treatment of them. With Maria Gravina he came close to being imprisoned for adultery (a criminal act under Neapolitan law). His fourth (and best-beloved) child, a daughter, Renata, was born, and nearly died. In old age he remembered the night he held her tiny body in his arms until dawn—his muscles cramping and his entire being concentrated on the effort of willing her fever to pass—as being charged with the purest and strongest emotion he ever knew.

His writing, increasingly popular and lucrative, was also increasingly controversial. As his reputation with the general public as the purveyor of thrilling wickedness grew, so did the respect of his literary peers. The French publication of *Pleasure* occasioned both a scandal in the popular press and a conference convened by his learned admirers at the Sorbonne.

These were d'Annunzio's helter-skelter years, a period when in public his reputation was consolidated thanks to bouts of hectic work, and in private he reeled, in a state of fecklessness and bad faith, from one desperate situation to the next. It was also the time when his reading and thinking began to coalesce into a political creed. Here are some glimpses of that period.

ROME. A WET NIGHT IN FEBRUARY 1889. D'Annunzio is in a closed carriage, waiting outside the house where Barbara lives with her mother. All day he has been passing and repassing her door, racked by desire for her. "It was raining almost as hard in the carriage as it was in the street, so violent was the downpour."

The life of an illicit lover can be wretched. Some time past midnight Barbara appears. She is with a man—her husband. D'Annunzio watches them go into the house, and waits on, hoping to see Count Leoni leave. After an hour and ten minutes he gives up and goes, not to the apartment where his wife and children are living, but to the rented room where he and Barbara meet. "Then began a new torment . . . My ear strained after every sound. Two or three times I went out into the street . . . I even imagined I could hear your voice." She doesn't come. At dawn he falls asleep, so exhausted that he feels "a physical need for death."

FIVE MONTHS LATER. Michetti's convent at Francavilla. D'Annunzio has arrived with a clear statement of intent. "This summer I absolutely must write a masterpiece." Now Michetti has found him in his studio down on the beach, in tears. He has a heap of fresh sheets of paper prepared, but so far he has written only on three of them: not the first pages of the new book, but three suicide notes, one to his mother, one to Barbara, one to Michetti. His knuckles are bleeding. He has banged them and his head repeatedly against the wall until he is half stunned. His forehead shows the bruise. Michetti is appalled and uncomprehending. D'Annunzio pours it all out. Barbara's "pathetic, sensual beauty, her sickness contracted in her marriage, the turpitude of her

husband . . . and all my incurable passion . . . the necessity of having her with me without delay, despite all that forbids it, or of dying."

One of his mentors, on reading *Pleasure*, remarked that it "smelt of sperm"—several of its most memorable passages are extended erotic fantasies—and advised d'Annunzio, before he wrote another, to take the sexual pressure off by providing himself with an undemanding concubine, "a sort of cow," for the duration of the work. Michetti, more sympathetic, undertakes to bring him, not a "cow," but Barbara. A true and generous friend, he finds d'Annunzio a hide-away, and persuades Barbara to join him there.

For two months the lovers live in the little house which d'Annunzio, still toying with the fantasy of a religious seclusion, dubs the "hermitage." This is his sketch of it (see above). It is a forty-minute walk along a rough path from the nearest railway station, on a cliff above the Adriatic, where, as d'Annunzio warns Barbara in advance, "all the comforts of life are lacking" but where they are completely secluded, able to enjoy the immensity of the sea before them, and to make love at all hours. D'Annunzio works on a new collection of poems, and begins the novel which will eventually be published as *Il Trionfo della Morte* (*The Triumph of Death*).

The first draft, written that summer with Barbara constantly beside him, traces the gradual slackening of his passion. The man who would wait all night in the rain for her is now sated. "The irreparable *ruin* that the constant presence of a woman wreaks on an exalted spirit," runs one of his notes. The novel describes two people in many ways resembling d'Annunzio and Barbara, alone in a house just like the "hermitage," swimming off the beach beneath, making love in an orange silk tent on the sand, observing the rituals of the peasants and fishermen who are their only neighbours, watching appalled (as d'Annunzio and Barbara did) as a family of fishermen mourns the death of a drowned child.

D'Annunzio later told Romain Rolland that he had sat by the bedside and taken notes on Barbara's appearance as she slept so that he could describe it in his novel with "terrible truthfulness." His heroine (who, as d'Annunzio explicitly tells Barbara, "is you"), blooms in the sea air (d'Annunzio preferred her sickly). She becomes tanned (d'Annunzio liked his women pale). With nothing else to do she makes a companion of their peasant-housekeeper, and busies herself with "low matters" like cooking. Her face becomes less spiritual, vulgar. Her pleasures are "animal." "She *lets herself go.*" The hero notices certain mannerisms, especially her way of rolling a cigarette, which strike him as "whorish."

The novel's hero has moods when he is revolted by sexual contact, by damp voracious flesh. Love, he reflects, "drags after itself an immense net full of dead things." D'Annunzio's liaison with Barbara will last another three years—his passion for her reignited by separation—but soon after they both return to Rome that autumn he writes the disenchanted elegy, *Villa Chigi.*

> All night—how long! (it seemed the dawn would never
>   come),
> With ardour, with mad anger, I had tried
> To revive the flame in our mingled bodies, in our kisses.
> She no longer drank my spirit in those kisses.
> She drank only her own tears in those kisses.

MARCH 1890. D'Annunzio's twenty-seventh birthday. He is passing it in a military hospital. After years of evading his national service (compulsory for all male Italians) on the spurious grounds that he is a student and therefore exempt, he has at last submitted. The soldier's life appalls him. He is tormented by bedbugs and nauseated by the close proximity of so many of his fellow men. Obliged to drill for hours of every day, he has stopped work on his novel. He has to groom his own horse and to help clean the stables. He barely has time to wash. "My worst enemy could not have imagined a more ferocious, inhuman torture for me."

For all his protests, he is being leniently treated. He has already been granted extended leave to visit his father. Now he is taking further time off for treatment for "neurasthenic disturbances." Seeking distraction, he goes to the hospital's dissection room and watches an autopsy. "Blood, so much blood, the stench of death, impassive doctors." He observes the admission of two badly injured soldiers. One of them is bleeding so profusely that all the onlookers are sprayed with gore. It is evening. "The shadows, the murmurs of the bystanders, the glitter of surgical knives, all these tragic things exalt me." Back in his room he writes to Barbara about the dissected corpse. "I still *see* that big body with the skull cracked, the chest ripped open."

D'Annunzio has an awareness of bodies—his own and others'—which is unlike that of any of his literary peers. In his love letters he likes to be right inside a woman, describing the inner folds of Barbara's vagina back to her. In his novels he gets near enough to his heroines to see their sweat and smell their breath. He writes about the pink, inner rims of eyelids, about armpits, about snot-clogged nostrils, about bare feet. When a group of young women crowd to a window in *Maybe Yes, Maybe No* to watch the swallows return in spring they are aware—pleasantly but a little awkwardly—of each other's legs as they stand flank to flank. These women are flesh, and so are we all—a fact which seems to d'Annunzio now marvellous, now disgusting, now pitiful, but which he never forgets.

In April 1890 in Pescara, Francesco d'Annunzio, cousin to the poet, shot himself dead. On 6 June, Maria Hardouin di Gallese, d'Annunzio's wife, threw herself from an upstairs window.

Maria survived, with two broken legs. Various possible motives for her attempted suicide have been proposed. She told one of her husband's early biographers that it was her father who reduced her to despair that day. Meeting him in the street while out walking with one of her boys, she tried to introduce him to his grandson. He rebuffed her, saying, "Who are you? I don't know you." Another source suggests that Maria was distraught after d'Annunzio had accused her of encouraging the advances of their mutual friend, a journalist who wrote under the Balzacian name of Rastignac. There was even gossip that she might be pregnant with her lover's child. All these accounts are credible, but Maria's worst trial must surely have been d'Annunzio's persistent infidelity. He had recently subjected her to a new humiliation, renting a new love nest for himself and Barbara in the self-same building as that in which he was living with his wife and children.

He visited Maria assiduously as she lay in hospital. He was always most attentive at sickbeds. "She would please me if she was always suffering, always ill," reflects his fictional Giorgio. But on the very day of her suicide attempt he wrote to Barbara suggesting that, since his wife would certainly be hospitalised for at least three weeks, she should hurry back to Rome. On leaving hospital Maria separated from him definitively.

The spectre of suicide stalks through d'Annunzio's fiction, and through his letters and diaries. *The Triumph of Death* (already partially written when Maria tried to kill herself) opens with a suicide. Giorgio and Ippolita are walking in the Pincio gardens when they see a group of men by a parapet overhanging a steep drop. On the road beneath, a carter pokes with a stick at traces of blood and blonde hair. A woman has thrown herself down. Her corpse has already been removed. "Blessed are the dead," remarks Giorgio as they walk away. "They doubt no more."

Suicide was a Romantic act. Death, as a consummation devoutly to be wished, was a concept d'Annunzio would have found over and over again in his reading. The English poets he had loved from his school days were death-besotted. Goethe's Young Werther, killing himself for love of an unattainable woman, had sparked a Europe-wide wave of copy-cat self-killings: in d'Annunzio's lifetime another wave of suicides swept over the German-speaking world. Arthur Schnitzler's daughter, Hugo von Hofmannsthal's son, three of Ludwig Wittgenstein's brothers and Gustav Mahler's brother would all kill themselves. Schnitzler suggested motives for suicide: "Grace, or debts, from boredom with life, or purely out of affectation." In 1889 the deadly fashion reached a peak when Crown Prince Rudolf, heir apparent to the Austro-Hungarian Empire, committed suicide after murdering his mistress Marie Vetsera, just seven months before d'Annunzio began writing the novel which would end with a similar double death.

In France in 1913, d'Annunzio wrote a novella whose narrator is the curiously named Desiderio Moriar ("Death Wish"). He signed his last work as "Gabriele d'Annunzio Tempted to Die."

·   ·   ·

His military service done, his marriage over, d'Annunzio spent the winter of 1890/91 living in a large ground-floor room near the Piazza di Spagna. There Barbara frequently visited, and d'Annunzio, his desire for her rekindled by abstinence, banked up the fire (d'Annunzio's expenditure on firewood was exorbitant) and lay with her naked on heaps of damask cushions in front of the great blaze.

Prompted by Barbara, he was reading the Russian novels which had begun to appear in French and Italian translation in the 1880s. From Dostoevsky he picked up a new tone of voice, and new subject matter. Rome in the last two decades of the nineteenth century was teeming with single men as alienated as Raskolnikov, many of them far from home, attempting to make a living in the booming city. During the spring of 1891, d'Annunzio wrote the novella *Giovanni Episcopo* set among such people.

An assorted group of men, ill-educated and coarse-mannered, live together in a boarding house. Each night they eat there and, sex-starved as they all are, each of them lusts after a good-looking wait-ress. "The heat becomes suffocating; ears turn red, eyes glisten. A base, almost bestial expression appears on the faces of those men who have eaten and drunk. I think I'm going to faint . . . I draw in my elbows to increase the distance between myself and my neighbours."

The brutalised peasants who surround the lovers in *The Triumph of Death*; now the bestial city workers: d'Annunzio's fiction was teeming with sub-humans. His Darwinism was becoming malignant: his imagi-nary world was filled with the unfit, those whose survival was unneces-sary and undeserved. In *Crime and Punishment*, Dostoevsky's murderer believes there are some superior beings who "have the absolute right to commit any kind of excess, any crime . . . to break the law in any way whatsoever, because they are not common men." D'Annunzio's next work was to be *The Innocent*, in which the hero Tullio kills a baby. The novel takes the form of a confession addressed to no one because, as Tullio asserts: "The justice of men cannot touch me. No tribunal on earth would know how to judge me." Tullio, like Raskolnikov, is laying claim to an exceptional status which allows him absolute licence, the status of the superman.

MARCH 1891. The bailiffs are breaking down the door of d'Annunzio's room. He has been declared bankrupt. The chief plaintiff against him is the maître d' at the Caffè Roma, where d'Annunzio has been eating on account for years. His financial affairs are complex beyond comprehension. He has debts covered by other debts, guarantors standing surety for each other in a web of illusory security designed to veil the horrid truth that he has spent far, far more than he has ever earned.

He has sent several containers full of his furniture and movables to Francavilla, where Michetti (from whom he has borrowed large sums) will accept it in lieu of payment, with a promise to return it all some fine day, and thereby keep it safe from other creditors. An extract from the inventory of those cases' contents suggests how d'Annunzio's money melts away so fast: "A damascened harp, two twisted ebony columns, a blue and gold Japanese tray, an etching of Botticelli's Primavera in a baroque frame, a large platter of bohemian glass, a length of Cordoba leather painted with figures, two boars' tusks, an altarpiece in the form of a sunburst, ten large antique oriental rugs ..." And so it goes on, and on, and on. There are eighty items in all, all salvaged from a one-room apartment.

Now he sees it all go, and leaves the city. "I departed ill, desperate, with no strength left, in a sinister dawn." He flees to his usual refuge at Francavilla. Michetti, his guardian angel and father abbot, takes him in.

Later he will boast of having written *The Innocent* in three and a half weeks. It takes him closer to three months in fact, but even so it is a prodigious feat of mind and will. He writes to Barbara, describing the budding fruit trees, the haze of grey-green veiling the distant woods, and then describes them again in his novel. He attends a village christening: the songs and rituals he observes pass straight into his narrative. Again he resists all Barbara's pleas for a visit, despite writing her letters in which he enlarges upon the state of unassuageable sexual arousal in which he lives. His "savage *gonfalon*," he tells her (the word is as archaic in Italian as it is in English), is permanently raised.

In mid-July he posts the completed manuscript to Emilio Treves. For months already he has been pestering Treves for an advance. He is, he says, a good investment. Treves can look forward to receiving a whole series of further books from him. Surely the publisher will not deny him now? "I await an answer accompanied by the money which is necessary to me." Treves will agree to nothing until he has read the novel. D'Annunzio sends it. Three weeks pass, and then comes the devastating response. *The Innocent* is "highly immoral." It is derivative (Treves, who has recently published Italian translations of *Anna Karenina* and *War and Peace*, is unimpressed by d'Annunzio's appropriation of Tolstoyan themes and techniques). Treves will not publish it. Now Barbara writes, threatening to break with him (they haven't seen each other for five months). His marriage over, his love affair faltering, his professional prospects dim, d'Annunzio leaves Francavilla for Naples.

The novel which Treves has just rejected will win d'Annunzio international acclaim. Its confessional form is innovative. Its protagonist-narrator Tullio Hermil describes himself as maintaining "an intensely clear-eyed surveillance" over himself. That self is so volatile that Tullio, tracing the currents of depravity and penitence, tenderness and sadism swirling through his own consciousness, describes himself as *"multanime"* (many-spirited). *The Innocent* is one of the most intricately nuanced of all the great psychological novels. It is also d'Annunzio's most compelling piece of story-telling.

Tullio, like most d'Annunzian heroes, is a contemporary Roman gentleman of leisure, intellectually sophisticated and emotionally jaded. He has been repeatedly unfaithful to his beautiful wife Giuliana and she, despairing of ever regaining his love, has allowed herself to be seduced by another man. At Easter time, while they are staying at his mother's house in the countryside, Tullio seeks a reconciliation, but Giuliana is by now pregnant with her lover's child. Together the couple spend a day at the deserted Villa Lilla, and in the garden, overcome by the scent of lilacs, Giuliana swoons into her husband's arms. Tullio is ardently in love with her again (not least because her difficult pregnancy makes her as pale and ill as d'Annunzio liked his women to be), but he is sickened by the prospect of having to rear another's man's child. A boy is born. In the dead of winter, when the rest of the household are in the chapel to celebrate the coming of Christmas, Tullio strips off the baby's shawls and holds him, naked, by an open window in the bitter cold until he catches a fatal chill.

Treves had been correct in fearing condemnation. When the novel was finally published the reviewer in the *Fanfulla della Domenica* deplored the "sour poison . . . which oozes from every pore of Gabriele d'Annunzio's new novel," and its nauseating "stench of corruption and depravity." It wasn't only the double adultery and the infanticide which shocked readers. There is a disturbing intimacy in the way d'Annunzio writes about the warm slime of kissing mouths, or crusted mucus on a baby's upper lip, or the softness of a woman's uncorsetted breasts.

He is equally forensic in his analysis of the impulses of desire, cruelty and squeamish revulsion alternating in a lover's mind as he caresses his partner. For many, this was a great deal too much reality.

To less nervous readers, *The Innocent* vindicates d'Annunzio's claim that the novel could be as verbally exquisite and emotionally suggestive as poetry. A network of repeated and varied images makes of the whole work a tapestry of words. Giuliana's hands, lying inert along the arms of a chair or over the sheets of her sickbed; a bunch of white chrysanthemums; Monteverdi's plaint of Euridice; the swallows' nests piled along the eaves of the empty villa: each of these motifs recurs, setting up a series of refrains which echo musically through the narrative. Henry James declared that *The Innocent* showed d'Annunzio reigning supreme over the sphere of "exasperated sensibility." "Other story-tellers strike us in comparison as remaining at the door of the inner precinct, as listening there but to catch an occasional faint sound, while he alone is well within and moving through the place as its master."

D'Annunzio aspires to "make his own life," but he is a man, not of decision, but of impulse. Michetti is going to Naples, so d'Annunzio, with no pressing reason for being anywhere else, goes there too. Their mutual friend Scarfoglio and his wife, Mathilde Serao, are living in the city. D'Annunzio reads *The Innocent* aloud to them over three successive evenings and they agree to publish it in instalments in their journal, the *Corriere di Napoli*.

If Rome is bustling with the energy of a new metropolis, Naples is grandly degenerate, the capital of a defunct kingdom (the Bourbon monarchs left hastily when Garibaldi advanced on the city in 1860). The drama of its situation between the volcano and the sea is breathtaking. Its government is corrupt: the authorities rule only with the consent of the Camorra, which is to the region what the Mafia is to Sicily. Its society is, in every sense of the word, decadent. D'Annunzio finds it congenial.

The celebrated author is soon frequenting the drawing rooms of at least two prominent hostesses. Meanwhile a notorious fixer is arranging meetings for him with the city's indispensable money lenders, and, at the offices of the *Corriere*, Scarfoglio and Serao are introducing him to the intelligentsia. He meets another brilliant Abruzzese, the philosopher Benedetto Croce, and two future prime ministers of Italy, Francesco Nitti and Antonio Salandra. A quarter of a century later Croce will be one of d'Annunzio's severest critics, and Nitti his political adversary; but for the time being they are both talented young men with whom he is pleased to keep company. He looks different now, more masculine. His fast-receding hair is cut short—no more of those dark curls—and he has grown a little, pointed, surprisingly blond, beard. He affects a monocle, and gets into a scuffle with a gentleman whose lady friend he has been eyeing up too brazenly.

He and Barbara exchange letters in which acrimony alternates with delirious pornographic fantasies. He tells her that he has with him always a "reliquary," a locket containing a photograph and a strand of her pubic hair. She visits. They bicker. He writes elegiac poems about the autumnal light and the gardens of Capo di Monte and the fading of love. Their affair, d'Annunzio tells a close friend, is at its finishing point. He receives anonymous letters informing him of Barbara's visits to a woman who is both a money lender and a go-between. Perhaps this woman is helping Barbara look for a new man wealthy enough to pay off her debts. Perhaps d'Annunzio would like to persuade himself so, in order to temper his own guilt.

He has already found her replacement. Shortly after arriving in Naples he meets the Princess Maria Gravina. Two years older than d'Annunzio, and several inches taller, she is married to an artillery officer, with whom she has two, or perhaps four children (accounts differ—however many children there are, she will anyway soon abandon them). She is Sicilian, a prince's daughter, dark-eyed, with a dramatic streak of red in her black hair.

Throughout the following winter, while still writing ardent letters to Barbara, d'Annunzio is wooing Maria. In the spring comes a sequence of unhappy events. Maria's husband Count Anguissola invests his money unwisely and loses it. He gives up his house in Naples and withdraws to his family's estate. Maria Gravina refuses to go with him. She leaves the marital home, taking her children with her, and asks for a legal separation. Her parents cut off her allowance. She discovers she is pregnant: d'Annunzio must be the father. She attempts to induce a miscarriage but fails. Her husband visits her house and surprises her and d'Annunzio *in flagrante*. The count brings legal charges. His prosecution takes nearly a year to come to court, during which time the lovers live with the knowledge that under Neapolitan law adultery is a crime carrying a mandatory prison sentence. D'Annunzio had not intended to prolong his relationship with Maria, but feels unable to abandon her now. Separated from her husband, estranged from her parents, she clings to him and her pregnancy "makes a break more difficult."

Naples and Rome are still separate societies. Gossip circulates slowly. Still oblivious of his new love, Barbara writes that she will come to visit d'Annunzio. He finds reasons why she should not. He has no money. Maria Gravina and her children move into his lodgings. D'Annunzio is accumulating debts in Naples as fast as he did in Rome. He is dogged everywhere by a "dreary procession of those to whom we owe money." Soon the bailiffs come to his lodgings. He is turned out. All the curios he has once more been accumulating are seized. He is homeless again, and this time he has a pregnant woman, her children and their nanny with him.

A friend of Maria Gravina's rescues the forlorn party by offering a wing of her castle in Ottajano, thirty kilometres out of Naples along the bay. Their setting is splendid: their circumstances wretched. As Maria Gravina enters the last trimester of her pregnancy, winter begins. "This immense feudal castle is an icehouse," writes d'Annunzio, the man who likes to keep his homes at such a temperature that his mistresses can comfortably lie naked on the floor at all hours, and whose male visitors repeatedly complain that to visit him is to risk being stifled. "These rooms are as high and long as the nave of a cathedral, and impossible to heat." Maria Gravina's children are noisy and demanding and a constant reminder to d'Annunzio of how long it is (nearly two years) since he saw his own boys. They cannot pay the milkman. They cannot buy bread. They cannot afford firewood. D'Annunzio cannot ask his former landlady to forward his mail because he hasn't paid his rent and she, too, is demanding money of him. He writes to Barbara (implying that he is alone), lamenting the curse of which he is victim, the fact that he (Duke Minimo! the arbiter of fashion!) has been stripped by his creditors of all his clothes but for one suit and a couple of nightshirts.

And yet, somehow, he gets by. He writes a teasing verse begging the Baronessa della Marra to buy him a Louis XVI writing desk he has seen in an antique-shop window, a lovely thing "in every way worthy of a famous writer," but which is, alas, beyond his own means. If she does so, then she is one of a number of aristocratic ladies ready to offer the poet expensive favours. Just as a princess offered him a rent-free castle, so, when that seems too cold, an obliging baroness lends him a villa. And when money comes in, as it intermittently does, d'Annunzio doesn't pay the milkman, he goes into town and dines out.

At last Barbara hears of the existence of Maria Gravina and the imminent child. She writes that she "knows everything." Unabashed, d'Annunzio replies that if that is so, she will know that "hustled along by the violence of events, trapped in a maze with no exit, I have done my duty." His last letter to Barbara is an astonishing exercise in self-delusion and self-regard. He has never lied to her, he says. He forgives her the words she has written in the blindness of her anger. He urges her to find another love—but not, please, in such a way as to embarrass him. As for himself, "I pursue my blind and vertiginous course towards who knows which precipice. I will not turn round to gaze, with eyes veiled with tears, at the great past love." He is the Dostoevskian exceptional being, beyond human judgement. He is also a helpless victim who cannot be held responsible for anything. He is unhappy. He is to be pitied. He is doing his best. None of this is his fault. Nothing has ever been; is ever; will ever be, his fault. "It is unbelievable how fate hounds me."

Through all this hubbub of wronged women, of bailiffs and criminal charges and precipitate flights, d'Annunzio keeps working. During his two years in Naples he produces a stream of poems, stories and journalism. He revises and completes the interrupted *Triumph of Death*, and gathers material for his next novel, *The Virgins of the Rocks*. He writes the poems to be published as *Poema Paradisiaco*, which includes some of his most abidingly popular verse.

He is encountering new stimuli. In Naples, there are people who knew Richard Wagner during his sojourn in Ravello during the 1870s, and it is now that d'Annunzio begins pestering van Westerhout to play *Tristan and Isolde* to him over and over again. He is also interesting himself in politics.

In Italy in the 1890s, political parties were defined not by ideology, but by shared interests. Administrations tended to be centrist coalitions, put together by means of the trading of favours. Alliances, based cynically on mutual advantage, were so tenuous that a new term "*trasformismo*" was coined to describe the process whereby deputies were tempted or intimidated into switching sides. Francesco Crispi gave an acerbic account of the process. In parliament, he writes, whenever an important vote was to be taken, chaos reigned. "Government supporters run all over the place, along the corridors, looking for votes. Subsidies, honours, canals, bridges, roads—everything is promised." Corruption was endemic, and commentators of every political persuasion called for change.

Edoardo Scarfoglio and Mathilde Serao were both loud in their condemnation of the feebleness of parliamentary government. The *Corriere di Napoli* was consistently critical of Italy's democratic institutions. D'Annunzio, in an article he wrote for the paper in September 1892, goes further, attacking democracy itself.

His piece is provocatively entitled *"La Bestia Elettiva"* (the electoral beast). The majority, he declares "will never be capable of liberty." The elite "sooner or later, will always regain the reins of power." He lays out his vision of the future. "Men will be divided into two races. To the superior ones, who have raised themselves by the pure energy of their will, everything will be permitted, to the inferior ones nothing, or very little." D'Annunzio is not talking about traditional class distinctions here. "The true nobleman in no way resembles the spineless heirs of ancient patrician families." Rather a member of the master race would be distinguished by his "personal nobility." Like the speaker in W. E. Henley's poem *Invictus* (first published in 1888), he is the master of his fate and the captain of his soul. "He is a self-governing force." His hands will never be dirtied by contact with a ballot paper. To participate in the democratic process would render him equal with the "plebs"—a degradation he will never accept.

At a dinner in 1895, d'Annunzio proposed a toast to "putrefaction," than which, he said, "there is no more fervid and violent manifestation of life." He explained himself by alluding to Darwin, but he was not really talking about biology. His toast was to the continuing debasement of political life, in the apparent hope that parliamentary democracy might destroy itself, leaving a land more fit for d'Annunzian heroes. "I drink to the roses which will flower from the blood."

In June 1893, d'Annunzio's father, Francesco Paolo, died. The news was brought to him as he sat in a café. "No rhetoric please," he said. He went to Pescara, but he went too late. For no good reason that we know of, he missed his father's funeral, arriving in time only to oversee the break-up of the estate. It was a sad and sordid business. He had hoped for an inheritance sufficient to pay his debts, but he was disappointed. The house in Pescara was preserved for his mother to live in, but all the other family property had to be sold, the proceeds used to pay the dead man's debts.

D'Annunzio introduces *The Triumph of Death* with an allusion to Friedrich Nietzsche: "We prepare ourselves, in art . . . for the coming of the *ÜBERMENSCH*, the superman." With his usual gift for sensing shifts in the cultural atmosphere, d'Annunzio had begun referring to Nietzsche's work some time before he had actually read any of it. But in 1893 an anthology of French translations of extracts from the philosopher's writing was published. D'Annunzio seized on it.

It has been customary for biographers and critics to allege that most of d'Annunzio's subsequent thinking was derived from Nietzsche's, but the truth is rather that both writers had been looking to the same masters, and arriving at the same conclusions. Like d'Annunzio, Nietzsche had been influenced by Dostoevsky, whom he called "the only psychologist from whom I have anything to learn." Like d'Annunzio, he had noted Darwin's suggestion that "Man" (none of these thinkers paid much attention to female humanity) might hope "for a still higher destiny in the distant future."

"What is the ape to man?" wrote Nietzsche. "A laughing-stock or a painful embarrassment. And a laughing-stock or a painful embarrassment is exactly what man should be for the *Übermensch*—the superman." A new race—a new species, even—was gradually coming into being. For Nietzsche, as for d'Annunzio, that "higher destiny" was reserved only for an elite. The great creative sprits, those exceptional beings whom Nietzsche saw as "bright lights" in the tragic darkness of life, could only display their brilliance at the cost of the oppression of lesser folk. "Mankind sacrificed en masse so that one single stronger species of man might thrive—that would be progress."

D'Annunzio, with his theory of the two races, was more than ready for these ideas. Years later in France, contemplating some porters lugging his furniture out of yet another house he was leaving, he was to ask himself in his notebook: "Am I of the same species as those men chattering as they carry the trunks?" The question expected the answer no.

The Nietzschean superman was the acme of biological evolution. More, he was a being so exceptional as to be beyond the reach of moral judgment, "beyond good and evil." Nietzsche extolled magnificent criminals. Humanity, he wrote, is "better off looking for a Cesare Borgia than a Parsifal." Discipline, ruthlessness and an inexorable will were required if one was to transcend the squalor and pettiness of most lives, and aspire, as Nietzsche did, to the condition of "no-longer-animals," those great philosophers, saints, warrior-heroes and artists whom he called the "Tyrants of the Spirit." He revered Napoleon, as the schoolboy d'Annunzio had done. All the bloodshed and mayhem of the French Revolution (which Nietzsche otherwise deplored) had been, in his opinion, amply compensated for in the emergence of such a "genius." "For the sake of a similar prize one would have to desire the anarchic collapse of our entire civilisation." He longed for the heroic, the colossal. He awaited the advent of the superman as an epiphany. "Imagine the bold step of these dragon-slayers."

In 1848, Thomas Carlyle, whose work d'Annunzio had known since his teens, had written: "Man is heaven-born; not the thrall of circumstance, of Necessity, but the victorious subduer thereof." Neither Nietzsche nor d'Annunzio considered heaven to have had any hand in the matter, but both of them agreed that to be "great," one must subdue necessity, imposing a value on life by the exercise of one's own will. Declaring that one must be not the "slave of life" but life's master, Nietzsche habitually slept only four hours a night. He was as ascetic as d'Annunzio was in his periods of "enclosure." His self-discipline, self-mortification even, was not a way of abasing himself but the means by which he lifted himself up. D'Annunzio had written that: "One must make one's own life as one makes a work of art." In Nietzsche he found his echo: "One should fashion an unequivocal work of art out of one's own life."

The hero of *Triumph of Death* is awakened one morning to find an unwelcome visitor already in his bedroom, an old school friend down on his luck, a whining, wheedling fellow who has come to beg a loan. The scrounger is described with loathing and contempt. D'Annunzio, a novelist capable of analysing his characters' most elaborate self-deceptions, must have been aware that this sketch was, among other things, a hideously caricatured self-portrait.

In Naples his debts grew ever larger, the shifts by which he managed to evade paying them more elaborate and opaque. Everything he earned was already promised away long before he received it. He could not even buy postage stamps. His friends had to pay the charges on letters in which he begged—or rather peremptorily demanded—loans which were unlikely ever to be repaid. There were days when there was no food in the house. "I can barely see," he wrote to a friend. "I have had no breakfast and I feel faint." He demanded sympathy with talk of suicide. "I would throw myself into the torrent so as not to suffer any more of this." He envied the poor fishermen bent over their nets; "I envy the beggars. I envy the dead." He even solicited money from Olga Ossani, his Febea, telling her he was so beset he might, at any moment, go mad.

In the event it was Maria Gravina's sanity which began to give way. The year 1893, in which he turned thirty, was d'Annunzio's *annus horribilis*. In January, Maria Gravina gave birth to Renata, but the event brought little immediate joy. The baby was sickly. Maria was unable to feed her. According to d'Annunzio unhappiness soured her milk. A court order took her older children from her: to d'Annunzio's relief they were returned to their father's custody. She could not endure the hardship and insecurity of the life she was being obliged to lead and vented her misery as rage. She was jealous (very likely with reason—Benedetto Croce complained that d'Annunzio broke an engagement with him for the sake of an amorous tryst). When d'Annunzio wanted to leave her to go into Naples for a few hours, she became frenzied. There were noisy, violent scenes.

Renata contracted whooping cough, and came close to death. She survived, but a couple of weeks later fell another blow. Count Anguissola's case against the errant couple came to court. D'Annunzio and Maria Gravina were obliged to appear and hear themselves sentenced to five months imprisonment for a crime, adultery, which d'Annunzio, by this time, most earnestly regretted. They were saved by a general amnesty, but the disgrace was mortifying.

D'Annunzio's debts were still unpaid. "It has begun again, the lugubrious line of people to whom we owe money. Twenty times I have heard the door knocker, twenty times the uncouth voices, twenty times I have been suffocated by a suppressed and most bitter anger." There were more crises: more humiliations. Creditors waylaid d'Annunzio on the street, and besieged him at home. Maria Gravina was jealous, reproachful, angry. One day, when he talked of leaving on his own for the Abruzzi, she became so frantic that he had to call the landlady to help him wrestle her to the ground to forestall her attempts to kill herself: "for a whole hour we had to make super-human efforts to prevent her breaking her head on the floor or against the walls."

Afterwards he was sick, miserable, unable to work. He left Maria for a few days in their little house in the suburb of Resina and hid out in the city. When he returned to Resina the bailiffs broke into the house again and stripped it of what little remained of their belongings—carpets, clothes, chairs. This time, as the wretched couple and their baby went in search of yet another borrowed home, Maria Gravina, the prince's daughter, took with her nothing but the dress she wore.

Rescue was, most wonderfully, on its way. Georges Hérelle, an Italophile French schoolteacher, visited Naples around the time d'Annunzio arrived there. The two didn't meet, but the Frenchman read and enjoyed the *Corriere di Napoli*, and when he left for home he took out a postal subscription. When *The Innocent* began to appear in the journal in instalments, Hérelle was "dazzled." He set himself to translate it and wrote to d'Annunzio, who encouraged him to continue. In September 1892, *The Innocent*, rendered into French by Hérelle under the title *L'Intrus*, began to appear in instalments in *Le Temps*. The following year, as d'Annunzio was being chivvied by his creditors up and down the Bay of Naples, it was published in Paris in book form. It was both a *succès de scandale* and a *succès d'estime*. Reviews were good. Sales were high. D'Annunzio had made his mark where it mattered.

Paris in the 1890s was the Western world's intellectual entrepôt. It was through French translations that d'Annunzio had discovered the Russian novelists and Nietzsche. It was through French translations that the rest of the world would first discover d'Annunzio. Payments began to arrive from France for d'Annunzio, steadily increasing both in size and frequency as more of his works appeared there. German and British publishers took note of this new name, and commissioned translations of their own.

This upturn in his fortunes, though, was too slowly accomplished to solve his immediate problems. When d'Annunzio and Maria Gravina were turned out of their house in Resina, the money coming from his French publication was still only a trickle. There were quicker, if less honourable, ways of saving oneself from debt than waiting for royalties. In October 1893, d'Annunzio somehow found himself in a position to pay his most pressing bills. According to Scarfoglio, Maria Gravina had obtained a large sum of money from a former lover. We do not know, although Scarfoglio drops heavy hints, what services she might have rendered in return. A respite had been granted. The besieging creditors placated, d'Annunzio escorted his troublesome mistress and their baby to Rome, left them there and went himself—with profound relief—alone to stay with Michetti in Francavilla.

Virility

W HEN D'ANNUNZIO LEFT NAPLES one of the city's pawn-brokers gave up hope of ever getting his money back and put d'Annunzio's pledges up for auction. One of them was a fur coat. The sale was crowded. The bidding was competitive. D'Annunzio was a celebrity, and his cast-off clothes were worth collecting as relics.

He was also, in his own estimation and that of his growing number of supporters, a genius, and the world—with prompting from him—was starting to take note of the fact. Ever the self-promoter, he saw to it that the positive French reviews of *The Innocent* were reprinted in Italian journals. "In Paris, *frenzy*. That's the only word for it," he reported gleefully, and he spread that word. One of his last tasks in Naples was to oversee the publication of a special magazine issue devoted entirely to the glorification of himself and his works. Called *D'Annunziana*, it included an enthusiastic essay by the young Austrian poet Hugo von Hofmannsthal. The essay had been "translated" (with the insertion of extra laudatory adjectives), by d'Annunzio himself. He sent copies to Treves, and to his French editor. Fame was a plant which needed careful nurturing, and harried as he was, d'Annunzio took care of it.

Back in the sanctuary of Michetti's convent during the spring of 1894, he at last concluded *The Triumph of Death*, laid aside four years previously, and published a new volume of verse. His public status, at home and abroad, and his earning power, were growing steadily. He had installed Maria Gravina in Rome in the borrowed apartment of a long-suffering friend (all his life d'Annunzio was to have an extraordinary gift for persuading other people to put themselves out on his behalf). After a few months, though, he succumbed to her pleas, and rented a house, the

Villino Mammarella, at Francavilla. He took the largest room for his study and filled it with the usual bric-a-brac: a photograph of that year shows him reclining odalisque-like among the cushions on a daybed draped in embroidered textiles. Maria Gravina and Renata came to live with him. They were not happy. D'Annunzio told his friends that living with Maria was "torture beyond imagining." She had lost her looks. Worse, she was "almost completely mad," subject to "terrible nervous attacks which make her almost demonic" (a fact confirmed by several of his friends). She did nothing, he said, but torment him. "What have I ever done to deserve this scourge?"

Maria is greatly to be pitied. She was mentally ill (possibly schizophrenic). She had sacrificed her social position, her children and her home for a man who no longer loved, or even liked, her. Her parents wanted nothing more to do with her. Her personal property had been confiscated and settled on her legitimate children. Isolated and insecure, she plagued d'Annunzio with her jealousy and frightened him with her rages. She invaded his study and tore up his manuscripts. She produced a pistol and tried to shoot herself. "What a disgrace that would have been!" commented d'Annunzio, "and there would perhaps have been people who accused me of causing her death."

In September 1894, d'Annunzio was in Venice to meet Georges Hérelle for the first time. He sat night after night in Florian's, receiving eager admirers. Each night there were more of them, until by the end of the evening a court of fifteen or twenty adulatory young men were gathered at his table.

One night, walking back to the hotel, d'Annunzio lamented the waste of the evenings. How much more agreeable it would have been, he said, to have hired a gondola and spent two or three hours exploring the "mysterious and fantastic obscurity of the little canals." So why, asked Hérelle, had he agreed to meet all those people? D'Annunzio replied, feebly but probably truthfully: "I am incapable of doing otherwise: I can neither refuse polite invitations, nor excuse myself from issuing invitations in return." It is true that he found it all but impossible to issue any kind of decisive rejection, whether it was saying no to half an hour in a café or ending a mutually destructive years-long relationship. His friends and relations were urging him to leave Maria, but he couldn't yet bring himself to make the break.

Actually he was probably enjoying the company of these acolytes (so different from the miseries of home) a great deal more than he admitted to Hérelle. Among the people he met, or re-met, that September were many who would remain close friends and collaborators. There was Angelo Conti, the art historian, whom d'Annunzio nicknamed Doctor Mysticus, and who would become his guide to the treasures of Venetian architecture and paintings. There was Mariano Fortuny, the designer of marvellous fabrics, gossamer-fine and pleated like the tunics seen on classical Greek statuary, which flowed over women's bodies with wonderfully modern immodesty. From this time forward the women in d'Annunzio's life, and in his fiction, would frequently wear Fortuny gowns (Marcel Proust was an equally enthusiastic admirer of them). There was the Austrian Prince Fritz von Hohenlohe and his mistress— the pair of them avid collectors of rococo ornaments for their miniature palazzo, the Casetta Rossa, which d'Annunzio would rent from them two decades later. There were hostesses both Venetian and foreign, many of them eager to entertain the famous poet. Another member of the circle in which d'Annunzio was moving was Eleonora Duse.

Soon after his sojourn in Venice, which left him, he said, in just the right frame of mind, with the vision of beautiful ancient things in his mind's eye, and imbued with the plangent sadness he wanted for "my musical book," d'Annunzio embarked on the writing of *The Virgins of the Rocks*. The novel is the nearest he was to come to his stated ambition of writing a modern prose narrative which played on consciousness as music might, blending "mystery with thought."

He had referred contemptuously to the "spineless heirs of the ancient patrician families." In this novel he brings them before our eyes. A family loyal to the dispossessed Bourbon monarchs of Naples and Sicily have retired to their labyrinthine country house, full of dim antique mirrors and relics of the *ancien régime*. The patriarch is a venerable representative of the old nobility, but his wife is mad: a sinister bloated figure who is occasionally glimpsed at the end of a garden alley, followed by two shadowy grey-clad attendants. The two sons are feeble-minded—one already "lost" to creeping dementia, the other pathetically afraid of suffering the same fate. The family are not, on the face of it, good breeding stock, and yet that is precisely how the hero, Cantelmo (apparently without any irony on d'Annunzio's part) sees them. There are three daughters, the virgins of the title, all princesses, all nubile, all beautiful. Cantelmo comes to the old house intent on choosing one of them to be his bride and the mother of the great hero whom he believes he is destined to sire.

The long first section of the novel sets out Cantelmo's world view. A fictional character's opinions needn't be those of his or her creator, but in this case we know that they are. Many of Cantelmo's sentiments are quoted word for word from articles and essays d'Annunzio had previously published over his own name. Cantelmo possesses a portrait of his ancestor, a condottiero, painted by Leonardo da Vinci. (While he was still in Naples, d'Annunzio had been reading an influential new biography of Leonardo by Gabriel Séailles.) He quotes Socrates, another fashionable past master. (Walter Pater's *Plato and Platonism* had been published just two years before d'Annunzio began work on *The Virgins*.) Like Nietzsche, like d'Annunzio, Cantelmo scorns the modern political process. He pronounces his belief that "Force is the first law of nature," that men are doomed to fight each other in each generation "until one, the most worthy, establishes dominion over all others." Plaiting together archaic concepts of hereditary nobility with the new one of evolution, he declares "each new life, being the sum of the preceding lives, is the condition of the future." The greatness of his forebears imposes a responsibility. Cantelmo is to be parent of "He who must come."

·   ·   ·

Maria Gravina's madness seeped into d'Annunzio's fiction. Frequently, as he sat writing of the way their mother's dementia lay like a curse over the lives of the "Virgins of the Rocks," the woman whose insanity was his own curse was in the next room. He described himself as living "like a tamer of wild beasts who would be devoured if for a moment he turned his head aside or allowed the whip to fall from his hand." He confessed to a male friend that Maria Gravina's sexual demands left him exhausted and afraid. She wishes, he told Hérelle, "to possess me entirely, like an inanimate object."

He saw no way of freeing himself. Far easier just to slip away. When, in the summer of 1895, Scarfoglio proposed an extended sea voyage to Greece and on to Istanbul, d'Annunzio accepted with alacrity.

This was the trip on which, as we have seen, d'Annunzio distressed Hérelle by parading around naked, and by telling smutty stories. Although the yacht was entirely Scarfoglio's, d'Annunzio pretended to have a share in it, and acted with host-like munificence. He had assured Hérelle that not much would be needed in the way of clothes—life on board would be informal and they would avoid dining ashore. The Frenchman, having taken him at his word and brought only one suit, was mortified to find that d'Annunzio himself had packed six, all white, as well as a dinner jacket, more than thirty shirts and eight pairs of shoes, and that he accepted all of the invitations which awaited them in Athens and elsewhere.

D'Annunzio was now an international celebrity, and enjoying the fact. But the term *multanime*, which he had coined to describe the vola-tile hero of *The Innocent*, could as well be applied to his many-spirited self. In Greece his manner was that of an indolent playboy, but his notebooks reveal a very different interior life. To Hérelle, sunbathing in the nude and complaining, as d'Annunzio repeatedly did, at hav-ing to do without daily sexual intercourse, might seem "puerile." But what looked to the Frenchman like preening indecency and silliness, was, to d'Annunzio's mind, perfectly in keeping with the spirit of their journey.

He was in pursuit of what Walter Pater called the "light-hearted religion" of ancient Greece, and hoping to make contact with the Dionysian vitality Nietzsche had described in *The Birth of Tragedy*. He improvised sacred rites. On board ship he burnt myrtle twigs as an aromatic offering to the beauty of the sunset. He was developing a neo-paganism of a kind which would shortly become fashionable every-

where from Cambridge to Munich. Nude, he exulted in his freedom from shame: "I feel as though Hellenism has penetrated me to the marrow . . . I should have been born in Athens, and exercised in the gymnasia with the young men." Gossiping and dozing on deck and exploring the sleazy backstreets in pursuit of whores, or dressing for dinner at an embassy in his nicely ironed shirts and shiny shoes, he may not have comported himself as Hérelle believed a poet should, but a poet he was. Within days of returning from this voyage he would begin work on *The Dead City*, his first play, its form borrowed from the Greek tragedians, its theme the glamour and potency of the myths and bloody histories archaeologists were then bringing back to light.

The cruise was curtailed. They were supposed to be sailing to Byzantium, but the yacht never reached the Bosporus, and d'Annunzio had anyway turned back several weeks before Scarfoglio and the others. He might pose as a pagan hedonist, shamelessly parading his sunburnished body, but that body let him down. He was seasick again.

When they sailed into a storm off Cape Sounion he asked to be put ashore and took the ferry home.

In the autumn of 1895, shortly after his return from Greece, Michetti painted a portrait of d'Annunzio (previous page). A photograph of the sitting shows the two friends in the studio, at ease and smiling in crumpled linen suits, but the resultant painting tells a very different story. Earlier paintings and photos of d'Annunzio had shown a romantic poet, pensive, introspective, melancholy. This one presents him in a new persona. The background is a turbulent skyscape, as though d'Annunzio were standing alone on a mountain top. His narrow, sloping shoulders have been broadened to heroic proportions. His hair (rather more of it than the photograph shows) and pointed beard are darker and more firmly defined than in life. The ends of his moustache have been waxed into ferocious vertical spikes.

In informal photographs he tends to hold his head on one side and watch his companions askance, half dropping his heavy eyelids, seductive and insinuating. Here he stands erect and glares upwards and outwards, his face in quarter-profile turned, not to the viewer, but towards his own great destiny. Hérelle, on being shown the picture, grasped its significance at once. "This is surely the first portrait of d'Annunzio 'Superman.'"

Eloquence

AMONG THE GRAFFITI ON THE WALLS of the yellow-papered office of the *Capitan Fracassa* were a crowd of caricatures. Among them was a profile of Italy's most celebrated actress, the beautiful Eleonora Duse, with her wide, soft lips, her exquisite bone structure and her pale mournful eyes. On St. Valentine's Day in 1885 the *Capitan Fracassa*'s twenty-two-year-old contributor, Gabriele d'Annunzio, was out on the pavement of the Corso, making notes on the grand ladies standing on the balconies of the palaces to watch the carnival frolics, and throw down sweets and flowers to the crowds seething below. He saw his lover, Olga Ossani, on the loggia of the Palazzo Tittoni and noted how beside her, "the strange Japanese hair-do of Signora Duse was outlined against the flower-patterned blinds as though against a decorated screen." For the time being he was interested in the actress only as an example of the fashion for *Japonaiseries* of which he was then so fond.

Nearly a decade later, in 1894, in Venice, d'Annunzio was introduced to the diva. Earlier that year she had written to her former lover, Arrigo Boito, reporting that she had read *The Triumph of Death*, and that she would "rather die in a corner than love such a soul as . . . that infernal d'Annunzio." Loving him was already on her mind. "I detest d'Annunzio, but I adore him."

It is unlikely that anything more than letters of admiration passed between them after that first meeting, but Duse obtained a copy of *Pleasure*, and read it on tour. The following September, shortly after returning from Greece, d'Annunzio, in Venice again, made a characteristically inscrutable but suggestive entry in his notebook, *"Amori. Et. Dolori. Sacra"* (Sacred to Love and Pain). According to a romantic account he gave many years later, he was climbing out of a gondola at dawn when he encountered Eleonora, each of them having passed a sleepless night. "Without a word," wrote Duse, "we framed a pact of alliance within our hearts." So began the most celebrated love affair of his life.

Eleonora was thirty-seven, nearly five years older than her new lover. Like him, she had lived in the public eye virtually since childhood, not because, like him, she craved fame but because she was born into a family of itinerant actors and needed the work. She was cast as Francesca da Rimini at the age of twelve, and Shakespeare's Juliet at thirteen. At twenty she was playing all the leading roles with a company in Naples. By the time she met d'Annunzio she had toured North and South America, England, Austria, France, Germany and Russia, playing a repertoire of suffering heroines, most notably Dumas's Lady of the Camellias, and being acclaimed everywhere as the finest, most beautiful, most exquisitely pathetic of all actresses, with the possible

exception of Sarah Bernhardt. She had had a succession of passionate relationships with sad endings. She was in her prime as an actress. Her audiences adored her. But she was discontented. The work she was doing, performing realist drama "among papier-mâché trees padded with green cloth," didn't satisfy her. After a successful season in London she wrote: "What an offence to the soul is this aping of life!" She wanted "the anguish and the promise." She longed to attain "that *deep* of life." D'Annunzio was just the man to help her reach it.

She was experienced, independent, high-earning. Always on the move (d'Annunzio was to call her "the nomad"), she was not a woman who would keep a man confined. An artist herself, she would be, not a drain on a man's energies, but an inspiration. As a woman whose fans were legion, she gave her lover the satisfaction of knowing he was the one chosen from among the multitudes who adored her. "When the theatre echoes with applause and flames with desire," wrote d'Annunzio, "he upon whom, alone, the diva gazes, upon whom she smiles, is intoxicated by pride."

They had a great deal in common. Words poured from her, as they did from him. His sentence structure is always perfect: hers is almost non-existent. In their letters he weaves flawless nets of words, she stammers and gushes, but they share the fantastic pretentiousness of two artists sure of their own genius. She wrote after their first night together: "Oh bless, bless, blessings on him who gives . . . I have felt your soul and I have again found mine—Alas I don't know how to tell you, but . . . do you know? Do you see? Clasp my hand tight!"

Duse was histrionic and totally humourless. "Everything about her was so artificial," wrote Tom Antongini, "that I never could understand how d'Annunzio . . . could put up for years with so patent and tiresome a lack of naturalness." But d'Annunzio relished being a part of the melodrama that was her life. They traded gnomic declarations which might have been gobbledegook, but seemed vibrant with implied meaning. They shared a greed for experience. As he trained the intensity of his attention on the world about him and on his own consciousness, so she (as he wrote approvingly) was ceaselessly intent on "living more and feeling more." "*Life*, life, free, *absolutely* free," was what she craved, "the thrill!"

Like d'Annunzio she was a hard-working artist, with the highest of aspirations. Like him she was a reader who knew her Shakespeare and her Sophocles, as well as being alert to the new: Ibsen's *A Doll's House* was a regular part of her repertoire. And like him, she loved to shop, buying precious old glass and secondhand books in fine bindings, dressing in tailored outfits from Worth or flowing robes designed for her by their mutual friend Mariano Fortuny. Each of them felt their identity and self-confidence confirmed by the other. "If you believe, I shall be," she told him. And he, in his turn, writing after her death, remembered how everything he did seemed to enchant her—"My way of biting a fruit . . . of kneeling to search for violets or four-leafed clover in the grass"; the way he tucked coins into his trouser pockets so that the warmth of his body might enhance their patina. "No woman has loved me like Ghisola, neither before nor after." (Ghisola was one of his many names for her.) "I lived in her gaze as a *pirausta* lives in the furnace." (A *pirausta*, according to Pliny the Elder, was a tiny filmy-winged fire-dwelling dragon.)

D'Annunzio had told Hérelle that he was responsible for Maria Gravina's troubles, and that he therefore had to stand by her, but, provided now with such an alluring alternative, he found that he was, after all, perfectly capable of overcoming his scruples. Not—being him—that he made a swift clean break. It would be another two years before he finally left Maria, but well before that she had sunk into the dim background of his increasingly busy and brilliant life. Over the winter of 1895/96, he was with Duse for weeks at a time in Venice, in Florence, in Pisa, returning to Francavilla only to write while she toured. They were to stay together, off and on, for eight years, the most settled and most creative of d'Annunzio's life.

The beginning of his liaison with the great actress coincided with the start of his career as a dramatist. There is no record of his having previously been much of a theatre-goer (though one of his early stories contains a sardonic depiction of a blousy actress on the provincial circuit). But Nietzsche's *The Birth of Tragedy* had set him thinking about drama's potential. His immersion in Wagner's music had suggested ways in which performance might be more immediately potent than literature on the page. Within three weeks of his return from Greece he was telling Treves about *The Dead City*, his first play.

He also made his debut as a performer. The International Arts Exhibition, the first ever Venice Biennale, opened in 1895. Michetti's painting, *Jorio's Daughter*, was on show, covering an entire wall, and won a prize. D'Annunzio had promised the organisers that he would come to "hymn" his friend's work. He was expected for the opening in April, but cried off, promising to speak instead at the close of the exhibition. In November he finally delivered his oration in a gilt and marble saloon in the opera house, La Fenice.

The talk was a sonorous piece of prose-poetry, a meditation on Venice, on Titian and Veronese, on sea and glass (d'Annunzio had visited Murano and was to become a discerning collector of the glass-blowers' work) and on the decayed splendour of Venice's ancient empire. D'Annunzio told an admirer he had written it in a single night, keeping himself awake by eating sugar lumps soaked in ether, a story which nicely combined his personae as heroic creator and as drug-taking decadent. In fact it was a reworking of a ten-year-old poem, *The Dream of Autumn*, and would itself be reworked for inclusion in d'Annunzio's next novel, *Il Fuoco* (Fire). (D'Annunzio liked to get plenty of use out of his material.)

D'Annunzio's work was cerebral and sedentary (or stationary at least, he often wrote standing) but to his mind it was physically heroic. He trained for it, as an athlete or warrior might, and in later life he was proud of the marks it left on his body: the writer's callus on his middle finger, the slight deformation of his shoulders, one raised above the other after a lifetime spent bent over a book. He boasted too of the effort he had put into developing his beautiful voice.

There are many testaments to that beauty. The English poet Arthur Symons, who was among the most eager champions of d'Annunzio's work, once heard him read from the Bible in Count Primoli's palace in Rome and was spellbound, just as Harold Nicolson would be by his recitation in Paris. And there are half a dozen accounts by women of how the disappointment of his less than lovely appearance was erased as soon as he began to speak, so enchanting was the "soft, supple, velvety" timbre of his voice, and so seductive his manner of using it.

He liked to stress that it was not something he had received as a gift, but his own creation. When, as a small child, he worried his mother by running out of the house, she would greet him on his return with a kind of chant of welcome and relief, wagging her head from one side to another as she crooned over him. "Enchanted, I imitated her manner, and tuned my speech to her speech, so that my voice become ever more beautiful." At the Cicognini he was teased initially for his Abruzzese accent. A proud and fiercely competitive boy, he rid himself of it in short order. Reading the classics, both then and later, he reflected on the way an orator could use speech to work on a crowd, writing about the way Cicero would "modulate his periods, almost as a singer would" to create a "vehement upheaval" in his listeners' emotions.

In his prose as well as his poetry, he was vividly aware that "an assembly of syllables has a suggestive and emotional power over and above their intellectual significance." Hence the repeated phrases and incantatory refrains laced through his novels. Hence the care he lavished on the rhythms of his splendidly elongated sentences. Hence the style of delivery he adopted for his speech-making, enunciating slowly and deliberately, as though "drawing a clear outline around each word." (Several of his contemporaries describe the effect: at first hearing "colourless," "without animation," "flat" or "monotonous," but rapidly establishing a hypnotic grip on his listeners.)

At La Fenice, he was able to see and feel for the first time how the word-music he created could be used as an instrument of power. His audience—aristocratic ladies in evening dress, a strong cohort of the admiring young men who had paid court to him in the Caffè Florian the previous summer—saw a dandy in a tailcoat, his moustache tips upstanding, gesticulating precisely with his small well-cared-for hands as he slowly read out his piece. What d'Annunzio himself saw was something more dramatic, "an ancient savage game in which the Herculean energies of the athlete revealed themselves, making his tendons quiver and his arteries swell."

The hero of *Fire*, Stelio Effrena, delivers the very same speech in similar but glamorised circumstances. As Stelio watches the audience intently following his words, he feels his own intellect distending and relaxing like an enormous snake. "He felt himself to be holding their minds, fused into one single mind, in his hand, and to have the power to brandish it like a banner, or to crush it in his fist." He is exultant. "In the communion between his soul and the soul of the crowd there arose a mystery, something nearly divine." D'Annunzio had discovered a new way of impressing his mark upon the world.

Cruelty

HANDS EXCITED D'ANNUNZIO. He once recorded his delight in the beauty of his own left hand as it lay relaxed "like an underwater flower" on the desk before him as he wrote with his right. The motif recurs persistently in his fiction and poetry. *The Virgins of the Rocks* contains a virtuoso passage describing the three heroines leaning on a balustrade, their three pairs of hands hanging gracefully before them. There are hands in d'Annunzio's love letters and hands in his domestic décor: the Vittoriale contains a room stencilled all over with hands.

Hands were erogenous. In *Pleasure*, a woman's leaving a glove on a piano is a signal of her sexual availability, and Elena Muti's permitting men to lap champagne from her cupped hands is an image of her depravity and allure. Sperelli makes a drawing of Maria Ferres's hands, a way of caressing her without touching. In real life d'Annunzio collected his lovers' gloves as trophies: there are drawers full of them still in his last home.

Hands were most interesting to him when mutilated. To Elda, his first love, he wrote: "Tell me something that would please you and I will do it . . . would you like me to cut off a hand and send it to you, in a box, by post?" In an early story he tells the tale of a peasant whose hand is crushed beneath a religious effigy. In a gruesome passage the man amputates it himself, and offers it as a tribute to the saint. Nearly thirty years later, d'Annunzio was thrilled to meet Umberto Cagni, the Arctic explorer who had cut off his own frost-bitten and gangrenous fingers.

Duse's hands were slender and pale. While they were together d'Annunzio dedicated book after book to her as "Eleonora Duse of the beautiful hands." But he also wrote a play, *La Gioconda* (the name is an alternative title for Leonardo's *Mona Lisa*), in which those lovely hands are horribly mangled. The character d'Annunzio created for

Duse is trying to save a toppling marble statue, her sculptor-husband's representation of his mistress. The massive figure, the image of her humiliation, falls on her hands and crushes them. It was widely said that d'Annunzio treated Duse cruelly: the way he depicted their relationship in his novels and plays suggests he was fully aware of it, and unabashed. Looking back on their love, after Duse herself was dead, the memory that moved him most was that of a curious gesture, peculiar to her. When he made her cry (as he frequently did), she would wipe her eyes with an upward movement of those long elegant hands, as though anointing her temples with her own tears.

Over the first two years of their liaison they explored the Veneto and were together in Milan, Venice, Florence, Pisa, Rome, Albano, Assisi. Those times left delicious memories—an afternoon in the Campo Santo in Pisa, when he picked violets for her in the rain, was still haunting d'Annunzio a quarter of a century later. For Duse, though, these brief snatches of happiness were a torment. A friend who knew them both well believed she was addicted to the sexual pleasure d'Annunzio gave her, and pitied her for it. He "held her by her senses . . . she couldn't do without him . . . it was lamentable." She described their time in Pisa as a "terrible convulsion of body and soul" and her reaction afterwards, when she was once more alone, craving his touch, as "Madness . . . Twenty days of atrocious fever." She fought her dependence by trying to reject him. "She is sobbing at the windowsill. 'Oh no, no, no: I know what would happen to me *afterward* . . . You will go always, you will go farther and farther from me.'" We know about this painful scene because d'Annunzio recorded it in his notebook, along with its aftermath ("she yielded in tears").

He loved to see her unhappy. With her downward slanting eyes and tremulous mouth, she was, said d'Annunzio approvingly, a "harmonious vision of creative suffering." One contemporary critic once described her as a "wounded Pierrot." To another she was "a torch of passion and of pain . . . On all her features, all her person, she carried written the word Melancholy." She was always unwell (she had tuberculosis), something which naturally interested d'Annunzio, and along with her physical frailty she offered him the thrilling prospect of a great star, a diva, prostrate at his feet.

They were frequently apart. Eleonora spent months of each year on tour. D'Annunzio returned periodically to Francavilla and Maria Gravina, alienated though they now were from each other. In the summer of 1897, Maria gave birth to a son, whom she named Gabriele Dante. D'Annunzio refused to acknowledge the child. He was not the father, he said: his servant was. Maria did not insist.

When he wasn't travelling with Duse he was frequently in Rome. He was now earning large sums (none of which he saved) from the French and German editions of his novels, and his reputation was sufficiently august to earn him the entrée to circles into which he had peered as an outsider when he was a young journalist. He was at last admitted into the exclusive hunting club, *Il Circolo della Caccia*, and rode recklessly after the foxhounds on the Campagna. He was invited, and went, to dinners and concerts, tea parties and balls. These periods of hectic gadding about, he liked to claim, provided stimulus for his imagination. "No day of drudgery was ever as fertile for me as a week of laziness." Romain Rolland met him during this period. One night, at the Countess Lovatelli's, Rolland heard a young man inveighing against d'Annunzio's vanity,—"he thinks he's a demi-god." The next night d'Annunzio himself was at the countess's, looking very *"snob"* in little pointed pumps, a white waistcoat with diamond buttons and, in his cravat, "an ugly pin in the shape of a jockey." Initially Rolland took against him: "This peacock with his tail constellated with eyes, followed around by gawping snobs . . . this smell of a low-life Adonis." Soon though, the two became close friends, united by a shared love of music. In Rome they attended concerts together day after day.

At the time of their first sacred night of love d'Annunzio had promised Eleonora his first play, *The Dead City*, but when he finally got around to writing it, a year later, he offered it instead to Sarah Bernhardt (whose acting he considered "more poetic," though Duse's was "more sincere"). The betrayal was very nearly the end of their affair. D'Annunzio wrote in his notebook that "the noble woman whose eyes are full of tears and infinity" had withdrawn from him. "Always in her sad step I hear the rustle of laurel leaves." He seemed to be resigning himself, with agreeable feelings of poetic melancholy, to having lost her. He was engaged, that winter in Rome, in two new love affairs, besides still living part of the time with Maria Gravina. He imagined Duse "far from me among the cypresses, carrying in her arms her love, like a lamb, its four feet tied by a rope." The romance which was to make the poet and the actress the most celebrated couple in Italy, if not in all Europe, was on the point of fading, almost before it had started, into a Symbolist image—delightful to d'Annunzio—of blood sacrifice and feminine grief. Friends intervened. Count Primoli, whose lacquered and cluttered salon d'Annunzio had so admired in the 1880s, invited them both to his house and effected a reconciliation.

Eleonora forgave. In ten days d'Annunzio wrote a new play, *Sogno d'un Mattino di Primavera* (Dream of a Spring Morning), as a reconciliation gift, and sent Duse the manuscript bound in antique brocade and fastened with green moiré silk ribbons. The play—like most of d'Annunzio's dramas—is wordy and static, and shot through with morbid eroticism. A wronged husband murders his wife's lover. She cradles the bloody corpse in her arms all night long and by morning she is raving mad. D'Annunzio had been reading about the stylised gestures of the classical tragedians and his stage directions (almost as verbose as the dialogue) suggest ways of emulating them, as well as giving detailed descriptions of his practically unrealisable setting.

In the summer of 1897, Eleonora performed the play in Paris. It was not a great success. That autumn d'Annunzio finally left Maria Gravina, and Duse took a house near Settignano, the town in the Florentine hills which was to be home to both of them for the rest of their time together.

Their relationship was fascinating to the public and fruitful for both of them. It was a love affair, certainly, but it was also a working partnership. Eleonora was not only a star, she was her own manager, hiring and firing fellow actors and setting up the exhausting tours on which she played before thousands all over Europe and America. For d'Annunzio, now launching himself as a dramatist, an intimate relationship with her could not but be useful. (His contemporary, Luigi Pirandello, had to wait years to see his plays performed.) Conversely Eleonora was tired of her repertoire; she was glad to have an author celebrated all over Europe writing plays especially for her. But if, professionally and artistically, they were partners, privately and emotionally they were a master and his abject devotee. In *The Virgins of the Rocks*, d'Annunzio had imagined a woman with "an unbridled need to be enslaved." Princess Massimilla confesses: "I am eaten up by a desire to belong entirely to a higher, stronger being, to dissolve my will in his, to burn like a holocaust in the fire of his immense spirit." In Eleonora Duse, d'Annunzio had found such a woman in real life. "I would like to unmake myself, wholly, wholly, wholly!" she told him, "to give my all, and melt away."

She added his plays to her repertoire, thus boosting his income but greatly reducing her own—her staples like *The Lady of the Camellias*, *Antony and Cleopatra*, Goldoni's *La Locandiera*, *The Second Mrs Tanqueray*, were far more popular at the box office. Bernard Berenson, the art historian who was their neighbour in the Tuscan hills, described d'Annunzio as a gigolo, a man paid for his sexual services. This was unfair: d'Annunzio was far too feckless and, in his own fashion, innocent, to make money out of women. But it is certainly true that Duse was ready to let him exploit her. Early in their time together she gave an interview to Olga Ossani (d'Annunzio's Febea, still working as a journalist) in which she insisted she would be happy to spend all she had in the service, not of her own art, but of his. "I have earned pennies, I will earn more . . . What do you want me to do with them? Buy a palace? . . . Can you see me, surrounded with liveried servants, giving the parties of an actress grown rich? No, no! Art has given me joy, intoxication and money; art shall have the money back." This was how Duse talked. She was "not an intelligent woman," said d'Annunzio cruelly after they had parted, but she was desperately serious. "I will die happy if I have made a beautiful thing, a *work of Beauty*." D'Annunzio—soon to be Beauty's parliamentary representative—benefited immensely.

She endured his infidelities. Her friends warned her against him, reminding her of his notorious promiscuity, but to speak ill of such a poetic spirit seemed to her like "slaughtering flowers . . . like pulling the hair of one who lies dreaming." He was a monster, but an adorable one, whom she could nurture and comfort. She was to tell a friend how he would come to her the morning after he had been with another woman, "exhausted, stupefied, spewing out his disgust at the night and his contempt for women." She appeared in the ignominious role of his handmaiden: a caricature of the period shows a scrawny-shanked d'Annunzio, posed as Botticelli's Venus, rising naked from the waves, while the much larger Eleonora, a buxom attendant nymph, holds out his bathing towel. When he was working he refused to admit her to his study. The great actress, adored by multitudes, waited meekly in the corridor until he felt like opening the door.

Her legions of admirers were soon indignant at d'Annunzio's treatment of her. But though their relationship was undoubtedly laced with cruelty (his cruelty to her), her masochism shaped it as powerfully as his sadism. He liked her abjection. When he heard the rustle of her dress and the sound of her breathing outside his door, he took pleasure in keeping her standing there. But she liked it too. She had no wish for independence, even for her own identity. She signed her telegrams "Gabrighisola" as though the two of them were one. She wanted to dedicate all the strength remaining to her to him, as the earth gives itself to nourish the peasant's sheaf of corn. "What would I live for if not to work for you?"

He repaid her with the privilege of being his chosen companion, and with sex. For Eleonora their sexual relations were ecstatic. "My soul is no longer impatient to go beyond my body . . . I have found *harmony.*" But if she was perpetually hungry for him, his desire for her was equivocal. In June 1896, only a few months into their love affair, d'Annunzio made some notes for the novel he was contemplating. "The clear and crude vision he has of her physical disintegration. Certain aspects of her face, her small pathetic chin . . . He is drawn towards the dawn when he leaves her house. She sees him so young and strong, taking deep breaths of the untainted air as if in the joy of *liberation*; he has just left the suffocating room where she oppressed him with her tears."

D'Annunzio had freed himself from Maria Gravina only to involve himself in another relationship with an emotionally dependent older woman who would be driven frantic by the pain he caused her. Something in him, this repeated pattern suggests, thrived on the presence of an imploring, adoring, despairing woman. And something in Duse predisposed her to accept that role. In the plays d'Annunzio wrote for her, she was blind (*The Dead City*), mutilated (*La Gioconda*), driven mad (*Dream of a Spring Morning*) and murdered (*Francesca da Rimini*). Their affair finally ended when he refused her a part in which she would have been burnt alive (*Jorio's Daughter*). She resigned herself to being exploited and hurt by him. He had an absolute right, she declared, to live according to a "law" formulated by himself to suit his own extraordinary nature.

The desires at play in their relationship were complex. D'Annunzio complained to his friends of Duse's jealousy and possessiveness, but he submitted to it, allowing her to make at once a god and a child of him. She, in turn, went along with him in exaggerating the age gap between the two of them. She called him "little son," "Gabrieletto," "Sweetness." She scolded him and chivvied him back to work—with the dual authority of a parent and a patron. "Life races by," she wrote to him. "Grasp it in your art." They played at being mother and son, but that doesn't mean that their relationship was any the less ardent. Over the next few years d'Annunzio would write a novel in which a widow has a sexual relationship with her much younger brother, and he would produce his own versions of the tragedies of Phaedra, the legendary queen of Athens, and the mediaeval Italian duchess Parisina d'Este, both of whom fall passionately in love with their stepsons. Incestuous relationships excited d'Annunzio, and so did the bond between sexually mature women and beautiful younger men.

D'Annunzio dedicated book after book to *"La divina Eleonora Duse."* He betrayed and humiliated her and made her cry, but her love was the inspirational fire in which he—the *pirausta*—renewed himself. He was, as he confessed almost ruefully, "mad about her."

Two vignettes, both real events that would find their way into d'Annunzio's fiction, and both involving damage to Duse's lovely hands. In January 1899, d'Annunzio accompanied her on tour to Egypt. He noted that in the theatre in Cairo the women's boxes were veiled with silk, so that from the stage it appeared she was playing to an empty house. They visited the Sphinx and the Pyramids. An archaeologist took them down into a newly opened burial chamber, and lifted the lid of a jar to show them that it was full of ancient honey, still glistening. As they marvelled, a bee flew in. The archaeologist tried to keep it from the pharaonic honey, and Eleonora helped. "The beautiful white hands, uplifted in the dimness of the sepulchre, seemed to compete in flight with that . . . bee of the morning and of two thousand years." Eventually—and this is what gave the memory its force for d'Annunzio—the bee stung one of those elegant pale fingers.

A few days later d'Annunzio and Eleonora visited the gardens of the Khedive's Palace. There was a maze of high myrtle hedges. They strolled in and became separated. D'Annunzio was enjoying himself, but Eleonora was frightened. "Suddenly I found myself all alone, in an alley between dense green walls." She felt as though she would never find her way out. "What silence, like a tomb." D'Annunzio re-created the scene in *Fire*, relocating it to the gardens of the Palladian Villa Pisani in the Veneto. In his account, his fictional alter ego, Stelio Effrena, is deliberately hiding from his mistress. He taunts her, laughing at her, calling out, "Come and find me!" but then staying silent as she calls frantically after him. He crawls under the hedge on all fours. He imagines himself a faun—goatish, feral, heartless. Pitilessly he refuses to help his wretched lover. The incident, for him, is charged with an intense and furtive pleasure.

In the Cairo garden, by her own account, Eleonora panicked, and sobbing, began to scrabble at the dense, thorny hedges, attempting to break out. "Look at these scratches on my hands that I thrust in vain through the myrtle!"

Silently watching from the other side of the hedge, d'Annunzio saw those lovely hands bloody and torn.

"I kept crying in anguish: 'Enough! Enough! I cannot stand it any longer! D'Annunzio!'"

D'Annunzio, still silent, took notes.

Life

HERE ARE SOME OF THE WAYS in which d'Annunzio described the Italian parliament. "A House which has trampled on the national dignity"; "a foul crowd of knaves and fools"; an assembly of "stable-hands of the Great Beast" whose "chatter is as vulgar and repulsive as the burping of a peasant who has eaten too many beans"; "a mephitic sewer." He had written that democracy was an absurd system. "You cannot treat human beings as though they were as alike as a row of nails awaiting the hammer." But in 1897 the parliamentary seat for his home district of the Abruzzi became vacant and d'Annunzio was offered the nomination. The man who could never turn down an invitation found this one irresistible. After taking careful soundings to ensure that he was not likely to be humiliated by an electoral defeat, he accepted. "The world," he wrote to Treves, "must be convinced that I am capable of *everything*."

It was a turbulent moment in Italy's history. In the previous year an Italian army had been defeated at Adua by the troops of the Ethiopian Emperor Menelik; 6,000 Italians were killed in one day. The disaster brought down the government of Francesco Crispi, whose bellicose nationalism had been much to d'Annunzio's taste. Crispi's followers looked to d'Annunzio as a new champion, and perhaps even as a leader. He himself, though, refused to be identified with any particular programme. He promised a "politics of poetry" and was content to allow the meaning of the phrase to remain obscure. "I am beyond right and left, as I am beyond good and evil," he declared (acknowledging his debt to Nietzsche with the phrase). He stood as an independent, describing himself as "The Candidate for Beauty."

Such a candidacy was neither as unworldly nor as innocuous as it might sound. When, in 1871, Nietzsche heard a rumour that the Louvre, one of the great treasure houses of European art, had been burnt down by the Communards, and all its precious contents destroyed (in fact the fire was in the Palace of the Tuileries) he wrote: "It is the worst day of my life." Nietzsche was an aesthete, and not only in a green-carnation-wearing, stained-glass-fancying sense of the word. He was one who valued beauty far higher than justice or human kindness. D'Annunzio would respond in the same spirit to the collapse of the campanile in Venice's Piazza San Marco in 1902. He was prostrated by grief, weeping, and pacing from room to room all day, unable to work. "And in the newspapers someone dares to be happy because there were no human victims!" To him the pain and death of his fellow beings would have been insignificant, by comparison with the loss of an harmonious architectural ensemble. "Innumerable human victims would not be enough to compensate."

The incompatibility of egalitarianism with the cult of beauty preoccupied nineteenth-century thinkers of all political persuasions. In the decade before d'Annunzio was born Heinrich Heine, utopian socialist and friend of Karl Marx, sorrowfully prophesied how the "red fists" of the communists with whom he sympathised would smash "all of the marble structures of my beloved art world." Beauty, genius, high culture could none of them coexist, Heine thought, with social equality. "The shop keepers will use my *Book of Songs* for shopping bags, to store coffee or snuff for the old wives of the future." What saddened Heine enraged d'Annunzio. He has one of his fictional heroes reflect with bitter irony on the function of poets in a democracy. How, he wonders, can they make poetry of the deplorable passing of power to the masses?

While writing *The Virgins of the Rocks* d'Annunzio had frequently escaped from Maria Gravina to spend time in Rome, staying—thanks to his friend de Bosis—in an enormous chamber in the Palazzo Borghese. Once the saddle room of the princely household, it was furnished only with a bed, a piano and a plaster cast of the Belvedere *Torso*. D'Annunzio loved its "splendid poverty." He dwelt on the image of Michelangelo, nearly blind, palpating with rough hands the *Torso*'s marble planes. Living alongside it, he was in contact with genius, both classical and Renaissance. Throughout the winter of 1894/95 he was there for weeks on end, feeling the "joy of breathing grandly" and working with his friend on the launch of a new journal, the *Convito* (the

Banquet). The title is an allusion both to Dante's *Convivio* and to Plato's *Symposium*. (In Paris in 1892, a journal with the same name, *Le Banquet*, was founded by a similarly minded group including the twenty-year-old Marcel Proust.) The *Convito* was lavishly illustrated and prohibitively expensive, a magazine for the elite, strongly advocating elitism. In the review's first issue d'Annunzio called upon "intellectuals" (a neologism he popularised) to gather up all their energies to fight for the "cause of intelligence against the Barbarians."

The *Convito* writers were united in lamenting that the realm of art and literature, once the *hortus conclusus* of a few rare spirits, was becoming a public playground for the unrefined many. D'Annunzio liked selling his books to the many, but, leaving that aside, he joined his voice to the others. The times, he wrote, were as disastrous as those in which Goths and Vandals rampaged through Italy but, while those invaders were a "whirlwind with tresses of lightning," with the grandeur of "bloody foaming rage," the "new barbarism" was mean and sordid. The Risorgimento had brought forth heroes commensurate with those who glittered off the pages of Plutarch's *Lives*, but the "Third Rome" they had created was now overwhelmed by "a thick grey sludge in which a deformed multitude bustle and trade."

These attitudes—elitist and misanthropic—were what underlay d'Annunzio's espousal of the cause of "Beauty," but to his constituents he was first and foremost a local man who had become a celebrity. He was greeted with cries of: "Long live d'Annunzio! Long live the Abruzzese poet!"

He campaigned vigorously. "This enterprise may seem stupid and extraneous to my art," he wrote to Treves defensively, but he submitted to the dust and discomfort attendant on rattling in overcrowded carriages over miles and miles of country roads through a hot Italian August. He attended banquets. He listened politely while the bands he detested played in his honour. He flinched, Coriolanus-like, from the "acrid smell of humanity," but nonetheless he visited town after town, village after village, delivering flowery and mellifluous speeches to crowds who may not have recognised his abstruse classical allusions but who responded with gratifying excitement to the performance he put on. Copies of his speeches were mounted on poles and carried through the streets—the word as icon. He ran his own press campaign, asking his writer friends to contribute laudatory articles on him to local papers, and adding his own (anonymous) comments. The publicity generated by his new political venture was made to serve his literary career. The halls in which he spoke were hung with posters advertising his novels and poems. While other candidates handed out cash bribes to voters, d'Annunzio found it sufficient to offer autographed volumes. The books were provided *gratis* by Treves; the autographs possibly, but not certainly, by d'Annunzio. (Book-signing was a chore he preferred to delegate—his eldest son was to become especially good at forging his signature.)

The Parisian journal *Gil Blas* had a reporter covering his campaign. It was Filippo Tomasso Marinetti, twenty-one years old, seeing d'Annunzio for the first time. Marinetti thought the spectacle of "the chiseller of precious dreams" addressing such rustic audiences a "savoury irony": "the haughty aristocratic minstrel stoops to address the shabby crowd." To Marinetti, watching from the back, d'Annunzio was a slight figure on the faraway platform, "elegantly narrow in a black suit, delicate, small, fragile." Marinetti described his delivery as "monotonous," but conceded that it was mesmeric. D'Annunzio, like an oarsman rowing on the "vast sea of the crowd," was drawing the people's spirits toward him "on a river of scintillating images" and on the "soft cadences of his voice." At the end of the speech his supporters had to clear a path through the crowd with their fists, before he could be ushered to his carriage and sent off at a trot. Marinetti was impressed. He recognised the "strident modernity" (a great compliment from the soon-to-be futurist) of what d'Annunzio was doing—converting literary fame into political influence, celebrity into power.

D'Annunzio won his seat. Having done so, he lost interest in it. To owe his position to the votes of others seemed to him demeaning. And that position, in so far as its main privilege was that of allowing him to cast a vote in turn, offended his self-esteem. When urged by the whips to lend his support to a new bill, he haughtily replied: "Tell the President I am not a number." He took his place in the chamber seldom (in this he was unexceptional, only about half of the elected deputies ever attended) and visited his constituency even less. After a year largely spent touring Egypt and Greece with Duse and overseeing the productions of two of his plays, he wrote to one of his Abruzzese relatives: "I do not understand how the constituents can complain about negligence on my part." Swanning around the Mediterranean, thinking and feeling and pursuing his art, he was serving his country in the way he knew best.

The year after d'Annunzio entered parliament was a stormy one in Italian politics. Socialist and republican groups had been gaining influence, especially in the industrial north. There were food shortages and price rises. On 5 May a general strike was followed by rioting in several cities. The following day the Prime Minister, Antonio Rudinì, declared a state of emergency in Milan. Filippo Turati, the socialist leader, was arrested. General Bava-Beccaris led troops into the city and fired on demonstrators. Over a hundred, perhaps as many as 400, people were killed.

D'Annunzio, true to his role as representative of Beauty, wrote an article for the *New York Journal* and the *London Morning Post* (his association with Duse had brought him far greater visibility in the English-speaking world). He called it "Bloody Spring." In it he laments, not the fact that troops have fired on unarmed citizens, but that Cellini's bronze *Perseus*, which stands in Florence's Piazza Signoria, has been hit by a demonstrator's stone. To him, damage to an artwork was infinitely more dreadful than any number of dead plebeians.

His only notable action as a member of parliament was his crossing of the house. He sat initially on the far right of the chamber, aligning himself with the monarchists and nationalists, but when, in the wake of the civil unrest, the government attempted to introduce ever more repressive legislation, d'Annunzio, more of a libertarian than a conservative, refused his support. He relates that one day, passing a room where members of the Socialist Party were holding an animated discussion, he went in, joined in the talk and was warmly received. He wrote in his notebook: "On one side there are many dead men howling, and on the other a few men alive. As a man of intellect I advance towards Life."

The socialists seemed dynamic: the establishment clumsy. D'Annunzio made his move. In the middle of a parliamentary session he left his place and, having ensured that all eyes were on him, he passed to the other side of the chamber. His secretary describes him springing from bench to bench "with the agility of a goat." His previous allies on the right were shocked, but d'Annunzio was defiant. His fictional heroes, he said, were all "anarchists" intent only on manifesting their will in bold actions. He was not of the right, or of any other fixed position. "I am a man of *life*, not of formulae."

"Life"—the word which d'Annunzio substituted for any conventional political value—had, like "Beauty," a complex meaning for late nineteenth-century aesthetes. It was the catchword of a political and philosophical creed—vitalism. Nietzsche had exalted *"zoe,"* the life that pulses through all animate things. Pater wrote of "that eternal process of nature, full of animation, of energy, of the fire of life . . . in which the divine reason consists." Life was amoral. "Life's sole aim is to multiply itself," wrote d'Annunzio. Life was violent, and paradoxically close to death. D'Annunzio liked to quote a punning tag from Heraclitus about a great bow "whose name was Life but whose work was Death."

A few days after his switch of allegiance d'Annunzio wrote an article calling out for "unending strife and unending world conquest" and explaining that he admired socialism not only for its "Life," but for its destructive potential. This was perverse of him: vitalism and socialism were not compatible. Pater, again alluding to Heraclitus, had made plain that only the "few" were capable of responding to and channelling life's divine energy, while the sluggish "many" were inert, "like people heavy with wine." "Life," like "Beauty," sounded grand, vague and surely unexceptionable, but for d'Annunzio and his like it had a particular meaning, and that meaning hardly accorded with a belief in the brotherhood of man.

"Do you really think I'm a socialist?," d'Annunzio asked a journalist two years later. "It pleased me to go for a moment into the lions' pit, but I was driven to it by my disgust with the other parties. Socialism in Italy is an absurdity . . . I am and remain an individualist, fiercely and to the uttermost."

In the most celebrated speech of his election campaign (celebrated because he persuaded Treves to put it out as a pamphlet, and saw to it that it was published in newspapers nationwide) he derided the concept of collective ownership as being suitable only to primitive nomadic herdsmen. Under socialism, he declared, the citizen degenerates. "His energy is enfeebled, his will is enervated, his dignity is lost." He is like the slaves whom the Scythians blinded and then chained in rows to churn great vats of mares' milk, day in, day out. Two impulses power every advance in the human condition, he maintained, the drive to own and conserve property and the companion drive to "dominion." Individual ambition; private property; a hierarchy with "infinite gradations" through which an exceptional spirit might rise: these were the essentials of a thriving state.

The words are unequivocal. Yet somehow d'Annunzio managed to persuade the socialists to accept him into their ranks, and even to support him in his next election campaign. Francesco Nitti, later d'Annunzio's political adversary, studied his speech and, overlooking its entirely explicit attack on socialism, described it as an exercise in emptiness, "which could lend itself to any interpretation, so much the more because it said nothing." For his peroration d'Annunzio launched into a eulogy of the hedge, the boundary which demarcates a farmer's land, protecting his property and asserting his pride. The hedge, recalled one of his listeners, was evidently a political metaphor, "but as he spoke, it became real—a lovely, flowery hedge." It appears that there was something about d'Annunzio's sweet seductive manner which so befuddled his constituents and his political associates that they missed what he was saying.

When parliament was dissolved in June 1900 he stood for reelection in Florence. He was defeated. His life in politics had hardly started, but his participation in parliamentary democracy ends here.

Drama

Fire, D'ANNUNZIO'S NEXT NOVEL, ends with the funeral of Richard Wagner.

Wagner died in Venice in 1883. D'Annunzio set his novel in that year purposely so that his hero can volunteer to be one of the great man's coffin bearers. The tributes include laurel branches brought all the way from Rome. It is winter (Wagner died in February) but the laurel leaves are "green as the bronze of fountains and rich with the odour of triumph." Back in Rome, the trees from which they were cut are putting out new buds "to the murmur of hidden springs." Wagner the barbarian is dead. D'Annunzio will be his Roman heir.

In the autumn of 1897, within weeks of his election to parliament, when his constituents might have expected him to be protecting their interests in the Chamber of Deputies, d'Annunzio was shuttling up and down the railway lines from Venice to Rome, drumming up publicity and patronage for the great new project he and Eleonora had in mind. They were going to construct an amphitheatre in the Alban Hills, and there they would found a "national theatre" (a novel concept at the time). Wagner had had his Bayreuth, where his works with their new/old Teutonic mythology were performed in an atmosphere of veneration. Reviving the legends of the *Nibelungen* and of the Arthurian knights, he had given Germans a nationalist mythology. Wagner's work, wrote d'Annunzio, supported "the aspirations of the German state to the heroic greatness of Empire." In *Lohengrin*, Henry the Fowler, the tenth-century founder of Germany, cries: "Let the warrior rise up from all the German lands." Thus inspired, in the 1860s and '70s, German warriors had triumphed over Austria and France. "The same victory had crowned both the effort of iron and the effort of metre." Now d'Annunzio craved a similar artistic-cum-expansionist triumph.

Drama offered him an enormous arena in which to display his talent. In late nineteenth-century Europe literature was for the entertainment of the educated classes only, but drama was popular. In the half century before d'Annunzio's birth over 600 new theatres were built in Italy. Marinetti estimated that ninety per cent of Italians went to the theatre (while in 1870 only twenty-five per cent could read).

From Nietzsche, d'Annunzio had taken a concept of tragedy as something both sacred and anarchic, full of amoral, ruthless vigour. A theatre was a furnace in which the base metal of ordinary people could be melted and bonded and recast as a "People," as hard and lustrous as bronze. He had read that when the Athenians left the theatre, exalted after a performance of Aeschylus's tragedies, they went from temple to temple, striking the shields which hung in the porticos like great gongs, and baying out *"Patria! Patria!"* That was the kind of effect he wanted his drama to have.

In Greece d'Annunzio had seen ancient statues recently excavated after lying underground for centuries, and had taken their return to the light as a precedent for a new Graeco-Latin renaissance. In *The Dead City* he blended the heroic project of modern archaeology with decadent passions (brother–sister incest, murderous possessiveness). The archaeologist hero, rummaging through the vestiges of a convulsed civilisation, releases a fearsome energy. So, writing brand-new plays based on ancient tragedy, d'Annunzio would unleash on the world the power of Dionysus. He would create a new drama, rooted, not in the dark northern culture of Wagner's dwarfs and dragons and maimed heroes, but in the dazzling light and tragic violence of ancient Greece.

Duse was beside herself. Enough of the realistic representation of modern life! Enough of light entertainment! "The theatre must be destroyed, the actors and actresses must all die of the plague. They poison the air, they make art impossible." A new mission was wanted, and a new architecture. "The drama dies of stalls and boxes and evening dress, and people who come to digest dinner . . . I want Rome and the Colosseum, the Acropolis, Athens." Away with the proscenium arch! Away with the pampered philistine socialites! "I want beauty, and the flame of life."

Count Primoli formed a committee. James Gordon Bennett, the proprietor of the *New York Herald*, gave enthusiastic support and published a lengthy interview with d'Annunzio. Fund-raising parties were organised. Titled ladies subscribed. A Roman marchese, noting that two noble ladies of his acquaintance had joined "the band of initiates to the new d'Annunzian aesthetic cult," predicted drily that "those gentlewomen and their intellectual acolytes will end by coupling like ancient nymphs with ancient fauns in the woods that shade the lake." The new theatre's repertoire would consist of the works of the great tragedians of antiquity and new works by d'Annunzio, all to be performed by Duse and the company she would assemble. It would open with a *Persephone* by d'Annunzio himself. The theatre would be charged with the "Latin spirit." The life-force celebrated by Nietzsche would throb through it. It would burn not as an oil lamp, "a pure and tranquil flame," but as a "smoky, resinous torch flashing with red sparks."

In the summer of 1897, Sophocles' *Antigone* was performed in the Roman amphitheatre at Orange in Provence. D'Annunzio was not there, but the tiresome little fact of his absence didn't deter him from giving an eyewitness account of the event. He wrote that peasants and labourers listened intent and mute. "Their rough and ignorant souls" were stirred by "the words of the poet, albeit not understood," with an emotion "like that of a prisoner on the point of being released from his heavy chains." Even the acridly stinking mob of the slave class might eventually be exalted by d'Annunzio's drama.

Nothing came of it. The theatre was never built. In *Fire*, Stelio writes a *Persephone*, but in reality d'Annunzio never did. Perhaps poor Eleonora was fortunate: the tragedy would have obliged her, as d'Annunzio's plays often did, to play a mournful middle-aged woman—Persephone's grieving mother Demeter—alongside a younger actress. In Paris fifteen years later d'Annunzio toyed again with the idea of founding a theatre: a collapsible and portable rotunda made of glass and wrought iron, to be designed by Mariano Fortuny and capable of holding audiences of up to 5,000 people. Nothing came of that idea either.

Scenes from a Life

IN SEPTEMBER 1897, reunited after an exhausting summer (he fighting his election campaign in the Abruzzi, she performing his *Dream of a Spring Morning* in Paris), d'Annunzio and Duse went together to Assisi, to visit the places sacred to St. Francis. As usual d'Annunzio was in tune with intellectual fashion: Paul Sabatier's recent life of St. Francis was an international bestseller. D'Annunzio's diary of the trip describes blue-green misty hills, soft rain and kindly light. He writes lyrically about the repose the place seemed to offer, the way the town felt cradled in the saint's pierced hands. D'Annunzio, the hand-fetishist, was, of course, fascinated by stigmata.

St. Francis was not only a holy man: he was also the instigator of Italian literature. His *Canticle of the Sun*, also known as the *Laudes Creaturarum* (Praise of the Creatures), has been called the first Italian poem. Soon after his visit to Assisi, d'Annunzio began work on the immense cycle of poems which constitutes his surest claim to a place in the literary pantheon. He called them *Laudi* (Praises), associating himself with the saint.

With Duse he visited Santa Maria degli Angeli, the white baroque church whose splendid dome is built over the fifth-century chapel, the Porziuncola, which the saint himself is said to have restored. D'Annunzio was pleased by the tiny, ancient structure, all hung about with gold and silver votive hearts: "It is like a chapel in a forest." He noticed the narrow door, as dry as tinder, cracked "like a heart consumed by suffering or rapture." Small though he was, he thought that to pass through it he would have to take a knife to himself and cut himself down.

A priest led them to the rose garden where St. Francis is said to have rolled naked on the thorns to subdue his fleshly desires, and showed them that the rose bushes still bear leaves spotted with blood-red. Poetry, roses, sexuality and pain: this was a combination to please d'Annunzio. Afterwards he dubbed the whitewashed villa Eleonora had recently rented in Settignano "the Porziuncola." The following spring he followed her there, taking the lease of a larger fifteenth-century villa across the way, the Capponcina, which was to be his base for the next twelve years.

Halcyon, the best-loved volume of his *Laudi*, begins with *La Tregua* (The Respite), a lyric in which the poet begs leave to withdraw from his political engagement with the mob, "the dark-minded dense Chimera whose stench was so strong my throat convulsed in the fetid air." Throughout the years he lived in Settignano, d'Annunzio kept up his interventions in public life, as an occasional orator and author of propagandist poems, but he spoke at a distance from the foul-smelling political arena. He lived on his hillside "like a great Renaissance lord," as he put it, with his dogs, his horses and his team of servants. His partnership with Duse brought him more money than he had ever had before. After two years of his newly settled existence he had paid nearly all his creditors. It also gave him the creative energy to produce much of his best work.

He was both very visible and very secluded. When he appeared in public he made a stir—people turned to stare at the famous author when he walked through Florence—but his outings were rare. For weeks on end, he was alone at his desk seeing no one but his staff and whichever woman or women he was bedding. When he left for France in 1910 nearly all of his best work was done. And while he worked, his reputation grew, a reputation which was as diverse and complicated as his oeuvre. He was the sexually promiscuous lover, the precious aesthete, the bellicose nationalist, the antiquarian who campaigned for the preservation of Italy's buildings, the embracer of the modern who courageously went up in one of the very first flying machines and who tore (at a shockingly speedy thirty miles an hour) along the dirt roads of Tuscany in a large, noisy, chronically unreliable motor car.

In old age, d'Annunzio told a visitor to his last home: "I am a better decorator and upholsterer than I am a poet or novelist." He was not

being self-deprecating (he was never self-deprecating), but proudly calling attention to his mastery of another art. Like Oscar Wilde with his Chelsea "House Beautiful," he took interior design very seriously. During his years at the Capponcina he at last had large sums of money coming in. And when he had money he always immediately spent it. Tom Antongini, who entered his life in 1897, explains: "If he has 500 lire, he buys flowers. If he has a thousand, he feels that he can afford ivory elephants. If he has 100,000, he immediately thinks of precious silks, gold cigarette cases, dogs and horses. If he is troubled with a million, he is interested in houses. D'Annunzio must buy!"

He insisted on paying a rent twenty per cent higher than that required for the Capponcina: such was his compulsion to spend money that a bargain distressed him. The house was furnished, but not to his liking. One of his most exasperating habits, to those charged with keeping his financial affairs straight, was his way of paying extra for furnished accommodation, only to strip his newly rented home of all its contents and spend a fortune (far more than the whole house was worth) in refurnishing it. The decoration of the Capponcina, a house which was to be seen by only a handful of people—d'Annunzio very seldom entertained—was indeed gorgeous enough to be worthy of a Renaissance lord. His dogs and horses and whatever furniture remained from the shipwreck of his previous homes were transported there and the house was soon thronged with "smiths, joiners, masons, stonecutters, glaziers, upholsterers, decorators, woodcarvers." His new major-domo, Benigno Palmerio (hired because he was an Abruzzese and because d'Annunzio liked both his face and his name—"Yes, you look benign") reports that d'Annunzio spent hours and hours with them, moving serenely through the hurly-burly and discussing the elaborate home improvements he had in mind "like the master of a laboratory or a factory."

Every sense was caressed. Perfumes, music, the touch of old silk, meals of perfect fruit. D'Annunzio was attentive to the least detail. He fussed about the design of his lampshades, nagging his supplier for his favourite pinks and peach colours. He pored over catalogues before ordering just the right bedlinen. Most of his furniture was made to order, massive pseudo-Renaissance pieces built to his scrupulous specifications. He kept the house heated to tropical temperatures which many visitors found all but intolerable, but in which he thrived.

By day and night he was at his desk, writing hour after uninterrupted hour. Between whiles he walked or sat in the garden, visited his dogs and horses or rode out, usually alone and in silence. "No one can ever have lived a life of such methodical discipline," wrote Palmerio. "We would see him wandering like a shade."

Here are some glimpses of those years: of the private man, of his public persona, of the workings of his mind.

1897. Romain Rolland has left a description of d'Annunzio at thirty-four years old. He looks like a slightly outdated man of fashion, an ambassador perhaps: "Small, oval head, a little pointed blond beard, his eyes focussed, attentive, clever, very cold and hard." They talk about books and Rolland, like Gide two years earlier, is astonished by how much of the new French writing he knows. D'Annunzio is genuinely well read, but he also knows how to make the most of his reading. Tom Antongini noted that he could talk for an hour about a book he had looked into for ten minutes. The talk turns to Rabelais. D'Annunzio claims to possess one of his letters, and—furthermore—a portrait by Leonardo that he never shows to anyone. Rolland, who doesn't believe him, remarks: "These little boasts don't shock. He is like a big child."

At the Capponcina, Rolland, a fine pianist, plays for d'Annunzio and introduces him to the work of French composers. He is quick to appreciate them. He is knowledgeable about early music: he will be instrumental in reviving the work of Claudio Monteverdi. He also keeps abreast of the new. He will collaborate with Debussy and write a poetic tribute to Richard Strauss: both composers are sufficiently avant-garde for their premieres to provoke outcries from conservative listeners. A decade later the composer Pizzetti, visiting d'Annunzio to work on the music for his play *The Ship*, will be surprised and impressed by his understanding of musical form: "He could talk about liturgical chant and polyphony as few others can."

JANUARY 1898. D'Annunzio is in Paris for the opening of Sarah Bernhardt's production of *The Dead City*. He is being fêted as the star he now is. Every night he returns to his hotel to find the lobby crowded with fans waiting to offer him flowers, or to demand an autograph, or simply to lay eyes on him. The two greatest living actresses are competing to perform his work. One of them, Duse, is his lover. Perhaps the other is too. According to Scarfoglio (over-fond of scurrilous gossip but unquestionably in the know: he is sharing a hotel suite with d'Annunzio), he has spent at least one night with Bernhardt.

This is Paris's *belle époque*. D'Annunzio is paying his first visit to a city through whose streets, it seems to him, "the fever of night burns as in the veins of a voluptuous woman" and he is, by his own account, "pouring out rivers of gold." His diary is crammed with appointments: a reception given in his honour by the Minister for Education, dinners and *soirées musicales* with hostesses like Princess Bibesco, private meetings with literary luminaries: Barrès, the poet Heredia, Anatole France. Marinetti sees him in a box at the theatre, "with his hand in the little ringed hand of an illustrious Parisienne." He is apt to finish the night in a *boîte* in Montmartre.

Hérelle visits him at the hotel. D'Annunzio has brought a servant with him, but nonetheless the sitting room is in chaos. There are bouquets of flowers everywhere. Tables, chairs, chests are all heaped with books sent in tribute by authors hoping for an endorsement. "But above all there was an incredible quantity of letters, hundreds, perhaps thousands of letters, in every style and every shape, satiny-smooth envelopes or envelopes of coarse paper, scented pages and pages torn from a school exercise book." Some of them are "lying half in half out of their envelopes for any passer-by to read." The rest are unopened. "It is impossible to pass through the room without brushing them with one's sleeve or one's coat tails." Soon they are spreading across the floor as well.

Duse is wretched. On the play's opening night, while Bernhardt is creating the role that she had believed was hers, she is at Count Primoli's house in Rome, lying on a couch with a hot-water bottle, then darting nervously around the room talking compulsively and tearing a flower to shreds. Now she sends dozens of telegrams. They are added to the drift of d'Annunzio's unread mail. At last she arrives in Paris, and sweeps him away to Nice. The great heap of fanmail is abandoned in the hotel.

D'Annunzio is fastidious to the point of neurosis. When he stays in a hotel he insists on having the bedcovers turned down and the sheets inspected before he settles in. His luggage always includes, along with the inevitable crimson silk cushions, a green damask cloth to be spread over a table onto which the contents of his dressing case—every item made of ivory and monogrammed in gold—is ceremoniously laid out.

Now he is in the dressing room at the Capponcina. It is "as light and white as a camellia," says Palmerio. A line from Pindar, in praise of water, is inscribed above the washstand in letters of gold and enamel. There is a large mirror, Bohemian crystal flasks and jars for scents and lotions, a set of Capodimonte porcelain figures of the Olympian gods, leather armchairs, hangings in flowered Venetian silk. It is a pretty room, a room to linger in. "I think," says Antongini, "if he had nothing better to do, d'Annunzio would be entirely happy bathing, dressing and spraying himself with perfume from morning until night." Every day he uses a pint of Coty's eau de cologne.

D'Annunzio is here changing his shirt for the fifth or sixth time today. From the wardrobe (an entire adjoining room lined with cupboards of polished walnut) he selects a fresh one. After he has left, a servant takes up the discarded shirt and, seeing that it is still perfectly clean, irons it and surreptitiously replaces it in a drawer.

·   ·   ·

In December 1898, d'Annunzio arrives in Alexandria to join Duse. The sea voyage has, as usual, made him fearfully sick. He feels weak and dizzy, but he is also excited. This is his first visit to Africa, or to the Arab world, or to anywhere outside Europe. It is not travel per se that inspires him, but history, and now he exults in being in a city founded by Alexander. Eleonora has sent a dragoman to greet him on the quay with a properly classical salutation—*"Ave!"* He regrets that, unlike the world-conquering Macedonian, he has no army and no baggage train, but he does have plenty of baggage. (Duse, who has been touring since childhood and knows how to pack, laughs at the exorbitant quantity of stuff he has brought with him.)

Back at the hotel he drinks a glass of champagne, noting the powerful effect it has when drunk on an empty stomach, and then, light-headed, takes Eleonora in his arms. He has already heard how her performance of the previous night has been acclaimed. Now he feels that the body he embraces is that of the whole people over whom she has scored such a triumph. He is Italy and, lying above her while she strokes his lips and eyelids with a posy of violets (he often employs flowers as aids to love-making), he is showing his mastery of "the barbaric and mixed race" of Egypt.

SPRING 1899, CORFU. D'Annunzio and Duse are in a rented villa, quarrelling over the young woman friend of Eleonora's whom d'Annunzio calls Donatella and whom he has attempted, perhaps successfully, to seduce. Duse is frantic: *"Horror!* . . . I had loved a monster . . . She and you—both of you—devouring my heart."

D'Annunzio is impervious. "What's wrong? Have you gone mad?" he asks. Tom Antongini maintains that d'Annunzio simply cannot understand the agonies of jealousy he causes. "He is capable of witnessing the most poignant manifestation of feminine sorrow with as little compunction as a dentist feels for a nervous patient."

D'Annunzio's mind is not on Eleonora, it is on the politically inflammatory play he is writing, *La Gloria* (Glory). His drama, as Mathilde Serao points out, does duty for the speeches he has never made in the chamber. *Glory*, he boasts, will "rouse the frogs in the putrid swamp that is Italy."

The riots of the previous year have left the government, widely accused of corrupt financial practices, unstable. Into this edgy political atmosphere, d'Annunzio launches a play in which the "men of yesterday" are challenged by young radicals whose political creed is ill-defined but whose impatience with the cautious, corrupt old establishment blazes out. Ruggero Flamma, a young leader who, as his name implies, "could set the world burning," leads a coup against an elder statesman, Cesare Bronte, only to be himself deposed by a furious mob. The play, d'Annunzio smugly tells Treves, "will have you shuddering in your conservative old skin."

Audiences see Bronte as a veiled portrait of Francesco Crispi, but more significant than any correspondence between the play's characters and real-life politicians is d'Annunzio's statement of a politics of violence. The earth itself, declares Flamma, cries out to be broken open and ploughed up so that the seed of hope can be sown. Change is to be effected by fighting in the streets. Corruption is to be washed away by blood. Battling by land and sea for its very existence, the nation will be purified and made magnificent. Only "a true man" with "a great destiny in his eyes" will be capable of effecting such a transformation, and whatever he does will be justified. Flamma loses power, according to his mistress, because he has sought his people's love. Instead he should have worked on the "brutal passions" released by the destruction of the old political order. "He who can exasperate their appetites and delude them, can drive them, head down, wherever he will."

A young man, being introduced to d'Annunzio five years later, recorded his awe at meeting "La Gloria himself." To d'Annunzio's admirers, it seems that Flamma, the charismatic demagogue calling for cleansing blood in "a clear, icy voice with something of frenzy and of menace in its depths," is the poet himself.

THE DINING ROOM AT THE CAPPONCINA. The little round panes of yellowish glass in the long windows create a dim and churchy light. Everywhere there are mottoes. D'Annunzio's cufflinks, his writing paper, his chairs and beds are all decorated with words. The jewellery he gives women is often engraved with the warning: "Who shall keep me chained?" A Latin motto is incised in gold into the wooden backrest of a row of choir stalls: "Read. Read. Read. And. Read. Again." "Per non Dormire" (so as not to sleep) is everywhere—on the glass of the windows, on the painted frieze, on the tiles of the floor. It is d'Annunzio's current favourite tag: he saw it on the façade of a Renaissance palace and adopted it for his own.

All around the room there are flowers, in vases of Murano glass or majolica or bronze. At the head of the table is the throne-like "Chair of the Guest" covered with a gold embroidered cloth. This, when she is in Settignano, is Duse's seat. To its right sits d'Annunzio. He eats little, but when the dessert is served he becomes greedy. He loves sweet things, and he loves fruit. When he has finished a servant pours water into a silver bowl, and d'Annunzio rinses his fingers, says Palmerio, "with the seriousness of one performing a sacred rite."

NAPLES, APRIL 1899. Duse is on tour and d'Annunzio is travelling with her. Each night, knowing himself to be a draw, he comes down to the footlights in the interval to take a bow, immaculate in white tie and tails, with a carnation in his buttonhole and a monocle in his eye (he is increasingly short-sighted). Duse is performing his latest plays, *La Gioconda* and *Glory*. The latter goes badly. The audience jeer at d'Annunzio, denying him his aristocratic persona by yelling out the name his father was born with: "*Rapagnetta*! Down with *Rapagnetta*!" D'Annunzio is unmoved. He withdraws while Duse struggles to regain the audience's attention and goodwill. Later Scarfoglio comes across him emerging from a dark corridor backstage, in the act of rebuttoning his clothes. He tells his old friend he has just enjoyed hurried sex with one of the company's actresses.

The Capponcina. D'Annunzio is working. The great church bell in the dining room doesn't ring to summon him to meals. When he is writing he eats only when it suits him, which may not be all day, stoking his energies with coffee. The servants move around on tiptoe. The word "*Silentium*" is carved into the lintel over his study door. A long work table from a Franciscan convent in Perugia is heaped with books and papers. Bundles of goose quills (he gets through up to thirty a day) stand in a bronze jar by a stack of fine paper, each sheet watermarked by hand with one of his favourite mottoes. This paper comes from Milani of Fabriano, where fine paper has been produced since the fifteenth century.

D'Annunzio is writing *Fire*. His mind is full of images of autumn and of Venice and of the ageing actress (called Foscarina or Perdita in the novel—but understood by everyone, despite d'Annunzio's protestations, to be Duse).

He lingers over descriptions of the master glass-blowers of Murano.

He conjures up fireworks, when the sky over the Grand Canal is a tissue of flaming gold. He mentally revisits the Eden garden on the Giudecca, with its paths paved with seashells, where he and Duse used to spend idle hours among the foxgloves and Madonna lilies. He writes of a demented artist and of a great lady immured by vanity in her own house (she cannot bear her wrinkles to be seen). He creates a fable of an underwater glass organ, a delicate piece of Symbolist fantasy. Alone in his room, pacing his garden, he is happy. Writing, he enters a trance-like fugue state in which he experiences "an uninterrupted series of epiphanies." When his concentration breaks he is left only with a distant sense of the state of mind he was in, "mysterious and frightening"—such as one might feel when shut out of a monumental cemetery, able to see only the white heads of the funerary statues, glimpsed above the wall.

Everything in the room looks old, but there are modern curiosities too. Some of the lamps are electric. D'Annunzio has recently taken up bicycling. He is delighted by photography. In the next door room, the library, along with some 14,000 books are stacked hundreds of photographs. D'Annunzio has been buying them from Alinari ever since his first years in Rome. They are reproductions of artworks, a compendium of images to add to the stout volumes of vocabularies which are his raw materials.

Visitors to d'Annunzio's homes may see clutter, but this is not mess, it is an arrangement. By the fire there is a painted chest emblazoned with a coat of arms. It is kept full of logs of pine and juniper wood, each piece cut to precisely the same length. When he works through the night, the poet will build up the fire himself, wearing gloves to protect his little hands.

D'Annunzio is writing, standing at a lectern. Duse is sitting near him on a choir stall salvaged from Santa Maria Novella. Each time he finishes a page he hands it over for her to read.

SEPTEMBER 1899. Once again Eleonora is on tour, and once again d'Annunzio is with her. They are staying in a hotel in Zurich where, by chance, Romain Rolland and his wife are also guests. Rolland finds d'Annunzio "simple and serious—tired of his meretricious glory." He seems to have aged rapidly over the preceding two years. His hair has almost all gone. He is wrinkled. He seems at once innocent and corrupt, "a youthful creature, almost a child, on whom debauchery has laid its wretched mark."

Duse stays in her room, coming out only to complain. "She is the eternal lamenter." She confides in Madame Rolland. D'Annunzio's life is like an inn, she says: "the whole world passes through it." One night, as she leaves for the theatre, she asks Rolland to sit with d'Annunzio, saying that he has been threatening to kill himself and needs music to soothe him. Rolland finds him apparently perfectly composed, but plays the piano as requested until d'Annunzio begins to talk. He is in one of the black moods that intermittently engulf him.

Another night the Rollands watch the other couple setting out for the theatre together. Duse strides ahead. "Little d'Annunzio followed her, running to keep pace."

JANUARY 1900. D'Annunzio has been invited to speak at the opening of the newly restored Sala di Dante in the Florentine church of Orsanmichele. He considers the occasion "a solemnity" with a "national character" and, as usual, takes pains over its publicity. He releases the text of his speech to the press in time for it to be published in full on the day, and is anxious for further coverage. "I don't know whether *Il Giorno* has yet arranged to have a report of the event sent over the telegraph," he writes to his friend Tenneroni. Tenneroni sees to it.

On the day the streets and squares around Orsanmichele are thronged with people. Before an audience of well over a thousand, d'Annunzio reads a canto of the *Inferno* and his own poem in praise of Dante, and then enlarges on a poet's role in a nation. "The artificer of the word" should be "first among citizens." Dante, he says, is like a mountain range, "home of the black eagles and lapidary thought." Dante was as much a part of Italy as the rocks of which the country was made. He brought Italy into being.

Tacitly d'Annunzio presents himself as the new peak in the mountain range of Italy's literature, and he predicts a great Italian renaissance. Dante wrote that the key to general felicity was strong autocratic government: he entertained a vision of a mighty emperor who would eliminate Italy's warring factions and impose order by force. D'Annunzio, awaiting "the necessary hero," thinks likewise. Italy will be great again, he announces. He is assuming his role of *Vate*—bard or prophet of the New Italy.

Between 1898 and 1903, d'Annunzio was composing poetry at a prodigious rate. In his *Laudi*—*Praises of the Sea, the Sky, the Heroes*—a veneration for the classical past blends with hopes for a grand and warlike future, and with the celebration of exceptional beings from the age of Homer to the present. Adding up to 20,000 lines of verse, the *Laudi* are inevitably patchy, but, as a contemporary critic puts it: "From the muddy sea of words emerge islands flowering in beauty, and rocky outcrops of rude and tragic grandeur."

They fall initially into three "books" (later d'Annunzio will add two more). *Maia*, the last written, is published as the first. It contains *Laus Vitae* (Praise of Life), a kind of modern *Odyssey*, drawing on d'Annunzio's memories of Greece and on classical mythology. The second, *Elettra*, is more overtly nationalist, containing twenty-six sonnets on the cities of Italy, verse eulogies to Italy's great men—condottieri, artists, thinkers—and bellicose visions of Italy's future. *Halcyon*, the third, is immediately and has remained the most popular. In its poems, d'Annunzio employs intricate forms and archaic vocabulary to create lyrics of limpid elegance which will be loved and memorised and anthologised for decades to come. In them d'Annunzio draws for his imagery on the Tuscan landscapes around him, all gilded by his imagination, stripped of intrusive modern buildings and vulgar modern people, and inhabited instead by nymphs and gods and hybrid mythological creatures.

He writes ceaselessly. "Nothing can compare with the intoxication of work. All the rest is mud and smoke." He breaks only for his daily ride and as he sets out, followed by his greyhounds, in the warm rain of an Italian spring (he loves rain) he feels ideas and poems forming in his mind, as plentiful and vigorous as the new leaves breaking on the trees around him.

MARCH 1900. *Fire* is published. The novel's hero, Stelio Affrena, is a dramatist who is writing a play which sounds just like *The Dead City*. Stelio is having an affair with an older woman, a world famous actress, Foscarina. He is young, brilliant, blazing with creative energy. She is beautiful but pathetic, constantly bewailing the loss of her youth and weeping over his obvious interest in other younger, more confident women.

D'Annunzio claims that Duse has sat beside him for weeks on end, reading each page as soon as it was written. In so far as the fictional heroine resembles her, he says, his depiction of her is a tribute to the real woman's greatness of soul. "I don't know a creature anywhere in modern fiction who can compare with Foscarina for moral beauty." Others disagree. Foscarina is in part a literary archetype like Pater's

Mona Lisa. She is "a night creature shaped by dreams and passions on a golden anvil." Her mouth has "tasted both honey and poison, the jewelled goblet and the cup of wormwood." So far, so safely non-specific. But she is also a tired actress who has—so d'Annunzio implies—had a great many lovers: "How many men had been singled out of the crowd to embrace her?" Her jealousy is tiresome and her breath is "cadaverous." In a passage which must have been unspeakably hurtful for Duse to read, Stelio and Foscarina make love. She is lying on top of him. She is heavy (Eleonora was taller and broader than d'Annunzio). He feels suffocated. "She fastened him down, with a grip that never slackened, as indissoluble as that of a corpse when its arms stiffen around the body of one living."

Duse's admirers are indignant. The impresario Joseph Shurmann begs her to forbid *Fire's* publication. She writes back grandly, "I know the novel and I have authorised its publication. My suffering, whatever it may be, counts for nothing compared with a masterpiece of Italian literature. Besides, I am forty years old, and in love!" According to Romain Rolland, when she read it she thought of killing herself, refraining only because of the damage her suicide would have done to d'Annunzio's reputation.

From this time onward d'Annunzio will be known as the man who exploited Duse, profited by her financially and then cruelly made public his vision of her as a worn-out degenerate. But if her fans cannot forgive him, she can. They will be together for another four years. She still adores him. And there is plenty of evidence that he is still, in his fashion, in love with her. Within a month of *Fire's* publication he joins her on tour. In his notebook he writes: "My heart pounds. In an hour I will see Isa." (Isa is one of his many names for her.) They meet, the reunion is evidently delicious for them both. Afterwards he writes to her: "Remember April 10 as the culmination of your life." He is writing in *Laus Vitae* about Helen of Troy, about the way the love of entire peoples has exhausted her, but also made her divine. When he describes Foscarina/Duse as having been desired by multitudes, he intends no insult, and what the public, outraged by his candid descriptions of her ageing, have not taken into account is how much he is moved by it. He loves "the faint lines that ran from the corner of her eyes up towards the temples, the dark veins that made her eyelids look like violets, all that in her which seemed touched with autumn sadness, all the shadow of her passionate face."

APRIL 1900. D'Annunzio is in Vienna, where Duse is performing *La Gioconda* before the Emperor and all his court. D'Annunzio is not at the theatre. Although he seldom misses a rehearsal, he never attends his first nights. He is out on the street at nightfall, admiring the "rumps" of the large blonde women and making notes. He feels good. He has eaten snipe—"magnificent colour . . . dark golden sauce in a silver dish"—and drunk gold-tinged Marco Brunner wine from fine glass. The aftertrace of recent sex tingles in his veins. All this physical well-being is stimulating his mind. "Great intellectual exaltation." He pauses to admire the window display of a florist's shop. He notices the deep dark red of a bunch of carnations, "a colour found only in the pictures of Bonifazio [Veronese]." He marvels at the extortionate prices. All around, the cafés and restaurants are noisy with laughter and raised voices. He is acutely aware of the prosperity and bustle of this great modern city, "the barbaric force of it, the power of trade and of work." He passes and re-passes in front the Burgtheater. Inside, a multitude of strangers is listening to his lover utter his words, but the odd thing is that no one turns to stare at him, as they do invariably now when he goes out in Florence or Rome. It is a little disconcerting. Travelling, he has temporarily shed the "glittering skin" of celebrity.

He follows Duse into Germany, and is impressed. The "miraculous" combination of Prussian militarism with a booming modern industry excites him. Nationalism, the "implacable yeast," is at work in the Austro-Hungarian Empire, disrupting and fragmenting it; but in Germany, the "instinct to dominate" is powered by commercial success. Temporarily forgetting his commitment to the conservation of fine old buildings, he praises German cities transformed into gigantic factories, German cathedrals "soot-blackened," German shipyards and railway depots.

He sees, with a clairvoyance unusual in 1900, where the "hurricane" of "the struggles of trade, the struggle for wealth" must surely lead. "Above the din of work can be heard the barking of the Dogs of War." The sound seems not to have alarmed, but excited him.

D'Annunzio is in his study again, rapt in concentration. He is delving into the literature of the distant past, mining it for verse-forms and models. For him, reviving Italy's mediaeval texts is a political project. He is quarrying them for words, because a developed literary language is the tool and badge of a great nation. The writing of poetry in the emergent cultures of modern Europe is a political act. "A poet is the creator of the nation around him," wrote Herder. D'Annunzio agrees. He works always with a dictionary at hand. Most Italians, he writes scathingly, use a vocabulary of barely 800 words. "I have so far used at least 15,000. Many I have called back to life, to many I have given a fresh significance." Out of all the thousands of books in his library, the one that is most essential to him is Niccolò Tommaseo's seven-volume dictionary of the Italian language.

D'Annunzio's teenage son Gabriellino is staying at the Capponcina and getting a little weary of the household's quietness. "It's like living in a Trappist monastery." It is lunchtime and Gabriellino is hungry. The servant, Rocco Pesce, rings a bronze bell which once sounded the hour of prayer in a monastic cloister. Gabriellino heads smartly for the dining room, but his father does not emerge and, despite Gabriellino's pleas, Pesce will not ring the bell again, or knock at the study door. He most certainly won't serve lunch until the master appears.

When d'Annunzio comes out at last it is as though he has wakened from a deep sleep. "There seems to be a veil over his face, his eyes are sightless." But once he sits down at table the cloud lifts from him. He has been writing about Homeric heroes, now he eats like one. He tucks into his veal cutlets with the kind of formidable appetite Ajax brought to meals of plump kids eaten by the sounding sea before Troy.

Across the broad courtyard in front of the Capponcina is a pretty little red-brick house. From its rooftop flies a green banner with the word *"Fidelitas"* written in red on one side, and on the other the figure of a greyhound. As evening comes on, the new-fangled electric lights are switched on inside and the building, with its stained-glass windows, glows like a jewel. This is d'Annunzio's kennel.

D'Annunzio confesses to loving animals more than people. At the Capponcina he initially has two horses. Soon he has eight, all of them handsome thoroughbreds, and ten (eventually rising to twenty-two) dogs, most of them borzois or greyhounds. He strips to his shirt-sleeves and squats in the kennel, a greyhound between his knees, running his hands over its feet, its ribs, its back, feeling with pride the musculature of its thighs, and the delicacy and power of its tendons. He will write one day that none of his syntactical constructions can rival the body of a greyhound for beauty.

Returning from an outing, he calls all the dogs by name and they come hurtling out of the kennel and race around him, leaping higher than his head, barking and yelping. He is delighted. He smiles. Then with a word he calms them (Benigno Palmerio, who was a vet before he become master of d'Annunzio's household, is impressed by his dog-handling skills). The dogs retreat to settle themselves watchfully around him. Now he turns his attention to his spaniel, Teli-Teli, and, holding the dog's gaze, launches into a long speech. Teli-Teli whimpers as though contributing to the conversation. When d'Annunzio leaves the Capponcina he will give the spaniel to one of his lady friends with a photograph captioned "Teli-Teli the philosopher."

When King Umberto I was shot dead by an anarchist in July 1900, d'Annunzio composed an ode to his successor, urging the young King to be worthy of the role to which he had been called, and darkly hinting that if he failed to be as martial and stalwart as his destiny required: "You will see close at hand among the rebels/Even he who today salutes you."

In his electoral campaign, d'Annunzio had proclaimed the "politics of poetry." Now, increasingly, he was writing the poetry of politics.

Other odes on patriotic themes followed, including one on the death of Giuseppe Verdi. He gave a public reading of it in Florence, prefacing it with a rousing oration "To the youth of Italy," urging them to be worthy of their glorious past. He wrote and recited his long poem to Garibaldi. He appeared on horseback at the funeral of Menotti Garibaldi (the hero's son), delivering an address to the assembled crowds in which he predicted a future glittering with blood: "The Latin sea is covered/with the slaughter of your wars …/Oh flower of the races!"

Every summer d'Annunzio and Duse rented a house on the Tuscan coast. These summers, passed between the long sandy beaches and the pine forests above which the mountains loom, formed the settings for the exquisite neo-pagan fantasies of d'Annunzio's *Halcyon* poems.

D'Annunzio was serene and productive. "These last few days, in my boat," he wrote to his publisher, "I have composed *Laudi* all penetrated with air and salt." He swam. He rode. "Furious gallops on the elastic sand, where the traces of the retreating waves are as delicate as the ridges inside my greyhounds' mouths." But even during these sojourns by the sea d'Annunzio was indoors working for most of the day and much of the night. Nothing, not even a life-threatening accident, could distract him long.

One August morning he was galloping along the beach when his horse stumbled. He fell. His foot was caught in the stirrup. The horse bolted, dragging him, bouncing. He struggled. The seconds seemed to stretch out interminably. At last he freed himself and lay stunned, his cheek pressed to the hot sand, hearing the vibration of his horse's hooves gradually distancing themselves. His perceptions were extraordinarily sharp. The cool slime of seaweed, the hardness of a stone, the corner of a piece of driftwood, the scent of the prickly flowers that grow in the sand; everything was hyper-real to him. As he stumbled down to the water to bathe his bleeding face the idea for an ode, "Undulna," a fantasy about a sea nymph, one of the loveliest of the *Halcyon* poems, sprang into his mind.

In the summer of 1901, at Versilia on the Tuscan coast again, d'Annunzio stood at his lectern day after day, working for up to fourteen hours at a stretch on his tragedy *Francesca da Rimini*. He was intent on giving Italy a back-story appropriate to the future he wanted for his country, that of a bellicose and expansionist great power. As Wagner had looked to the past to inspire the future, reviving the stories of the *Niebelungenlied* to give Germans an heroic tradition, so d'Annunzio, bard of modern Italy, expanded Dante's poignant brief tale of forbidden love into a grand five-act tragedy full of sound and fury.

The thirteenth-century wars between the Guelphs and the Ghibellines rage onstage and off. The kernel of the narrative is the well-known story which had already inspired fourteen operas in Italy alone, as well as numerous pre-Raphaelite paintings, Tchaikovsky's symphonic poem and Rodin's most famous sculpture (*The Kiss* was originally entitled *Francesca da Rimini*). Francesca is married for dynastic reasons to Gianciotto Malatesta, a fabled warrior but lame and unlovely. She was tricked into the marriage. She thought her husband was to be Gianciotto's handsome brother Paolo, with whom she is in love. Reading the story of Lancelot and Guinevere together, Paolo and Francesca can no longer restrain their passion. Finding them together Gianciotto kills them both.

D'Annunzio sat (so he tells us) elbows on knees, head in hands, eyes clenched in concentration until he could see in his mind's eye "the very bones and flesh" of Gianciotto, the ferocious one-eyed killer he was conjuring up. At nightfall he would appear in the hallway, shouting for a light (the Capponcina had electricity, but by the sea he still needed a servant and a lamp). When he took his daily gallop along the beach he singed his horse's mane, to have in his nostrils the acrid smell in which—according to him—the warriors of the Malatesta family had delighted.

His play is spectacular. He embellishes the simple plot with a Shakespearean jester and a chorus of attendant women who perform folkloric dances and provide a salacious commentary on their mistress's love life. There is a scene with a cloth merchant which allows him to display his knowledge of mediaeval textiles and to fill the stage with swirling lengths of gorgeous fabrics. There are brothers palpitating with incestuous desire. The play's tone owes much to d'Annunzio's early reading of Keats, with his pseudo-mediaeval fantasies full of jewel-bright colours and his pot of basil fertilised by a buried human head; but it is animated by a zest for violence which is d'Annunzio's own. There is a scene in which the heroine, in ferocious mood, plays dangerously with "Greek fire" (a form of early napalm invented in Byzantium) and talks wildly

of immolating herself and her enemies. There are lascivious lines about the "lips of a fresh wound." There is an off-stage torture chamber from which awful howls emanate. There is a great deal of noisy and technically elaborate business to do with siege engines and catapults. There is a severed head brought, dripping gore, onto the stage.

D'Annunzio's stage directions make inordinate demands on his performers. In *Glory* his female lead is required to speak in a voice "whose indefinable melody seems to prolong itself in the most remote mystery of being." Her smile, moreover, must "arrest time and abolish the world." Even from an actor of Duse's calibre, this was asking a lot.

Designers were set equally impossible tests. Each of the sets for *Francesca da Rimini*, as d'Annunzio describes them, are multiplex. Arches open onto further vistas, galleries and alcoves provide subsidiary acting spaces, windows show distant landscapes and sea battles afar off. Trap-doors, curtained doorways, flights of stairs and raised terraces further complicate the geometry. And these elaborate structures are crowded with objects. Walls hung with weapons, tables spread with wine and bowls of fruit, rose bushes and embroidered hangings, all clutter the space, which must yet be left clear enough for a dozen men at arms to assemble or for a bevy of handmaidens to perform a "swallow-dance," waving gold-entwined garlands of narcissi and carved wooden birds.

D'Annunzio recruited Mariano Fortuny as his production designer and wrote him long letters about each detail of the costumes, the props, the lighting, the complicated machinery required. In these years he was campaigning for the preservation of Italy's artistic heritage, lobbying for the protection of Piero della Francesca's frescoes, writing an ode on Leonardo's *Last Supper*. Now he was putting Italy's past on stage for the glory of the race, and he wanted it to look right.

Perhaps unsurprisingly, Fortuny found the job undoable, and dropped out, to be replaced as design supremo by d'Annunzio's old friend and illustrator de Carolis. The costumes were eventually made by the couturier Charles Worth, from fabrics woven to order after mediaeval patterns. (Duse as Francesca, previous page.) The production was to be the most expensive ever yet seen in the Italian theatre.

The first night was bedevilled by d'Annunzio's insistence on a realistic battle. He had demanded real smoke: the audience, as a result, were half-asphyxiated. He had wanted real missiles: a boulder, hurled from a catapult, demolished one wall of the stage. But once the machinery was brought under control, the play was acclaimed. Romain Rolland called it "the greatest Italian work since the Renaissance."

Liane de Pougy, one of the most celebrated courtesans of Paris's *belle époque*, is visiting Florence. D'Annunzio invites her to the Capponcina and sends a carriage, filled with roses, to collect her. As she descends from it his servants pelt her with more roses. "There before me was a frightful gnome with red-rimmed eyes and no eyelashes, no hair, greenish teeth, bad breath, the manners of a mountebank and the reputation, nevertheless, for being a ladies' man." She rejects his advances and leaves. Two days later the carriage comes for her again but this time she sends her maid—"my sniffy old Adèle"—with a long note full of excuses.

De Pougy is one of many who testify to d'Annunzio's ugliness, yet photographs show a trim and perfectly presentable-looking middle-aged man. He was no Adonis, and certainly no Hercules, but no "frightful gnome" either. It appears that just as his charm could transfigure him, and make him irresistible to some, so—to those who were resistant to it—there was something repugnant about his incorrigible impulse to seduce. De Pougy, a professional well known for her book-keeping, and who was accustomed to being paid a fortune for her favours, was aware of his reputation as "a man who was, to say the least, ungrateful to the ladies." Great man he might be, but a debt-ridden poet had nothing to offer that could interest her.

1902. D'Annunzio is in Turin overseeing the production of *Francesca da Rimini*, conversing with an old acquaintance from Rome, the writer de Amicis. As he holds forth a servant keeps coming in, each time bringing a calling-card or a note from someone hoping to see the great man, or asking him to address some gathering. "In two days he has been asked to make eight public speeches." Each time d'Annunzio replies that he is unwell, and lays the card down on a table already strewn with them. He is a master of evasion. None of these interruptions cause him to lose the thread of what he is saying.

Their conversation over, d'Annunzio allows those who have been waiting in the outer room to come in for a kind of public audience. Again his performance is impeccable. De Amicis writes: "He wears the royal mantle of celebrity as though he had been born to the throne."

Now he is in Milan, at the house of his editor Treves. He is playing the new-fangled game of ping-pong. (Celluloid balls and rubber-stippled bats first went on sale in Europe in the previous year.) He is very fit. He needs to be, he says, for the heroic labour of writing his books. He rides most days when he is at home, returning, after hours in the saddle, in a kind of ecstasy: he feels himself a centaur, wild and not wholly human. He plays tennis and golf. At the Capponcina there is a large wood-panelled room on the first floor which he uses as a gym. There, every day, he practises fencing and lifts weights and dumbbells. His face may be ageing—in these years people describe it as looking like wax, or like ivory, covered all over with tiny wrinkles—but his body is smooth and muscular.

He loves ping-pong. He plays for hours, his mouth tense with concentration, his eyes shining.

1902. Duse is touring the Austrian-controlled territories of Venezia Giulia and Istria. D'Annunzio is with her, and the two of them are received with a wild excitement which is more about politics than about their theatrical gifts. To d'Annunzio and like-minded Italian nationalists, these territories, still under Austrian control, are *irredenti* (unredeemed) parts of the true Italy.

Twenty-seven curtain calls (with d'Annunzio on stage) in Gorizia. Flowers and scraps of coloured paper bearing the titles of his works raining from windows as he passes through Istria. Delirious crowds roaring their approval in the theatre, and then taking to the streets to roar some more, in Trieste, where a deputy describes the couple's progress as a "sacred pilgrimage"—sacred, that is, not to any celestial divinity, but to the cause of Greater Italy. Wherever they go they are shadowed by the Austrian police.

D'Annunzio asks his book-finder to provide him with books on Istria and Dalmatia. He invokes Dante's lines "to Pola by the Bay of Carnaro/ which bounds Italy and washes its edges." (Pola and the Carnaro are at this time deep into Austrian territory.) He writes an ode to the Bronzetti brothers, a pair of Italian partisans from Trento executed by the Austrians as "martyrs" to the irredentist cause. "As the white sap surges through wood, hidden by the bark," writes d'Annunzio, so should the people of unredeemed Trento "in silence make ready your heroes." The Austrian authorities protest at what they (correctly) interpret as incitement to rebellion, and confiscate copies of *Il Giorno*, in which the poem is published.

1903. The bedroom at the Capponcina. The walls are covered with fine old green damask. The ceiling is hidden by a sixteenth-century canopy with flower-embroidered hangings, fixed at the centre with a gilded garland. The room contains the usual profusion of precious things, a gilded harp, a silver Arabian sword inlaid with ivory and gemstones, columns and tables covered with vases and caskets and old morocco-bound books. At the bed's foot, two bronze copies of the *Winged Victory* of Samothrace stand on green-veined marble pillars. D'Annunzio has completed the *Laudi* and Eleonora Duse's celebratory gift is being delivered. She has already given him a full-size plaster cast of one of Michelangelo's *Prisoners*. Now, into the bedroom, porters carry a terracotta copy of the *Charioteer* of Delphi. They set it up at the food of the bed.

In this room, in the previous month, d'Annunzio awoke on the morning of his fortieth birthday with, as usual, a dagger beside his pillow, and a sense that his youth is struggling like a soldier of fortune whose adversary kneels on his chest, ready to give the death blow. "Now I must embalm the corpse of youth. I must wrap it in bandages and enclose it between the four walls of a coffin. I must make it pass through the door, where the spectre of old age has appeared between the slats of the blinds and with an almost familiar nod has wished me a good day."

1904. Eating alone in a hotel in Lucerne, d'Annunzio overheard a group of diners telling each other that the plot of *The Innocent* was all factual: Gabriele d'Annunzio had really and truly killed a baby. He once aspired to make his life into a work of art. Now others—journalists, fans, gossips—were doing it for him. D'Annunzio the public figure had become an imaginary construct, one over which d'Annunzio the man was struggling to retain control.

Fame was a tool which he used with cunning. It was also a burden. Celebrity worship, then as now, was a volatile emotion which included fault-finding vigilance, a perverse joy in the adored one's flaws and furious envy. There were plenty of people who disapproved of d'Annunzio. There were others who exhausted him with their admiration, their craving for a piece of him. They rummaged through his intimate affairs and "the poet himself and his life are made ugly by the filth of those hands."

He was talked about as an inveterate socialite, but the inscription on the lintels of the Capponcina's rooms—"Silence," "Enclosure," "Solitude"—give a truer account of his daily life. Rolland, visiting him this year, was struck by the isolation in which he and Duse lived. They never seemed to go out. "She has no friends. He, not many."

MILAN, 1904. D'Annunzio has turned back to his Abruzzese origins to write a rustic tragedy. Two decades after the event, nine years after Michetti's painting of the same name took a prize in Venice, d'Annunzio has finally converted into drama the scene they witnessed of the young girl hounded by drunken peasants. He has made of it an Italian myth. Now *Jorio's Daughter* is going into rehearsal and d'Annunzio is reading it to the cast. It takes him four hours. He enunciates with perfect clarity: he chants. The leading actress is trying to commit to memory every one of his inflections so that she can reproduce it exactly in her performance "I *phonographed* his rhythms. My Mila was his."

He wrote the play, he claims, in eighteen days (it seems, in fact, to have taken him about six weeks) "obedient to the daemon of the race, which chanted its songs through me." The story is that of a girl—a feared outsider, the daughter of a sorcerer—hunted down by a crowd of harvesters intent on rape. She is saved, but inadvertently brings death and disgrace to the family who rescues her. There is a wedding, a murder, terrible penalties (drowning in a sack with a savage dog: live burial). The language is archaic but simple, a blend of traditional songs with echoes of Dante and phrases from the Bible and the Catholic liturgy. Much of the dialogue is in verse. There are choruses, constructed like fugues (d'Annunzio's understanding of music was one of the most useful tools he brought to his playwriting). Earthy naturalism is disrupted by the entrance of characters with overtly symbolic functions— a miracle-working saint, an old wise woman who can provide poisons and cures.

D'Annunzio fires off almost daily letters to his folklorist friend de Nino, asking his opinion of costume sketches and bits of stagecraft and greedily demanding more detail. He has recruited Michetti, who in turn has set several of the *Cenacolo* to scouring the Abruzzi for old pottery and embroidered costumes and archaic musical instruments. The two friends correspond earnestly about carved stools and goatskin bladders. The resulting spectacle is to be a grand mélange of poverty and colour, of crude materials and beautiful workmanship.

In the persecuted girl d'Annunzio has created a luminous heroine. Duse exults. Here is the dramatic masterpiece of which she has always believed him capable. But Mila, the play's heroine, is an innocent girl in her teens, and Duse is now forty-five, an ailing woman whose love life has been a topic of prurient public gossip for a quarter of a century. The company to whom d'Annunzio has granted the first performance rights has their own leading actress, who would like the part. There are edgy negotiations. The gossip columns are full of rumours. Duse feels obliged to issue a statement denying that "there is any truth in the stories about artistic differences between herself and d'Annunzio."

As the play goes into rehearsal she is ill again, shaken by an uncontrollable cough. Nobly, at the last moment, she agrees to waive her claim to the role. The production must go ahead without her. She writes to d'Annunzio, in her usual staccato style: "Gabri—sweetness strength— hope—the sole strongest and most painful thing in my life . . . I have given it to you, for you, for your beautiful destiny—and if the heart

shatters into tiny pieces—it doesn't matter!" With her own hands she folds the costumes that have been made for her—wonderfully elaborate as d'Annunzio likes them to be—and sends them to Irma Grammatica, who will take her place.

Mathilde Serao visits Duse in the hotel in Genoa where she lies sick, coughing and spitting blood. D'Annunzio has not been to visit her, although he has taken a few days off from attending rehearsals in order to go to Rome for some fox-hunting. As Duse suspects, he has a new love whom he will see there. Serao asks her about the play. "A cry burst from her: 'It was mine, mine, and they have taken it from me!'" She brings the script out from under her pillow and, struggling to sit up, begins to read from it. Feeble as she is, "her voice strengthens; her face changes; she recites as though she were on stage, in front of a thousand spectators." Fearful that she will bring on another fit of coughing, Serao tries to stop her, but Duse reads it all.

A week later the play opens in Milan. The production has been put together at great speed, but it is splendid. D'Annunzio's drama describes a brutal, misogynist society, whose people live in terror of their comrades' disapproval and of supernatural vengeance. But it seems to his first audiences that he has given it the grandeur and mythic resonance of Aeschylus' Mycenae or Sophocles' Thebes.

As the curtain falls at the end of the first act there is a sepulchral silence. The actors wait in suspense. Then, according to one of them, "suddenly, as from far off, like a great wave of the sea, resounds the immense applause." D'Annunzio is called to take a bow ten, twelve, fifteen times.

For reasons both financial (too many creditors trying to get in the door) and romantic (too many women claiming an exclusive right to the visitor's bedroom), d'Annunzio has found it expedient to leave home for a while. He is staying near Florence with the sculptor, Clemente Origo. The poet (so health-conscious, so obsessively clean) is a non-smoker himself, but he is amused by Origo's prodigious intake of nicotine—120 Turkish cigarettes a day.

Origo is very tall and lean. One day the friends exchange jackets and pose for a photograph. Origo towers. His shoulders are hunched together in an attempt to squeeze himself into d'Annunzio's trim little linen blazer, his bony forearms extending well below the cuffs. Beside and below him stands d'Annunzio. The broad shoulders of Origo's tweed jacket droop half-empty on him. Its sleeves dangle. The hem reaches the poet's knees. He is beaming, like a child dressing up in the grown-ups' clothes.

D'Annunzio could be playful. Those of his household who wrote their memoirs recall his pranks and teasing: so do several of his friends. His work, though, and his public persona, are totally devoid of humour. Of all the dozens of pictures of d'Annunzio in existence—most of them carefully posed—this is the only one which suggests that he had it in him to make fun of himself.

An episode from d'Annunzio's life with Duse, one described by himself.

They are outside the Capponcina. Eleonora is on a raised terrace, leaning over the ivy-covered railing. Beneath her d'Annunzio is check-

ing his horse's girth. He rides for hours every day along the lanes and tracks of the hills above Florence, flanked with olive groves and vine- yards, crowned with woods, rich in associations with artists and ancient wars. His poetry is full of his sense of the old and new of what encircles him, the freshness of blossom and rushing water, the deep timbre of a beauty already and so often hymned. As he writes he alludes to those who have described this landscape before him—Dante, Michelangelo, Lorenzo the Magnificent. This is the kind of company he likes to keep.

"Where are you going?" asks Eleonora.

"At random."

"But in which direction?"

"Don't ask."

The very word, "fidelity," in his opinion, has a tone as phoney and theatrical as that of false chains (since his plays' heroines were fre- quently manacled, this is a sound with which d'Annunzio is familiar).

"No couple is faithful for love's sake . . . I am unfaithful for love's sake." Perhaps this is cynical self-justification: perhaps he really doesn't understand the pain his promiscuity causes.

He takes the old road skirting the hillside towards Fiesole. Florence's Duomo and Campanile seem to float on the haze beneath. He dismounts, he tells us, at the gate of a villa surrounded by neatly clipped hedges, where he is awaited by two sisters, both musicians, both "expert in perverse games" (these obliging girls sound like figments of d'Annunzio's erotic imagination, but there certainly were women on whom he paid such calls). Three hours later he goes home.

As he comes up the road he begins to call out to his "one and only companion." He drops the reins and leaps down onto the gravel. He is still shouting "Ghisola, Ghisolabella!" (his tenderest name for Duse).

She appears, surprised and slightly frightened. "What's the matter with you?"

Indoors he strips and bathes. His desire for her is urgent, "the fleeting infidelity gave love an intoxicating novelty," but, fastidious as ever, he won't omit his bath. From the tub he calls out to her incessantly. "Ghisola, I love you. I love you, only you for ever. Wait for me. You wait for me." Clean at last, he goes to the guest room. What follows, he tells us, is like dying without death.

Poor Eleonora has different views on fidelity. Benigno Palmerio, the major-domo, tells the story. She summons him one day at the Capponcina (d'Annunzio being away in Livorno). She is in the music room, seated in an armchair "in an attitude which could have been that of a dead woman or a medium." There is a surviving film showing Duse acting out grief and outrage. In it she leans against a wall, head thrown back, mouth trembling, eyes half-closed, her lovely pale face as smooth and yet mobile as turbulent water, her throat exposed as though to an assassin's knife. This is how she looks as Palmerio comes in.

Speaking "like an automaton," she announces: "We must set fire to this house immediately." On stage or off, Duse is always dramatic. Palmerio stammers and temporises. He is a practical man, an inhabitant of the real world, and now he finds himself obliged to act out a scene from a melodrama opposite the world's greatest tragedienne. It is embarrassing. Duse begins to circle the room, moaning: "The Temple has been profaned. Only fire can purify it." She is looking for matches.

Palmerio warns her that if she sets light to the house he will call the fire brigade. He pleads. He soothes. He leads her outside. He asks what is the matter. She opens her clenched hand to reveal the two hairpins— the kind of pale-coloured ones a blonde would wear—she has found in the guest room. Palmerio, who knows very well whose the hairpins are, and also whom (yet another woman) d'Annunzio has gone to meet in Livorno, cajoles and flatters and gradually calms her until her tragic grandeur collapses and she bursts into tears.

MAY 1904. D'Annunzio's landlady and neighbour in Settignano, the Marchesa della Robbia, witnesses a curious ceremony. Women are strewing the road through the olive groves to the Capponcina with rose petals. Servants in livery are dawn up in line. D'Annunzio appears, in a white silk suit, with a tall, blonde, elegantly dressed woman on his arm. They walk towards the house with the solemnity of a bridal pair approaching the altar. D'Annunzio's romance with Duse is over, and so is the period of comparative tranquillity in which he has done so much work. The lady is the Marchesa Alessandra di Rudinì, an independently wealthy twenty-six-year-old widow and mother of two children (whom she is now abandoning), daughter of a former prime minister and, for the next three years, d'Annunzio's acknowledged mistress.

Speed

D'ANNUNZIO'S LAST FULL-LENGTH NOVEL, *Forse che sì, Forse che no* (Maybe Yes, Maybe No) opens with a couple hurtling across the northern Italian plain towards Mantua in an open-topped red car. She (wayward, seductive young widow Isabella Inghirami) is tantalising him (dashing explorer and aviator Paolo Tarsis) with the title words. Goaded, Tarsis speeds up. The car roars along the dead-straight Roman road, the pulse of its engine as warlike as the beating of a vast metal drum. He tells her that her life is in his hands:

> "I could in an instant dash it into the dust, crush it against the stones, make of you and of me a single bleeding mass."
> "Yes."
> They are both feverish.
> "Close your eyes, give me your lips."
> "No."
> "We are going to die."
> "I am ready."

A cart is lumbering towards them, laden with massive tree trunks, drawn by four oxen, blocking the road. Tarsis keeps accelerating. Isabella is intensely aware of her own body, of her legs "as smooth as those of a silver crucifix which has been kissed by thousands upon thousands of pious lips." A swallow careens across their path: it falls shattered. Isabella is watching Tarsis in the wing mirror, the image of his face—bronzed, clean-shaven, his lips swollen above his silk scarf—distorted by the convex lens into a streamlined futurist icon.

> "You want this?"
> "Let it come!"

242 · GABRIELE D'ANNUNZIO

They are right upon the cart. At the last possible moment Tarsis swerves. The car judders over the rough verge, narrowly avoiding toppling into the canal full of water lilies which runs alongside the road. Isabella begins to laugh wildly, a great sobbing laugh hinting at her incipient madness.

Speed, risk, sexual cruelty, suicide, insanity: these were themes which beat through d'Annunzio's work and haunted his life in the years between his break with Duse and his departure for France. His financial affairs became increasingly desperate, his lifestyle more preposterously extravagant and his love-life more hectic. An awareness of his own age was growing on him, and it depressed him profoundly. His wrinkles, his bald pate, his discoloured teeth, all felt like disfiguring injuries. His literary output slowed: the miraculous years when poetry flowed through his veins like blood were past. His fame, its novelty exhausted, had become irksome. He called the journalists who tracked his comings and goings "mingy little scribblers." He felt lonely. Pursuing younger women for the first time in his life, he knew he was chasing his own fast-escaping youth.

He always courted danger. He was a duellist when he needn't have been. (He fought another duel in 1900 when his election campaign in Florence gave rise to what he considered an unforgivably *ad hominem* newspaper article.) He rode fast and hard, and fell frequently, not because he was a bad rider but because he was such a reckless one. When he was going fox-hunting he would feed his thoroughbred sugar lumps until the horse was so "drunk" he couldn't control it. He once set a record by jumping forty-four walls in succession out on the Roman Campagna. Fellow huntsmen made a joke of the way he breached hunting etiquette, unable (or disinclined) to prevent his hyper-stimulated mount overriding the hounds. "The poet has an urgent message for the horizon!"

Hunting near Rome in the autumn of 1903, while Duse was on tour, performing his *Francesca da Rimini* (to her own substantial financial loss) in Germany and England, d'Annunzio met Alessandra di Rudinì. A few weeks later he met her again in Florence at her brother's wedding and within days he had written to tell her he loved her. That winter, as *Jorio's Daughter* went into rehearsal, d'Annunzio repeatedly excused himself and slipped away, not to Genoa, where Duse lay ill, but to Rome to go hunting again, and to see his new beloved.

Alessandra was fifteen years younger than d'Annunzio, twenty years younger than Duse. She was tall and athletic, a blonde Amazon known in Roman society as a fearless horsewoman who (shockingly) wore breeches and rode astride. "I love horses, dogs, hunting and all those things which give me the opportunity of proving to men that not all women are animals to be preyed upon," she told d'Annunzio, shortly before becoming his prey. Always attracted to androgynous women, and admiring her for her aristocratic independence of spirit, he called her Nike (Victory) and set about encompassing her defeat. She was exultant and reckless. "How long will your love last? I fear terrible sufferings are in store for me. But it does not matter . . . I tremble at the thought of seeing you again."

D'Annunzio was still a married man. Alessandra's family were aghast at her degrading herself by becoming the mistress of a bankrupt poet who was, for all his fame, a mere bourgeois. Her father cut off her allowance. Her husband's family took her two small sons from her. She was undeterred. "Remember always to dare," was one of d'Annunzio's mottoes. "So as not to sleep," was another. There was nothing sleepy or timid about Nike. She was as exciting and dangerous as a thoroughbred horse high on an excess of sugar lumps.

No more, wrote Benigno Palmerio, of the "harmony and serenity, so propitious to work" that had prevailed in Duse's time. The actress, careful of her reputation, had only ever been a visitor in the Capponcina, for all the hundreds of nights she had spent there. Nike, grand

and self-confident enough to defy convention, moved in and set about expanding the household. The number of servants rose from six to fifteen and then to twenty-one. "Money wasn't spent," writes Palmerio, "it was thrown away." A blacksmith came all the way from Milan twice a month, with an assistant, to shoe the horses (as though there were no farriers in Tuscany). Enormous bills for Nike's clothes arrived from Paris couturiers. Antongini claims to have seen with his own eyes Persian carpets laid in the stables for the horses to bed down on. "It looked as though d'Annunzio and his adorable companion . . . were trying to compensate themselves in one wild flight for the austerity and reasonableness of some previous existence." But for all their fortune-defying behaviour, the disaster that soon overtook the couple was not of their own making.

In the spring of 1905, Nike developed an ovarian tumour. She underwent three life-threatening operations under general anaesthetic (extremely dangerous at that date). D'Annunzio moved into the hospital with her, staying there for weeks on end, and attended her assiduously. He stood by as the chloroform was administered. Three times, he wrote: "I have held in my hands the hands of the victim, while her soul plunged into the dark abyss . . . I seem to have been present at three death agonies."

He saw her illness as his own ordeal. "Sufferings horrible torture never ending," he telegraphed to Antongini. "My anguish indescribable." Nike's survival was evidence of his own heroic fortitude. "The doctors are astonished by my endurance. For six weeks I have watched all night." Her operations were his "martyrdom." "Each time I waited standing upright on my legs of stone, transforming pain into a sacred vow." For all that, the writer in him remained alert. While the potentially fatal surgery was performed he took notes about the mechanics of his lover's ordeal—the gleaming scalpels and forceps, the wheeled "bed of torture," the surgeon's deft movements and the protocol of the operating theatre. His next play would include a detailed description of a similar operation.

Moved and elated by Nike's illness, he contemplated freeing himself so that he could marry her. But divorce would not become legal in Italy until 1974. The only way he could end his marriage would be by adopt-

ing Swiss citizenship, something that, as the voice of the Italian race, was unthinkable for him. Anyway, the moment passed. As Nike recovered, his love for her dwindled.

She had been given morphine to ease her pain. By the time her body was mending she was dependent on the drug, writing to d'Annunzio: "Nike has succumbed to her despair and has injected enough morphine to forget for an hour the torment of having Gabri far away from her." D'Annunzio had loved her for her audacity. Now she was abject, he sought solace elsewhere. The more morphine Nike took, the more tiresome her lover found her; the more he stayed away from her, the more wretched she became and the more she took. Their affair ended in a style fitting to its inception. One evening—distraught—she took d'Annunzio's strongest horse and galloped off, soon losing control of her mount. D'Annunzio raced after her and with difficulty managed to bring horse and rider safely back.

The next day she wrote him a note. "The life we lead in common has become a weight upon you." She could sense it in the "deaf irritation (as last evening when you took my horse in hand)—and more, your words (like yesterday), cruel disenchanted tired words which reveal your boredom." Recovering her dignity at last, she took herself off to Rome. Palmerio watched d'Annunzio drive her down to the station, kiss her hand and say goodbye as impassively as though he were parting from "any guest who might have come for a day's visit." D'Annunzio's emotions were intense, but when they were over they were over entirely.

His spending was now completely out of control. *Jorio's Daughter* had been translated into Spanish, English, Norwegian, German, Russian and half a dozen other languages, but still d'Annunzio's income fell hopelessly short of his outgoings.

His financial affairs were teetering: his private life was equally hectic. His liaisons multiplied: the longer-lasting love affairs overlapping, the brief encounters becoming more frequent. Women all over Europe fantasised about him. As an author he had admirers who longed to experience the waves of erotic ecstasy he described in his lyrics and novels. As a celebrity he had fans who wanted a share in the decadent glamour that hung around his name. He could invite a woman whom he had only just met to visit him alone at the Capponcina, and she came. He could pick up a girl in a café and suggest she take "a rest" with him in his hotel, and she consented. He could meet a respectably married woman at a formal party and make no move whatsoever, and she might yet appear at his door, set upon "abandoning herself." Seduction was something he did almost without willing it. Bernard Berenson noticed that he talked quite sensibly when in male company, but that as soon as a woman came within earshot his voice and manner changed, as though he were a "trained monkey" responding to a command.

One woman who became a lasting friend was the Marchesa Luisa Casati, heiress to an immense fortune. Orphaned at thirteen, and married before she was twenty to a Milanese aristocrat from whom she soon separated, Casati was an unconventional beauty, whom Marinetti described as having "the satisfied air of a panther that has devoured the bars of its cage." Her style was studiedly bizarre. She surrounded herself with animate accessories expressive of exoticism—Afghan hounds and ocelots, parrots and peacocks; black servants whom she dressed for parties in costumes copied from Tiepolo. Very tall and thin, she painted

her face dead-white, outlined her long green eyes with kohl or with glued-on strips of black paper, and wore her hair dyed red and teased into a Medusan tangle of curls standing out several inches around her head. She posed for artists as diverse as Boldoni, Augustus John, Giacomo Balla and Man Ray. She gave d'Annunzio a rare black greyhound and sent him cryptic telegrams: "The glass-maker has given me two large green eyes as beautiful as the stars, do you want them?" She was, wrote d'Annunzio, "the only woman who ever astonished me."

He was trying out another version of the role of superman. In his next play *Più Che l'Amore* (More Than Love), he created the figure of Corrado Brando, a magnificent brute of a man, square-shouldered—as d'Annunzio was markedly not—an explorer and fighting man. Brando has done battle in African wars and, when captured on the "black heap" of his slaughtered foes, laughed and sang under torture.

Ever since the calamitous invasion of Massaua in 1887, Africa was seen as the place where Italians went to die or prove their manhood. Besides, d'Annunzio had been reading Henry Morton Stanley's account of his African adventures, and Stanley, another shrewd manipulator of the press (who, according to Sir Richard Burton, "shot negroes as if they were monkeys") appealed to him. When small-minded authorities deny him the funding for a new expedition, Brando robs and murders a money lender, a person he considers as dispensable as the grubs in a rotten loaf. D'Annunzio is reprising the plot of *Crime and Punishment*, but while Dostoevsky's Raskolnikov is a desperate and pitiful character, d'Annunzio's Corrado is a force of nature, not to be judged or condemned.

More Than Love caused an outcry. One spectator recalled that the last scenes were "shipwrecked in a furious sea of hostility." The curtain fell to a "hurricane" of hissing. As the audience poured out of the Costanzi Theatre in Rome someone yelled to a passing troop of *carabinieri*: "Arrest the author!"

D'Annunzio reacted furiously, publishing a polemical afterword describing his critics as dung-eating beetles (his researches into archaic or arcane vocabulary had given him a terrific command of scatological invective, a weapon he would employ with increasing gusto over the next decade). He spoke vaguely of a "being who was forming himself, son of our marvellous anguish and of divine myth." Any opposition to that development he dismissed as being the revolt of "drunken slaves." Writing in his own person, he sounded alarmingly like-minded with the square-shouldered superman of his fantasy, to whom a person who got in his way was no better than a grub.

Madness haunts d'Annunzio's drama and fiction. As in his imagination, so in his life. There are aspects of d'Annunzio's own psyche which smack of mental abnormality—the swings from obsessive hard work to equally driven frivolity, the bouts of depression, the dazzling intelligence combined with extreme obtuseness about practical matters and others' feelings. Maria Gravina was at least intermittently insane, and Nike's wildness might well be considered pathological. D'Annunzio's next lover was, by the end of their association, to be incarcerated in a madhouse.

She was Giuseppina Mancini, a Florentine countess whose husband, a prosperous landowner and wine producer, was initially gratified to welcome the great author into his house. D'Annunzio called her Amaranta, and adored her pallor, which he likened to that of a white rose or to the marble of Delos, "which the temple servants used to tint with a mystical synthesis of attar of roses and just a little gold." He called her a witch or a cat. He addressed her as "little one," and as "*titiva*," naughty. But she was not really the mischievous animal of his fantasies. Months elapsed between their first meeting and the beginning of their sexual relationship, and their affair—ardent as it was—was never light-hearted or easy.

On 11 February 1907, a date whose anniversary he would celebrate for the rest of his life, she came secretly to the Capponcina and made "the great gift." There was a power cut. The benign darkness seemed to d'Annunzio a happy omen. He heaped their bed with white roses and then made love to her among the petals (one hopes he remembered to remove the thorns). He adored her ampits smelling of sandalwood and myrrh, her tongue dripping honey (he had been reading the "Song of Solomon"). He worshipped her "rose" which she revealed to him for the first time with delicious slowness, drawing aside the folds of her silk underwear to expose "the infinitely precious thing." Their love-making, he told her, was "*perfect*"; their pleasure like an infinite melody passed from her to him, from him to her. "A kind of *mystic* happiness . . . because everything that is perfect is divine."

These divine trysts, though, were furtive and fleeting. D'Annunzio was discovering all over again how wretched it was to be a married woman's other man. Their sexual encounters were frequently hurried and uncomfortable. On the way back from an ostensibly innocent outing they stopped for two hours in a hotel, while a servant whose discretion could not be guaranteed waited below. When d'Annunzio was a guest in the Mancinis' country estate they contrived to meet in the middle of the night, and made love on a landing. D'Annunzio was in his forties now, an acknowledged great man and the father of adult sons. Yet he was obliged to play the undignified role of a lover in a farce; lingering outside doors or recklessly climbing through bedroom windows.

He could not be sure of Amaranta's love. When they saw each other in company she was discreetly cool (although they did once hold hands while listening to Beethoven) and he would go home distraught. He tried in vain to persuade her to leave her husband. Lacking, for once, the upper hand, he described himself as her "prey" and "possession," her "wretched slave." He thought (perhaps not very seriously) about suicide. "Tonight I must take a narcotic, or take poison."

He waited for her in a closed carriage on a bridge over the Arno; she joined him in it dressed in black lace. He rented an apartment in Florence for their meetings. The bedroom was hung with green damask: he called it the "green cloister." He kept it amply supplied with flower vases and kimonos—"in two years of passion and pleasure none of our days was without elegance and beauty" he wrote—but he was frequently miserable there, waiting through lonely evenings with only a stray cat for company on the off chance that his lover might come to him, or lying awake, chilled and aching with frustration, in a solitary bed. Amaranta, devoutly Christian, was oppressed by guilt, and terribly afraid of discovery. The apartment was on the ground floor, overlooking a garden with a creaking iron gate onto the street. When they were together there she flinched at every rasp of the gate's hinges.

In February 1907, Carducci died. Four days later the *Corriere della Sera* published d'Annunzio's poem, *For the Tomb of Giosuè Carducci*. It ended with the words: "The living torch which he entrusted to me,/I will brandish on the sternest peaks."

Luigi Pirandello considered the lines presumptuous. D'Annunzio was not the only surviving great Italian poet—Giovanni Pascoli was another—but here he was "lighting a funeral torch at the death-bed" and pushing his way to the highest peak alone. A month later he consolidated his claim, delivering an oration in the course of Carduccci's memorial ceremonies in Milan.

The theatre was packed. Wherever d'Annunzio went now he caused a stir. Arriving a few minutes late to hear a new oratorio around this time, he was aware of a great whispering and rustling as he took his seat. When he found the music was not to his taste, and left before the end, "I believe I caused a scandal." From Milan he wrote to Amaranta: "Everyone wants to chew on a scrap of me: there's nothing left but a few aching bones." But for all his claims that he would much prefer to have been at home, enjoying the violets in the Capponcina's garden and the "soft ears of my dogs," he had to confess that the task of offering himself up "as a meal to the mob" had been lightened by two moments of elation.

One came as he stepped out on stage. "Never have I seen such a deep human sea." The second was his visit to the newly modernised printing works of the *Corriere della Sera*. Editor Luigi Albertini had devoted the whole of the front page to the text of d'Annunzio's oration. Seeing his words flowing off the presses, 300,000 copies destined to be distributed all across Italy, d'Annunzio exulted in the power and reach the paper had granted him. He was to become one of Albertini's most prized contributors.

He was supposed to be delivering a eulogy to Carducci. In fact, the speech is his own manifesto. Mingling the discourses of devotion and of nationalism, he talked about the "eternal spirit of the race." He spoke of the Roman consuls, of the bloody but noble wars of the Ghibellines, of the Medici, of Michelangelo, of a history full of "arduous beauty and violent destiny." Naming Italian hero after Italian hero, Italian city after Italian city, he seemed to be ushering a nation into being by naming its parts. He alluded to Rudyard Kipling, whose Puck, summoning ghosts of past Britons out of Pook's Hill in a book published the previous year, performed a similar function for Great Britain.

His speech was a call to arms. Half a century before, the land had been "irrigated" by the "rich blood" of brave Italians, but the great adventure of the Risorgimento had petered out. Now, like Crispi before him, d'Annunzio was looking for a pretext for a fight. The identity of the opponent was unclear—it might be the internal enemy, the "grey democratic flood." It might be a foreign power. No matter. Repeating the sentiments he had given his imaginary dictator in *Glory*, d'Annunzio declared that the contaminated land must be violently ploughed up. He called for Italy to become industrialised, to arm itself with modern weapons, to develop an aggressive new "national consciousness." He praised Germany, a nation as young as Italy, where the prowess of a new generation of heroes was made concrete in massive ships and manufacturing plants. He conjured up a modern world of iron and fire as dangerous and majestic as the mediaeval one he had tried to create on stage in *Francesca da Rimini*.

All this bluster availed him nothing in his love life. In the "green cloister" he would lay out the robe patterned with violets which bore the scent of Amaranta's body, or the wonderful pleated Fortuny tunic, blue-black and printed with Mycenaean motifs, which he liked so much he

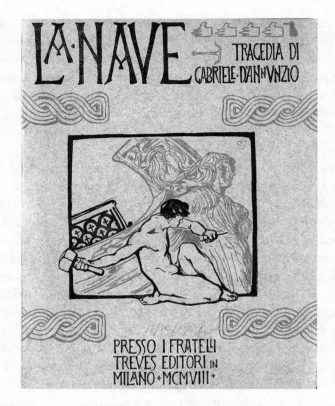

would dress two of his fictional femmes fatales in it. He would light the incense burner. He would strew the bed with petals and scented handkerchiefs. He would yearn for Amaranta's presence, for the chance to bite her nipples, which he had named Muriella and Fragoletta ("blackcurrant" and "little strawberry"). But time and again something would prevent her arrival.

He was happier at his desk. He was writing *The Ship*, his most ambitious drama to date. Its protagonist, he wrote, was "an entire race." Its central image was the construction of a warship, the sixth-century equivalent of the ironclads being constructed in Germany's Baltic shipyards, or those he wished that Italy would build. Throughout the autumn of 1907 he wrote flat out, staying at his task for twenty hours nonstop, eating only fruit and raw eggs, working, not like a dog (he loved his dogs for their aristocratic idleness), "but like a labourer on the road."

Set in AD 552, the play gives a lurid account of the Venetians' struggle to make themselves free of Byzantium. A basilica (which, we are to understand, will be St. Mark's) is rising from the watery ground of an island in the Venetian lagoon. Built into its fabric are Roman fragments—pillars, pieces of carved marble, golden mosaics. In this new state Romanità will be preserved and revitalised. Also in view is the half-built ship (the production team included a master shipwright) and enough large vistas to accommodate the enormous cast. At several points in the drama there are three choruses simultaneously onstage.

D'Annunzio had required his composer, Ildebrando Pizzetti, to provide a musical equivalent for the "rush and roar of rivers in spate." Sailors belt out triumphal anthems, Christian zealots sing Latin hymns. Pagans challenge them with Dionysian paeans. Soldiers march on in victory. Prisoners of war are driven into a pit, where they are killed, one by one, by a fatal woman with a bow and arrow. This woman, Basiliola Faledra, is an avenging demon. Her father and brothers have all been blinded for their treachery in dealing with the eunuch-Emperor of Byzantium. Now she hopes to destroy their rivals, another pair of brothers whom she seduces one after another with a lascivious ballet-cum-striptease in which she unsheathes her body like the lethal weapon it is, slithering out of layer upon layer of gorgeous Fortuny-inspired silk.

The play's language is a sequence of seductions, outpourings of religious fervour and war cries. The action is a-throb with cruelty and sex. The five blinded Faledri cower on stage. Basiliola is "shaken by the craving to see blood flow." As she fits another arrow to the string she licks it lasciviously and the infatuated prisoners in the trench beneath her beg her to kill them. "Another arrow!" "To me!" "To me!" At the end the hero cries out that she must be the figurehead of the new ship, her body nailed, still living, to its prow. She thwarts him by leaping into the great fire blazing before the altar, living sacrifice to the project which d'Annunzio announced in his prefatory verses: that of making all the oceans (but most particular the Adriatic) *"Mare Nostro,"* our sea.

D'Annunzio went to Rome to supervise rehearsals. He was in one of his black moods. The city whose stirring glamour he had once chronicled seemed "appalling" to him. The faces he saw in the street expressed "weakness, cynicism, savage envy, useless love." He complained that the actors' voices gave him headaches. "To have my skull trepanned without chloroform wouldn't have made me shudder as much as Traba's trombone of a voice." The hugger-mugger circumstances and perfunctory manners of back-stage life were repellent to him. "I had to eat lunch there, at a dusty table, in view of all the actors!"

D. H. Lawrence, who saw *The Ship* a decade later, called it "bosh." D'Annunzio's first Italian audiences, though, were exhilarated by it. Most overtly polemical of his plays, it triggered an uproar, immensely gratifying to its author. The King and Queen attended the opening night and called d'Annunzio into their box to congratulate him at the end of the evening, while a noisy crowd spilled out of the theatre and marched through the streets of central Rome chanting the catchline—which at once became an irredentist slogan: "Arm the prow and set sail for the world!"

At a grand banquet given in his honour a few nights after the opening, in the presence of a government minister, d'Annunzio proposed a toast to the "most bitter Adriatic." He explained the phrase to a reporter: "the *bitterness* of the Adriatic relates to our diseased left lung" by which he meant the land on the eastern shores of the Adriatic, those once-Venetian dominions of Venezia Giulia, Istria, Croatia, Dalmatia, which were still in Austrian hands.

The production ran for weeks, and then transferred to Venice. D'Annunzio offered to donate the manuscript to the city. There was further, publicity-generating controversy when the mayor demurred on the grounds that *The Ship*'s blend of sexual perversity and Christian liturgy might upset the Church. Eventually his objections were overcome and d'Annunzio, spruce in top-hat and tails, arrived at the municipal offices by gondola, carrying the manuscript tied with a crimson ribbon and wrapped in fine old red velvet (a piece, he claimed, of the state robes of a magistrate of the mediaeval Venetian Empire). The presentation was followed by a banquet for over a hundred prominent irredentists at the Hotel Danieli. The tables were decorated with flowers picked inside the Roman amphitheatre at Pola, the "unredeemed" Istrian port. Speakers prayed that d'Annunzio might "sound the paean of victory over our sea." He responded by paying tribute to those who tended "the hidden Roman flame" on the "other shore."

His speeches in Venice were incitements to war. When Giolitti, President of the Council, met the Austrian Chancellor von Bülow a few days later, it was noted that d'Annunzio's words had created "ill humour" between the two powers. The Austrian Foreign Minister thenceforward kept a copy of *The Ship* always on his desk, as a reminder of how dangerous Italy might be.

The play's production was profitable enough to cover its immense costs and leave d'Annunzio with a substantial sum of much-needed money. More cheerful now, he basked in his success.

In 1908, the year of *The Ship*'s premiere, Filippo Tommaso Marinetti, driving through the outskirts of Milan, swerved to avoid two bicyclists and overturned his car in a ditch. Marinetti wrote up the incident as a prologue to his "Futurist Manifesto," published the following year, and noisily appointed himself the spokesman for a new aesthetic of sleek metal and powerful machinery.

Marinetti was seizing upon and popularising a cultural trend that had been extant for at least a generation. Huysmans's des Esseintes queries whether there could be any human being "more dazzlingly beautiful than the two locomotives recently put into service on the Northern Railway" and d'Annunzio too, despite being a conservationist and celebrator of the Italy's past glory, had, for years, been celebrating all that was new and fast and efficient. "In the carriages which race along the steel rails, in the ships which slice through the rivers and seas, and in all the machinery of work and wealth, marvellous beauties are preparing themselves."

He had a telephone installed in the Capponcina at the earliest opportunity. As soon as motor cars became available he bought himself one, a red Florentia with a ninety horse-power engine, the biggest and fastest then available. He bought motoring manuals, and talked about patenting a new kind of steering wheel. (Of his three sons it was Veniero, who became an engineer, for whom he seemed to feel most respect.) He drove so recklessly that Clemente Origo insisted he made a will before accepting a lift to the seaside. D'Annunzio filled the car with red roses when he took female friends for a drive in it—so abundantly, remarked one lady, that there was scarcely room to sit down. He was soon known to the Tuscan police for speeding along the region's narrow dirt roads.

Like her lover, Amaranta was excited by the new technology of speed. Contemporaries who knew them both saw Isabella Inghirami, the death-defying heroine of *Maybe Yes, Maybe No*, as a portrait of her. In this helter-skelter decade of d'Annunzio's life women's fashions changed utterly. The high-necked, lace-adorned dresses, with their capacious skirts and boned bodices, gave way to slim lines and fluid fabrics. D'Annunzio's heroine, her legs outlined in motion by her narrow satin skirts, her face shaded by a hat as sleek and angular as the wing of a predatory bird, is a modernist vision of female elegance.

With Amaranta and her husband, d'Annunzio attended a motor rally at Brescia in 1907, a sensational event. The sight of such speed, previously undreamt of, was intoxicating. The drivers were so resolute, so likely to die. Marinetti was inspired to write his prose-poem, *Death Takes the Wheel*: "Transmission of my nerves, throwing into gear the planetary orbs!/Divining instinct, oh gear-box!/O my explosive and detonating heart!"

All this enthusiasm for the whizz and zoom of modern machinery found its way into heroic fiction in d'Annunzio's *Maybe Yes, Maybe No*, but in real life it was converted into the blackest farce. The ending of d'Annunzio's relationship with his Amaranta was wretched, and in it a ridiculous spectacle recurs: that of the poet who had welcomed the machine age with such enthusiasm standing fuming at the side of the road by a broken-down car.

Giuseppina might look as shiny and trim as a metallic car mascot, but she was psychologically frail. She craved danger but, guilty, she also craved punishment. Her liaison with d'Annunzio was an ill-kept secret. She was afraid both of her husband and of her father. For all d'Annunzio's ardour, she suspected him of infidelity (she was right). When she reproached him, he cruelly turned the tables on her, accusing her of denying their sacred love. She couldn't make a decision. She couldn't reconcile all the claims being made on her. In September 1908 her mind gave way.

One morning she precipitately left home, leaving a letter for her husband announcing that she was abandoning "all things which were once my life and my every good," but saying as well that her heart rebelled against d'Annunzio—"he who is the cause of all this ruin." She took a train, but her resolve failed. At Compiobbi, not far from d'Annunzio's home at Settignano, she left the train and telephoned him. He came to her, but not fast enough. We have only his fragmented recollection of what followed: "the pursuit, the engine blowing up in the middle of the road, the butcher's cart, running through the dust, the crowd gathered at the station. Amaranta with a look of madness, trembling, babbling, shuddering." Waiting for him, she had become so agitated as to attract a crowd of gawping villagers. The more they stared, the more frightened she was, the more crazy her behaviour became. How the episode ended we don't exactly know, but soon thereafter she was back in her marital home, on her own, her husband having left for the country after terrible scenes during which he had called her a *puttana*, a whore. She met d'Annunzio in the "green cloister" but refused to spend the night. D'Annunzio let her go, and the next morning, feeling a "need to be elsewhere," he drove to Bologna. From there he sent her a flurry of telegrams, and tried to telephone her, but failed to get through.

At 2:30 in the afternoon he received a telegram from her. "Dying of grief and love. Come, come, come for pity's sake." He sent her three more telegrams, but didn't go to her. Once more his car was out of action (a problem with the ignition). The following morning he telephoned her again. She was incoherent: she didn't know where he was, or what she herself had been doing. "The breath of madness blew on my face, and froze me." This time he set out instantly but his journey, which should have been easily accomplished in three hours, became a long-drawn-out farce. The car broke down repeatedly. Eventually d'Annunzio hitched a ride with some friends who providentially passed by. It was nightfall by the time they reached Florence. They stopped for ten minutes just outside the city to light the oil-fuelled headlamps. Those ten minutes—as d'Annunzio subsequently tormented himself by thinking—sealed Amaranta's fate. Just before he finally reached the "green cloister," she had been there with two strange men, calling themselves police officers, who had been beating noisily at the door, and who, as d'Annunzio eventually discovered, were in fact known criminals.

The police eventually pieced a story together. The two strangers had found Giuseppina, confused and vulnerable, in the piazza only a few minutes walk from her home. Somehow they had coerced her into getting into a carriage with them. It seems that initially they had taken her for a prostitute and when she gave the address of d'Annunzio's hideaway they assumed it was a brothel. Failing to gain entrance, and beginning to understand the real situation, they saw the chance of blackmailing her. It was now about nine o'clock. Later that evening they were seen with her in a café. They finally deposited her at her own home very late that night. D'Annunzio never discovered what had happened to her in the intervening hours.

By the time a doctor saw her the following morning she was raving. She had hidden herself in a little room on a landing which she refused to leave. She claimed she had been poisoned. She talked about her "enemy," by whom she meant, as the doctor gradually understood, d'Annunzio. She didn't wish to see him or to hear him spoken of. She threw away the jewellery he had given her, and took to wearing her wedding ring again, and a bracelet her husband had given her (with multicoloured stones, in horridly "strident" taste, according to d'Annunzio). When her father arranged for her to be confined to an asylum, d'Annunzio left bunches of wild cyclamen on the outer windowsill of what he believed was her room. He suspected a plot by her family to deprive her of her liberty and so separate her from him; but he resigned himself to never seeing her again.

Nike, Amaranta and numerous less significant others, this hectic succession of love affairs, complicated by drugs and insanity, by prodigal luxury and near-fatal illness, was accompanied by the gradual crescendo of d'Annunzio's financial problems. He was always demanding payment—he was not a disinterested artist—but he was an inept businessman. There was something in him, it seemed, that recoiled from commercially promising assignments.

Giacomo Puccini proposed a collaboration. The composer, disappointed by the poor reception of *Madame Butterfly*, hoped to do better with a libretto from "the first genius of Italy." Flattery got him nowhere. D'Annunzio demanded such an extortionate fee that the plan foundered. In 1908 Puccini tried again, visiting d'Annunzio in his summer retreat by the sea. D'Annunzio proposed the subject of Parisina (on which he would in fact write a libretto, to be set by Mascagni, four years later) but privately doubted that Puccini had the creative force "to raise such a tragic weight." Puccini responded by suggesting the poet might write more concisely. As soon ask the sea to be less wet. D'Annunzio was almost too incredulous to be affronted. "He actually told me that he needed a little thing, something light to be set to music in a few months! And for this he turned to the poet of *Francesca da Rimini!*"

The Capponcina, writes Palmerio, had become a place of pilgrimage. Processions of creditors trooped up the hill to it. "There were those who were cordial and patient, and there were those who showed their teeth." D'Annunzio remained insouciant. When Palmerio tried to explain his situation to him, he interrupted to exclaim at the beauty of a blossoming tree. That he was short of funds he certainly knew, but he made no consistent attempt to reduce his expenditure. He spent all his earnings from his latest play on a hunter. He won the lottery—an amazing stroke of luck—but his prize money, boon though it was, was very soon gone. To avoid the duns now virtually besieging the house, he went to stay for months on end with his friend Origo. In 1909 he flitted from Genoa to Cap Martin to Rome, staying in hotels he could not afford.

In public he appeared suave, with the bloom of success on him. But "melancholy" darkened his world view. He fell from his horse, breaking his shoulder, and newspaper reports hinted the accident might have been a suicide attempt. Even sex sometimes failed him, generating only fatigue and self-disgust. His apartment in Florence was next to a workshop. Sometimes, in bed with a woman there, hearing the productive clash and bang from next door, he felt ashamed of his compulsion to "the sterile carnal work."

D'Annunzio's affair with Giuseppina was, he wrote when he was near death, his "last felicity." After the catastrophe, the world around him seemed "a sewer" and love "a drunken clown." He had written to her: "There is no desire in my blood which is not for you . . . I see in my life no other companion. I see no other joy." But it was not quite true. Several months before her breakdown, in Rome for the premiere of *The Ship*, d'Annunzio met a Russian visitor from Paris, Nathalie de Goloubeff, the wife of a diplomat from whom she was amicably separated. Nathalie was a gifted singer. She had modelled for Rodin. She loved dogs and horses as much as d'Annunzio did. A photograph (overleaf) shows her superbly androgynous in large felt hat and riding breeches, her soft leather boots laced up to mid-thigh, with the kind of large-boned face d'Annunzio admired. In Rome she became a protégée of Count Primoli, who—once more acting the go-between—introduced her to d'Annunzio. For several months she hung back, thinking of her husband, her children, her social position, but a few days after Giuseppina's incarceration she telephoned d'Annunzio late one night and boldly asked if she might visit him.

He was uncharacteristically diffident. A decade earlier he had written cruelly about Foscarina's withering and softening skin, now he was five years older than Duse had been then. The mirror appalled him. "I am ashamed of my kisses." All the same he bid Nathalie come.

"She arrived pale, trembling, determined to give herself . . . blind to all the rest." He called her his "Spikenard," after the herb whose oil is an ancient remedy for pain. "One passion is extinguished," he wrote, "another passion flames up."

Once again a sexual relationship revived him, both emotionally and creatively. He laid claim to Nathalie by calling her Donatella or his "Caucasian Diana," and soon he was writing a play, *Fedra*, dedicated to her. She was his "red rose," his "young archer." He wrote to tell her how he longed to kiss "the wound of St. Sebastian"—meaning her cunt. This was to be a relationship in which, more even than was usual for d'Annunzio, pain was the spur to passion. He liked to think of Nathalie as a descendant of Tamburlaine—a wild conqueror. He called her "a great naked bee with beautiful tresses" (bee stings were still sexual for him) and longed to suck her honey. The relationship would be full of unhappiness for Nathalie, but it would last, intermittently, another seven years.

In February 1909, while d'Annunzio was writing *Fedra*, in Paris *Le Figaro* gave its entire front page over to the publication of Marinetti's "Futurist Manifesto." This was Marinetti's cultural coup, the moment when he transformed himself into the spokesman for an international artistic-cum-ideological movement whose art (uneven in quality) and ideology (incoherent) were both eclipsed by the sheer *élan*, to borrow one of his favourite words, of the front man.

Born in Egypt, educated in Paris, Marinetti was rich, cosmopolitan and provocative, the self-described "Caffeine of Europe." He was a journalist, an entrepreneur, a performer, an agitator and a polemicist. Like d'Annunzio, he understood and used publicity. (One of the futurist artists, Carlo Carrà, was to call the movement an "advertising machine.") And, like d'Annunzio, Marinetti had a pike-like talent for snapping-up the ideas of others and making them his own. Many of the notions laid out with such a provocative flourish in his "Manifesto" had been expressed, in several instances years earlier, by d'Annunzio.

Marinetti had been writing about d'Annunzio for over a decade. An advocate of all that was modern and vigorous ("a roaring motor car, which seems to run on shrapnel, is more beautiful than the *Victory* of Samothrace"), he had for a while been vociferously anti-d'Annunzio, the man who kept a reproduction of the *Victory* in his bedroom. He described d'Annunzio's oeuvre as the Monte Carlo of literature: "that false decorative verdure, those ideas sick and plaintive beneath a weight of futile opulence." He berated the older man for peddling "the intellectual poison of sickly nostalgia" and condemned his "obsession with lechery . . . and mania for antiquity." Over the years, though, he had come to recognise that, for all his fondness for classical art and mediaeval knick-knacks, d'Annunzio was a fellow modern, a poet who rhapsodised over warships and steelworks, and who set a higher value on energy than he did on virtue.

Through the first years of the century Marinetti had been staging "futurist evenings," uproarious events each of which was a political demonstration, a satirical cabaret, a publicity stunt and (nearly always by the end of the evening) a bloody brawl. One of them had honoured d'Annunzio. When Duse's production of *The Dead City* was badly received in 1901, Marinetti took it upon himself to defend it. He and "hundreds of others" invaded the theatre "delivering boxes to the ears and blows to the bellies of the conservative spectators"—not, one would have thought, an efficient method of helping them to enjoy the play, but one which attracted plenty of attention. D'Annunzio and Marinetti shared a sophisticated understanding of the serious uses to which showmanship could be put. Marinetti was drawn by "a violent personal sympathy," he said, to "the distinguished seducer, the ineffable descendant of Cagliostro and Casanova."

In early 1909, thousands of copies of his "programme" (a condensed version of the "Futurist Manifesto" reduced to bullet points, to make it more handy for journalists), were sent out to opinion-formers around the world, from Mexico to Romania. A friend of Marinetti's father, who happened to be a shareholder in *Le Figaro*, got him the front page of the paper. Back in Milan he published the manifesto in his own journal, hung a huge white sheet bearing the single word "FUTURISM" from his balcony on one of Milan's main thoroughfares, and had billboards in cities all over Italy plastered with his manifesto blown up to ten foot by three foot and printed in fiery red letters.

The manifesto is an eccentric document—part tirade, part fantasy. It opens with a thoroughly d'Annunzian fictional episode. A young man is discovered lounging around in an interior cluttered with oriental rugs and brass lamps, his fingers glittering with Byzantine rings. Abruptly galvanised, he leaps into his motor car, drives recklessly through the city streets, crashes and climbs unruffled from the wreck. The juxtaposition of fin-de-siècle languor and machine-age velocity was one d'Annunzio had been living long before Marinetti wrote it down. The polemic which follows is full of sentiments d'Annunzio had already expressed. D'Annunzio had proclaimed the tenth muse, whom he named Energeia, and announced: "I advance towards life." Now Marinetti—following Henri Bergson—worshipped *élan vital*. D'Annunzio had written of an awful beauty in the newly industrialised world: "The omnipotent machines . . . proclaim an unknown poetry, an unhoped-for joy, an august liberation." Now Marinetti wrote admiringly of "violent electric moons," of "bridges that straddle the rivers like giant gymnasts, flashing in the sun with the glitter of knives." D'Annunzio had been writing for over twenty years about the advent of the superman. Now Marinetti proclaimed "the hour is nigh when men with broad temples and steel chins will give birth magnificently, with a single thrust of their bulging will, to giants with flawless gestures."

In 1901 d'Annunzio had prophesied an imminent war which would cleanse Europe. Now Marinetti hailed war, "the world's only hygiene." D'Annunzio had deplored the meanness of lives governed by prudence and economy and had run his own affairs and written his dramas with a Dionysian disregard for moderation. Now Marinetti wrote: "Let us break out of the horrible shell of wisdom and throw ourselves like pride-ripened fruit into the wide, contorted mouth of the wind!" Marinetti never acknowledged it, but he was d'Annunzio's noisiest and most brilliant disciple.

In the summer of 1909, d'Annunzio was intent on throwing himself into the wind, quite literally. He wanted to fly. He was in Rome, enjoying himself (while Nathalie awaited him on the coast) with the Marchesa Beatrice Alvarez de Toledo, who signed a kind of contract: "I belong soul and body to Gabriele d'Annunzio, now and for ever ready for him in life and in death." By day he was visiting the Centocelle airfield, where Wilbur Wright was teaching the first Italian aviators how to construct and pilot a flying machine. D'Annunzio describes it:

the hangars, the din of roaring engines and whirring propellers, the mechanics, silent and intent. He observed the aviators: an edgy tribe, with their own jargon and their distinctive style, the wide breeches, the tight leather caps, the incessant cigarettes.

The now-familiar form of a winged tube had yet to establish itself as the best one for an aircraft. Early flying machines came in many shapes. D'Annunzio lists them: "Assemblages of quadrangles like heaps of bottomless boxes, flimsy hulls laden with scaffolding." Others which reminded him of windmills and ceiling fans and butter churns. And in each bizarre structure sat an aviator, like a spider in his web, pulling levers, desperate with the nearly-always-frustrated longing to feel his machine rise. After hours of preparation someone would achieve lift-off, propellers whirring until they were visible only as "stars of air in air." Each flight, however brief and clumsy, was a miracle.

"We stand on the extreme promontory of the centuries," wrote Marinetti in his manifesto. "Why look behind us?" But look behind him Marinetti, like d'Annunzio, repeatedly did, ransacking ancient myths for imagery. Motorists were centaurs. Aviators were angels. D'Annunzio repeatedly likens manned flight to the assumption of the Virgin Mary. He writes again and again about the myth of Icarus. He invokes the bird-headed gods of ancient Egypt with their immense wings. Marcel Proust, watching flying displays in France in the same year through "eyes brimming with tears," felt the same need to "look behind." He was as moved, he wrote "as a Greek might have been upon seeing a demi-god for the first time."

God-like though they may have been, the aviators were not immortal. The danger they faced fascinated d'Annunzio. Death was constantly on his mind. He was attending séances and listening to fortune-tellers. He told friends that three separate clairvoyants had predicted that he would die violently on 17 July 1909. He at least partially believed it. He wrote to Treves, listing his works in progress and referring to them as his "posthumous books." His son Gabriellino recalls seeing him on the dread day "playing crazy tricks" on horseback and at the wheel of his car, as though daring fate. But the disaster that in fact befell him that month wasn't death, but financial ruin.

All the contents of the Capponcina had been mortgaged to guarantee a bank loan. When it became obvious that d'Annunzio would not and could not pay up, bailiffs broke down the door of the house that had once been the "serene haven of dream and thought." D'Annunzio had taken his horses and dogs down to the coast in the vain hope of retaining possession of them. The bailiffs caught up with him at his borrowed villa in Marina di Pisa and took the animals too. "Perhaps tomorrow they will confiscate my shoes and superfluous shirts," he wrote flippantly to his old friend Scarfoglio. They did.

There is something liberating about calamity. The Capponcina and all its contents—its hundreds of damask cushions, its lecterns and choir stalls and death-masks and shelves full of crystal cosmetics jars—were lost. (D'Annunzio's books were bought and eventually returned to him by a syndicate of his friends and admirers, but it would be years before he had them with him again.) The house into which he had poured so much money and creative energy was being dismembered. Yet, Palmerio, his faithful steward, was astonished to see him leave the house for the last time as carelessly as he might leave a hotel where he had briefly stayed. "To be separated from old things impregnated with useless memories doesn't hurt me." He carried his fortune in his head.

The only thing that bothered him was that all the kerfuffle made it hard for him to concentrate on the novel he was writing. Looking out of his window, he envied the hens spreading their feathers to catch a downpour of rain, and wished he were one of them, "then nothing would prevent me laying my egg." He found a money lender willing to oblige him, and set to work making "improvements" to his seaside villa, squandering money he would never repay on a house he would shortly leave. He went on a series of excursions—to Mantua and Volterra, which would provide the settings for the new novel, and most importantly, back to Brescia for the air show.

Air shows were the new circuses, as deadly as those performed 2,000 years previously in the Colosseum: two of the most celebrated pilots would die that summer. The one at Brescia was a great event. The rich and fashionable arrived in their motor cars, ploughing ruts into the dirt roads and rendering them impassable. Kafka and Brod, gazing up at the stands, could have seen d'Annunzio's brother-in-law the Duke di Gallese, the Marchesa Luisa Casati in one of her striking monochrome outfits, and the Countess Morosini, whom he would meet again in Venice on his way to overfly Trieste. Puccini was there, and so was the King, and so were perhaps 100,000 others. Afterwards people would spend up to twelve hours trying to travel back along the clogged roads to Brescia, twenty-five kilometres away. D'Annunzio's description of the chaotic scene must be the first-ever literary account of a traffic jam.

The American aviator Glenn Curtiss won the Grand Prize and then consented to take d'Annunzio up as his passenger. In his fictional account of the event d'Annunzio would describe his heroic aviators flying so high that their planes were specks in the sky, or so far that they vanish over the horizon. The reality was less sublime, more often ridiculous. Luigi Barzini, covering the show for the *Corriere della Sera*, described d'Annunzio—in a tight-fitting motorist's cap with a chin strap like a baby's bonnet—perched on a narrow bench, his dainty feet resting on a bamboo pole, caged in by the rigging of steel cords. The crowd let out a great shout when Curtiss's plane moved forward with the "first genius of Italy" aboard, but all they could actually see of the poet were his legs.

"The aeroplane set off, its wheels wavering over the uneven ground, raising and lowering its tail with the motion of a boat in the water; then it lifted a few feet off the ground, but soon it fell back again and continued its humble gallop over the ground for a while before coming to a stop." Not exactly the soaring trajectory d'Annunzio had hoped for, but he was nonetheless ready for the crowds who pressed around the grounded plane clamouring for his impressions.

"He was glittering with enthusiasm," reports Barzini. "It's divine," he announced. "I can think of nothing but my next flight." Someone pointed out that the Italian aviator Calderara was still on the field. At once d'Annunzio hurried off to beg him for a ride. Calderara agreed, and this time d'Annunzio remained airborne for eight minutes. Once again he was mobbed on landing by journalists and admirers avid for his account of the experience. "D'Annunzio," wrote Barzini, "is the representative of human sensibility, taken on board like a precision instrument of the psyche." Afterwards, Curtiss's mechanics staged an auction, selling the bench on which d'Annunzio's backside had rested to the highest bidder among his clamorous fans.

Having flown, d'Annunzio wrote his novel of flight. *Maybe Yes, Maybe No* was written at high speed during the autumn of 1909. His home closed to him, he worked all day and all night in his villa by the sea, going to bed at five in the morning, only to rise again at ten to continue writing. By the end of the year he had written over 900 pages. Treves

decided to publish the work in two volumes—apparently in the hope that the first half might have a cordial reception before the more shocking aspects of the plot—brother-sister incest, sadism, prostitution—had been made explicit.

The novel contains some of d'Annunzio most effective prose-poetry. Gorgeous settings and gothic plot devices—incest, a suicide pact, mysterious intruders glimpsed only in a mirror, a ruined abbey, a lunatic asylum, a prison, an ancient tomb—alternate with scenes of modern high life as sophisticated as anything in *Pleasure,* and with passages of haunting Symbolist landscape-writing. Its heroine Isabella Inghirami is a volatile character, a kind of group portrait of d'Annunzio's recent mistresses. Her gift for performance is Eleonora Duse's: her independence as a young widow and her physical daring are Nike's; her heavy eye make-up and Fortuny robes recall Luisa Casati; her pathetic descent into madness is not just like Amaranta's, it actually is Amaranta's. Page after page of the novel are taken, word for word, from d'Annunzio's journal of the terrible end of their affair.

The fictional lovers take to the air, flying above the Tuscan coast in their little plane. She wears sandals and a straw hat for their aerial outings, during which they converse comfortably. Few people, d'Annunzio not yet among them, had enough experience of flying to know how cold and noisy it was in an open plane. The seashore tilts beneath their wings. They look down on the quarries from which Michelangelo's marbles were taken, Pisa's Campo Santo with its leaning tower, the walls of Lucca, seeing it all from an angle at which it had never yet been seen by human eyes.

Marinetti raved furiously against modern Italy's subordination to its own past. Italy was too full of ancient beauty to have space for the new glories of speed and energy. "So let them come, the gay incendiaries with charred fingers! . . . Heap the fire with the shelves of the libraries! Divert the canals to flood the cellars of the museums! Take up your pickaxes, your axes and hammers, and wreck, wreck, wreck the venerable cities, pitilessly." D'Annunzio's strategy was less delinquent, more subtle. He sought to preserve the past's legacy, but make it serve the new cause of nationalism.

The novel's hero, Paolo Tarsis, is a copybook superman, with "the bone structure of audacious will, the gaunt face of one possessed by the ardour of victory, the flashing eye of a predator . . . the hard jaw which held the red flesh of the mouth like a soft fruit gripped by steel pliers." He and his friend Cambiaso have served together on battleships, fought in submarines. Impatient of discipline, they left the navy together and travelled the world, going lightly clad through Korean snows and the flaming tropical heat of Mindanao. They have starved for days on end in the desert: they have ridden for eighteen hours a day over the steppes. (D'Annunzio had been reading the English traveller A. Henry Savage-Landor and granted Tarsis and Cambiaso many of his adventures.) Eventually they arrive in Egypt where they gaze at ancient paintings of winged, bird-headed gods and dream of adventures in the sky. They come home at last to Italy to become members of the new aristocracy of the air.

D'Annunzio had friends aplenty, but most of them were more properly disciples of whom he made use. Tarsis and Cambiaso are true comrades. Their feeling for each other is a "great and virile sentiment," which, as d'Annunzio makes explicit, greatly surpasses the love of women. While Isabella Inghirami toys with Tarsis's nipples, he is abstracted, impassive. When he sees her approaching over the airfield at Brescia, his first impulse is to prevent her meeting Cambiaso, so as to protect his friend from the debilitating effects of sexual love. She, and the other fashionable young women who hang adoringly around the aviators at air shows, are Sphinxes, Hydras, visions of corrupting pleasure that could have been lifted from Swinburne's *Ballad of Death*, futurist versions of the fin-de-siècle archetype of the femme fatale.

Shortly before he began work on *Maybe Yes, Maybe No*, d'Annunzio told an interviewer: "Contempt for women is the vital condition of the modern man: just as . . . disdain for men is the distinguishing quality of the modern heroines." He was not a conventional misogynist. The two female characters in the novel are both considerably more interesting than the hard-as-bronze Tarsis or the women's effete, if divinely beautiful, adolescent brother. But feminism and its obverse, misogyny, were dominant themes of public discourse, and d'Annunzio had to have his say on the subject. Love, he told the same interviewer, is incompatible with modern heroism (which, five years before the outbreak of the Great War, he thought found its only modern outlet in sport). The shoulder of a beloved woman "takes on the dimensions of a Himalaya, it cuts us off from the horizon."

So he said publicly, but privately he was writing to Nathalie: "Remember the inimitable hours of yesterday? . . . Your lovely laugh in the musical instrument shop, the concert, the interrupted caress, the white rose . . . the voice that I shall never forget, the tears, the fury, the voluptuous pleasure that was more than human?" D'Annunzio was inspired by the ideal of the adamantine male, taciturn and celibate, but it was not one he chose to emulate.

His novel finished, d'Annunzio embarked on a lecture tour of the cities of northern Italy, speaking on "The Domination of the Skies." He foresaw, long before the military establishment did, how aerial reconnaissance and aerial bombardment could alter the nature of armed conflict. So did his British contemporary H. G. Wells. "I do not think that numbers are going to matter so much in the warfare of the future," wrote Wells after Blériot's cross-Channel flight. "I fail to see what [the common soldier] can do in the way of mischief to an elusive chevalier with wings." Only eight years later, hundreds of fighter planes would be deployed over Verdun. D'Annunzio predicted that explosive development. In the 1880s he had urged the Italian government to build up its navy. Two decades later he was calling for the creation of an air force.

The organiser of his lecture tour was paying him handsomely, but d'Annunzio—as destructive of his own financial interests as ever—

quarrelled with him. The audiences were insufficiently large, the venues insufficiently grand. Halfway through the planned programme d'Annunzio announced he would speak no more.

Another impresario, Giovanni del Guzzo, approached him. Del Guzzo's appearance in d'Annunzio's life was an amazing piece of luck. An Abruzzese who had emigrated to South America and made an immense fortune there, del Guzzo wanted d'Annunzio to tour Argentina, speaking in city after city in celebration of the hundredth anniversary of the country's independence from Spain. The fee would be so prodigiously generous as to make it possible for d'Annunzio to do what had previously seemed beyond the bounds of possibility, and pay off all his debts. This was salvation, unlooked for and absolute. Even d'Annunzio, snobbishly referring to del Guzzo as the "tenacious colonial," acknowledged his own good fortune. He gave del Guzzo a copy of *Maybe Yes, Maybe No*, inscribed: "To the Messiah, invoked and come . . . with Hosannas." He signed a contract.

In *Maybe Yes, Maybe No*, Tarsis goes to the airfield at dawn and sets off, alone and unobserved, on what was, at the time of writing, a flight of impossible ambition. Amidst a flurry of references to the *Aeneid*, he sets his course over the Tyrrhenian sea towards Sardinia. Lines from Tennyson's *Crossing the Bar* toll through his mind, but he rejects the English poet's pious hope to meet his divine "pilot." Rather, "he was his own pilot; his spirit was the guide of his own spirit." When his engine falters he sustains it by the sheer force of will. He is a raptor. He is the iron-headed god Horus. The sea he crosses is like the River Lethe, expunging memory, and erasing all the "filth" of love and the emotional complications of his past life. He is free.

With this fictional vision of escape still fresh in his mind, d'Annunzio said goodbye to del Guzzo. The millionaire messiah left for South America to start making the arrangements for the lecture tour (12,000 d'Annunzio dolls were to be manufactured for sale in the lecture halls. The poet's fame was capable of shifting merchandise as well as drawing crowds). Del Guzzo took with him seventeen of d'Annunzio's manuscripts and his cherished red motor car, which had been kept out of the hands of his creditors only by dint of being hidden in the grounds of a clinic. D'Annunzio was supposed to follow him across the Atlantic in due course.

He never went. Perhaps he balked, poor sailor that he was, at the thought of the long sea voyage. Perhaps he decided that delivering lectures to a "colonial" (and therefore, to his mind, negligible) public, was not worth his while. Perhaps he just wanted to be with Nathalie. Two days after del Guzzo sailed, d'Annunzio announced that he urgently needed to see a French dentist. Taking what was for him the exiguous luggage of three trunks and three suitcases, a dressing case and an edition of Petrarch's *Rime Sparse*, he boarded a train to Paris. He would stay in France for the next five years.

Kaleidoscope

N EVER ONCE IN HIS LONG ADVENTUROUS EXISTENCE," wrote Tom Antongini, "did d'Annunzio pass through a more phantasmagoric period, or a more useless one, than his first few months in France." Antongini, a young lawyer and aspiring writer, first met d'Annunzio in Florence in 1897, in the Caffè Doney, where d'Annunzio went to eat ice-cream. Great-nephew of Cesare Fontana, the wealthy Milanese aesthete with whom d'Annunzio had corresponded as a boy, Antongini attached himself to d'Annunzio as the latter had perhaps hoped to attach himself to Fontana. D'Annunzio encouraged him to set up a literary journal, then contributed to its collapse by failing to produce copy on time. Antongini moved to France and for the five years of d'Annunzio's residence there, he was to be d'Annunzio's right-hand man and confidant and, for part of the time, live-in secretary and factotum. In his relations with d'Annunzio (about whom he wrote three books of reminiscences) Antongini was at once amused and exasperated, a sceptic and a devotee.

In Paris in 1910 he watched his newly arrived patron go day after day, night after night where sensationalism called, or where prurient adventure awaited . . . from a lunch at the Rothschilds, to the racecourse at Auteuil, from an intimate tête-à-tête to a first night at the Opera, from a fancy-dress ball to the reception of a new member at the Académie Française."

D'Annunzio in France was a different, lesser man. He had left his political eminence behind in Italy along with his possessions. He continued to address his Italian nationalist admirers, sending polemical poems to the *Corriere della Sera*. He met French nationalist authors. He acquired some contacts in the military and diplomatic establishment. But in Paris he was more fin-de-siècle decadent than futurist patriot. A cartoon of the period by Sem shows him dancing in the steam ris-

FORSE CHE SI, FORSE CHE NO

ing from a plate of pasta—trim, airy and frivolous. Outrageous stories circulated about him. Within days of his arrival it was being said that he had had sex in the lift at the Hôtel Meurice. (He may have left Italy to escape his debts, but he immediately checked into a preposterously expensive hotel.)

Nathalie was to remain part of his life throughout the five years of his French "exile," but she had to compete with a legion of his other mistresses. In memoirs of the time her tears of jealousy are mentioned as often as her extravagantly large jewels. Laying aside his mission to revive and expand the Italian language, d'Annunzio wrote in French, impressing French readers with his fluency not only in the modern language but also in the archaic vocabulary and constructions of mediaeval French verse. He dredged his memory and his notebooks for material for intimate, introspective prose-works. Like Marcel Proust, who began *À la recherche du temps perdu* the year before he arrived in Paris, he turned his gaze inward, experimenting with a kind of fictionalised autobiography in which the author's prime subject matter is his own consciousness, his declared aim "to illuminate myself."

The five years he spent in France were divided between Paris, where his life was crowded with people and public events, and the Landes, a region of pine forests and sand dunes on the Atlantic coast. Once again d'Annunzio had found for himself a landscape closely resembling that of his childhood. There he rented a fantasically ornate wooden chalet overlooking the beach near Arcachon, and ensconced himself in rooms cluttered with the usual bric-a-brac, and his dogs in a specially constructed kennel, the columns of which were topped with carved wooden hares.

The five years of his French sojourn are a kind of hiatus in his life. Superficially they were brilliant—never before had d'Annunzio enjoyed such a busy social life—but as an author he was reworking old ideas or experimenting with forms he would fully master only later. He made friends but they were peripheral to the core of his life story, which would seem in retrospect (to him anyway) to be a story about Italy. He had a number of lovers, but no great love. To him, as for all Europe, these are the pre-war years, a prelude to an as-yet-unannounced drama. They will seem afterwards to most of those who live through them either a gracious age of lost beauty and optimism, or a period of culpable irresponsibility, of a time when everyone played silly games with their backs turned to the approaching dark.

D'Annunzio was forty-eight when he arrived in Paris, but he seemed both older and younger, physically wizened, intellectually ebullient. Hérelle, who had not seen him for twelve years, was shocked by how "old and ugly" he had become. His complexion was pale, his skin dead-looking. Several French observers commented on his large "semitic" nose. (Casual anti-semitism was widespread in snobbish French circles at the time: d'Annunzio himself became infected with it. He had never before shown any interest in the subject, but the diplomat Maurice Paléologue reported "d'Annunzio . . . hates the Jews.")

His many admirers (his fiction was immensely popular in France) were now laying eyes on him for the first time. Several were taken aback by how effeminate the superman seemed. Marinetti, contemplating his "dear little figure," was put in mind of courtesans, of foaming lace and posies of violets and Gloire de Dijon roses, and detected an odour of chanciness and cunning emanating from his "feminine gestures." There were men who found him sinister. The poet Henri de Régnier wrote: "He's ugly, energetic. Something cunning and cruel about him, like the Harlequin who killed Pierrot."

D'Annunzio's supposed ugliness was no obstacle to his social success. Nor was the fact that the fine-tuned snobbery of Parisians detected his merely bourgeois origins. "At first sight," wrote René Boylesve, "he seems a bit common, a little man who could easily become ridiculous." But let d'Annunzio only begin to speak and his spell was cast. He was courteous and apparently self-effacing. He dominated gatherings by stealth and charm, not by a noisy imposition of himself. A sharp-eyed girl not yet in her teens (the daughter of the composer Pietro Mascagni, with whom he collaborated in Paris) described his winningly confidential manner: "When Signor d'Annunzio speaks, it always seems as though he is telling one a secret. Even if he is only saying good morning."

Two women were waiting to introduce him to Parisian society, his mistress and his wife. Nathalie had had new gowns, inspired by Persian miniatures, made so that she could astonish him on his arrival. She lived in some splendour near the Bois de Boulogne and frequented a circle which the poet André Germain (who was a part of it) described as being made up of "false marquises, dubious princesses, upstarts, ambitious pederasts and knowing pimps" but which also included a number of fine musicians and artists. In this milieu d'Annunzio was easily made welcome.

Maria Hardouin di Gallese was also in Paris. It was nearly twenty years since she and d'Annunzio had separated and they were on amicable terms. She gave a reception for him, and introduced him to Count Robert de Montesquiou-Fézensac. De Montesquiou, nobleman, dandy and author, now aged fifty-five, had been painted by Whistler and Boldini. He was the primary model for Huysmans's des Esseintes (as he would shortly be for Proust's Baron Charlus). D'Annunzio, who had learnt so much from *À Rebours*, now had the piquant experience of meeting for the first time, in real life, the man who had indirectly inspired some of his own fiction.

De Montesquiou seems to have become besotted with d'Annunzio. He called him "Beloved Master," "Divine Friend," *"Porfirogenito'* (born to the purple). He invited him to his chateau, and laid Persian carpets along the drawbridge in honour of his arrival. He volunteered to enter into a sort of contract, "a sentimental, almost religious bond for a period of one year," vowing himself to d'Annunzio's service as a vassal might pledge his service to his liege lord. He also observed him perceptively. The Italian was not, he thought, "a man to whom one could become attached; attachment must be reciprocal, and he did not seem to desire it." He may have meant simply that d'Annunzio was not homosexual, but he also saw that d'Annunzio would "put himself out to please," not out of any feeling for another, but "for the pleasure he took in excelling in this skill, as he excelled in his art."

Another new friend was Comte Boni de Castellane, another of Proust's circle (de Castellane is one of the models for Proust's Robert St. Loup). Man about town, giver of extravagant parties and decorator of fantastic homes, de Castellane had much in common with d'Annunzio: "He even dared to claim he was more of a spendthrift than I." De Castellane was initially surprised by the other's reputation as "a dangerous man"—"a few reddish hairs on his head, pale face, green eyes; in a word, he looked sickly"—but de Castellane looked on as one woman after another succumbed. D'Annunzio's allure was "like that of a perfume: it captivated, it attracted, it prostrated."

D'Annunzio soon met some of his French literary peers: Anatole France, Anna de Noailles, Maurice Barrès. But he had always sought out visual artists or musicians rather than fellow authors. When he arrived in Paris, Diaghilev's Ballets Russes was beginning its second season. At de Montesquiou's urging he went along to see Ida Rubinstein in *Scheherazade*, and stayed at the theatre bar afterwards until four in the morning expatiating on the "plastic perfection" of her legs. He saw her again in *Cleopatra* and—as we have already seen—went backstage and kissed those legs from toe to crotch.

Rubinstein played only mime roles, but though she couldn't dance and spoke only with a heavy Russian accent, she had, by all accounts, a compelling stage presence. "She is a fabulous being," said the Ballets Russes designer Léon Bakst. "I adore her." Tall and stick-thin, with long golden eyes, dark hair and a theatrical dress sense, she was like a tulip, said Bakst, or "like some heraldic bird'; the same delicate bone structure, the same combination of flexibility and long-lined angularity. Mascagni's daughter conveys, again with innocent directness, how sexy she was. "I had the impression she was naked under her black tunic embroidered with gold . . . When she talked she made strange snake-like movements. She looked as if she were gesticulating with her legs and hips." D'Annunzio loved Rubinstein's exoticism, her *grande dame* manner, her rumoured bisexuality. She was to other Parisian actresses, he declared, as a Russian icon is to the sparkly trinkets in a modern jeweller's shop.

She was also rich enough to be, like Duse, her own impresario, and d'Annunzio must soon have been aware of the fact. Shortly after meeting her, in July 1910, he left Paris for Arcachon. According to Antongini, debauchery had left him "debased, tired, weakened, disgusted and spineless," but the facts suggest rather that he had recovered his creative energy. At once he set to work to write *Le Martyre de Saint Sébastien*.

Here are some episodes from the period between d'Annunzio's arrival in Paris, and the night, over four years later, when he was seen at the Trocadéro theatre on 27 June 1914. On the latter date he sat in the box of the Comédie-Française's leading actress, Cécile Sorel, whom he had first met playing charades with Isadora Duncan, and to whom he had paid what—from him—was the highest possible compliment, telling her that she could hold her own in a beauty contest with a greyhound. They watched Isadora Duncan's troupe performing a programme of "Botticellian" dances. The following day the Archduke Franz Ferdinand, heir presumptive to the Austro-Hungarian Emperor, was shot dead in Sarajevo and what d'Annunzio called *"la vita leggera"* was over.

In coming to France in 1910, d'Annunzio has arrived at the hub of the aviator's world. At Issy-les-Moulineaux, just north of Paris, the great Blériot—to d'Annunzio a modern avatar of the Frankish knights who once dominated all southern Europe—presides over the growing number of novice pilots and engineers. Their exploits fascinate the intelligentsia. Proust makes the trip with his chauffeur Albert, and soon he will send his fictional narrator out to the airfield with Albertine. Maurice Maeterlinck, Pierre Loti, Anatole France and Henri Bergson are among those who, like d'Annunzio, travel out to watch the flying. D'Annunzio affects to despise Maeterlinck ("artificial and monotonous") but he has frequently imitated him. Anatole France is becoming his friend. Soon he will rent the Dame Rose farm conveniently close to Issy and ensconce Nathalie there with their dogs.

Artists are as excited about flight as the writers. It creates new perspectives. The aviators see terrestrial life from further off than anyone has previously done and from an unprecedented angle. The pioneers of cubism, Pablo Picasso and Georges Braque, make model aircraft, and frequently visit Issy-les-Moulineaux to watch the planes take off. D'Annunzio does not know them. He writes with fervent enthusiasm about the classical statuary and Renaissance paintings in the Louvre, and about a Pisanello medal in a private collection, but nothing about the post-Impressionists, nothing about Picasso. He is in Paris at a time of tremendous artistic innovation, but it passes him by.

THE BOIS DE BOULOGNE. De Montesquiou has arranged a dinner at Le Pré-Catelan. Newly restored, the restaurant is a place of swagged silk curtains and crystal chandeliers, grandiose bow windows and discreet private rooms. The damask and the silver are heavy, the food rich. Cécile Sorel is playing hostess. During dessert another actress reads out passages from *Fire*. D'Annunzio sits next to Sorel and sets out to charm her. Nathalie, watching from the other end of the table, bursts into tears. Sorel is embarrassed but d'Annunzio, unperturbed, tells the assembled company: "She is beautiful only when she cries."

The purpose of the dinner is to introduce d'Annunzio to Maurice Barrès, one of the lions of the Parisian literary world. Born within a year of each other, the two have, in their separate countries, been following parallel paths. Barrès began as an aesthete and an individualist, instigator of a *"culte du moi."* His early novels were among those from which d'Annunzio was lifting ideas, images, even whole sentences, in the 1890s. He has written a book about Venice with the d'Annunzian title of *Amori et Dolori Sacrum*. He has been a member of parliament, but only so that he could complain about parliament's shortcomings. For the last decade—increasingly convinced that the individual could thrive only in full consciousness of his race, his blood, his soil—he has been writing novels full of mystical nationalism. He and the Italian, so like-minded, should be allies, and d'Annunzio, by means of a flattering dedication, will see to it that they soon are, but Barrès is initially wary, watching d'Annunzio with a perspicacious eye and a grudging mind. D'Annunzio affects "the fading tradition" of the Symbolists and Oscar Wilde, thinks Barrès, but there is nothing languishing about him. "He is a little Italian with a hard face . . . A businessman looking for providers of funds."

Every Friday afternoon the American whisky-heiress Natalie Barney is at home to her friends in the Rue Jacob, in a room hung—d'Annunzio-

style—with red damask and decorated with mottoes. Into the lace curtains are woven the words: "May our drawn curtains shield us from the world." Barney, a lesbian, has had a shamelessly public affair with Liane de Pougy, the beautiful courtesan who thought d'Annunzio a "frightful gnome." She calls her salon the "temple of friendship." She serves strawberry tarts and invites an eclectic group. There are writers—Cocteau, Rilke, Tagore—and there are, according to Sylvia Beach, a quantity of "ladies with high collars and monocles," although Barney herself wears long white lace dresses.

D'Annunzio is fascinated by lesbians. He gains an entrée to Barney's cosmopolitan circle of self-confident homosexual women. Soon he meets another American heiress (destined to become the love of Barney's life), the painter Romaine Brooks (above).

Brooks crops her dark hair and wears trousers. Her clothes and the décor of her apartment are all black, white or shades of grey. D'Annunzio dubs her *Cinerina* ("little ashy one"). She has just had her first solo exhibition: de Montesquiou, paying tribute to her stark monochrome portraits in *Le Figaro*, calls her "the thief of souls." D'Annunzio is impressed by her talent and her beauty (she reminds him of Eleanora Duse) and titillated by her bisexuality. "Although she is an American," he says— the New World, in his opinion, is inhabited entirely by barbarians— "she is both intelligent and a true artist." She notices that he uses his knife and fork "like weapons" and likes him for ignoring gossip and talking instead about English poetry. They ride together in the Bois de Boulogne. He gives her a dog named Puppy, and then writes a story in which he imagines it savaging her face. She senses in him a "supernatural force." When he leaves Paris for the Atlantic coast in July, she is with him. It is probably she who pays the rent on the house.

D'Annunzio leaves Paris clandestinely. Antongini and de Montesquiou—enjoying the prank—have been complicit in a scheme whereby his luggage is moved by night from one hotel to another and thence to the railway station (perhaps to avoid his creditors, perhaps to baffle Nathalie and any other women who might be pursuing him). For a while he succeeds in vanishing. He and Brooks go for drives together. He falls asleep in the passenger seat and she watches "your dear face, enclosed in a leather helmet and a great fur collar." She imagines a tranquil shared life of work and begins on her first portrait of him, but after two weeks they are interrupted. D'Annunzio is dressing himself in his hunting clothes—white breeches, high, black boots, pink coat—to pose for her when they hear a rumpus outside. Nathalie—whom d'Annunzio has taken to calling "the tormenting woman"—has tracked them down and, on being told by Brooks's chauffeur that d'Annunzio is not at home, is trying, in tears again, to climb over the garden gate.

Brooks is one of the few women with sufficient self-possession to enjoy an affair with d'Annunzio without being shattered by its ending. Too dignified to dispute possession of her lover, she returns to Paris. D'Annunzio writes her one of his self-pitying farewell letters. She replies tartly that he has no cause to be sad since he has precisely what he wanted. "In heaven, dear poet, there will be reserved for you an enormous octopus with a thousand women's legs (and no head)." Their friendship survives.

Early in their relationship, d'Annunzio took Nathalie to see Benozzo Gozzoli's painting of St. Sebastian in San Gimignano. He addressed her as St. Sebastian. With her long legs and ephebic body, Nathalie made a plausible boy. Their letters to each other are full of quasi-mystical allusions to rough sex. "My suffering is like carnal magic, oh St. Sebastian!" he wrote. She replied that St. Sebastian was reliving "his martyrdom" with intense pleasure. She/he "calls to the archer who loved him— come to St. Sebastian stretched on his burning couch." In the autumn of 1910, d'Annunzio settles to making of that private fantasy a dramatic spectacle.

He orders photographic reproductions of every known painting or statue of St. Sebastian. He despatches Antongini to the library in Bordeaux to hunt out material on the saint. He walks at night through the pine woods. Each tree has a cup strapped to its trunk to collect the resin oozing from a gash the foresters have made. The trees are bleeding, he thinks, like the martyred saint stuck full of arrows.

Around him as he works in his first floor library, on walnut bookcases, are some 5,000 books, all purchased since he arrived in France, all luxuriously bound, with gold lettering, by the celebrated Parisian bookbinder Gruel. He calls them, with a Latin flourish, his *Bibliotecula Gallica*. Everywhere in the room, on the cornices, on the mantelpiece, on the walls, are mottoes, his old favourites in Latin and Italian augmented now by others in Old French pleading for peace and quiet: *"Tais Toy,"* and *"Laissez Moi Penser a Mon Ayse."* D'Annunzio will stay here, eating his dinner alone, until four in the morning, before retiring to his bedroom number one. Bedroom number two, on the second floor, is for private assignations. No visitor other than his sexual partners sees it, and servants enter only with express permission.

Ida Rubinstein is his producer, and she will play Sebastian. She and d'Annunzio address each other as "Brother." She urges him on: "Brother, send me a word with fire in it!" She and Romaine Brooks are now having an affair. With d'Annunzio they make up a perverse androgynous trio, three incestuous "brothers." Rubinstein comes to Arcachon to visit. D'Annunzio buys six longbows with arrows and they practise archery among the dunes.

D'Annunzio is broke again. His expenditure on firewood, oil and candles is exorbitant. He has just spent half of his remaining funds on flowers, and there's not enough remaining to pay the rent. He hands Antongini his gold watch and chain, a gold pencil and several small gold charms. Antongini—devoted follower—adds a ring of his own, and sets off to town to pawn the lot. When the next crisis comes d'Annunzio rummages through the pockets of his winter clothes, which have been put away in camphor, and finds 500 francs. His inability to live within his means seems—literally—insane. He writes that he is so weary of money troubles he is "seriously considering retiring to a Trappist monastery," and then, in the self-same letter, orders an expensive green morocco binding for a run of journals.

The Martyrdom of St. Sebastian is a "mystery" or a "choreographic poem" or an almost-opera, with music by Claude Debussy. D'Annunzio may be ignorant of modern French painting, but when it comes to music he is discriminating and well informed. In France he listens to Franck and Ravel. Reynaldo Hahn becomes his close friend (providing another link with Proust, Hahn's one-time lover) and sings to him one evening, a cigarette hanging from a corner of his mouth: d'Annunzio loves the nonchalance of this.

Debussy is a congenial collaborator. Described by a contemporary critic as one who reclothed "the old French beauty" in "modern garments," he is entirely in sympathy with d'Annunzio's aim of creating modern work in an ancient idiom. D'Annunzio (like Ezra Pound, who arrived in Paris in the same month that he did) has been making a study of the Provençal troubadour poets, and now he employs their intricate verse-forms and archaic language with a fluency that even French critics find prodigious.

The production, funded by Ida Rubinstein, is spectacular, with sets and costumes designed by Bakst. There are over 200 performers on stage, a hundred musicians in the pit. The mood of the piece is Byzantine and sado-masochistic, full of glittering imagery and eroticised pain. It is heavily derivative of the works of Flaubert (*The Temptation of St. Antony, Hérodias, Salammbô*), Oscar Wilde (*Salomé*, another foreign-written French drama), Swinburne (*passim*) and, above all, of d'Annunzio himself. The victim who trembles with desire as he/she begs the archers to shoot, the stage thronged with choirs, the chanting, the lascivious focus on wounds and blood, the detailed stage directions calling for silken banners and beautiful weaponry and crowds of persecuted victims, all recall *The Ship*. So does the merging of the languages of sex and of religious ecstasy. The difference is that the earlier play employed all this gorgeous antique flummery to modern political ends.

Now, distanced from his *patria*, d'Annunzio is writing only about his own psyche.

Debussy's music is generally admired, the lighting is magical, and the choruses so movingly sung that the composer is seen repeatedly wiping away tears. But Ida Rubinstein is no actress. "You are the Prince of Youth," the Emperor tells Sebastian. "Power and joy are yours/And wonder woven of dream/To clothe your ambiguous form." There is nothing wrong with Rubinstein's ambiguous form: whether encased in golden armour or stripped almost naked for death, she looks the part perfectly. But, for all that she has hired a professor to improve her French, her elocution is not up to the task of making d'Annunzio's convoluted lines dramatic. Jean Cocteau thinks she looks like a stained-glass figure animated by a miracle but not yet in command of its newly found voice.

Marcel Proust, making a rare excursion out of his cork-lined room, is at the premiere, sitting next to de Montesquiou, clasping his wrist and feeling how the count is vibrating with emotion. Proust himself is unmoved. He praises d'Annunzio's language—"How many Frenchmen write with such precision?"—but nonetheless the play, which lasts until past one in the morning, is, he says, "very boring." The two authors don't meet. D'Annunzio, as usual on his first nights, stays away from the theatre. Antongini finds him in the small hours, in a nearby café, fast asleep.

D'Annunzio is a connoisseur of early ecclesiastical music—Palestrina, Monteverdi. In Paris he kneels in St. Séverin, and is moved to think that Dante once knelt there too. He has made friends with the organist Louis Vierne, who invites him into Notre Dame by night and plays Bach's Toccata and Fugue in D Minor for him, the two of them sitting in a single pool of light alone in the enormous edifice. It is, writes d'Annunzio years later, the most exalted moment of his "exile." He attends the Lenten sermons of a famous preacher, and takes note of the flirtations for which the service is cover, especially the closeness of two young girls. "The hair of the one is the colour of tea, cool in a 'famille rose' bowl, and the hair of the other like coffee, steaming in a cup of dark blue saxe." He watches as one of "these sinful girls" kisses her friend's hand "with such an ardour of desire that I half expected the cherubim to drop their tinsel-paper skirts, and fly away, shrieking in holy horror."

So he is a church-goer, of an impious kind, but he is not liked by the Church. A priest once refused to give Nike the sacraments so long as she was living with him. Now the Archbishop of Paris has warned all good Catholics to stay away from *The Martyrdom of St. Sebastian.* The fact that the martyr is played by a woman is shocking enough, but that Ida Rubinstein is Jewish is worse, and so is the fact that she appears on stage with her famous legs fully exposed. D'Annunzio, fully aware of the way controversy can be transmuted into useful publicity, gets Debussy to keep the fuss going by writing a letter to *Le Figaro,* insisting that the work is "profoundly religious." The Church does not agree. D'Annunzio has compared Jesus Christ with Adonis, the beautiful young man whom Aphrodite loved, and who died to rise again. The similarity between the two myths is now a commonplace of comparative theology, but in 1911 it is shocking to clerics. All of d'Annunzio's works are placed on the Vatican's Index of forbidden reading.

D'Annunzio is back in Arcachon. Nathalie is there with him, and he has hired a housekeeper who will remain a part of his household until his death, Amélie Mazower, whom he dubs Aélis. She is no ordinary servant. She is d'Annunzio's occasional concubine, and she suffers intensely from jealousy whenever he and Nathalie retire to the bedroom reserved for sex. Aélis's origins are working class, but her manners are grand. One visitor, to whom she opens the door wearing elbow-length white gloves, likens her to a Swedish princess. D'Annunzio also has a groom he hired in Pisa—he may be broke but he still keeps horses—and there is a witch-like woman servant, who rides briskly about, not on a broomstick, but on a bicycle.

Henri Régnier, whose poetry d'Annunzio has imitated in his earlier work, is visiting. His wife leaves a description of the house. Much of it is predictable—hot, perfumed air; silk curtains and shaded lamps; full-size plaster casts of statues. But there are two new details: the *Charioteer of Delphi* now holds in its outstretched hand "a sort of blue stone which, it appears, is a violent poison" and on d'Annunzio's desk lie "dense rows, like a thousand thin blue piano keys, a veritable keyboard of telegrams."

D'Annunzio takes great pleasure in the new medium of wireless telegraphy. He still writes copious letters, but telegrams have become his preferred method of communication. He likes to make them tiny imagist poems which must frequently have left their recipients flummoxed. On arriving at Arcachon he gave Antongini four telegrams to transmit, each one to a different woman, each one suggestively opaque. To one: "The melody of the waves cradles my regrets. Everything is distant and everything is near." To another: "I am thinking of you as the richest bronze for my statues."

D'Annunzio is writing about himself. He is sending autobiographical fragments, which he calls "*Faville del Maglio*" (Sparks from the Anvil), to the *Corriere della Serra*. His sources are his notebooks, dozens of them, which he brought away with him from the Capponcina in his smart pigskin suitcases. Through them he revisits his past, converting it into prose more intimate and direct than any he has previously published. These pieces owe something to the works of the Renaissance essayists Michel de Montaigne and Sir Thomas Browne, both of whom d'Annunzio admires, but, as he often did, d'Annunzio is doing something both old and up-to-the-minute. As he begins his "Sparks," Marcel Proust, James Joyce and Virginia Woolf are all, like him, experimenting with new forms of narrative, in order to explore the working of their own and their characters' minds.

AUGUST 1911. The *Mona Lisa* is stolen from the Louvre, and remains missing for over two years before the thief, an Italian named Peruggia, is found with it in Florence. The robbery is the talk of Paris. Guillaume Apollinaire and Pablo Picasso are both arrested as suspects. According to Antongini, the thief brings the painting to d'Annunzio at Arcachon and asks him to hide it. The story seems far-fetched, but d'Annunzio confirms it in a letter to Albertini, and tells a reporter from *Le Temps* that he knows something about the theft that he cannot reveal.

D'Annunzio, the playwright of *La Gioconda*, has frequently written about Leonardo, implicitly comparing himself with the great Renaissance polymath. Perhaps Peruggia really did see him as someone who might help. The famous painting's presence in France is as much of an irritant to Italian nationalists as Lord Elgin's removal of the Parthenon marbles is to Greeks. When Peruggia is finally arrested he becomes a hero in nationalist circles.

D'Annunzio claims that he urged the man to return the masterpiece to its true owners, the people of Italy. The theft—viewed as a piece of political theatre or propagandist performance art—appeals to him. He also sees it as a way of making a bit of money. He announces his intention (never realised) to write a detective story titled, "The Man who Stole the *Mona Lisa*." Claiming that he himself is implicated in the crime is a piece of advance publicity for the proposed work, as audacious as his long-ago faked death in a riding accident.

OCTOBER 1911. Italy is at war with the Ottoman Empire in North Africa, fighting over the territory which will afterwards become the Italian province of Libya. The action foreshadows Italy's African ventures of the succeeding two decades but for now the future instigator of those wars, Benito Mussolini, still a socialist and anti-imperialist, disapproves. He writes: "Let a single cry arise from the vast multitudes of the proletariat . . . down with war!" He serves a five-month jail term for rioting in protest against the "mock-heroic madness of the warmongers by profession." By contrast d'Annunzio, who is unlikely to have yet heard of Mussolini, is fiercely excited.

The conflict is ugly. Turks and Arabs kill over 500 Italians in one engagement, and nail their mutilated corpses to palm trees. The Italians retaliate by massacring thousands of Arabs, and sending thousands more to penal islands. Undismayed, d'Annunzio settles down to write ten *Songs of Our Exploits Overseas*. A colonel obtains the manuscript of one of them and keeps it in a kind of improvised shrine along with the regimental colours. D'Annunzio receives packets full of admiring letters, some signed by whole companies of soldiers, many of them illiterate and able only to make their mark.

These new *Songs* are diatribes against the Turks and their allies—most particularly Italy's "hereditary foe" the Austro-Hungarian Empire. In them, d'Annunzio turns his aversion to dirt against whole nations, smearing them with imagined filth. The *Song of the Dardanelles* is so vitriolic that the government intervenes. Austria is still officially Italy's ally, yet here is d'Annunzio describing the Emperor Franz Joseph as a hangman and an angel of death and Austria as "the two-headed eagle which vomits back up, like a vulture, the undigested flesh of corpses." (This disgusting image haunted d'Annunzio—he used it repeatedly.)

Albertini says he cannot print the poem in the *Corriere della Sera*. Treves, who is to publish the *Songs* in book form, implores d'Annunzio to cut the offending lines. D'Annunzio refuses. The text is censored. When the book appears some of the lines have been deleted, and in the blank space where they ought to have been d'Annunzio inserts the words: "This song of the deluded fatherland was mutilated by order of Cavaliere Giolitti, head of the Italian government."

Giolitti, careful and pragmatic, had succeeded Crispi as the dominant figure in Italian politics. He was a realist, a practitioner of the art of the possible and adept at the practice of *trasformismo*. Socialism was to be placated by gradual reform and the alleviation of poverty. Trade unions were to be tolerated. International affairs were to be conducted with tact, and deference to rivals' wishes. If Crispi had wanted to baptise Italy with blood, Giolitti sought to soothe it with the oils of prosperity and diplomacy. His opponents accused him of being too "empiricist." He replied that "if by empiricism you mean taking account of the real condition of the country and the population . . . and proceeding as best one can, without grave danger," he was happy to own up to it. Such an approach to government "is the safest and even the only possible method." Giolitti was the master of compromise and caution. D'Annunzio detested him.

D'Annunzio's foreign admirers, accustomed to seeing him as one of the international fellowship of artists, are dismayed by the violence of his *Songs*. Hugo von Hofmannsthal, who has been one of his greatest admirers, publishes an open letter to him saying: "You were a poet, an admirable poet . . . Now I do not see a poet, or an Italian patriot. I see Casanova whose luck has run out, Casanova at fifty, Casanova tricked up as a warrior, in a badly fastened dressing gown." The philosopher Benedetto Croce, with whom d'Annunzio was on friendly terms in Naples in the 1890s, is repelled by the way d'Annunzio appears to "enjoy war, even to enjoy slaughter." The "politics of beauty" is beginning to reveal itself as a politics of blood.

D'Annunzio is entertaining an editor. He is all sweetness and affability, smilingly conceding point after point as they discuss his latest contract, but whenever sums of money are mentioned he flinches away from the subject as though, observes Antongini, he wished to say, "I implore you to leave this revolting and painful discussion to our secretaries."

A couple of days later, Antongini, acting as d'Annunzio's agent, conveys his demands to the editor, who turns pale, and fidgets, and points out that other eminent authors—Tolstoy, Kipling, Rostand—are all content with far less. D'Annunzio is immovable. The deal is done.

APRIL 1912. There is a solar eclipse. Viewed from Arcachon, the sun's disc is almost completely obscured. The weird, dreary light suits d'Annunzio's mood. Here is an image of the Landes, he writes in his notebook. Here is a leafless tree. Here is a mummified corpse with a blade of grass between its teeth. He is contemplating mortality. Two deaths—those of his fellow poet Giovanni Pascoli, and his sweet-natured octogenarian French landlord—have shaken him. Writing in his new introspective mode, he composes a meditation in which the repugnant bodily facts of death are squarely confronted.

The previous year he saw the corpse of a drowned fisherman washed up on the beach, "a poor naked thing, more wretched than broken debris, more squalid than a pile of seaweed." Now he recalls the pale, emaciated arms "weak as a woman's," the blue fingernails, the legs pale beneath "the bestial hair," the mottled feet. He has been haunted by the memory. Working late at night he has a *frisson* of dread—imagining the corpse standing in the corner of his dimly lit study. Horror and fear diffuse themselves through his mind, as a cuttlefish's black ink darkens water.

In the winter of 1911/12 he writes the libretto, all 5,000 lines of it, for an opera, *Parisina*. This is the subject for which he doubted Puccini's music would have the requisite tragic heft. The story, of incestuous love set against a backdrop of mediaeval warfare, has been covered in a long poem by Byron, and in an opera by Donizetti. But for his version d'Annunzio draws directly on mediaeval lyrics and on the thirteenth-century chronicler Panfilo Sasso. He laces the work with allusions to *Tristan and Isolde* and to his own *Francesca da Rimini*. The composer is Mascagni, whom d'Annunzio once dismissed as a "band-leader" but with whom he now works amicably. The pivotal moment is that where the hero, arriving hotfoot and gory from the battlefield, embraces his stepmother in the sanctuary of the miracle-working church at Loreto, thus staining her beautiful robes with blood.

1913. The Marchesa Casati is in Paris, staying at the Ritz, and requiring the staff to supply her with live rabbits with which to feed her boa constrictor and fresh meat for her Borzoi dogs. Seven years after they first met, she and d'Annunzio are now lovers. D'Annunzio calls her "the divine Marquise," an allusion to de Sade. They dine together in the garden of a restaurant in St. Germain, where a band plays the tango. Afterward he notes "the stinging kiss on the neck, the mad return to the hotel, the red mark displayed."

Luisa smokes cigarettes in a long diamond-studded holder and wears enormous pearls and Persian trousers of heavy gold brocade fastened around the ankles with jewelled bangles. She has several homes, all fantastical. Her house in Rome is decorated all in black and white, with an alabaster floor lit from below. In Venice, she lives in the single-storey palazzo on the Grand Canal which is now the Guggenheim Museum, lining its main saloon with pale gold leaf, and draping the widows with gold lace. She looks like one of the etiolated seductresses Gustav Klimt is painting in Vienna, swathing them in jewel-coloured fabrics and setting them, as Casati set herself, against a background of shimmering gold.

Come winter, she moves on to St. Moritz (winter sports are beginning to be fashionable). She writes d'Annunzio a letter in gold ink on a sheet of black parchment, crested with a death's head and a rose (his watermarked stationery is sober by comparison). She summons him to meet the film producer Giovanni Pastrone.

D'Annunzio is interested in the cinema. Nearly thirty years earlier,

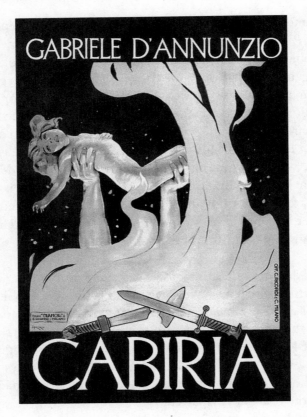

he was already fantasising about a way of preserving a theatrical performance, and guessing that, just as a still image could be captured by a camera, so some day movement, and even sound, might be similarly recorded. Now that his prediction is coming true he foresees a new art of the "marvellous." In 1911 he sells the film rights to four of his plays, and reworks a libretto he once offered to Puccini as a film script. But d'Annunzio's most successful excursion into film-making will be the work he does on Pastrone's epic of ancient Carthage, *Cabiria*.

He has nothing to do with the film-making, being brought in at a late stage to rewrite the captions and "inter-titles," a simple task for which he is paid so much that when the offer is first made Tom Antongini, acting as his agent, literally cannot believe his ears. Despite the fact that he is making a huge sum for very little work, d'Annunzio—characteristically—is so dilatory about it that Pastrone, with the scheduled opening looming, eventually plants himself in the hall of his apartment, prevailing upon the porter to bring him up sandwiches, to ensure the poet doesn't go out until he has finished. In three days the task is done.

Cabiria is marketed as "a film by Gabriele d'Annunzio." Certainly it is d'Annunzian enough. Set in ancient Carthage, it celebrates Roman virtue, while titillating audiences with human sacrifice. Scarfoglio, reviewing it in Naples, summed it up: "the ruin of men, the fall of a civilisation, the riot of passions in the blazing heat of a terrible conflagration . . . the Fates, and, opposed to them a lovely curly-haired girl, armed only with her fragile beauty." It is the most successful of all pre-war Italian films, running for six months in Paris and a year in New York.

D'Annunzio pockets his fee and accepts the credit and the compliments. ("Your genius," says the director of the Vaudeville Theatre, has produced "a masterpiece.") But he never goes to see the film. He tells Treves it is "rubbish," good enough only for the "silly crowd." Ever since he was electioneering in the 1890s d'Annunzio has been anxious to reach a mass audience, but he has no wish to join the masses in the confined space of a cinema. He does not like the way they smell.

In the Landes, d'Annunzio goes boar-hunting, becoming acquainted with the local gentry, and with the Duke of Westminster, who has a hunting box in the forest. Once the hunt lasts from seven in the morning until the early hours of the following day, and fifteen years later he will still be dwelling on the long ride home at walking pace through the night-dark pine forest, and the vigorous massage his Pisan groom gave him when he returned home at long last, filling the house with the smell of embrocation. He persuades the local fishermen to take him out on their boats, several times braving ferocious seas.

The climate is supposedly healthy for tubercular lungs. A "winter quarter" has sprung up along the shore and in the town there are concerts, which d'Annunzio attends. The Villa St. Dominique is agreeably remote, but not so far removed that d'Annunzio cannot walk through the woods at night, lantern in hand, to visit a mistress, sometimes Nathalie, who lives in a separate villa, sometimes another.

Without sex, even for a few days, he is wretched. Alone in Arcachon he writes to Antongini in desolate mood, and then writes again a few days later, much happier, reporting that he has found "a most delectable stray cat" in a nearby village. André Germain comes to visit him and is gleefully shocked to meet "a veritable maenad of the Landes, who was nearly always on a horse and only dismounted to fall into the arms of d'Annunzio." D'Annunzio takes the woman off into the woods. "As he pushed his maenad before him . . . he made the whinnying sounds of a faun who . . . rushes off to seduce a nymph."

Aélis, the "housekeeper," later claims that he requires her to have sex with him three times a day. Soon she is acting as his procurer as well as his concubine, finding him willing local girls.

FEBRUARY 1913. D'Annunzio writes *La Pisanelle, ou la Morte Parfumée*. The story, which he offered to Puccini years earlier (he is using up all the scraps left in his cupboard), is set in Cyprus under its twelfth-century crusader kings. Two men, uncle and nephew, both love a mysterious woman, who is eventually murdered, buried under a heap of rose petals. D'Annunzio might have found the idea in Suetonius, who accuses Nero of smothering some unwanted guests with roses, or in the *Satyricon*. Or he may have seen a print of Alma-Tadema's *The Roses of Heliogabalus*, in which a melee of smooth-fleshed young men and women, tunics slipping suggestively, are overwhelmed by a wave of pink petals.

Later in the year he follows it with *Le Chèvrefeuille* (Honeysuckle), a modern tale of a ruthless superman and seducer, and the havoc he causes in a family of neurasthenic aristos. Paul Poiret makes the costumes, and there is a fracas when D'Annunzio refuses to pay extra for a particularly elaborate outfit. Poiret sues.

Neither play is a success.

AUGUST 1913. D'Annunzio has written a novella for magazine publication, *Leda without Swan*. Its setting is modern and the plot concerns a disreputable woman with a pearl-handled revolver and a hobble skirt (d'Annunzio was intensely appreciative of the increasing visibility of women's legs). The unnamed lady is a femme fatale whose fortune-hunting adventures are squalid and provincial, involving a life-insurance policy, morphine, and a sequence of loveless flirtations with men picked up in small-town casinos or a spa. This is the kind of life, where promiscuity and prostitution merge, into which d'Annunzio feared Barbara might lapse, and which Maria Gravina was, by this time, living. It is also a little too close to his own—the lady's problems all have their origin in debt.

D'Annunzio was writing a "thriller," a "mystery," something intended to be popular and enticing, but into it he poured a toxic dose of depression and misanthropy. He didn't like his fellow beings. There were certain moods in which didn't like his life. This is the book in which he gives his narrator the name Desiderio Moriar (Death Wish).

In the autumn of 1913, d'Annunzio returned to Paris, renting an apartment on the Avenue Kléber. His creditors had caught up with him again. He was behind with his rent. The Villa St. Dominique was under siege. There was really no prospect of his being able to repay his debts, but meanwhile he had his windfall from *Cabiria*. He made the most of being back in the great city. He attended race meetings at Chantilly. Nathalie was now installed at the Dame Rose (Pink Lady) farm near Villacoublay to the north of Paris, where she cared for her dogs and d'Annunzio's. Between them they had some sixty greyhounds, including some champion racers, most of them bred by themselves. D'Annunzio had a win in the greyhound racing at St. Cloud with his "White Havana." He went to boxing matches. He had been a keen boxer since his school days. Now he set up a punchball in the hallway of his apartment, dressing it up with a curly black wig so that visitors were startled by the apparition of a Medusa.

He attended performances: one night he and Auguste Rodin are among the invited audience at a tango demonstration staged by Valentine de Saint-Point, author of the "Futurist Manifesto for Women." According to Natalie Barney, that winter d'Annunzio "was all the rage. The woman who had not slept with him became a laughing-stock."

D'Annunzio is taking tea and cakes in Rumpelmeyer's patisserie. People are looking and whispering: everywhere he goes in Paris his bald pate and curious waxen complexion are noticed. A strange gentleman approaches and asks if the maître would consent to meet his employer, the Queen of Naples. D'Annunzio is delighted to do so. The Queen, driven off her throne by Garibaldi half a century earlier, has featured several times in his work. She is the "Bavarian eaglet," the embodiment of the royal warrior caste now being rendered obsolete all over Europe by the rising tide of democracy which d'Annunzio deplores. Bowing low to the old lady, he kisses her hand.

D'Annunzio steps out of his front door on the Avenue Klebér, and gives twenty francs, as he does every day, to the Italian tenor begging there. His companion protests, telling him that the man has been seen drinking in a fashionable café with a pretty woman. "What do you expect him to do with twenty francs?" asks d'Annunzio. "Buy a motor car?" He is as generous with others as he is indulgent to himself.

Antongini, who knows all too well how little he can afford to throw money around, observes his prodigality with mixed dismay and affection. "He tips the man who punches his ticket at the railway station; he tips the man who looks at the ticket on the train; he tips the servants who open the doors in the homes of his friends; he tips the attendants in museums; he tips the urchin who picks up the handkerchief he has dropped; he tips the urchin's friend who is sneering at such wasted energy."

FEBRUARY 1914. D'Annunzio is in England. He is travelling with four women: Nathalie, Aélis (who is keeping a diary of the trip) and Mesdames Boulanger and Hubin, who are, respectively, the wife and mistress of his good friend Marcel Boulanger, all of them united by their shared passion for dogs and horses.

Aélis records that she and Nathalie both share his bed in the Savoy. The superfluity of sleeping partners doesn't prevent him from appreciating the view from the hotel window, and jotting in his notebook a Whistleresque riverscape in words. "A red sun in an opal sky. The bridges are veils of lace—a symphony in grey." They visit the National Gallery and then travel to Altcar in Lancashire, for the premier event of the hare-coursing calendar, the Waterloo Cup. D'Annunzio makes notes about the sodden green landscape, the huge horses dragging carts laden with coal, the Englishmen "returning from a day's sport, red-faced as if varnished," and the sheep grazing incessantly, like leeches sucking sustenance from the wet ground.

SPRING 1914. The flower-sellers' stalls are filling the air with the scent of violets and lilies of the valley. There is a concert of early choral music in the Sainte Chapelle. D'Annunzio is excited. To hear such singing in that marvellous Gothic building, with its jewel-coloured glass, will, he promises, be sublime. Also present is the young Russian artist Catherine Barjansky. "I saw a small, thin man with a strange face that looked as though it had been moulded in yellow wax. There was not a single hair on his scalp, and his narrow face was sharpened by a tiny, pointed beard." He is escorting the Princesse de Polignac (née Winaretta Singer, American sewing-machine heiress, lesbian and noted musical patroness: she commissions Satie, Stravinsky and Poulenc). He introduces himself to Barjansky. "He approached with an odd dancing step, holding one shoulder slightly higher than the other . . . He was dressed too elegantly in a pale grey suit, an incredible necktie with a huge emerald, the same large stones in the cuffs of his silk shirt, patent leather shoes, and an eyeglass on a black cord."

He presses her hand meaningfully. She feels the rings on his fingers. He gazes into her eyes. His glance is "singularly penetrating." He says: "I hope to see you again."

A few days later Barjansky receives an invitation to dinner. She goes, and describes the evening.

'A heavy perfume, a mixture of incense and amber, assailed me as I entered." The clothes she is wearing will smell of it for months. "On a couch of silver brocade, amongst a quantity of gold and black velvet cushions, sat a slim woman of remarkable beauty." This is Nathalie, her dress cut very low in front, her jewels large and plentiful, her dark blue eyes swimming, as usual, with tears. There are some "Parisian society people," and an actress-cum-courtesan with an over-loud laugh and strings of pearls dangling from neck to knee. Swathes of embroidered Indian fabrics are suspended from the ceiling. Black-framed mirrors glimmer. Orchids, masses of them, a concert grand piano, numerous statues of the Buddha, vases full of peacock feathers, a malachite dish heaped with peaches and grapes.

There is music: Bach, Beethoven, Gluck. D'Annunzio, monocle fixed, sits listening intently, "as though turned to stone." Afterwards dinner is served at a round table, surrounded by a tall gilded Japanese screen. There is a black bowl full of white roses on the table, and a number of little black or white glass horses from Murano.

D'Annunzio holds forth until, after a particularly extravagant anecdote, Catherine Barjansky asks: "Was that really true?"

"Oh no," replies d'Annunzio.

His fame has become something he plays with. He contrives tableaux, using all Paris as his stage. He and Ida Rubinstein drive down the Champs Elysées in an enormous white motor car, both dressed entirely in white (she has a wonderful ermine coat). Now he says to Barjansky: "Don't you know that I'm the greatest liar in the world?"

While d'Annunzio was posturing in Paris, back in Italy his ideals were finding new supporters. He would later cast himself as a lone voice, keeping the lights of nationalism and heroic endeavour bright among the vapours rising from "the swamp of abjection and compromise" which was Italy under Giolitti's cautiously liberal-leaning administration. But the truth is that other voices were adding themselves to his in decrying democracy and glorifying violence.

The futurists were the most clamorous. "We exalt aggressive acts," declared Marinetti, "the perilous leap, the slap and the blow with the fist . . . We want to glorify war . . . militarism, patriotism . . . the beautiful ideas which kill." Marinetti's zest for violence was matched by his contempt for the elected government: he called democrats "democretins." There were others who thought likewise, and who were calling out for a renaissance of Italian vigour. One of their mouthpieces was the journal *La Voce*, published in Florence. In 1907, Giuseppe Prezzolini, one of *La Voce*'s editors, described his generation's state of mind: "Dissatisfaction and bitterness." Prezzolini put forward no political programme, but he was clear that the unheroic reality was not acceptable. "Our opposition must be radical and irreconcilable. With implacable intransigence we have to say NO! to the present state of affairs."

Georges Sorel's *Reflections on Violence* was published in Italy in 1909, and found more admirers there than it did in France. Sorel's theory of the symbolic power of violence, and the creative potency of mass hysteria and mob action, appealed to those Italians who, like d'Annunzio, had made an idol of the tenth muse Energeia. In 1913 the philosopher Giacomo Donato wrote, under the pseudonym Spartaco, "the young generation wants to live, LIVE, LIVE, their own life, a life that is intense and strong . . . LIIIVVVEEE!!! (Fighting + Enjoying) A life of true freedom, of courage, strength, paroxysm, sport, desire, lust, pride, recklessness, of madness if necessary." D'Annunzio, the mandarin stylist with a gift for unrolling enormously protracted, but syntactically perfect, sentences, would have put it differently, but to live, *LIVE, LIIIVVVEEE!!!!* was something to which he too aspired (had he not, as a member of parliament, "advanced towards Life"?).

In March 1914, d'Annunzio announced, via the social columns of the French press, that he would be accepting no more invitations after an injury sustained while playing hockey in the Italian ambassador's garden. From March to May he stayed in, and kept largely to his bed. In fact it was a sexually transmitted disease (probably syphilis)—which had incapacitated him. "The shameful mark of the Parisian branding-iron," he called it in a letter to a friend, "the ignoble scourge."

He felt jaded, physically and emotionally. "A continual feeling of precariousness" prevented him writing. Ordinary life felt remote. The people around him were like insubstantial ghosts. He was seized by acute spasms of homesickness. "I don't know how I can live here, how I can open my eyes every morning on this low, grey world." His disease was as degrading as it was uncomfortable: his allusions to it are sheepish, he felt unclean. More, the world around him seemed soiled and rotten morally, spiritually and politically.

In April, the French elections resulted in a landslide victory for the left. The new, anti-militarist government reduced the requirement for military service. Meanwhile the public was riveted by *l'affaire Caillaux*—a tale of adultery, murder, blackmail and political corruption involving the Minister of Finance and the editor of *Le Figaro*. D'Annunzio's evocation of the atmosphere in the city and (indirectly of his own state of mind) is full of revulsion. He imagines the judges in the Caillaux case dipping brown-striped fingernails into the murdered man's bullet wounds and then, with the same bloody nails, picking their own noses and wiping the mucus on their neighbours' sleeves. He thinks of carcasses crawling with maggots and buzzing with flies, of beggars' hands so repulsive that after touching them he needs to clean himself not only with water but with acid.

The news from Italy was troubling. A general strike, called by the socialists, had occasioned a week-long series of violent demonstrations. Hundreds of workers had been killed in street-fighting, buildings were burned, telegraph wires cut, railway stations occupied. D'Annunzio was appalled. The "Latin genius crawls through the mud." Summoning up his erudition to provide an image for his disgust, he recalled how, when Rome was in its decline, the sacred geese came down from the Capitol to honk and squawk in the city's great sewer. On 16 June 1914 he told the French ambassador to Russia, Maurice Paléologue, "We live in an infamous era, under the reign of the multitude and the tyranny of the plebs." Paléologue had been talking about the dire international situation. D'Annunzio told him, "This war that you seem to fear—I summon it with all the force of my soul."

27 JUNE 1914. D'Annunzio takes his seat next to Cécile Sorel at the Trocadéro Theatre. Isadora Duncan's dancers are barefoot and dressed in skimpy "Grecian" tunics. As he sits, apparently so immaculate in white tie and patent leather pumps, d'Annunzio is feeling a little seedy. Sitting is uncomfortable. He is irritated by an outbreak of haemorrhoids.

The Archduke Franz Ferdinand of Austria and his wife Sophie, Duchess of Hohenberg, are travelling through Bosnia. In a café in Sarajevo, Danilo Ilić, leader of the Black Hand, is distributing weapons to his associates. He hands a gun to Gavrilo Princip.

The Dogs of War

ON 27 JULY 1914, one month after the assassinations at Sarajevo, d'Annunzio went to the races at Chantilly with his friends Marcel and Susanne Boulanger. That day the French Minister of War issued standby mobilisation orders. The ships of the British fleet, returning from manoeuvres, were instructed not to disperse but to take up war stations. The Serbian authorities were considering Austria-Hungary's impossible ultimatum. The day was overcast. The racehorses were as superb as ever, but what few spectators there were seemed all to be walking with downcast eyes "as though searching for magical herbs in the grass."

After the races d'Annunzio went to dine at the Boulangers' house nearby. Arriving, he was met by a boisterous crowd of greyhounds: eyes shining, muzzles pointing, glossy hides rippling and changing in the light like shot silk. D'Annunzio and Marcel Boulanger had already talked about the impossibility of feeding their dogs in wartime. Most of these treasured creatures would have to be killed; so would many of d'Annunzio's pack. "Sacrifice had taken its place among the household gods."

Boulanger brought out the military tunic and cap he had worn as a young soldier. Moth-proofed and stored away for decades, it smelt of camphor. Touching it, d'Annunzio imagined it drenched in blood. At nightfall "not only a day ended: a world dissolved."

The following morning Austria-Hungary declared war on Serbia. A week later Germany declared war on France. Marcel Boulanger put all his beloved greyhounds on leashes and led them out into the forest, the dogs, as usual, prancing joyfully around him. Deep in the woods, he killed them. D'Annunzio writes that "he himself laid the noble bodies side by side in the ditch in the middle of the forest; and he came back by the same path, head low, with the collars empty and the leads dangling."

Earlier in the summer it had seemed to d'Annunzio that the air was infected. Rain was like sweat. He felt himself trapped in a ship becalmed, its bilges stinking, amidst a loathsome colony of gigantic octopuses. How to purge this nauseating mess? Violence on a massive scale was the only remedy. Now, at last, the torrent of cleansing blood was about to flood across Europe. "Is this the last day of humiliation? Are these the final hours of shame?"

D'Annunzio's relief at escaping from the "impure" complexities of peacetime life was widely shared. In Germany, Thomas Mann wrote an essay entitled *"Gedanken im Kriege"*—thoughts in time of war—in which he asked how an artist could fail to praise God "for the collapse of a peaceful world with which he was fed up?" Rainer Maria Rilke called war "a deadly enlivening" and exulted in his loss of personal freedom, "the battle-god suddenly grasps us." In Austria, von Hofmannsthal published a patriotic poem and the twenty-five-year-old Adolf Hitler, "overpowered by stormy enthusiasm," fell on his knees and thanked God for the cataclysm which would release him from "the painful feelings of my youth." In England, Rupert Brooke wrote: "Now, God be thanked,/who has matched us with his hour."

As the German invaders marched in from the north, Paris emptied. At about four o'clock in the afternoon on the day France went to war, Luisa Casati, staying in one of Paris's grandest hotels, rang for her breakfast (she was not a morning person). There were no staff left to serve her. Catherine Barjansky reports: "I found the Marchesa Casati screaming hysterically . . . Her red hair was wild. In her Bakst-Poiret dress she looked like an evil and helpless fury." In such deadly times decadent posturing was no longer amusing. "War had touched the roots of life," thought Barjansky. "Art was no longer necessary." D'Annunzio concurred: "Who am I?" he asked himself. "What have I ever done?"

As the clash of nations began, Giolitti announced that Italy would remain neutral, observing the terms of the Triple Alliance. D'Annunzio might believe war to be the crucible in which a great future could be formed, but Giolitti saw it as "a misfortune that must only be faced when the honour and great interests of the country require it." The arguments of the pro-war party were all emotional and, although "anyone is free to throw his own life away for an emotion," no one, in Giolitti's considered opinion, had the right to imperil the country on such grounds.

D'Annunzio found himself the expatriate citizen of a country with no part in the drama. He was the wrong age in the wrong place, and his *patria* had, in his opinion, the wrong policy. He wrote to Albertini asking, "What should I do? . . . My situation is terrible." He was overtaken by a most uncharacteristic diffidence. As Parisians stampeded southwards he felt himself stranded like the pitiful debris left on the bed of a channel at low tide, as useless and squalid as an empty bottle or the shoe of a drowned man. For the next six months he was to write a stream of polemics in prose and verse, but to be a writer no longer seemed to him an adequate calling. Meeting General Gallieni, commander-in-chief of the French forces in Paris, he told him: "At this moment I would give all of my books for one of your actions."

The new intellectual fashion was anti-intellectual. Prezzolini had written in *La Voce* earlier that year: "One doesn't make revolutions with scholars, or people who wear white gloves. A *teppista* [thug] counts for more than a university professor when it comes to opening fire on a barricade or breaking down the door of a bank. And if what's needed now is breakage and violence, on whom should we call?" Not, clearly, on a short-sighted middle-aged poet still feeling down after a dose of venereal disease.

The banks were closed. Travel was circumscribed. Driving out to Dame Rose, d'Annunzio passed new aircraft-hangars, "the black nests of the fighting-planes." A man who had always treasured his solitude, he found himself, in those first weeks of war, unable to remain alone. He was out on the streets at all hours, exploring Paris on foot as he had never done before, with a compulsion to "*know*" the city (his emphasis) which he recognised as an anxiety that it might soon be totally destroyed.

In 1897, visiting Assisi, the place sacred to St. Francis, lover of all God's creatures, d'Annunzio was acutely aware of the distantly audible bellowing of cattle in a slaughterhouse. Animals, ignored in the majority of wartime reminiscences, are everywhere in d'Annunzio's.

Horses were being requisitioned for military use. The Bois de Boulogne was full of them, and the park at Versailles had become "an equine city." Ropes were strung between the trees, and row upon row of horses were tethered there, ready to be taken to the front. The alleys and vistas of the palace's grounds were littered with straw and dung. The fountains were stilled, and horses crowded around the basins to drink from the green scummy water.

The roads were thronged with cattle. D'Annunzio found himself surrounded one day by perhaps 3,000 bullocks—a great mass of moving flesh spilling over the roadside and the riverbanks. Periodically they became entangled with "herds" of troops going north towards the front. The young men were, to d'Annunzio, all too obviously, dead men walking, just as those bullocks were, for all their noisiness, ambulant meat. He saw a soldier pushing a red-haired child in a pram. The woman with him wore a black dress "as though," wrote d'Annunzio, "she was already a widow." He watched lorries pass by, their flat-beds filled with seated soldiers. They wore the uniform of blue jacket and red breeches. Tight-packed, their lower bodies lapped in red cloth, they seemed to him to be sitting waist-deep in blood.

Such hallucinatory prescience of the horrors to come did nothing to reduce d'Annunzio's determination that Italy should enter the war. His *Ode to the Latin Resurrection* was a call to arms. France had already "donned the purple robe of the warrior," ready to sing "like a lark on the summits of death." Italy should be at her side.

> This is your day, this is your hour
> Italy . . .
> Unhappy be you who hesitate
> Unhappy be you who do not dare to cast the dice.

Romain Rolland, now a pacifist, noted gloomily that d'Annunzio, along with Rudyard Kipling, was "writing hymns of war."

Throughout August the Germans advanced. D'Annunzio remained entranced by Paris's "marvellous agony"—"the city has never been so beautiful." On 24 August the Germans broke through the French defences at Charleroi and advanced on the Somme. D'Annunzio was seen in the street with tears in his eyes. On hearing that one in twenty-five of those French soldiers who had run from the battlefield had been shot, he was disappointed that the executions had been so few. That evening he walked outside after dinner, contemplating for the first time the possibility of a German victory: "Profound melancholy, thoughts of the distant horror."

With France on the verge of defeat, he was preoccupied with his dogs. Some had already been put down ("breaking my heart"). Over the next few days at the Italian embassy, where despairing lines of would-be refugees queued for exit permits, he was using his considerable influence to try (in vain) to get two covered carts to transport his pack south.

On 2 September, with the French army still retreating, he found his road out of Paris jammed with people in flight, "beautiful fresh women glimpsed through the windows," but arrived at Dame Rose in time to take Nathalie out to lunch in Versailles, and with enough of his peacetime persona intact to object to her outfit. She was fresh and pretty in a summer dress, suitable enough for a restaurant, but not—he judged—for the visit they planned to make afterwards to the hospital for the wounded. They ate an omelette and cold chicken, and a punnet of wild strawberries which d'Annunzio had brought with him from Paris. The maître d' told them, to d'Annunzio's disgust, that although he had already hidden his best wine he would stay put, and was ready to serve German officers.

The battle lines were now very close. The Boulangers' house at Chantilly was overrun. Nathalie insisted she would not leave Dame Rose without the dogs; she would rather die. D'Annunzio indulged in an admiring fantasy about his "Caucasian Diana" going into battle, "unleashing with her guttural cry the fearsome pack against the invader, commanding the strange battle amid the red glow of flames." He loved his greyhounds for their ferocity as much as for their well-muscled beauty. "The urge to kill is terribly strong in them," he wrote. "They tremble with the desire to kill."

At the beginning of September, the French government decamped to Bordeaux and over 800,000 Parisians fled south. D'Annunzio would have been safe at Arcachon. Tom Antongini reports he had received an invitation from a lady with a house on the Côte d'Azur offering refuge and, as Antongini coyly puts it, "all the rest." But d'Annunzio stayed. He went shopping, stocking up on sardines, condensed milk and jam sufficient for himself and his two servants, and bird seed for the twenty-two canaries he had acquired that year. He dined with Luigi Barzini, the *Corriere*'s celebrated war correspondent, and envied him his freedom to travel to the front, but he wrote ruefully to Albertini, admitting he was not a reporter. His subject matter was "sentiments and ideas." "In the present moment, could that interest your readers?"

By 3 September the German army was less than forty kilometres from Paris. The city's trees were being cut down, and trenches dug at its gates. Life was simplified. D'Annunzio saw the cartloads of flour being brought in past the barricades at the city's gates—basic provisions in a situation where luxuries would be inappropriate (no more *fraises du bois*). Night after night he went to the railway stations, which seemed to him like gigantic pumps, ridding the city of cowardice (those fleeing to safety), sending the courageous out to fight. He saw women, their make-up looking lurid against their white faces, struggling with piles of suitcases and boxes. He noticed other women in high heels—prostitutes getting ready, he supposed, for new German clients. He was still sufficiently himself to appreciate the "knowing play of knees and thighs in the tight skirts." But what he went for primarily was to see the wounded being brought back from the front, and to exult in the "splendour of the blood."

He despatched another article to the *Corriere*, one in which public indignation—"the enemy's horses trample on the very heart of France"—alternates strangely with poignant expressions of his own state of mind. "I have lost my world and I do not know if I can conquer a new one." He spent evenings in the Café de la Paix. There were no horses for cabs and no fuel for private cars: for the first time he began to use the metro, and marvelled at its efficiency. Obliged to stay home all day to complete an article, he felt jumpy and miserable until, at dusk, he set out with his favourite greyhound, Fly, for a stroll up the Champs Elysées. He was seen in the Bois de Boulogne, lost in thought on a bench, with the dog at his feet.

By night the blacked-out city seemed newly beautiful to him, lit only by the criss-crossing blades of the searchlights and by the moon. Previously he had lived mainly amidst the *grands boulevards* of western Paris. Now, in those summer nights, he paced the not-yet-fashionable streets and alleys of the mediaeval city, of the Marais and St. Michel, of the Îles de la Cité and St. Louis, noticing the mean shops, the beggars and prostitutes, the shrines with little lamps, the stale-smelling taverns. He read the *Life* of Benvenuto Cellini, who worked for the French kings. He conjured up France's sacred heroes—St. Louis, Philippe le Bel, Napoleon. He was projecting a visionary city onto the darkened stones of the real one, one full of martial symbolism, and traces of a Franco-Italian "Latin" culture under threat from the "Huns" and "Vandals." He dwelt on stories of Italian ladies who had become, by marriage, members of the aristocracy or the royal family of France. One night, pausing to take notes on the view from the Pont des Arts, he was accosted by two officers under suspicion of spying and taken to the police station. He went quietly but first, according to Barzini, he begged his captors to wait: "Would you allow me to add an adjective?" His identity established, he was released with profuse apologies. As the most famous Italian in France, and one who was repeatedly and emphatically promising that his country would soon come to France's aid, he was a man the French authorities were anxious not to offend.

By 12 September, French and British troops had at last halted the German advance on the Marne. The Germans fell back. Both sides dug in. D'Annunzio, brought so close to modern warfare, was in two minds about it. Publicly he declared it was magnificent. Privately, though, he was surprised to find it tedious. "For two months we have been going round and round a single little group of ideas and sentiments. When it comes down to it, war is the most monotonous of human activities."

After the Germans drew back, d'Annunzio obtained a permit to drive out into the territory they had occupied in the weeks before. On a day of pouring rain he set out towards the front with three friends, one of whom recorded his "bizarre" get-up: a long yellow waterproof, goggles and a "kind of helmet of waxed cloth which covered his ears." He was in high spirits. On this, and subsequent sallies into the war zone, he comported himself as though going on a jaunt. His companion found his gaiety and "verve" quite "extraordinary."

A few days later he made another such excursion, this time taking Antongini with him. On each occasion he made copious and careful notes. They drove through devastated villages and abandoned fields. D'Annunzio concentrated on intimate details—grubby toys, a vase of artificial flowers and a "toothless" piano in an abandoned house; shutters flapping in the wind, blackened stooks of corn; the thinness of the cows and their distended, unmilked udders—sad remnants of blasted lives. He saw human corpses "as stiff as cardboard puppets," but he paid more attention to the dead horses with which the roads and fields were littered, all lying stiff in the same ungainly pose, their bellies inflated by gas, their hind legs hoisted into the air, prey to carrion crows and clouds of flies. His notes are dispassionate, acutely observant, honest. Not so his published accounts of his explorations of the war zone.

On his second expedition he reached Soissons. Antongini reports that on the outskirts of the town a soldier examined d'Annunzio's papers and told him "the city is being shelled. If you want to go on, you can, but you will probably be killed." In the main square they found a horse and driver, both lying dead in their own blood. An officer ran out of a house, shouting at them to take cover or get out. This officer turned out to be a fervent admirer of d'Annunzio's works, and—mollified—allowed him to stay for two hours and to distribute fifty packets of cigarettes to the soldiers. As d'Annunzio left he asked where the battle was, and was drolly pleased to be told that he was in the middle of it.

So much for Antongini's laconic account of what happened. Here is d'Annunzio's report, all puffed up with poetic sentiment and lies. Arriving at the brow of a hill, on a road crowded with cartloads of the wounded, he reached out his arms "with a gesture of love" towards the city. He could see the cathedral's twin spires, which seemed to him to reach for the sky like imploring hands. The Germans were shelling the road. He was under fire, and so were all the helpless, mangled men around him. "Everything appeared beautiful to me." Bloody bandages were like red and white rose bushes. He seemed to see an angel balancing between the cathedral's two spires.

A sudden dazzling flash. A tremor of the air.

"There was a human and superhuman silence everywhere, in everything, as when the multitude gathered in the square falls silent to hear the innocent's head roll from the platform into the executioner's basket.

One of the two spires was broken. The town raised to heaven only one arm and a stump.

I cried out to the carts. Now all the wounded were bleeding on behalf of that bloodless stone."

The truth is that d'Annunzio never saw the paired spires of Soissons' cathedral rising like two hands to heaven. He didn't see the stricken one fall. It was destroyed by German shells several days before he visited.

The night before d'Annunzio set off for Soissons, another cathedral, that of German-occupied Reims, was burned, its timbers all consumed, its soot-blackened walls left a roofless skeleton. As we have already seen, d'Annunzio first visited Reims and saw the ruins in March 1915, half a year later. But that didn't prevent him from giving a sombrely beautiful "eye-witness" account of the event. "I saw another cathedral, the most solemn, the place of the great sacred rites, fulfil itself in flame."

D'Annunzio had been a writer of fiction: now he was a propagandist. Truth-telling, the accurate expression of facts, was not something by which he set much store. He was out to stir emotions and alter minds and to tell his readers how to understand the chaotic violence of the war. On the one side were the Latins (he never mentions France's British and Russian allies)—the inheritors and defenders of a civilisation dating back, via the mediaeval cathedral-builders, to the ancient Greeks; on the other, Hunnish barbarian vandals. "This war," he wrote, "is a struggle of races, a confrontation of irreconcilable powers, a trial of blood, which the enemies of the Latin name conduct according to the most ancient iron law." He contrasts the French troops—"shining children"—with those of the enemy—"stinking beasts."

Every bit of land in the environs of Paris was being taken over for the war effort. D'Annunzio's precious kennel at Dame Rose was overrun, not by German invaders but by the French authorities, and handed over to literally stinking beasts. The close-mown grass of the walled meadow where his dogs had been exercised was churned into mud by the 600 cattle foisted on him. The hungry animals stood up to their bellies in muck, and bellowed. Nathalie was frightened by the herdsmen. D'Annunzio protested. "That the refuge of a poet should be made to serve the belly, that meat and butchery should overwhelm it, is not very *Apollonian.*"

Now the meadow was lost, he and Nathalie and their kennel hands walked the greyhounds for hours on end, on leashes, through the forests around the farm. If a hare crossed a clearing in front of them the dogs would take off, their "ferocious clamour echoing in the shadows." One day they pulled d'Annunzio off his feet and he was dragged though the mud, the leashes wound around his wrists, until at last he managed to stagger upright, bruised and bloody, his mouth and nostrils full of earth. His imagination, full of images of trenches and mass graves, made the undignified incident the starting point for an appalling new cult of the earth as a deity greedy for human flesh.

The image of soil watered and fertilised by the blood of warriors, has been a part of the poetry of war at least since Homer, but while the heroes of the *Iliad* grieve over it, d'Annunzio dwelt on the idea with sombre joy. His writings that winter are full of related images: of Joan of Arc "armoured in mud"; of troops coming from the trenches so fouled with mud they are identifiable as human only by their eyes. The soldiers fighting and dying in deep slits in the ground were children of the earth, who now reclaimed them. The earth was the foundry in which they were to be broken down so that a new race could be forged: it was the god who demanded their death as a sacred holocaust. Carnage is the necessary prelude to renaissance. "Where flesh putrifies, there sublime ferments arise." Even d'Annunzio's own mishap—falling over and getting muddy while out dog-walking—was transmuted into a kind of eucharist, a communion with "the insatiable voracity" of the "divine" earth.

Nietzsche had written that there were too many low-grade people in existence, dragging down their superiors. "Far too many live." To d'Annunzio it seemed that, swallowing human flesh, the earth opened up "mystical space." As the felling of trees creates a light-filled clearing in a forest, so the killing of large numbers of people opened the way for "sublimity." Even his own dramas, *The Ship* with its tortures and mass executions, *Glory* with its paeans to the purifying power of violence, were puny compared to the spectacle to which he was now witness. In Paris he watched "the great tanks . . . heading northwards, full of sacrificial flesh and drunken singing" and thought "Destiny ordains events like a great tragic poet."

In the last week of September 1914 ships of the French navy attacked the Austro-Hungarian fleet in the Gulf of Cattaro (now Kotor in Montenegro), a part of the eastern Adriatic coastline which d'Annunzio wished to reclaim as Italy's lost "left lung." This was his cause. It was intolerable to him that it should not be his, and his country's, war. On 30 September he published a great tirade of anger and disgust and self-aggrandisement, quoting the most furious lines from his own past work, laying out the themes which would clang again and again through his rhetoric over the coming years. The "senility" of the cautiously pragmatic Italian authorities who would not commit themselves to war. The "corruption" that a pacific foreign policy engenders in a state. The "necessary hatred" all good patriots must feel against those who deny their nation's greatness. The grandeur of "action," regardless of its purpose. With each one of his public utterances the essence of his philosophy was becoming more naked. Killing and being killed, pouring out the blood of myriads of young men, only by doing these things could a race demonstrate its right to respect. What d'Annunzio was saying is appalling: what is worse is how few people there were to disagree.

He had sounded his trumpet. He didn't quite know what to do next. At Dame Rose he walked his dogs. In Paris he visited the wounded daily in the Franco-Italian hospital, for which he helped to raise funds. Hearst Newspapers proposed to employ him as a war correspondent, but he instructed Tom Antongini to demand an enormous retainer, plus a correspondingly enormous fee for each article published, plus reimbursement of all travelling and hotel expenses for himself, his secretary and his servant. Furthermore he must be allowed total freedom of action, including the freedom to fight. Hearst demurred.

Inactive, he sank into one of his cyclical depressions. He wrote to friends complaining that he was "dying of sadness." His house at Arcachon was now off limits to him: he was behind on the rent, and creditors were waiting for him there. Still he shopped. A notebook of his expenses reveals that he was spending prodigally on flowers, perfumes, taxi-cabs, new suits and laundry. It was in this desperate winter that he bought the painting which might, or more probably might not, have been by Watteau. He boasted he had got it cheap, presumably from a refugee, "true booty of war."

He found a new home. In a street of old houses in the then-unfashionable quarter which lies along the right bank of the Seine between the Hôtel de Ville and the Marais, a line of shops is interrupted by a magnificently sculpted portal surmounted by a roaring lion and a heraldic cartouche. Behind it lies the exquisite baroque Hôtel de Chalons-Luxembourg. D'Annunzio wooed the leaseholders, a Madame Huard and her artist husband, by inviting them to dinner, and presenting them, at the end of the evening, with a pair of greyhounds, each dressed in a blue coat with red trimmings which d'Annunzio had had tailored for them by Hermès. The deal was agreed. D'Annunzio rented five high-ceilinged, wood-panelled rooms on the ground floor.

At once he set about "improving" the place. He removed all the Huards' antique furniture and filled the apartment with sofas and chaises longues piled high with cushions. He arranged his collection of oriental artefacts. He installed a lavatory in what Madame Huard (aghast, on reclaiming her home, to find how it had been altered) called a "black redoubt" lit by candelabra, and he hung enormous mirrors on the panelled walls. His rooms lay between a courtyard and a garden with a portico and statues. The nights were silent, the days full of birdsong. There were blackbirds in the garden: indoors d'Annunzio kept his canaries in lacquered and gilded Japanese cages. He reverted to his peacetime pastimes. An Italian visitor reported that he was "quite happy in an exquisite house," concocting perfumes and experimenting in glass-blowing. He developed his interest in the making of musical instruments (there was a clavichord and spinet in the salon) and was overjoyed to find that the wood-panelled salon had a perfect acoustic. There he listened to hired musicians play Frescobaldi and Couperin. He wrote: "Ivy covers the walls. The silence is interrupted only by the bells of churches and neighbouring convents." The man who, in the first weeks of war, had been out on the streets by day and night, unable to bear solitude, now retreated. "It is like being in a small cathedral city in a distant province. When I go out I 'go to Paris' as though to Hell."

In January 1915 central Italy was shaken by an earthquake. In Rome the British ambassador saw chandeliers swinging. On the other side of the peninsula, in the Abruzzi, the tremor's violence was devastating: 29,000 people were killed. The town of Avezzano was totally destroyed, L'Aquila partially so. (The latter would be rebuilt in the 1920s, becoming one of the most complete examples of fascist architecture and town planning, only to be flattened again by the earthquake of 2009.) The earthquake aroused in d'Annunzio neither concern for his family nor pity for his fellow Abruzzesi. Instead he appropriated the natural disaster as a parable supportive of his newly synthesised mythology. He suggested that the earth, impatient for Italy's entry into the war, and the feast of human blood and bone on which it could subsequently gorge itself, had claimed "a preliminary sacrifice." "It drags us back, it reclaims our flesh and our breath . . . it bends over us with voracious love."

Negotiations between Austria and Italy continued, the former being ready to offer generous territorial concessions in exchange for the latter's continued neutrality. Giolitti, ever reasonable, argued that Italy might thus gain more advantage than from fighting, however victoriously (he was right). Such thinking was anathema to d'Annunzio. He was not interested in "advantage." He quoted his own line from *More Than Love*, "the fit place for a coin is between the jaws of a corpse."

On 12 February, d'Annunzio took part in a conference on "the defence of Latin civilisation." In the grand amphitheatre of the Sorbonne, before an audience of 3,000 people, an actress read his *Ode to the Latin Resurrection*. D'Annunzio, who should have been on the platform with her, arrived late, and slipped into a seat on the benches. (Antongini, whose job it frequently was to get him to the right place at the right time, has droll stories to tell about d'Annunzio's aversion to conforming to someone else's timetable.) The next day, though, he was present, ready for his turn to take the stage. His speech was his usual blend of erudite references (Pallas Athena, Delphi, François Rude's sculptures on the Arc de Triomphe), self-congratulation and calls to arms. He assured his audience that Italy would soon enter the conflict (an assurance that was grounded solely in wishful thinking). He prophesied an "heroic spring." His Sorbonne speech was widely published in the French press: in Italy, Albertini dared to compromise the *Corriere*'s neutralist stance by reprinting it. D'Annunzio was becoming, in absentia, the spokesman for the Italian interventionist party. The Queen Mother wrote him a letter of congratulation and encouragement which he proudly displayed.

There were an increasing number of Italians who thought like him. For a civilisation to become "fecund," wrote Luigi Federzoni, "hatred is no less necessary than love." Federzoni was one of the nationalists who drew on the ideas of Charles Maurras and Action Française, and who argued that Italy, expanding demographically, was a "young nation," like Germany, and therefore must fight to enlarge its place in the world. In 1910, at the first Nationalist Congress, Enrico Corradini said: "Let nationalism arouse in Italy the will to a victorious war." That war's aims were immaterial. The Nationalist Association initially agitated for Italy to observe the terms of the Triple Alliance and enter the war alongside the Central Powers, but by the beginning of 1915 they were with d'Annunzio in urging Italy to fight on the other side.

Syndicalists agreed. It was Georges Sorel's belief that a "great foreign war" could put new vim into the sluggard bourgeoisie, and either trigger proletarian violence—"real" and "revolutionary" and therefore preferable to the dullness of peace—or open the way for a seizure of power by "men with the will to govern," men who combined the attributes of the condottieri, the warlords for hire who rampaged through mediaeval Italy, with those of a messiah. Giovanni Papini and Giuseppe Prezzolini, co-editors of *La Voce*, wrote in 1914: "While the mean-spirited democrats cry out against war as against the barbarous onset of ferocious deaths, we see it as the greatest awakener of the enfeebled, and a rapid and heroic way to power and wealth."

In November 1914 the war party received a new recruit. In August of that year, Benito Mussolini, as a good internationalist vociferously opposed to imperialist wars, had argued vehemently for Italy's neutrality. A flag, he said, was "a rag to be planted on a dunghill," and he declared that the *Patria*, like God, was "a spook . . . vindictive, cruel and tyrannical." But a man can change his mind. In November, Mussolini wrote: "Those who win will have a history . . . If Italy is absent she will be the land of the dead, the land of the cowards." He was immediately expelled from the Socialist Party, whereupon he started a new paper, *Il Popolo d'Italia*, funded by French and Italian industrialists, and began to campaign vigorously for intervention. "Mussolini is a futurist!" wrote Marinetti approvingly, adducing as evidence "his lightning-swift conversion to the necessity and virtue of war."

Another who believed in that "necessity and virtue" was one Ettore Cozzani, editor of a nationalist/interventionist journal, *L'Eroica*. In March 1915, Cozzani wrote d'Annunzio a most flattering letter, addressing him as "Maestro." He invited d'Annunzio to contribute a piece to a forthcoming issue on "all that is noblest and greatest about Italy." He also mentioned a monument to Garibaldi on which a sculptor friend of his was working, soon to be unveiled at Quarto. D'Annunzio put the letter aside unanswered.

His financial affairs in Italy had finally, thanks to Albertini's good management and help from other friends and well-wishers, been settled. It was time to go home, but characteristically, he was finding it hard to make a decisive move. In the first weeks of the war, as the Germans swept towards Paris, his mother wrote to him imploring him to return. He replied that he could not leave France in its time of "tragedy."

In November 1914 the municipality of Pescara had invited him to attend a ceremony in his honour: a plaque was to be fixed to the "hermitage" where he and Barbara had passed their summer together. This was too petty an occasion for the return of the hero. He refused, saying: "You know what I await before returning. All my wishes hasten the great day." When friends pressed him to grace his stricken homeland with his presence after the earthquake he told them: "Not now. I will come for the war." In February he declined to attend the premiere of Ildebrando Pizzetti's musical version of his *Fedra* at La Scala. "My return should be reserved for a higher purpose." He wanted to storm back into his homeland, harbinger and herald of the sublime conflict. Only a "Roman javelin" could free him, he said, a javelin "stained with blood."

He was in danger of becoming entrapped in his own rhetoric. But then came another letter from the obliging Cozzani, this one enclosing photographs of the Garibaldi monument, with its d'Annunzian imagery of heroes resurrected to fight anew in a patriotic cause. D'Annunzio liked the pictures. He was conferring now with Peppino Garibaldi about the return to Italy of the Garibaldi Legion. At last he read Cozzani's letter, with its invitation to speak at the ceremony at Quarto. It was a grey morning, the sky over Paris ashen, but all his twenty-two canaries, scenting spring, were singing their hearts out. He would return to Italy. From now on he would "create not with words, but with human lives." His life as a hero was about to begin.

In the next few days, as though in a valedictory splurge on the pleasures of civilian life, d'Annunzio bought a prodigious number of cravats, and a painting that he thought (erroneously) was a Rembrandt. He composed four sonnets "On an image of France crucified." The image in question, reproduced alongside the poems in *Le Figaro*, was a painting by Romaine Brooks, showing a uniformed Red Cross nurse. The model was Ida Rubinstein. The three androgynous "brothers"— Brookes, Rubinstein and d'Annunzio—brought together by art and polysexual desire, were now united in the glorification of war.

On Maundy Thursday, Fly, who had been lame and ailing for some weeks, became too weak to stand. In the evening d'Annunzio took her to the vet and stayed with her, her dainty head cradled between his knees, until the following dawn. On 4 May 1915, he took the train to Italy, and to war.

· III ·

WAR and PEACE

War

A YEAR AFTER HE RETURNED to Italy d'Annunzio was lying supine, his bandaged head lower than his feet, in a blacked-out room in Venice. He was blind.

On 16 January 1916 the plane in which he was flying had been hit by anti-aircraft fire. D'Annunzio was violently thrown about, his head smashing against the machine gun mounted in front of him. One of his eyes was irreparably damaged: he would never see through it again. He was told that if he was ever to recover the use of his other one he would have to remain absolutely still for months on end.

He saw nothing real, but hallucinations flickered behind his closed eyelids—deserts shimmering with mirages, monsters carved into walls of rock. For weeks on end he lay, he tells us, with his elbows pressed to his sides, as though the darkness were the nailed planks of a coffin enclosing him. He was as rigid as the basalt carving of an Egyptian scribe he used to admire in the Louvre (sightless, he had memories of three decades of sightseeing to draw on for his visual imagery). But all the same—because he too was a scribe—he was writing.

His knees were slightly raised, to support a board which served as a desk. Using the smallest gestures and the least pressure possible (his head must not move), he wrote in pencil on tiny slips of paper, one line to a slip, guiding himself by feeling the edge of the paper with a thumb and finger. Aélis was with him, and so was his twenty-two-year-old daughter Renata. When she was his little "Cicciuzza" he had doted on Renata, but he hadn't seen her for years, and he had not been reliable in paying her school bills: when Duse once gave him money for the purpose he had spent it on a horse, and Renata had had to work as a pupil-teacher in order to complete her education. When she arrived in Venice he initially arranged for her to stay in the Danieli Hotel, an unwarrantable extravagance, but he didn't want her inhibiting his erotic adventures. Now that he was helpless, though, she was living with him as his nurse and amanuensis. Groping in the darkness, she gathered up the paper slips, carried them into the adjacent room, collated and copied them. The text thus produced would form the nucleus of d'Annunzio's post-war memoir *Notturno*, the most emotionally direct and formally original of his prose works, the one for which Ernest Hemingway admitted one had to honour him, despite his being, in Hemingway's opinion, such a "jerk."

He was living in the Casetta Rossa, a miniature palace on the Grand Canal, taken for a peppercorn rent in October 1915 from his friend Fritz von Hohenlohe. Austria might seem to d'Annunzio a vulture vomiting human flesh, but he had no compunction about accepting favours from an Austrian prince. He took on Hohenlohe's staff, including a gondolier pleasingly named Dante. He planted a pomegranate tree (his emblem) in the garden, but, marvellous to relate, he left the house's décor untouched. Hohenlohe and his mistress were collectors of eighteenth-century French furniture and ornaments. In their house, d'Annunzio's base for the remainder of the war, the walls were hung with pearly pale silk or flower-patterned painted panels. The mantelpieces and side tables were crowded with porcelain figurines and little patch boxes in gold, silver or enamel. A collection of eighteenth-century purses—embroidered, beaded, filigree-clasped—hung on one wall. A small painting by Guardi, an iridescent waterscape, on another. In the dining room, mirrors in rococo frames multiplied the shimmering reflections of the canal outside. Hanging in the hallway were a tricorne hat, a crimson cloak and a domino, as though an eighteenth-century masquerader had stepped out of one of the prints by Pietro Longhi (there were several in the house) and come to call. D'Annunzio made only one substitution. Hohenlohe's gilded spinet was removed to make way for a proper piano. At all times, and most especially in his blindness, d'Annunzio had to have music.

Over and over again d'Annunzio set out from this "doll's house" (as he called it) to go to war. In it he faced the possibility of having lost his sight, recovered the use of one eye and then set out again, defying his doctors' warnings, to risk losing it once more. He was a war hero, but he was also still an aesthete and a voluptuary. His public life coexisted with a private one with which it often seemed to have as little relation as the tesserae of a mosaic viewed too close to see the overall design. Soon after he had participated in the deadly fighting along the River Isonzo, he was writing to Antongini in Paris asking him to buy and send him some high-heeled slippers in gold brocade (he liked his women to wear high heels in the bedroom). Repeatedly he took off on flights during which, passing through anti-aircraft fire, he flew further than had previously been considered possible, returning to Venice, as he explained to his publisher, "to take a bath" and to dine out in one of the city's great palaces.

Here are some of the tesserae—the themes and episodes—that made up that wartime life.

In the last days of May 1915, while he waited in Rome for instructions as to where he was to serve, d'Annunzio made an excursion with his friend Guglielmo Marconi to see the radio station at Centocelle airfield. A couple of years earlier, in Paris, he had found himself staying in the Hôtel Meurice with Marconi as a fellow guest. There was a problem with the electricity. D'Annunzio quipped that he was untroubled—after all he had a world famous inventor to fix his lightbulbs for him. Now, in Italy and in wartime, his friend was no longer someone to joke about, but the "magician of space" who had slung a radio-telegraphic net around the world. Now he and Marconi were wearing their country's uniform and their creations—d'Annunzio's poetry, Marconi's radio—would soon be employed as instruments of war.

They travelled by car, as befitted two men of the future, but each of them wore a sabre, as befitted heroes of the past. They drove through a landscape dotted with ancient tombs, to an airfield full of spanking new machinery. Surrounded by the ruins of antiquity, they talked of things the future had yet to bring forth: about television—Marconi was already experimenting with the transmission of images; about radar— he was searching for ways of using radio waves to "see" underwater. Arrived, they listened to the rat-a-tat of the telegraph transmitting messages from France, Italy, Russia, America, and one, most startlingly, from enemy Austria. Marconi stroked the metal shell of the transmitter as an enchanter might lightly touch an animal he had placed under a spell. Both men held their sabres awkwardly to avoid trailing them along the floor. Old/new, novelty/antiquity, a recurrent theme of d'Annunzio's thought was to be given full expression in this war, where humans were slaughtered, for the most part, by efficient modern industrial methods, but where, on the mountainous Italian Front, soldiers rolled rocks down enemy lines—killing their fellow humans in the way Neanderthals must have done.

It was a blustery day, d'Annunzio recalled later, and "the whirling wind, lifting the ash from the sepulchres, transformed it into the seeds of the future."

Within thirty-six hours of arriving in Venice in July 1915, d'Annunzio was on board the *Impavido* (Fearless), flagship of a flotilla of torpedo boats, sailing under cover of darkness into the waters off the Austrian-held Istrian port of Pola. The fleet, based on Venice, was commanded by Umberto Cagni, the Polar explorer (he of the self-amputated fingers) whose exploits d'Annunzio had celebrated in one of his *Laudi*. Ever since his first arrival in Venice, as a shipwrecked dilettante yachtsman rescued by a warship, the poet had been a friend to and advocate for the Italian navy. Now he was made welcome by naval officers and allowed to accompany manoeuvres. On 12 August he was in a submarine when it submerged, sinking to the sea bed thirteen metres down. On 18 August, on what he would afterwards describe as one of the most beautiful nights of his life, he was with the *Impavido* again, when it was one of six ships sent to loose sixty torpedoes on the enemy's base in Monfalcone, east of Trieste.

He was an observer, the literary equivalent of the war artists the British sent to the battlefields in France. His notes demonstrate the quality of his attention. He has seen barges laden with the poison-yellow sulphur crystals (used in the manufacture of explosives) passing towards the Venetian Arsenal. Now he notes that the new moon burns yellow in the sky like a fistful of sulphur, and that the officer shielding a flashlight with his hand while reading the chart seems to have a fistful of sulphur too.

He is wearing light shoes, easy to slip off should the ship sink. He notices that the sailors' lifejackets are already inflated. The mate orders that biscuits and dried meat be placed in the lifeboats. "Death is here . . . it is as beautiful as life, intoxicating, full of promise, transfigurative." An officer treats his fellows to champagne. "It could be the last glass," thinks d'Annunzio.

They steam eastwards. The vessel is cramped. "To pass from the bow to stern involves stepping over a recumbent sailor, knocking one's shins against the casing of a torpedo, pressing oneself against a burning-hot funnel." Everyone is silent. All lights and cigarettes have been extinguished. As they approach their target (and the enemy's guns) the minutes seem to lengthen into hours. Searchlights cross in the sky like white swords. "We could be discovered at any moment. The coast is barely a mile off. Always the funnels are our despair; they make too much smoke, too many sparks." At last comes the order to fire. The enormous torpedoes slink down their tubes. At once the ships wheel. Relief. Hot coffee which tastes ambrosial. Cigarettes. Then comes a radio signal. There are two enemy submarines lurking near their homeward route. "And once again we fill our lungs, breathing in peril and death, in the first shivering of the dawn."

D'Annunzio's wartime notebooks are full of physical detail: the glint of a nail in a soldier's boot sole as he kneels to pray; the grain of the wood—as diverse as the markings of animals' pelts—in the rough trestles on which the wounded are laid out. But when he came to work these notes up into fine prose for publication, he surrounded these sharp particular facts with a glittering miasma of past glory. The deadly weaponry was modern but the men who operated it were from a timeless tradition. One sailor is "a true companion of Ulysses." An officer issues orders in the same Tuscan accent as that in which a great Renaissance sea lord would have spoken. Another man, a Sicilian, might have been an Arab from the thirteenth-century Palermitan court of the Emperor Frederick II. D'Annunzio was always looking for historical analogies, but in these war-writings the practice is more than just a stylistic quirk. In likening these young servicemen to mythical heroes or the great men of Italy's golden age he is imposing a new meaning on the war.

During the war years, d'Annunzio went often to the garden of the Palazzo Contarini dal Zaffo. In the north of Venice, in what is even now a secluded district of tall dilapidated palaces and dead-ends, the garden extends down to the water on two sides, overlooking the lagoon. It was a place where he could be alone, unpestered by admirers. He was by this time not only a celebrity but a hero, and liable to be mobbed in the streets. The words "I am recognised, alas ..." recur in his diaries. He dreamt wishfully that his public persona was like a colourless cloak, which he could take off and fold up. He dreamt again that he was hanging it from a nail on the wall.

The garden's architecture was formal. Brick walls, battered by time and the salty air, surrounded it. Pergolas supported on ancient columns and draped with wisteria traversed it. There were flights of steps, a wrought-iron screen overlooking the lagoon, a gazebo at the centre, paths paved in red and white and edged with hedges as low and fine-clipped as garlands. "We passed through a sequence of adjoining rooms, rooms of box, of hornbeam, of myrtle, of laurel, of honeysuckle." He would bring his pilot and beloved friend Miraglia here after some of their most hair-raising flights, to meditate and to allow the adrenalin to subside.

Miraglia was the first of the young comrades-in-arms whom d'Annunzio, during the war years, was to befriend, to idealise and eventually to mourn. His relationships with these young men were emotionally intense. He himself freely used the word "love" to describe his feelings for them. He appreciated their beauty; he revered their courage; he basked in their admiration. They were sons more satisfactory than the ones he had actually fathered, fellow warriors who renewed his youth by accepting his friendship, sacrificial victims whose bodies he could cast into the flames of war.

At the northern end of the Contarini garden, steps lead down to a wrought-iron grille which affords a view across the Lagoon to the cemetery island of San Michele. There d'Annunzio and Miraglia used to sit, the latter in a blue cloud of cigarette smoke. On one occasion a woman (perhaps Miraglia's mistress, perhaps one of d'Annunzio's) was with them, coyly asking them to compare her beauty with that of a water lily in the marble basin. On another Miraglia, who had learnt from d'Annunzio to appreciate the "poetry of the extreme Orient" and whom d'Annunzio repeatedly describes as looking like a bronze Buddha or a *bonze* (a Buddhist monk), composed an approximation of a haiku as he watched a white butterfly settling on the rusty screen. "Its wings still flutter/Already it has landed." A few months later, when Miraglia was buried on the island of San Michele, d'Annunzio would reflect that the lines might have made a fitting epitaph for him, but that the memory of his subtle smile had been darkened by the "severity of his fate." Gardens and butterflies, Japanese verse and subtle smiles were all very well as private pleasures, but for the duration of the war, rigor and severity would be the key notes of d'Annunzio's public utterances.

Venice was in peril. D'Annunzio went one night to a scruffy little *pensione* frequented by artists and intellectuals who had volunteered to act as air-raid wardens, protecting the marvellous city. There the composer Gian Francesco Malipiero was playing the music to which he had set d'Annunzio's play *Sogno d'un Tramonto d'Autunno* (Dream of an Autumn Sunset). One of the audience reports that "the room, which was horrible, and the piano, which was worse, upset the musician, who played badly," but d'Annunzio was gracious, and made a lifelong friend of Malipiero, a fellow enthusiast for early music in general and Monteverdi in particular.

Before he left Italy in 1910, d'Annunzio had been calling upon his government to form an air force. Slowly they did so. In Libya in 1911 planes were used, initially for reconnaissance and then in actual combat. Marinetti, who was there, wrote of one of the pilots: "Higher, more handsome than the sun, Captain Piazza soared, his bold, sharp-edged face chiselled by the wind, his little moustache crazy with will." In Libya the first ever aerial bomb was dropped on Turkish troops. Marinetti waxes ferociously enthusiastic as he describes wings "slicing brutally" through the halo of the sunset and a pilot singing as he opens fire on the "torrential sea" of the enemy army. D'Annunzio celebrated Piazza in one of his *Songs* on the war.

From 1914 onwards, people all over Europe, dismayed by the horrors of modern mechanised war, fixed on the exploits of the pilots as evidence that one aspect at least of the ghastly conflict allowed scope for gallantry. D. H. Lawrence, watching a zeppelin over London, had apocalyptic visions of "light bursting in flashes to burn away the earth." This was terrible, but at least, unlike the wasteland of mud and decomposing body parts and trashed towns which was the Western Front, it was brilliant and grand. At high altitude, wrote d'Annunzio, "nothing mean or fearful can survive." The upper air was the domain of heroes, and a dashing show. Miraglia, in helping him to a starring role in it, had given him his heart's desire.

We have seen how the two of them overflew Trieste on 7 August 1915. On the twenty-fifth they flew to Grado, passing low over the waters near Monfalcone to drop a bouquet over the spot where the submarine *Jalea* had sunk, becoming a gigantic iron coffin to the dozens of men drowned in her. On 28 August they were over Trieste for the second time. On 20 September, this time with a different pilot, d'Annunzio took off from Asiago to drop leaflets over Trento, the Austrian enclave in the foothills of the Alps which was one of the territories Italians were most anxious to "redeem." In October he was in the sky above Gorizia, near to what is now the Slovenian border, which would be a battlefield throughout the war. These flights were bombing raids: they were also important for reconnaissance. At the outset of the war military commanders had sent observers scrambling to the top of church towers in a futile attempt to see the Austrians' mountain-top positions. D'Annunzio and his fellow aviators were able to bring back far better information.

On each flight d'Annunzio made notes on the landscape beneath. "The shore is cut like a high-curved saddle." As he jotted down poetic similes there were bombs beneath his feet. Repeatedly he passed through anti-aircraft fire. On one occasion the damaged plane dropped 1,800 metres before the pilot recovered control. Risking death, he felt intensely alive. "The mocking wave at the enemy gunner; the indifference to the pain in the half-frozen right hand; the mad urge to sing." He had no desire to protect himself. "Life's value is that of a spear to be thrown." All that mattered was the next planned sortie, and that was "everything."

Back on the ground he frequently dined at Montin's, usually in company with assorted writers, artists, journalists—almost all of them in uniform now. He was particularly partial to the chef's zabaglione.

"One does not advertise ideas as though they were laxatives or toothpaste," said the Emperor Karl, last of the Hapsburg Emperors of Austria-Hungary—a mistaken opinion which was one of the contributory causes of his own downfall and the disintegration of an empire which had endured (in various forms) for a millennium. D'Annunzio knew better.

Advertising was a fast-growing cultural phenomenon of the early twentieth-century world and the most acute artists were already employing its techniques and questioning its strategies. In Paris, Braque and Picasso were incorporating adverts into their collages. In Trieste, when the war started, a language teacher named James Joyce was working on an immense novel based, like d'Annunzio's *Maia*, on Homeric epic, whose hero is a seller of small ads. D'Annunzio was well aware that the things of the mind—whether poems or political programmes—needed to be marketed every bit as energetically as material merchandise, and he had no compunction about employing all of advertising's tricks for the purpose. He used public readings to promote his poetry: he turned his political speeches into book-selling opportunities. When his *Life of Cola di Rienzo* was being published in Tom Antongini's journal, d'Annunzio, anxious about sales, had urged Antongini to pay more attention to publicity. "Why don't you '*hustle*' your review?" he asked. "Take an example from TOT." (TOT was a remedy for indigestion.)

Advertisers use the military word "campaign." D'Annunzio's war-making was real and deadly. But it was also a "campaign" in the advertisers' sense of the word. Flying, he was flyering. The conventional phrase "theatre of war" was one which he was sophisticated enough to take literally. His flight over Trieste was the first of a sequence of exploits—part performances, part acts of derring-do—with which d'Annunzio demonstrated how close acting (as in staging a show) is to action (as in violence). He knew that winning sympathy was as important as winning redoubts, that small-scale acts of terrorism could have a bigger effect than massed attacks, and that an army fights not only on its stomach but on its convictions.

Dropping pamphlets over Trieste he was applying a double strategy of menace and cajolement which he would employ repeatedly. The text was an attempt at persuasion. The act of dropping it (and so demonstrating how easy it would have been to bomb the city) was a threat. As his pilot Miraglia banked and turned, d'Annunzio looked down at the grandiose white stone buildings around the waterfront piazza and inwardly vowed: "We shall not harm them" (he was still the conservationist), but the implied meaning of his "action" was, precisely, that harm them he might.

Around dawn on 19 September 1915, the day before his flight over Trento, d'Annunzio dreamt he was in a plane crash, and that his thigh was sliced open from hip to knee, laying open the muscles, veins and tendons.

He had listed the things he needed to take with him. The usual aviator's leathers and fur-lined boots, plus woollen dressing gown, woollen pyjamas, woollen underclothes and socks—d'Annunzio was the human

salamander and he was going to spend the night in a military base in the mountains where adequate heating could not be relied upon. Dressing case with soap and so forth, clothes brush, beard brush (he no longer needed a brush for the hair on his head), shoe-cleaning kit, jars of face powder. Now that he was constantly in the public eye appearances mattered and he kept them up assiduously. Ugo Ojetti confirms that when addressing the troops he did so "powdered and perfumed." He had redeemed Duse's two immense emeralds from the London bank to which he had pawned them, and wore them always in rings on his right hand, and a fellow officer was amused to notice how his shiny high-heeled boots twinkled as he clambered into a plane. His enemies seized on the unmanly care he took over his grooming. An Austrian wartime cartoon shows him as a raddled woman in a gauzy negligee, powdering his nose at a dressing table laden with cosmetics.

His son Gabriellino and the captain of the *Impavido*, by now a close friend, accompanied him in the motorboat to Mestre (Venice's mainland port) where his car and driver awaited him. He was driven along the Brenta Canal, passing the gardens and villas he had explored with Duse and described in *Fire*, and he felt a wave of nostalgia for the richness of peacetime life. In Vicenza he stopped to go shopping. (Had something been left off the list?) He was recognised and a crowd gathered to cheer him as he proceeded on his way.

The road wound up into the mountains, the long motor car negotiating the precipitous bends with difficulty. At Asiago, d'Annunzio was received by officers and escorted to the airfield in an alpine meadow, where he tried out the plane waiting for him. Tiny, a flimsy frame held together by steel cords and covered only with canvas, it pleased him. He would have nothing in front of him but the machine gun. He fired a few test rounds. He had brought pamphlets attached to little sandbags, and red, white and green streamers. He and Beltramo, his new pilot, talked seriously about how to avoid getting the streamers tangled in the propellers, or in the steel rods of the plane's armature. He noticed the tiny mauve flowers growing in the closely mown grass.

That night, dining in the mess, he proposed a toast to the assembled officers, asking them to receive him, not as a speaker, but as a soldier on active service. Nonetheless, at great length and with unmistakable pleasure in his own fluency, he spoke.

The following afternoon, after hours of waiting on the weather, he took his seat in the plane. Cameras were clicking and snapping. Everything d'Annunzio did provided useful images for propaganda, and thrilling stories for the press. Photographers were as essential to these exercises as the pilots and mechanics were. He and Beltramo flew up through cloud, and then into a head wind. On the peaks beneath them pointed rocks stood like the columns of primitive temples, or Nibelungen castles. Passing the notebook back over his shoulder to the pilot, d'Annunzio had—unusually for him—a moment of vertigo, feeling how easily the book, and by extension the plane and its occupants, might drop into the abyss.

Safely back on land, having reached Trento and dropped his pamphlets, d'Annunzio addressed the officers at the airfield again. More words, and with many more to follow. The next day he spoke to engineers constructing trenches. Three days later he delivered a harangue to the survivors of a battle in which over a thousand men had been killed. In

October he was speaking again, this time at a Mass attended by the royal Duke of Aosta. His major speeches were carefully prepared, and published afterwards in the *Corriere della Sera* and subsequently all over Italy. Others, toasts proposed to his fellow officers, addresses to crowds who gathered round his car—were delivered *ex tempore*.

The themes were constant. Combatants were heroes (and so, depending on his audience, were sappers or mechanics). They were martyrs. They were as noble and constant as the heroes of classical mythology or the legions of ancient Rome. They would never retreat or surrender. Their blood would drench the disputed ground. They owed it to their dead comrades to fight on until all "Greater Italy" was liberated. The dead would haunt them forever if they proved unworthy. They would fight to the death, and so would he. "This we swear, this we will do, for the holy spirit of our dead."

He flattered and cajoled. He shamed and inspired. His speeches were incantatory, designed to work, not on their hearers' intellect, but on their emotions. "Soldiers of Italy, gunners of a great destiny, today begins your heroic symphony, the tremendous symphony of victory and of glory." If the war was a symphony, his orations, too, were musical compositions full of virtuoso displays and insistent refrains. Words toll through them like leitmotifs—words like blood, dead, glory, love, pain, sacred, victory, Italy, fire—and again blood, dead, Italy, blood, dead, blood. They build slowly, in great hypnotic swells of language, wave after wave of charged rhetoric succeeding each other, crest after crest of rousing calls, culminating at last in great crashing climaxes of acclamation—d'Annunzio's acclamation of his hearers' supposed "heroism," their acclamation of his hero status.

Italy's opponent was its neighbour and "hereditary enemy," the Austro-Hungarian Empire which had, within living memory, ruled over much of the Italian peninsula. (Italy's declaration of war against Germany didn't come until August 1916.) For most Italians the Great War was, first and foremost, a war of Italian liberation.

The Hapsburg army was manned by the Empire's subject peoples. Many of the troops whom the Italians faced were Slovenes, Croats, Serbs and Bosnians, the people who, after the war's end, would form the state of Yugoslavia. The line of battle ran all the way along the border for some 600 kilometres from the Swiss frontier down to the

Adriatic coast west of Trieste. Inland the Italians were fighting in the mountainous region to the south of the Alps which the Austrians called the Tyrol and Italians Trento, or the Alto Adige. In the mountains the peaks were snowbound even in August. Soldiers were given inadequate boots. The first consignments had cardboard uppers and wooden soles: frostbite was almost unavoidable. Before they even came under fire, men lost their feet. At the southern end of the line the disputed territory included the coastal plane of Friuli, cut by rivers which flood in winter, forming—turn by turn—useful lines of defence or insuperable obstacles.

The major battlefield was the Carso (now Karst), a limestone upland stretching inland from Trieste, eastward into Slovenia and northward towards the Alps. Deeply eroded, it is riddled with fissures and caverns, its upper surface pitted, its lower layers such a baffling complex of sharp

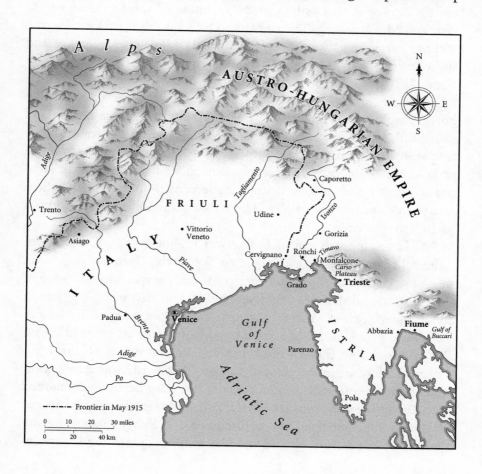

rock and deep holes that it has been likened to a petrified sponge. Water drains through it in underground rivers, which d'Annunzio repeatedly used rhetorically. The Carso, he said, was "greedy for blood."

There is no constant water supply on the plateau, but there are floods which fill the potholes with liquid mud. A griddle in summer, where men were blinded by the glare off the rock and parched by the lack of spring water, in winter it became a treacherous three-dimensional maze of snowdrifts and crevasses and red mud. Swept by a wind ferocious enough to have its own name, the Bora, the Carso is an inhospitable terrain for any purpose. For trench warfare it is hellish. Unable to dig, troops hacked shallow grooves in the rock or sheltered behind loosely constructed dry-stone walls, often no more than knee height. A bursting shell filled the air with shards of broken rock.

All along the line the Italians were attacking, nearly all the time, uphill, on slopes that only a properly equipped mountaineer would now consider climbing. They advanced by scrambling up forty-degree inclines carrying packs that weighed thirty kilos, often slipping and slithering back down twenty or thirty metres of desperately hard-won slope. This war was horrific both in its primitivism and its modernity. D'Annunzio, in his *Francesca da Rimini*, had dwelt with relish on the horrid machinery of mediaeval warfare. Now men were killing and being killed with implements that were equally crude, equally grotesque. Blades mounted on iron wheels, spiked maces, fireballs made of resin and bitumen. Newer technology added to the horror. Isolated peaks were mined and blown to smithereens. Poison gas left whole companies dead in their holes. The Italians scrambled upward into a hailstorm of grenades.

The landscape was infernal. The war fought in it was made even more murderous by human stupidity. When the Germans dug in on the Western Front, Lord Kitchener confessed he was baffled. None of the conventional theories could help him: "This isn't war." The Italian commander-in-chief, General Cadorna, was faced with an even more intractable problem. His Austrian opponents had also adopted defensive positions, but theirs were on the peaks and ridges of mountain ranges. Cadorna simply ignored the problem, ordering attack after attack against entrenched mountain-top positions defended by barbed wire. Discipline was rigorous. On freezing nights men were tied up and left outside for minor breaches of discipline. "Ordinary soldiers," wrote a conscript condemned to six months' imprisonment for complaining about conditions, "were treated worse than beasts." In the opening months of the war officers led from the front, brandishing useless swords: only in January 1916 did an order go out permitting them to bring up the rear, as Austrian officers did, with revolvers at the ready to shoot deserters. The men advanced in close order, presenting the Austrian machine guns with a conveniently easy target. "It looked," said an Austrian officer, of one of their advances, "like an attempt at mass suicide."

Once d'Annunzio began to spend days on end in the battle lines he needed a forward base, and rented rooms in a house in the garrison town of Cervignano. His landlord was an ornithologist, and the rooms were cluttered with stuffed aquatic birds. D'Annunzio disliked them and, according to Tom Antongini, bought eighteen screens over six feet high. "Through a cleverly contrived arrangement the birds disappeared from his sight, but he was only able to reach his bed by devious paths through a sort of labyrinth." In this eccentric billet he lived well. He had brought with him forty damask cushions and a terracotta figure of Melpomene, the tragic muse. Every morning he enjoyed what he described to Miraglia as a "tribute paid by my hosts to the Maestro"—a lavish breakfast of milk fresh from the cow, thick cream, jam, marzipan and the finger-shaped little cakes known as *savoiardi*.

War hadn't cured him of his profligacy. He was still sending money to Nathalie at Dame Rose for herself and the dogs (at least twenty-four of them still surviving) and maintaining, for no good reason, his household at Arcachon, as well as the Casetta Rossa and his rooms in Cervignano. Albertini paid him handsomely for anything he wrote, but he would "sing" if he felt moved to, not for sordid mercenary motives. "If I must earn my daily bread singing, then I renounce my bread."

There are certain days of d'Annunzio's war which he recorded in detail, so that we can know not only what he was doing, hour by hour, but also the fluctuations of his mood and the eddying of his thought. One such day was Sunday, 17 October 1915, the day preceding the beginning of a major Italian offensive along the River Isonzo.

A priest was to celebrate mass for a brigade encamped near Cervignano, and d'Annunzio drove out to attend, his motor car cutting through the long files of troops on the road like a ship's prow slicing through water. The soldiers were drawn up in formal ranks, bayonets fixed, in the slanting October sun. A crude altar—a table covered with badly holed wool blankets of the kind in which the men wrapped themselves to sleep—had been set up beneath a row of yellowing poplar trees whose leaves trembled continuously.

A general shouted an order, the soldiers knelt, leaning on their rifles as they dropped to their knees. There were crows cawing in the trees and insects circling. A young officer kneeling next to d'Annunzio murmured "excuse me," captured a wasp that was about to sting his neck, and showed it to him smiling. He contemplated the soldiers tenderly. Some of them were as beautiful as classical statuary. Kneeling, they showed the soles of their boots, a part of them as intimate and usually secret as the warm damp crannies of groin and armpit and knee that he loved in his mistresses. When they stood at the end of the service their knees were earthy. But, for all his awareness of their physical particularity, d'Annunzio still valued them primarily as matter to be sacrificed. As they dispersed across the meadow he saw them as "a mass . . . a torrent" of "flesh ready for the shambles."

The Duke of Aosta was present. Tall and handsome, an infinitely more impressive figure than his cousin the King, the duke was a vociferous nationalist and an effective commander: d'Annunzio respected him. After the service they talked briefly about aeroplanes. Afterwards d'Annunzio was driven up to the duke's observation post on a nearby crest. An enemy aircraft was circling overhead, trailed by anti-aircraft fire. D'Annunzio, who knew, as few others did, the view from the sky, told an officer he should cover the glass windows: their glint would be easily visible from above. He was taken down into a redoubt. With surreal incongruity the wood-panelled walls of the bunker were being decorated with painted garlands of flowers. The painter, an admirer of d'Annunzio's writing, asked the poet to propose some mottoes to complete the design.

Back in Cervignano, d'Annunzio lunched with his old friend Ugo Ojetti (soon to be appointed head of the military command's press department). They ate fresh sea bass. Then he took out his horse, named Doberdò after one of the unredeemed regions, and set off in search of open country. He followed a stream away from the road, away from the smoke and dust and din of trucks and troops and ambulances, along a bank lined with willows. The October afternoon light on the dying leaves was gold on gold. D'Annunzio, like Keats before him, imagined autumn personified. For him it was a portrait by Palma il Vecchio, "something feminine and docile." Arriving at a secluded meadow curtained by rows of poplars he put his horse into a gallop.

He was melancholy but calm. He thought he might die the following day and the thought left him undisturbed. "It is time to die: *tempus moriendi*." The Latin tag (from the Book of Ecclesiastes) was one which had recurred throughout his work.

He went back to his apartment, read with some irritation a letter from Nathalie, and then took a bath. This was an elaborate ritual. His manservant rubbed him down with a horse-hair glove and scrubbed his back with hard brushes. He was still in the *"tub"* (his English) when the pilot Beltramo tapped on his window. He thought "perhaps he has come to offer me an heroic death."

Spruce and scented once more, he joined the pilot on a bench outside the door. Beltramo told him that he had just spent an hour of "ferocious voluptuousness" with a Red Cross nurse. "What," thought d'Annunzio, as he thought frequently, "would I not give to be twenty-seven years old!" Then, getting down to serious matters, they discussed flights. The offensive would begin the following morning. Two days later they would fly over the enemy lines, to reconnoitre and to do what they could to protect the troops on the ground. "He offers me peril, as one offers a flower." They talked a little longer, about their dream of flying over Vienna (it would be nearly another three years before d'Annunzio achieved it) and about Beltramo's girl. All the time d'Annunzio was appraising his companion's appearance—his white teeth and dark curly hair, his suppleness, but also his gloves, which were too tight ("he has no real elegance") and thinking that in a day or two they might each be reduced to a handful of charred meat.

Beltramo left and d'Annunzio was at a loose end. It was evening, but he didn't want to dine in the mess. "I could perhaps rape the servant," he thought, watching the stocky girl empty his bath tub in the garden. Beltramo's boasting must have aroused him sexually, but it was just a passing thought. (This is one of several fleeting suggestions in d'Annunzio's private writings that he liked the idea of forcing himself on working-class women.) Instead he strolled out along the road, barely able in the black-out to see the river running alongside it. There were passers-by: a line of cavalry on foot, each man leading his horse; a lorry with its headlights dimmed by blue gel; a prisoner in rags, driven along the verge by a mounted lancer. Finally came a brigade of infantry singing, going up towards the front. D'Annunzio stepped into their ranks

334 · GABRIELE D'ANNUNZIO

and walked with them, unnoticed in the darkness. An elbow nudged him, a rifle butt bumped against his hip, he could feel heavy breath on his cheek. He was, momentarily, intensely aware of these soldiers' physical reality. "They weighed on me as though I was carrying them, as though I personally was taking them to their death."

The following day over 1,300 Italian guns opened fire along a fifty-kilometre front, shaking the earth as far away as Zagreb. The ensuing fighting, over mountainous terrain and in continuous rain, was ferocious and inconclusive. The trenches became "quagmires of filth." In one brigade two-thirds of the men were killed. By the time snowfall put a stop to the fighting seventeen days later, 67,000 Italian soldiers had died to gain a strip of land about a hundred metres across.

On the first day of the offensive d'Annunzio was on the island of Morosina, at the mouth of the River Isonzo, where a company of sailors, whose ship had been sunk, manned a battery. He picked his way over planks laid across the mud, and climbed a wooden lookout tower "like a pagoda." He admired the view of the castle at Duino, where he had passed "delicious days" in the "time of idleness." (The castle's chatelaine, Rainer Maria Rilke's patroness, Princess Marie von Thurn und Taxis, was sister to his landlord.) When he arrived at dawn he heard larks singing. Then the Duke of Aosta's order of the day blared out of megaphones all along the line, the din of the artillery began, and "little by little even the air became metal."

D'Annunzio stayed on the island all day, while all around him men were being wounded or killed. Seconds after he had moved away from a position, a shell exploded there. He was gathering instances of heroism, and jotting down in his notebook the phrases in which he would celebrate it. He followed the wounded to the dressing station. The boardwalks were splashed with blood. He found an Abruzzese with terrible abdominal wounds. The man was naked but for his ragged shirt. His exposed genitals moved d'Annunzio, so vulnerable did they seem. D'Annunzio knelt in the mud beside him. Years later he would still be haunted by the way the man, in his agony, flexed his bare feet spasmodically, poking them into d'Annunzio's thigh. An officer, so chopped about by shrapnel he seemed almost shapeless, was agitated because he could not hear his battery firing. "He begged to return there, and wept with bitterness and promised to be better, and he didn't know himself to be sublime."

Always a devoted sick-room nurse, D'Annunzio stayed with the wounded, soothing them and telling them that they were heroes. On the drive back to Cervignano that evening, their blood was still beneath his fingernails. The poplars along the roadside, "like the arches of a cathedral," induced a feeling of hushed solemnity. He thought of Titian, of his mother, and of angels. The fact that he himself had escaped death by a matter of seconds hadn't shaken him. "The incomparable music of the divine war" was sounding through his mind.

Over the next two weeks d'Annunzio was repeatedly on the front line. Around him he saw the mountains thick with gun emplacements spouting fire, like volcanoes, or wreathed in smoke, as though in the aftermath of an eruption. He stood in a church-tower-turned-observation post, hearing bullets thwack into the walls near him, as he trained his binoculars on a hillside and watched soldiers running up it, their bayonets glittering like water, while enemy machine guns drilled into them with the stabbing efficiency of a sewing machine.

Three times he and Beltramo flew over the battle zone. He was using his machine gun to fire on the Austrian troops, but he doesn't mention any killing in his notebook, although he does recall looking down through his binoculars and seeing soldiers, limp and helpless as discarded rags, tossed into the air by an exploding shell. Instead he dwells on the marvellous effects of the light.

Repeatedly he addressed the troops. He talked at mass funerals. He harangued soldiers who had fought all day and must fight again the next day. He talked of banners flaring in the wind over Italy, of rivers full of corpses, of the earth's terrible thirst for blood. He flattered the soldiers in terms they might not have recognised, but which fired them nonetheless. Dante had imagined no such tortures: the Carso was an inferno beyond all inferni. "You chewed poison, you bit on flame, you wept black blood." Mazzini, instigator and rhetorician of the Risorgimento, had devised an oath whereby all those joining Young Italy must swear loyalty "in the name of all the martyrs of the holy Italian cause." Now, applying the same kind of emotional pressure, d'Annunzio insisted that the living owed it to the dead to fight to the uttermost. He declared the dead were crying out from beneath the earth: "Forward! Forward!" He said that they would never rest easy until all the unredeemed territories of Greater Italy had been redeemed.

In his notebooks there is a constant fluctuation between the appall-

ing and the pastoral. Sun on the grass. Birdsong. "Dry leaves fall delicately, like a love letter dropped furtively at the feet of the beloved."
Other witnesses record the foul stench of the battle lines. Many men
found it almost impossible to eat, so nauseating was the atmosphere
in which they lived. Corpses lay unburied. Many units neglected to
construct latrines, and even if they did so the conscripts, untrained
and terrified of snipers, failed to use them, defecating wherever it felt
comparatively safe to do so. Soon, as a volunteer from Trieste records,
the hillsides were covered with human excrement. D'Annunzio says
nothing of this. Instead he records the light of the setting sun filling a
forward base in a hollow in the Carso with a purple glory, making the
shells in their wooden crates glow, turning bits of broken bottle-glass
to emeralds.

In 1921, when the war was safely over, d'Annunzio described what
was actually happening in that rocky dell where the glass sparkled so
brightly. The Italian artillery, firing from behind the advancing soldiers, had misjudged the range. Sheltered for once from enemy fire, the
soldiers in the hollow had been hit by their own guns. Soon a heap of
mangled corpses lay to one side of the space. To the other the captain
was addressing the survivors. The guns were still firing; a lieutenant
was sobbing. D'Annunzio, in as much danger as the rest of them, was
observing as intently as ever—the soldiers' socks and shirts hanging on
a washing line, the row of mess tins and worn cooking pots, the way
the captain's voice trembled, the fact that he wore too many rings. But,
for once shocked out of his usual cool acceptance of mass death, he was
imagining the dead dragging their entrails and slithering towards him.
"I heard it, as you hear the advance of a company crawling flat between
rocks and bushes." The captain fumed and cursed, then suddenly col-
lapsed and rolled, convulsing hysterically, down into the bottom of the
hollow.

D'Annunzio did not choose to pass on scenes like this to his wartime readers. He saw for himself how muddled and disgusting war
really was, but he continued to preach his faith in its purifying virtue, to tell the troops that they were superhuman. "I see them scaling
the mountain crests, alone with the flash of steel and the gaze of the
fatherland . . . They are like the teeth of the ferocious rock. They bite
eternity."

Ernest Hemingway, who worked as a volunteer in the Italian ambu-
lance service in the last year of the war, wrote afterwards in *A Farewell*

to Arms: "I was always embarrassed by the words sacred, glorious, and sacrifice and the expression in vain . . . I had seen nothing sacred, and the things that were glorious had no glory and the sacrifices were like the stockyards at Chicago if nothing was done with the meat except to bury it. There were many words that you could not stand to hear." The narrator of Hemingway's novel hears those words, "standing in the rain almost out of earshot, so that only the shouted words came through." D'Annunzio was foremost among those doing the shouting.

By 6 November the battle was over, and d'Annunzio was back in Venice. He went to visit Admiral Thaon di Revel to discuss his plan to fly over Zara (now Zadar) on the Dalmatian coast—an 800-kilometre round trip in one day, a phenomenal distance for aircraft at that time. Thaon di Revel was enthusiastic and promised to have torpedo boats in the area in support.

The following day d'Annunzio called on Miraglia, recovering after four days in bed with gastric flu. The two friends walked back to the Casetta Rossa to smoke cigarettes (d'Annunzio had taken up smoking while at the front, preferring the smell of tobacco to that of his fellow men). They looked at maps and pictures of Zara, and fantasised about aerial battles. They talked about "warrior chastity" and about "contempt for women" (d'Annunzio sometimes calls Miraglia "the misogynist").

D'Annunzio proposed a shopping trip. They went to Alinari, supplier of photographic reproductions of works of art, and he chose pictures to paste up on the screens in his rooms in Cervignano: a selection of warriors—Carpaccio's St. George, Donatello's great bronze statue of the condottiero Gattamelata—and of sculpted lions (the symbol of Venice). For Miraglia he bought an image of the Marciana Leda, the relief of which he would have a plaster copy in his bedroom in the Vittoriale. They moved on to a curio shop, where d'Annunzio was tempted by some glass, but finally allowed himself "to be seduced by a little red morocco binding." The book was an eighteenth-century edition of the *Dubious Loves and Luxurious Sonnets* of the Renaissance pornographer Aretino. D'Annunzio was delighted. "It's a poisonous little book, disgustingly obscene. And the morocco is so lovely!" He bought it, and carried it off discreetly concealed.

Miraglia left—to meet a woman, d'Annunzio supposed, because he stopped to buy a box of bonbons (so perhaps his praise of "warrior chastity" was as hypocritical as d'Annunzio's own). D'Annunzio went home and had supper with his son Gabriellino and Tom Antongini. They were interrupted by a group of friends, with whom d'Annunzio had recently shared a "droll Casanovan adventure." A woman he refers to as his "little friend" Melitta sat down next to him, surreptitiously nudging his leg with hers, despite the fact that her jealous husband was present. Afterward he escorted Melitta and two other ladies to the end of the alley. She rubbed herself against him like a cat, and murmured that she would come back tomorrow when her husband was on guard duty. "I see with terror a dangerous new adventure beginning," wrote d'Annunzio afterwards. Celebrity that he was, he was often now, in his erotic adventures, the trophy rather than the hunter.

That night he slept fitfully. His mind was busy. The "Ode on the Serbian Nation" which he would shortly deliver to the *Corriere della Sera* pulsed through it in "lyrical waves." He had been reading his new Aretino and was troubled by "voluptuous visions."

The following day he woke depressed. His morning went by in tiresome business related to "the eternal source of trouble: vile money." An art dealer came round, hoping to sell him some chalk drawings attributed to Watteau. (D'Annunzio, a famous big-spender, was a target for the dealers of Venice.) He was irritable, bored; he thought longingly of shells and shrapnel.

In the afternoon he wrote more letters, then prepared for Melitta's arrival. White roses, perfumed lozenges smouldering in a censer, fine linen handkerchiefs drenched in more perfume tucked under the cushions. He thought about her pubic hair, which was even redder than the hair on her head. A bath, a massage, a fine silk shirt. But when Melitta arrived, looking like a big brown velvety moth in her fur coat, it turned out that all these preparations had been a waste of time. She was mistaken. Her husband was not on duty. He was waiting for her. She was so sorry.

D'Annunzio was angry, but also icily indifferent. He realised he didn't care for her at all. It was just annoying to have taken so much trouble over futile scene-setting. Miraglia's view of sex, as of a nine-minute phenomenon not worth troubling oneself about, came to his mind. Melitta begged him to walk her back along the narrow dark alleyway. He agreed, but coldly. As they went along he had a vision of her not as the graceful twenty-five-year-old she really was, but as an ancient crone dressed in spider webs, with long claw-like nails, leading him by the hand to a well in the middle of a secluded little square, in which he would see Nothingness. Sensing his alienation Melitta started to whine.

"Don't you want to see me again?"

"No."

"Haven't you ever had a married woman before? Don't you understand what it means to be married?"

She was irritating, but she was still elegant, and her red hair smelt of verbena. Suddenly he wanted very much to have her right there, leaning up against the damp wall of the alley, but someone with a lantern was coming towards them and Melitta hurried away. D'Annunzio walked home, sadistic lines from his new ode running through his head.

He had three male friends to dinner. They talked about planes and bombs and new weaponry. D'Annunzio was exhausted (had he caught Miraglia's virus?) and contributed little. He slumped in his armchair, too inert even to move his leg when the fire began to scorch it. When the others left he went to bed but the cries from the lookouts on the *altane* repeatedly woke him. At midnight he got up again to write.

His sour mood translated into a furious verse-polemic. Within a week he had sent off an ode to the *Corriere della Sera* containing a vicious personal attack on the Emperor Franz Joseph, whom he described as putrescent, with slavering mouth, worms crawling through his nostrils and revolting slime dripping from his brow. In addressing the troops he never alluded to the gross physical facts of death, but what he had seen at the front made its way into his invective. The censor cut fifty lines.

On 21 December, the year's midnight, Giuseppe Miraglia was killed. At the time d'Annunzio was posing for Romaine Brooks, who had followed him to Venice and was painting his portrait, this time as military hero, uniformed and resolute, clutching a distinctly phallic baton. On the previous day he had gone to the airbase at Sant'Andrea taking his suitcases and a bag of flyers ready to be dropped, hoping that he and Miraglia would take off the following morning for the long-planned aerial sortie over Zara. But the weather was wild: the expedition was postponed for two days. D'Annunzio stayed and lunched in the mess. Miraglia had shown him a talisman, saying he would take it up in the plane for good luck. The conversation became general as all the assembled officers told stories about fetishes and charms (their lives depended, almost every day, on luck—no wonder it was a preoccupation for them). They talked about explosives: several of them were engineers. They discussed the "psyche" (a modish word) of the Chinese and Japanese. The company of these young men, a well-educated elite who shared his nationalism and taste for risk, was delightful to d'Annunzio. As they talked he watched a black cat eating from a bowl beneath a couch, its tail switching with pleasure "as cats' tails do when they are in love." After lunch he parted from Miraglia, inviting him for supper the next day.

That night he took Renata out to dinner, along with two young officers. After he had escorted her back to the Danieli, he walked home past the church of Santa Maria del Giglio, whose seventeenth-century façade is decorated with reliefs depicting some of Venice's Dalmatian colonies, and touched, as he always did (it was one of his superstitious rituals) the comical little depiction of a walled town: his target, Zara. He was awake much of the night, falling asleep after dawn, and he came down near midday on the twenty-first to find that Renata (as profligate a buyer of flowers as her father) had arranged red roses, violets, carnations and narcissi to make a gala of their supper party. After breakfast he went to Brooks's studio on the Zattere. Renata followed him there with the dreadful news. Miraglia had gone up on a test flight. The lookouts had seen his plane drop into the sea.

Over the next three days d'Annunzio kept watch over his friend's corpse. He returned home only to sleep briefly before taking up his post again. This vigil left him physically and emotionally exhausted. He was beside himself with grief. But to one like d'Annunzio, who called it "a beautiful fate" to be killed young, it was perfectly possible to love someone, while finding a satisfying consummation in his death.

He described the ordeal in writing three times. D'Annunzio's syntax in his intimate memoirs is stark, his expressions of emotion terse. He writes about the chill in the dismal chapel of rest. He mentions the transgressive intimacy of touching Miraglia's dead legs, cold and solid, as he lays flowers alongside them. He describes the way his own teeth chatter as four soldiers lift the corpse into the coffin. He records the sense of a further, more absolute loss as the lead casket is soldered shut. He describes not only the visiting dignitaries and the masses of flowers (in his opinion only Renata's white roses and his own enormous wreath—so big it takes two strapping sailors to carry it—escape vulgarity), but also the man with a mop wiping the blood from the tiled floor. He has not lost his taste for obscure, high-sounding verbiage: "The man in a coffin encompasses the horizon, is the ring of the universe." But he is also very clear about what death entails. He records with grim exactitude the way, as the second and third day pass, the body becomes blotched and begins to smell.

A few days later, d'Annunzio asked another pilot to undertake the flight to Zara with him. The man replied: "With a single motor. In an unreliable contraption. Around nine hours of flying. We would certainly fall, and land on the sea. One cannot count on being picked up by a torpedo boat." He firmly believed, he concluded, that there was no chance whatsoever of success, but if he was ordered to attempt the flight he would, as a good soldier, obey. D'Annunzio was disappointed. With Miraglia gone, "I feel that never again will I find my equal in the love of risk," he wrote. The expedition to Zara was, for the time being, abandoned.

That wartime mid-winter, Venice was even more melancholy, more haunted by spirits of dead revellers, than ever. D'Annunzio, from the little garden in front of the Casetta Rossa, looked almost directly across the Grand Canal at the shuttered house of his friend Luisa Casati, setting for so many extravagant parties, now as silent as an abandoned palace in a fairy tale. There were no longer white peacocks screeching in the garden, only seagulls flying back and forth, back and forth, "like large pale supple hands repeatedly rearranging a pearly veil."

Soon after Miraglia's death he escorted Renata, one foggy evening, through the blacked-out alleys back to the Danieli. "We chewed on fog," he noted. People passing seemed insubstantial. The bridges were identifiable only by the rims of white stone edging the steps. "Dream city, other-worldly city, city bathed by Lethe or Avernus." St. Mark's Square was as full of opalescent mist as a pool is full of water. Returning home alone, d'Annunzio was amazed to be overtaken by a family talking at a normal pitch of ordinary things. They passed and became shadows. The eerie silence resumed.

Entering the narrow alleys which led past Miraglia's lodgings and on towards the Casetta Rossa, he became conscious of someone walking beside him, silently, as though in bare feet, and with an extra silence about him "as though there was neither voice nor breath in him." D'Annunzio didn't believe in ghosts, exactly, but he dreaded seeing one. He slowed: the other, grey all over, walked ahead. His stature, his shape, his gait, were all Miraglia's. D'Annunzio's heart fluttered. Skeins of mist wound themselves about him. He hurried to keep up with the other. "Beneath the house where, in the evenings there was always a piano playing, beneath the house where there was an antique shop, he suddenly vanished." There was no exit from the narrow alley, no canal to fall into, no doorway in which to hide. Silence. And then, in the distance, the bellowing of a group of drunks.

On 27 December 1915, d'Annunzio had a visitor, an archaeologist now working in the commissariat. He had been in the Alps near Trento, distributing white winter uniforms to men living virtually without shelter. That winter was one of the coldest on record: five metres of snow had fallen in the first half of the month. On the Carso, he reported, things were even worse. The men were required to stand for days on end up to their knees in foul water. "Three days, he says, are enough to finish off even a tough man."

From the contemplation of these horrors, the conversation shifted. The visitor told d'Annunzio a story about their mutual friend Miraglia, about how once, when flying alone at sunrise, the pilot had folded his arms, leaving his plane to coast unguided while he sang, words and music flowing spontaneously from him. The war afforded both horror and joy, the one somehow enabling the other. To d'Annunzio, Miraglia's dawn song recalled St. Francis's canticles, his great *Praise of Life*.

Later in the war W. B. Yeats wrote his famous poem about an Irish airman, driven to volunteer not by any sense of patriotic duty but by a "lonely impulse of delight':

> I balanced all, brought all to mind,
> The years to come seemed waste of breath,
> A waste of breath the years behind
> In balance with this life, this death.

D'Annunzio wasn't alone in thinking it was death's constant imminence which gave lustre to "life"—the quasi-religious ecstasy of the lone pilot singing to the rising sun.

· · ·

D'Annunzio was still seeing the red-haired Melitta, his "frenetic little friend." One misty evening in early January he agreed, without enthusiasm, to wait for her in a gondola. The water was low and Venice smelt rotten. He had been reading Kipling, and Casati's half-built palace reminded him this time of a ruined temple in a jungle. He didn't like the gondola's little cabin. Cushions, rugs and perfumes could have made it charming, he thought, but as it was it was like a third-class coffin.

Melitta arrived. She had told him she would come "without pantaloons" and she was as good as her word. Beneath her fur coat she wore only stockings and a man's woollen shirt, which she promptly removed, allowing her hair to fall down over her bare torso. She smelt—obligingly—of d'Annunzio's own Acqua Nuntia. Kissing; biting; "Hurt me! Hurt me!" The gondola rocked; d'Annunzio's knees ached. Melitta came twice, grinding her pretty teeth. D'Annunzio "was as though absent from what I was doing. I felt not pleasure but anger. I could barely refrain from violence." The water around them reeked, the tiny compartment was stuffy. Soon Melitta had to get back.

On the outbreak of war Rupert Brooke wrote that it provided men like him with an escape from "all the little emptiness of love." Walking home that night through alleys full of distorted shadows and echoing footsteps, d'Annunzio was left desolate by that "little emptiness." He yearned for Miraglia. "Why don't you console me. Why don't you take me away?" There was nothing dashing or romantic about such adventures: he was allowing himself to be used as a sexual toy by a woman half his age whom he didn't much like. Everything around him seemed slimy and foul-smelling. He thought of the white roses he had put in Miraglia's coffin and wondered whether they, and his friend's flesh, were already putrefying. He wanted to be back at the front, or dead.

On 15 January 1916, d'Annunzio went up in a trial flight of a new aircraft with Luigi Bologna, a pilot who had stood beside him, shuddering with grief, by Miraglia's corpse. The plane was sluggish: Bologna couldn't get it to rise high enough to be safe from artillery fire. Nonetheless, the following day, they went ahead with a planned raid on Grado. On the way there they were pursued by two Austrian planes and fired on from the ground. The aircraft was damaged. Bologna succeeded in bringing it down on the water, but he hadn't seen a submerged sandbank.

D'Annunzio was flung upwards by the force of the impact, then fell back, receiving the blow to the head which would blind him.

His vision was immediately affected, but he mentioned the fact to no one. Ojetti suggests that, "at his age, alongside his very young companion, he was ashamed to admit to being tired or in pain." They returned safely to the airbase but he insisted on taking off again, and carrying out the planned mission. He wrote that the flight back westward into the sunset that evening was "divine." The following day he was airborne once more.

He travelled to Milan and spoke at La Scala, the great opera house which holds over 2,000 people, describing what he had seen on the Isola Morosina during the autumn offensive in grandly sonorous sentences sharply contrasted with the pithy immediacy of his diaries. The speech was published in the *Corriere della Sera*. Two days later he was back in Venice speaking in the cemetery of San Michele for Miraglia's *trigesimo* (the Mass celebrated thirty days after a death) and mourning his friend as a second Icarus: his private mythology was proving neatly adaptable to wartime circumstances.

It wasn't until over a month after the accident that he finally sought help. On 21 February, he was due to fly in a three-man plane to Laibach (now Ljubljana), but was late arriving at the airfield. Another officer took his place, and was killed, along with the pilot, when the plane came under fire. The third man aboard succeeded in flying the damaged plane back to base (but was killed in his turn two years later). D'Annunzio had been keeping his eye trouble secret, in anticipation of the Laibach raid. Now he finally faced up to what was happening to him. His right eye saw only a purple cloud, his other very little. Looking in the mirror, all he could see of his face was a small part of his forehead. He reported to a doctor and was taken directly to a field hospital for those with injuries to their eyes.

Here everyone was blind. Soldiers turbanned with linen and gauze clustered around him murmuring timidly as he lay on a stretcher. The arrival of the hero had caused a stir in the hospital. One of the blind men, shaking his bandaged head, said softly, in a tone of reverence and amazement: "This is *that man*!" They didn't annoy d'Annunzio: he pitied them as they pitied him. One of his favourite mottoes, "I have that which I have given," sounded through his head. It had had other meanings for him. He had used it to describe kissing: the greater the pleasure given, the greater the pleasure received. But now he meant it piously—

he was happy in the greatness of his loss. Those blinded in action were generally accorded especial respect: they were the aristocrats among the wounded.

The doctor examining d'Annunzio told him that his right eye was damaged irreparably. To save the left eye he would have to remain absolutely still for a long time, perhaps months. D'Annunzio insisted, against all advice, on being driven back to Venice and there, cared for by his daughter, he took to his bed. While he lay in the dark, writing on his little strips of paper, the approaches to the Casetta Rossa were crowded with admirers come to leave tributes. Telegrams arrived from Prime Minister Salandra, from commander-in-chief Cadorna, from the Duke of Aosta. The Mayor of Venice called in person, and so did the senior naval and military officers in the region. Thousands of letters and tokens arrived from d'Annunzio's lesser admirers. At the front a soldier had told him that while anyone else was dispensable, he must at all costs be protected. "Because if you are killed, who will make another like you?"

Immobile on his sickbed, d'Annunzio repeatedly imagines himself buried. Sweating, dehydrated, his mouth tasting of iodine and steel, and filling with the tears streaming continually from his damaged eye, he struggles with claustrophobia. The darkness seems to press in on him like the walls of a sarcophagus.

He doesn't know whether he will ever see again. The blind woman in *The Dead City*, the one-eyed Malatestino of *Francesca da Rimini*, the whole family of blinded brothers in *The Ship*; with shuddering relish he has inflicted on these imaginary beings the fate he is now actually suffering. He doesn't know whether he is in his right mind. The drugs he is being given are powerful and disorientating. He is hallucinating almost continuously. The insane, too, have haunted his fiction: the gibbering mother of *The Virgins of the Rocks* and her sons, prey to creeping dementia. The writer in *The Innocent* who succumbs to a neural disease which leaves him paralysed and dribbling and, worst of all, aphasic. These images of madness return to d'Annunzio as he lies in the dark. He recalls his friend, a sculptor, who lost his reason, and seems to see him struggling up a steep and stony slope surrounded by devilish goats.

He composes a hymn to death. The dead beat their wings like wounded eagles, bloodying the light. He fantasises about his own end

346 · GABRIELE D'ANNUNZIO

as it would have been if only he had died rather than Miraglia. "The heroic pilot brings back to the fatherland the bloodless corpse of the sacrificed poet . . . All the shores of Italy ripple like the margins of his banner."

Waking dreams chase themselves through his head. He is driving into an abandoned village near the front. The houses are all ruined. The mountains, visible at the end of a row of shattered trees, are sapphire blue. A young soldier appears, chewing a piece of bread. D'Annunzio asks to see Colonel Barbieri (the man who was killed in his stead over Laibach). The soldier leaves, and returns with a bundled up leather jacket streaked with blood.

Another dream. He is at the airfield from which he should have flown, inspecting the damaged plane. It is covered with blood, still liquid and dripping. It is a miraculous liquefaction, like that of the saints' blood kept as relics in numerous Italian churches. D'Annunzio clambers into the plane. His hands are bloody as though he is receiving the stigmata. He sees the place where his neck should have rested as he sighted his targets. It is like an executioner's block.

He seems to have a butterfly trapped in his eyeball, its fluttering a torment to him. He sees something like a fern, obscuring his vision. Gradually the fern becomes a black spider squatting on his eye, blocking out the world.

Renata wipes his face, and murmurs an endearment. His daughter is acting as his mother. He feels himself the dead Christ of a Pietà.

Sightless, d'Annunzio is even more than usually sensitive to sound and scent. A dripping tap maddens him. The scent of hyacinths overpowers him. Music is consolation. He is listening to a Trio by Beethoven, whom he describes as "Flemish." This is not the time for professing an admiration for a German composer. The music moves him to tears.

These recitals are frequent. D'Annunzio has what he calls his "Wartime Quintet," peacetime musicians now turned soldiers and stationed at the gun batteries on the Lido. Their commanding officers are lenient in granting them time off to soothe the wounded hero. With one in particular, a cellist, d'Annunzio likes to discuss the manufacture of fine instruments. He dwells on the piquancy of a man's working half the day with heavy guns, instruments of destruction, and half the day with an equally cumbersome but fragile contraption designed only to create beauty. While he lies in the dark, the musicians play in the next room, their audience of one (plus Renata and occasional privileged guests) is invisible to them, as they are to him.

The pianist Giorgio Levi comes to play Frescobaldi for him. D'Annunzio's taste is catholic. He loves, as he always has done, Renaissance and baroque music. But since his sojourn in Paris he is interested too in modern experimental work. He listens to Debussy and to Scriabin.

Like Scriabin, and like Baudelaire before them, d'Annunzio is interested in correspondences between different sensory pleasures. At the Capponcina he used to scent his rooms with perfumes appropriate to the music he was listening to. Scriabin drew up a table of equivalences between musical notes and the colours he thought had affinities with them. As d'Annunzio listens blindly, the coloration of his visions changes periodically. The world he sees behind his closed eyelids is suffused with violet and purple. He sees a forest of amethyst trees. Flocks of birds swoop between them and perch on their branches. Now everything turns yellow, and all the birds are suddenly canaries.

By day Venice is silent, as lifeless, thinks d'Annunzio, as Angkor Wat. But at night come the sirens and the thunder of anti-aircraft guns.

As spring began, soldiers picked flowers on the killing fields of the Carso, dried them and sent them to d'Annunzio. Peasant women from the Abruzzi posted him packets of medicinal herbs and jars of ointment. Magical objects—talismans hallowed in some cases by a priest, in others by sorcery—accumulated in his dainty house with its décor dating from the age of enlightenment.

Fruit, sweets and other delicacies arrived in such quantities that d'Annunzio arranged for the surplus to be taken to the military hospital and given to the wounded. When his generosity became known, as it quickly did, even more gifts began to arrive.

On 2 April, by which time d'Annunzio had been laid up for five weeks, two of his young aviator friends came to visit him. On the following day they were to test a new aircraft that one of them, Luigi Bresciani, had designed himself. It would have a longer range than any currently in use. With d'Annunzio they talked excitedly about where they might go in it, what Austrian bases they could bomb. Bresciani was pale and slight, with long side-whiskers and thin lips. D'Annunzio thought he looked "like a little English officer of the time of Horatio Nelson." Nelson, small, one-eyed, valiant, was someone about whom d'Annunzio liked to think.

Bresciani's plane failed, and dropped into the sea. Both men were killed. Bresciani's body was brought back to Venice. The other, Robert Prunas, was drowned, his body lost. Afterwards, as d'Annunzio dozed and dreamed, it seemed to him that the coffins of Miraglia and Bresciani were close on either side of him, walling him in. At high water d'Annunzio would hear the boats in the canal beneath his window jostling and thudding against the steps. Now the insistent dull thump became Prunas's corpse, battering against the walls of his room as though begging to be taken in.

He wrote a poem, a variation on his favourite Icarus theme. Fifty winged youths have been confined to a quarry: the word d'Annunzio uses is an archaic one recalling the infamous quarries of ancient Syracuse where, according to Thucydides, prisoners taken during the Peloponnesian war were kept so tightly penned that the dead remained wedged upright among the living. D'Annunzio's imagined boys are unable to fly, their wings (not made of wax like Icarus's, but real and sentient) are painfully crushed—there is no space for them to be spread. The "enemy" appears, darkening the sky, wielding a great axe. He begins to lay about him, hacking off the beautiful tremulous wings. Blood spurts. Feathers are spoiled by gore, the boys are bleeding to death. As they drop, a space is cleared. One of them, stepping up on the mutilated bodies of his brothers, opens his wings, and flies up. "And all our eyes were full of sky,/As we lay supine on the feathers/And our race, unvanquished, took flight."

Mass slaughter clears the space from which the superman can soar. D'Annunzio mourned the flyers, his friends, but he did not regret their deaths.

At night comes the sound of male voices singing. Three barges tugged by a motor boat are passing up the Grand Canal, full of new recruits on their way to the front. D'Annunzio is moved. The boatloads of fruit that arrive at the Rialto market are beautiful, but this "cargo of the fatherland"—flesh to be sacrificed—is more beautiful still.

D'Annunzio is recovering. He sleeps better, and has happier dreams. His subconscious (a term fast gaining currency) is as literary as his

waking mind. He dreams he is in Scotland, or rather in the land of Walter Scott—his oneiric Scottish castle is a great deal better upholstered than the real thing would be. "Velvets in emerald green, straw-yellow, crimson, crow-black, and a dark green shot with gold." D'Annunzio is pleased by the sofas (such comfortable items of furniture are rare in Italy) and by the rosy-cheeked ladies and little spaniels as lovely as those painted by Gainsborough and Reynolds. He wakes back into reality with regret.

He is allowed to remove his bandage for short periods. He gets up and walks across the room for the first time. He holds his head back, and keeps it as steady as possible. He thinks of paintings of the martyr St. Lucy, regularly depicted carrying her gouged-out eyes on a platter.

Easter is come round again. A year ago d'Annunzio buried his dog on Good Friday. Now he invokes the Christian rituals of sacrifice and mourning in describing his own "Passion." The purple mist over his damaged eye is like the purple cloth which hides the altar during Passion Week. His confinement to bed has been like being nailed to a cross.

At last he is allowed to go outside. He insists on dressing in his uniform and notices with annoyance that the breeches, previously a perfect fit, pucker inelegantly around his shrunken knees. He wears a black silk bandage, a blackout against the daylight. Slowly, slowly. Down the stairs. Out into the garden. Instead of illusory flashes of amethyst and violet, he sees (through one carefully shaded eye) the real mauve of wisteria. He can take in the sweep of the Grand Canal, from the Palazzo Dario to the Salute. He is seeing again. Never one to balk at hubris, or at blasphemy, he makes the obvious connection. "It is Easter." (Actually it's the week after.) "It is the Resurrection."

While d'Annunzio lay in his imagined tomb, the slaughter on the Italian Front went on, men dying in their tens of thousands while the line barely shifted.

D'Annunzio's Easter rising was premature. Throughout the early summer of 1916 he was still convalescent, but able now to work, writing the autobiographical *Licenza* before the end of June. While he wrote, General Cadorna successfully resisted an attempt by Prime Minister Salandra to remove him from his command. Backed by the King, who was now spending more time in Cadorna's base in Udine than he was in Rome, and by the press, the general held on to power, and Salandra lost it. Italy's parliamentary democracy, never strong, was being catastrophically weakened by the war. People began to refer to Cadorna's headquarters as the "second government." Employing an ancient Roman title which had been revived and popularised by Garibaldi, his supporters called him *Il Duce*. The word means guide as well as commander, and it conveys profound respect.

In August, Cadorna launched a series of attacks, and succeeded in driving the Austrian army back beyond Gorizia, gaining control of the right bank of the River Isonzo and the western Carso. Over 150,000 men (two-thirds of them Italian) were killed in eleven days. A strip of land between four and six kilometres wide changed hands. Italian troops arriving at last on Monte San Michele, the hill over which the two armies had been fighting for a year, wandered dazed among the blackened boots, spent cartridges and empty knapsacks. One officer recorded his disgust at the maggots which seemed not only to infest the unburied bodies, but to sprout out of the ground, so numerous and revolting were they. For those on the spot victory felt bathetic, its cost grotesque; but d'Annunzio, still in his dainty floral-sprigged refuge, was jubilant. He celebrated what he called "the sacred days of Gorizia" with a poem:

> Swift as the wing that stoops in a streak,
> The first shout rang out from victory's peak.

D'Annunzio was awarded another silver medal for valour. The presentation was made before assembled crowds in St. Mark's Square by the naval commander-in-chief. D'Annunzio, appearing in public for the first time since his crash, was heavily bandaged, but fit enough to make a stirring speech.

Temporarily out of action, he could still put his image to use. Romaine Brooks completed the portrait for which he had been sitting when he heard of Miraglia's death. Convalescent, he sat for another one, by Ercole Sibellato, showing him as the wounded champion, with bent head and bandaged eye. He saw to it that a lithograph of Sibellato's picture was made, and that hundreds of copies were distributed. He wrote to Antongini: "I perform the function of a mascot."

He was called upon to endorse the newfangled "war bread." Proper bread was virtually unobtainable. Now d'Annunzio declared the almost uneatable ersatz version the "bread of communion where the entire fatherland lives transubstantiated." His vocabulary and syntax were becoming ever more liturgical. When America at last entered the war it was d'Annunzio who took it upon himself to welcome the new allies with an article syndicated all over the United States. "You were an enormous dull mass of wealth and power. And now behold how you have been transfigured into ardent, active spirit." (Members of the "dull mass" were tolerant of being so described: d'Annunzio was a popular contributor to Hearst's publications, his articles being telegraphed to Paris, where Antongini, whose English was passable, translated them and telegraphed them on.)

He was receiving visitors. Ojetti came and d'Annunzio received him "like a king." His French friends, Susanne Boulanger and Madame Hubin, came in May. (Following page, with Aélis on left.) He escorted them around his favourite places in Venice. Maurice Barrès arrived.

D'Annunzio entertained him to a *soirée musicale à la Française*, ordering his quartet to play Franck, Ravel and Scriabin. "He is true to his nature," wrote Barrès afterwards, still "immersing himself in an atmosphere of the precious and the rare."

On 13 September 1916, against medical advice, d'Annunzio flew again. Bologna was his pilot. Their plane was one of a squadron of bombers making a raid on Parenzo. D'Annunzio, his head still heavily bandaged, had four bombs tucked into the cockpit alongside his legs. The doctors had warned him that the fluctuating pressure at high altitude could blind him permanently and completely. As the plane rose, he alternately checked his eyesight, and released a smoke signal designed to help the squadron keep together. The notes passed between him and Bologna (Bologna's in italic here) have survived:

2,200?
I can see.
2,600?
I can see, I can see.
3,000?
I can still see—climb, climb.
3,400?

I can see. Climb.
We're coming down to 1,600.
Over the piazza. All four ready to hand.

They were right above the batteries. Bologna ducked and weaved between the trajectories of the shells. D'Annunzio pulled the pins from the bombs and lobbed them over the side.

Returned to base, d'Annunzio was helped from the cockpit by a crowd of young aviators who carried him shoulder high, celebrating his "rebirth."

D'Annunzio dropped pamphlets, but he also dropped bombs. The machine gun that had blinded him was there so that he could kill people with it. He never mentions it, either in his public speeches or his private writings, but he must have been responsible for many deaths.

Kafka, watching aeroplanes fly at Brescia in 1909, wrote afterward of a troubling thought that had come to him: that to the pilots in the air, the great crowd of people of which he had been part must have melted into the plain, so that the people of which it was composed were no more human-seeming to the pilot than the guideposts or signalling masts. Though Kafka didn't pursue the idea further, its psychological implications are clear. To the eye of the pilot—literally an *Übermensch*, an "above-person"—cities are no more than geometrical arrangements, and human beings mere sludge.

Men fighting on the ground could not escape from what was being done to them, and the more imaginative could hardly avoid making the small shift which allowed them to comprehend what they in turn were doing to their enemies. For the aviators it was different. The physical danger they faced was extreme, but they weren't driven mad, as so many soldiers were, by the horror of mutual slaughter. Far enough up to be spared the sights and smells of battle, they never needed to know how many people they killed or mutilated, how many homes they destroyed. In the cleanliness of the upper air they could, like Miraglia, fly singing, pitiless and guiltless, in the sun.

An aesthete's night out. D'Annunzio wanted to try out a famous echo purportedly to be heard in the Sacca della Misericordia, the enclosed harbour on the northern edge of Venice. Taking with him his "wartime quintet" and a celebrated soprano, d'Annunzio visited the place by gondola. The narrow craft was crowded. The cellist remained standing, with his cello upright beside him. He had swathed the instrument in his cloak and playfully stuck his hat on top of it. In the gloaming it looked like a human being, or like a ghost.

As they circled the Sacca, the singer cleared her throat and sang an aria. Then the gondoliers ceased to row and as they drifted silently she began trying single notes, first high, then low, pausing after each to listen for a response. Nothing. A fleeting echo. Again nothing. It was a breathlessly still night, with no stars. The hulking *zattere*, floating wooden quays, reminded d'Annunzio of rafts crowded with the shipwrecked, or with quarantined plague victims.

They were about the leave when, abruptly they heard a sombre, distant bellowing. D'Annunzio raised his hand (just visible as a pale shape) to still the rowers. His companion were all grey in the almost-darkness, as spectre-like as the weird cello man in their midst. Someone said: "It's the guns on the Isonzo."

D'Annunzio had a new lover, Olga Brünner Levi. She was in her thirties, a talented singer and pianist whose husband had one of the finest private music libraries in Italy. The couple lived in the splendid sixteenth-century Palazzo Vidal, a short walk from the Casetta Rossa. D'Annunzio was often there, alone or bringing along his dinner companions with the easy licence of an intimate friend of the family. Olga's husband was complaisant. (Aélis, who was well informed about anything relating to her master's intimate affairs, believed that the marriage was unconsummated.) Soon d'Annunzio had given Olga new names—Balkis, after the legendary Queen of Sheba, Vidalità, after her house, and Venturina, after the gold-spangled brown Murano glass which reminded him of her eyes—and was writing her the first of over a thousand letters.

Olga was from Trieste. Her father and other relatives were cut off in the "unredeemed" city: she shared d'Annunzio's determination to see it annexed to Italy. They shared their politics, and their love of music. He called her "crazy little one," and adored the way she lisped over her "s's, but he wrote to her as to an equal and friend. His letters are full of riddles and coded jokes. He pours out his thoughts and feelings unself-

consciously, playfully tossing off obscene or satirical couplets, composing mock haiku and punning mottoes, all with an apparent confidence
in Olga's being able to follow his flow through Latin and Spanish, to
appreciate his humour, to catch his allusions and sympathise with his
sombre reflections on war and on Italy's future.

He enjoyed watching her take off her long black stockings, enjoyed
it so much that he seldom allowed her to finish. Stockings—newly on
show as hemlines rose to several inches above the ankle—were much
on his mind. There are a lot of mentions of them in his notebooks for
this period: the way they at once hide and reveal the skin, the way
downy hairs poke out through the weave, the way peeling them off
Olga's legs was like unsheathing a sword. Flying over Lake Garda he
thought that the promontory of Sirmione was like a brown silk stocking into which a woman had thrust her arm in order to turn it inside
out, an image which tells us more about his preoccupations than it does
about topography. He added one of Olga's stockings to the collection of
magical objects he took in his pockets when making a dangerous flight.

Olga permitted him plenty of pleasures. "Pentella has never been
so soft and hot and velvety as during those *four orgasms* [his empha-
sis] before Saturday lunch." No more furtive sore-kneed fumbling in
gondolas. She would come to his house and lie on his couch while he
sniffed and licked every part of her, dwelling especially on the shadowy
hollows of her body. His letters to her are full of sexual gusto. "Last
night the taste and smell of you drove me crazy. You smile, because
each time I say the same thing. But each time *you please me more.*" She
gave him a kitten, whose playfulness and little pink nose delighted him
in much the same way that his "brown tail-less Triestina" did.

To her he wrote long accounts of his exploits, but he preferred her
letters to be concerned exclusively with "Ordella, Muriella and Pentella" (her nipples and cunt). This was not one of the great loves of
d'Annunzio's life. But the tone of their correspondence suggests that
with Olga he enjoyed an uncomplicatedly happy affair, beginning without difficulty and ending without rancour. Olga was "the prize" of his
combat, he told her, "the rose" of his war.

Having established that he could still fly, he remained grounded for
months. His bandages made it hard to wear a helmet and goggles.
Instead of flying over the lines, he came to know them on foot. In

October and November 1916 he visited the battlegrounds over and over again, rising long before dawn to reach the observation posts before the troops' day had begun, picking his way along boardwalks blocked by corpses, hearing the wounded whimpering and crying out for their mothers, inhaling the odour of death.

He was present during the fighting on Mount Veliki and Mount Faiti. One-eyed, his balance was disturbed, his ability to judge distances poor. He stumbled over the pitted ground of the Carso. In trenches and tunnels he struggled to stay upright in his heavy nailed boots. Once on Faiti he fell and injured his leg so badly he was sent back to the dressing station, but insisted on returning to the front with a soldier to lead him by the hand. His sight, even in his still-functioning eye, was distorted. By day everything was veiled in a sickly yellow. By night whatever he looked at was ringed with light. He turned the annoyance into a symbol of glory. His comrades, he liked to say, were haloed.

At the front he was constantly in danger, and passed days on end in circumstances so wretched that he would normally have found them insupportable. He stood in trenches, knee-deep in "dysentery-coloured filth." He spent the night in foul-smelling caves, his only covering the standard grey-green uniform cloak, sleepless, listening to the scrabbling of rats and the moaning of the wounded. In the cramped dugouts and rocky hollows he was jostled ceaselessly by unwashed men. Worse, he was unwashed himself. "I have accustomed myself to the impossible: I go five days without a change of clothes, without so much as washing my face." He endured hunger and thirst and extreme cold. He lived in the din of bombardments, and he was happy.

An officer of the engineers was hit standing beside him. D'Annunzio helped bandage the man's leg. He went down on his hands and knees in the hole where a badly wounded man had hidden; the man whispered to him that he was his "disciple." He dreaded nothing except a loss of dignity. To be killed with his mouth full, he thought, would be horrible: to die in the "bestial act" of nourishing the "sad sack" that was his body. Otherwise he was fearless.

He travelled from battle line to cemetery, from field hospital to base in his new motor car, a grey Fiat 3Ter Torpedo, "as slim and pointed as a little torpedo boat," addressing men who may not have understood much of what he said, but who responded to the presence of the hero-poet with adulation.

The soldiers came from all over Italy. In his notebooks d'Annunzio specifies their regional origins. They are Sardinian, or Pugliese, or Tuscan or Sicilian. Each region had sent its tributary stream to the great torrent of sacrificial blood poured out on the harsh rocks of the Carso. In its army, Italy finally appeared to be one. Every foot soldier's face reminded d'Annunzio of some episode of the heroic past. Each exhausted teenage peasant could be likened to an intrepid Venetian mariner, to a Roman legionary, to a mediaeval knight, to a martial saint recreated by an Italian Renaissance master. His vision of Italy's glorious past overlaid the ghastly modern conflict like a theatrical gauze, lending a shimmering glamour to the excrement, the din and the heaps of dead boys.

Officers worried about his being taken prisoner, a tremendous propaganda coup for the other side, but he reassured them. He would never be taken alive. He had his little enamel vial of poison with him at all times. Everywhere he went he was recognised. An order of battle ended with the announcement: "The Great Poet of the New Italy is with us."

His notebooks record his serenity and exaltation. Stepping out of the cave in which he had spent the night he found himself in moonlight, and noted his "marvellous feeling." In the devastated landscapes of foul mud and trees shredded by shellfire he was on the lookout for beauty, noticing the flash of a green woodpecker at an observation post, the shimmer of a blue and silver dragonfly on a hillside where the infantry advanced on their stomachs, crawling past the dead. To him the shells, exploding with sounds like the striking of great bronze cymbals, seemed to signal a dance.

Looking up at the mountains around, he thought that the pinnacles of rock were like crosses made ready for the crucifixion of thousands upon thousands of Christ-like martyrs, the troops. The young men around him—wretched conscripts or callow young officers alike—were beautiful. He loved them. He rejoiced in the thought that they had been brought here, by him and those like him, so that they might all die.

By the end of 1916 he had been awarded his second silver medal. He cared about such things. A year earlier he had hinted to Albertini that the latter might, in his turn, hint to General Cadorna that the blue ribbon of a decoration would make a very pretty Christmas present for

Italy's bard. He pestered Antongini, still in Paris, to see what he could do about getting him a Croix de Guerre. He also asked Antongini to translate the citation for his Cross of the Military Order of Savoia for circulation to other nations who might wish (or be prevailed upon to wish) to decorate him, and for publication in *Le Figaro* and *Le Temps*. The motive for his medal-hunting was not pure vanity—to some of these honours a stipend was attached.

D'Annunzio was back in Venice in January 1917, in bed with a fever, when he received a message from the commander-in-chief, Cadorna himself, breaking the news of his mother's death.

D'Annunzio's last sight of Luisa in reality, when he visited Pescara in 1915, had been distressing. He hadn't seen her for the five years of his sojourn in France and he found her unrecognisable, "a poor, poor, bent, formless thing" who could barely see or hear or speak. When the peasant woman who cared for her had repeatedly told her that Gabriele was there she had lifted her hands and laid them on his head as he knelt before her. The hands were a dead weight. Afterwards he admitted he recoiled from the sight of her, but at the front he repeatedly claimed to have seen visions of her, strong and beautiful, and watching protectively over him. When he had moved away from a battery seconds before it was shelled he claimed afterwards that his mother had taken him by the hand and led him away from danger. Now he received sacks full of telegrams and letters of condolence, from unknown admirers and from powerful ministers of state.

He rose from his sickbed, and arrived in Pescara (as he had not done for his father) in time to be present at her funeral.

In May 1917 he began flying again, and in the same month he wrote a long and detailed letter to General Cadorna, laying out his vision of aerial warfare. Hundred-strong squadrons of Italian planes, he wrote, should be bombing the armaments factories of Germany. He had the technical knowledge to back up his suggestions. His proposals went into minute details about bombs and fuel capacity, instruments and wing structure. The Italian aeronautical industry, which had produced its first plane in 1911, was expanding prodigiously; by the end of the war it would provide employment to 100,000 people. D'Annunzio had made a friend and collaborator of Gianni Caproni, whose factory had produced the first Italian-made aircraft in 1911, and who was soon supplying bomber planes not only to the rapidly expanding Italian air force, but to the British and the French as well. Veniero, d'Annunzio's son, was working for Caproni as an engineer and test pilot and was a regular visitor to the Casetta Rossa. Conversations in the rococo-mirrored dining room were now as often about fuselages and fuel tanks as they were about poetry.

Cadorna was impressed. D'Annunzio was given command of a squadron of Caproni bombers. He was now not just a mascot, but an officer with wide responsibilities. When he bombed Pola in August 1917 he did so at the head of thirty-six planes, all of them under his command. He called his squadron the *Serenissima*, and designed insignia for their fuselages and mottoes for their proclamations. As their leader he was as glamorous and deadly as the condottieri he so much admired. Marcel Proust, watching an air raid over Paris, was enthralled by the gallantry of the aviators, who seemed to him like "human shooting stars" or Wagnerian Valkyrie. D'Annunzio, risking death repeatedly on his sky-high missions, had become one of those superhuman beings.

One after another his fellow aviators were killed. Luigi Bologna crashed into the lagoon not far from where Miraglia had died, and died in his turn. D'Annunzio, flying two missions a day during major offensives, was as vulnerable as any of them, protected only by his amulets. (He was now carrying a pocket-sized Roman terracotta phallus and Duse's emeralds for luck.) Flying over Pola he saw shells whizzing past his plane "like moles burrowing through the air." Over Mount Grappa guns were firing before, behind and to the sides of him. On one occasion he returned with his plane hit in sixteen places: on another there were twenty-seven bullet holes, including one in his wrist.

Returning from a reconnaissance flight one evening before the searchlights were lit, his pilot miscalculated his angle of descent and the plane crashed on the airstrip, but both men escaped unhurt. On another the pilot lost control of a plane while attempting take-off. Instead of becoming airborne it careered across the runway, crashing into the earthworks around the gun emplacements. The plane was loaded with bombs. The engineers were standing by, as they did for each take-off, ready to see off the aviators with a war cry. Instead they whimpered, and d'Annunzio saw that they had all turned away and hidden their heads in their hands, not wanting to watch the inevitable catastrophe. But somehow, amazingly, the bombs didn't explode: the plane didn't catch fire. D'Annunzio and his companion stepped insouciantly out of the wreck, brushing earth off their cheeks and clothes. The pilot was killed soon afterwards, but not d'Annunzio.

War brought him peace. To set out on a dangerous mission was, for him, to achieve "an ecstasy" he compared with that known by the great mystics. Leaning out from the prow of a plane he felt such joy it seemed to him it must overflow and fill the sky.

He was alternating his flights with exploits on the ground. In May 1917 he joined the fighting at the mouth of the Timavo, a short, deep river which flows into the sea west of Trieste, and which formed an important line of defence for first one side, then the other. D'Annunzio was attached as liaison officer to the romantically named brigade, the Tuscan Wolves. He had met the commanding officer Major Giovanni Randaccio, an admirer of his poetry and sharer of his nationalist fervour, during the fighting of the previous autumn. Then, in his order of the day, Randaccio told his troops: "You are all heroes!" D'Annunzio approved. Randaccio joined his pantheon of god-like young men. He called him the "soldier of soldiers," and wrote that to "make war with him was a sublime intoxication."

Now the two were reunited in a war-littered landscape—yellow-flowered meadows cluttered with hulking iron wreckage; marshes strewn with abandoned helmets and dead men. For two days and nights the "Wolves" fought their way towards the river. On the third day came the order to suspend operations. D'Annunzio was indignant. He had arrived bearing banners, including an enormous tricolour made for him by Olga, embroidered with the words "Beyond the Timavo." He drove to headquarters, demanded an appointment with the Duke of Aosta, and persuaded him to countermand the order. Then, having taken time off to revisit his apartment in Cervignano for a wash ("extraordinary voluptuousness"), he returned to the battle line.

The plan was that at midnight the men would cross the river—thirty metres wide, deep and in full spate—on a narrow pontoon bridge, then advance on the hill known as Quota 28, on which there was an Austrian battery. Having taken it, they would storm on to Duino. On both banks

of the river, and during the crossing, the men would be within range
of enemy guns. Randaccio was anxious. D'Annunzio "comforted" him.
It is not clear who had first come up with this reckless plan, but it was
certainly d'Annunzio who saw that it had to be carried out.

The bridge was made up of single planks about forty centimetres
wide, bobbing and bouncing on floating oil drums. The men had to
cross it in single file, in the dark. The planks wobbled and tilted. They
sank, so that men walked hip-deep in water, unable to see where to
place their feet. Beyond the river stretched two kilometres of marshes
providing no cover from the Austrian guns on the wooded hill. The
first men over managed to cross the marshes unnoticed and reach
Quota 28, occupying it briefly. But meanwhile Austrian gunners had
begun to fire on the bridge and the men assembled on both banks.
D'Annunzio records that the officers, by this time, had not eaten, nor
drunk clean water, for thirty-six hours. Neither had the men. Now, seeing what was being required of them, forty of the troops on the far side
of the river decided they had done enough. When their officers, yelling
and threatening them with revolvers, tried to keep them in position
they fired on them, shouting: "We don't want to be sent to the slaughter
again." Waving white handkerchiefs or tying strips torn off their shirts
or underwear to their bayonets, they surrendered, and allowed themselves to be taken prisoner.

The Italian troops on Quota 28 had been driven back, pursued by Austrians troops who were now closing on the bridge. Of the Italian troops
trapped on the far side some of those who had not surrendered managed to swim back across the river. D'Annunzio (who had not crossed)
helped pull them onto the bank. Randaccio was hit. D'Annunzio was
by him, pillowing his head on the useless banner. Randaccio could not
feel his legs. He was numb from the waist down. He was growing cold.
D'Annunzio followed him to the dressing station. As he was dying he
repeatedly asked d'Annunzio, "Have we held Quota 28?" and repeatedly d'Annunzio lied to him, telling him the hill was won because, he
explained afterwards: "The hero cannot but die victorious."

He had loved Randaccio living. He referred to the two of them as
a "couple," and he told Olga that Randaccio was his "peer"—the highest compliment he could pay any man. But as he had frequently fantasised about how lovely his women would be on their death-beds, so
now he made a cult of Randaccio dead. "He was intensely beautiful, as
though that same artist of the race, who had formed his flesh, had now

sculpted him in marble." He spoke at his funeral, his words competing with the din of an enemy bombardment, having covered his body
with the banner destined for Duino. The dead officer was to become
a key figure in d'Annunzio's mythology of war, as hero, martyr and
sacrificial victim. D'Annunzio's eulogy to him was published as a pamphlet distributed throughout the Third Army. The banner which had
pillowed his head and draped his coffin became one of the most used
props in d'Annunzio's political theatre—at once relic of the dead saint
and promise of future glory.

As Randaccio lay dying and the last of his troops retreated across the
Timavo, d'Annunzio ordered a battery to fire on those remaining, now
prisoners of the Austrians, on the other side. General Cadorna counted
any soldier who was taken captive as a deserter and issued a directive
instructing his officers that "deserters" were to be shot down, using
machine guns or artillery where necessary. To discourage its soldiers
from surrendering, the Italian government, alone among the combat-
ant nations, refused to send aid parcels to its soldiers held as prisoners
of war abroad: as a result one in six died of cold, hunger or disease. In
ordering his men to fire on the captive Italians, whom he called "sin-
ners against the fatherland," d'Annunzio was following his general's
lead. But he need not have done so. It is because of this incident that
historian Mark Thompson described d'Annunzio as "vicious." In his
repeated retellings of the story of that night, d'Annunzio tended to
leave it out.

D'Annunzio is in Venice, in the Casetta Rossa. Behind a screen in the
music room stands Evandro, a bittern. Two soldiers snared the bird
at the mouth of the River Timavo and presented him to d'Annunzio
as a memento of the battle. Now Evandro has the run of the house
and stalks through it with, thinks d'Annunzio's secretary, a "severe self-
respect and a measured correctness towards others" which would be
appropriate were he a president. The composer Gian Francesco Malipiero comes in. D'Annunzio invites him to play one of his own pieces.
He sits down at the piano. As he sounds his first notes, Evandro comes
out from behind his screen, crosses to the door and exits (he can't abide
music). "Look how refined he is!" says Malipiero. "He walks on the tips
of his toes."

.   .   .

More flights. More orations. D'Annunzio was tirelessly criss-crossing the war zone, bringing the drug of his oratory to troops preparing to kill and be killed. He spoke at mass burials. He spoke on the eve of battles. His addresses were designed to manipulate his hearers' emotions and alter their minds, tuning them in to his patriotic fervour, turning them on to the rage of battle, encouraging them to drop out of the benign contract which binds one human community to another. The military commanders approved. "If d'Annunzio could speak to the soldiers before every battle," wrote General Diaz, "that battle would be three-quarters won."

Some way of boosting the soldiers' morale was badly needed. Of the five and half million Italians who fought in the war, barely 8,000 had volunteered, the rest were conscripts. On trains carrying troops to the front, men opened fire on the military police, and tens of thousands of men deserted or went into hiding to avoid the draft. The troops who had surrendered on the night of Randaccio's death were not the only ones to be fed up with the whole bloody business of warfare. In some parts of the line men could only be chivvied into marching on the guns in front of them, by more guns behind. Military police to the rear of the trenches fired on any soldier who seemed reluctant to advance. After one battle a doctor recorded treating eighty men shot by the enemy, and twenty-five shot in the buttocks by their own police.

Most of the troops were uneducated, very far from home and very young. Many of them complained that they could not understand what the war was about, and even those who had set out with some comprehension of, and allegiance to, irredentist ideals, had been nonplussed by the way the people of Friuli had received them. Far from welcoming the Italians come to "redeem" them, the ethnically mixed people, whose villages had become billets and whose fields were battlegrounds, had retreated behind closed shutters, and watched the progress of the war in sullen misery. For many of them united Italy—barely two generations old—meant less than the empire which had dominated the region for centuries. A journalist reported that north Italian peasants were ready to welcome an invasion, believing the Austrians would "chop off the heads of the gentlemen who wanted the war, and then help the poor."

Colonel Angelo Gatti, the high command's official historian, was told by an infantry commander that, when ordered to attack, his men obeyed. They allowed themselves to be pushed out of their trenches. "They went; but they wept." They had cause to weep. In some battalions, during this dreadful summer, seventy per cent of the men were killed.

Not all the soldiers went meekly to their deaths. In July 1917 a brigade whose men had been counting on longer leave and a less deathly posting, were ordered back onto the Carso after only a few days' rest. There was muttering in the barracks, and then armed mutiny. The rebels killed three officers and four military policemen, before being overwhelmed by cavalry, armoured cars and artillery. They were in revolt against the war, and the irrational ethos which had inspired it, and their particular target was the man who had made himself the voice and the embodiment of that ethos. A group of them tried to break into the house of a local aristocrat, mistakenly believing d'Annunzio was there, shouting: "Down with war! We want peace! Death to d'Annunzio!"

D'Annunzio was in fact at a nearby airfield, and made his way to the troubled base the next day. Thirty-eight men were to be shot, some of them identified as instigators of the mutiny, others chosen by lot to die. D'Annunzio, fully aware of the hostility the condemned men felt towards him, chose to be present at the executions.

His notes made on the day are starkly factual. "The grey wall with pebbles visible in the mortar . . . The airless heat. The song of the larks. Corpses lined up face down . . . pale ears . . . the sounds of hoes and spades digging the deep ditch . . . nettles against the tragic wall." The gifts he had employed in his fiction to describe the complexities of human emotion hadn't atrophied in wartime. He was perfectly capable of inciting men to make war while pitying them for having to do so. The condemned men, he recognised, were peasants "bled white by too much fighting." Their punishment was cruel. As the firing squad awaited the order to fire, d'Annunzio saw their gaze fixed on him and felt himself pale. For all that, he welcomed their deaths as a necessary sacrifice. In a private letter he expressed his disappointment that the commanders had executed so few of the rebels. "Not even decimation!"

Cadorna—the commander against whom the men might more justly have directed their anger—still sent troops marching up mountainsides in tight formation which made them perfect targets for enemy artillery, still insisted on attacking every peak and ridge, however inaccessible and strategically unimportant, and on holding every position gained, whatever the cost. Those costs were enormous. An officer with a critical view of his commander-in-chief's strategy calculated that to maintain a garrison of a hundred men on a 3,000-metre peak required 900 porters working in relay, and that on one occasion Italians had fired the equivalent of four tons of steel per dead man in the process of driving a dozen Austrians off a pinnacle of rock. The highest price of all was that paid in human lives.

August 1917 saw another massive attack along the River Isonzo, one which initially seemed so successful that Ambassador Rodd telegraphed Lloyd George, telling him to expect the "complete smashing of the Austrian army," and Arturo Toscanini, who was visiting the front, led a military band to the top of the newly conquered Monte Santo to play patriotic songs "in the Austrians' faces." Soon though, the advance halted again. The Austrians had sited their artillery and their base camps in caverns deep in the rock. The Italians bombarded their positions in vain. One mountain lost ten metres in altitude, so heavily was its summit shelled. But for all the fire, for all the air filled with shells and shattered rock, and for all the thousands upon thousands of dead young men (40,000 Italians were killed in less than a month), nothing much was gained. "I feel something collapsing inside me," wrote Colonel Gatti. "I shall not be able to survive this war, none of us will; it is too gigantic . . . it will crush us all."

A little to the west of the Casetta Rossa along the Grand Canal is the splendid baroque Palazzo Pisani, home to the College of Music. Working one afternoon at home, d'Annunzio heard in the distance the opening bars of one of Frescobaldi's *canzone*. He hurried over to the Palazzo and slipped into the grand salon, which was deserted but for the celebrated organist Goffredo Giarda, then recovering after the motorboat on which he was a volunteer had been wrecked in the lagoon.

Giarda looked round, without interrupting his playing. D'Annunzio murmured, "Am I disturbing?" Giarda shook his head and played on. At the end of the piece d'Annunzio introduced himself and the two had an animated conversation about how much Bach owed to the Italian master. Thereafter d'Annunzio went frequently to the Palazzo Pisani to listen, sometimes alone, sometimes with lady friends, and sometimes, in the evenings, with a pair of soldiers whose job it was to wind the generator, in case of power cuts, so that the music need not be interrupted.

One night, when d'Annunzio had brought along an English-woman in a white dress, the sirens sounded an air-raid warning. The lights went out. The lady, terrified, huddled moaning in a corner of the room, visible only by flashes of anti-aircraft fire from the gun emplacements on the palace roof. To calm her d'Annunzio asked the maestro to keep repeating the piece (a Frescobaldi *toccata*) until the all-clear. Giarda played it twenty-four times. A bomb fell just across the canal from the Casetta Rossa. "That," said d'Annunzio (quite possibly correctly—the Austrian high command were longing to be rid of him), "was meant for me."

In September 1917, d'Annunzio was in the Casetta Rossa preparing to depart on a raid on Cattaro. This was to be his most ambitious aerial attack yet. Two squadrons would fly south by stages to an airbase in Puglia, and then cross the Adriatic, returning on the same night. D'Annunzio had been working for months, with Veniero and other engineers, to refine the aircraft that were to undertake the flight, but on the eve of his departure his mind was elsewhere.

He had fallen out with Olga. She had been jealous (almost certainly with good reason: the historian Damerini, who was living in Venice at the time, reports that gossip linked d'Annunzio with at least six other women) and they were parting on bad terms. D'Annunzio posed in the garden for a sculptor who was making his portrait bust, but felt so dejected he could take no pleasure in the process. He packed, assisted by the red-eyed Aélis, who wept as she folded his shirts. It was on his mind as well as hers that he might well not come back. His doctor brought a new vial of poison for him to take in case of capture. Renata and her husband (she had recently married one of his officers) escorted him to the station by gondola. He held his daughter's hand all the way. In the stuffy sleeping compartment of the train he opened his overnight bag and found some flowers pinned to his pyjamas, with a touching note from Aélis.

In Rome he visited the Ministry of War and talked to staff officers about extending the air force, but all the time he was thinking of his love trouble. "I am dying of sadness. The very will to live withdraws from me, like warmth from a corpse." From Rome he flew on southwards, and was pleased to believe that those waiting on the airstrip were surprised by his nimbleness in springing from the cockpit.

After several frustrating days waiting for equipment and ammunition, he and his squadron were finally ready to depart, and at once his depression lifted. He wrote a farewell letter to Olga (quoting from Wagner's *Tristan*) to be read in the event of his death. Feeling a "savage need to drink from a woman's mouth before passing on," he pressed himself on a woman with slim ankles whom he had met at the base, and then led his men in a "Francescan litany':

> For Brother Wind, that he be not against us, *Eia Eia Eia!*
>   *Alalà!*
> For Brother Fire, that he does not burn us,
> *Eia Eia Eia! Alalà!*
> For Sister Water, that she does not drown us,
> *Eia Eia Eia! Alalà!*

At last they took off, and he stood up in the prow to yell out his *Alalà!* while all his fellow aviators yelled back and waved as they swooped upward. His single eye seemed to see prodigiously well. This "adventure" was his latest creation: war was his new poetry. He entered a kind of ecstasy. For the rest of his life he was to recall the experience with wonder. He had found a transcendental "third way" of being, beyond life and beyond death.

The flight was long and dangerous; the raid successful. All of the fourteen planes involved returned safely (although three of them had to turn back before reaching Cattaro). Jubilant, d'Annunzio gave the squadron its own motto *"Iterum rudit leo"*—the lion, Venice's symbolic beast, roars again.

Some two weeks after d'Annunzio's aerial attack on Cattaro, Italian troops on the mountainsides above the Isonzo Valley saw a column of Austrian soldiers marching two abreast up the valley towards the town of Caporetto (now Kobarid in Slovenia). The Italians assumed they were watching prisoners being escorted behind the lines. They were wrong. A century earlier Napoleon Bonaparte had noticed that the otherwise insignificant town of Caporetto lay in a gap in the mountains through which an army could flood down onto the Friulian plain. The next defensible line to the west, judged Napoleon, was the River Piave, barely thirty kilometres from Venice. Over the next catastrophic fortnight the Italians were to discover that he was right.

The Austrian army had been reinforced for the first time by German troops. On 24 October 1917 they attacked, beginning with a devastating bombardment along a thirty-kilometre front, following it up with poison gas shells, and then with an advance so rapid that one Italian unit after another found itself surrounded. Where Cadorna had sent his men plodding up heavily defended mountains, the Germans simply skirted them, leaving the rock fortresses isolated and useless. Italian troops surrendered en masse.

Caporetto was a defeat which rapidly became a rout. On the afternoon of 25 October, Cadorna wrote to his son: "the men are not fighting . . . A disaster is imminent . . . I shall go and live somewhere far away and not ask anything of anyone." He had given up, and so had nearly all of the men under him. As the line broke Italian troops turned and streamed to the rear, throwing away their rifles as they went and chanting: "The war's over! We're going home!" while their officers, weeping or enraged, looked on helplessly, or did likewise. An officer who refused to surrender was shot dead by his own troops. For days on end the narrow roads through the mountains were clogged with exhausted men, who jettisoned their equipment, burnt their stores, blew up bridges behind them and pressed doggedly homewards. One of them recalls it: "They move on, move on, not saying a word, with only one idea in their head: to reach the lowland, to get away from the nightmare." Back on the plain they spread out through muddy fields, units dissolving, officers and men losing each other.

Cadorna hoped to reform the line on the west bank of the River Tagliamento, but the Austro-German forces were too close behind. On 4 November he ordered a general retreat to the Piave. Four days later, with the Italian armies on the river's western side, the rout was finally halted and all the bridges over the Piave were blown up, leaving the enemy in possession of the entire Friulian plain. Of the million or so men who had been fighting for Italy on the Isonzo, 40,000 had been killed or wounded during the previous two weeks, 300,000 had been taken prisoner, and 400,000 had vanished, most of them having set off on a long walk home.

It was a military disaster, maybe more. Curzio Malaparte described soldiers rampaging—part modern anarchists, part ancient Bacchae. "Often they hoisted on their shoulders, cheering, along with prostitutes, some fat, pot-bellied senior officer—Bacchus and Ariadne—while the orgy of the *sans-fusils* dissolved into brawls and riots, cries of lust and lewd songs." Coming as it did within days of the Bolsheviks' seizure of power in Russia, to many contemporary observers Caporetto looked like the beginnings of a revolution.

In public, d'Annunzio coped with the calamity by denying it. Later he was to write about the "wretched herds of deserters," and about cowards as "vile" as the "sludge of mules' excrement and liquid clay through which they shuffled." But at the time he was still devoted to the task of conjuring glory from failure. He repeatedly referred to Caporetto as a "Victory."

His apartment in Cervignano was now way behind the lines (an Austrian officer, who had taken it over, courteously offered, two years later, to return all of his forty damask cushions to him). He found a new mainland base in Padua, as guest of a friendly Contessa, from which he repeatedly visited the troops on the Piave, promising national resurrection and new victories. He told the army which had just stampeded for home, letting slip an entire province, that it was composed of indomitable heroes, and that he knew it would never bend by so much as the breadth of a fingernail. He addressed the latest batch of recruits, all of them seventeen years old, elaborating a metaphor of Italy as an effigy repeatedly battered and cast down, but tirelessly renewing itself. "From the ashes of all the shattered idols it has once more raised the deity of its Genius." His speeches of that month were published and distributed to the troops in a pamphlet wishfully entitled *"La Riscossa"* (The Reconquest).

The front line was now only thirty kilometres from Venice. Artworks, archives and government offices were all hurriedly moved out of the city. Many of the citizens went as well. In Venice, in December 1917, d'Annunzio went to watch Verrocchio's equestrian statue of Bartolomeo Colleoni being lowered from its plinth by the church of San Zanipolo (Giovanni e Paolo). Colleoni was one of the Renaissance condottieri whom d'Annunzio saw as personifying all that was boldest and most virile about Italy's history. Verrocchio's magnificent bronze was a technological marvel in its time, and remains one of the world's grandest monuments. The warrior's stern face and armoured body surmounting the great, high-stepping horse convey dauntless resolution and physical force. Viewers, obliged to peer upwards, are dwarfed by it. It is everything that futurist and subsequently fascist art aspired to be—a hard image of power and obduracy, metallic, beautiful and overbearing. D'Annunzio admired it immensely.

Now it was to be taken down and removed to a place of safety. Grounded, it could be viewed from close-up as never before. D'Annunzio noticed the normally invisible fudging whereby the artist had made up for flaws in the casting, the little divot of wood keeping the helmet steady. He was impressed by the confident negligence of detail, the way the warlord's frown is made with three slashing lines. There were a flock of little boys bowling tin hoops noisily over the square. Being d'Annunzio, he noticed the children's hands, how small they were, and the "imperious power" of the colossal hands of the bronze horseman. One-eyed, he noticed the eyes—the pupils were two "terrible holes," one deeper than the other.

Peering at the bronze as it lay on the cobbles, d'Annunzio was the craftsman and connoisseur of the applied arts. Back at his desk, drafting his next speech, he became once more the bombastic orator, harnessing the heroes of the past to his present project. What he had actually seen was the warrior downed, an image of defeat, but what he wrote was that Colleoni, personification of Italian valour, was back in his saddle and riding once again to war.

Venice was emptying. For those who remained, wrote Damerini (who was among them), d'Annunzio "symbolised the spirit of resistance." In the almost deserted streets he was repeatedly stopped by "outbreaks of affection and respect." His passage across the piazza would be met with applause and shouts of *"Evviva!"*

He and Olga had made up their quarrel. D'Annunzio would send her a note telling her he was free and within minutes they could be meeting, as it were by accident, on the short route of alleys and little bridges separating their two homes. And because for d'Annunzio to experience something was to be moved to set it down on paper, those meetings didn't deter him from writing to her, sometimes several times a day. He told her: "When you said those unsayable words in my ear . . . when I was deep inside you, I was *burning* in all my bones like a bundle of resinous branches." He was also seeing a young woman whom he called Nerissa, a Red Cross nurse, whose nun-like demeanour and obvious infatuation with him was deliciously gratifying to his vanity. "I am aware of her thrilling to my voice as to a searching caress." For all that, he wrote nostalgically to Giuseppina Mancini on the anniversary of their first night together telling her: "I am alone . . . I can never be loved again."

The war on the ground had stalled. The Austrian armies occupying Friuli, their supply lines impossibly long, were starving. They were ordered to live off the land, but after two months there was nothing left to steal. Bread and polenta were mixed with sawdust or sand. Men boiled grass. Horses died of exhaustion, and soldiers traded in their weapons for a cut of meat. They were in no more of a fit state to attack than the Italians were to defend themselves.

With no fighting on the ground, for his next adventures d'Annunzio looked to the sea and air. Italian naval engineers had developed a fleet of small, light attack craft called *Motoscafi Armata Svan* (MAS). D'Annunzio was much taken with them, perhaps seeing that, like the little planes, they were a fit vehicle for an individual hero and his intrepid band. He laid claim to them as he habitually laid claim to a woman, with a name. The sailors had taken to calling the MAS *Motoscafi Anti Sommergibile* (anti-submarine motorboats). D'Annunzio went better: the initials he declared, stood for *Memento Audere Semper*— remember always to dare. His friends in the naval command told him of a planned raid, using three MAS, on the Austrian naval base in the Bay of Buccari (now Bakar), a deep indentation into the mountainous Croatian coast just south-east of Fiume, a kind of fjord running nearly five kilometres inland with only a narrow and heavily defended opening to the sea. D'Annunzio obtained permission to join the expedition.

The boats didn't carry nearly enough fuel to make the trip to Buccari from Venice. They were to be towed by destroyers a distance of over a hundred kilometres through Austrian-patrolled waters, until they were near the coastline. Then, by night, they would thread their way between the offshore islands, pass through the strait and travel up the long inlet, overlooked by mountains thick with armed lookout posts, to the harbour. On arrival they would torpedo the enemy ships (thereby inevitably revealing their presence), before making their way back by the same dangerous route, constantly in range of enemy guns. D'Annunzio was delighted with the plan. The most intense experience of life, he believed, was "to be bought only with the coin which has life on one side and death on the other." He set himself to write a defiant message to the Austrians. While his companions loosed their torpedoes, he would drop sealed bottles overboard, each one containing his text, and decorated with tric-olour streamers.

This was to be one of the great adventures of his life. He called it the "*Beffa di Buccari*," the Buccari prank. Like his first flight over Trieste, it was an act of impudent provocation, a snook cocked at the enemy. He saw that it would make a great story. In the days preceding it he kept a detailed diary, which he subsequently published in the *Corriere della Sera* virtually unchanged, judging correctly that the intimate details there recorded (a tiff with Olga, their voluptuous reconciliation, his nostalgic observation of the anniversary of his first night with Giuseppina) would make the exploit all the more exciting to the public. He wrote a ballad with an insistent beat and a stirring refrain, and ensured its wide circulation among the civilian public and the servicemen alike:

> We are thirty with one fate,
> and thirty-one, counting death.
> *Eia!* That last one! *Alalà!* ...

For several anxious days the pranksters waited for clear skies: they needed at least twenty hours of fine weather if the little boats, not designed for open seas, were to twice cross the Adriatic successfully, even under tow. At last, on 10 February 1918, the expedition was launched.

> All of us will return, or none.
> *Eia!* Depths of the Carnaro! *Alalà!*

They made it safely to Buccari, eating en route a good picnic, packed by Aélis, (chicken in aspic, cakes and marmalade, biscuits, mandarins, liqueurs). For the rest of his life d'Annunzio would be revisiting the memory of that night: the darkness, the "pride and intoxication of

being few against many," the comradeship he felt with his handful of companions, together defying the massive technological might of the Austrian Empire in their wobbly little vessel.

D'Annunzio dropped his bottles. The torpedoes were launched. Most of them were caught in the nets protecting the harbour. The three MAS turned and chugged back to open sea, rejoining their escort safely while the Austrian gunners, apparently unable to believe what they were seeing, let them pass unscathed.

No enemy warship was damaged (the only vessel to be hit was a commercial ferryboat) but the *Beffa* was a hugely successful propaganda exercise. For Italians, demoralised after Caporetto, and for Austrians alike, it was a sign that the fight wasn't over. The plan had not been d'Annunzio's (as the raid on Cattaro really was), but he made it his own. In the message in his bottles he called himself the *Nimicissimo* (the supreme enemy), and announced he had come to make a mockery of the price the Austrians had placed on his head. He posed for photographs (previous page) in oilskins and sou'wester, looking like a shiny little water sprite, next to strapping sailors nearly twice his height.

After the debacle of Caporetto the King visited General Cadorna at his headquarters to inform him that he was to be replaced. The conversation lasted two hours. At the end of it Cadorna, the man who had caused the deaths of tens of thousands of his own men by refusing ever to relinquish a position, was, true to his own obstinacy, still refusing to stand down. It was only the next day, on receipt of a written dismissal and with his successor already in his office, that he left at last.

That replacement was General Armando Diaz, the man who believed that a battle before which d'Annunzio had harangued the troops was already three-quarters won. Where Cadorna had expected his men to do or die in deaf and dumb obedience, Diaz was solicitous about their morale. He knew they needed food and boots above all else, but he also believed in the efficacy of "a healthy fortifying word." He made propaganda a priority, setting up the new "P Service," to coordinate it. Posters and leaflets, talks, theatre and cinema, "trench newspapers" edited by servicemen for their peers, all played a part in his effort to resurrect the army. Minister Martini wrote sourly in his diary that d'Annunzio's *Beffa* was an adventure "without common sense," but the new commander understood the value of the flamboyant gesture, the grandstanding performance in the theatre of war. With his encouragement, d'Annunzio was called upon to speak to the troops lined up along the Piave again and again.

More conferring with technicians and manufacturers over new weapons of war. Six and a half thousand planes were built in the last year of the war (up from under 400 in 1915), and d'Annunzio was consulted by ministers and manufacturers alike. He was in contact with Caproni, and also with Giovanni Agnelli, founder and managing director of Fiat, whose company had grown sixfold during the war years, turning out trucks and lorries by the tens of thousands and Italy's first tanks. "My little one would be amazed," he wrote to Olga, "to see me talking straight-faced and ardently about engines, as though a steel piston was the most important thing in the world."

More daring excursions by air and sea. In April, d'Annunzio joined a naval expedition to bombard Pola. In June he flew over the Piave, dropping bombs on Austrian batteries. In July he was bombing Pola again. Day after day he flew, sometimes making two or even three sorties in a day. "Action rejuvenates me," he told Albertini. "I barely have time to sleep." Between raids he was participating in more test flights in preparation for his best ever prank.

For over a year d'Annunzio had been urging the supreme command to authorise an air raid on Vienna. Repeatedly he had been denied. The round trip from Venice, weaving through and over mountains, would be some thousand kilometres, at unprecedentedly high altitudes. The planes would be continuously in the air for ten hours, with no chance to refuel. Such a flight had never yet been attempted.

Throughout the summer of 1918, while the armies faced each other over the Piave, d'Annunzio was conferring with Caproni about ways of increasing fuel capacity and strengthening aircraft to withstand the buffeting they could expect while overflying the Alps. At last he was able to demonstrate, with a ten-hour, thousand-kilometre flight over Italian mountains, that the thing could be done. General Diaz gave his approval. On 8 August, d'Annunzio spent the evening in the College of Music listening, alone, to a recital of baroque music. On 9 August, eleven monoplanes took off from Treviso, d'Annunzio riding in one which had been especially constructed to accommodate a passenger (see overleaf). Three had to turn back almost immediately. A fourth came down in Austrian territory, but the remaining seven arrived safely in the skies over the imperial capital.

In 1908, H. G. Wells wrote a novel, *The War in the Air*. In it Wells imagines the aerial bombardment of a city. "No place is safe . . . bombs drop in the night. Quiet people go out in the morning, and see air fleets passing overhead—dripping death—dripping death!" At the time the story was received as improbable fantasy. Now, only ten years later, the Viennese faced the possibility that it could be realised in their own city. Austrian bombers had been targeting Venice, but no one in Vienna had expected their own capital, so far behind the lines, to be under such a threat. The Italians, appearing overhead, were terrifying.

In the event d'Annunzio dripped not death but words. He and his squadron let fall 50,000 copies of a text by d'Annunzio printed on red, white and green paper. Giving his address as "The Sky over Vienna," d'Annunzio announced: "On the wind of victory arising from the rivers

of liberty, we have come only for the joy of the daring deed . . . Viennese! We could now be dropping bombs on you! Instead we drop only a salute." The people of Vienna were urged to reject their own government, and to plead for peace. "If you wish to continue the War—continue it! You will thereby commit suicide." A further 100,000 copies were dropped of a rather blunter and more explicit message, composed by Ugo Ojetti, written in German and urging the citizens of Vienna to save themselves and their city by surrendering.

On the return trip the engine of d'Annunzio's plane cut out three times. Each time he reached for his little damascened box of poison. Each time the pilot, Natale Palli, managed to restart it. Returning safely to the airfield near Venice, d'Annunzio was received rapturously. His exploit was lauded not only in Italy but in all the Allied countries as well. *The Times* of London (British journalists clearly being better conversant with European literature then than they are now) called him "a new Ruggiero," alluding to Ariosto's hero and his gallant flight astride a hippogryph. The French awarded him the Croix de Guerre. The enemy was equally impressed. "And our d'Annunzios," asked the leader writer of the Viennese *Arbeiter Zeitung*, "where are they?"

.   .   .

Throughout September 1918 the Italian administration was pressing General Diaz to move. Italy's seventeen-year-olds had been drafted to replenish an army emaciated by the desertions of Caporetto. British and French divisions had arrived to lend support. But still Diaz insisted the army was not ready.

On 19 October word came that the Austrians were about to make a peace offer, agreeing to withdraw from all Italian territory. The prospect of Italy's gaining what it wanted with no further loss of life seemed intolerable to Prime Minister Orlando. In 1864, when the Austrians offered to restore the Veneto to Italy in return for their neutrality, Nino Bixio, the Garibaldino whose sword d'Annunzio had brandished on the Capitol, vociferously opposed the deal, telling parliament that he would rather 100,000 Italians died for Venice than accept it without a fight. Irrational, self-destructive and wickedly careless of human lives, that mind-set lived on. In the first months of the war d'Annunzio had written that territory obtained peacefully could never become a true part of Italy. Unless it was "watered with our own blood" it would remain an alien limb, subject to gangrene. Prime Minister Orlando was of like mind. He telegraphed Diaz: "Between inaction and defeat, I prefer defeat. Get moving!"

On 24 October, the anniversary of Caporetto, "the Virgin Victory shook the frost of Autumn from her wings" (or so d'Annunzio put it) "and, flexing her bare foot upon the blood-nourished grass of the river's margin, soared aloft from the right bank of the Piave in her stupendous flight." In other words, the Italian counterattack began. A battalion of Gordon Highlanders were ferried across the Piave by Venetian gondoliers (the fact that the Italians had Allied support in this final campaign is one d'Annunzio never publicly mentioned). Soon the Austrians, by now so starved that the average weight of a soldier in their armies was down to eight stone, were retreating so fast their pursuers could barely keep up with them. For ten "lacerating and divine" days, d'Annunzio and his squadron flew above the advancing Italian troops—d'Annunzio on his feet in the unsteady plane so as to be able to see, and be seen by, all of his pilots. They dropped seventy bombs on the retreating Austrian troops, needlessly killing men who only wanted to go home. D'Annunzio was, once again, nearly killed when his plane, still loaded with bombs, crashed soon after take-off (the bombs didn't explode; he was unhurt).

By 31 October the Italians had reached the town of Vittorio (now

Vittorio Veneto), by whose neatly appropriate name the Italian victory would be known. On 1 November the Austrian governor of Trieste left hurriedly, by train. Two days later an Italian warship entered Trieste's harbour, bringing the new Italian governor who announced "our dead are dead no longer." On 4 November, with almost all the territory lost at Caporetto redeemed, the armistice between Austria and Italy came into effect.

Early in October, d'Annunzio told Marcel Boulanger: "I adore war," and wrote to another friend: "For me and for you and for those like us, peace today is a disaster." On the day that Diaz ordered his armies to advance, d'Annunzio's *Prayer of Sernaglia* was published in the *Corriere della Sera*. It's an incantation full of disdain for Italy's allies (President Woodrow Wilson, although not named, comes in for some withering invective) and rage against Italy's enemy. Austria is still the vomiting vulture who has fouled Italy's houses, contaminated its springs, flogged its old men, raped its women and mutilated its young men. But the real adversary is peace, which comes to grieving men, "not like a snowy dove but like a clammy serpent."

War had brought d'Annunzio adventure, purpose, a cohort of brave young comrades whom he loved with a love beyond the love of women, a new and manlier brand of fame, and the intoxication of living in constant deadly peril. His contemporary, the Austrian novelist Robert Musil, who was serving on the other side in mountains near Trento, wrote about the giddy joy he felt while facing mortal danger, as if the fear of death "which lies on top of man forever like a stone" were rolled back by the fact of death's probable imminence, and "an unaccountable inner freedom blossoms forth." D'Annunzio had felt that freedom: civilian life seemed like a stinking jail to which he was about to be forcibly returned. While millions of people all over Europe hoped that at last the stupid killing might be at an end, he wrote: "I smell the stench of peace."

Peace

I N DECEMBER 1917, with the nation traumatised by the rout from Caporetto, Benito Mussolini proclaimed a new order. "The music of tomorrow will have a new tempo . . . the brutal and bloody apprenticeship of the trenches will mean something." A year later, on 1 January 1919, Mussolini wrote to d'Annunzio suggesting that a meeting between them might be of use to the cause they shared. But in the first weeks of peace, d'Annunzio had other things on his mind than making the acquaintance of the editor of one of the several journals that published his speeches. Another six months would go by before the two men came face to face.

Mussolini served in the war first as a private soldier and latterly as a corporal. He was in the front line for over nine months and took part in fighting on the Asiago—the Alpine plateau where d'Annunzio had admired the little mauve flowers on the airstrip. In 1917, Mussolini was injured when a mortar bomb exploded in his trench, and invalided home with some forty shards of metal in his body.

Mussolini's inspirations were d'Annunzio's. As a young man he used to walk the streets of his home town declaiming passages from Dante. Nietzsche filled him with "spiritual eroticism." He had learnt from Sorel. He called himself "an apostle of violence." Resuming his editorship of *Il Popolo d'Italia*, he celebrated the "moral force" generated by the war and prophesied that the future belonged to a new elite of battle-hardened veterans, the "trenchocracy."

It was true that the war had altered Italy's political composition. General Cadorna had repeatedly resisted attempts by the elected government in Rome to prevail upon him to change his tactics, or to replace him. Facing down the government with the King's tacit approval, Cadorna created a split between the parliamentary democracy and the military, which weakened the government and left the troops disgruntled and suspicious of their civilian masters. In the summer of 1917 there were demonstrations in Milan during which people called upon Cadorna to make himself dictator.

The interventionists who had swept their reluctant government into the war never fully trusted the civilian authorities. Over a hundred deputies had remained loyal to Giolitti in 1915. Like him, they saw the war as wasteful and unnecessary. As the years of attrition went by, and the pointless expenditure of Italy's economic resources was joined with the killing of hundreds of thousands of young men, and the wounding or capture of hundreds of thousands more, the civil administration became ever more alienated from the apostles of violence who were, effectively, running the country. On the other hand the military made the usual complaints about the parsimonious bureaucrats stinting on supplies of food and equipment, and so failing to support the gallant young men so bravely sacrificing their lives. There was talk of the army's being "betrayed" by a timorous administration.

Then came the ignominy of the flight from Caporetto. The rout shocked and humiliated the entire nation and, for those who lived in fear of a socialist revolution, the spectacle of mass desertion and mutiny in the very month in which the Bolsheviks had seized power in Russia was terrifying. People searched for others to blame. The military blamed "defeatists"—those who had been, in the first place, insufficiently enthusiastic about the war and who had continued to question its usefulness and likely outcome. There were secret societies whose members vowed to assassinate leading socialists, or to blow up the Vatican (Pope Benedict—dubbed "Pope Pilate" by Mussolini— had refused to declare the conflict just). "Resistance committees" and "*Fasci* of national defence" were formed (the word *fascio* was becoming increasingly popular in political circles). Their functions included the harassment of the "enemy within"—meaning neutralists, socialists, Giolittians.

General Cadorna was ousted. For a whole year Italians lived with the awareness of defeat. When victory finally came it was too late to restore the nation's morale. The exhausted troops redeemed themselves with their counterattack in the last weeks of the war, but it was increasingly evident that their efforts were to be wasted: the triumphant advance on Vittorio Veneto would never be translated into equally splendid terms in the peace treaty.

As the Italian army pushed easily through Friuli in October 1918, the famished Austrians throwing away their guns and racing homewards ahead of them, d'Annunzio exulted, as though the ground on which Italian boots now trod, must therefore and forever be Italian. "Those of us who flew over Trieste, passing between fires, took possession of Trieste. Whoever challenged the inferno of Pola seized the port for Italy . . . I was of that breed." But that is not the way territorial disputes are resolved in the modern era. Negotiations between the Allies and the moribund Austro-Hungarian Empire were already under way when the advance began. By the beginning of November the roads into Istria, or over the Carso into Slovenia, lay undefended. D'Annunzio was one of many Italian officers raring to follow those roads, to continue southwards into Dalmatia, to flood the unredeemed territories with Italian troops, to make the Adriatic an Italian sea at last. But when the armistice was signed in November 1918 the Italian advance was halted.

At Caporetto the army (so civilians thought) let the civilians down. A year later the civilian government, in agreeing to the "armistice line," (so thought the army) let down the army. The shocking defeat; the truncated victory. Between them they left a nation riven by resentment and distrust.

D'Annunzio sank into one of his cyclical depressions. He had seen hundreds of bewildered teenagers slaughtered for a cause they barely understood. He understood all too clearly that their deaths had been almost entirely futile. But the experience had left his appetite for violence unappeased. War was music: war was religion. He could not bear to be without it.

On 3 November 1918, the night before the armistice, *The Ship* was staged at Milan's La Scala, with new music by Italo Montemezzi, but the author was not celebrating. He told Antongini he regretted that he had finally given up his house in Arcachon. He didn't want to live any longer in Italy "where the rabble is incorrigible." He was awarded a gold medal for valour, and felt no pleasure in it. He thought about entering a monastery. He wrote to Romaine Brooks: "Even heroism is exhausted and blood no longer has the brilliance that once thrilled us . . . I am thirsty for bitter water . . . I have so much sadness in me." Repeatedly he declared that he wished he had been killed, that to survive was disgraceful, that his vial of poison was always with him and he was tempted to use it. He adopted a new slogan. Clothing his glumness in Latin dignity he declared himself *in hilaritate tristis*—sad amidst rejoicing—and used the phrase as epigraph to all his letters.

He wrote to Olga breaking off their liaison. He dwelt voluptuously on their past pleasures, on the whiteness of her leg when he peeled a stocking off it, as the calyx is turned back from a rose, and told her: "We will both be unhappy for ever." (Olga suspected that he had already found consolation.) He fell ill, and was laid up for several days with a high fever, cheered only by a new puppy named Sva (after the motorboats). He wondered how he was to spend the rest of his life. He wrote flippantly that he might apply for a commission in the regular army, "or I may end as a Bolshevik, not without making a considerable splash. Or I may die on Sunday from Spanish flu." The existence of a desk-bound author seemed intolerably dull. "Must I return to telling fairy tales and scanning verses?"

Soon after the armistice, Costanzo Ciano, naval commander on the *Beffa di Buccari*, came to lunch at the Casetta Rossa. The two men ate "excellent tagliatelle" and "exquisite pink trout" while they talked about their unhappiness at the ending of the war, and of "vague hopes of starting up again. Bold plans." Ciano's son would eventually marry the daughter of Mussolini, who, in December 1918, was still a long way off being invited to such exquisite lunches, but who was thinking along the same lines. While d'Annunzio and Ciano discussed their "contempt for the little men who rule us," Mussolini was calling on soldiers to "break the fetters of decrepit institutions" and become a "political avant-garde" ready to effect "a profound renovation of our national life."

The British and French had lured Italy into the war with the promise of substantial grants of territory on the Dalmatian coast. In 1915 that territory was still a part of the Austro-Hungarian Empire and the Allies had no compunction about promising away their enemy's land. By the time of the armistice in 1918, though, the map of Europe, and the Allies' war aims, had changed drastically. The Empire was falling apart. The United States, which had not been party to the Treaty of London and whose president, Woodrow Wilson, had repeatedly declared his disapproval of such secret agreements, had entered the war and established itself as main arbiter of the peace. In the unredeemed territories to the east of the Adriatic, the new Kingdom of Serbs, Croats and Slovenes (subsequently Yugoslavia) was coming into being, and laying claim to the territory, from Istria southwards down the Dalmatian coast, that d'Annunzio had for so long been calling a part of the Greater Italy, and much of which had been promised to Italy in the Treaty of London.

Before arriving in Paris for the peace talks, Woodrow Wilson declared that "all nations have a right to self-determination." He was inclined to look favourably on the Yugoslavs' claims. The British and French each had their own reasons for seeing the new state as a potentially useful friend. To them Croats and Slovenians and Serbians were peoples freed at last from the defeated Austro-Hungarian Empire, their new independence evidence that the war had been necessary and that its outcome would be benign. Italians, who had slogged through the long and bloody war against Austro-Hungarian armies, including large contingents of Croatian and Slovenian troops, and commanded—for the last year of the war—by a Croatian general, saw the southern Slavs quite differently, as their defeated enemy.

Wilson announced his "Fourteen Points" according to which the peace settlement was to be determined. One of them was that "a readjustment of the frontiers of Italy should be effected along clearly recognisable lines of nationality." There were no such lines. Along the eastern shore of the Adriatic—in the port cities of Pola, Zara, Spalato and Fiume—there were sizable and influential Italian communities (in some cases forming a majority of a city's population) hemmed in by Croatian hinterlands. To the peace-makers in Paris, struggling to find equitable solutions to controversies over places they had never seen and ethnic groups of which they had no knowledge, the claims of such isolated settlements seemed more like a nuisance than a just cause. As Giolitti had foreseen, the Italians stood to gain almost nothing for their participation in the war.

"Victory of ours, you shall not be mutilated!" d'Annunzio wrote in October 1918 (before that victory had actually taken place). The line became one of his slogans. For him—the man who had slept for years with a plaster cast of the headless and armless *Victory* of Samothrace in his bedroom, and named one of his mistresses after it—the slogan had a secret erotic significance. For his public it was a ringing call to further conflict. Three days after the armistice he was raging against the Allies' decision not to allow the Italians to lay claim to the Austrian ships in the harbour at Pola. "Already they are cheating us!" He talked wildly of a new front, of bombarding Berlin. He had proved himself a useful, and surprisingly docile, servant of the high command. The citation for his final medal declared that: "He wholeheartedly dedicated his noble intellect and his tenacious will . . . to the sacred ideals of his native land, in the pure dignity of duty and sacrifice." Now he repeatedly signalled that he was about the exchange the "pure dignity of duty" for the turbulence of political confrontation.

In Genoa back in May 1915 he had addressed a gathering of Dalmatian Italians, promising them that their home was a part of Italy "by divine right and by human right" and in all the speeches he had made that month he had made plain that his own war aims (whatever his government's might be) included the recovery of the "lost" cities of the eastern Adriatic. During the final weeks of fighting, as it became increasingly clear that those cities were unlikely to be restored to Italy, he gave a series of incendiary speeches at soldiers' funerals in which he promised those who had been killed in battle not to dishonour them by accepting a "mutilated Victory." He called these orations "prayers." He was the high priest of a cult of the bloodthirsty spirits of the fallen. Following Garibaldi, who had prayed "Give us this day our daily cartridges," he composed a new version of the Lord's Prayer. "Our dead, who art in earth as you are in Heaven . . . Deliver us from every ignoble temptation, Free us from every cowardly doubt . . . Keep aflame in us our holy hatred." He declared that civilisation was a splendour generated only by ceaseless conflict, and vowed to the war dead: "We will fight not only to the last drop of our blood but, with you, until the last grain of our ashes . . . Amen."

Italy was on the winning side. Italians' dogged endurance had fatally weakened the Hapsburg Empire. The "hereditary enemy" had fallen apart. The Italian nation could have congratulated itself on its success. But victory had come only after a year during which Italy had felt what it was like to be ignominiously beaten. Its post-war mood was as resentful and vengeful as any loser's, and d'Annunzio was foremost among those shaping the story of the war's end as one of Italian humiliation, Italian victimisation. It was a story which would have long-lasting and disastrous consequences. The nation was to develop politically in ways as pathological as did those countries traumatised by defeat.

D'Annunzio wrote a tirade for the *Corriere della Sera*. Albertini refused to publish it: "You speak the language of those who believe our exploits can be measured by the quantity of our booty . . . I wish with all my heart that you would repudiate these violent ideas." To the regret of both men, it was the end of their collaboration.

On 31 October 1918, with the war not yet ended, representatives of the victorious "Big Four"—Britain, France, America and Italy—agreed that the Italian army should occupy the territory along the eastern shore of the Adriatic promised to them in the Treaty of London. This occupation would be strictly provisional and temporary, pending decisions on the region's future to be made at the peace talks, and it would be undertaken on behalf, not of Italy, but of the Allied high command.

Warships loaded with Italian troops landed in Pola, Zara and Cattaro. An Italian admiral assumed the title of "Governor of Dalmatia." Very soon Italian troops, over-enthusiastically laying claim to territory they believed to be theirs by right, were finding themselves opposed initially by the Serbs (their wartime allies) and subsequently by the militias of the new state of Yugoslavia, which came into being on 4 December. A British officer reported that "Italians only supplied food to those who signed a declaration of loyalty to Italy." When the Yugoslavs protested, other Allied forces were sent to dilute the Italian presence, but since the Italian General Diaz was the senior Allied officer in the region they came under his command. To the dismay of the Croat, Slovenian and Serbian people of Yugoslavia, and to the delight of many Italians, this felt not like Allied peacekeeping, but like an Italian invasion.

D'Annunzio was determined to make that illusion real. Italy, he said, was like one of those exotic flowers which bloom overnight "with a violent magnificence." The country's late victory had made it, abruptly, gigantic. Its future destiny, and in particular the territory to be granted it, must be commensurate with its new grandeur.

In January 1919, President Woodrow Wilson declared that the Treaty of London was invalid. Two days later, d'Annunzio published a "Letter to the Dalmatians," promising the Italian inhabitants of Dalmatia that they would soon be united with their homeland. Rejected by the *Corriere della Sera*, it appeared instead in Mussolini's *Il Popolo d'Italia*. In it d'Annunzio attacked the Allied leaders—Woodrow Wilson, Clemenceau, Lloyd George—in vitriolic terms. They were quack doctors preparing to amputate Italy's limbs, or wild beasts with slathering jaws agape, ready to devour territory that was Italy's by right. He swore to fight on for the cause of an Italian Dalmatia, with bomb in hand and blade between his teeth. "You will have me with you *to the end* [his italics]."

Italy in 1919 was politically unstable and financially depressed. The economy was shattered by the costs of the war, which had been covered, not by taxation, but by reckless borrowing. The national debt increased eightfold between 1916 and 1919. The lira dropped to twenty-five per cent of its pre-war value.

The vast majority of the troops had been peasants. Farms, without the young men to work them, were dilapidated, while women—mourning their sons and lovers—turned furiously against the landowners whom they blamed for the pointless war. Soldiers were reluctant to go back to impoverished villages. Cities were swarming with unemployed men. There were stories of uniformed generals shining shoes on the streets. In a revival of ancient Roman practice, each veteran had been promised a plot of land if he wanted it, but the land grants were never made.

Italians back home received the returning army with trepidation. The "victors of Vittorio Veneto" had expected a heroes' welcome, instead they came home to averted faces and locked doors. The land was full of men without occupation or income, and trained to violence. Worse, they fell into two mutually hostile groups. Parades of returning combatants were disrupted by anti-militarist protests. Soldiers in uniform were assaulted. Amerigo Dumini, who five years later would head the gang of thugs who killed Giacomo Matteotti, was converted to fascism, so he claimed, after being set upon by a socialist mob outside Florence's Duomo. Soldiers' anger against the government that had shown so little care of them festered. "Discontent began to snake its way through the ranks of the veterans," recalled one of them.

During the war the word *"imboscato"*—wooded-up, gone to the woods—had become a term of abuse used by the trenchocracy against anyone who was not fighting, be they deserters or those who had been legitimately excused military service. As the war dragged on, and the age of conscription dropped, more and more families hid their boys, more and more soldiers deserted. Even before Caporetto the countryside was full of men on the run from the military police, staying alive by robbery and scavenging. After the rout some 400,000 more soldiers went missing. To those men who had stayed and fought, and now came home to no satisfactory reward, the *imboscati* were hateful.

Returning soldiers formed *"Fasci di Combattimento"*—combatants' groups. Their aims were nebulous, their mood was violent. By the end of February 1919, some twenty such groups had sprung up. They were spoiling for a fight, and their natural opponents were the socialists, whom Mussolini had identified soon after Caporetto as constituting a more dangerous enemy than the Austrians had been.

"When I returned from the war, like so many, I hated politics and politicians," wrote Italo Balbo, aviator and leading fascist, in 1922. To return to "the country of Giolitti, who offered every ideal as an object for sale," was intolerable. "Better to deny everything, to destroy everything, so as to rebuild everything from scratch." He, and hundreds of thousands of men like him, craved violence and radical change, almost regardless of its direction. "Without Mussolini, three-quarters of Italian youths who had returned from the trenches would have become Bolsheviks." Fascism saved Italy from a socialist revolution, in Balbo's opinion, not by beating up socialists (though fascists did plenty of that) but by providing an alternative outlet for the anger the war left behind.

In the cities food shortages triggered riots. Shops and warehouses were plundered. In the countryside peasants marched on land-owners' homes, and landowners employed thugs to intimidate or forcibly suppress them. "Now the war against the foreigner is over," wrote the futurist Mannarese a month after the armistice; "class war has flared up again, more violent, more fierce." Demobilised soldiers and deserters alike were resentful and hungry. Landowners looking for fighting gangs to protect their property, socialists hoping to foment revolution, nationalists intent on ridding the *patria* of socialism—all could draw from an immense and toxic pool of disaffected manpower.

On the day the armistice was declared Mussolini chose to address the celebrating crowds from an armoured car manned by *Arditi*. The *Arditi* were the elite troops of the Italian army. Modelled on the German *Sturmtruppen*, they were better paid and better fed than the ordinary troops, and, used for the most dangerous assaults, they died quicker. They carried not guns but grenades and daggers. Their task was to rush, unencumbered by packs, on enemy positions and fight there, hand to hand, until the heavily laden regular troops came up. They had a fearsome reputation. Their black uniforms were strikingly hand-some, decorated with embroidered flames. Their flag was black, and bore the skull and crossbones. They affected a distinctive hairstyle, growing their hair long in front until some of them achieved forelocks as long as horses' tails. One contemporary observer called them *"mafi-osi,"* using the word in its original sense of a swaggerer, "a brave and assertive man who does not tolerate insult." They were the ruthless dandies of the war.

The futurist Mario Carli, who was one of them, wrote proudly that they were "legendary warriors, exempt from common law . . . blood-thirsty assassins, dagger between their teeth, provocative, hooligans, brutal as orangoutans." They were well educated, self-confident. Politi-cally unpredictable, they tolerated only minimal "formal discipline, no bureaucracy, the most flexible of hierarchies." Some had been, or remained, futurists. Others were anarchists or anarcho-syndicalists. All had a penchant for violence and a dislike of authority. Carli coined the term *"Arditismo"* to describe their spirit, and defined it in images: "a deep black background against which the musculature of an acro-bat glistens . . . the gay power of a twenty-year-old youth who throws a bomb while whistling a song from a Variety show."

So long as the fighting lasted the *Arditi's* violence was rewarded, their anti-social tendencies condoned. But once the war was over the public wanted no more to do with them. As one of them wrote bitterly, after having risked their lives for the fatherland they were "received by the fatherland . . . as undesirable guests." They were "believed to be wild and ferocious animals." They were "refused work . . . slandered by the press. Persecuted by the police. Irritated by the totally unjust and ungrateful attitude of the Nation." A contemporary observer describes them drifting from bar to bar in Milan, fearsome-looking but aimless, "talking loudly until boozed into silence." They still wore their black shirts, still sang their anthem *Giovinezza* (Youth), still chanted *"a noi"* meaning that something (Italy, or tomorrow, or the world) belonged to them. But one of them wrote: "We have no direction any more . . . The war has become our second nature . . . Where shall I go? What shall I do?"

General Caviglia, who became Minister for War in February 1919, judged that in the current state of unrest, such a body of fighters might be useful "because they were greatly feared for their inclination for swift and violent action." If they were disbanded on the other hand, "they would reinforce the revolutionary parties." He was right to fear it. The *Arditi* were seen as potential recruits by activists of right and left alike. Mussolini flattered and wooed them, inciting them to "break the fetters of decrepit institutions," and make of themselves a political "advance guard."

D'Annunzio had great respect for the *Arditi*, and the *Arditi* in turn admired him. Whenever he made the transition from speech to action he would be able to count on their support. Like them, he was intolerant of all the argy-bargy of negotiated settlements and democratic debate. He represented, as Carli wrote that they did, "the true Italy, the young Italy, the Italy which marches in the vanguard and cuts through diplomatic labyrinths with a good dagger-blow."

In January 1919, cabinet minister Leonida Bissolati addressed a meeting at La Scala. Bissolati was proposing a compromise. Italy would renounce its claims to the predominantly Croatian region of Dalmatia, asking only for the cities of Zara and Fiume, each of which had Italian majorities. Bissolati's proposal had the backing of General Diaz, who, like his predecessor Cadorna, believed that Italian bases elsewhere on the Dalmatian coast would be "militarily useless and dangerous." But despite the endorsement of these unimpeachably patriotic and militarist figures, the plan was too modest to please those assembled in La Scala. Marinetti and his futurist cronies led the heckling from their box. An "infernal symphony . . . Squeaks, shrieks, whistles, grumbles . . . A patriotic cry became distinguishable now and then, and ruled the inarticulate mass with the rhythm of a brutal march." Elsewhere in the auditorium Benito Mussolini, with a "pale, spade-like face," added to the hullaballoo with an "unmistakable voice, dishearteningly wooden, peremptorily insistent, like the clacking of castanets."

Mussolini was not yet sufficiently influential for d'Annunzio to have taken much notice of him, but his power base was growing. On 23 March 1919 he invited the leaders of the *Fasci di Combattimento*, along with some like-minded nationalists, futurists, and *Arditi*, to a meeting in a rented hall overlooking Milan's Piazza San Sepolcro. Over the next two decades this assembly was to assume, in fascism's myth of origin, the haloed significance of a nativity. At the time, though, it was just an incoherent gathering of some hundred widely assorted malcontents.

All those present had been interventionists, all believed ardently that warfare was glorious, and that those who had fought were being denied the honour that was their due. Beyond those shared tenets, they had little in common. Marinetti was there, so was Ferruccio Vecchi, leader of a movement he called *Arditismo Civile*. So were spokesmen from almost every point on the political spectrum, republicans and monarchists, anarchists and authoritarians calling for the strong leadership of a charismatic dictator. In a great deal of fiery talk, their differences remained unresolved. The first task must be the creation of a new ruling class. There would be time later on to think about "administration, the law, the schools, the colonies and so on." Mussolini said: "We have the luxury to be aristocrats as well as democrats. Reactionaries as well as revolutionaries, defending legality while committing illegal acts." Such a movement, lacking internal coherence, needed a leader, a *Duce*. There were better-known people at the San Sepolcro meeting, but Mussolini already saw himself in the role.

Three weeks later, Marinetti and Ferruccio Vecchi met up in a fashionable pastry shop in Milan's *galleria*—the splendid glass and wrought-iron shopping mall in the heart of the city—and, with a group of their followers, moved on to break into the offices of the socialist newspaper *Avanti!*, smashing machines and furniture. Mussolini was not present, but after the raid a stolen *Avanti!* signboard was carried as a trophy to his office. Two days later he declared in print that he "accepted the whole moral responsibility for the episode," adroitly laying claim to an exploit (or outrage) with which he had actually had nothing to do.

The authorities seemed incapable of maintaining order: some overtly condoned the violence. After the raid on *Avanti!* the Minister of Defence went so far as to congratulate the aggressors, warning the socialists: "You are up against men who for four years risked their lives every day, a thousand times a day." The government, desperate to prevent the socialist revolution they feared, were sanctioning the erosion of the law. It was a fatally dangerous strategy. Soon the *Fasci* were effectively at war with the socialists, in a conflict which the civil powers did nothing to halt.

On Easter Sunday 1919, Frances Stevenson, secretary and lover of the British Prime Minster David Lloyd George, was watching the window of American President Woodrow Wilson's apartment in Paris. Inside the apartment the Council of Four, the heads of state of the victorious

Allied powers, were attending an emergency session called in a final attempt to reach agreement on Italy's demands. Stevenson was hoping it would be over in time for the picnic Lloyd George had promised her. "Suddenly [the Italian premier] Vittorio Orlando appeared at the window, leaned on the bar which runs across it, and put his head in his hands. I thought it looked as though he was crying, but I could not believe it possible until I saw him take out his handkerchief and wipe his eyes and cheeks." Lloyd George's valet, watching beside her, asked: "What are they doing to the poor old gentleman?"

What they were doing was flatly refusing to grant what he demanded: all the concessions promised in the Treaty of London, and Fiume as well. Orlando, and his Foreign Minister Sonnino, were as intent as d'Annunzio on claiming territory for Italy, but they had failed to make their case. Orlando was convinced that a secret society of nationalists was pledged to assassinate him if he returned from Paris without having gained Dalmatia for Italy. He warned the other delegates that if he could not bring back terms that his electorate would accept Italy was likely to collapse into civil war (he was not exaggerating). Waxing extravagant, he declared that denying him Fiume would be fatal to the peace of the world. He would not modify his demands. He would face the consequences of his inflexibility "up to and including death." He wrung his hands and wept. Clemenceau and Lloyd George looked on stonily. (Sir Maurice Hankey, the conference secretary, said afterwards he would have spanked his son if the boy had behaved in such an unmanly fashion.) Woodrow Wilson offered Orlando a consoling arm across the shoulder, but no concessions.

Orlando was a lawyer and a skilled politician who had held his country together through a difficult war and the first months of an almost more difficult peace, but in Paris he was outclassed. Lloyd George patronisingly described him as "attractive and amiable," but the young British diplomat Harold Nicolson thought him "a white, weak, flabby man." Sonnino, described as "hawk-like and ferocious" by Wilson's aide Edward House, might be less flabby, but his obstinacy was no more useful than Orlando's wheedling. The two of them had allowed the question of Italy's entitlement to new territories to be postponed until the peace talks were already well advanced. When the discussion at last began they were dismayed to find how reluctant their allies were to grant their demands.

They had failed to allow for the other peace-makers' low opinion of them. The British ambassador in Paris reported that the general attitude to Italy among the delegates "has been contempt." The British and French had bought Italy's support with the concessions made in the Treaty of London, and—greatly though they had benefited from the deal—the representatives of both countries despised a nation that would so sell itself. Their distaste was powered as well by simple irrational prejudice. When Clemenceau described Orlando as "very Italian" he intended a racist insult. Lloyd George agreed, calling Italy "the most contemptible nation." Sir Charles Hardinge, Permanent Under-Secretary at the British Foreign Office, referred to his Italian counterparts as "the beggars of Europe," well known "for their whining alternated with truculence." Italian seamen, said the British First Sea Lord, were useless "organ-grinders." American attitudes were scarcely more positive. President Woodrow Wilson brought to Versailles the preconceptions of a nation receiving, with increasing reluctance, an enormous influx of Italian immigrants. In America—a polyglot society where divisions of class and race, rather than intersecting at right angles as they do in Europe, run parallel—Italians were seen as being among the lowest of the low: untrustworthy, if not downright criminal.

One of d'Annunzio's most often-repeated arguments for Italy's entering the war had been that by fighting the nation could prove its valour and so earn the respect of others. To him, and to all his fellow patriots, it seemed that the Italian servicemen's fortitude throughout the terrible conflict, and their ultimate success, had demonstrated that this was a nation of heroes, as courageous and virile as any other. The world had failed to take the point. The defeat of an empire, the hundreds of thousands of men killed on the Italian Front, had not been enough to prompt the delegates in Paris to re-examine their prejudices.

Four days after that emotional Easter morning Orlando and his foreign secretary walked out of the peace talks. D'Annunzio hailed their intransigence. "Italy is not afraid to stand alone against everyone and everything . . . And so I say that today only Italy is great, and only Italy is pure." Diplomacy had failed to bring back Italy's lost left lung. There were some prominent militarists, including more than one high-ranking general, who were saying that Italians should seize by force what the peace-makers in Paris refused to grant them. D'Annunzio agreed.

That April he embarked on a series of speeches as bellicose and incendiary as those he had made four years before. In Venice he spoke in St. Mark's Square. Venetians, he declared, were still being denied what was theirs. Italy was victorious, but her ignoble representatives were allowing her to be cheated of her prize. He appealed to the people to prepare to fight to renew the greatness of Venice's mediaeval empire.

Moving on to Rome, and tailoring his message to suit his audience, he called for the revival of the Empire of Rome. Speaking on the Capitol, he played at being Mark Antony, who had there displayed Caesar's torn and blood-stained garments to the susceptible crowds. On the spot where, four years earlier, he had reverently raised aloft Nino Bixio's sword, d'Annunzio now unfurled the flag which had covered Randaccio's coffin, and which was stained with his blood. He spoke fervently of the debt that all survivors owed to the "glorious martyrs" of the war. Repeatedly he kissed the stained and tattered flag and then released it, now bordered with a black ribbon, sign of mourning for the still-unredeemed territories. As though intoning the creed of his new sect, he called out, slowly and sonorously, the names of all the cities and territories for whose "redemption" he was now calling. His listeners trembled and wept.

In May, Orlando and Sonnino returned to Paris, the former looking, according to an American delegate, "very white and worn . . . without much pep . . . and ten years older." D'Annunzio was speaking repeatedly, his rhetoric becoming increasingly seditious. He preached that it was no sin to take up arms against elected politicians, the "parasites" whose "weakness, ineptitude, idleness and egoism" threatened to compromise Italy's victory. On 26 May, the anniversary of Italy's entry into the war, he was due to speak in the Theatre of Augustus, but he was forbidden to do so. Within days his speech was published instead. It was a great drum roll of prose about how Italy's smoking blood had been offered up as a sacrifice to the greatness of its promised future, how the sky over the battlefield had glowed with courage and sacrifice, yearning and fire.

Increasingly now d'Annunzio was using religious rhetoric, drawing on the hypnotic rhythms of the liturgy by which, in his youth, he had seen peasants worked into states of frenzy. He claimed to see visions. He told his public 80,000 dead soldiers were flying over Rome transporting the mountain on which they died. "I see it. Don't you see it too?" He saw the "Christ of our battles." He said that Christ was calling out to the Italians to "rise up and be not afraid." He led his listeners in chants in which the word "blood" tolled repeatedly—the blood shed already, the blood which yet must flow to cleanse Italy of the filthy shame of a negotiated peace. He was blasphemous, unreasonable, electrifying.

The military authorities ordered him out of Rome, and back to Venice. As an officer he was bound to obey. He resigned his commission. He would take orders from no one.

The conjunction of a war hero and a returning army is a danger to any civilian state. As one of d'Annunzio's most perceptive biographers remarks: "the Rubicon has never really been forgotten in Italy." The Italian authorities placed d'Annunzio under close surveillance. The watchers found plenty to occupy them.

One of his slogans was *Ardere non Ordire* (To Dare Not to Plot), but plot he did. He had new friends. One was Giovanni Giuriati, a prominent figure in the irredentist movement who had been twice wounded and twice decorated in the war. Giuriati was as passionately committed to the creation of a Greater Italy as d'Annunzio was, and as impatient with the Italian government's caution. His power base was the National Association of Trento and Trieste. An energetic administrator and a subtle diplomat, Giuriati saw that he could make use of d'Annunzio's charisma, and—himself no showman—he was content to play the modest grey eminence in d'Annunzio's brilliant drama.

In June the peace conference ended with the question of Italy's claims unresolved. Orlando returned from Paris for the second time to be voted out of office on 23 June and was replaced by Francesco Nitti, not a warrior, not a superman, but a professor of economics. Nitti was to become d'Annunzio's prime hate figure, the butt of his grossest humour, the target of his most excoriating verbal abuse. A canny politician, Nitti had entered parliament as a radical, and held ministerial posts under Giolitti and Orlando. Giuriati described him as "anti-war, anti-victory, our enemy by definition." He was a pragmatist who preferred negotiation to warfare, and who saw the restoration of Italy's economy as being more useful than the defence of its honour. He had no sympathy with the new political order of which d'Annunzio was to be the harbinger. In 1924 he would leave Italy, going into exile after courageously opposing the fascist regime.

Seven months after the armistice, the expensive and dangerously recalcitrant army still numbered over a million and a half men. The majority of them were deployed along the northern frontiers, the high command believing, as d'Annunzio did, that fighting there might, and perhaps should, soon resume. The rest were stationed around the country, supposedly to guarantee public order. Nitti made his first priority the reduction of men under arms to pre-war levels. The Italian army was top heavy. By the end of the war there were over a thousand generals, and they all now vehemently protested against their own enforced retirement. Those plotting to destabilise the civilian government, or to lead an unauthorised invasion of the unredeemed territories, could now count on the sympathy of a considerable proportion of the military hierarchy.

An enquiry into the catastrophe of Caporetto ended with Nitti declaring a general amnesty for deserters. Given the vast numbers of men involved, it was the only feasible outcome. Nitti wasn't interested in hunting the deserters down. He wanted them back home, working, supporting their families, paying tax. The trenchocracy was outraged. Were cowards and traitors to be treated the same as those who had valiantly risked death? It was to this amnesty that d'Annunzio was later to trace his determination to rebel. If the law protected "the booty of deserters" then he would have no compunction about breaking it.

D'Annunzio now had followers very different from the earnest young scholars who used to crowd around his table in Venice in the 1890s. One night in 1919 in the Caffè Greco, a young poet and admirer of d'Annunzio saw a group of people arguing loudly, among them *Arditi* with bushy beards and great falls of black hair. He was told they were "d'Annunzians." The *Arditi* might not fit with that part of d'Annunzio's life which included Gothic bibelots, Murano glass and china tea, but he prized them as he had prized his greyhounds, for their physical splendour and their appetite for killing. He flattered them by giving them a new mythopoeic character. If the Carso was Inferno, he announced, they were its demons: if the sky above the battlefields was Heaven, they were its angels. He made innumerable puns on the words *ardire* (to dare), *ardore* (ardour) and *ardere* (to burn). He dined in their mess and told them "to be among you is to enter the fiery furnace." He admired the medal which showed an *Ardito*, grenade in each hand, enveloped in flame. He told them that he had carried with him on all his wartime exploits a dagger, which had been given him on the battlefield by one of their number, still dripping with Austrian blood.

The day after Nitti assumed office d'Annunzio published an article entitled "The Command Passes to the People." He was now openly inciting Italians to reject their elected government.

The police files for the spring and summer of 1919 report that d'Annunzio was involved in a series of conspiracies with a varying combination of allies—with senior army officers, with the Duke of Aosta, Peppino Garibaldi and other assorted nationalists, with futurists, irredentists and anarchists, with *Arditi*, and with Mussolini and his fascists.

One evening in June, half a year after d'Annunzio had ignored Mussolini's initial request for a rendezvous, the two of them met face to face for the first time. They sat in the Grand Hotel in Rome talking at length about how the Italian state should be restructured. That same month a police report on Mussolini was delivered to Nitti. It described him as very intelligent, with a gift for swiftly divining men's strengths and weaknesses, and as an orator who could hold audiences gripped.

D'Annunzio saw the fascists as crude imitators of himself. They were potentially useful supporters, but they were lamentably brutal in their methods and unrefined in their thinking. Mussolini was a "companion in faith and violence," but he was a subordinate partner, when he was included at all, in the conspiracies of those months. Those conspiracies' aims were variously to seize Spalato and/or the rest of Dalmatia, or to stage a coup against the insufficiently irredentist government in Rome and form a revolutionary assembly with d'Annunzio at its head.

That summer of 1919 was perhaps d'Annunzio's political apogee. Every intrigue and conspiracy made use of his name, every projected coup d'état was to lead to his installation as dictator. In Paris, when Orlando told Lloyd George he foresaw his own downfall, perhaps as a result of a parliamentary rebellion, perhaps as the result of a popular revolt, Lloyd George asked who he imagined would assume power. "Perhaps d'Annunzio," he replied.

There were plenty of people seeking to destabilise the Italian democracy. Few would have guessed by whom, just over three years later, the thing would be done. "The Italian people is a mass of precious materials. It needs to be forged, cleaned, worked. A work of art is still possible. But a government is needed. A man. A man who, when the situation demands it, has the delicate touch of an artist and the heavy fist of a warrior . . . A man who knows the people, loves the people, and can direct and bend it—with violence if necessary." The author of those words was Mussolini, but in 1919 the man with the miracle-working charisma, and the enormous popular following which might make a regime-change possible was not him, but Gabriele d'Annunzio.

D'Annunzio was still living in flamboyant style. He made time to visit Luisa Casati on Capri, where he hung all the bushes in her garden with flowers made of Murano glass, but Venice was still his base. Everywhere he went he was fêted. When the statue of Colleoni was returned to its position, d'Annunzio was there, batting away applause with studied modesty as he permitted the assembled enthusiasts to draw parallels between himself and the legendary warrior. When he returned to Venice after a brief absence the railway station was mobbed by his admirers. War veterans, students, the mayor and his officials, all crowded round him, while the sky filled with aircraft: the pilots of d'Annunzio's squadron were flying spirals in his honour.

In Rome, when he wanted to meet the King, one telephone call secured him an audience that very afternoon. Poet and monarch—two small men with a shared taste for small metal objects (the King was as keen on old coins as d'Annunzio was on Renaissance medals)—paced the paths of the royal Villa Savoia's gardens for three-quarters of an hour while d'Annunzio talked. The King was quieter—a British ambassador once said of him: "He is thought to have ideas but has never propounded them to anyone"—but he probably enjoyed the conversation. Unlike his father and grandfather, who each boasted of having never read a book, he liked poetry. As they parted he pressed d'Annunzio's hand warmly and said something about how the constitution constrained his freedom, words which d'Annunzio and his followers interpreted as meaning that Victor Emmanuel would have appointed him president if only he had had the power to do so.

The young Belgian poet Léon Kochnitzky met d'Annunzio for the first time at a party in Rome in July, and has left a vivid description of his sitting in an armchair at the centre of a room crowded with his hushed and reverent admirers, talking ceaselessly of Shelley, Rasputin, Renaissance painting and his preferred routes for nocturnal strolls around Rome. He was—as he had been when he sat, a tiny child, on a little stool at the centre of a circle of his mother's friends—the centre of attention. His voice was melodious. He used little hand gestures and smiles to keep each listener entrapped and they all, old and young, obscure or very powerful, sat silently listening while he talked and talked and daintily ate ice cream—first strawberry-flavoured, then banana, then strawberry again.

There was an American-born princess at the party who claimed to be clairvoyant. She offered to read the cards for d'Annunzio. He accepted. They were highly auspicious. "Then," d'Annunzio said lightly, "I shall march on Fiume."

Fiume (now called Rijeka), which was about to become the setting for the climactic act of the drama of d'Annunzio's life, was a city with a staccato history and a mongrel population. Dramatically sited at the northern end of the Adriatic, in the crook of the angle formed by the Istrian peninsula's meeting with the Dalmatian coast, it is backed by mountains and overlooks the island-dotted Gulf of Carnaro. Badly damaged by subsequent wars, its centre is now patched with ruins, but Alexander Powell, an American who visited it just after d'Annunzio got there in 1919, described it as "shaded by double rows of stately trees" with "numerous surprisingly well-stocked shops; and rising here and there above the trees and the housetops, like fingers pointing to heaven, the graceful campaniles of fine old churches."

One of the Austro-Hungarian Empire's two great Adriatic ports, Fiume had been, for the previous two centuries, Budapest's outlet to the sea, as Trieste was Vienna's. Roads and rail tracks converged on it from Budapest, Prague, Belgrade and Zagreb. Alongside it the river from which it takes its name hurtles down a ravine, powering the mills which were among the sources of the city's prosperity. In the mid-nineteenth century, Fiume's industrial output constituted half of all Croatia's. By 1914 it boasted an oil refinery, a British-owned torpedo works, foundries, chemical plants, tanneries, timber yards, factories producing soap and candles, pasta and sail cloth. Most important of all were the docks and shipyards. "Miles and miles of concrete moles and wharfs," reports Powell, "equipped with harbour machinery of the most modern description, and adjacent to them rows of warehouses as commodious as the Bush Terminals in Brooklyn."

As it had increased in prosperity, so Fiume became a more desirable prize and its political status more controversial. The eighteenth-century Empress Maria Theresa had granted it the status of a *corpus separatum*, a quasi-autonomous free city. Thereafter it was ruled in turn by Hungary, by Napoleonic France, by Austria, by Hungary again and then, after 1848, by Croatia, before the Hungarian monarchy once again gained control of it in 1867. From that time onward, it was a Hungarian outpost, some 300 kilometres from the capital, ruled directly from Budapest by a Hungarian governor resident in the city.

On all its landward sides it was closely surrounded by Croatia, which had a measure of constitutional independence within the Empire. Uncomfortably conscious of how vulnerable Fiume was, during the last three decades of the nineteenth century the Hungarian authorities encouraged Italian merchants to settle in the city, partly in order to facilitate trade across the Adriatic, partly to provide a counterbalance to the restive Croat population. By 1915 Italians formed the majority in the inner city.

Over twenty years the population of the city had doubled, and the traffic passing though its ports had increased sixfold. Banks opened. Fiume was flourishing. The narrow alleys of the Venetian-built old town were now encircled by suburban boulevards with neo-classical villas and gardens filled with roses. But the Italian Fiumans proved no more docile than the Croats. They formed the great majority of the city's middle class: they were prosperous and successful, but they were governed and policed by Hungarians. Soon they were nearly as discontented as the Slav communities. In 1892 they tore down a statue of the Emperor Franz Joseph.

Fiume was a city obsessed with its own destiny, and known for its crowded cafés, where people sat arguing all day long, and for the multiplicity of its printing presses. During the war years there were 346 journals published in the city. A visitor describes it: "The public life of the city centres on a broad square on which front numerous hotels, restaurants, and coffee houses, before which lounge, from mid-morning until midnight, a considerable proportion of the Italian population, sipping *caffè nero*, or tall drinks concocted from sweet, bright-coloured syrups, scanning the papers and discussing, with much noise and gesticulation, the political situation and the doings of the peace commissioners in Paris. Save only Barcelona, Fiume has the most excitable and irritable population of any city that I know."

In the autumn of 1918, as the defeat and dismemberment of the Austro-Hungarian Empire came to seem inevitable, the people of Fiume faced encompassment by the brand new state of Yugoslavia.

There were those in the city (most of them Croatian or members of the smaller but vocal Serbian community) who welcomed the prospect, but they were opposed by the Autonomists (mainly socialist, and including members of all ethnic groups), who wanted Fiume to be once more a *corpus separatum*, and by the Italian or Italophile "annexationists" who hoped it would become part of a Greater Italy.

A small place with a strategic importance disproportionate to its size, and a highly politicised, mixed-race population, Fiume posed problems for the peacemakers in Paris. It had not been one of the territories promised to Italy in the Treaty of London: its future was not predetermined.

On 28 October 1918, as Italian troops chased the Austrians past Vittorio Veneto, the last Hungarian governor of Fiume informed the mayor that Magyar rule was over, and that he was leaving the city. Over the next three days rival groups tussled for control. The pro-Yugoslav Popular Committee, backed by Croatian troops with Hapsburg-issue machine guns, claimed that power had been transferred to them. They took over the Governor's Palace and hoisted the Croatian flag. At the same time the Fiuman-Italians formed the National Council, electing the septuagenarian Dr. Antonio Grossich as their president, and announced they were the city's *de facto* government. A third would-be administration, a workers' council, challenged them both. There were rowdy demonstrations and counter-demonstrations. The rival groups fought it out in the streets.

On 30 October the National Council conducted a plebiscite which resulted, so they claimed, in an overwhelming vote by the city's people in favour of annexation to Italy. Some pro-Yugoslav sources deny this plebiscite ever took place; if it did it was probably more of a noisy rally, with a resolution arrived at by shouting, than an orderly democratic process. But for the Fiuman-Italians and their supporters on the Italian mainland it was to become a key moment in their story.

As the war ended the city was occupied by Allied forces, most of them Italians who heartily agreed with d'Annunzio that Fiume was, and forever after should be, Italian. An Italian warship appeared in the harbour on 4 November. The admiral in command ordered that the Croatian flag flying over the Governor's Palace be taken down. Soon matters were complicated by the arrival of a battalion of the Allied

Army of the Orient, made up of French and Serbian forces, who had been fighting the Turks on the Eastern Front. On 15 November they moved into the suburb of Susak, just across the river from Fiume. The Serbs (allies whom d'Annunzio had described two years earlier as "our future enemies") were not welcome to the Fiuman-Italians. Nor were the French contingent, most of their troops being actually Vietnamese or North African; in contemporary accounts suspicion of the French, as being likely to support Yugoslav claims, is overlaid by simple racist hostility to the "chinks" and "niggers."

The atmosphere in Fiume became so explosive that the Serbian troops were rapidly withdrawn. An hour after they left more Italian troops began to pour into the city, disembarking from ships or walking over the inland frontier. Croatian and Serbian flags were torn down and the Italian *tricolore* hoisted in their place. Croatian shop signs were defaced and the sale of all Slav newspapers banned. British and American ships arrived in the harbour in a belated attempt to impose some kind of neutral interim government, but they were unable to annul the fact that Fiume was well on the way to becoming a *de facto* Italian enclave.

It was an edgy time, but an exciting one. One of the Italian soldiers with the Allied force occupying Fiume was the young poet Giovanni Comisso. He liked the place at once. "Americans, English, French crowded the streets: it seemed that every day there was a victory celebration." After months on the battlefields, Fiume seemed to him a garden of earthly delights: beautiful girls, shops full of perfumes, marvellous cakes; cafés with deferential waiters; illustrated magazines, coffee with cream, delicious zabaglione (Comisso, who dedicates a whole page of his memoirs to a custard tart he once ate in Trieste, had as sweet a tooth as d'Annunzio himself). Best of all was the way the Fiuman-Italians welcomed the Italian troops. Every night officers were invited to parties in the locals' houses, where they ate and drank and danced until morning.

Over the next months, Fiume's Italian inhabitants became ever more clamorous in their appeals to the Italian government to offer them its protection. Meanwhile the Yugoslavs appealed to the Allied leaders to cede the city to them. Geographically it seemed naturally to form a part of their new country. The French were sympathetic: a strong new state would help to contain Germany, and to keep Italy (which Clemenceau considered an untrustworthy ally) from dominating the eastern Mediterranean.

The Italians of Fiume turned to d'Annunzio. Within a week of the armistice in November 1918 he had received a letter from the President of the National Council full of assurances of the "burning faith" of the Fiuman-Italians in their imminent "liberation" by their great Mother, and asking for his help in hastening on the happy day. Initially he temporised, but on 14 January 1919, he published his "Letter to the Dalmatians" in which he publicly and fervidly dedicated himself to the cause of the *Italianissimo* (very, very Italian) city.

"Why they have set their hearts on a town of 50,000 people, with little more than half of them Italians, is a mystery to me," wrote Edward House, Woodrow Wilson's adviser. But as months passed with no good news from Paris for Italian nationalists, Fiume became a symbol of all that Italy aspired to, and all that it was being denied. Orlando promised the Italian parliament he would be true to "that most Italian city, the jewel of the Carnaro." D'Annunzio took up the theme. Hitherto Fiume had been, for him, just one of the many cities for whose redemption he called. Now, in the mesmeric sequences of call and response with which his speeches climaxed, he began to include the new slogan: "Fiume or death!"

In the spring of 1919, a Fiuman *Ardito* officer, Captain Nino Host-Venturi (who was to become one of d'Annunzio's most important associates over the next two years), assembled a fighting troop which he initially described as a "gymnastic club" but which was soon openly referred to as the Legion of Fiume. Men and women alike began to wear red, white and green rosettes. Streets were given new Italian names. The atmosphere is described by Father J. N. Macdonald, a Jesuit priest living in the city. Unlike the great majority of the other foreign visitors who left descriptions of the next two years' events in Fiume, Father Macdonald spoke Croatian and sympathised with the city's Slavic peoples. He saw "postboxes, lampposts, house doors . . . daubed with liberal quantities of red, white and green paint. Wherever one looked the word *Italia* struck one in the eye and even at night it was outlined with electric lamps." Host-Venturi's Legion of Fiume kept growing (one recruiting trip to Rome raised another 400 volunteers).

When Orlando and Sonnino withdrew from the peace talks in April, the Fiuman-Italians shouted: "Down with Wilson! Down with redskins!" Meanwhile, back in Rome, Orlando was greeted with cries of "Viva Fiume!" and in Turin students tore down the street signs along the Corso Wilson, exchanging them for new ones reading Corso Fiume. Mussolini came to Fiume and gave an inflammatory speech. The newly formed association of Young Fiume issued a declaration. "Citizens be prepared! The battle is now beginning against everything and everybody, on behalf of our rights and our dead. We write this with blood on our banners."

The battle against everybody took the form of racist bullying. Father Macdonald describes gangs twenty strong roaming the streets at night, terrorising non-Italians and beating them up. They muscled their way into the cafés and ordered the musicians to play the Italian national anthem, while the customers were forced to stand up. One night in May the legionaries went out in force, defaced non-Italian shop signs with tar, and daubed the doors of the Slav population with skull and crossbones, or black crosses. In June, the National Council declared its intention of raising an army, and decreed that it was high treason to question Fiume's "political union" with Italy.

There were numerous high-ranking Italian officers willing to serve the Fiuman-Italians' cause. Giuriati put the resources of his irredentist Trento-Trieste Association at Fiume's service, organising a recruitment drive across Italy for a "National Fiuman Army." But while Wilson and the other peacemakers were inclined to recognise the independence of communities who had risen up against their former rulers, they were far less likely to acknowledge a regime imposed by an invading force. The Fiumans had to stage their own coup. Before they could get up the nerve to do so they had need of a inspirational leader. They cast around for one among the prominent nationalists. Peppino Garibaldi, the Duke of Aosta and the futurist poet Sam Benelli were among the people Host-Venturi and his associates considered. But their choice was for d'Annunzio. On 29 May he received a telegram from one of the leaders of the National Council of Fiume. "We look to the only firm and intrepid *Duce* of the Italian people. Command us. We are ready."

Here at last was d'Annunzio's chance to play the condottiero. He sent a telegram accepting the role of Fiume's liberator with characteristic portentousness: "Await me with faith and discipline. I will fail neither you nor destiny. Long live Italian Fiume!" On Whit Sunday, 8 June, he published a polemic entitled "Italian Pentecost," calling Fiume "the only living city, the only ardent city, the only city of the spirit, all wind and fire . . . the most beautiful holocaust which has ever, throughout the centuries, been offered up." Two days later posters appeared overnight in public places all over Fiume announcing: "Gabriele d'Annunzio the fervid assertor of your rights is today the symbol of the mind and soul of Italy," and "Tell the faithful that their faith will be rewarded."

Their faith was first to be sorely tried. D'Annunzio was dividing his time between Venice, where music and philandering kept him busy, and Rome, where he was being offered other roles. Nitti hoped to neutralise him with a job offer: he could be high commissioner for aviation. D'Annunzio does not appear to have responded. From somewhere came the idea that he might fly by stages to Tokyo. This was more tempting. D'Annunzio addressed a group of aviators, calling on them to turn their backs with him on the West, which was at once so "infected" and so "sterile." While the Fiuman-Italians awaited him with "faith and discipline," he apparently forgot them, busying himself with meetings with chiefs of staff to discuss the complex logistics of the proposed flight.

It is unclear who, if anybody, seriously expected this voyage to take place. It is possible the government offered it as a lure to keep d'Annunzio harmlessly busy on the other side of the world. It is equally possible that d'Annunzio himself was only pretending interest in order to deceive the police agents by whom he was, by this time, ceaselessly watched. More likely, he simply hadn't made up his mind which of the two roles offered him appealed to him most. Again he dithered. Again he waited for a sign. Several more weeks were to go by before the fortune-telling princess inspired him to action.

In July 1919, Fiume passed from tension into lethal violence. The city was still garrisoned by a mixture of Italian and French troops under Allied command. The multi-ethnic French troops would cross over in the evenings from Susak, and parade through Fiume, provocatively wearing rosettes of ribbons in the Yugoslav colours. Meanwhile Fiuman-Italian girls would hand out rosettes in the Italian colours, and at evening, when everyone assembled along the city's waterfront for the *passeggiata*, there were scuffles. After an incident when a French soldier was alleged to have torn a rosette in the Italian colours off a girl's dress, the jostling and bullying which had become commonplace tipped over into murder. Thirteen Vietnamese-French soldiers were killed—stabbed or shoved off the quays into the water to drown. Some fifty more were injured. An American oil man who was staying in the grand waterfront Europa Hotel saw it all from his window and told one of his colleagues: "Believe me, friend, that was one hellish business . . . they literally cut those poor little Chinks into pieces." The Croatian Club was trashed by Italian nationalists. Italian troops were seen taking part in the riots and allowing, if not actually participating in, the killing.

This was too much. When reports of the massacre reached Paris, four Allied generals were despatched to Fiume to set up a commission of enquiry. Giuriati, visiting the city, found it "in an indescribable state of exaltation." The prospect of having their affairs decided by a panel of outsiders had the citizens in uproar. Wild talk, bells ringing, patriotic songs. "No one cared any more about his own business. Timetables no longer existed. News, true or false, spread like lightning." At every flying rumour people poured into the streets. "An orator, leaping onto a chair or a table in the Caffè Commercio would find his every word underlined by waves of enthusiasm or explosions of fury." Giuriati met Host-Venturi of the Legion, Grossich, leader of the National Council, and other prominent Fiuman-Italians. They were all, he reported, ready to risk their all for annexation to Italy.

The Italian government's attitude to the Fiume question was ambivalent. The stridency of d'Annunzio's invective was an embarrassment, but his speeches, which were widely reported throughout Europe, were useful to the Italian negotiators in Paris as evidence that without substantial concessions in Dalmatia the government would find it hard to keep the peace at home. Orlando would not overtly sanction a coup in Fiume or anywhere else, but it is quite possible that he would have covertly welcomed one. With Nitti's accession to the premiership though, the situation changed. The Duke of Aosta, who had been in command of the Third Army stationed around Fiume, was recalled, and replaced by General Badoglio, who had been Diaz's deputy for the last year of the war.

Badoglio had a lot of sympathy with d'Annunzio. Three months earlier he had written to him: "Your image, as a Great Italian, will be for ever a radiant example of faith, of heroism and of sacrifice to the army and to the whole nation." He had drawn up a plan to blight the beginnings of the Yugoslav state using black propaganda and *agents provocateurs*, encouraging Italian soldiers to seduce the "susceptible local women," and stirring up conflict between the Serbs, Croats and Slovenes. He seemed like a natural ally for the irredentists. Late in July, Giuriati approached him, hoping at least for "discreet complicity." But Badoglio was still a loyal soldier. He would not condone the creation of a private army like the Legion of Fiume. He certainly would not tolerate mutiny in his own ranks. "In barely educated minds and simple souls, like those of most of our soldiers, the concept of discipline expresses itself in a single word 'I obey'." On 31 July he issued orders that the approach road to Fiume was to be watched, and that no one attempting "movements contrary to the government's orders" was to be allowed to pass, not even "noti uomini"—famous men. (He meant d'Annunzio.)

With the Italian high command refusing to sanction their plans, the Fiuman-Italians prepared for open revolt. On 19 August, Host-Venturi, commander of the Legion, declared: "I no longer speak to you as an Italian officer, nor even as an Italian citizen, but from today onwards as a revolutionary."

In August the Allied commission on Fiume decreed that the city's Italian-dominated National Council should be replaced by a governing body under Allied control which better represented the Croat population of the city's suburbs, that the Legion of Fiume should be disbanded and that the Italian troops, a regiment of Sardinian grenadiers, who formed a part of the Allied garrison, should be moved out of the city and replaced by British and American troops. These orders caused an uproar. Italian officers were greeted with thunderous applause on every street corner and the church bells clanged all day. More parties, more romances between Italian officers and obliging Fiuman-Italian girls, more laughing and kissing and (according to Comisso) more "exquisite cakes."

The Sardinian Brigade had been the first Italian troops to enter Fiume the previous November. They were seen, by themselves and the Fiuman-Italians, as the city's liberators and guardians. The Allied command, hoping to avoid a demonstration, ordered them to march out of the city before dawn, but the Fiuman-Italians saw to it that the demonstration took place anyway. The town hall's bells were rung at 3 a.m. Boys ran through the city yelling and clashing hand bells. People, many of them brandishing, or wrapped in, the Italian flag, poured onto the torch-lit streets.

Trumpets sounded. The President of the National Council addressed the departing troops: "Tell our brothers that we have been Italian for centuries . . . Though rent from our mother we are her devoted sons." The Sardinians found their route blocked by kneeling women entreating them to stay and by children who grabbed at their knees and hung on their coat tails. They hesitated. Like most of the military, they were convinced irredentists. They had been idling in Fiume for several agreeable months during which they had become fond of the Italian citizens who hailed them as heroic protectors, who drank and danced and had sex with them. Only the resolution of their commanding officer—who would have faced court-martial had he allowed them to linger in the city—got them moving. They left at last, shouting: "Long live Italian Fiume!" in chorus with the crowds who pelted them with flowers.

They withdrew across the Istrian peninsula to the military base at Ronchi, but the boldest among them immediately began to make plans to return and claim Fiume for Italy. Then, like the Fiuman-Italians before them, they made contact with d'Annunzio. Seven officers, hereafter known portentously as the "Ronchi Seven," signed a letter: "We have sworn upon the memory of all who died for the unity of Italy: Fiume or death! And you do nothing for Fiume? You who have all of Italy in your hands?" One of the signatories carried it to Venice in person.

Still d'Annunzio hesitated. Another emissary, one Attilio Prodam, set out from Fiume to Venice and the Casetta Rossa, taking his pretty daughter with him and vowing he would not return to Fiume alive unless he brought d'Annunzio with him.

Day after day Prodam visited d'Annunzio, staying with him for four or five hours at a time. Persuasion failed: perhaps an erotic-cum-patriotic spectacle might succeed? General Diaz came to Venice to be presented, amid much pomp and ceremony, with a sword of honour. Prodam arranged for his daughter to present the general with a bouquet. Wearing a ribbon with the words "Fiume or Death" embroidered on it, she made a speech begging permission to present Diaz with the "flowers of the passion of my city." The following day, 6 September, Prodam visited d'Annunzio again. His daughter (still wearing her ribbon) was with him. This time, at last, d'Annunzio agreed to go.

Yet more days went by. D'Annunzio wanted to wait until the eleventh, a date he considered particularly auspicious, because it was on the eleventh that he had first had sexual intercourse with Giuseppina Mancini and on the eleventh that he had perpetrated the Buccari prank.

Besides, he had some dinner engagements. Ida Rubinstein was in Venice preparing a film version of *The Ship*, to be directed by d'Annunzio's son Gabriellino. On 9 September she gave a party at the Danieli for guests including d'Annunzio and two of his painter friends. Rubinstein herself danced to music by Florent Schmitt, and a gifted young pianist, Luisa Baccara, played the piano wearing, at d'Annunzio's express request (he was still taking an interest in his women's clothes), a silver dress and black and white shawl.

D'Annunzio had met Luisa at Olga's house (which he continued to frequent) and was struck by her playing, her lovely voice, her narrow brown face and wild hair prematurely streaked with silver. On 10 September he invited her to the Casetta Rossa again, this time so she could sing the Garibaldi hymn, with its rousingly xenophobic refrain: "Get out you foreigners," for himself and emissaries from the Sardinian Brigade at Ronchi. Luisa, nearly thirty years younger than d'Annunzio, stayed the night. ("Do you remember," he wrote afterward "the extreme voluptuousness, and the terrible mirror, and the final moments when I made you a drink with my own hands?") She would be d'Annunzio's mistress and the keeper of his harem until he died nearly two decades later.

At last, on 11 September, d'Annunzio rose early despite a high temperature, took a boat over to the mainland and set out, in his brand new, bright red Fiat 501 motor car (a sporty model launched that season), on what he was to call his "penultimate adventure."

The City of the Holocaust

I N FRANCE BEFORE THE WAR d'Annunzio witnessed a forest fire. His house at Arcachon was on the seaward fringe of a pine forest stretching for miles along the coast. At summer's end the woods were suddenly ablaze. D'Annunzio rode out to watch. Behind the line of the advancing fire, the black tree skeletons, stripped bare of all their needles and twigs, stood upright like "undefeated martyrs" at the stake. A gusty wind raised whirling man-high funnels of ash, veering, dipping and dissolving among the ruined woods like ghosts.

Fires blaze through d'Annunzio's work. In both *The Ship* and *Jorio's Daughter*, a heroine leaps voluntarily onto a pyre. One of his favourite words was "holocaust," meaning a sacrifice in which the victim is wholly consumed by fire. He had found the word used with relish in *Salammbô*, where Flaubert describes the killing of scores of children as sacrifices to Moloch. He had made it a part of his wartime rhetoric. The conflict was a fire in which all the filth and corruption of peacetime would be utterly destroyed, leaving a world cauterised and pure. Dead wood must burn so that new can grow. The millions of deaths would create a transformative blaze out of which would emerge a new form of humanity. Arriving in Fiume with a vanguard of *Arditi* known as the "black flames," he had come to set the match of his personality to a conflagration which would scorch the eyes of the watching world.

On the morning of 11 September 1919, d'Annunzio wrote to Mussolini to announce that he was setting out for Fiume. Nine years later Mussolini would publish part of this letter, declaring: "I too had been living this drama—day by day d'Annunzio and I had been close together," and claiming that it was one of many "brotherly letters" that had passed between them. He was lying. This was not a letter between brothers, but a set of instructions from a world famous author delivered, without a please or thank you, to his subservient editor. The part which Mussolini did not publish reads: "Summarise the article which the *Gazzetta del Popolo* will be publishing, giving the last section in full. And support our cause vigorously." Having thus seen to the all-important business of publicity, d'Annunzio set out, bundled up in rugs, on his great adventure.

The march on Fiume was set to begin from the cemetery of Ronchi at midnight. The "Ronchi Seven" had managed to recruit 186 men to their cause. Arriving at the base, d'Annunzio, still feverish, passed the early part of the night stretched out uncomfortably on four small tables (no damask cushions here). Years later he remembered how thirsty he was, and how his fever made him too weak even to reach out for the bunch of grapes an old peasant woman placed on a chair next to him.

The hour came, but the lorries to transport the men did not. Ronchi is over a hundred kilometres from Fiume. An aviator named Guido Keller, a notorious wild man who would play an important role in d'Annunzio's Fiume, took charge. Keller had flown with d'Annunzio's squadron in the raid on Pola in August 1917. He kept an eagle as a pet and habitually slept rough. According to one of the mutineers, Keller leapt into a motor car and "hurled himself at breakneck speed" towards a military depot. There, revolver in hand, he faced down the captain of the guard. The captain was an *Ardito*, one of the black-clad killer elite, but on this occasion he was either timid or, more likely, complicit. Announcing that he "ceded to violence," he allowed Keller and his band of hijackers to drive away twenty-six lorries. Several hours after the appointed hour, the column was ready to move. At last, recumbent in his red car, his damaged eyes protected by dark glasses, d'Annunzio set out for Fiume.

The Italian army occupying Istria on behalf of the Allies lay ahead. As dawn turned the sky what one of his followers saw as a "Garibaldian red," d'Annunzio stepped out of his car and addressed a group of thirty officers, telling them that from this moment on they were entirely his—"mine *perdutamente*." Like the leader of a religious cult, he was requiring them to abandon their separate identities. He was deathly pale. His little blond moustache and his chin were all caked with dust. He said they were about to confront the guns of the regular troops barring the road. He would not turn back, and nor would they. He was offering them death. His voice was weak at the outset, but it gradually became as "sharp and penetrating and resonant as a blade of steel."

The Allied garrison in Fiume was under the command of the Italian General Pittaluga, who had assumed command only ten days previously. He had told Nitti he felt unequal to a post of such political delicacy. Nitti had assured him that the administration's policy was quite straightforward and he would face no difficulty. This was nonsense. Pittaluga was out of his depth. His troops' loyalties were divided and he found the people of Fiume "bellicose and intolerant." Now he drove out to meet d'Annunzio's oncoming column.

A group of *Arditi* had placed themselves in the vanguard. Pittaluga ordered their commanding officer to turn around and shoot d'Annunzio. The officer flatly refused. Pittaluga drove on until he found d'Annunzio himself. He implored the poet to turn back, "for Italy's sake." D'Annunzio, regressing at this heroic moment to memories of his boyhood hero, unbuttoned his overcoat to reveal the row of medals on his chest as he said: "All you have to do is order the troops to shoot me, general." Just so had Napoleon, returning from exile on Elba, opened his coat and invited French troops to fire on him if they would. D'Annunzio, like Napoleon, was armoured by his fame. It was as impossible in 1919 for an Italian soldier to kill the "poet of slaughter" as it had been in 1815 for a French one to kill his Emperor.

Pittaluga gave up. "I will not shed blood nor be the cause of a fratricidal war!" he announced. According to the account in *Il Popolo d'Italia* (Mussolini was dutifully supporting the cause) the general took d'Annunzio by the hand and said: "Great Poet, I am honoured to meet you. I hope that your dream will be fulfilled and that I may shout with you, 'Viva Italian Fiume!'" He then turned around and headed back towards the city he was supposed to be defending, meekly following in the invaders' train.

Of the thousands of armed men within range of d'Annunzio that morning, all of them under orders to stop him by any available means from reaching Fiume, not a single one opened fire. D'Annunzio's little band proved magnetic, and the more recruits were drawn into it, the greater its magnetism. D'Annunzio himself described it in an interview in the *Corriere della Sera* five days later. "Armoured cars were awaiting us to stop our column. I reached them, passed them by, and the cars followed me under my orders. A staff officer tried to stop me. I ordered him to fall in at the rear of the column, and he obeyed . . . It was really rather funny." By the time he reached the city he had a following of over 2,000 men.

The first of the armoured cars crashed through the barricades at the city's outskirts. One after the other, machine guns at the ready, the lumbering vehicles passed into the centre through streets which the Fiuman-Italians had carpeted with branches of laurel. Two decades earlier d'Annunzio had written: "Imagine the flash of desire in the eye of the adventurer when, at a turn in the road, at the crest of a mountain, appears the face of a promised city." Then he was thinking of the condottieri of mediaeval Italy. Now he had a city of his own.

As he approached it, Fiume was in uproar. The departure of the grenadiers for Ronchi hadn't ended the turmoil in the city. Members of the Autonomist Party had been beaten up in the streets. There had been anti-British demonstrations, suppressed only when an officer trained a Lewis gun on the protestors. The planned march from Ronchi was no secret. Giovanni Comisso, serving with the garrison in Fiume, overheard girls chattering excitedly about the return of their boyfriends in the Sardinian Brigade. Throughout the day of 11 September, according to Father Macdonald, "a strange spirit of unrest seemed to pervade the town . . . a bubbling over of a long pent-up excitement, and the expectation of Signor d'Annunzio's arrival."

D'Annunzio was expected at dawn. One of the Italian warships in the harbour, the *Dante Alighieri*, was under orders to sail at first light, but its crew were all ashore, ignoring the sirens summoning them on board, detained, according to one source, by the kisses of female members of "Young Fiume" playing at being sirens of a different sort, "sealing their ears with the wax of their kisses." A young man came up to Comisso at a party in Fiume and asked to borrow his revolver, explaining that he had heard there would be a revolution in the morning.

At 11 p.m., Captain Host-Venturi informed the officers of the Legion that d'Annunzio was on his way, and led them in reciting an oath pledging themselves to defend Italian Fiume at all costs. At 3 a.m. a group of legionaries marched out of the city, ostensibly for a session of physical training, in fact to meet d'Annunzio's approaching column. Other legionaries were standing by to seize the Allied command post. As the sun rose all the bells in the city were rung and the Fiuman-Italians, few of whom had been to bed, poured out into the streets.

Delayed by the missing trucks, d'Annunzio was still many miles off. No one in Fiume knew where he was or whether he would come. The morning dragged by. Host-Venturi gave up hope, and attempted to disperse the crowds, but no one wanted to go home.

And then, at last, came the advent of "the necessary hero"; of "He who must come." Crowds, who had poured out of the city to welcome the marchers, began to flood back into it, singing hymns and patriotic songs, with the armoured cars of the *Arditi* following behind. D'Annunzio deferred his own arrival until the film crew had come up: this was a show he was staging for a world audience.

He rode into town standing up in an armoured car, wearing the uniform he had abjured earlier in the year, his medals flashing. Lorries full of *Arditi* followed, all on their feet and yelling "Fiume or Death!" They were welcomed by Fiuman-Italians wild with patriotic ardour and lack of sleep. Women and children were waving laurel branches. D'Annunzio's followers describe "ovations without end" and "thousands hailing us as saviours."

The column passed the Allied barracks; the machine guns mounted in the windows remained silent. D'Annunzio, according to one of his aides, "almost disappeared beneath a rain of flowers and laurels: his motor car became a living pyramid: soldiers, citizens clambered onto it from all sides, yelling, weeping, crushing around the condottiero, who was kissed, on his face and his hands, by a thousand mouths." He was to call this his *Sacra Entrata*—his sacred entry.

So astonishing was the success of the march that contemporary observers and subsequent historians alike have found it literally incredible. The rulers of the newborn nation of Yugoslavia assumed that the Italian government must surely have secretly authorised the coup. American and British diplomats came to similar conclusions. Father Macdonald was convinced of it.

In fact the regular army's failure to stop d'Annunzio seems to have been the result not of a conspiracy, but of a muddle. Afraid to provoke a general mutiny, the generals hesitated. As d'Annunzio's column moved towards his troops, General di Robilant, in command of the Italian Third Army, wrote to Nitti: "I am not certain I could induce our soldiers to open fire against colleagues shouting 'Viva l'Italia, Viva the Army, Viva Italian Fiume'." Even the very high-ranking were unsure what was expected of them. Di Robilant wrote later that various circumstances—the fact that the government agents shadowing d'Annunzio had been withdrawn a few days before the coup; the fact that the "Fiumanised" grenadiers had been stationed so dangerously close to the city at Ronchi instead of being withdrawn from the area altogether—"created in me the grave suspicion that something . . . had been organised by the government for ends which I could not imagine by myself and which I did not wish to hinder." His inaction in turn appeared to others evidence that d'Annunzio had protectors in high places and should therefore be allowed to pass unchallenged.

And so those who might have moved against d'Annunzio, seeing others fail to do so, drew back. While they did so he made Fiume his.

The Sacred Entry accomplished, feeling his fever after a short night on a row of tables, d'Annunzio made straight for the town's best hotel and went to bed for the afternoon, leaving it to others to decide how the newly emancipated city was to be governed.

While he slept, his followers merged with Host-Venturi's Legion and overran Fiume, taking over the Governor's Palace and the telephone exchange, forcing their way into public buildings while the Italian troops of the Allied command stood by and allowed them to do so. All the Allied flags, except that of Italy, were lowered. The insignia of the Hungarian monarchy were hacked off the carved furniture in government offices. *Arditi*, looking to one observer "superhumanly beautiful" with their black and silver uniforms, their battle-hardened features and their sweeping forelocks, stood guard at each crossroads and in every piazza. Many of the Italian troops in the city deserted their posts and joined d'Annunzio's following. Meanwhile Guido Keller, representing d'Annunzio, had a meeting with Grossich, the president of the Italian-dominated National Council of Fiume, and easily persuaded him to welcome the new order. It was resolved that the poet should be asked to accept the role of the city's "Commandant." The National Council would continue to be responsible for the day-to-day government of the city, but they would be subject to d'Annunzio who would have his own administration, known as "the Command," and his own cabinet of ministers.

When he was wakened towards evening to be told that he was to rule the city, d'Annunzio is said to have exclaimed, "Who? Me?" This could have been play-acting. But it is conceivable that he had never looked beyond his seizure of Fiume to the power that might follow it. The drama of the Sacred Entry was exactly to his taste. The excited crowds, the air full of flung flowers, the stern elation of the fighting men, the dancing, the armed women in their party clothes: it was on this moment of Dionysiac liberation that he had fixed his eyes. He spoke the language of ecstasy and conflagration, not of five-year plans.

Fiume's Governor's Palace, which d'Annunzio soon made his headquarters, forms the upper side of a sloping semi-circular piazza, a perfect auditorium. The palace, a nineteenth-century neo-Renaissance building constructed as a symbol of Hungarian power, has a grand balcony, some twenty feet deep, which became, for the next fifteen months, d'Annunzio's pulpit, his rostrum and his stage.

Awakening from his nap, d'Annunzio arrived at the palace in a car covered with flags and flowers, with *Arditi* riding on its running boards, its boot, its bonnet. The piazza was packed tight with people. There were more people on the rooftops, or hanging out of the windows of the houses around. Every balcony was hung with banners. *Arditi* perched precariously on the ledges along the palace's façade. D'Annunzio was still tremulous with fever and visibly exhausted but his ringing voice seemed to echo off the walls as he presented himself to his people. "Italians of Fiume," he began. "Here I am." He repeated himself insistently. "Here I am . . . Here is the man . . . *Ecce Homo.*" He was the new Messiah, the god of a new cult, and this was his epiphany.

He pledged himself to stay in Fiume while he still had breath. He brought out the banner he had carried to the Timavo, the banner with which he had draped Randaccio's coffin and which he had spread on the Capitol that summer. He called upon the crowd to confirm the vote of the plebiscite of the previous October, when they had resolved to become a part of Italy, intoning questions to which they answered, in an ever-increasing crescendo of hysterical noise: "Yes!" "Yes!" He climaxed with the declaration that Fiume was for ever reunited with Mother Italy. "The crowd," wrote Comisso, "was totally carried away."

Giovanni Giuriati, driving to Fiume from Trieste that night in a late dash to catch up with events, kept passing troops marching the same way by the light of the full moon. He stopped and asked an officer: "Have you orders to go and fight d'Annunzio?" and was told: no, orders were of no account, all the men he saw were going to join d'Annunzio in liberating Fiume. They were all singing. "They were like crusaders in sight of Jerusalem."

In Fiume the cafés and restaurants were overflowing. Flags waving, orators shouting—their voices drowned out by the roars of the crowd, officers carried shoulder-high, hats and handkerchiefs thrown, women dancing as though possessed. Arriving after midnight Giuriati thought the main square looked like the crater of a live volcano, "a tumult of sound and movement, a whirlwind, an uproar which took you by the throat." Sirens wailed, bells rang. "The crowd was frightening—a force of nature, a cyclone unchained." There was jubilation: there was also violence. Some French soldiers who had taken refuge in a brothel were dragged out and killed, and so was the prostitute who had sheltered them.

By noon the following day, after a long tête-à-tête with d'Annunzio, General Pittaluga had handed over the government of Fiume, telling the other Allied commanders present in the city that he was "yielding to superior force." He then left town in a hurry by car. Some of his men obeyed orders and followed, but a substantial number of his younger troops deserted, and remained in Fiume. Of the officers commanding Italian ships in the harbour one obeyed orders and sailed away, but the two others submitted to d'Annunzio. That afternoon the Italian high command in the region (based only a few miles away in Abbazia—now Opatija) asked the British and French contingents to withdraw from Fiume on the grounds that their presence would be a hindrance should it become necessary to blockade or even bombard the town. Judging that this bizarre situation was probably best treated as an internal Italian affair, they agreed to do so. D'Annunzio was left in undisputed possession of his little city-state.

No one was certain what would happen next. D'Annunzio appointed Giuriati his prime minister. Host-Venturi, leader of the Legion of Fiume, would be his military chief. Guido Keller was his "Action Secretary." Giuriati believed that, although the Italian government would ostensibly disown them, it would be secretly glad of what they were doing and would find ways of covertly supporting them. D'Annunzio foresaw conflict. But come what may, he announced that they would resist "to the last drop of blood" any attempt to drive them from Fiume.

He instructed his Command to begin preparing for the expected influx of thousands of volunteers.

Nitti, handed a telegram with the news as he sat in Rome's parliament, was visibly beside himself with rage, pounding the table with his fist. Only days earlier General Diaz had assured him that a "high sense of discipline" obtained in the army, and any orders would be "obeyed in perfect obedience." Now the army's failure to stop d'Annunzio signalled a degree of insubordination that posed a real threat to the stability of the state. The ground beneath Nitti's feet, as he put it, had been mined. He looked to General Badoglio to deal with the problem.

Badoglio, mimicking d'Annunzio's own strategies, had a plane overfly Fiume, dropping leaflets announcing that those soldiers who did not return to their units within twenty-four hours would be considered traitors. D'Annunzio was undaunted. Out on his balcony again he told his followers they were not deserters; the deserters were those who had failed to stand by Fiume. "The true army of Italy is here." They roared out their devotion. "I have overcome," he wrote exultantly to Albertini. "I have everything in my power. The soldiers obey only me. The city is tranquil. There is nothing to be done against me."

Fiume's wharfs are massive, its harbours deep, but it is possible to walk from one side of the city centre to the other in thirty minutes. D'Annunzio liked to tell the story of the Venetian Doge outraged on being shown a terrestrial globe and finding that Venice showed barely the size of a falcon's eye. Little Fiume, he implied, could, like Venice, have a world-historical destiny. For the time being though, it was cramped and encircled. There were still Allied troops based in Susak just across the river, and more in Abbazia, the resort which had been the seaside playground of the Hungarian nobility throughout the *belle époque*, and whose palatial pastel-coloured hotels were visible over the bay. One of d'Annunzio's officers tapped into their telephone lines and overheard the generals in charge of the two bases agree that d'Annunzio was "crazy" and his legion a gang of "delinquents." But surrounded though it might be by scoffers, d'Annunzian Fiume was proving magnetic.

Thousands of Italian soldiers—whole battalions—deserted their posts and flocked to Fiume, stowing away on trains, chugging down the coast in little MAS boats, or walking over the Carso to join him.

Sailors mutinied and steered their ships there. Fighter pilots flew in with their planes. Léon Kochnitzky, arriving in Fiume a few days after the Sacred Entry, describes the scene on the train. As they cross the armistice line there are no soldiers to be seen but then, as they approach their destination, "fake railway men shake off their fancy dress, uniforms come out of suitcases, young men black with soot burst out of the tender." As the train drew into the station the stowaways all let out the war cry d'Annunzio himself had taught them *"Eia, Eia, Eia! Alalà!"* Along with the young soldiers, a cosmopolitan host of artists, intellectuals, revolutionaries and romantics were drawn to Fiume as to the one bright light in the dreariness of post-war Europe.

Of the thousands who poured into the city over the following weeks, few could have articulated precisely what they were doing there, and those who did would put forward wildly differing accounts of their motives. The Fiuman-Italian merchants and industrialists who dominated the National Council favoured the city's annexation to Italy because they believed that as part of a Greater Italy they could resist Yugoslav attempts to take over the lucrative traffic in and out of the harbour, and re-establish Fiume's prosperity. Many of them were patriotic Italians, but their primary interests were local and practical. In the instability of post-war Europe they sought safety, and a way to do business.

Most of the incomers had much larger aims. For irredentists like Giuriati, Fiume was only the first step. Inspired by the glorious "march of Ronchi," Italians at home would clamour for a more expansionist policy and Italians in Dalmatia would rise up and insist on their Italian identity. Nitti's government would fall. Caution and parsimony would be cast aside. Diplomatic negotiations would give way to violence. Italy would be great again, and those who had laid claim to Fiume would be hailed as the heroic instigators of this glorious revolution.

The first programme was simple, with realistic, achievable aims. The second was wildly ambitious, and wildly subversive. There were others, though, even wilder. Some of the new arrivals in Fiume were looking to found, not a newly independent Fiume, not a Greater Italy, but a new world order. Others simply sought excitement. Kochnitzky spoke for many when he described his state of mind: "There was nothing anywhere in the world but gold, iron and blood. *The very light of heaven is venal.* [his English]" In the general mood of dreariness and disenchantment, d'Annunzio's action was thrilling: "Behold, a beacon had been lit at the end of the Adriatic."

Within days of taking over the city, d'Annunzio was obliged to close it. He had more volunteers than he could feed. On 23 September he published a proclamation asking all regular Italian troops to stay at their posts. Those who had already joined him, he averred, had done something marvellous. "The blessed smile of the dead" shone upon them. But the rest must stay with the regular army and defend the armistice line against the Yugoslavs—that way, too, they would be serving the cause of the City of the Holocaust.

The weather was as beautiful as it always ought to be in September. The sea was warm, the hills behind the town covered with vines, the shops—initially anyway—full of luxuries, and the cafés, despite the blockade, still serving coffee with cream. Fiume faces the sea. Its pink and white stone, the scallops and ogees of its remaining Gothic windows, its narrow pedestrian streets and paved squares, all bear the stamp of Venice. Grand mountains rise behind it. The glittering bay, dotted with islands, is its prospect. "The city was stupendous," wrote Comisso. "My youth was at its peak, summer was closing slowly, with glittering sunsets over the sea."

The legionaries, now joined by around 9,000 new recruits, were a motley bunch of dandies. There were so many officers that a high proportion had no troops under their command, and were free to spend their nights playing cards, their days strolling in the sun down the stone-flagged Corso with its pretty Venetian clock tower, or arguing about politics in the cafés. These superfluous officers were much decorated. One of d'Annunzio's first actions on arriving in the city was to present medals to all those who followed him there. Vividly aware of the potency of what the historian David Cannadine has called "Ornamentalism," he bound his followers to him with honours and titles, anthems and ceremonies glorifying their exploits. His officers' uniforms were swagged with gold braid, their chests adorned with a rainbow of ribbons.

The rank and file were as colourful. All the legionaries cultivated eccentricity. "Gait, cries, songs, daggers, hairstyles, all were unusual." They raided the abandoned depot of the Vietnamese-French troops and decked themselves out with fezzes and silver stars. They were as gaudy and hyper-masculine as a crew of stage pirates. "Infantry undid their jackets, opened their collars and revealed necks and chests bronzed by the sea wind . . . Everyone wore a dagger in his belt."

There was little discipline. The soldiers who had obeyed Pittaluga and left the city were the older ones, trained to obedience. Those who remained were young, many of them still teenagers, juveniles proud to be delinquent. The *Arditi*'s marching song extolled youth: *"Giovinezza, Giovinezza, Primavera di Bellezza"* (Youth, Youth, Springtime of Beauty). Youth was splendid, wrote the futurist Mario Carli (soon to arrive in Fiume), because the young have no past and therefore none of what others might see as the wisdom of experience but which to a futurist was simply "corrosion." Marinetti, already past thirty when he published the "Futurist Manifesto," had exulted in being young (or youngish) and sanguinely anticipated that, in ten years' time, he and his coevals would be hunted down, "crouched near our vibrating aeroplanes, warming our hands at the wretched fire on which our books of today are flaming" and slaughtered by those who came after them. "Injustice, strong and sane will break out radiantly in their eyes." The slogan of the 1960s counterculture—"trust no one over thirty"—looks forgiving by comparison.

"On the verge of old age I have been reborn as the Prince of Youth," announced d'Annunzio in Fiume. He flattered his followers by repeatedly praising their white teeth (so unlike his black and yellow ones), their "ruthless merriment," their "marvellous purity" and their contempt for the dirty compromises of old age. His admirers returned the compliment by pretending that he was one of them. "What rapid steps, what swiftness of movement, what vivacity in his glance! He is of an age with his soldiers, he is twenty again!" wrote Kochnitzky. (The last point would not, of course, have been worth making had it been true.)

For Italians, Fiume had a sexually louche reputation. The city's legal system—anomalous as so much about the place—was still that of Hungary, under which divorce was permitted (as it would not be in Italy until 1974). A sceptical observer reported that the city was full of deceived husbands and discontented wives, and that the only business flourishing was that of ending marriages. Like most ports it was renowned for its brothels, and even respectable Fiuman-Italian young women were, by several accounts, unusually easy-going. A young volunteer, forgetting his tact in his amazement, wrote to his fiancée: "everyone enjoys himself here . . . and makes love with the Fiuman girls, who are famous for being beautiful and not difficult." Another wrote "Each soldier had his lover and lived at home with her."

D'Annunzio himself claimed to be living with "Franciscan chastity," and amused his officers (all fully aware of his priapic reputation) by rebuking them for their promiscuity. They could at least, he suggested, avoid going to brothels where the men would see them. He himself was writing ardently to Luisa Baccara, who would soon give up her promising career as a concert pianist to join him. Meanwhile Lily de Montrésor, resident chanteuse at one of the bars on the waterfront, entered the Governor's Palace nightly by a concealed door to sleep with him, leaving again at dawn.

Secret agents and ambassadors alike assumed d'Annunzio must aim to make himself Italy's ruler. A week after his *Sacra Entrata* he had a private meeting with Riccardo Zanella, leader of Fiume's Autonomist Party. According to Zanella, he revealed his master plan: the annexation of Fiume to Italy, to be followed by an Italy-wide uprising, the occupation of Rome, the dissolution of parliament, the deposition of King Victor Emmanuel, and the installation of a new regime headed by himself as military dictator. "If I wanted to I could march on Rome with 300,000 soldiers," he announced. It was probably true. The combatants' associations, for whom he was a hero, could alone have provided at least that number of volunteers, and, in the opinion of a senior general, had d'Annunzio called the "loyal" troops in Istria to march with him on Rome they would have deserted their posts and followed him. "Nor would there have been much resistance from troops in the rest of the peninsula." In late September a British admiral with the Allied occupying force reported pervasive rumours of an imminent Italian revolution, and the American high commissioner in Rome warned that the Italian government "cannot hold the army any longer." General Badoglio wrote to tell his political bosses that even those of his troops who were still ostensibly loyal were "infatuated" with d'Annunzio. He urged Nitti to proclaim the annexation of Fiume, warning that the alternative might well be civil war.

Had d'Annunzio really wanted executive power he might well have found, as Mussolini did three years later, that he had only to go to Rome and get it. But while his followers all over Italy waited for him to make a decisive move, he stayed put, waiting, in his turn, for sparks from his "holocaust" to set the world alight. He declaimed and then published addresses to the people of Trieste and Venice, to the Seamen's Union and to Italians in general, calling upon them to set the nation ablaze with the cauterising fire of armed revolt. But, for all the generals' anxieties, no insurrection took place.

D'Annunzio vented his disappointment in a letter to Mussolini, whose *Fasci* had not, as he had assumed they would, risen up all over Italy in his support. The heavily edited version of this letter published in Mussolini's journal is all heroic boasting. "I have risked all, I have given all . . . I am the master of Fiume . . . I hold Fiume for as long as I live . . . ." And so on, and so forth to the final *"Alalà!"* Mussolini would have his followers, then and throughout the fascist era, believe that the *Duce* of Fiume had turned to share his triumph with the *Duce* of the future, as though acknowledging him his companion in glory. The excised passages speak of a very different relationship. D'Annunzio upbraids all those Italians who have let him down, attacking Mussolini as being among the idlest and most craven of them all. "I am amazed at you . . . You tremble with fear! . . . You stay there chattering, while we struggle . . . What about your promises? Can't you at least punch a hole in that belly that weighs you down, and deflate it?" The *Fasci*'s frontman is a gross windbag, almost as despicable as the "piggy" (*porcino*) Prime Minister against whom he has failed to rise up.

Francesco Nitti had known d'Annunzio for a quarter of a century. In Naples in the early 1890s they had both been contributors to Scarfoglio and Serao's journal. Nitti, five years younger than the poet, had admired the latter's immense capacity for work. He had also noticed "how methodically and assiduously d'Annunzio cultivated publicity." There was, thought Nitti, "something artificial about everything he said or did."

Finding that his old acquaintance's flamboyant action threatened to undermine his administration, Nitti attempted to belittle it. He scoffed at d'Annunzio's much-vaunted patriotism: "Italy is just the latest of the many women he has enjoyed." He told the world that d'Annunzio had "no programme, nor true passion, nor any sense of moral responsibility." He made fun of d'Annunzio's made-up title, of his acting like "a little King." He gave the name Fiume to his dog. Writing his autobiography years later he claimed that the "so-called legionaries" of Fiume included numerous government agents, that all the talk about marching on Rome was promptly reported back to him. "The matter didn't worry me much . . . I never took d'Annunzio's threats seriously." Fiume was just a comedy, he said, and d'Annunzio a showman.

Nitti was right about the showmanship, but wrong to mock it. In Fiume, d'Annunzio was developing a new and dangerously potent politics of spectacle, from which others would learn. When Mussolini "marched" on Rome three years later, his coup was just a comedy too, a civil change of government pranked out as an armed revolution, a march headed by a leader who found it more comfortable to take the train. But as d'Annunzio had long known and repeatedly demonstrated, play-acting can have substantial consequences. His reign over Fiume outlasted Nitti's premiership by half a year.

D'Annunzio was a man who composed whole novels in his head and then couldn't be bothered to write them down. Noble concepts and grand gestures excited him. The quotidian business of government was less congenial. Despite all his dreams of a national theatre, he had never yet run anything larger than his own household, and no one would entrust a state's economy to a man who had proved so spectacularly incompetent—dishonest even—in the management of his own finances. General Badoglio thought his patriotism *nobilissimo*, but his talent for organisation minimal. "He was just a stirrer-up of energy, an outstanding generator of mass excitement." It was necessary to set someone else to work to run Fiume.

On 20 September, with much ceremony, Grossich formally resigned the National Council's power to d'Annunzio, addressing him as "divine leader." D'Annunzio, in turn, graciously invited the Council to remain in being, and to continue to undertake the daily business of government, with the proviso that all issues relating to law and order or to politics would be referred to d'Annunzio and the members of his Command.

The National Council continued to collect taxes, clean the drains and administer the law under the supervision of Giovanni Giuriati. As chief minister Giuriati served d'Annunzio loyally, effectively running Fiume on his behalf, but had no great opinion of his practical capabilities. D'Annunzio couldn't be bothered with budgets, and he was almost equally insouciant about the law. "I was interrogated by him endlessly about legal matters," wrote Giuriati later, "but always with a lightly ironic tone . . . he considered the subject beneath the altitude at which nature had placed him." This was, after all, the superman whom no human tribunal could judge.

Nor did he have the adroitness necessary for keeping all his disparate followers onside. Four days after d'Annunzio's arrival, Marinetti, along with one of his futurist comrades, came to Fiume. By the end of the month they were gone again, ordered out by d'Annunzio lest their republican rhetoric incense the monarchists among his supporters. Marinetti, always glad to make trouble, boasted "our mere presence in Fiume is sufficient to alarm the timid and the foolish to the point of nervous collapse." Marinetti noted d'Annunzio's lack of political nous: "Although he is very cunning and full of his own importance, he is guileless and forgets to act, to eliminate the spies, the indifferent, the traitors."

A deputation of nationalists arrived in Fiume hoping to persuade d'Annunzio to march on Rome and make himself dictator of all Italy. Giuriati deflected them, not because he was opposed to such a coup in principle but because he judged it wasn't enough to have a leader charismatic enough to trigger a revolution, "it was also necessary to have ready a dictator capable of making a new regime work." D'Annunzio was a poor administrator, said Giuriati, he was financially incompetent. He vacillated. His decisions were arrived at impulsively and frequently too late, prompted more often by superstition than by reason. In brief, he simply wasn't up to the job. Better perhaps to wait until a more competent leader presented himself? Three years later Giuriati became a minister in Mussolini's first cabinet.

The American vice-consul in Trieste reported that Fiume was "completely beflagged." Lights blazed all night. Portraits of d'Annunzio hung from the upper floors of houses all around the main piazza. Banners reading "Italy or death" were suspended over every street. The stage was dressed. The star was on. D'Annunzio was everywhere, speechifying, reviewing troops, posing on the docks alongside a destroyer, tirelessly displaying himself to the crowds who filled the streets night and day, and for the two film crews who followed his every move.

Another American observer describes him, "his beautifully cut clothes, which fit so faultlessly about the waist and hips as to suggest the use of stays, but partially camouflage the corpulence of middle age. His head looks like a new-laid egg which has been highly varnished; his pointed beard is clipped in a fashion which reminded me of the bronze satyrs in the Naples museum; a monocle conceals his dead eye. His walk is a combination of a mince and a swagger; his movements

are those of an actor who knows that the spotlight is upon him." The American thought d'Annunzio "unimpressive-looking," but to Marinetti, he seemed *"elegantissimo"* in white gloves, his hands raised in an almost perpetual salute.

Every day he would appear on the balcony to address the hundreds of people—most of them legionaries or local women—gathered in the square beneath. He treated them as a conductor treats his chorus, or a priest his congregation. He gave them their cues; they responded. His speeches were repetitive—designedly so. He would ask an inflammatory rhetorical question: "To whom the victory?" and the crowds hollered out the expected answer: "To us!" He recited great Homeric lists of names—of his supporters, of the illustrious dead, of the Italian wartime victories, of the cities he proposed to "liberate." These lists became devices whereby he slowly, notch by notch, ratcheted up the intensity of the crowd's excitement.

Before these appearances he would spend half an hour of intense concentration in the grand saloon which opened onto the balcony. "The people stormed and howled, calling out for me." Words and phrases flashed in his mind. His chest was tight. The very air he breathed seemed phosphorescent. "I'd let out a shout. My officers came running, flung open the doors, fanned out on either side of me like wings. At a pace as violent as a bolt fired from a crossbow I went to the balustrade."

He would become transported by his own oratory. He describes the "maelstrom" he felt within and around him, the hallucinatory images of blood-red flags and of battle which flickered before him as he spoke. At intervals he would begin to intone the Oath of Ronchi, the vow to fight "against everybody and everything" for Fiume's right to be Italian. The sequence of question and answer was punctuated by his war cry *Alalà!* and thousands of voices would cry back to him, *"Eia, Eia, Eia! Alalà!'*

D'Annunzio referred to these "colloquies" as his "parliament in the open air," and the "first example of direct communication . . . between the people and their ruler . . . since Greek times." But this was not political discussion. It was the deliberate stimulation of mass hysteria. In Fiume he was experimenting with a new medium, creating artworks for which the materials were marching men, cheering crowds, masses of pelted flowers, bonfires, stirring music—a genre which would be developed and elaborated over the next two decades in Rome, in Moscow and in Berlin.

Nitti ordered that Fiume's electricity supply should be cut off, and began a blockade of the city. The Italian Third Army surrounded the city on its landward sides. Italian ships blocked the entrance to its harbour. But within days Nitti had realised that to be overly aggressive towards d'Annunzio, Italy's bard and national hero, would be politically dangerous. The blockade was relaxed. Later the director of the Red Cross paid tribute to the humane and efficient way Fiume was kept supplied with food and medicines, with Nitti's covert assistance. "He [Nitti] has always forbidden me to reveal how much he has done." In the first months of d'Annunzio's sojourn in Fiume, one of his most ascetic acolytes recalled with amazement that he had eaten sugared rose petals there.

D'Annunzio's household was run with his usual profligacy. "All the members of your staff order food in profusion," protested an official charged with the thankless task of managing the Command's budget, "for a consumption that evidently you can not sustain." D'Annunzio had taken over two rooms in the otherwise austere palace for his private apartments and filled them with carpets and incense burners, rows of banners, and two more-than-man-sized plaster casts of sculpted saints from Florence. His bed, according to Father Macdonald, was surrounded with massed flowers like the catafalque of a dead hero. The flowers were changed three times daily—white in the morning, pink at noon and red for evening.

Foreign journalists tended to see d'Annunzio's great symbolic drama in conventional terms, as an ordinary debauch. A typical story from Fiume in a London paper was headlined "Chorus Girls and Champagne." Another English newspaper reported: "Unnameable orgies inspired by Satanic libations amid the fumes of incense." In the words of a disapproving Italian socialist, Fiume was being transformed into "a bordello, a refuge for criminals and prostitutes of more or less 'high life'." A British agent reported it as "a known fact, that Gabriele d'Annunzio spends most of his evenings at the Restaurant Ornitorinco with his mistress, where he drinks numerous bottles of champagne, and from where he seldom returns before late in the morning." D'Annunzio never drank to excess but he did like to stay up late. The Foreign Office official who filed the report noted, "D'Annunzio seems to be having the time of his life at Fiume." That at least is true.

D'Annunzio had made no plans as to how his fast-growing horde of volunteers was to be fed. "When vile lucre was scarce," wrote Giuriati, "he considered himself the victim of a patent injustice . . . The sources of revenue in Fiume were not, as in all other states in the world, taxes and loans, but *colpi di mano*—acts of violence." Fiume was provisioned by piracy.

D'Annunzio established a force of raiders under Guido Keller's command, whom he called the *"Uscocchi"* after the pirates who had operated in the Adriatic in the sixteenth century. They sallied out of Fiume's harbour in motorboats and raided the depots of the Allied armies across the bay, bringing back food, weapons, horses and even sometimes hostages. They drove lorries round to the military base at Abbazia, and loaded them up with stolen boots. They seldom needed to use their weapons. Many soldiers from the blockading army, sympathising with their cause, were willing to look the other way.

Further afield, they stowed away on cargo ships. *Arditi* in civilian clothes would leave the city in small groups, to reconvene in a port and hide themselves on board. When the moment came they would strip off their nondescript jackets to reveal black shirts spangled with medals, and allow their fearsome forelocks to swing out from concealing caps. In most cases the crews allowed their officers to be overpowered and altered course without much argument, bringing their ships into Fiume laden with supplies.

D'Annunzio had once complained of the tedium of a life in which tame commercialism had replaced the "magnificent crimes" of a grander, bloodier age. During the war the *Arditi* had adopted d'Annunzio's motto *"me ne frego"*—I don't give a toss—which Mussolini would later describe as being the summation of the fascists' "new style of ideal life." Now d'Annunzio had it embroidered on a banner which hung over his bed. He had become the insouciant ruler of an outlaw state.

D'Annunzio dubbed Nitti *"Cagoia,"* an invented term of abuse which translates approximately as "shitty." The filth, which he had so deplored when he saw it engulfing Italy's political system, now gushed through his own rhetoric. Alongside his exalted talk of sacrifice and fatherland ran another stream, that of scatological abuse. He became a verbal cartoonist, ribald and jeering, as disgusted by Nitti's body as he had once been by his own father's. His invective is full of excrement and blubbery flesh, of belches and farts.

Nitti retaliated by putting it about that d'Annunzio had lost control of his own adventure. The poet "has been overcome by madmen," he told a reporter. D'Annunzio was no longer responsible for his actions. He was senile (or childish); he was being held prisoner by his officers; he'd fled from Fiume on a sailing boat; he'd accepted a massive bribe and was about to surrender. All of these rumours were intended to undermine d'Annunzio with apparent sympathy. The poet's popularity was such that any direct verbal attack on him would only rebound on its perpetrator.

D'Annunzio was not so tied. Over and over again he accused the Prime Minister of cowardice. Reaching back to his memory of the "cowards" on the Timavo, tying strips of torn clothing to their bayonets as they surrendered to the enemy, he elaborated a grotesque image of Nitti using his soiled underpants as a white flag. He berated him for being interested only in "eating and swilling." D'Annunzio was not anorexic—he could write with hearty gusto of roast quail and of strawberries and ice cream—but now he equated eating with degradation. He was ferocious. He called upon his followers to pillory Nitti. He was blasphemous. He called upon them to "baptise" Nitti by spitting on him. He was flattering. He told his listeners they were free, unlike the "slaves" who remained loyal to Nitti's government.

In Rome, on 25 September, two weeks after d'Annunzio's Sacred Entry, the King called a meeting of his privy council. It was agreed that d'Annunzio's annexation of Fiume could not be accepted. Nitti, encouraged, dissolved parliament, calling an election for 16 November. D'Annunzio's seizure of Fiume was perhaps not such a bad thing. It vividly demonstrated what Orlando had been trying to argue at Versailles the previous spring—that the Italian administration was obliged, by its own people's wishes, to ask for concessions in Dalmatia. Unable to dominate d'Annunzio, Nitti, whose pragmatism d'Annunzio considered so dishonourable, sensibly made use of him.

Fiume, always bustling, was now crowded with armed young men. Four bands patrolled the streets, playing by day and night, trains of followers forming up to march or dance along behind them. D'Annunzio himself passed daily through the city at the head of his troops with a flower in his hat, their progress accompanied by the sound of trumpets. Each morning he reviewed his personal bodyguard of *Arditi* on the waterfront. Modelled on the "black band" attendant on a Renaissance Medici prince, they wore tight black tunics and were drilled in a way most of the Fiuman troops were not. They had a showy new salute, a straight arm raised skywards. "The company files past him in the greatest solemnity. He claps his hands and two hundred daggers are raised on high on extended arms." Randaccio's banner dips in salute "and the fateful cry, breaking from two hundred breasts, resounds by the sea. *A NOI!*'

Every day the Legion marched out into the surrounding countryside. They ran and wrestled in the pine forests along the seashore, and marched, singing now the Garibaldi hymn, now the battle song of the *Arditi*, through the orchards and olive groves that climb the hills backing the town. They would cut leafy branches. At nightfall, still singing and garlanded with greenery, they marched back into the city, lit great fires along the waterfront and roasted sheep. Feasting off charred mutton, their fantastic costumes glittering in the light of the flames, they made an archaic and stirring spectacle. As d'Annunzio appreciated, it was as though Achilles and his myrmidons had returned to encamp once more before Troy.

Léon Kochnitzky had been an admirer of d'Annunzio since he read *Fire* at the age of sixteen. "Ecstasy! Enchantment! The excruciating joy of discovering treasure destined to render all our lives more beautiful!" Before the war he glimpsed d'Annunzio at the Paris opera, immaculate in a starched cravat and with pearly-white cuffs and monocle gleaming. In the summer of 1919, by this time a published poet himself, Kochnitzky made his way to Rome and there at last he contrived to meet the bard who had meant so much to him. A true fan, he stole one of d'Annunzio's gloves and kept it as an "amulet."

Kochnitzky arrived in Fiume towards the end of October 1919. D'Annunzio kept him waiting for two full days for an appointment, but then he was all affability. Of course he remembered their encounter in Rome, the card game they had played, the flowers that had scented the room, everything about the night. Kochnitzky was dumbfounded by the honour. Only later did he realise d'Annunzio greeted every acquaintance as though welcoming a dear friend, "but really, he couldn't care less."

Kochnitzky was an adoring disciple. "I breathed in the light which radiated from Gabriele d'Annunzio: in this light I lived." Self-mocking but candid, he committed to paper the self-abnegating emotions which thousands of hero-worshipping legionaries shared. "I am an instrument without a will, a tool which sees and feels nothing but the marvellous craftsman." He didn't feel degraded by his infatuation, on the contrary: "I give thanks to God for having put me in direct and daily contact with the most perfect of his creations."

For Kochnitzky, a Belgian of Russian-Jewish descent, Italian irredentism was of little interest. "Where are we going? Nobody can say . . . What are our war aims? Hard to define them . . . So be it! . . . Above us we have Gabriele d'Annunzio to guide us. Beyond Gabriele d'Annunzio the UNKNOWN and the destiny which drives him on."

D'Annunzio set Kochnitzky, and another enthusiastic young poet, the American Henry Furst, to work scanning the foreign press for him. Furst revered d'Annunzio for his poetry and also because he was a great "pagan." Paganism had been fashionable in Anglophone poetic circles since Pater, and Rupert Brooke, beautiful dead idol of the pro-war British, had been at the centre of a group of "neo-pagans." D'Annunzio was happy to accept the characterisation, and literary young men with language skills were useful to him. Kochnitzky and Furst drafted press releases. They were affronted by how frequently he returned their drafts to them, with their syntax corrected or a word changed.

When d'Annunzio was not speaking to his people he was writing to them. He took over control of the city's Italian newspaper *La Vedetta* (The Lookout), and made it his mouthpiece. It appeared daily, printing verbatim every one of his speeches. He would convey his resolves to the populace on proclamations fly-posted all over town or in leaflets handed out in the streets or showered from the sky by low-flying aeroplanes. In times of crisis new posters reflecting his changing state of mind would appear in public places four, or six, or even eight times a day. Fiume was for d'Annunzio both stage and page, the platform on which he postured and a surface on which he could inscribe the marvellous story of himself.

That story had to be broadcast, as well, beyond Fiume's confines. The City of the Holocaust was to be a beacon visible around the world. D'Annunzio's publicity department was organised with thoroughly modern efficiency. His speeches were rushed off the administration's own printing presses within hours of their first delivery and distributed to newspaper offices across Italy. A journalist went with the Uscocchi on each of their most daring raids, writing up their exploits. D'Annunzio's pilots overflew the disputed cities of Trento and Zara dropping leaflets. He ordered the citizens of Fiume out to form up in an open space along the waterfront so that their massed bodies formed the words *"Italia o Morte,"* had them photographed from the air, and circulated the pictures.

On 7 October, two of d'Annunzio's aviators were killed when their plane's engine failed during a reconnaissance flight. D'Annunzio seized upon the deaths of Fiume's first "martyrs" as the occasion for an awe-inspiring ceremony. The city's florists' shops and its public parks were stripped of their flowers. The funeral procession wound its way through Fiume for several hours, observing a solemn and impressive silence but for the blaring of the bands. Troops of little children from the orphanage led the way. Then came the legionaries, both wounded veterans and frightening black-clad young warriors. Almost the entire Fiuman-Italian population paced after them. As night fell the coffins were displayed in the main square. Randaccio's banner was draped across them by the dead men's fellow pilots and, as a full moon rose, d'Annunzio spoke. He talked of the "sign of the cross that is made by the shadow of the winged machine" and described the dead men as "burnt confessors of the faith." A legionary recalls it: "The words of the poet rang high and clear in the great piazza . . . It seemed that those thousands and thousands of persons who listened did not breathe, did not live: it seemed that they were a people of mournful shades."

From the night of its inception, d'Annunzio's Command had included an intelligence service called the "Office of Information." "Within a week," records Giuriati, "the officer in charge had established a network of most trustworthy informers." These agents were instructed to be on the lookout for "Yugoslav intrigues" and to report on the behaviour of all the citizens, but most particularly of non-Italians. *La Vedetta* called for the expulsion of "foreigners," i.e. native Fiumans of non-Italian origin. "We have tolerated them long enough . . . [they] have nothing to do here." The Fiuman-Italians wanted to be locked in an exclusive embrace with the "brothers" come to defend them. The actual racial diversity of their "*Italianissimo*" city complicated the simple, glorious story of their "redemption."

In d'Annunzio's supporters' accounts of their sojourn in Fiume, the city's non-Italian inhabitants are all but invisible. The Italians ignored them, or feared them as an enemy within. Other less partial observers testify that the harassment of one ethnic group by the other, which Father Macdonald had seen as constant throughout the summer, continued. As trade faltered and stuttered during d'Annunzio's reign, there were food shortages. Seeking scapegoats, some of the Fiuman-Italians began to blame their Slavic neighbours. It was said that the Croatian butchers of Susak would sell meat only to those who spoke Croatian, or who would swear fealty to Yugoslavia. In Fiume proper, Croats were evicted from their homes in the city to make way for incoming Italians. The city of fiery brilliance had from the outset its dark and hidden channels.

Luisa Baccara, the young pianist d'Annunzio had met just before leaving Venice, was soon visiting him regularly in Fiume.

Simple, clear-cut, severe, classical—these are some of the words
d'Annunzio uses to describe Luisa's beauty. Powerfully arched eyebrows, strong shoulders and neck which reminded him of a swan
exhaling its death song. She put others in mind of birds, too. Guido
Keller, who was jealous of her hold over d'Annunzio, once presented
her with a cockatoo, a gift which was intended as an insulting allusion
to her beaky nose.

Luisa was thirty years younger than her lover. He called her Siren-
etta, the name he had also given his daughter. But like so many of her
predecessors, she was a strong-willed and talented woman, a fêted
artiste, not quite a star like Eleonora Duse but a performer who played

with confidence to full theatres. He loved to watch her at the keyboard, to see the waves of energy passing through her from the nape of her bowed neck to her foot on the pedal, as though the music was issuing not from the piano but from her body. That body, as he knew from their love-making, was finely constructed and responsive as a violin from the hand of a master lutenist. He called her his "dark rose," his "olive-skinned melancholy," his "golden, poisoned grape." He applauded her taste for metallic embroidery and silver lamé. His letters suggest that she was not just compliant but sexually demanding. Self-confident and poised, Luisa made d'Annunzio hers, not exclusively, but for life.

In Fiume she gave recitals for his officers and for visiting dignitaries, finishing with a rendition of the *Song of Ronchi*, while, as d'Annunzio describes it, "the *Arditi*, long-haired like the Achaeans, would brandish their daggers at each refrain, making her a crown of vengeance."

Relations between d'Annunzio's Command and the National Council were strained. In mid-October, d'Annunzio dissolved the Council and called elections, putting forward new candidates of his own. On the day of the vote he spoke in the theatre, telling his listeners: "You are asked to vote for your soul. You are asked to vote for an act of love and fervour." Over seventy per cent voted for his candidates. Four days later the reconstituted National Council reconfirmed his absolute power.

Father Macdonald scoffed. "The stage chorus of loose women and licentious soldiery, which the poet-actor had succeeded in attaching to his touring party, could be relied upon to vote to order." It is true that women played a large part in the political life of d'Annunzio's Fiume. Just before his arrival they had been enfranchised, a fact which several contemporary observers considered to have been a great help to him. In the view of his detractors, he had not so much stepped out of the bou-doir into the real, tough, male world of political action as transformed the political arena, by dint of his incorrigibly decadent and voluptuous ways, into another boudoir. His phenomenal success in establishing his ascendance over a turbulent city was, when it came down to it, just another seduction.

In Fiume, under d'Annunzio's rule, drugs were as readily available as sex. One artist attempted to make a living in the city by selling psychedelic art, advertising "Fantastic impressions 'morphine style'" in the evident expectation that his public knew just what that looked like.

D'Annunzio wrote, in a moment of exasperation, that he was wearing himself out on behalf of a "rabble stuffed with phrases and crammed full of drugs." He was as guilty on both counts as any of his followers. While he was recovering from his eye injury he took painkillers and sleeping pills and afterwards always kept stocks of opiates by him. We know that soon after he left Fiume he had a greedy cocaine habit. He was probably already a user while there.

In the pre-war years cocaine was seen as an aid to courage and endurance. Shackleton and Scott each took a supply of it with them on their polar expeditions. During the war, a number of pilots, in Italy as elsewhere, used it to keep themselves alert. Many retained the habit afterwards. Others imitated them, despite the fact that it was becoming all too obvious that the drug was not, as Freud had thought, good for the health. Marcel Proust called cocaine one of time's special express trains bound for old age (a good haircut, he considered, was an equally fast train running back towards youth).

In Fiume a pharmacist was arrested for selling cocaine. D'Annunzio asked that he be released (perhaps the man was his own supplier). Osbert Sitwell, who visited Fiume later, mocked the British reporter who took the "glassy glitter" of d'Annunzio's "snake-like eye" as evidence that he was "drug-crazed." Did the hack not know that one of the Commandant's eyes was glass indeed? It wasn't, actually, and it is more than likely that the hack was right.

Italy was boiling with discontent. Ex-soldiers, or the bereaved families of the war dead, were demanding compensation for their sufferings or their lost men. Combatants' associations rallied them. Beating drums and waving flags, they marched onto uncultivated land and began to dig for themselves, to the consternation of landowners, many of whom, unable or afraid to reclaim their property, were obliged to sell. The socialists were increasingly belligerent. Socialist labour unions had quadrupled their membership in two years during which more than a million people (including the waiters at Florian's, where d'Annunzio had spent so many evenings) went on strike. At their National Congress in the autumn of 1919 the Socialist Party voted in a new constitution calling for the "violent conquest of political power."

436 · GABRIELE D'ANNUNZIO

The Italian authorities could no longer trust their armed forces. In October two of the army's highest-ranking generals arrived in Fiume to dedicate themselves to the service of d'Annunzio, one of them being the charismatic General Ceccherini. D'Annunzio, on first meeting Ceccherini at the front in 1916, described him as a "famous fencer, of Herculean stature, square shoulders . . . with a fine mouth beneath grey moustaches. He seems to be dressed in leather, like a warrior who has removed his armour." Now he became commander of the "Fiuman First Division."

Every day in Fiume there were parades. Every night there were torchlit processions and firework displays. The funeral of the two airmen. The ceremony to endorse General Ceccherini's command. The solemn inauguration of the re-elected National Council. A military review to honour the visiting Duchess of Aosta. The lamentations over the death of a legionary killed by regular troops after visiting a restaurant in Abbazia. March pasts. Fly pasts. Yelling crowds. Flags, bells, dancing. But still the Italian revolution failed to happen. Still Nitti held on to power.

Resigning himself to a long stay, d'Annunzio sent for his winter clothes. Boots and shoes, cravats, a variety of uniforms and an overcoat lined with Astrakhan were despatched from the Casetta Rossa, along with ten boxes of his favourite chocolates and 500 grains of strychnine. He was at war again, and again in need of the wherewithal to kill himself.

Fiume's economy was foundering. What had been a busy port and manufacturing town found itself cut off from its suppliers of raw material and its markets. The port was closed, the docks were silent, the factories were abandoned. No rice arrived to be milled. No seed came to be pressed for oil. Increasing numbers of the Fiuman working class were unemployed.

Money was unstable and confusing. Nobody knew to which political entity, if any, Fiume now belonged. Nobody knew therefore, which of the several currencies (Hungarian, Italian, Yugoslav) circulating in the city was valid. The Command issued their own notes, but these were so easily forged that shopkeepers soon refused to accept them. Taxes were paid in one currency, prices paid in another. Exchange rates fluctuated wildly. A satirical journal summed up the situation. "The moneychanger will give 7.10, the café 6.50, the hat store 6, the stationer's store 5, the pizzeria 4, and so on. This is all done with the noble intention of enabling the youth of Fiume to learn mathematics without going to school."

Tradesmen were desperate. The price of bread was fixed, but bakers demanded the right to raise it and threatened to go on strike. Giuriati put legionaries on standby to run the bread ovens. The bakers backed down and returned to work, but they began producing two grades of bread: the expensive white and the gritty, grey "economic." Giuriati was photographed munching an "economic" loaf for public relations purposes, but nobody ate it out of choice.

Mussolini had kept his distance from d'Annunzio's adventure. In September he wrote with a five-part plan for the overthrow of the monarchy by "faithful" (i.e. mutinous) troops and announced that he would get up a subscription in support of d'Annunzio's Fiume. (A large sum was raised but there is no record of Mussolini ever having handed the money over.)

On 7 October he finally flew in, remaining closeted with d'Annunzio for two hours, but two days later (still in his aviator's outfit) he was attending the first National Congress of the *Fasci* in Florence. Since its inception in March, his movement had spawned 150 local branches, with some 40,000 members. He publicly announced the fascists' solidarity with the Fiuman legionaries, but his mind was not on the Adriatic. It was on the imminent elections.

On 15 November 1919, Italy went to the polls. Defiantly acting as though Fiume was a constituency entitled to return a member to the Italian parliament, d'Annunzio staged a ballot. Luigi Rizzo, gold-medal-holding war hero, who had been with d'Annunzio on the night of the Buccari prank, was elected the "member for Fiume." More celebratory marches, more dancing in the streets. Rizzo never went to Rome to take his seat.

The outcome of the national elections was a shock to d'Annunzio and his associates. Mussolini and Marinetti had joined forces to oppose Nitti's administration. Mussolini campaigned vigorously, loudly singing *Giovinezza* at repeated rallies, but to no avail. The fascist-futurist alliance received derisorily few votes. Not a single one of their candidates was elected. The socialists paraded through Milan carrying a coffin with Mussolini's name on it. The six-month-old fascist movement appeared to be dead and done for. When the results were announced there was fighting on the streets in Rome and Milan. Police searched Mussolini's lodgings and found an illegal cache of weapons. Both Mussolini and Marinetti were briefly jailed.

Nitti was confirmed in power with an increased majority. It looked as though the Italian people had decisively rejected fascism and, incidentally, had turned its back on d'Annunzio and a blind eye to his beacon. It was a severe blow.

After the election, Nitti, feeling secure with his greatly increased mandate, offered d'Annunzio terms. His proposal, known as the *Modus Vivendi*, stopped short of any firm promise that Fiume would be annexed to Italy, but it guaranteed the people of Fiume's right to decide their own destiny. The city was to be an independent *corpus separatum* under Italy's protection. Italian troops would resist any Yugoslav attempt to take over the city by force and the government undertook "not to welcome or agree to any solution which separated Fiume from the motherland."

For most Fiuman-Italians the proposal was entirely satisfactory. The National Council were ready to accept it. So was Giuriati, so was Major Reina, foremost among the "Ronchi Seven." So was Rizzo, Fiume's supposed MP. D'Annunzio was not. For him acceptance of the terms would be bleakly bathetic. The Legion of Fiume was to be disbanded forthwith and he himself was to leave the city, handing it over to a garrison of regular Italian troops. His mystic City of the Holocaust would dwindle back into a moderately important industrial port and he himself would lose his city-wide theatre, his worldwide audience and his leading role. He wrote, "a beautiful thing is about to end. A light is going out."

He struggled to find a way of refusing the deal. He made unrealistic counter-proposals. He repeatedly declared that he would never leave Fiume until it was a part of Italy. He told one of his ministers: "I am ready for anything, including a new coup in the Adriatic." His emissaries went back and forth to Badoglio's headquarters and to Rome. They got no further concessions.

The atmosphere in Fiume was becoming increasingly edgy. For months the legionaries had been chanting "Italy or Death!" at d'Annunzio's prompting. They didn't want to be robbed of their adventure and returned to the dreariness of peacetime unemployment. Meanwhile the Fiumans were impatient to make peace. People were accusing each other variously of cowardice or of stupidity. In the overcrowded encircled city there were shouted altercations, brawls, injuries, near riots. Giuriati foresaw the imminent onset of a "popular cyclone."

On 12 December, d'Annunzio told Nitti's representative that he would accept the *Modus Vivendi* if it was approved by the National Council of Fiume. On 15 December the councillors met to deliberate. While they did so d'Annunzio, never happier than when on stage, interrupted a performance in the town's main theatre. Striding down to the footlights he shocked the audience by announcing that he and the Legion of Fiume were about to be ordered out of the city. His supporters carried the news through the streets. D'Annunzio was deliberately inciting the people to riot in an attempt to intimidate the Council. "People talked of killing," wrote Giuriati, "as though human life had lost all value."

The Council, staunchly ignoring the uproar, voted by forty-eight to six to accept the *Modus Vivendi*. By the time they announced their decision some 5,000 people had crammed into the square outside the Governor's Palace, crying out for d'Annunzio. He appeared on his balcony, holding the text of the agreement. He read it out, pausing histrionically after each point to ask: "Do you want this?"—a question expecting, and receiving in a massive yell, the answer "No!" Yet again Randaccio's banner was unfurled. D'Annunzio declared that the Council's decision must be tested by a plebiscite. The people must decide. Once again, as in Rome in 1915, he was defying constitutional authorities and appealing directly to the masses.

The *Arditi* launched into their battle songs. Throughout the night and into the following morning the square and surrounding streets were full of people shouting, singing, fighting. The President of the Council was waylaid in the street and beaten up by a gang of *Arditi*. A mob burst into the Governor's Palace. The next day d'Annunzio issued a proclamation: "Never of my own free will shall I abandon this city nor you my brothers-in-arms and in faith." Later in the day he softened— in this crisis he was simultaneously stubborn and wavering—and a new series of posters announced his willingness to allow the people of Fiume to "release" him and his legionaries from the oath by which they had bound themselves to the City of the Holocaust. "We came to serve the Cause of Fiume. We will leave to serve the same Cause . . . We only await your word."

The plebiscite took place on 18 December. During the preceding two days d'Annunzio's cooler, more realistic associates had pleaded with him to concede defeat. Meanwhile the legionaries had taken over the printing presses, destroying any pamphlets or posters advocating acceptance of the *Modus Vivendi*. Citizens who dared declare themselves in favour of it were roughed up in the street, or their houses were staked out. On the eighteenth the officials in charge of the voting were threatened and forced out and the polling stations were manned—menacingly—by *Arditi*, the black-shirted warriors whom Kochnitzky called "the dark seraphim of another Apocalypse."

As the people of Fiume went to vote, d'Annunzio was in the Ornitorinco ("Platypus"), the restaurant where he took his favoured officers to eat crayfish and drink a cherry brandy cocktail which he called "blood." The place had got its name when Guido Keller stole a stuffed platypus from the natural history museum, and placed it as a tribute on the Commandant's table because, said Keller (in his role of licensed jester), its horny bill was as smooth as d'Annunzio's ivory-coloured pate.

On the night of the ballot, young Comisso, the patisserie-eating poet, was for the first time one of those privileged to sit at the Commandant's table. D'Annunzio's bared head glimmered pale in the dim light of red-shaded lamps. His face looked as lifeless as wax. He took Comisso's hand in his own, which was icy cold, and invited the younger man to sit beside him. His command was perhaps about to be terminated, the room was full of his officers, their nerves strung to breaking point, making a great anxious hullabaloo. But d'Annunzio chatted serenely. Noticing Comisso's engineer's badge he flattered him, praising engineers in general and reminiscing about the heroism of those who had set up telephone lines in battle, working steadily under "homicidal" enemy fire.

An officer arrived with news. There were violent scenes at the polling stations. Officials announcing the results were being shouted down by angry legionaries. The urns in which the votes were cast were being smashed or seized. But it was impossible to obscure the fact that the people of Fiume were voting by approximately four to one in favour of the *Modus Vivendi*, and therefore for d'Annunzio's expulsion. There was much loud indignant talk in the Ornitorinco, in which d'Annunzio himself took no part. Some of his people were saying angrily that the wording of the proposition to be voted upon was ambiguous. An officer suggested they should all embark at once on a destroyer and leave the "ungrateful" city. Others were in favour of sending out more *Arditi* to close down the polling stations.

D'Annunzio listened quietly. Other messengers arrived, confirming the news of defeat. Eventually he got up, smiling, and remarked pleasantly that he felt like a French *littérateur* waiting to hear whether he had been admitted to the Académie Française. Then he left, to return to the palace, walking alone through the alleys of the old town, jotting in his notebook as he went: "Officers singing in the lower room." "Weeping women . . . Sense of tragedy in the city . . . The atrocious song."

The "electoral beast" had rejected him, but since he had never had any respect for it, he would not be discomposed by its decision. On his balcony again the following morning he declared: "We came here to win, we have sworn to win. If this agreement is signed, we will leave without a true victory." He prayed. He lamented. "Must we part? Must we bid each other farewell? Must we leave the axe embedded in the trunk of destiny?" His answer to his own questions was "No!"

He had called the plebiscite: now he chose to ignore it. He declared the vote null and void. The future of Fiume was to be decided by him and him alone. He would never abandon the city (however clearly it might express its wish that he should do so). He was more steadfast than Christ. "I will not say, Let this cup pass from me." He would drink it (and force all Fiume to drink it with him) without wavering, to the last drop.

The Fifth Season

IN THE FIRST WEEK of January 1920, d'Annunzio wrote to Dante, his gondolier and factotum at the Casetta Rossa, asking for a further supply of his favourite Fiat chocolates and a pot of lotion for his fingernails. He was staying put.

On New Year's Eve he proclaimed the beginning of a new season, one hitherto unknown in human history, "the fifth season of Fiume." In this time out of time, anything was possible. The true Italy might turn out to be a beleaguered little city in Croatia. A one-eyed man in late middle age might be a Prince of Youth.

The fifth season was celebrated with a night-time festival on the Field of Mars, with bonfires blazing and d'Annunzio haranguing the crowd, his voice competing with crashing waves and the rattle of machine guns. His language was incantatory, his images biblical. "As the new year begins, before the cock crows, let us all spring to our feet shouting out 'I believe!'" He told his legionaries that together they would build a new city. The blood and sweat of hundreds of thousands of war dead would anoint it. The sun would gild it, and feed them with its honey-sweet light. They would live a new life, singing perpetually, brothers united in daring. He was calling into being a Never Never Land, an unregulated space out of the continuum of cause and effect, where lost boys could enjoy dangerous adventures untrammelled by good sense.

He records the occasion: "The blue black winds snatched away my voice . . . Fists raised flames to the incorruptible stars and the machine guns opened their formidable fans over the contested sea."

Giuriati wept when he failed to persuade d'Annunzio to accept the *Modus Vivendi*. The morning after the plebiscite he resigned as his chief minister, and left Fiume. Major Reina, the man who could claim to have launched d'Annunzio on his great adventure, followed him out of town in early January. D'Annunzio now ruled Fiume in direct contravention of its people's proclaimed wishes, and Reina was one of many who refused to support his doing so. Reina had never wished—as he now believed d'Annunzio did—to draw the whole army into insubordination. He had no patience with the Uscocchi's "idiotic *colpi de mano*." He detested wild talk of a coup d'état in Rome and he wanted no part in the flummery about the "fifth season." Many other officers, no longer willing to defy their own government after the offer of such reasonable terms, left Fiume too, among them Luigi Rizzo. So many of the legionaries went with them—some 10,000—that d'Annunzio, who in September had had to turn away volunteers, was obliged to begin recruiting again.

The nature of d'Annunzio's Command was changing, and so was the atmosphere in the city. New arrivals were wilder than those who had left. General Caviglia (who had taken over from Badoglio as commander-in-chief for the region) reported that it had become "a refuge for foreign adventurers and agitators and shady people who had unfinished business with the police of their own countries." In his notebook d'Annunzio wrote: "The feeling that we are acting at the very heart of the world. The remoteness, the anxiety, the hostile nations."

The legionaries, erstwhile liberators, became enforcers. Ruling now without the consent of the ruled, d'Annunzio governed his city-state by intimidation. According to Father Macdonald, "the prisons were full to overflowing. The Carabinieri proved admirable spies and secret detectives and 'adjustments' were nightly carried out by the *Arditi*."

D'Annunzio issued an ambiguously worded proclamation which seemed to threaten the death penalty for anyone who "professes sentiments hostile to the cause of Fiume." No executions are recorded as having taken place, even though the local socialist journal continued to publish articles critical of d'Annunzio's Command; but censorship became rigid and hostile foreign journalists were expelled from the city. At the end of January 1920, d'Annunzio had over 200 socialists deported. According to a persistent oral tradition, it was d'Annunzio's *Arditi* in Fiume who first made punitive use of castor oil, a powerful laxative. The "golden nectar of nausea," as a leading fascist later called it, caused severe diarrhoea and dehydration. Forced to drink it, helplessly soiling themselves, victims were sickened and grossly humiliated. It was a technique of which the fascist squads would make extensive use over the next few years.

As d'Annunzio had once sprung like a mountain goat across the parliament chamber towards the socialists—"the Party of Life"—so now, deserted by monarchists and military men, he looked to radicals and revolutionaries for support. His finite political ambitions (the unseating of Nitti, the annexation of Fiume to Italy) seemed, for the time being anyway, to have failed. He reacted by enlarging the scope of his enterprise. He was no longer in Fiume to redeem a bit of Italian territory. He was building Utopia. The man whom he invited to succeed Giuriati as his first minister and to help in its construction was Alceste de Ambris, a revolutionary syndicalist, and the secretary of the Italian Union of Labour.

Syndicalism represented a supposedly pacific third way between capitalism and socialism. In a syndicalist world, instead of unending conflict between workers and bosses, there would be association and consensus. Employers and employees alike would belong to "corporations" working for the prosperity of all. Everyone's interests would be fairly represented. The theory was attractive to both left and right. It was only a few years later, under Mussolini, that the potential repressiveness of a state so constituted became evident. The "corporate state" was necessarily totalitarian—if all were to be included, then no one could be allowed the right to secede. De Ambris was seen as a socialist. But, like Mussolini, he had been strongly in favour of intervening in the war, and he was a follower of Georges Sorel, whose thinking was soon to be appropriated by the extreme right.

Sorel proclaimed the subordination of all ideologies to the pure, transformative power generated by violent struggle, by general strikes and terrorism. Industrial society was corrupt and democracy had failed. What was needed to replace it was a free association of heroic individuals. ("You are all heroes!" Randaccio had told his troops, and d'Annunzio in turn had told the people of Fiume.) Sorel stopped short of the anarchism to which logic seemed to be leading him. The people were noble, yes, but they needed leaders, great men untrammelled by irrelevant morality or outdated conventions; leaders with the swagger of condottieri and the charisma of a messiah, men like the imaginary dictator Corrado Brando in d'Annunzio's *Gloria*.

D'Annunzio invited de Ambris not only to help him run the city, but to assist him in drafting its new constitution. Father Macdonald—who disliked everything about d'Annunzio—intended only to express his disapproval when he wrote that in their plans he and de Ambris seemed to "depart from time-honoured methods and to aim at the production of something akin to the cubism or futurism of modern art." But his observation was accurate. The "charter" on which d'Annunzio was now working was a product, not of practical thinking, but of the artistic imagination. Long ago d'Annunzio had promised a "politics of poetry." Now he and de Ambris would produce its manifesto.

20 JANUARY 1920. The feast of d'Annunzio's favourite Saint Sebastian. A solemn rite presided over by an *Ardito* priest is celebrated in Fiume, in the cathedral of St. Vito. A troop of women process up the aisle to present their Commandant with a bayonet ornamented with gold and silver. Accepting the weapon, d'Annunzio delivers an oration in which the imagery of weaponry and sexualised pain overlap ecstatically. The tortured saint, d'Annunzio claims, cried out under the rain of arrows: "Not enough! Not enough! Again!" So Fiume cries out for more suffering: "I want to believe, my sisters, that this proffered bayonet was made with the steel of the first and last arrows." The blade is presented by the priest on behalf of the women with the decidedly un-Christian wish "that with it you may carve the word *victory* in the living flesh of our enemies." The Autonomist Party leader Riccardo Zanella believes that the weapon is destined for his murder and leaves town, shifting the offices of his journal to Trieste.

After the ceremony d'Annunzio reviews his Legion in yet another march past. Fiume's mayor, deeply moved, declares: "He's a saint!" Kochnitzky reports that "in the impoverished homes of the old city the women had removed the sacred images. The tiny light glowed in front of the figure of Gabriele d'Annunzio."

The priest officiating at the St. Sebastian's Day ceremony was subsequently reprimanded by the Vatican, and ordered out of Fiume.

On the mainland the fascists and socialists were fighting each other, to the death in many cases, but d'Annunzio, with his gift for shape-shifting accommodation, was still friend to both parties.

On 10 October 1919, just a month after he arrived in Fiume, he had received some unlooked-for aid. The crew of the *Persia*, an Italian cargo ship carrying some thirteen tons of weapons and ammunition destined for the supply of the White Russian armies, refused to support the enemies of their "brothers" the Bolsheviks. In the Straits of Messina they mutinied and sailed the ship to Fiume, handed its lethal cargo over to d'Annunzio and placed themselves under his command. They, and especially their leader Giuseppe Giulietti, head of the Seamen's Union, were given a properly Fiuman welcoming ceremony. D'Annunzio was jubilant. Most of the crew stayed—their presence in the city shifting the political character of the place leftwards—and d'Annunzio told Giulietti their politics might merge, inspiring "insurrections of the spirit against the devourers of raw flesh."

In early January 1920, Giulietti (now back on the mainland) was writing to d'Annunzio about another planned coup. This one was to be of a very different political colour from those monarchist-militarist plots in which d'Annunzio had been involved the previous summer. This would be an uprising of Italian socialists, its leaders to include the veteran anarchist Enrico Malatesta, its rank and file to be provided by Giulietti's Seamen's Union and by the Legion of Fiume. D'Annunzio havered. His heart was not in the venture. He may have felt the projected uprising's political complexion was uncongenial to him, but all he said was that he didn't want to leave Fiume: "Here the new forms of life are not only conceived, but are fulfilled."

As a man who believed the "the art of command is not to command," d'Annunzio was creating a space in which those new forms could flourish, and where the most unlikely alliances could be attempted. Fiume in 1920 was a bazaar of the mind.

In the cafés, on the waterfront, along the stone-paved Corso with its pretty Venetian campanile, noisy groups of disputants passed days and nights in planning new world orders. Communists preached world revolution. Futurists leapt on café tables, holding up placards, or harangued passers-by from the back of carts—calling on them to "smash to pieces all altars and pedestals," to destroy "banks, beards and prejudices," to explore every possible option in the city "where everything is possible in an atmosphere of geniality and incandescent madness." Bolsheviks formed soldier soviets. Anarchists and syndicalists and anarcho-syndicalists set up varying versions of the producers' networks prescribed by Proudhon. There were groups vehemently declaring elitist views like those d'Annunzio had been espousing since the 1890s: "We denounce the tasteless and unworkable system of parliamentary representation . . . We rejoice in beauty, in elegance and courtesy and style . . . we want to have over us miraculous, fantastic men." Marinetti had envisioned an era "when life will no longer be a simple matter of bread and labour, nor a life of idleness either, but *a work of art*." In the spring of 1920, another futurist, the *Ardito* Mario Carli, announced that that time had come to pass. In Fiume "today reigns poetry . . . the old antithesis of Life and Dream has finally been overcome."

D'Annunzio had a new, world-bestriding vision. He had spent decades extolling the grandeur of the Roman and Venetian Empires; he had enthusiastically lauded Italy's invasion of Libya. Of other, non-Italian empires, though, he disapproved.

It was time, he declared, for sparks from the Holocaust of Fiume to ignite "desires of revolt the world over," against Western colonialists in general, and Great Britain in particular. He announced his support for "the indomitable Sinn Féin of Ireland," and "the Egyptian red banner where the crescent and cross are united." His mission was directed against all the world's evil, "from Ireland to Egypt, from Russia to the United States, from Rumania to India." It was universalist. "It gathers the white races and the coloured peoples, reconciles the gospel with the Koran." The Fiume adventure, which had started out as a nationalist project with regressive aims—the recreation of an ancient empire— had transmuted into something resembling a Socialist International.

In January 1920, Léon Kochnitzky, poet and copywriter in d'Annunzio's press office, was appointed his Minister for Foreign Affairs, with fellow poet Henry Furst as his deputy. D'Annunzio proposed a union of all the people oppressed by the capitalist-imperialist powers, a League of Fiume. This league would be set up in pointed opposition to the League of Nations, which had its first meeting in Paris on 16 January. Kochnitzky, a communist sympathiser, embraced the idea enthusiastically. It was, he said (still as star-struck as he had been when he gazed at d'Annunzio's gleaming shirt front at the Opéra), a "shimmering globe that is worthy of the hand of Gabriele d'Annunzio alone."

By March, Kochnitzky could report that he had promises of support not only from the various ethnic populations of Dalmatia and the inhabitants of the Adriatic islands but also from Egyptians, Indians and Irish. He had had promising responses from Turks and Flemings. He had made overtures to the Catalans. He was in contact with Chinese labourers in California. Emissaries from all of these groups came and went in Fiume, or attended secret meetings on the Italian mainland.

British spies and diplomats kept a sharp eye on the League of Fiume, with its links to anti-British nationalist movements worldwide, as the copious Foreign Office memos on the subject demonstrate. So did the Italian Ministry of the Interior. There was much exhilarating talk, many ardent promises of cooperation and solidarity, but d'Annunzio never had the resources to transform the League's policies from hot air into arms or men.

D'Annunzio's deputy as ringmaster of Fiume's intellectual circus was his Action Secretary, Guido Keller. Keller, who got to know d'Annunzio in Venice in the months after the war, was an artist and an aviator who was said to paint a landscape or defy death with equal insouciance. "Like all true heroes," wrote Giuriati, "he disdained to boast . . . Like all the great comedians, he seldom laughed." Keller travelled light and

liked to walk naked along beaches; before the war he had been arrested several times for indecent exposure. He had been awarded three silver medals (the maximum) for his wartime exploits but he never wore them. He was striking looking, with the sharpest of black eyes, a luxuriant black beard and a great tress of hair growing, *Arditi*-style, from the crown of his head and falling like a horse's tail before his face.

He introduced a streak of night-black humour into the high solemnity of d'Annunzio's Fiume. In Zurich during the war, the Dadaists had begun to create anti-art and gibberish poems as their way of unmaking the world order which had concluded in the stupid slaughter. Keller certainly didn't share their pacifism, but he did share their insolence and their taste for obscenity and absurdist pranks. Once, on a surveillance flight over Serbian territory, his engine failed and he brought his plane down abruptly in the grounds of a monastery. There he met, and took a fancy to, a little donkey. While the monks shouted at him from the doors of their cells, he coolly mended his aircraft and then—strapping the poor beast to the plane's struts—took off with it and, having landed it safely, presented it to d'Annunzio.

It was Keller who enabled the Sacred Entry by stealing twenty-odd trucks, and it was Keller, continuing as resourcefully thievish, who recruited and commanded d'Annunzio's Uscocchi. In the fifth season the Uscocchi graduated from piracy to terrorism. On 26 January 1920 a party of them crossed the armistice line and ambushed a general of the Italian army on the road to Trieste, taking him captive and bringing him back to Fiume. There he was held for a month in the palace, treated with sarcastic courtesy and intimidated into declaring (despite his well-attested hostility towards d'Annunzian Fiume) his "faith in the sanctity of the cause and his high esteem for the defenders of the threatened city."

Fiume was like a city in the throes of Dionysiac possession, and d'Annunzio was its god. "The word 'd'Annunzio' shouted in a theatre or in any other public place was sufficient to cause the entire audience to rise to its feet and shriek frenzied *Evvivas*," wrote Father Macdonald sourly. Women pelted d'Annunzio with flowers when he marched out with his legionaries. His men vied for the right to be near him, to touch him, to get his autograph, to speak to him if only for a few seconds. Most evenings he dined in an officers' mess, or sometimes made a performance of sitting down to eat among the ordinary soldiers. "Evenings of noise and shouting, of frenetic adoration, of craziness." He had to be careful to distribute his favours with an even hand: after he had visited one division too often legionaries of another division, crazy with jealousy, attacked the barracks of the highly favoured ones waving machine guns.

In Paris, nearly a decade earlier, he had told a French lady who had been indelicate enough to commiserate with him on his hairlessness that he was proud of his "superhuman cranium," and told her, "Madame, in future, beauty will be bald." Unlikely as it may have seemed, his prediction was realised. In Fiume his devotees became, as the Bishop of Fiume noted, "so many caricatures of the Commandant." They shaved off their hair (initiating skinhead fashion). They grew little pointed beards. They wore white gloves and monocles and moved, as d'Annunzio did, in a miasma of strong perfume. One reported that "officers ate candies . . . and pursued the charms of women," all in imitation of their adored master.

Kochnitzky noticed how florid and verbose conversation in Fiume became, as the acolytes strove to emulate the fantastic circumlocutions of their master. Two months became "sixty days of passion and sixty nights of anguish." D'Annunzio's verbal mannerisms were catching, and so was his way of thinking. The bishop wrote: "The contagion of greatness was the greatest peril for anyone living in Fiume; a real contagious madness which everybody caught."

To Mario Carli, futurist, *Ardito* and spokesman of *Arditismo*, Fiume seemed a good base from which to aim "a monumental kick" at a "thousand mouldy traditions." In one of his first speeches in Fiume, d'Annunzio had removed his feathered cap to show his shining pate. The god of armies, he said, had given him a head harder than his enemies and now, he told his listeners: "You are Iron Heads all!" *Testa di Ferro* (Iron Head) became a Fiuman catchphrase, one of those which d'Annunzio only had to utter to get a bellow of appreciation from his adorers. Carli took it as the title of the journal he launched in Fiume, its first issue appearing on 1 February 1920.

For Carli there were two "centres of World Revolution"—Moscow and Fiume. He described Fiume's political ethos as "our Bolshevism" and sought to establish links with the Russian variety. So did Kochnitzky, who considered it essential to get the backing of the Soviet

Union for the League of Fiume. Communist Russia was one of the "spiritually alive elements of our time."

Lenin and his cohorts, struggling to control their immense domain, had no interest in involving themselves in d'Annunzio's little venture, but they viewed it benignly. An Italian Communist Party deputy declared: "The d'Annunzian movement is perfectly and profoundly revolutionary," and went on to assert that "Lenin even said so at the Moscow Congress." But when d'Annunzio made overtures to the Soviet Union, attempting in March 1920 to set up a meeting between Kochnitzky and one Engineer Vodovosoff, described as "official messenger" of the USSR, Vodovosoff declined.

It was increasingly hard to pin down d'Annunzio's political position. Comisso was amused to watch him courteously hearing out Kochnitzky and Furst as they talked of the inevitability of the worldwide communist revolution. "He listened attentively, then went off and he did whatever he had previously decided to do."

"All the ancient faiths are renegade, all the ancient formulae are rent," proclaimed an editorial in the *Testa di Ferro*. "We shall put our faith in and obey no man but our sole and marvellous leader Gabriele d'Annunzio." His worshippers (the word is not too strong) served not a cause but a man.

It was difficult for d'Annunzio to go out alone. The minute he set foot outside the Governor's Palace a shout would go up, a crowd would gather. Immured by his celebrity, he created a den for himself in his apartments. His bedroom was hung about with banners and military standards. There was a table covered with flasks of perfume. There was a couch heaped with cushions on which he stretched out to allow his imagination to play, or on which he and Luisa Baccara enjoyed "ultimate voluptuousness," their love-making shown back to them by a strategically placed mirror. Often, when he was conferring with his ministers, ostensibly intent on logistics or diplomacy, or quick-marching his soldiers over hills ("Today we almost ran," he reported), his mind, or so he told Luisa, was in these intensely private rooms.

The days of wine and sugared rose petals were drawing to a close. There were fuel shortages. Rations were becoming shorter, for officers as well as rank and file. In March 1920, d'Annunzio had to tell Luisa that there were no flowers in Fiume, that his vases all stood empty.

D'Annunzio's old habits of extravagance remained unchanged,

and his followers imitated him. And if the financial administration of d'Annunzio's household and staff was corrupt, that of the city as a whole was frighteningly ill-planned. D'Annunzio's Command paid and provisioned the legionaries, the municipal expenses were the responsibility of the Council; there were incessant arguments over the balancing of the two separate budgets. De Ambris seemed almost as negligent of economic affairs as his Commandant. In February 1920 he announced that the economic situation was under control. A month later he had to admit that the food and fuel which had kept Fiume going through the winter had all been bought on credit, that the suppliers were now demanding payment and that the warehouses were "virtually empty, with no possibility of resupply."

In February 1920, d'Annunzio created perhaps the most sentimentally potent and callously irresponsible of the artworks he made with the material of human lives. Declaring that—as a result of Nitti's cruel blockade—Fiume could no longer feed its children, he called upon patriotic Italians to provide homes for hundreds of Fiuman babies whose lives would otherwise be at risk. A group of Milanese ladies representing the *Fasci di Combattimento* duly arrived in Fiume with an enormous banner and took away with them some 250 babies for fostering on the mainland. Nitti—a novice playing here against a grand master of public relations—initially refused to allow the children to land, but after a public outcry they were permitted to enter Italy and delivered to their foster families. D'Annunzio, the man who had abandoned his own children, had successfully cast himself as the good and loving father of hundreds, and forced Nitti into the role of one who refused succour to starving Innocents.

Rivals for Luisa Baccara. On 21 February 1920, d'Annunzio was enjoying "voluptuousness, deep kisses, oblivion" and "savage sex" with a woman named (repeating himself) Barbarella and on the following day he had three female visitors—"little Bianca," someone "brown and soft" but nameless and a third whom he called "the little mistress of Merano." The four of them engaged in partner-swapping sexual games, the number of his bedfellows making the pleasure, d'Annunzio noted, more than usually acute.

Fiume, its civilian population swelled by some 20,000 fighting men, had become a military encampment, administered along military lines. But the legionaries, most of whom had come to Fiume in direct disobedience to orders, didn't take kindly to discipline. Delinquent young men clustered around Guido Keller. Keller was drawn to the "most unhinged" because he considered them the most daring. There was "the Red Pirate," who embezzled a large sum of money sent to the Command by supporters back in Italy, but who was nonetheless taken up by Keller, immediately on his release from prison, as a promising "action man." There was the legionary whom Keller employed as his personal servant until one evening the man, getting hold of a gun, began to fire it at random out of the window. There were the three young anarchists whom he came upon one day passed out on the floor of a "lurid inn" after smoking too much hashish.

There were people living rough in the idle shipyards—deserters, criminals, underage runaways or other fugitives who had arrived in Fiume without documents. Nitti's agents reported that these "turbid elements" lived in vast warehouses alongside armoured cars, whose engines they kept turning over day and night, despite the chronic shortage of fuel. Keller, paying a visit to investigate, found a titanic adventure playground full of half-naked men, heavy metal and aggressive song: a Vorticist underworld peopled by hell's angels. Amidst the fumes and incessant mechanical din, men dived into the harbour from the bows of the abandoned ships, others attempted to drive the immobilised engines of the Fiume-Budapest railway line, others scrambled up the immense cranes along the waterfront, all "beautiful and proud, crazy and joyful." Keller thought they could be of use. He formed them into a troop of irregulars variously known as the "Centurions of Death" or *La Disperata* (the Legion of the Desperate), and offered them to d'Annunzio, who made them his private guard. They became a highly visible part of Fiume's public life. Handsome, rowdy and violent, they paraded through the streets bare-chested. At night they played war games, using live grenades. Some of them died.

D'Annunzio and Keller teased and riled each other. Their relationship was prickly and flirtatious. D'Annunzio, so portentously earnest in public, was playful in private and with Keller, the latest of his beloved young men, he could relax. Keller absented himself from headquarters and took a room in a hotel with a sea view. There, despite the February chill, he basked naked on his balcony, accompanied by his eagle, who liked to groom him, plunging its beak into his thick black hair. D'Annunzio, on being told how he passed his time, sent a legionary with instructions to wait until Keller was taking a bath, and then to abduct the eagle. The deed was done. Keller, distraught, ran out into the street in his towel. There was (as so often) some sort of a rally going on. A column of marching *Arditi* all acknowledged the semi-nude Action Secretary by giving him the salute—arm outstretched, dagger in hand.

Keller went back indoors, having guessed there was only one person in Fiume who would dare to cross him so, and wrote out a challenge. There must be a duel. The robber—whoever it might be—would have to face him. The missive was carried to the palace by his seconds. D'Annunzio cheerfully admitted his crime and handed back the eagle, now wearing a ribbon in the Italian colours around its neck and a label proclaiming in Latin that it brought tidings of a future empire. The duel was averted. The Commandant placed his car at the disposal of Keller's two friends and the restored eagle. As they made the short journey back through the crowded streets, *Arditi*, clustering as they did every day around the famous motor car, found themselves hailing a bird.

No one expected Yugoslavia to last. It was not a nation, said d'Annunzio, it was a monster, an earthly version of Dante's imagined Malebolge; a place part Byzantine, part Roman, "where Belgrade commands, Sarajevo conspires, Zagreb threatens, Lubliana froths, and Catholic and Orthodox and Muslim tear each other to pieces." Hardly any well-informed commentator would have predicted in 1920 that the botched-up new country, with its mutually hostile populations and its bloody history, might survive for nearly seventy years.

The Italian government was looking for ways to provoke conflict among its constituent parts. So was the rogue outpost at Fiume. During the autumn of 1919, Giuriati encouraged d'Annunzio to see the Slavs encompassing Fiume, not as a sea of undifferentiated enemies, but as a pool of possible supporters. The Command was in contact with Montenegrins and Croatians, and Giuriati worked tirelessly behind the scenes to foment hostility to the over-dominant Serbs among their fellow Yugoslavs. After he left, at the beginning of 1920, d'Annunzio told one of his correspondents that: "Even the Croats, wishing to unshackle the Serbian yoke, turn to me." Throughout the spring he worked to effect an uprising which would have shattered Yugoslavia back into its constituent ethnic groups, and left the way open for Italy to grab what territory it wanted. A revolution, he said, would shortly "explode." "I can lead the movement. I can enter Zagreb as a liberator. All is ready."

Luisa Baccara was not popular with the young men around d'Annunzio. Fiume was a place of boyish adventure, not adult sexual partnerships. When a risky expedition down the coast was discussed Luisa didn't want her lover to go. What if they met Allied ships? What if they were torpedoed? Guido Keller and Comisso, his adoring sidekick, deduced, entirely irrationally, that she must therefore be an agent of the government in Rome. They resolved to be rid of her.

When carnival time came round Keller offered to organise a *festa*, and Comisso suggested they revive the ancient game of the Castle of Love. In mediaeval Treviso, a wooden castle would be built and the town's prettiest young women shut themselves up in it and were "besieged" by suitors throwing food and flowers. Keller planned a party-cum-mock battle on the beach, during which a troop of Fiuman women headed by Luisa Baccara would be similarly imprisoned in a "castle" (actually a bathing pavilion). Each nationality represented in Fiume would have its own boat. Hungarians, Slavs and Italians would compete in a sea battle and in a "tournament" on the beach to decide who would carry off the disputed women.

D'Annunzio refused to sanction the idea on the interesting grounds that it would be "too d'Annunzian." He was the Commandant now, not the precious antiquarian poet, and, with his ever-alert awareness of how a story would play, he no longer wished to be associated with pseudo-mediaeval erotic frolics.

It was just as well he withheld his permission. Keller and some of his fellow radicals had formed what they called a Committee of Public Safety; the menacing historical echoes were fully intended. A Dadaist Robespierre, Keller intended the Castle of Love to be a purge, in the not-yet-current Stalinist sense of the word. In the frenzy of the dancing, those identified by Keller as the "men of the past" would be "seized, put on a boat and carried away," while Luisa would be "put in a cage like a hen" and marooned on an uninhabited island in the bay.

D'Annunzio's legionaries were ebbing away: 750 left in one week. In *La Vedetta* he reminded the erstwhile legionaries how bravely they had come to Fiume, and how, in entering the marvellous city, "all of a sudden you were changed into a single flame." But now—Oh, what a change! He heaped up reproachful words: infamy, perjury, violation, abandonment. The defectors were like St. Peter, who denied Christ three times. Let them go. Those who remained would share his death and his glory, as the true disciples had shared Christ's.

Each time he reiterated one of his phrases it acquired an extra patina, an extra authority, until his legionaries would bellow them back to him, like rock fans recognising and singing along to the opening riff of a beloved anthem.

D'Annunzio and de Ambris were working on their constitution, the Charter of Carnaro. By March 1920 its outline was complete.

The political institutions it describes are modelled variously on the Athenian assembly, on the governments of the mediaeval Italian commune, and on the institutions of the Venetian Republic. True to the doctrines of anarcho-syndicalism, it decentralises power, granting "collective sovereignty" to all its citizens "without regard to sex, race, language, class or religion." There were to be two parliamentary assemblies, both elected by universal suffrage, but they were to meet only once or twice a year. Remembering the tedium of his few visits to Montecitorio, d'Annunzio required their meetings to be of "sharply concise brevity." The great speech-maker had no desire to hear others speak.

The real work of government would be done by the nine "corporations," each of which represented a section of the community defined by the work they did—one for seamen, one for artisans, one for "the intellectual flower of the people" (teachers, students, artists), and so forth. Every citizen had to belong to one or other of them.

A College of Ediles would be responsible for "the Beauty of the City" (as in Ancient Rome) and for civic ceremonies, of which there would be many. Creativity became a public duty. Every corporation was "to invent its insignia, its emblems, its music . . . to institute its ceremonies and its rites; to participate, as magnificently as it can, in the anniversary festivals and the games; to venerate its dead, honour its leaders, celebrate its heroes."

A great edifice was to be constructed, an enormous theatre akin to that which d'Annunzio and Duse had once planned in the Alban hills, where 10,000 people at a time could attend concerts "gratis, as the Church fathers termed the grace of God." In this Utopia, music, not religion, would be the opium of the masses.

The constitution described in the charter had no place for a Commandant. There was, however, another vacancy in the political structure which d'Annunzio might fill. There was a "tenth corporation . . . represented in the civic sanctuary by a glowing lamp," whose nature and function is so veiled by mumbo-jumbo that it can only be described in the constitution's original words. "It is reserved for the mysterious forces of the people. It is a figure of offering to the unknown genius, to the appearance of the new man, to the ideal transfiguration of the works and of the days, to the fulfilled liberation of the spirit." The unknown genius sounds a bit like Nietzsche's superman, and the only available incarnation of the ideal was, of course, d'Annunzio himself.

Many of d'Annunzio's contemporaries mocked the charter's apparently disproportionate stress on appearances and ceremony as evidence that d'Annunzio was nothing but a frivolous old mummer. There were others, Mussolini and the many future fascists who were present in Fiume among them, who grasped the importance of the art in which he was so adept, the manipulation of a community's collective emotions. Political doctrine was impotent without the art to promote it.

In April, the Uscocchi turned horse-thieves, a band of them seizing and bringing back to Fiume forty-six well-fed cavalry horses belonging to a recently disbanded regiment of the regular Italian army. D'Annunzio greeted them exultantly: "My young corsairs!" Herding their catch into Fiume in the small hours they were "luminous in the shadowy morning, as though you had seized the horses of the Sun from the cavern of the furthest Orient."

To d'Annunzio their raid was an exploit worthy to be celebrated by a new Tasso. To General Ferrario, now in command of Italian troops in the region, it was a breach of the tacit understanding whereby d'Annunzio had been allowed to remain in Fiume for so long. Ferrario demanded the horses back, and announced that if they were not returned within three days the hitherto-perfunctory blockade would turn serious. Trains would cease to arrive in Fiume. No flour or other foodstuffs would be allowed across the line. For historians the interesting point about these threats is the clarity with which they show how lenient the so-called blockade had previously been. But for d'Annunzio they were "brutal," the "cruellest cut" inflicted upon the "tortured and famished body" of the "martyred" city. "The hospitals would have no more medicine; the exhausted children would have no more milk." He raged against Nitti and pelted the soldiers of the regular Italian army with pleas and reproaches. He presented the episode as a story of brutish oppressors overreacting to the high-spirited teasing of "merry predators."

The episode ended with another prank. D'Annunzio had forty-six horses delivered to Ferrario's headquarters—not the original, glossy animals, but an assortment of scrawny beasts from Fiume's own dwindling stock. It was a way of mocking the general, and of advertising what d'Annunzio claimed to be Fiume's desperate straits, deprived not only of milk for its babies but even of fodder for its nags. He issued a statement—jeering, mystical, nonsensical, highfalutin and defiant.

> We have stolen forty-six quadrupeds.
> We deserve only to be starved, manacled and executed.
> We shall resign ourselves.
> But I must further confess that last night I stole the Horse of
>   the Apocalypse . . .
> *Cum Timore.*

With the coming of spring the Legion of Fiume's daily marches became more festive. The legionaries traversed meadows full of violets. They cut branches of almond and peach blossom and carried them like banners. Clumping heavy-booted, they sang out loudly, and d'Annunzio, the smallest and oldest of the party, always aware of his "devastated face," sang along, jubilant.

D'Annunzio's was the politics of poetry and his poetry the poetry of sensuality. In Fiume under his command a political rally might segue smoothly into a street party and thence into a love-in. To be young and passionate was a patriotic duty. "It was a period of madness and bacchanal," wrote a participant, "ringing with the sounds of weapons and those, more subdued, of love-making." With so many unattached young men crammed into the town there were not enough women to go round. Homosexuality was tolerated. D'Annunzio, looking out of his window one day and watching couples of *Arditi* walking hand in hand toward the hills behind the town, said fondly: "Look at my soldiers, going off in couples as in the time of Pericles." Father Macdonald was shocked to see Italian officers "painted and powdered like street-walkers." An Italian medical officer reported there were 150 cases of venereal disease for every fifteen patients with other complaints. It was widely rumoured that d'Annunzio himself had contracted syphilis (or more likely brought it with him, mark of the Parisian "branding iron").

As the spring of Fiume's "fifth season" turned to summer, the *Arditi* stripped off and bathed in the river, and strutted through the streets in short shorts. "There was no limit to the number of love affairs," says Comisso. The cemetery on the hills behind the towns was full, at night, of couples making love.

Rations grew tighter. In March 1920 the sale of cakes, biscuits, chocolate and caramels were banned. No more delicious patisserie. Basic foods were rationed, and even when provisions were available in the shops the workers often had no money to buy them. To demonstrate his solidarity with the hungry troops, d'Annunzio put on the uniform of a humble corporal and took his place in a ration queue for a photocall (overleaf).

In April the Fiuman unions called a general strike to back up their demands for a minimum wage. D'Annunzio acted as arbitrator in negotiations with the Employers' League. His sympathies were with the workers (he was still corresponding with Giulietti about labour relations) but he was bored by the whole affair. Sitting in on rancorous discussions he fretted at being confined in a stuffy meeting room when he might have been out picking violets. He hadn't come to Fiume to talk about the cost of living (a subject he'd always preferred to ignore). He wasn't interested in securing a decent wage for the workers; he wanted to make them burn with a hard, gem-like flame.

He was increasingly estranged from the National Council, most of whose members were industrialists or businessmen. They were annoyed by his espousal of the workers' cause. He in turn was incensed by the way they acted without consulting him, expelling so-called troublemakers (most of them union officials) from the city. Five hundred workers were arrested. The local police, led by Captain Rocco Vadalà,

sacked and then closed down the offices of one of the main unions, all apparently without d'Annunzio's consent. He was losing his grip on Fiume's civil administration. In April 1920 the mayor and other members of the National Council went to Rome to meet Nitti and tell him they were exasperated by the "disorder, corruption and craziness" d'Annunzio had brought to their city.

In May a party of Uscocchi stowed away on board a Hungarian grain ship outward bound from Trieste. They hid in the ship's tender, all but buried in coal, appearing after several days, black all over, to persuade the crew to mutiny and alter course for Fiume. "We have bread for eight months!" exulted d'Annunzio. It was the miracle of the loaves and fishes all over again. It was a new Eucharist. "In dark grief yesterday we made our communion in blood. Today, with manly serenity, we make our communion in the bread that God has sent us." It was a respite, but it was not enough to stop the defections.

In May 1920, Captain Vadalà left Fiume at the head of 750 men. D'Annunzio rewrote their defection as a purge: "We are no longer nauseated by the fetor of bad consciences." He was not being rejected, rather he was rejecting traitors whose moral degeneration made them as horrifying as walking corpses, slimy and putrescent.

His odious rhetoric stirred his followers to violence. As the departing men approached the armistice line they were set upon by *Arditi*. Three men were killed and several wounded. The entire front page of

La Vedetta was given over to an account of how the *Arditi* had punished the "traitors," nobly shedding their own "robust blood."

Back in Italy, with the government's authority gravely undermined by d'Annunzio's continued defiance, Italians were fighting among themselves. Socialists claimed that 145 of their supporters were killed by police in the year up to May 1920.

The fascist movement, badly shaken by its electoral defeat, died down, then mutated and grew back in more virulent forms. Its revival began in Italy's northeastern corner, in Trieste and the surrounding region, just across the Istrian peninsula from d'Annunzio's Fiume. Trieste had only been Italian again since the armistice, and its population was as mixed as Fiume's. "Border fascists," as these groups were known, were as interested in race as they were in ideology. They inveighed against socialism, but their prime opponents were the Slavs who lived among them. Throughout the last months of d'Annunzio's "five seasons," fascist violence around Trieste become ever more frequent and more ugly. Newspapers' offices trashed; Slovenes and Croats harassed and bullied; socialist rallies disrupted; labour offices torched; socialists shot dead.

Elsewhere, fascism's second wave of recruits were of a different mind from the original trenchocracy. A military ethos, with its glorification of discipline and hierarchy, gave way to an outlaw mentality. In the immediate aftermath of the war there had been much talk of sacrifice and dedication. New fascists were motivated more by the intoxication of violence perpetrated with impunity.

The economy was as volatile as the public mood. The cost of living was four times what it had been before the war. In May there were violent demonstrations in Turin. "Workers' councils" took over factories. Moderates were as alarmed as the nationalist right: these workers' councils were seen as versions of the Russian soviets. Nitti called on the army, sending 50,000 soldiers into the city. The fascist squads were not the only people reacting with violence to the perceived threat of a red revolution.

While at home in Italy politics became ever more polarised, in Fiume d'Annunzio embraced any idea that took his fancy. "Do not be surprised at anything; tomorrow he could be celebrating a fakir's ritual or dancing the light fantastic with the most civilised Arabs of Egypt," wrote Carli. "It is the privilege of genius, this transition into a thousand forms, and it is his secret how he remains immutably and miraculously himself."

Others, less privileged by genius, grew alarmed. The Charter of Carnaro was not made public until September, but rumours about it spread: that it was shockingly egalitarian, and that it described an independent republic, implying that d'Annunzio was no longer holding Fiume for Italy, but for himself. General Caviglia, observing from Abbazia through the eyes and ears of his numerous informers, heard that many of d'Annunzio's "finest officers" were moved to leave him, "disgusted with the revolutionary attitudes of the Command."

Fiume's intellectual life was becoming ever more active and unconventional. The "Union of Free Spirits Tending Towards Perfection" met under their fig tree to debate alternatives to prison and "the beautification of the city." There were nationalists calling for a purer *Italianità*; there were internationalists borrowing doctrines from the farthest reaches of the earth. Like their Californian counterparts half a century later, the thinkers of Fiume's counter-culture looked to India for enlightenment. YOGA, an association motivated by "ardour of action . . . genius and mystic ire," was the brainchild of a Venetian officer with an enthusiasm (shared by d'Annunzio, who had been reading the Bhagavad-Gita in the 1880s) for Hinduism. For the members of YOGA, the Nietzschean division between supermen and slaves could be formalised according to a Hindu model. They proposed the adoption of the caste system, people to be allotted their status according to their "spiritual potency." There were the Brown Lotuses, proto-hippies who reviled capitalism, money, modern industry and the city, exalted Eastern mysticism and aspired to get back to nature and live a simple life following the rhythms of the earth. There were the Red Lotuses, modern Dionysiacs who proclaimed the advent of a new world transformed by sexual love. There was a group whose markedly homoerotic manifesto announces their oneness in "Sacred Love" and their dedication to "squandering it like saints and madmen."

Guido Keller, who knew how to throw a party in tune with the Nietzschean spirit abroad in Fiume, organised a *Festa Yoga*. The invitation promised "a dance in the abyss of the profound sea. A dance in the African forests. A dance beyond good and evil. Rally! Free spirits."

In June 1920, Nitti fell from power. D'Annunzio celebrated with a mock funeral and a paean to the God of Vengeance, reprising all the insults he had hurled at *Cagoia*, the "putrid blown-out windbag" who had "used our dead as manure for turnips." But Nitti's loss of office was a disaster for him.

Giolitti, whom d'Annunzio had denounced in 1915 as a traitor, was recalled from retirement (he was now seventy-eight years old) to head the government. In Paris, the Allied powers had finally decided not to decide anything about Fiume, leaving it to the Italians and the Yugoslavs to arrive at a settlement between themselves. Ignoring d'Annunzio, Giolitti, a more confident statesman than Nitti, entered into negotiations with Yugoslavia.

In Fiume the atmosphere of carnival was turning darker. "It is impossible," said Kochnitzky, "to be sublime for so many months without danger." On that summer's hot nights, the shouts of *"Eia, Eia, Eia! Alalà!"* rising from the public gardens and the waterfront were as threatening as they were jubilant. Fiume reeked of violence. Father Macdonald describes it: "Cries of *Fiume o Morte*, frightfulness, bomb-throwing in the streets, imprisonment of respectable people for no other reason than because they are suspected of not being supporters of d'Annunzio—such are the methods by which Fiume is governed. How long will the disgusting comedy last?"

Most of those victimised were non-Italian. In the charter, d'Annunzio and de Ambris had allowed for the existence of Croatian citizens, fully integrated into their visionary state, but allowed—if they so wished—to create Croatian communes enjoying equal rights and freedoms with their Italian counterparts. In practice, though, d'Annunzio, raging against Yugoslavia ("a Balkan pigsty," or a "beast" born from the vomit of the dying Austrian vulture) allowed his fury to spill over onto the ethnic groups of which the new state was made up. Serbs were "ferocious," they "cut off women's breasts and kill babies in their cradles." He referred to his Croatian neighbours pejoratively as "Croataglia," while he sneered at Slavs in general as "swineherds."

Croatian or Serbian citizens were arrested on the street and locked up in the theatre before being expelled to Susak. Their homes, thus brutally vacated, were allotted to Italians. Unemployment and hunger fuelled racial tensions. Industrial disputes between Slav labourers and Italian employers merged with ethnic conflicts. The legionaries crossed the river into Susak and swaggered through the streets, terrifying the Croatian citizenry. Showing forged papers and claiming to be members of the secret police, they barged into people's homes and "confiscated" their valuables. Zanella, observing from Trieste, wrote that Fiume "groans under the yoke of a domination which is mediaeval, absurd and ridiculous. Citizens are no longer safe in their own homes . . . peasants have to guard their animals in their bedrooms."

An Italian officer and his driver were attacked and killed by Serbian troops in Spalato (Split), provoking angry demonstrations in Fiume, and invective from d'Annunzio directed at the Serbian filth sullying the halls of Diocletian's palace. Another ceremony: the dead men were buried in Spalato, but that didn't prevent d'Annunzio ordering funerals for them in Fiume.

Primed for violence, told insistently by their adored "capo" that their neighbours were their enemy, the legionaries went on the rampage, wrecking and burning Croats' shops and houses. D'Annunzio ordered them back to barracks, but announced that the Command would be practising "special vigilance" in regard to "politically suspicious persons"—by which was meant, almost invariably, Slavs.

If most of the city's pre-war industries were temporarily defunct, one form of production was still lively: the manufacture of hand grenades. Military exercises were conducted with real ammunition, and real injuries. The legionaries fought duels with flame-throwers, returning from exercises bloodied and singed. The tenth month of d'Annunzian Fiume was celebrated with a massive military exercise with shelling from batteries at sea, on the mountains and along the shore. D'Annunzio reviewed the entire Legion, taking hours over it, passing along the lines, holding the eyes of each man in turn, telling them they were as beautiful and violent and swift as tawny beasts, as impenetrable as a wall of flame.

More anniversaries celebrated with rallies and shouting, with legionaries marching with laurel branches in their rifles, and with d'Annunzio on his balcony whipping up a storm of hero worship and martial ardour. More fanfares. More flags: the red, white and green of Italy; the violet, yellow and crimson of Fiume. Awards ceremonies. Welcome parties at the railway station, with women pinning rosettes on the lapels of newly arrived volunteers.

In June, for the festival of San Vito, Fiume's patron saint, the streets were brilliantly illuminated and the harbour was crowded with boats garlanded with flowers and hung about with lanterns. "They danced everywhere," recorded Kochnitzky, "in the piazzas, in the streets, on the dock; by day, by night, they danced and sang." There were fanfares and fireworks. "One's gaze, wherever it was fixed, saw a dance: of lanterns, of sparks, of stars." It was an orgy (a word d'Annunzio used approvingly and often). Kochnitzky "saw soldiers, sailors, women, citizens in bohemian embraces." It was also a *danse macabre.* "Starving, in ruin, in anguish, perhaps on the verge of death in the flames or under a hail of grenades, Fiume, brandishing a torch, danced before the sea."

D'Annunzio was preparing for a decisive move. "Patience has no more to say: I cut her throat last night. Now courage speaks."

On 30 August, to an audience of Fiuman citizens, and again next day to officers of the Legion, he read aloud the new constitution, the Charter of Carnaro. These addresses were made, not from his balcony, but in Fiume's Teatro Fenice. Crammed to capacity, the theatre was swelteringly hot. Making a metaphor of adversity, d'Annunzio described it as the furnace in which a new order would be smelted. He told his listeners: "These pages are yours . . . Your spirit has written them with an eagle's feather, trimmed and sharpened with the edge of your short sword."

Some of his ministers protested that the charter's Article Nine (which implied that property rights were not absolute) must be dropped, or farewell to any hope of outside investment in Fiume. The corporations, which sounded alarmingly like trade unions, would "give the city into the hands of the workers." D'Annunzio didn't care. In the midst of a landscape scored with trenches, he told his legionaries: "We have established the foundations of a city of life."

He ended his address to the citizens with a rousing cry for "annexation to Italy, sooner or later, but certain. *Eia, Eia, Eia, Alalà!*" There were those who wondered, as the ululating drowned out criticism, why, if Fiume was to become a part of Italy, it needed its separate constitution? In de Ambris's first draft the charter described Fiume as a "Republic."

To soothe the monarchists among his supporters d'Annunzio subsequently changed the word to "Regency," but he was moving further and further from the state to which he claimed he wished his city to be joined. To think "Italianly," he now said, was to think ignobly, deviously, cravenly.

There were people around him urging him to rebel. Carli's "Iron Head" announced that Fiume was an "island of wonder" and its people were "the advance guard of all nations on the march to the future . . . a handful of . . . mystic creators, who will sow through the world the seed of our force."

That force might be figurative. It might be actual. For de Ambris, as for many of those who stayed with d'Annunzio into its fifth season, the political transformation of Fiume was a try-out for a larger revolution. De Ambris told d'Annunzio that Fiume should "annex Italy," and establish there a new society organised along the lines of their visionary charter. "In Italy a saviour is demanded and awaited, and the most illuminated identify him as Gabriele d'Annunzio." Only d'Annunzio could unite the proletariat, the bourgeoisie and the military. Guido Keller agreed; he was barely interested in Fiume per se. For him it was simply the first step towards an Italian revolution "and after Italy, the world."

For decades d'Annunzio had been toying with visions of dictatorship: his admiration of Plato, whose republic is ruled by all-powerful philosopher-kings; his poetic reinvention of Garibaldi as a marmoreal figure, master of the elements and of the mob; his play *Glory*, whose hero Flamma is "a true man suited to the great emergency, a vast free human spirit." *Glory* was subsequently much admired by fascists for its apparently miraculous prescience, but d'Annunzio, in writing it, was not prophesying the coming of Mussolini: he was creating a role for himself. In France before the war he had visited a sorceress who had told him (or so he maintained) he would become "a kind of king."

Despite urging from his supporters though, he was not ready to cross his Rubicon. De Ambris proposed a pact with Mussolini for a joint uprising in Italy in which d'Annunzio would provide the "genius" and Mussolini the manpower. But Mussolini, more confident now of his own authority, wasn't interested in raising a revolt on someone else's behalf, and d'Annunzio, true to form, couldn't make up his mind.

. . . .

The National Council of Fiume was not pleased with the Charter of Carnaro. Nervous of confronting d'Annunzio and his Legion directly, its members resorted to legalistic temporising. On 8 September the Council dissolved itself, and reformed as a "directive committee" with the declared intention of calling for a new election within six weeks for members of a "constituent assembly" which would "consider" the Charter of Carnaro. D'Annunzio was having none of this pussy-footing. He issued a proclamation through *La Vedetta* requiring all the people of Fiume to gather that very evening beneath his balcony. "Today you will decide the fate of the city!" Alarms sounded, bells rang, Randaccio's banner was unfurled. The piazza filled. D'Annunzio called out that it was a "decisive hour" for the future of Fiume. There and then, on his own authority, he proclaimed the inception of the "Italian Regency of Carnaro." The "act of life" for which he had been calling turned out to be a coup d'état.

Grossich, representing the National Council, protested. D'Annunzio answered him defiantly:

The party of slaves dissents and opposes us.
Excellent.
Let fighting begin.
We will fight.

The Council, helpless to oppose his Legion, acquiesced. But the charter never made the transition from words to action. From this time on, d'Annunzio called his administration the Regency, but nothing else materialised, no corporations, no immense concert hall, no "palpitating fact."

12 SEPTEMBER. The first anniversary of the Sacred Entry. D'Annunzio raised a new standard, a purple flag with gold stars framed by a serpent eating its own tail, and announced the issue of a new set of Fiuman postage stamps.

20 September. The fiftieth anniversary of the unification of Italy. More bedecking of the streets with flowers and strewing of the cobbles with laurel branches.

22 September. A city-wide demonstration-cum-street-party to celebrate the visit of Guglielmo Marconi. D'Annunzio gave his old friend a solemn public welcome, addressing him as a "dominator of cos-

mic energies," and lauding him for having spread the genius of Italy through the universe at the speed of starlight. Marconi had come to build a radio mast, so that the voice of Fiume could sound out over the world's airwaves. D'Annunzio went aboard Marconi's ship, the *Electra*, and from its little onboard studio made his first broadcast to the world.

Kochnitzky's adoration cooled. D'Annunzio was no longer interested in his League of Fiume, and he was losing his place in the inner circle (Osbert Sitwell, a privileged visitor, called him "the only bore in Fiume"). He still had the glove he had stolen on his first meeting with d'Annunzio but sometimes he was tempted to use it as a pen wiper, just to vent his exasperation.

There came a day when Kochnitzky's deputy and friend, Henry Furst, criticised another of d'Annunzio's protégés and the Commandant—still fit, still a boxer—put his fists up as though to strike him. There came another day when, on bidding goodbye to Kochnitzky, d'Annunzio gave him his hand briefly and then swivelled to the right and abruptly turned his back. Everyone knew what that meant. His favour had been withdrawn. The Office for External Affairs was closed.

As Kochnitzky and Furst were packing up their files they heard Luisa Baccara playing one of Bach's fugues in d'Annunzio's apartments on the next floor up, and then, the final indignity, his bath water began to drip through their office ceiling. Over their heads their erstwhile idol, distracted by his mistress, had left the tap running. Kochnitzky went straight to the railway station, so anxious to leave that he ran down the tracks after the train he had just missed, and mounted it as it stopped at the armistice line.

In September 1920 a miniature civil war began. Rival officers of the Legion, in competition for new recruits, ordered their men into battle against each other. One of d'Annunzio's ministers told the Commandant the officers were behaving like drunken looters. D'Annunzio took heed, but the reforms he instigated were hardly designed to reinforce discipline.

One of the topics for discussion under the YOGA group's fig tree through the summer had been the idea that in Fiume, the city of youth and fire, military hierarchy was absurd and military discipline oppressive. YOGA's members vowed "to attack senior officers publicly and violently." Keller drew up some resolutions: the uniform to be redesigned, abandoning the prissy stand-up collar and the useless sword still worn by officers. The *Ardito*, a heroic individual operating alone, would be taken as the model for all soldiers. Keller was envisaging a fighting force made up of insubordinate individual warriors, something like the bands of armed knights who had made mediaeval battlefields such scrimmages.

D'Annunzio agreed. On 27 October he published his plans for his army. He described his ideal troops, few but each man as fit for lethal action as a torpedo. A legionary must be able to run, leap, swim, ride, lift weights, throw stones, climb trees. He must be ready to break down a door with his shoulder, or to fling himself from a cliff. He must be able to sing, dance, whistle and "imitate the voices of men and of beasts." Killers and performers at once, the legionaries would be the star actors in d'Annunzio's ideal theatre of war and they would operate, as the heroes envisioned by Sorel would do, as individuals, violent, noble and grand.

There would be no more officers. Every intermediate rank between the Commandant and the troops was abolished. The entire army answered directly and exclusively to d'Annunzio. "To the Commandant alone is reserved the power to deliberate . . . He alone has the right to declare war." D'Annunzio was setting his men free: each one was entitled to a vote in a military council in which the most junior recruit had as good a voice as the most senior officer. But he was also binding them tightly to him. "To him is owed obedience without limit, and total faith."

The military reforms, like the Charter of Carnaro, remained unimplemented. All the same, after the publication of the new military code, many of the officers remaining in Fiume defected.

The men were leaving, to be replaced by boys. Osbert Sitwell, arriving in Fiume, found himself sharing a railway carriage with two sixteen-year-olds whose pockets were weighed down with volumes of d'Annunzio's verse, who told him that if they were put off the train they would walk to Fiume over the mountains. Their heads full, not of solid iron, but of poetry and adolescent discontent, they were typical of the Legion's new recruits—fervent, devoted, but perhaps not very useful.

D'Annunzio's blind eye was hurting, as it would for the rest of his life. Worse than completely sightless, it baffled and distracted him with light flashes and blurred hallucinations.

Keller and his wild crew were getting restless. They called d'Annunzio "Calypso," after the nymph who kept Odysseus captive and idle for years. On 4 November, the second anniversary of the armistice, Keller, without consulting d'Annunzio, took a plane and flew by stages to Rome. Circling over the city he dropped a chamber pot full of carrots and a jeering message over the parliament building. The Vatican got a white rose addressed to St. Francis. Over the royal palace Keller let fall a bouquet of red roses addressed to the Queen and the people of Italy. The most pointed of these symbolic gifts was to have been the battered boot of an infantryman, to be dropped on the Capitol as the armistice celebrations got under way there, but the ceremony was abandoned for fear of violence. Italy was increasingly unstable.

The messages fluttering down from a low-flying plane, the flowers, the invocation of St. Francis, the boot, the menace converted into a glittering joke—this was a d'Annunzian action. But it wasn't d'Annunzio who perpetrated it. Falling prey to one of his periodic depressions, he had withdrawn from sight.

There are moments when one glimpses through contemporary accounts something in d'Annunzio's manner like the disquiet of an actor who has wandered onto the wrong stage and is obliged to improvise his way through a drama for which he never auditioned. A few days after he first took Fiume, Marinetti wrote of him: "He does not see the revolutionary and decisive greatness of his undertaking"— which may just mean that d'Annunzio saw his undertaking differently from the way in which Marinetti did, but may also be perspicacious. D'Annunzio was still the man who couldn't be bothered to attend parliamentary sessions, for whom the mass of humanity was as uninteresting as a railway siding, who avoided gentlemen's clubs because talk of men's topics—business, politics, diplomacy, money—found him at a disadvantage. At the outset of the war for which he had so longed, he had written to Albertini, complaining of the monotony of warfare. In Fiume, too, he sometimes found his great adventure tedious.

He was lonely. His legion of young men—so callow and unruly— were splendid accessories to his glorious vision, but they were trying company. Luisa was delightful, but she came and went according to her own schedule. D'Annunzio repeatedly reproached her for cancelling a visit to Fiume in order to perform. "You know you are my only delight in a joyless struggle; and yet you consider a concert more important than my spirit! I don't understand, I can't understand." In her absence he felt bereft. He complained to Osbert Sitwell of "how he, who loved books, pictures and music, had remained there for months surrounded by peasants and soldiers." The ruler of this extraordinary little state, this political laboratory in which a dozen different ideologies were being tested out, was bored.

Giolitti was moving surely to bring an end to the Fiuman embarrassment. "The betrayal is near," declared d'Annunzio. He further developed his famous phrase "mutilated victory." Italy's victory was now in agony. Her wings mere stumps, she could not fly. Her feet lopped off, she could not march. She was carried, a helpless offering, grotesquely dressed up and made up, to a shameful altar.

On 12 November 1920, the Italian and Yugoslav governments signed the Treaty of Rapallo. Under its terms Fiume became an independent city-state linked to Italy by a strip of land. Italy gained the Julian Alps and the Carso, Zara, nearly all of Istria, and a few Adriatic islands. Italians living in the rest of Dalmatia were granted the right to Italian citizenship.

Most of what d'Annunzio had been demanding for years had been granted, but it had been done behind his back and without his sanction. No Italian blood had drenched and sanctified the soil of the newly acquired territory. This was not a victory, but a deal. Worse, under its terms he would be obliged to hand over the government of Fiume, and leave. He was back to where he had been a year ago, at the time of the *Modus Vivendi*, and every bit as intransigent as he had been then.

Again, his supporters urged him to accept the situation. Fiume was to be independent of Yugoslavia: how much more could he reasonably ask? Mussolini advised him to recognise the treaty. General Ceccherini implored him to do so. But d'Annunzio, now fixed on the unattainable, continued to call for Fiume's annexation by Italy. His motives are hard to read between the lines of his increasingly vehement and incoherent proclamations. Certainly one of them was his reluctance to give up power. "I must maintain my prerogative," he told one of his officers. "It is the only joy in all this tedium." Besides, the very fact that so much had been offered seemed to distress him. He and his Legion had been offered "walkways of silver, bridges of gold," but he refused to be bought off. Steeped now in his own rhetoric of martyrdom and purifying blood, he insisted on seeing his "sacrifice" through to its end.

He shut himself in his room for fifteen hours at a stretch, his only companions the cockatoo Keller had given Luisa Baccara and the greyhounds whom Marcel Boulanger, visiting him earlier in the year, had been surprised to find he kept "in the most secret recesses of his palace, like the sultan who keeps a favourite hidden in his tent." He communicated with his officials only through one favoured officer. He fired off letters to former supporters (Mussolini among them) who left them unanswered. It was said that he had attempted to fly out of Fiume, that he had shifted his quarters from the Governor's Palace to a ship in the harbour which was kept continually under steam. (These rumours were probably based on the wishful thinking of those who wanted him gone.) He bewailed his isolation. "We are alone again, alone against all . . . alone, alone with our courage . . . Alone against a vast conspiracy." His announcements became ever more opaque, his political position more unstable. He would die for "the cause." He would not spill a single drop of his blood for such an ungrateful people as the Italians. He was ready to negotiate; he would never compromise.

Dismayed by his irrationality, the Herculean General Ceccherini, whose presence had been vital in reassuring the militarists that Fiume's cause was a legitimate one, left the city, despite d'Annunzio's reiterated pleas.

A last opportunity for action presented itself. Giuriati, still working for the irredentist cause, suggested d'Annunzio's legionaries should be transferred from Fiume to Zara, where the Italian Governor Admiral Millo—as unhappy about the treaty as d'Annunzio—would support an uprising. Millo was ready. The legionaries, many of them eager for action, were singing: "Treacherous government, it's you, it's you, it's you/Who sold Dalmatia/While we believed in you."

Once more d'Annunzio dithered until the moment passed. Giuriati arrived in Fiume but d'Annunzio kept him waiting, and when he finally granted him an appointment declared he was too busy to stage an insurrection. He was planning a ceremony to celebrate the granting of a new banner to his artillery corps. Giuriati suggested that the ceremony could perhaps be performed on board ship en route for Zara? D'Annunzio thought not. Giuriati gave up on him and left for Venice.

Having failed his would-be collaborators, d'Annunzio sent his legionaries to occupy two islands off the Dalmatian coast, Veglia and Arbe, granted to Yugoslavia under the Treaty of Rapallo. They brought back a massive bronze bell, taller than a man, to which he had often alluded in his speeches. He had it installed in his private study and added it to his store of totemic objects: "O bronze rich with mysterious gold!"

General Caviglia reinforced the troops of the Italian army along the lines around Fiume, drove the legionaries off the islands, and brought further ships into the gulf of Carnaro to enforce the naval blockade of Fiume. Giolitti, whom d'Annunzio had dubbed the "slobber-lipped hangman," was tightening his noose.

Emerging from his *clausura*, d'Annunzio spoke again and again. He told his followers: "We have not suffered enough." From his balcony, with the blockading ships visible out to sea, he compared himself favourably with Christ, who had begged that the cup might pass from him. He would never flinch. He would never yield. He would die (over and over again he said it) rather than abandon his cause.

He was priming himself and his little army for a fight to the death, but all his rhetoric was based on a false premise. "Fraternal blood shall not be spilt," he said, meaning that a conflict between his Legion and Italy was unthinkable. He ranted again and again about filthy Slavs, about "Croataglia" and dirty Serbian pig-keepers. But no such enemy presented itself. The ships blockading the city, the guns trained upon it, the troops mustering along the armistice line, all served Italy, the *patria*. D'Annunzio, the national hero, had become an enemy of the Italian state, but he seemed incapable of comprehending the fact.

Guido Keller urged him to break through the lines of the Italian army now surrounding Fiume and march first on Trieste, then on Rome. But when Keller's proposal was debated by d'Annunzio's officers, one of them, a minor member of the royal family, declared that he would never "play the brigand" in Italy. D'Annunzio, it seems, was of the same mind. The Legion remained in Fiume. Keller blamed Luisa Baccara for softening d'Annunzio. Meeting her on the stairs of the Governor's Palace, he frightened her by throwing a knife between her feet.

It was cold now, but even in the wintry rain or late into the nights, the piazza was thronged. In the atmosphere of crisis, what little discipline the Legion had ever observed was breaking down. On 1 December, de Ambris wrote to d'Annunzio reporting that the legionaries were making themselves odious to citizens by arrogance and robberies. Their officers took no steps to control them, and refused to hand thieves over to the police.

4 DECEMBER 1920. The feast of St. Barbara. The legend relates that Barbara's own father cut off her head when she refused to deny her Christianity. D'Annunzio requisitioned her story for use in his propaganda. His Fiume was the maiden-martyr; Giolitti's Rome the unfeeling parent. The blockade was becoming painful. The legionaries were hungry. D'Annunzio offered them no comfort—only exaltation. They were like wood heaped up for burning, he told them.

5 DECEMBER. The first shipload of Italian troops left Zara in accordance with the Treaty of Rapallo, while the Italian citizens of Zara rioted, attempting to block their embarkation. In Fiume the legionaries were in a fighting mood. D'Annunzio told them that the balustrade on which he leant was now as odious to him as the bars of a cage. He wanted only to smash it, and use its stones as missiles. Someone responded by yelling that there were tons and tons of rusty iron down in the port that could be used for the same purpose. "Before you rid yourself of old iron, you should rid yourself of the old people," retorted d'Annunzio (using the phrase "old people" as the Russian revolutionaries were using "people of the past"). His listeners took the hint. "Death to the Traitors!" D'Annunzio, working in his favourite medium of human lives and emotions, was creating a lynch mob. "We are with the Commandant. We are his faithful . . . Anywhere, with him! To the death!"

6 DECEMBER. The crews of two of the blockading ships mutinied and brought their vessels, a destroyer and a torpedo ship, into the harbour at Fiume. D'Annunzio greeted the new arrivals sombrely. "Comrades, it is evening. Soon night will fall." They had come, he told them, to die with him.

Back in Italy his prestige was dwindling. Giolitti had, by any rational measure, negotiated a good deal for Italy at Rapallo, and he knew how to use d'Annunzio's tools of propaganda and invective. Antonio Gramsci, co-founder of the Italian Communist Party, thought Giolitti's propaganda about Fiume "extremely violent." Gramsci summarised it: "The legionaries are represented as brigands thirsting only to satisfy the basic passions of human bestiality." D'Annunzio was characterised as "a madman, a performer, as an enemy of the *patria*." The entire campaign, thought Gramsci, was strikingly successful. By playing on stock themes, "fraternal blood coldly spilt, personal rights and liberty threatened by a horde of soldiers crazy with alcohol and greed, girl-hood sullied by unbridled lust," Giolitti had successfully shifted public opinion.

In autumn 1919, high-ranking officers had judged it impossible to ask their men to fight d'Annunzio. A year later that was no longer the case. Even his admirers were puzzled or impatient. He received a missive signed by eighty sympathetic members of the chamber of deputies urging him to accept the Treaty of Rapallo. On the same day he issued a proclamation to his legionaries:

> Have your weapon in your hand, at all times.
> Be proud to call yourself rebels
> Spit in the face of cowards . . .
> Blessed are the dead.

Giolitti set a deadline. He ordered d'Annunzio to leave Fiume, with his Legion, by 6 p.m. on 24 December, and he promised an amnesty to all those who left in time. D'Annunzio prepared to resist. He had taken as his motto *"Semper Adamas"* (always hard). He talked of turning Fiume into his own pyre. It was rumoured that he had ordered the fuel stores should be set alight if he were killed or captured, so that the City of the Holocaust might live up to its name and be utterly consumed behind him.

On 21 December he summoned all his officers to a conference. They crowded into the palace's grand salon, shouting their *"Eia, Eia, Eia, Alalà!"* as he took his place at the centre of the long table. "During those days," wrote Comisso, "he was truly amazing . . . Besieged by the troops of a government intent on finishing him off . . . he knew, even in the bitterest moments, how to find a profound, poetic word." He declared that Fiume was at war. Twice over that day he addressed the crowd from his balcony. Jeeringly he invited all those unwilling to die for his cause to take themselves off, to join the "amnestied deserters" on the other side. For those who remained with him, he said, a mas-sacre awaited. "Fratricide has been ordered."

The Legion prepared their defences. Fishing nets were slung across the approach roads and barbed wire closed off the city streets. Carts were dragged together to form barricades. The road to Abbazia was blocked with antiquated Austrian cannon. Fiume was sealing itself off from the world.

On 24 December, Christmas Eve, Giolitti's troops took up positions along the frontiers of Fiuman territory and an Italian warship moved into the harbour. There were 20,000 regular troops, opposed by some 6,000 legionaries. D'Annunzio ordered his men to prepare to fight from house to house. One of his planes dropped flyers over the "brothers who besiege their brothers," appealing to them in the names of their mothers and of Christmas, to lay down their arms. The watchword for the day was "Ungrateful Italy."

The hour appointed by Giolitti for d'Annunzio's withdrawal came and went. The regular troops crossed the line, marching into Fiume along the railway tracks. D'Annunzio ordered his men to fall back on the city. This was a conflict he had never wanted, perhaps never really believed possible; a conflict not with the "vulture's vomit" of the former Austria, or with Slavic "swineherds," but with the army of his beloved *patria*.

That evening Giovanni Comisso, dining with some fellow officers, met a woman who told him: "You shouldn't shoot. They are Italians like us." Comisso was irritated, partly because he, like his Commandant, was in denial about the nature of the enemy and didn't want to hear that the opponents were compatriots and fellow soldiers ("they are just cops"), partly, as he records, because he couldn't stand women butting in on serious manly conversations. He snapped at her. She cried. He gave her a flower. He and the other men continued to tell each other how excited they were about the imminent battle. An explosion shook the restaurant. D'Annunzio had had the bridge over to Susak blown up. Unable to think any more about food, or flowers, or women (especially a woman who spoke the truth), the men poured out into the street. Comisso found his unit out towards Abbazia. He positioned his machine-gunners on terraces overlooking the road, and settled down to wait, listening to a woman in a nearby house singing an *Arditi* song. That night the fighting began.

It lasted for three days, days which d'Annunzio called the "most glorious in human history" and the "Christmas of Blood." He harangued his troops repeatedly, ordering them to leave if they were not happy to be slaughtered. He cried shame on the soldiers of the regular army "walking on corpses" to defeat their Italian brothers. He led the legion-aries in yelled-out litanies:

To whom the victory?
To us!
To whom the victory?
To the Heroes!

He was ecstatic. He was beyond himself. According to the director of Fiume's main bank: "He never went near the fighting, despite declaring every half hour that he wanted to run to the line of battle and die there: his officers managed every time to stop him leaving the palace." But he was ready for martyrdom. He would never surrender.

Luisa was staying in the comparative safety of the mayor's house. D'Annunzio sent her notes, reporting hour by hour on events. In the early hours of Christmas morning he wrote: "I believe the assassins [his word for the loyalist troops] will attack at 6.30. We will resist." It wouldn't take long. He would be able to join her for lunch.

His optimism was unfounded. On the morning of Christmas Day the regular cavalry attacked from the hills above Fiume, unsuccess-fully resisted by mounted *Arditi*. Torpedo boats appeared in the har-bour, machine guns trained on the quays. On the outskirts of the city, *Arditi* fired from houses on troops crouching behind low walls. An arsenal was hit, triggering a devastating explosion. A cloud of black smoke obscured the sea. By afternoon d'Annunzio was weeping over his dead and wounded legionaries, and writing to tell Luisa that from now on he would love her better because "grief sharpens and revives love." But for all the fire and noise, it was a half-hearted battle. Offi-cers on both sides threw away the advantage of surprise by calling out warnings to their opponents and begging them not to advance—they didn't want to have to shoot. Comisso gave away his revolver, saying that he couldn't have used it at a distance because his eyesight was poor and "close-up I would have embraced my adversary." In three days of fighting a total of thirty-three men were killed.

Towards evening on Boxing Day, when sunset, as d'Annunzio noted, was bathing the sea and the skies with blood red, the warship *Andrea Doria* fired on the Governor's Palace. A shell slammed through a window of d'Annunzio's quarters and exploded in the room below that in which he sat. The windows caved in. Plaster fell from the ceiling. D'Annunzio, seated at a table, was flung forward and temporarily stunned. According to one witness he panicked, screaming: "Help! Save me!" Two of his officers, stumbling over the debris, rushed to grab hold of him. They hustled him out of the room and down the stairs. The courtyard was crowded with *Arditi* running hither and thither brandishing daggers, rifles and grenades. Pushing though the melee, d'Annunzio's aides half-carried, half-dragged him to a house safely screened from the waterfront.

D'Annunzio was to claim that when the shell hit his palace, women, distraught to think of their Commandant in danger, came out onto their balconies, holding up babies and crying out: "This one Italy! Take this one! But not *HIM*." Another, more plausible, story goes that there were women beating on the Mayor of Fiume's door, imploring him to persuade d'Annunzio to spare their children by surrendering.

The shell had been a warning of what might be to come. The Italian commander delivered an ultimatum. Either d'Annunzio must leave or he would order a further bombardment. The mayor, the bishop and members of the National Council came to beg d'Annunzio to save the city and its people by admitting defeat. He hesitated. According to Antongini, unable to decide the issue, he tossed a coin. Perhaps he really couldn't make up his mind. Perhaps he preferred to pass some of the responsibility for the humiliating decision on to blind fortune.

Hundreds of times now he had led massed crowds of people in the chant *"Fiume o Morte!" "Italia o Morte!"* He had been prepared to fight to the death: the Italian troops who afterwards entered Fiume found enough ammunition to have kept the Legion firing for weeks. The heroic death about which he had so frequently rhapsodised was imminent. The martyr's crown hovered ready. But as the guns on the *Andrea Doria* prepared to fire again, d'Annunzio's tossed coin came down for capitulation. The people of Fiume were to be spared the awful splendour he had for so long been offering them. The apostle of death and glory chose ignominy and life. D'Annunzio agreed to go.

There were, of course, plenty of voices quick to sneer that for all his valiant speeches it had taken only one shell to make d'Annunzio turn and run. But he was no coward. "I have offered my life a hundred and a hundred times in war, smiling," he said, and it was true. He would have been glad to die, he said, but the people of Italy, "wallowing in their Christmas debauch," were unworthy of such a sacrifice.

He had never quite believed that Italians would open fire on him. When they did, he lost in an instant the magical invulnerability which had allowed him to pass unscathed through an opposing army on the day of the Sacred Entry, and he lost his capacity for self-deception. Almost exactly a year after the people of Fiume had expressed through the plebiscite their disinclination to sacrifice themselves for him, the *Andrea Doria*'s shell had finally awoken him from his dream of their compliance. He had announced that where he was, was Italy. It took an Italian shell to make it plain to him that on the contrary, he was Italy's opponent.

Giolitti, who understood as well as his opponent did how to manipulate the news, had timed his attack carefully. No papers were published during the three days of the Christmas battle, but d'Annunzio, still unsurpassed as a propagandist, had made sure that the radio station Marconi had set up for him in Fiume kept the world informed, hour by hour, of the Legion's brave resistance. Now he prepared to make a dignified spectacle of defeat.

The legionaries laid down their arms reluctantly and slowly. They were furious at their own people's "betrayal" of them. How could Italian troops have agreed to fight them? Why had the Italians at home not risen up in protest against the attack? Why had they been left to be slaughtered? They tore any remaining military badges off their uniforms and replaced them with Fiuman postage stamps.

D'Annunzio called them all together in the main square. The weather was bleak. The Governor's Palace stands on a hill above the main square down by the waterfront, with a long flight of steps leading from one to the other. Very slowly d'Annunzio walked down those stony stairs, his wrinkled ivory face paler than ever, wearing a yellow raincoat over his uniform. Seeing the banner he himself had given to *La Disperata*, he stopped and called on them to keep themselves in readiness. A voice answered him: "You haven't seen anything yet, Commandant!" Fighting words, but this was the end.

On 2 January he led a funeral procession several thousand strong to the cemetery on the heights above the town. The coffins of the thirty-three men who had been killed during the "Christmas of Blood" were decked with laurel and Randaccio's banner laid across them. D'Annunzio spoke sombrely and with the kind of gracious gentleness with which, in his time, he had undone so many women and won over so many men. There were both "loyal" and "rebel" troops among the dead men. D'Annunzio, not strident now but generous in mourning, voiced his belief that if they were to rise again they would "weep, pardon one another, and throw themselves into each other's arms." He knelt down. The whole enormous crowd knelt with him. Finally, in silence broken only by the sound of weeping, he led the Italians of Fiume back into their city.

He had taken up arms against the Italian state, but he still had a greater following in Italy than the government did. He was allowed to go with impunity. His defiance of the law had been outrageous. Giolitti chose to overlook it. There was to be no trial, no punishment.

The legionaries departed by the train load. Groups of officers came to say farewell to d'Annunzio, who gave each of them a memento. Many of them wept, but few, perhaps, felt as desolate as he did. Looking back as they descended the steps, they saw him at the window, his face pale behind the glass, waving them out of sight.

He left Fiume on 18 January. Even in defeat he was still an idol. The majority of Fiume's inhabitants may have been relieved to see the last of him but nonetheless thousands of them turned out to watch him go, and the leader of Trieste's *fascio* begged to be allowed to kneel in the dust along the roadside and kiss his hands as he passed by.

In one day he dwindled from the god-like Commandant into a tired old man. That evening, a misty and bitterly cold one, he arrived in Venice, to be met, as we have seen, by Antongini. Arriving at his apartment, large, gloomy and cluttered with a jumble of stuff salvaged from his various past homes, he went straight to his room. He had nothing to say.

Clausura

IN SEPTEMBER 1920, while d'Annunzio was celebrating the proclamation of his new constitution in Fiume, workers in Italy rose up. Some half a million of them went on strike and occupied factories and shipyards, running up red (socialist) or black (anarchist) flags and demanding worker control. For nearly a month Italians lived with the possibility of an imminent revolution. Leon Trotsky was only partly exaggerating when he told the Fourth Congress of the Communist International two years later: "the working class of Italy had, in effect, gained control of the state, of society, of factories."

But their leadership was divided. Each factory was an isolated fortress. There was no consensus as to the strikers' ultimate aims. Largely thanks to Giolitti's adroit mediation, they were eventually prevailed upon to accept generous terms—higher pay, shorter hours, better conditions. Work resumed, but huge caches of arms and explosives were found in the factories. Nervous capitalists concluded (correctly) that the occupation might have been the beginning of a larger and more violent insurrection. In the face of such a threat the authorities were ready to use any weapon, however questionable. A circular sent to the chiefs of staff suggested that the fascist gangs might be serviceable "against subversive and anti-national forces."

In November, while d'Annunzio cast around for pretexts to reject the Treaty of Rapallo, there were local elections all over Italy. The socialists further alarmed their opponents by making considerable gains. Bologna was one of several cities whose councils they would now dominate. On 21 November the council's new socialist administration took over. Their opponents responded immediately: 300 armed fascists marched on the town hall. Grenades were thrown. Eleven people were killed.

Further such attacks followed. The fascists were now organising themselves in squads, and were evolving a style they had taken from d'Annunzio. Like the "corporations" d'Annunzio and de Ambris proposed, the squads had their own banners, their own slogans and rituals. They dressed in black. They poured libations in cherry brandy before a raid. They gave their squads names—honouring dead heroes, or their own prowess. There was one called *La Disperata*, in knowing reference to Keller's gang in Fiume. Many of the *squadristi* had been in Fiume themselves.

The socialists appeared to be flourishing: fascism was comparatively weak. But, as Mussolini boasted, "a million sheep will always be dispersed by the roar of one lion," meaning that force will always prevail. Fascist squads, riding in lorries, prowled the country in search of socialists to assault. Mussolini supported them in print. "The Socialist Party is a Russian army encamped in Italy. Against this foreign army, fascists have launched a guerrilla war, and they will conduct it with exceptional seriousness."

The communist leader Antonio Gramsci derided fascists as "monkey people" who "make news, not history." But many Italians agreed with the editor of a Ferrara paper who wrote: "New, young, courageous forces are needed . . . the Fascists. Only they can arrest the wave of madness which is breaking over Italy." In the five months following the deadly fracas in Bologna, the Fascist Party's membership increased tenfold.

During the war years, and at Fiume, d'Annunzio repeatedly alluded to his previous life as a "mere poet" with incredulous contempt, as though literature was something he had toyed with in the past but then outgrown. He was a warrior, a Commandant. He told his legionaries that there was no melody in him but that of their marching songs. Returned from Fiume, though, he was suddenly in a hurry to get back to work. *Notturno*, begun in his blindness five years before, had to be revised and amplified and he wanted to get on with it. He needed the money, of course, but he also needed the rapt pleasure he took in the exercise of his literary gift. He wrote to de Ambris: "I am eager for silence after so much noise, and peace after so much war."

On the morning after his defeated return to Venice, when he ordered his six helpmeets to find a home for him forthwith, d'Annunzio paused from pacing irritably around his cluttered apartment, fidgeting with papers and trinkets, to take Tom Antongini aside. Each of the searchers was to be dispatched to a different part of northern Italy. D'Annunzio had assigned Lake Garda to Antongini, because, he told him, with that flatteringly confidential air of his, "I feel that my fate impels me to live there."

Garda was border country: the frontier with Austria ran through the mountains only a few miles to the north of the lake. Italian nationalists complained that the region's principal town should be known as "Desenzano-*am-See*," so full was it of German tourists and German-speaking residents. In choosing it d'Annunzio was keeping himself close to the field of a dispute which, for him, was as yet unresolved. But there were other reasons for wanting to live in an area where mountains meet water to create a landscape of tremendous natural beauty and a playground for Europe's leisured cosmopolitans. The poet murmured to his old friend that whereas the other searchers knew only the Commandant of Fiume, Antongini knew Gabriele d'Annunzio, "my tastes, my vices and my virtues."

Antongini found him the Villa Cargnacco, an eighteenth-century farmhouse secluded on a steep hillside, screened by cypresses and beech trees, but with immense views of the lake and the mountains on its opposite shore. Way beneath lay the resort town of Gardone Riviera, with its balconied and stuccoed grand hotels, its restaurants and gardens full of magnolia and jasmine, its jetties for pleasure boats. But d'Annunzio's only neighbours would be the inhabitants of the mediaeval village of Gardone di Sopra (Upper Gardone) and he was surrounded by the kind of landscape—dry rock and terraced olive groves—he had loved in Settignano.

The house was modest, remarkable only for its setting, for the profusion of roses around it and for its associations. Its previous proprietor, Henry Thode, had been married to Daniela Senta von Bülow, who was Liszt's granddaughter and Wagner's stepchild. Confiscated by the Italian state in 1918, the house was still full of its dispossessed owners' stuff, including Thode's 6,000-volume library, and the Steinway grand piano on which Daniela, and her mother, Cosima Wagner, had played. D'Annunzio was delighted. He saw his move as a patriotic act: in "Italianising" a German-owned property he was serving his country.

He moved in on St. Valentine's Day. He would devote much of the remaining seventeen years of his life to transforming the house out of all recognition. It was his ultimate artwork, purpose-made to outlive

him as his memorial and his shrine. Initially he called it the Porziuncola, after St. Francis's retreat and Duse's house in Settignano. Later, as
its function shifted from refuge to monument, he renamed it the Vittoriale. The word was archaic: d'Annunzio claimed that it came to him
by divine inspiration while he listened to a choir. In fact he had found
and underlined it in a military dictionary. Whatever its provenance, its
significance was clear—of victory, victoryish, victory-thing.

Work on the house never ceased. D'Annunzio's architect, Gian Carlo
Maroni, became a permanent member of his household. Masons and
glaziers, sculptors and plasterers, painters and goldsmiths, smiths and
woodworkers were kept busy for years refining and elaborating the
poet's extravagantly detailed and bizarre vision. The Vittoriale (which
has been preserved as he left it) became the outward and visible manifestation of his peculiar personality: all his brilliance and all his perversity rendered in concrete form.

All the rooms have names: the Room of the Leper, the Dalmatian
Oratory, the Corridor of the Way of the Cross. They are dark and
thickly ornamented, each one a piece of installation art dense with
significance. The Room of the Lily represents d'Annunzio's extraordinarily well-furnished mind: it contains over 3,000 books, fastidiously
arranged, a harmonium and tiny dark niches that he called "thinking places." The Room of the Stump, tucked away up a flight of stairs,
expresses a more unsettling aspect of his psyche. It is another study,
lined with books in dark-panelled bookcases, but its ceiling is patterned
with the image of a severed hand.

Everything in the Vittoriale is placed on something else. A rosary is
draped over a statuette which stands on a piece of embroidered velvet,
which covers a majolica box which is set upon a carved table which
stands on an oriental rug. Every window is filled with stained glass
and curtained with heavy, rich fabric; every available wall or ceiling
space is encrusted with plaques and painted mottoes. There are casts of
the Elgin marbles. There are Buddhas and Madonnas. There are reli-
quaries and swords, bronze animals and ecclesiastical furniture. There
are vases and shawls and tapestries and numerous glass lampshades
shaped like bowls of fruit. And in among all the artsy clutter there are
modern relics—the steering wheel of a speedboat, a paintbox, a rusty
nail. Max Beerbohm, who visited the Vittoriale in the last months of

d'Annunzio's life, wrote: "If Aladdin could come back to life and were admitted to the house and domain he would say to himself, rather rue-fully: 'My palace was comparatively insipid. *My* palace was rather *pot-au-feu.*'"

On 28 October 1922, Mussolini seized control of the Italian state. That very day he wrote to d'Annunzio: "I do not ask you to line up at our side, though this would avail us greatly; but we are sure that you will not set yourself against this marvellous youth which is fighting for your and our Italy." D'Annunzio, never one to line up at anyone else's side, sought refuge in incoherence. His letter in reply refers to his "sadness and spiritual uneasiness" at the news but he promises to put his "robust and resolute shoulder to the wheel." He further promises (as though addressing a criminal), "to see nothing, to hear nothing." This latter promise he kept. "With the advent of fascism," wrote Tom Antongini, "Gabriele d'Annunzio's political activity came to an end . . . The proclaimer of the war, the hero of the heavens, of the sea, of the slopes of the Carso and of the miraculous gesture of Fiume entered the realms of Legend." For the rest of d'Annunzio's life he stayed at home and cultivated his garden, his collections, his house, his private museum, his literary reputation, his wardrobe, his increasingly deviant sexual tastes, his escalating drug habit and the cult of himself.

He worked. He wrote little that was absolutely new after his return from Fiume, but he diligently revised and edited and expanded his existing oeuvre. Luisa Baccara was there. She stayed with him to the end of his life, and so did Aélis, the housekeeper-concubine he had employed in France in 1912. His wife joined him from time to time, living intermittently in a separate house in the grounds. He continued to amuse himself with speedy machines. He raced motor boats on the lake. He acquired an enormous bright yellow car.

He received many visitors although, skulking unseen like the Minotaur in the private chambers of his labyrinthine dwelling, he was hard of access. Admirers, disciples and old friends alike were kept waiting for hours, days, or sometimes even weeks, at a time, housed in the Vittoriale's guest rooms or a nearby hotel, before d'Annunzio would deign to grant them an audience. Some of the less-favoured went away without ever having laid eyes on him. But though the distinguished might be disappointed, others, more obscure, were welcomed. Like the Minotaur, d'Annunzio required his regular shipments of youthful sacrifices. A stream of new young women passed through his bed, many of them prostitutes, some local girls, some enthusiastic admirers who travelled from all over Europe to offer themselves to the poet and hero. He had always prided himself on his sexual vigour, now his notebooks are full of self-celebratory descriptions of his "orgies': nights when, powered by drugs, he would fuck for hours on end.

His domain became ever more fantastical as his foibles were actualised in plaster and stone. He planned an amphitheatre, a version of the one he and Duse had wanted half a lifetime earlier. He built a paved piazza surrounded by curved loggias and marble benches with a flagstaff at its centre adorned with a tragic mask. There he staged concerts and performances which were part ritual, part drama. The garden was designed to delight the nose as well as the eye. Antongini estimated that d'Annunzio planted 10,000 rose bushes there over the years. He converted the modestly proportioned house's outbuildings into showrooms and shrines which towered over it, and filled them with trophies celebrating his exploits.

The house itself took on the character of a claustrophobe's nightmare. It had never been spacious. D'Annunzio's remodelling converted it into a disorienting warren of overcrowded little rooms. "One can imagine secret passages behind the panelling," wrote an early visitor, "an alcove behind a tapestry. Everything is padded, smothered, cluttered like a seraglio." Wherever there might have been some open space, d'Annunzio introduced an oversized sculpture or a marble screen. Even the entrance hall was all but blocked by a marble column. The whole was overheated, heavily scented and swathed even at midday in a crepuscular gloom. The only bright room was d'Annunzio's study, and even there any sense of openness was negated by a doorway so low that even its diminutive master had to bend down to pass through it.

While d'Annunzio wove his extraordinary cocoon about himself Mussolini warily scrutinised his agents' reports on his activities and the company he kept. It suited Mussolini that the Italian public should believe that d'Annunzio was wholeheartedly behind the new regime, but in truth dictator and poet remained suspicious of each other. At times d'Annunzio assumed a paternal stance, pointing out (correctly) how much Mussolini and his followers had learned from him. Mussolini was more than happy to agree. But still the poet withheld any public demonstration of support. He was untrustworthy and dangerously influential: he had to be kept on side. Mussolini granted him every favour he requested, with one exception. He was refused permission to build a private airfield near his villa. He was to have anything he wished for except an escape route.

Strange stories circulated about the life he led in his seclusion. One visitor reported that he liked to sit naked under a fountain reading an edition of Dante especially printed for the purpose on sheets of rubber; another that he had had two ribs removed to allow him to perform fellatio on himself. Some of these stories are credible, others were invented by imaginative reporters or by d'Annunzio himself, who liked to have his own eccentricities talked about. Once, at a pre-war dinner party, he had remarked musingly, to the thrilled consternation of his fellow guests, that the meat of human children tasted remarkably like spring lamb. He hadn't lost his taste for teasing. The story goes that when a Russian emissary visited him at the Vittoriale he entertained him to a splendid dinner *à deux*. As they sat at table two fearsomely accoutred *Arditi* entered carrying a damascened scimitar. They handed it to d'Annunzio and went out, locking the dining room doors behind them. D'Annunzio, in tones of polite regret, informed the visitor that he had resolved to decapitate him. Some minutes passed before he announced that after all he wasn't in the mood.

His health was deteriorating. He was fifty-seven when he came to the Vittoriale, half blind, and even his prodigious energy undermined by five years of exhausting activity. He almost certainly had syphilis. While he was in Fiume, Father Macdonald had written: "The Poet's constant orgies, and the disease from which he was commonly reported to be suffering, so affected his brain as to render him irresponsible alike for his words and for his actions." Behaviour normal to d'Annunzio might have appeared pathological to the priest, but Macdonald was probably right. Over his years at the Vittoriale, d'Annunzio's letters became increasingly incoherent: something was playing havoc with his mind. Drugs didn't help. He took various opiates to control the pain in his eyes, and to help him sleep, and certainly by the mid-1920s—probably earlier—he was taking copious quantities of cocaine.

Lurking in the self-created lair which was also to be his mausoleum, he seemed to outsiders as baleful and forlorn as a fairy-tale beast. "Poor decrepit old bard! I pity him," wrote Walter Starkie. But the truth is he was often happy during these last years. His notebooks are full of evidence of his continuing zest for pleasure. He writes with gusto about lamb cutlets, about the exquisite gradations of colour on the mountains at sunrise and about his sexual experiments. He entered with enthusiasm into his role as patron to a new legion, one not of warriors, but of artists and artisans. His letters show him playful and funny. Hidden from the world behind his high walls he dropped the grand roles of *Vate* and Commandant and indulged a sense of humour of which, as he himself remarks, his published works allow no inkling.

The coming man was modelling himself ever more markedly on the "decrepit old bard." In October 1922, the month of Mussolini's seizure of power, an article in the fascist magazine *Gerarchia* (Hierarchy) described the distinguishing marks of public life under fascism: "The banners fluttering in the wind, the blackshirts, the helmets, the songs, the cries of '*Eia, Eia, Eia, Alalà!*' the Roman salute, the recital of the names of the dead, the official feasts, the solemn swearing-in occasions, the parades in military style." It could be a description of d'Annunzio's Fiume. Margherita Sarfatti, editor of *Gerarchia* and Mussolini's mistress, paid tribute to d'Annunzio as the originator of the "rites that under fascism became an art form and a way of life . . . at once gay and austere, carefree and pregnant with religious and moral content."

D'Annunzio had often been accused of plagiarism. Now the tables were turned. Angelo Tasca, one of the founders of the Italian Communist Party, observed how, "the occupation of Fiume . . . furnishes fascism with the model for its militia and its uniforms, the names for its squads, its war cry and its liturgy. Mussolini commandeers from d'Annunzio the whole of the stage scenery, including the dialogues with the crowd." He had commandeered as well much of the poet's mindset. D'Annunzio, concluded Tasca, became under fascism, "the victim of the greatest piece of plagiarism ever seen."

D'Annunzio's decline. Mussolini's ascent. Here are some of the stations along their two trajectories.

JANUARY TO MAY 1921. During the five months after d'Annunzio left Fiume, over 200 people were killed and about a thousand wounded in clashes between fascist squads and socialists. Like Keller on the night preceding the Sacred Entry, the fascists got hold of lorries—legally or otherwise. They roared around the countryside, terrorising anyone who was, or in their opinion might be, socialist. They did so with impunity. "The *carabinieri* travel around with them in their lorries . . . sing their hymns and eat and drink with them," reported a priest. A lot of those lorries were provided by the army, many high-ranking officers being kindly disposed towards the squads. People were being killed on both sides of what was fast beginning to look like a civil war. Judges were partisan: a disproportionate number of those fascists accused of murder were acquitted, while socialists received maximum sentences. Anti-authoritarian, scattered through the countryside, the squads were a loose association of independent groups, each obeying only their local *capo* or *ras* (the latter word borrowed from the Ethiopian tribal chieftains). Mussolini didn't create the wave of violence, but he was good at riding it.

1 FEBRUARY 1921. D'Annunzio, waiting to move into his new home, writes to de Ambris lamenting the state of Italian political life. "It is all corrupted. It is all gone astray."

De Ambris has been instrumental in setting up the National Federation of the Legionaries of Fiume. There was a *Fascio di Combattimento* in Fiume. D'Annunzio joined, but he kept his distance, staying away from the *fascio*'s rallies. Fascism was not his movement; he wanted nothing to do with it. Now he writes that he wishes his legionaries' Federation to keep itself from contagion by any other organisation. "Today in Italy there is no sincere political movement."

MARCH 1921. In Florence, fascists break into the offices of the socialist journal *La Difesa*, smashing everything they find. Between February and May, 726 buildings—libraries, print shops, employment offices, socialist headquarters—are attacked and wrecked by fascist squads. Those who used them are beaten up, or murdered.

5 APRIL 1921. Mussolini visits d'Annunzio. There is an election in the offing. Mussolini proposes that d'Annunzio stands as a candidate for Zara, and that he writes something—a proclamation, a programme—of which the fascists can make use in their campaign. D'Annunzio declines both proposals. He disdains parliament: he has no desire to "line up" in another man's phalanx.

APRIL 1921. A story appears in a Roman newspaper, and subsequently in the *New York Times*, claiming that d'Annunzio, having instituted new, permissive divorce laws in Fiume, has freed himself from his first marriage and made Luisa Baccara his wife. This is not true, but Luisa is with him as his mistress, hostess, resident musician, librarian, procuress and companion in games of dressing-up. Her clothes are becoming increasingly fantastical. Tall and thin, she wears mediaeval-style gowns in silver tissue and cut velvet, with floor-sweeping pointed sleeves, "Romanesque" embroidery and braided girdles. D'Annunzio has taken to calling her the *Papessa* (the female Pope).

24 APRIL 1921. Elections in Fiume. Riccardo Zanella's Autonomist Party wins the majority of votes. His opponents—fascists, nationalists and followers of d'Annunzio—invade government offices, smash the ballot boxes and seize power regardless. D'Annunzio fires off congratulatory telegrams to the insurgents, and sends Mayor Riccardo Gigante the gilded bayonet that was presented to him in San Vito the previous year, the one that Zanella claimed was to be used to assassinate him. D'Annunzio does not, however, go to Fiume, as many of his legionaries are urging him to do. He writes to a friend that "these are sad and clouded days." (To his chagrin, he never gets the bayonet back.)

15 MAY 1921. General elections in Italy. Giolitti, in a characteristic attempt to subsume and control the fascists by a process of "transformism," has invited them to form a part of his "national bloc." "The fascist candidates will be like fireworks," he says privately. "They will make a lot of noise but will leave behind nothing but smoke." It is the worst mistake he has ever made.

The results are excellent for Mussolini. He is one of thirty-six fascist deputies elected to parliament. They promptly renege on their deal with Giolitti, and join the opposition. Mussolini is no liberal: he announces that he has "lead and fire" ready for the bourgeoisie, and that most parliamentary business is "useless chatter."

Now he is within reach of legitimate power he makes well-publicised efforts to control the violence of the squads, telling them the "civil war" is over and Bolshevism is defeated; but when the fascist chief Roberto Farinacci beats up a communist deputy Mussolini does not disown him.

JUNE 1921. D'Annunzio collaborates in the making of a documentary film about himself. He poses at his desk. He is a writer now, not a Commandant.

Eleonora Duse, aged sixty-three, is touring again. He writes in his usual florid style to tell her that he had thought he *might* be capable of bestirring himself to come and watch her performance, that he *might* have had the courage to allow her to see him, "injured by years" as he is, but he finds that actually, no, he can't do it. He can't face the crowds.

On 19 June he sends a message to the *Arditi*, who are gathering for a congress in Rome, reiterating his advice that they should hold themselves aloof from any existing political formation—meaning, by clear implication, from fascism.

AUGUST 1921. D'Annunzio tells his friend Boulanger that he aspires to being the person of whom, one day, people will say: "Come then! There is no one but him!" When that day comes though, he lets the opportunity pass.

Mussolini, more interested now in extending his power than in terrorising his opponents, has proposed a "pact of pacification" with the socialist unions. His more militant followers are outraged, the bullyboys of the squads and the powerful local bosses alike. After furious disputes, Mussolini resigns from the fascists' executive committee. "If fascism does not follow me, no one can force me to follow fascism." The fascist *ras* resolve to find a replacement for him. Two of the most prominent among them, Dino Grandi (who first vents his fury by beating up the socialist leader in the parliamentary chamber) and the celebrated aviator Italo Balbo, visit d'Annunzio at the Vittoriale. They invite him to assume the leadership of "national forces." As usual when confronted with a decision, d'Annunzio dithers, and takes refuge in real or pretended superstition. He must first consult the stars, he says. The night sky is overcast. His visitors will have to wait.

Perhaps changing their mind about his suitability, Grandi and Balbo leave unanswered. But the possibility that d'Annunzio might one day come out of seclusion continues to haunt the minds of both those who long for and those who dread it. Two years later, the socialist historian Gaetano Salvemini, is worrying that Mussolini could be ousted by d'Annunzio, "the maddest of all," with a "Superfascist programme."

10 SEPTEMBER 1921. Three thousand fascists, led by Italo Balbo, converge on Ravenna for a brutal attack on the city's socialists. Afterwards they celebrate their victory over the unpatriotic Reds by filing solemnly past the newly erected monument to Dante. They have learnt from

d'Annunzio how politic it is to claim that Italy's great poet is on their side. He frequently quotes a line from Dante—"Up in beautiful Italy there lies a lake ..."—as an endorsement of his choice of home.

D'ANNUNZIO IS STILL SHOPPING. A year earlier Tom Antongini was Fiume's emissary to the Paris peace talks. Now, back in Milan, he is once more d'Annunzio's errand boy. D'Annunzio writes to him frequently. "Please collect my parcel from *Vogue*. Please ask Corbella for six pairs of blankets, wool, and six pairs, linen. Please bring dead-leaf-green varnish. Please bring me 20,000 lire."

D'Annunzio tells Antongini he is in a very good mood and *"libidinosissssimo"*—verrrrry randy.

1921. Mussolini is making a speech. Ugo Ojetti, d'Annunzio's old friend, is watching. As Mussolini finishes, two blackshirts, with tears of emotion in their eyes, take him by the waist and lift him above the crowd "with the air of a priest elevating, within a monstrance, the sacred host." Like d'Annunzio in Fiume, Mussolini is becoming an idol.

OCTOBER 1921. With the help of a bank loan which will not be repaid in his lifetime, d'Annunzio buys the Villa Cargnacco, with its gardens and olive and lemon groves, and renames it the Vittoriale. It is the first house he has ever owned. He has already met Gian Carlo Maroni, the architect who will work with him for the next seventeen years on the expansion and remodelling of the house and grounds.

It is the latest of his many homes to be nicknamed the *Eremo* (the Hermitage). He refers to it also as the Canonica, the house of the Canon. The central wing is called the Priory. He calls himself the *"poverello,"* dresses on occasion in vaguely Franciscan-looking robes and alludes to the women of his household as "Clarissas" after the nuns of the order of St. Clare. Paul Valéry, visiting him, finds he is required to ask for "my sister water" or "my brother bread," as though dining with St. Francis.

There is still no evidence to suggest d'Annunzio has any religious feeling. He is dressing up and teasing his public with the decadent frisson of blasphemy (those "Clarissas" are far from chaste).

NOVEMBER 1921. At a congress in Rome, Mussolini renounces his "pact of pacification" with the socialists and reclaims control of the fascist movement. For years he has been insistent that fascism is a fluid, ever-creative phenomenon not to be confined within the old-fashioned terms of party politics. Now he changes his mind, and proclaims the founding of the "National Fascist Party."

D'ANNUNZIO'S STUDY IS CALLED THE "WORKSHOP." The Vittoriale at large is a workshop in the wider sense. It hums with activity. The never-ending process of construction and decoration keeps a troop of artisans on the place. This is d'Annunzio's new court. He is at ease with the people working to realise his fantasy. He teases them and calls them by nicknames. He sends them little notes of praise and encouragement. He makes jokes.

DECEMBER 1921. The programme of the National Fascist Party is published. It is full of sentiments and proposals which d'Annunzio has been espousing for years. The nation as an "organism" enduring through history, and therefore far greater than the sum of its living members. Corporations as the proper unit of social organisation. Italy as a "bulwark of Latin civilisation." The imperative need for Italy to attain "geographical unity," and to defend the rights of Italians abroad. The necessity of building up Italy's armed forces, and training its young people to be ready at all times for "danger and glory."

The squads and their violent practices are not disowned—quite the reverse. "They are a living source of strength in which and through which the fascist idea embodies itself and defends itself."

D'ANNUNZIO'S POLITICAL POSITION IS UNCLEAR. His legionaries, he complains, pester him, looking to him still for leadership, but he has no appetite for public life.

He publishes an account of himself in which he seems to take on the roles of Virgil's Aeneas and of Jesus Christ. Like Aeneas he has fled from a burning city "with a few of the faithful" (the fact that his little band consists not of warriors but of lovers and domestic servants is glossed over). The Vittoriale, he says, is a palladium and a shrine. There he will honour those who died at Fiume and keep alive the spirit that moved them. There is nothing left of his "city of life" but "a stain of dark blood." But that stain may yet spread, as the blood dripping to the foot of Christ's cross has spread across the world.

4 NOVEMBER 1921. On the third anniversary of the armistice, *Notturno* is finally published. D'Annunzio has made a myth out of its composition: out of his blindness and prostration in a still room encircled by the hubbub of war; the little slips of paper; the daughter as devoted as

Milton's were to their sightless genius of a father. In fact what he wrote in those dire months in 1916 was a scrappy kind of journal. Now he has expanded and shaped it, keeping intact its unconventional cut-up structure, and its intense inwardness. Through it d'Annunzio's consciousness streams as fluidly and inconsequentially as that of any of Virginia Woolf's characters, veering from childhood memory to hallucination, from wartime reportage to erotic fantasy.

À la recherche du temps perdu was already partially published when d'Annunzio embarked on *Notturno*. Given that he and Proust had such a good mutual friend in de Montesquiou, d'Annunzio was probably aware of it. But he didn't need to have read Proust in order to write with Proustian solipsism. In his Dostoevskian novels of the 1890s he was already minutely attentive to fluctuations of emotion. A long sentence wavering, via multiple subordinate clauses, towards an inconclusive main verb was already in his repertoire in the 1880s. As for an attentiveness to the fine detail of life, including some of the gross facts not conventionally included in fiction, he needed no one to teach him that. As he overflew wartime Trieste, James Joyce was in the city writing *Ulysses*, modernising classical epic just as d'Annunzio had done in *Maia*; making connections between smutty-minded modern prostitutes and the temptresses of Homeric legend, just as d'Annunzio had done; deploying languages ancient and modern in a word symphony in which the sharp ping of up-to-date allusions sounded over the grand subterranean rumble of ancient myth: d'Annunzio had been employing these strategies for decades. Now, with the book's publication, Ernest Hemingway, who loathed d'Annunzio for his glorification of war, pays tribute to "the great lovely writer of *Notturno* whom we respect."

Nearing sixty, d'Annunzio writes poignantly: "Now that at last I have perfectly mastered my art I have only until tomorrow morning to sing."

Sales figures are splendid. D'Annunzio is making money. He is writing for Hearst's *New York American*, and being paid enormous fees. He is also doing nicely from the sale of his autographs.

JANUARY 1922. In a glade among his garden's magnificent old magnolias, D'Annunzio creates what he calls his *"Arengo"* (an archaic word for a parliament or assembly). Stone benches are arranged in a circle, with a carved marble throne for d'Annunzio raised on a dais. There are seventeen stone columns, for the seventeen Great War battles which were (in

d'Annunzio's opinion anyway) Italian victories, and a broken column signifying Caporetto. There is a specially commissioned bronze figure of Victory wearing a crown of thorns (pagan triumphalism merging with the Christian idealisation of a suffering victim). Here d'Annunzio holds court, and addresses the legionaries who come to the Vittoriale to pay their respects.

Now it is the anniversary of one of d'Annunzio's battles and he is conducting a ceremony. A fire burns beneath a wrought-iron grill. D'Annunzio lays branches of laurel over the flames. Afterwards he distributes the ashes to his old companions-in-arms.

23 FEBRUARY 1922. D'Annunzio writes to Luisa Casati, inviting her to visit his "Franciscan garden." He alludes only with vague distaste to what is happening elsewhere. "The whole world is drowning in the

murkiest vulgarity." Casati accepts his invitation, only for d'Annunzio to put her off. He is wary of reunions with women from his past. It distresses him to see how they have aged. It distresses him even more to allow them to see what age is doing to him.

Ugo Ojetti, however, is permitted to visit on 24 February, and finds the house heated like a furnace and perfumed with sandalwood. D'Annunzio, looking "slim, agile, dapper," is full of energy and good cheer. He wants to show Ojetti around at once. He has been reading a chicken-breeders' manual: now he requires Ojetti to admire the "rational poultry house" in his garden, stocked with rare breeds. He introduces him to the gardener, pleasingly named Virgil.

The construction works which will transform the Vittoriale have barely begun. Ramshackle and built over a drop, the old house is desperately unstable, its walls riven by cracks and precariously propped up by an exoskeleton of scaffolding. A chunk of plaster has fallen from the bedroom ceiling onto d'Annunzio's pillow: he escaped a nasty blow to the head by a matter of inches. His writing table is set by a window so that if the floor gives way he will be able to jump onto the balcony and cling to the railings until someone comes with a ladder to rescue him. Ojetti, to whom he explains all this, listens with amused scepticism. "He enjoys exaggerating the decrepitude of his house." As a war hero, d'Annunzio went on at great length and with great solemnity about his love of risk, his fortitude in the face of danger. Now he reprises the same themes for a laugh.

SPRING 1922. The fascists gain control of trade unions—displacing the socialist organisers—and of large sections of the press. Five national newspapers and eighty local papers are now run more or less directly from the fascist headquarters in Rome. Mussolini has abandoned hope of forming an alliance with the socialists and tacitly encourages his followers' violent attacks on them. The third anniversary of the meeting in Piazza San Sepolcro, now grandiosely described as the foundation of fascism, is celebrated with rallies in Milan and other northern cities.

The architect Gian Carlo Maroni is twenty-eight when he first begins to work for d'Annunzio. Soon he has become the latest of d'Annunzio's beloved young acolytes. With him, d'Annunzio is teasing. He gives him nicknames: Gian Caro (Dear Gian) or Gian Carnefice (Gian the Executioner). He addresses him as Brother or Magus or as the "Master of the Living Stones."

5 APRIL 1922. Mussolini visits d'Annunzio in Gardone. He has a high regard for literature. One of his mottoes is: "Book and rifle—perfect fascist." He has even written some books himself.

Ten days later d'Annunzio publishes an open letter to the actress playing the lead in a new production of *Jorio's Daughter* in Rome. He will not be in the audience, he writes. "All the rights and all the privileges of the free citizen have been revoked for me for some time." Whether Mussolini has threatened him—or whether his decision to cling to his home and his silence is freely taken—is unclear. "I am now reduced to making a hole in my little piece of land in which to place my secrets."

21 APRIL 1922. More fascist rallies, this time to celebrate the foundation of Rome. Fascist orators have taken over d'Annunzio's insistence that modern Italy should model itself on, and aspire to be worthy of, the grandeur of ancient Rome. Mussolini writes: "In Rome we see the promise of the future. Rome is our myth."

D'ANNUNZIO'S HOME—like so much of his written work—is an idiosyncratic and original creation made up of allusions and reproductions. The house's rooms are full of plaster casts of famous statuary and photographic prints of famous paintings. There are oddities of scale and tone. The *Mona Lisa* dwindles to a black and white postcard. Classical Greek sculptures, known for centuries only as pristine marble, have been gilded. Michelangelo's tragic *Dying Prisoner* is festooned with necklaces, its truncated legs kilted with a silk shawl.

The buildings are as much of a collage of imitations as their contents. The cornucopia which recurs on stone seats all over the garden is copied from a Roman tomb in Lucca cathedral. The eagles perched on pillars are replicas of those in the gardens of the Villa d'Este, where the youthful d'Annunzio once heard Liszt play by moonlight, and where he and Barbara were happy. The façade of the original farmhouse, now the Prioria, is covered with plaster escutcheons in direct imitation of the mediaeval Palazzo del Podestà in Arezzo. The colonnades lining the driveway are copied from Roman aqueducts.

D'Annunzio has encountered modernism in the white cubes of

Luisa Casati's Roman villa, in the black and grey austerity of Romaine Brooks's rooms. Now, half a century before the term becomes current, he is creating a piece of post-modernism, sprinkling his enormous work of installation art with fragments of the great buildings and statuary of the past.

27–28 MAY 1922. D'Annunzio receives Georgy Chicherin, the Soviet Union's Commissar for External Affairs, who stays with him for two days or more. The *squadristi* have torched houses which communists are known to have visited. "Thank you," says Chicherin on arrival. "You show greater courage by receiving me than I do by coming to visit you." D'Annunzio wilfully misunderstands. "I have never feared contagion," he announces. "The plague victims of Fiume know it." (He is proud of the fact that when there was an outbreak of bubonic plague in Fiume, he visited the victims in hospital, as fearless of disease as Napoleon at Jaffa.)

He is interested to receive the commissar, but he is not impressed by his doctrine. "The Russian people have freed the world for ever of a puerile illusion," he writes. "The dictatorship of a class has proved incapable of creating the necessary conditions for a tolerable life." It is during this visit that d'Annunzio allegedly pulls the trick with the scimitar and the threatened beheading.

MAY 1922. Tens of thousands of *squadristi*, led by Italo Balbo, converge on Ferrara for the funeral procession of a fascist "martyr." The procession clashes with anti-fascist demonstrations. People on both sides are killed. Mussolini writes, "To all Italian fascists: consider yourselves materially and morally mobilised from this moment on." They are to move with the speed of lightning. "Everything will crumble under your blows." Ten thousand fascists pour into Bologna, camping out under the colonnades. They drive out the city prefect, and install a sympathetic general as head of police.

1922. Thanks to the efforts of a syndicate of d'Annunzio's devoted friends and admirers, the library of the Capponcina, all those thousands of books which he has not seen for twelve years, are at last restored to him. Mining his past again, he begins to rework and expand his *Faville* for a collection of semi-fictionalised autobiographical fragments covering his childhood and schooldays.

He is still spending. He asks a friend, travelling to Milan in February, to buy him at least a dozen Californian peaches: "Don't be terrified by the price." The army of decorators and craftsmen at work in the house wait months, even years, for payment, but he gives extravagant presents to his servants on their saints' days. He commissions Antongini to buy "two or three" trinkets for presents. Antongini sends twenty-odd pieces from which to choose: cufflinks, gold and silver cigarette cases, some rings, a few tie pins. D'Annunzio keeps them all. He has drawers full of such things to give to guests.

JULY 1922. The socialists have called a nationwide strike. It provokes a terrible response. Fascists led by Italo Balbo sweep through north-eastern Italy, burning socialists' houses and smashing up their meeting places. Balbo writes in his diary: "It was a night of terror. Our passage was signed by plumes of smoke and fire. All the Romagna plain up to the hills became prey to the exasperated reprisals of the fascists, determined to finish for ever the Red terror." Balbo's aim, he writes, is to "destroy the present regime and all its venerable institutions. The more our actions are seen to be scandalous, the better."

AUGUST 1922. Duse is in Milan, performing *The Dead City*. Back in 1909, d'Annunzio asked her to play the part of Fedra. She wrote back firmly refusing. When he left her, she said, it was as though he had smashed her to pieces with his own hands. She can no longer read his work. To speak to him would be harder for her than to rise from the dead. "I have given you everything. I have nothing left."

Thirteen years later, though, she feels differently. She has written to d'Annunzio asking his permission to make changes to the text of the play, and suggesting they might meet. D'Annunzio replies, telling her that he has come to realise "certainly and mystically" that no relationship with any other human being "is worth the communion that I had with you, that I have with you."

He goes to Milan. Accounts of their reunion vary. D'Annunzio's servant claims afterwards that he peeped through the keyhole of the hotel room and saw d'Annunzio and Duse facing each other, both on their knees like the donors in a Renaissance altarpiece, both in floods of tears.

Duse herself gives unmatched accounts of their conversation to two different female friends. To one she says she snubbed him:

D'Annunzio: "Even you cannot imagine how much I loved you."

Duse: "Even you cannot imagine how much I have forgotten you."

This kind of sharpness wasn't Duse's style. Her other version sounds more like her, and (with its breathtaking arrogance) more like him:

D'Annunzio: "How you have loved me!"

Duse (silently to herself): "He is still deluding himself. Had I loved him *as he thinks*, I would have died when we parted. Instead I have lived."

In the first days of August 1922, some 5,000 *squadristi*, singing *Giovinezza* and brandishing revolvers, rampaged through Genoa, destroying printing presses, trashing the offices of a socialist journal and driving the president of the shipowners' association out of his office. There were similar scenes in Ancona and Livorno, where the fascist squads were led by d'Annunzio's beloved comrade Ciano. In Parma d'Annunzio's former associate, de Ambris, courageously resisted the fascist onslaught, fighting back at the head of the socialist "People's *Arditi*" against thousands of *squadristi* led by the fascist heavyweights, Balbo and Farinacci.

Milan had a socialist city council. On 3 August the squads swarmed through the city, drove the councillors out of the city hall in the Palazzo Marino and occupied it themselves. The mayor, turning for guidance to the government in Rome, was advised not to intervene.

3 AUGUST 1922. D'Annunzio is in Milan seeing Duse and chivvying his publisher, Treves, over the production of his *Complete Works*. Several of his wartime comrades, now with the squads, come to seek him out at the Hotel Cavour. According to Antongini, who is with him, their black shirts are drenched in sweat, and their "burning faith" shows in their every gesture and in their shining eyes. With thousands of fascists milling around the city, d'Annunzio allows himself to be carried along to the Palazzo Marino. Going out onto the balcony he speaks in public for the first time in the twenty months since he left Fiume.

His speech is long and evasive, one of his luminous word-clouds from which no meaning flashes clear. He does not use the word "fascist." He does not mention Mussolini. He speaks in the gnomic liturgical style he perfected in Fiume: "It is not we who breathe but the nation which breathes in us. It is not we who live but the *patria* which lives in us."

His apologists will maintain that this is an act, not of commitment, but of political naïveté. He withholds any explicit verbal endorsement of fascism, and perhaps he does not realise how potent an image his presence on that balcony, alongside a phalanx of blackshirts, provides. The argument doesn't stand up. D'Annunzio is a master of political theatre. He surely understands how he is being used. Perhaps he is afraid to refuse the blackshirts' invitation. Perhaps he can't resist the chance to be once more onstage in front of a roaring crowd. But whatever his motives for going to the Palazzo Marino, he rapidly comes to regret it.

The fascists assail the offices of *Avanti!* for the third time, using bombs, rifles and electrically charged barbed wire. The journal's warehouse is set on fire. The Communist Club is broken into and smashed up. There are battles in the streets between the civil authorities' tanks on the one hand, and the fascists' forty armoured trucks on the other. Mussolini sends a message from Rome, approving "the grand, the beautiful, the inexorable violence of decisive moments."

D'Annunzio is not paying attention to the public commotion. Safely back in the Hotel Cavour, he fires off a sequence of telegrams to Luisa instructing her to prepare for a visit from Duse, whom he now sanctifies as the great love of his life.

Back in Gardone he waits in vain for Duse, but he receives a telegram from the Fascist Party Secretary. "The National Fascist Party echoes your cry of 'Long Live Fascism!'" D'Annunzio, who has pointedly refrained from uttering any such "cry," replies indignantly that his only *Evviva* is for Italy: "I know of no other." Too late. The fascists are as adept as he at disseminating their own versions of reality. A copy of the telegram has been sent to their paper *Il Popolo d'Italia*, which promptly publishes it. D'Annunzio is now indelibly marked by his apparent association with fascism. Three weeks later Mussolini publishes a bellicose article: "Our recruits want to fight, not to argue." He entitles it *"La Fiumana."* He is keen to emphasise the affinity between d'Annunzio and himself. D'Annunzio is not. In his notebook he makes a Latin note to himself, *"Tempus tacendi"*—time to be silent. He will never speak in public again.

SHORTLY AFTER HIS RETURN FROM MILAN, d'Annunzio received a surprising letter. It was from ex-Prime Minister Francesco Nitti—*Cagoia*—the man whom he had so virulently abused. For the country's sake Nitti was prepared to overlook all d'Annunzio's past insults: "It doesn't matter about me." He proposed they should work together to save Italy from the violence engulfing it. "All our forces must be united . . . You see the danger and you can work on the youth, setting it alight, and leading it back to the right path." Nitti invited d'Annunzio to meet him and Mussolini in a villa in Tuscany on 15 August. It is hard to imagine what kind of accord they could have reached, but a quarter of a century later Nitti would write that if only that meeting could have taken place, the history of Italy might have taken a different path.

It is two days before the appointed date and d'Annunzio is enjoying a musical evening. Luisa is playing the piano in the Music Room on the raised ground floor of the Vittoriale. It is around eleven o'clock at night. D'Annunzio, in pyjamas and slippers, is sitting on a window seat, with the windows wide open behind him. Accounts differ as to who else is in the room. One suggests that Luisa's younger sister Jolanda, a cellist, is sitting beside him and she and Gabriele are fondling each other. There are certainly a number of people in the house, servants and guests. Among them is Aldo Finzi, who was one of the pilots who flew with d'Annunzio to Vienna. Finzi is now an influential member of the Fascist Party's central office.

Somehow d'Annunzio falls head-first out of the window onto the gravel some ten feet below. His skull is fractured and for the next three days he lies in a coma while no fewer than six distinguished doctors attend him.

Many theories—none of them proven—have been advanced to explain how a man might suddenly topple out of a window. Three people at least see what happens: a lawyer who is visiting, Finzi, and the gardener's boy; but none of them ever gives a conclusive account of the event. D'Annunzio's children accuse the Baccara sisters of trying to murder him, but it is hard to imagine their motive for doing so. D'Annunzio is later so outraged by the suggestion that he forbids his son Mario and even his dear Renata ever to visit the Vittoriale again. Anti-fascists allege that it was Finzi who pushed him. The Fascist High Command see d'Annunzio's political interventions as dangerous meddling. His public following is still substantial (his fall is front-page news, and once he is on the way to recovery the *Corriere della Sera* publishes cabled messages of goodwill from dignitaries ranging from Francesco Nitti to Giacomo Puccini). He is unpredictable. They might have wanted to forestall his meeting with Nitti. They might simply have wanted him eliminated.

But Finzi has been, and remains, a friend and admirer of d'Annunzio's. Besides, if this was a failed assassination it was a remarkably clumsy one, and one which the victim himself was at pains to cover up. D'Annunzio claimed in his semi-fictional, semi-autobiographical *Libro Segreto* that his "fall" was a suicide attempt. Perhaps it was: he had been toying with the idea of killing himself for years, and his ill-advised appearance at the Palazzo Marino might have precipitated one of the bouts of depression to which he was subject. Or perhaps—and this seems the most likely explanation—he just fell.

One-eyed, he occasionally complained of disorientation, or disturbances to his balance. Besides, according to the local pharmacist, he was, by this time, consuming large quantities of cocaine. He was also taking sulfonal, an addictive hypnotic drug whose side effects include problems with balance and a tendency to stagger. Perhaps he was unsteadied by drugs or alcohol (always an abstemious drinker, he nonetheless enjoyed fine champagne). Perhaps Jolanda, disliking his advances, gave him a shove which was harder than she meant it to be. At all events—whether it was a sinister attack, an act of despair or the undignified accident of a drug-fuddled lecher—the incident was soon to be transformed to golden fable by d'Annunzio's Midas-like way with stories. Something about the incident shamed or alarmed him, so he baffled enquiry by wrapping it in a haze of glory. He ascribed his escape from death to supernatural intervention. He entitled his fall his "archangelic flight." He noted that on the third day he rose again.

26 SEPTEMBER 1922. The Fascist Party has thousands of new members, so many that the party secretary maintains that it cannot continue as an independent institution, it must "become the state." Mussolini delivers an ominous speech, warning the King that he should not oppose the "fascist revolution" which is ready to shoulder its "responsibilities"—in other words, to seize power. For decades d'Annunzio has been inveighing against the filth engulfing Rome, and calling for it to be cleansed. Now Mussolini volunteers for the job. "It is our intention to make Rome the city of our spirit, a city that is purged and disinfected of all the elements that have corrupted it and dragged it into the mire."

4 OCTOBER 1922. Fascists have occupied Trento and Bolzano near the Austrian border. Still the government makes no move to curtail their rampages. Mussolini addresses his followers in Milan. The liberal state, he announces, is "a mask behind which there is no face; a scaffolding behind which there is no building." One of Mussolini's closest associates writes that the government is "useless . . . We are forced to take over. Otherwise the history of Italy would become a joke."

11 OCTOBER 1922. Mussolini pays d'Annunzio a visit. D'Annunzio, apparently fully recovered from his fall, has been negotiating with Mussolini on behalf of the Seamen's Union headed by Giuseppe Giulietti, who did so much for him at Fiume and who is losing his members to the rival fascist Mariners' Union. These negotiations are long-drawn-out and frequently ill-tempered. It is a frustrating wrangle, to which d'Annunzio is giving attention he might have better employed observing more significant developments in Italy's political life. After their meeting Mussolini agrees to close down the fascist union, allowing Giulietti's association a free hand. D'Annunzio is exultant. He owes Mussolini a favour. He agrees to disband his legions, who have been massing at Fiume.

14 OCTOBER 1922. Mussolini writes to General Badoglio, now chief of the general staff, warning him that any attempt to put down the fascists by military means will result in a massacre.

21 OCTOBER 1922. D'Annunzio writes to Antongini saying: "I am not, and I do not want to be, anything but Italy's *poverello*. I live only for my work." He has five books in progress, including a memoir of his childhood, and Hearst has given him an advance of a million lire for an autobiography. (He will never deliver it.) He has done seven years' "forced labour" in the public arena. He has "stooped" to "repugnant mingling" with hoi polloi on the battlefields and in the piazzas. "No one can imagine with what anxiety I sought out this refuge, with what a need to steep myself in myself, and in the secret springs of my poetry."

24 OCTOBER 1922. At a Fascist Party conference in Naples there are repeated calls for a march on Rome. Mussolini, who enters the conference to three blasts on a trumpet, seems to concur. "Either the arrow must leave the bow or the string will break." The delegates parade

through the city in their black uniforms for three hours, singing war songs. They call their groups now not "squads" but "legions" (another d'Annunzian borrowing). Shouts, salutes, blaring music. An especially noisy cheer for the representatives of Fiume. Yells of "On to Rome!" At last, in a "religious" silence, Mussolini speaks. "Either they will give us the government or we will take it by descending on Rome. It is a question of days, of hours perhaps . . . Go back to your towns and await orders." Those orders are likely to be for violent action, for "in history, force decides everything." Like d'Annunzio motoring into Fiume three years earlier, Mussolini is about the make his "Sacred Entry."

The representatives of liberal democracy are hopelessly disunited. The incumbent prime minister, Luigi Facta, is longing to be ousted. "I have great hopes to be free of all this in the next few days," he writes to his wife. "Oh darling . . . the day I will leave I shall be indescribably happy." Over the next four days ex-premiers Salandra, Orlando and Giolitti fail to agree on a strategy to keep the fascists out. On the contrary, each indicates he would prefer the premiership to go to Mussolini than to one of the others. Meanwhile there is much talk of a strategic alliance between the socialists and the Catholic *Popolari* Party who could, between them, have formed a government. Many of the moderate "reformist" socialists are in favour of the alliance, but the hardline "maximalists" cannot stomach a partnership with the purveyors of the people's "opium." Keeping their principles unsullied, they open the door to fascist dictatorship.

26 OCTOBER 1922. The fourth anniversary of the fightback across the River Piave. All fascist leaders are ordered to mobilise their squads. Fascist sympathisers in the army and police are warned not to intervene.

27 OCTOBER 1922. Fascists swarm through major towns all over Italy, taking over telephone exchanges and telegraph offices, police stations and town halls. It is cold and rainy. The *squadristi* wander without good maps. All the same, some 16,000 of them reach assembly points in an arc around the periphery of Rome. Mussolini stays in Milan, going to the theatre, disconnecting his telephone at bedtime, making a display of his sang-froid. Later this crisis will be repeatedly described as a "revolution" led by the valiant *Duce*, but at the time Mussolini is careful to stay well away from any potential violence. He is aiming, not at the glamour of an insurrection, but at solid, incontrovertible, legitimate power.

28 OCTOBER 1922. In the early hours of the morning, Prime Minister Facta meets his ministers and senior generals. Very few of the fascists encamped around Rome have weapons (apart from their clubs) and they have no provisions. General Badoglio offers to disperse them. Just before 8 a.m., Facta resolves to declare a state of emergency and impose martial law across the whole country from midday. Officials all over Italy are informed by telegram. At 9 a.m. Facta goes to the King, and asks him to sign the declaration. Victor Emmanuel refuses. His reasons for doing so remain, to this day, uncertain. Perhaps he is afraid the troops will mutiny if asked to take action against the fascists, just as he and his generals feared they would if asked to attack d'Annunzio in Fiume. Perhaps he suspects a move to launch a military coup and replace him with his more dashing cousin, the Duke of Aosta. Perhaps he is unwilling to sanction bloodshed and afraid of triggering a civil war. Perhaps he prefers the possibility of a fascist government to the one he has: he remarks later that he had no desire to order the army to fight for "a cabinet of poltroons."

Facta resigns. Martial law is revoked. The fascists enter the capital, not in the kind of awe-inspiring "March on Rome" that fascist mythology will later describe, but sporadically, and in no particular order. Many of them arrive by special trains chartered with the connivance of the army. The King calls upon Salandra to form a government. Mussolini, still at his editorial desk in Milan, writes: "Central Italy is completely occupied by blackshirts . . . The government must be unequivocally fascist." He needs a ringing phrase. He takes it from d'Annunzio. "Our victory must not be mutilated!"

STEEPED IN HIMSELF and the secret springs of poetry, d'Annunzio plays no part in the day's events, but Mussolini, uneasily aware how much influence he has, keeps him informed. In the morning a telegram arrives at the Vittoriale. "We have had to mobilise our forces to cut short a wretched situation. We are absolute master of the larger part of Italy, and elsewhere we occupy the essential nerve centres of the nation." Then comes the assurance that d'Annunzio is not expected to "line up" and finally a request. "Read the proclamation! . . . You will have some great word to speak." D'Annunzio utters no word.

Mid-afternoon. Mussolini sends another message. "The latest news consecrates our triumph. Tomorrow's Italy will have a government. We will be intelligent and discreet enough not to abuse our victory."

He is sure, he says, that d'Annunzio will salute this marvellous development, and "consecrate the reborn youth of Italy." He ends with a bit of sycophancy which is not intended to be taken seriously. Mussolini has seized power, he tells d'Annunzio, "To you! For you!"

At nightfall d'Annunzio responds at last. He has had an awfully busy day, he says, and only just got around to reading the telegrams. He makes no clear comment on Mussolini's news. Instead he sends him a volume of his own wartime speeches, with a gnomic caution: "Victory has the clear eyes of Pallas Athena. Do not blindfold her."

29 OCTOBER 1922. It is still raining. Thousands more damp blackshirts have converged on Rome, but the fascists' seizure of power is an act, not of force, but of robbery with menaces.

Salandra informs the King that he cannot, or dares not, assume power. At last Mussolini receives the telephone call he has been awaiting. He is one of only thirty-six fascist deputies, but Victor Emmanuel is proposing that he attempt to put together a coalition. As keenly aware as d'Annunzio has always been that the media coverage of an event will have a wider impact than the event itself, Mussolini delays his journey in order to draft a press release. He is going to Rome, he tells the world, "wearing his black shirt, as a fascist" and he has the support of 300,000 men "faithful to my orders." Belatedly he places himself in the van of the "March" by taking the night train south.

30 OCTOBER 1922. Arriving after a fourteen-hour journey, Mussolini goes to the Quirinal Palace, wearing a bowler hat and spats and a formal suit over his black shirt, and introduces himself to the King with another verbal flourish taken from d'Annunzio. "Sire, I bring you the Italy of Vittorio Veneto." Victor Emmanuel invites him to form a government and implores him to send his blackshirts home. Mussolini agrees to the former request but rejects the latter: his "legions" must be allowed to celebrate their Roman Triumph.

31 OCTOBER 1922. Mussolini is sworn in as prime minister and 50,000 fascists celebrate on the streets of Rome. They break into Nitti's house, smashing and robbing things from the man d'Annunzio taught them to despise as *Cagoia*. Giovanni Giuriati, d'Annunzio's prime minister in Fiume, is Mussolini's minister for "recently liberated lands," meaning the former Austrian territories along the Dalmatian coast. General

Diaz, who set such a high value on d'Annunzio's wartime rhetoric, is his chief of staff.

For five hours the King reviews the blackshirts who pass by the palace cheering, flapping banners, and yelling, as d'Annunzio taught them to do, *"Eia, Eia, Eia, Alalà!"* They sing *Giovinezza*. They give the stiff-armed salute. For those many of them who were with d'Annunzio in Fiume it seems as though sparks from the City of the Holocaust have at last ignited an answering blaze in Rome.

2 NOVEMBER 1922. D'Annunzio publishes a statement in the journal of his legionaries' association. It is non-committal. He praises the King, but in nebulous terms. He says that the "experimental government" is to be "tolerated" until an election can be called in the spring. He mentions labyrinths and rainbows. He sprinkles his text with Latin tags. He is lining up neither alongside Mussolini and the fascists, nor in opposition to them.

He writes more candidly to Antongini. He complains that his name is being improperly made use of. He does not want the fascists exploiting his reputation for their advantage. He is, however, quite willing to exploit their newly acquired power for his own ends. Once again he gives Antongini a list. This time he is not sending him out shopping for household fixtures and fittings. He is asking him to convey some proposals and requests to the new premier and his ministers. Military bases in Trentino must be strengthened. The convent in Assisi which has been converted into government offices must at once be restored to the Franciscans. And so on and so forth. For the rest of his life d'Annunzio will ceaselessly demand favours of Mussolini: some on a grand scale (changes of policy), some trivial (jobs for his protégés). Mussolini receives them patiently, and grants those to which he can easily agree.

16 NOVEMBER 1922. Mussolini's first speech to parliament. He is crowing over the parliamentarians' discomfiture. He harks back to May 1915, the month when d'Annunzio had all Rome in uproar, and when Italy went to war without the consent of parliament. "So now a government has arisen without parliamentary approval." Like d'Annunzio reminding the people of Vienna that it is only thanks to his magnanimity that they are not being bombed, Mussolini tells the assembled deputies, that he could have turned "this grim grey chamber into an armed camp

for blackshirts, a bivouac for soldiers. I could have nailed up the doors of parliament and formed an exclusively fascist government." That he didn't do so is a token of his forbearance, and the clear implication is that nobody should count upon its lasting. He has learned from d'Annunzio the efficacy of the theatre of what might have been.

D'ANNUNZIO'S SILENCE IS MUSICAL, he writes. Those of his former comrades who have "lined up" with Mussolini, would prefer a more audible music. On 24 November, Aldo Finzi, who is now Mussolini's High Commissioner for Aviation, writes to him reproachfully. How can he, "superb prophet of the destiny of our beautiful Italy," withhold his support from those who are converting his prophecies into reality? Finzi has followed Mussolini "blindly" because he is persuaded that Mussolini is the one man who can realise d'Annunzio's visions. "How are we mistaken? How do our ends differ from those you have predicted and desired?" A letter from d'Annunzio to Luigi Albertini provides an indirect answer. He recognises the fascist "ideal for the world" as being a version of his own, but it has been "squandered and falsified." He wants nothing to do with it.

MUSSOLINI LEAVES FOR LONDON. He stays at Claridges and is received by the Prime Minister and the King. He lays a wreath at the Cenotaph. Crowds follow him around, some British blackshirts singing *Giovinezza* in a deplorably bad accent. By the time he returns his mood has hardened. On 15 December he demands his cabinet's authorisation to act "by whatever means I hold necessary" against a variety of untrustworthy political elements including "pseudo-Fiumanism."

D'Annunzio has been bombarding Mussolini with instructions. Construct airfields. Build "a beautiful pediment around the temple that is Italy." He has insisted on his role as fascism's inventor. "In the movement which calls itself 'fascist' has not the best been engendered by my spirit? Was not the present upheaval heralded by me forty years ago and set in motion by the condottieri of Ronchi?" He is disappointed by the slowness and curtness of the *Duce*'s replies. On 16 December he writes to Mussolini: "I have resolved—today—to retreat into my silence and give myself up again entirely to my art." A refusal, a promise and a surrender.

Three days later comes the crackdown on d'Annunzio's legionaries. Anarchists and "subversives" are questioned roughly. The legionaries' armed groups are broken up. De Ambris and others with trade unionist connections are bullied and harassed until they go into exile. D'Annunzio protests, but ineffectually. By the end of the month Mussolini has switched his attention to the Communist Party. Most of the Central Committee, including Gramsci, are arrested and thousands of socialist and communist workers leave Italy.

DECEMBER 1922–JANUARY 1923. The Fascist Grand Council is created, an extra-constitutional body, not answerable to the electorate, which will gradually assume many of the powers and functions of the conventional ministries. At the same time the fascist militia is formed. It is Mussolini's own private war host, as the Legion of Fiume was once d'Annunzio's.

It is unclear to what extent d'Annunzio's withdrawal from the world is voluntary. He tells Luigi Albertini: "I am a perpetual prisoner here." He fumes intermittently at his confinement. "Why can I not run along a level road, or pass through a populous city, or enter a library, or rest in meditation before the works of art I interpreted and loved?" Certainly he is closely watched, and certainly he acts as though an invisible fence keeps him by the lakes, far from the centres of power. Fifteen years after his death, Ernesto Cabruna, who was among his trusted lieutenants at Fiume, writes: "History will reveal how fascism diabolically kept d'Annunzio prisoner at the Vittoriale in the last years of his life . . . D'Annunzio had twenty-one persons in his service, six of them members of the fascist police."

MARCH 1923. Mussolini writes: "Mankind is perhaps tired of liberty. It has had an orgy of it." He proposes sterner, more bracing ideals: "order, hierarchy, discipline." The British ambassador to Rome reports back to London that although Mussolini is "hasty and violent" and prone to "fits of ungovernable rage," he is nevertheless a "statesman of exceptional ability and enterprise," and really quite gentlemanly. He has been "driving about through Rome in a two-seater with a well-grown lion cub sitting beside him." The ambassador finds this "strange," but concludes: "Italians seem to like this sort of thing."

6 MAY 1923. D'Annunzio is becoming more and more reclusive. His typist reports that he stays shut up in his room. He sees no one. He wants to see no one. For days on end he doesn't even go out into the garden.

He does, however, find time for sex. Now he is writing to Luisa, who is in the house but refusing to see him. Some visiting woman has provoked Luisa's jealousy. D'Annunzio apologises. "I know I am incomprehensible," he writes. "I know that what I have sometimes asked of you is perhaps inhuman." He reassures her. "Nothing is taken from you. You are always the highest in my heart and in my thoughts. I do not know how I would live without you." So far, so ordinary for an erring lover. But then d'Annunzio takes a further, outrageous step. Really, he writes, *she* should pity *him*. Her "silent rancour" is very trying to him. Her "bitter words" are even worse. He is not responsible for his own promiscuity. The trouble, he explains, is his "hereditary infirmity," which makes him more wretched than she can possibly be. He deserves—he demands—her "fraternal compassion."

15 MAY 1923. Over a week has gone by and Luisa is unappeased. She has let d'Annunzio know that their love affair is "dead." He protests. He never wants to part from her. Has he not given her endless proofs of his tenderness? He becomes querulous. Has he not explained over and over again that he takes other sexual partners, not for pleasure, but in a spirit of "voracious curiosity"? They stimulate his imagination—bedding them is a form of research, just part of his work. "We've talked about this so many times." (Poor Luisa!) He reminds her that after he has had another woman he and she have especially exciting sex. "Our delirium goes beyond all limits."

Perhaps that is why Luisa stays, "imprisoned by her senses" as Duse was before her. For the next fifteen years she will live with d'Annunzio, playing the piano for his pleasure, running his household, procuring other women for him, entertaining his guests, leaving a rose in the keyhole of her bedroom on nights when she wants him in there with her.

JUNE 1923. D'Annunzio is still cultivating his increasingly peculiar garden. This month he takes delivery of boulders from the various mountain tops where Italy's Great War battles were fought. He arranges them around the *Arengo* and decorates them with mottoes.

He turned sixty in March, and he has a new sexual partner, a twenty-two-year-old Frenchwoman named Angèle Lager who is living on Lake Garda as paid companion to an old acquaintance of his from Paris. She will be his lover, off and on, for the next three years. He enjoys biting her neck, revealed by fashionably cropped hair. He calls her *Jouvence*

(Youth). He sends her strawberries and peaches and—so she will allege after their affair has ended—introduces her to the use of cocaine, and infects her with venereal disease.

BACK IN 1915, Marinetti hailed Mussolini as an exemplary futurist. Now he adores everything about the *Duce*: his contempt, his audacity, his pugnaciousness; the way he "spits on everything which is vain, slow, cumbersome, useless"; his massive head, his "ultra-dynamic eyes like speeding cars"; his bowler hat like "black clouds which hang heavily over the inky blackness of ravines in the Apennines"; his resemblance to a torpedo.

The feeling is not mutual. Mussolini doesn't much like the futurists. He doesn't trust Marinetti, and has him closely watched.

24 SEPTEMBER 1923. D'Annunzio asks Mussolini for a "guard," ostensibly to keep off the importunate legionaries who are still turning up at the house with tiresome frequency to salute their Commandant. Mussolini is delighted to comply, sending him Giovanni Rizzo, a police officer who subsequently plays the triple role of protector, jailer and spy. D'Annunzio is fully aware he is under surveillance. Fascist agents have been loitering around the village under various transparent pretexts. Now, in voluntarily accepting a spy into his household, he takes control of his own situation which is, from now on, virtually one of house arrest.

Rizzo sends regular reports back to Fascist Headquarters. D'Annunzio, knowing this, uses him for the transmission of messages to Mussolini. He is a good master to Rizzo, using his influence on Mussolini to obtain repeated promotions for him. Rizzo, in turn, apparently growing fond of his master/charge, protects d'Annunzio by putting, in his reports to Mussolini, a harmless gloss on the poet's more dangerous public utterances. He is also very helpful in persuading the local police to ignore d'Annunzio's motoring offences, which are many and flagrant.

D'Annunzio is undressing. He washes. He dabs scent onto himself. He is trying to resist his craving for cocaine. He fails. "Like a thief, like an assassin, fleeing the light, I go to fetch the poison from the cabinet." As well as cocaine and sulfonal, he is regularly taking laudanum and a painkiller he calls "Adalina."

The door to Luisa's room is ajar. The "orgy" lasts until dawn.

23 NOVEMBER 1923. Mussolini has been taking an interest in the Bavarian "fascists" led by one Adolf Hitler, but after the failure of the Beer Hall Putsch he decides they are "buffoons." The visiting Spanish general, Miguel Primo de Rivera, is more congenial: he salutes Mussolini as "the apostle of a world campaign against dissolution and anarchy."

22 DECEMBER 1923. D'Annunzio graciously offers to donate the Vittoriale to Italy, giving a new meaning to his favoured motto: *"Ho quel che ho donato"* (I have what I have given). He has the words incised in the arch above the entrance gate. Their ambiguity is teasing. D'Annunzio is fully aware what a good deal he is proposing. The house will remain his home, but he will no longer be financially responsible for its upkeep.

27 JANUARY 1924. Fiume finally becomes a part of Italy under the terms of a new treaty with Yugoslavia, and d'Annunzio is named Prince of Monte Nevoso (Snowy Mountain). He writes to Jouvence: "I am, oh delicious Maldestra, a 'great man' and a 'public man' alas, alas, alas!"

Whatever he may say, he is very pleased with his new title and commissions one of his favourite artists to design him a coat of arms—a laurel wreath, a mountain and seven stars—which will soon be carved in stone on the Vittoriale's grand portico. Rizzo reports to Mussolini that d'Annunzio wants only two things: the first is a great name to be remembered by posterity; the second is enough money "to live as he has always lived, without anxieties of any kind."

6 APRIL 1924. Another general election. Campaigning is rough. Rallies deteriorate into brawls. The fascists employ fraud, intimidation and murder. To ensure their impunity, Mussolini purges the police force, forcing 340 commissioners and deputies to retire prematurely. The opposition parties—socialist, communist, liberal—again find it impossible to overcome their differences in order to stand together against fascism.

Mussolini's supporters win two-thirds of the votes, and now easily dominate the chamber. The fascist deputies are new—eighty per cent of them have never sat in parliament before—and young, two-thirds of them being under forty. Like d'Annunzio in Fiume, Mussolini is now a "Prince of Youth."

12 APRIL 1924. Paul Valéry visits the Vittoriale. He is met in Desenzano by a "diabolical motorboat" and whizzed up the lake in a flurry of

wind and spray which comes near, he complains, to stripping him of his clothes, his hair and his skin. Arrived at the Vittoriale ("heated like a furnace"), he is greeted by d'Annunzio, who has shaved off all his facial hair, eyebrows included. They embrace, but not on equal terms. As Valéry tells it, d'Annunzio's embrace is the "accolade of a King."

D'Annunzio tells Valéry he has been trying to re-enter that "third place," the state that was neither life nor death, which he glimpsed on the night of his perilous night flight over Cattaro. His cocaine consumption and his compulsive promiscuity are not just self-indulgence. By means of drugs, of sex, of the arrangement of his bizarre but meaningful domestic spaces, he is trying to attain a mystical self-transcendence. He is reading ancient authors on the cult of Dionysus. He quotes St. Paul on *"sobria ebrietas."* He has been studying the Rig Veda, Socrates, Nietzsche, the prophet Hosea.

He is interested in self-denial as much as in self-indulgence. He makes a note about Mahatma Gandhi: he is impressed by the way Gandhi survives on a kind of thin porridge.

24 APRIL 1924. John St. Loe Strachey, a British journalist who will become Oswald Mosley's parliamentary private secretary, visits Mussolini in the Palazzo Chigi. Mussolini is hunched behind his desk: his only greeting is a brusque nod. Strachey is sufficiently impressed to employ a metaphor frequently used by d'Annunzio of himself. "Imagine Vulcan interrupted at his forge." Mussolini is the Vulcan who is hammering out the new Italy on his anvil. "You can feel the heat of the furnace, the strain on his body, in the set of the muscles of his face, in his heavy shoulders, and in his regard." Strachey shares his impressions with Ambassador Graham, who agrees about Mussolini's "smouldering force," but has reservations. "I fear that he does not really, in his heart, disapprove of the violence used towards his political opponents."

22 MAY 1924. D'Annunzio takes delivery of Mussolini's biggest gift yet—the plane in which the poet flew over Vienna in August 1918. He will eventually construct an enormous domed room for its display.

21 APRIL 1924. Eleonora Duse dies, in a hotel in Pittsburgh, while touring America. On receiving the news d'Annunzio writes to Mussolini: "Far from Italy, the most Italian of hearts has been extinguished." He

asks that her "adored body" should be brought home at the state's expense. It is. Mussolini, who fully understands the symbolic useful- ness of celebrities, needed no prompting.

Sure now that she can make no further demands on him, d'Annunzio mourns Duse unreservedly. He asks his favourite sculptor to make a bust of her and keeps it—veiled—on his desk. Every year, for the rest of his life, he marks the anniversary of her death. He has always enjoyed imagining his beloved women dead.

Duse's daughter Enrichetta destroys all her mother's letters from d'Annunzio. She claims Duse "commanded" her to do so, but it seems strange, in that case, that Eleanora did not destroy them her- self. Enrichetta must have been shocked by them: no doubt, like all d'Annunzio's other love letters, they contain explicit accounts of the couple's love-making. D'Annunzio writes furiously to her "the destruc- tion of my letters to Ghisola is an unjustifiable crime against the spirit." He knows Duse's mind better than Enrichetta does. "She is ever near me, speaking without words."

30 MAY 1924. Giacomo Matteotti, the new leader of the Socialist Party, addresses parliament, denouncing the "obscene violence" whereby the fascists have won the recent election. There is noisy barracking. Musso- lini sits silent, frowning, immobile; but his supporters shout and shake their fists and attempt to drag Matteotti from the podium. A voice from the government benches yells: "We will teach you to respect us by kicking you or shooting you in the back!" Matteotti waits until he can be heard again above the hubbub and then continues his indictment of the government. He protests against the formation of the illegal mili- tia. He declares: "You want to hurl the country backwards, towards absolutism."

He knows exactly what he is risking. In conclusion he turns to his friends and says, smiling: "Now you can prepare my funeral oration."

26 MAY 1924. D'Annunzio has a new pet, a tortoise that Luisa Casati bought for him from a zoo in Hamburg. The gardeners call it Caro- lina. D'Annunzio, aiming for a higher tone, names it Cheli (Greek for tortoise).

10 JUNE 1924. Matteotti is walking along the Tiber, in the centre of Rome. Not only has he challenged the fascist government in parliament,

he is an accomplished lawyer with important connections abroad. It is widely believed that he is gathering evidence of corruption within the fascist government, and particularly of bribes paid by an American oil company to secure control of petrol distribution in Italy.

As Matteotti walks alone, five men surround him and drag him into a car. They all belong to an undercover group of fascist hitmen known as the *Ceka* (after the Soviet secret police). Matteotti is stabbed to death. His killers drive around the city for several hours, before eventually taking his corpse out into the countryside and burying it in a shallow grave beside the road, where it will be found two months later. It is rapidly established that their car was parked the previous night in the courtyard of the Ministry of the Interior. Late in the evening, one of the men visits Mussolini and shows him a small piece of blood-stained upholstery.

Mussolini denies any responsibility for the murder and orders his associates to create "confusion" about the facts of the case. He announces that the investigation will be conducted, not by the independent magistrates but by the fascist chief of police. He tells his staff: "If I get away with this we will all survive, otherwise we shall all sink together."

Throughout the next two weeks d'Annunzio is at work revising his autobiographical essays for publication, working, so he tells Treves, from two each afternoon until five o'clock the following morning. He makes no recorded comment on Matteotti's death.

13 JUNE 1924. Some one hundred anti-fascist deputies—democrats, socialists and members of the Catholic Popolari Party—declare that the fascist government is "unconstitutional" and walk out of Montecitorio, boycotting parliament to signal their condemnation of the killing of Matteotti. Their withdrawal, known, after the fifth-century BC revolt of the Roman *plebs*, as the "Aventine Secession," is a disastrous mistake. Mussolini calls for a vote of confidence, and with all the opposition absent, easily wins it.

G. Ward Price writes in the *Daily Mail*: "Not in our time only, but down through history Mussolini will remain an inspiration to all who prize freedom and love their native lands."

D'ANNUNZIO COMMUNICATES WITH HIS DOMESTIC STAFF IN WRITING. Now he writes in playfully salacious mode to his cook, whom he addresses as Sister Albina. He loves her pastries and cream cakes, to each variety of which he gives a sacred name. The "five eyes of St. Ninfa" is a chocolate and chestnut confection topped with five dollops of whipped cream. Now he tells her that he has been informed by Aélis ("the Abbess") that the biscuits she produced the previous evening are known in France as "nuns' breasts." He signs his letter "Father Prior."

15 JUNE 1924. The fascist government pay d'Annunzio an enormous sum (the price, perhaps, of his silence) for the manuscript of *Glory*, the play in which—it is generally agreed by fascist critics—he described the kind of leader with whom Italy has now been blessed, Mussolini.

D'Annunzio writes to Antonietta Treves, his editor's wife, asking her to buy him two large garden umbrellas, one with red stripes, one with blue, and a quantity of the very best opoponax for the concoction of perfumes. This summer he acquires the house next door, the handsome Villa Mirabella with its balconies and apricot-coloured stucco, as a guesthouse. For all his talk of hermitages and melancholy, he is quite the host. Ida Rubinstein comes to stay. No sooner has she left than Luisa Casati arrives. And a week after Casati's departure d'Annunzio's wife takes her place: he takes pleasure in welcoming her as the Principessa di Monte Nevoso. Four decades ago their elopement opened a way for him into the aristocracy: now he has conferred a title on her.

23 JULY 1924. D'Annunzio writes to one of his former legionaries describing the political situation as a "fetid ruin." It is the nearest he will ever come to commenting on Matteotti's death. When the letter is made public Rizzo reports to Mussolini that neither this, nor any other public statement of d'Annunzio's, should be taken at face value. Rizzo thinks d'Annunzio may have written the letter as an "alibi" in case anti-fascists ever return to power. The poet "has never been fascist," says Rizzo, but he is now politically quiescent.

SEPTEMBER 1924. A fascist deputy is shot dead in a Roman street. Roberto Farinacci, most aggressive of the fascist *ras*, blames the communists and calls out for vengeance: "The land of Mazzini and Dante must not be consigned to Lenin." The squads are out in force, bullying and beating suspected socialists and trashing their property.

Luigi Pirandello, Italy's other famous playwright, sends a telegram to Mussolini. "If Your Excellency deems me worthy of entering the National Fascist Party, I will consider it the greatest honour to occupy the post of your most humble and obedient follower." D'Annunzio is to blame for saying nothing about Matteotti's murder, but at least he does not say this.

4 OCTOBER 1924. The painters Guido Marussig and Guido Cadorin have joined d'Annunzio's more or less permanent staff of craftsmen and artists. With Maroni they are busy transforming d'Annunzio's rickety old house into a sacred space—part Franciscan, part Buddhist, part nineteenth-century decadent, entirely solipsistic. D'Annunzio announces in an open letter to the Province of Brescia that he is not interested in anything occurring outside the walls of his property.

Now he writes to Cadorin, who is working on the "Room of the Leper," which contains a coffin filled with earth from the cemetery at Fiume. Cadorin has produced to d'Annunzio's order a painting entitled *Saint Francis Embracing d'Annunzio the Leper.* Cut off from the world, speaking to multitudes while himself unseen, d'Annunzio identifies with lepers.

The dark little chamber is turning out to be frightfully expensive, for all its supposed Franciscan austerity. The walls and couch are covered with deerskin, which may have been easy to come by in the woods around Assisi in the twelfth century, but which, in the 1920s, is an extremely costly furnishing fabric. The skins are laced together with gilded thongs. Cadorin has made a black lacquered wardrobe decorated with paintings of some of d'Annunzio's favourite motifs—a nude archer, a greyhound, a rearing horse, an aeroplane, a woman bound and naked.

Writing to Cadorin, d'Annunzio addresses him as "Brother Guidotto" and signs himself "Brother Fire."

BETWEEN 27 DECEMBER 1924 AND 2 JANUARY 1925, tens of thousands of armed blackshirts rampaged through Italian cities, wrecking anti-fascists' houses and breaking into the prisons to release their fellows. Further evidence linking Mussolini to Matteotti's murder was made public. Salandra, the wartime prime minister whose support had seemed to legitimise the fascist government, went over to the opposition. The commanders of the militia told Mussolini that unless he broke the opposition, the fascist movement would do so without him. It was widely expected that the King would dismiss Mussolini and declare martial law.

In this crisis Mussolini made a move to silence at least one potentially dangerous critic—he confirmed the contract declaring that the Vittoriale was a "National Monument." This was perhaps the greatest of his gifts to d'Annunzio. Henceforward the cost of the building works on the property would be borne by the state.

D'ANNUNZIO ACQUIRES A GRAMOPHONE. Initially its poor sound quality—"just barking"—seems "horrendous" to his fastidious ear, but he quickly grasps its potential. All his life he has sought out musicians; now he can have music night and day. Choral singing, issuing mysteriously from a hidden source, will greatly enhance the seduction scenes he stages in his oratory-cum-boudoir.

30 DECEMBER 1924. Mussolini calls all deputies to return from their Christmas holidays by 3 January to hear him make an important speech.

3 JANUARY 1925. He addresses parliament. He acknowledges, or rather boasts, that the violence now endemic in Italian life is the result of "a particular climate" that he himself has created. (So he denies his debt to d'Annunzio, that "climate's" true originator.) "I declare that I, and I alone, assume political, moral and historical responsibility for all that has happened."

Like d'Annunzio defiantly advocating lynch law on the Capitol in 1915, Mussolini goes on: "If fascism has been a criminal association, I am the head of that criminal association." He is effectively admitting to having murdered an opposition leader, and threatening to repeat the crime as often as he deems necessary. "Italy wants peace, tranquillity and calm industriousness, gentlemen." He will grant Italy that peace "with love, if possible," but, "when two powers clash and are irreconcilable, force is the answer." He is laying claim to the dictatorship and announcing that he will defend it brutally.

His speech is greeted with tumultuous applause and cries of "Viva Mussolini!" Farinacci strides across the chamber and shakes him by the hand. Prefects throughout the country are ordered to close down forthwith any organisation suspected of "undermining the state." By nightfall, fascist militia and police are arresting members of opposition parties.

JANUARY 1925. More presents for d'Annunzio are arriving from Mussolini. D'Annunzio is a small man who feels comfortable in confined spaces and cherishes precious objects that can be held in the palm of a hand. Mussolini, whose taste is always for the outsize, presents him regardless with Brobdingnagian souvenirs.

First comes the MAS in which he carried out the "Buccari prank." D'Annunzio will have a hangar for it built on the hill above his house.

Then comes a seaplane in working order. D'Annunzio calls it *Alcyone*, after his own poem-cycle. General Diaz gives him more mementoes, the casings of several unexploded shells. D'Annunzio has some of them mounted on a bridge, the Bridge of the Iron Heads. The others are placed on plinths and columns around the grounds.

Next comes the prow of the *Puglia*. Set into the steep slope, the demi-battleship looms over d'Annunzio's rose garden like an alarmingly apt political allegory—the poet's playground overshadowed by lethal might.

2 FEBRUARY 1925. D'Annunzio is in his dining room, eating, and making notes. On the table are violets and narcissi, the first of the year. He meditates on the contrast between the soft loveliness of the ephemeral petals, and the hard, shiny durability of the enamelled peacocks.

He is still troubled by hallucinations in his damaged eye, and his vision in the other is distorted. Flat planes appear to be sculpted in relief. Colours are oddly pronounced. He sees double: an object seen up close has its copy on the horizon, one in the distance has a duplicate looming close by. He is stoical about these annoyances, but one-eyed, he finds it hard to judge distances. Pouring a drink, he misses the glass and spills wine or water on his papers. This is something about which he seldom complains, but which may explain his preference for eating alone.

He keeps Great Danes now, dogs as tall as his waist, whose names all begin with the same letters as his own—Danki, Danzetta, Dannaggio, Dannozzo, Dannissa.

In the Vittoriale women come and go: an actress he knew in Paris, whom he entertains to a Franciscan-style supper of red and yellow beans, served in the Room of the Leper; the Italian film actress Elena Sangro, with whom he first made love in Rome in 1919 in the hectic weeks before his march on Fiume.

29 MAY 1925. Mussolini visits the Vittoriale again. D'Annunzio has placed an inscription in the antechamber. "To the Visitor: Are you

carrying the mirror of Narcissus? . . . Fit your mask to your face/But consider that you are glass against steel." If a minatory message is intended, Mussolini ignores it. D'Annunzio takes him across the lake on the MAS. Mussolini keeps his mackintosh tightly belted, but manages to look politely entertained. In the evening a string quartet plays Beethoven and Debussy. After Mussolini leaves, d'Annunzio comes out onto a balcony and reads to an assembled crowd a telegram he and the *Duce* together have sent to the King, announcing their mutual regard. "So," notes Rizzo in his next report, "the last hopes of those who had obstinately attempted to set the two patriots against each other vanish."

D'ANNUNZIO IS IN HIS GARDEN. He is lying on the grass. Around him are rocks from the battle sites, a captured Austrian machine gun, a stone lion from Sebenico, but his sight line is so low he sees only tiny flowers, blue, yellow and white, like those on which an angel might tread in a painting of the Annunciation. His dogs find him there. He orders them to lie down and gradually they quieten around him until man and dogs seem to be breathing in accord. From an upstairs window Luisa calls to him in Shakespearean English, "Come with a thought, delicate Ariel."

22 JUNE 1925. Mussolini announces that the entire nation must be "fascisticised." He boasts of his own "intransigence" and declares that he will "ferociously implement" his "ferocious will." Anti-fascist politicians and intellectuals are leaving the country. Those who stay are intimidated, bullied, or beaten up. Giovanni Amendola—the liberal journalist and politician who courageously published the evidence incriminating Mussolini after Matteotti's death—is beaten to death.

1925. Throughout the summer d'Annunzio is expanding his estate. He buys a tower down on the lake. He sets Maroni to work on a grand portico, dedicated to his "parent" Michelangelo, at the entrance to his property. He buys another adjoining house, the Hotel Washington. In July his wife visits him (Luisa Baccara and her sister are packed off to Cortina for the duration of her visit). Other visitors, including Toscanini, come and go. D'Annunzio escorts them around his domain, which is by now famous for its eccentricities. He takes them on to the *Puglia* where the sailors parade for their inspection. Visitors of sufficient importance are honoured by the firing of the ship's guns.

OCTOBER 1925. Mussolini announces his special contribution to political theory—the doctrine of totalitarianism. All opposition parties, unions and associations are banned: henceforward Italy is a one-party state. Five years earlier d'Annunzio and de Ambris finished drafting the Charter of Carnaro, with its corporations within which every citizen was to be contained. Back then Mussolini, still casting around for a political programme, was declaring: "I start with the individual and proceed against the state." The state was "asphyxiating," so he then thought, it "causes nothing but harm." Now, exactly reversing his position, he delivers his tolling declaration of the death of individualism: "Everything in the State, nothing outside the State, nothing against the State."

4 OCTOBER 1925. D'Annunzio, who has been complaining vociferously about the noise of the village's church bells, makes a noise of his own,

personally firing a twenty-one-gun salute from the *Puglia* to celebrate the anniversary of his bombing raid on Cattaro.

The décor of d'Annunzio's bedroom is finally ready. Black lacquer, gilded carving and blue-and-gold striped wallpaper provide the background to the usual superfluity of textiles and vases and figurines. In a marbled niche over the fireplace stands a gilded copy of an intensely erotic Greek stele of "Leda with the Swan." The room is full of phallic symbols—columns and spears, ears of wheat and elephants' tusks.

NOVEMBER 1925. The party of the reformist socialists is proscribed.

D'ANNUNZIO IS THINKING OF DEATH. He writes to Mussolini proposing a one-way expedition by airship to the North Pole. "Think of planting our banner in that inaccessible place, and remaining there, at the foot of the flagpole, watching, with unflinching eye, the victorious dirigible departing for the fatherland!"

Mussolini ignores the death wish, takes the proposal literally and invites d'Annunzio to come to Rome to discuss it further. D'Annunzio doesn't budge. He will never see Rome again. Instead of becoming an explorer-hero, he entertains one. The aviator Francesco Pinedo, who has accomplished the flight to Tokyo d'Annunzio himself contemplated in 1919, visits the Vittoriale, and adds the propeller of his seaplane to d'Annunzio's collection of heroic hardware. Speeches, *Alalàs* and so much ceremonial firing of the *Puglia*'s guns that afterwards d'Annunzio has to apply to Mussolini for a further supply of gunpowder.

IN DECEMBER 1925, Luigi Albertini—who has spoken out in print and in person against Mussolini—is sacked from the editorship of the *Corriere della Sera*. Mussolini declares that Italy is "in a situation of permanent war." Alceste de Ambris is stripped of his citizenship and leaves for France.

JANUARY 1926. Mussolini announces that this will be fascism's Napoleonic year. Napoleon is one of his role models. He has even written a play about him. D'Annunzio, who has been a Bonapartist since his schooldays, has a shrine for Napoleonic memorabilia at the Vittoriale—Napoleon's death mask, his hour glass and a snuff box he used on St. Helena, all displayed on a lectern whose base is a Roman eagle sculpted in travertine.

The deputies of the Popolari Party attempt to resume their seats in Montecitorio. They are driven away by fascist guards.

SPRING 1926. D'Annunzio is promoted to the rank of general. He celebrates by ordering himself three fine new uniforms, and high boots to go with them. When Mussolini makes a bellicose speech saying that the Austrians must be driven out of Trento, d'Annunzio signals his agreement by firing twenty-seven rounds from the *Puglia*.

Ida Rubinstein is performing *The Martyrdom of St. Sebastian* at La Scala in Milan, with Toscanini conducting. D'Annunzio, wearing his new general's uniform, watches from a box.

CLEMENTINE CHURCHILL MEETS MUSSOLINI and finds him "quite simple and natural, very dignified . . . [with] beautiful golden brown piercing eyes." She is one of numerous women entranced by the muscular *Duce*, whose image is now omnipresent. Like d'Annunzio, Mussolini understands the political power of a picture. An estimated thirty million photographs of him, in 2,500 different poses, are in circulation.

On 28 March he addresses 50,000 blackshirts at a hippodrome. The uniforms of these new "dark angels of the apocalypse," the salutes, the songs, the incantatory exchanges between orator and crowd, all are in the style d'Annunzio set in Fiume. So are Mussolini's death-besotted sentiments. "It is beautiful to live, but if it is necessary it will be still more beautiful to die."

OUT OF THE PUBLIC EYE, surrounded by his little court, d'Annunzio becomes playful. He teases. He sends himself up. He writes the following note to his cook:

> Dear, dear Albina, [he also calls her "Sister Sauce"]
>
> It is years and years since I ate a boiled egg cut into four.
> Yours is cooked to absolute perfection.
> It is sublime.
> When I was a child, I used to ask for the egg to be spread with a small amount of anchovy paste. I used to lick my fingers and sometimes I went so far as to swallow them up to the first joint. Tonight I experienced that divine ecstasy again. I slide under the table in a faint no woman will ever provoke in me.
> Albina, may you be praised for evermore. And shine in eternity in the Constellation of the Egg and Nebula of the Anchovy! Amen.

7 APRIL 1926. A middle-aged Irish lady, Violet Gibson, shoots Mussolini at point-blank range on the Capitol. Turning his head aside to acknowledge some students who are singing *Giovinezza* (signature tune of the legionaries of Fiume—now the fascist anthem), he escapes with a slightly nicked nose. That afternoon, wearing sticking plaster, he makes another stirring speech. D'Annunzio urges his followers: "Remember always to dare." Mussolini tells his to: "Live dangerously" and to follow the soldier's code: "If I go forward, follow me. If I retreat, kill me. If I die, avenge me."

JUNE 1926. A state-funded Institute for the Publication of the Complete Works of d'Annunzio is founded: the volumes in question, all forty-four of them, are to be published by Arnaldo Mondadori (whom d'Annunzio, revelling in this new source of income, dubs Monte d'Oro—mountain of gold). This is immensely gratifying to d'Annunzio's vanity. It will keep him happily occupied for the remainder of his life, editing, revising, collating, fussing over paper quality and page design.

SEPTEMBER 1926. Paola von Ostheim, Princess of Saxe-Weimar, visits d'Annunzio at the Vittoriale. She first caught his eye twenty-one years previously, when she was in Rome for treatment of a damaged ear drum. Returning from the doctor after an agonising procedure, she was half-carried to her hotel room, passing by d'Annunzio, who was chatting in the corridor with a princely acquaintance. A beautiful stranger, faint and in evident pain, was a bait to which d'Annunzio could not but rise. She looked, he noted, as tender and long-legged as an antelope.

He wheedled his way past the small crowd of her attendants into her room, where he feasted his eyes on her—"white rose and gold-flecked Murano glass"—as she lay barely conscious on the bed. He slipped away but sent her a little golden box with an invitation to visit him in Settignano. The Princess never took up the invitation, but now she publishes her memoirs, sends d'Annunzio a copy, and is invited to the Vittoriale. This time she accepts.

She is picked up from the station by an aviator driving a huge red sports car, and taken at breakneck speed up the hill to the Vittoriale. Ushered into the Prioria's cramped hallway she waits until a gust of Eau de Coty announces the appearance of her host. White uniform. Flabby cheeks powdered white. Eyes damp and slightly shifty.

In her account the Princess glosses over what follows, but d'Annunzio's notes record their love-making in cruel detail. Her antelope-like legs are still beautiful, but the rest of her is so much aged he prefers not to see it. "My cunning in covering her torso with a gold shift, and hiding her face in the shadows of many cushions."

The Princess has brought him a marvellous offering: a gold clasp from Mycenae, a piece of ancient treasure which is also a delicate tribute to the author of *The Dead City*. In the morning she sends it to him by the hand of one of the "Clarissas." He sends it back to her, in a golden box. She protests that she intended him to keep it. He returns it again, this time with a testy note. "Excuse me. I was in the bath. I do not—do you understand?—want this gift."

1926. Margherita Sarfatti, Mussolini's Jewish mistress, publishes her biography of him, *Dux*. She portrays Mussolini as a genius, the quintessence of Italian virtue, and a martyr. His body, when he was invalided home from the war, she writes, was like that of "Saint Sebastian, his flesh pierced as with arrows." This is a conscious borrowing: Sarfatti knows d'Annunzio's writing. She calls the poet the "Lord of Fiume," the father of futurism and the originator of the "stormy gladiatorial attitudes" of virile nationalist literature.

THE REFURBISHMENT OF D'ANNUNZIO'S MUSIC ROOM IS COMPLETE. It contains fifteen columns—red marble, black marble, ebony—none of which have any structural function. They are arranged asymmetrically: their placement, according to d'Annunzio, is the concrete expression of a musical fugue. Atop them are vari-coloured glass lamps in the shape of gourds or fruit baskets, made for d'Annunzio by Napoleone Martinuzzi, a master glass-blower from Murano whom he calls "Brother Nape." Here the "Vittoriale Quartet," a group of Venetian musicians whom d'Annunzio patronises, perform on their frequent visits.

AUTUMN 1926. After surviving another assassination attempt Mussolini dismisses his Minister for the Interior, and adds the ministry to the many he already holds. Those members of the opposition who withdrew as the "Aventine Secession" are formally deprived of their parliamentary seats. The communist leader Antonio Gramsci is arrested again and tried by Mussolini's "special tribunal." He will die in prison. Francesco Nitti, d'Annunzio's *Cagoia*, is stripped of his citizenship and goes into exile. The fascist-friendly newspaper *L'Impero* goes further, calling—in terms as virulent as d'Annunzio's once were—for Nitti to be condemned to death, "the sentence to be executed by any Italian citizen who can succeed in catching him."

Mussolini is proclaimed "Caesar of the Modern Empire." The ceremony involves much deployment of Roman eagles, fasces and a gilded throne. A textbook designed for the *Balilla*, the fascist boys' movement, announces, "Caesar has come to life again in the *Duce*; he rides at the head of numberless cohorts, treading down all cowardice and all impurities to re-establish the culture and the new might of Rome."

D'Annunzio, who has been calling since the previous century for a revival of what Mussolini calls *Romanità*, receives another big present: a pair of Roman arches donated by the city of Vicenza. Maroni has them re-erected in the Vittoriale's grounds.

14 JANUARY 1927. Winston Churchill meets Mussolini and is charmed by the dictator's "gentle and simple bearing."

The wild men of the squads are being eliminated. Their violence was useful in bringing Mussolini to power, but they are too anarchic and unpredictable to form part of his new regime. Thousands of them are expelled from the party. Fascism is now respectable.

Mussolini has learnt another lesson from d'Annunzio. He tells parliament that he intends to strengthen the navy and to "make the air force—in which I believe increasingly—numerically so strong and powerful that the roar of its engines will drown out every other sound in the peninsula, and the surface of its wings will blot out the sun across our land."

11 SEPTEMBER, 1927. The anniversary of the march from Ronchi is celebrated with a performance of *Jorio's Daughter* in the gardens of the Vittoriale. The Duke of Aosta is there, representing the King, and so are luminaries of the theatrical world including Meyerhold, Stanislavsky and Max Reinhardt. D'Annunzio is in his general's uniform, and the opening of each act is signalled with cannon shots. The poet's retreat is becoming—despite his insistence on his desire for tranquillity and solitude—a performance venue. He is planning a pond in the shape of a violin, with a platform at one end on which he can stage dances.

1927. A new fascist calendar is introduced, full of days sacred to Italy's glorious past or to its tragic dead. The new year begins on 29 October, and the years are numbered as beginning in 1922.

War memorials are springing up all over the country. As d'Annunzio has done so many times before, Mussolini repeatedly invokes the 600,000 war dead, urging Italians to be worthy of their sacrifice. Schoolchildren were invited to feel pride in being "born on this soil bathed by so much blood, sanctified by so many martyrs."

MORNING, 21 SEPTEMBER 1927. D'Annunzio is in his bedroom. A woman has just left. A disordered bed. An overturned scent bottle. A little gold box in which a few traces of cocaine remain. A cold supper laid out on a table. D'Annunzio hasn't yet touched the food, but the woman ate some of it during the night, while he returned to his own room mid-"orgy" to wash and change into a fresh silk nightshirt. Now, alone, he eats ravenously: the figs and the prosciutto each remind him of his visitor's cunt.

16 MARCH 1928. A new law decrees that in future elections all parliamentary candidates will be selected by the Grand Fascist Council. Giolitti, now aged eighty-six, is the only deputy to speak out against it.

D'ANNUNZIO'S DEPRESSION, which he gives its Latin name "*taedium vitae*," has many causes, but one is the fame which he once so assiduously courted. He says he is a *mostro*, an ambiguous word meaning both "monster" and "show" (as in freak show).

Three former legionaries reach the Vittoriale, having travelled all the way from Naples on foot, like pilgrims. D'Annunzio refuses to see them. Another devotee is injured falling from a tree which he has climbed in the hope of catching sight of d'Annunzio walking in his garden. Maroni is set to work to build a girdle of high walls around the domain.

1929. Mussolini moves his office to the Palazzo Venezia in the heart of Rome. He sets up his desk in a room called the Sala del Mappamondo, which also happens to be the name d'Annunzio has given his library in the Vittoriale. D'Annunzio estimates that he has 75,000 books. Increasingly secluded from the living, he keeps company with those of the dead he considers his peers. He reads Montaigne and Dante. He argues with them in his jotted notes, and agrees with them warmly when they lend their authority to his own opinions.

D'Annunzio's "World Map Room" is small, dominated by a collection of fine editions of the *Divine Comedy* and a five-foot-long model of a Venetian galley suspended from the ceiling. Mussolini's is immense. One journalist remarks that you need a pair of binoculars to see him across it. The two rooms are both freighted with significance and knowingly designed for their occupants' glorification. Mussolini's mosaic floor shows Europa being raped by Jupiter in the form of a bull, just as the world is now to be dominated by the bull-necked *Duce*. His private secretary reports that women, a different one almost every day, are brought to him in his office for brisk bouts of sex.

The Palazzo Venezia is Mussolini's stage, as the Governor's Palace in Fiume was d'Annunzio's. Day after day he speaks to his people from his balcony. His gestures are deliberately exaggerated, as d'Annunzio required his actors to be after he had read about the gestural language of the ancient Greek drama. Mussolini grimaces and clenches his fists and throws his arms around. His body language looks impetuous, but it is carefully rehearsed.

12 MAY 1929. D'Annunzio spends a night with a lesbian. They have thrilling sex, but in the morning he has her taken unceremoniously away. While she is sitting on her suitcase in the station, he eats little cakes with marmalade. He loves these tranquil post-coital breakfasts. He asks for a glass of Mumm champagne, and his sensations, on a fresh morning filled with birdsong, seem to him to transcend human experience.

10 NOVEMBER 1929. Guido Keller, d'Annunzio's action secretary from Fiume, is killed in a car crash. D'Annunzio has his body brought to the Vittoriale, keeps vigil over it on the deck of the Puglia, and then buries it in his grounds. He talks to Maroni about plans for a mausoleum.

The Marchesa Casati visits again. D'Annunzio tells her that the tortoise she gave him has died after eating a surfeit of tuberoses. In a knowing allusion to the tortoise which made its way from de Montesquiou's reality into Huysmans's fiction, d'Annunzio has had his favourite animal sculptor Renato Brozzi give it bronze legs and head, and it is placed at the head of the table in the new dining room as a warning—d'Annunzio explains—against gluttony. This room, in his opinion, is the only one in the Prioria which is not "sad." Scarlet and gold walls, brilliant blue and gold barrel-vaulted ceiling: everything lacquered shiny bright. This is a modern room, hard-edged, slick and jazzy.

MARCH 1930. Mussolini addresses party leaders. He is parroting d'Annunzio again. The world believes, he says, that Italians cannot fight. It is their task to disprove the slander, by reviving the culture of the mediaeval condottieri who "had temperaments of steel, and brought all their courage, their hatred and their passion to bear in war." Modern Italians must do likewise because "the prestige of nations is determined almost exclusively by their military glories, their armed might." This is why d'Annunzio wrote Francesca da Rimini, and why he wanted Italy to go to war in 1915.

D'Annunzio is working alongside the craftsmen embellishing his Wildean "House Beautiful." He mellows the stark white of new plaster by brushing it lightly with a mixture of tea and coffee (a trick he learned from an American woman in the first years of the century in Venice, when he was happy there with Duse). He paints a length of silk with the signs of the zodiac, a realisation in the real world of the marvellous bedspread he described nearly half a century earlier in his first novel. It is a wedding present for Mussolini's daughter Edda, who is marrying the son of d'Annunzio's old friend Ciano.

He has a collection of scarves and shawls and slips and kimonos and stockings with which to dress up each "Clarissa of passage." He is a stylist as a well as a lover. Hard to know which he enjoys more, the dressing of a new woman, or her undressing.

D'ANNUNZIO AND AÉLIS are both crazy about jazz. He sends a servant to Milan to buy records by the dozen. *"Jazz-band. Jazz-band. Jazz-band!"* (his English). He tells a friend: "We dance every night."

The Vittoriale is covered with words—mottoes, warnings, instructions, couplets from d'Annunzio's own poems. There are snatches from the canticles of St. Francis. There are unorthodox beatitudes: "Blessed are those who die in a just war." A Latin inscription in the entrance hall introduces the host. "I am Gabriel who stands before the gods/Among the winged brothers uniquely sighted."

Mussolini likes mottoes too: "Who dares wins." "War is to a man what motherhood is to a woman." "He who hesitates is lost" (this is an old saying, but Mussolini probably lifted it from d'Annunzio's *Glory*). "Fidelity is stronger than fire." "Mussolini is always right." "Let us have a dagger between our teeth, a bomb in our hands and infinite scorn in our hearts." "Hang the weak."

JUNE 1930. The Italians are in Libya. Pietro Badoglio, who played such an equivocal part in the story of d'Annunzio's Fiume, is the governor. Telling his men they must be "ferocious and inexorable," he and his military colleagues round up over 100,000 civilians—women, children and old men—march them across the desert (in some cases for over a thousand kilometres) and intern them in barbed-wire compounds near Benghazi. Over the next three years over forty per cent of the internees will die of disease or malnutrition. Libyans resisting the occupation are bombarded from the air with poison gas.

In celebration, d'Annunzio commissions a medal from Renato Brozzi. Ivory and gold (d'Annunzio relishes the word "chryselephantine"); an elephant, trunk raised; the words *Teneo te Africa.*

AUGUST 1931. D'Annunzio is an avid reader of *Domus*, a magazine devoted to interior decoration and edited by the architect and designer Gio Ponti. Many of the craftsmen working on d'Annunzio's house first came to his attention through its pages. Now Ponti himself is refurbishing d'Annunzio's bathroom, which has marbled walls and lapis blue sanitary ware. Glass-maker Pietro Chiesa contributes a Japanese-inspired Art Deco window with a swirling design made up of the outstretched wings of herons in shades of blue from darkest indigo to brilliant ultramarine. D'Annunzio is still delighted by new technology, still keeping up with aesthetic fashion.

He likes to shuffle his possessions. He balances an ancient green glass alembic on a damascened Persian helmet. He likes the effect.

OCTOBER 1931. Giovanni Giuriati, d'Annunzio's erstwhile first minister, is Mussolini's party secretary. Now, as in Fiume, Giuriati is loyal but open-eyed. He is dismayed by Mussolini's boastfulness and his cynical acceptance of corruption.

SEPTEMBER 1931. D'Annunzio, who came to Gardone, he said, in search of silence, has now been living for a decade in the hubbub of a building site.

Maroni is dispatched to Pompeii to study the amphitheatre, and then set to work designing his patron another one big enough to accommodate 1,500 people. He is also building a garage. D'Annunzio still adores cars, and regularly receives Fiat's latest models as gifts from his wartime associate Giovanni Agnelli. Cars are female, he rules. His favourites are as graceful and lively as women, but much more obedient. He is particularly pleased with his bright yellow one.

18 FEBRUARY 1932. D'Annunzio asks Mussolini for funds for more building. He is not expanding his living space. Far from it. Antongini likens the Vittoriale to Versailles, that vast palace where visitors are startled by the tininess of Marie Antoinette's private apartments. D'Annunzio is planning a museum of war, with a concert hall, a cinema and a hanging garden (the latter is never to be realised). There must be a great many Persian carpets and "other beautiful, rich things." And there must, of course, be first-rate bathrooms.

All these will be housed in d'Annunzio's new "citadel" designed by Maroni in the style of Giorgio de Chirico's architectural fantasies.

D'Annunzio calls it *Schifamondo*—escape from the world—an allusion to the seaside villa in which a part of *Pleasure* was set, which in turn was named after the fourteenth-century d'Este Palace in Ferrara. Far larger and more pompous in style than the sprawling over-decorated Prioria of which it is an offshoot, it has tall, smooth, vertical surfaces, unadorned arches, the grandeur of height and space and implied power. D'Annunzio hasn't seen any fascist architecture—he never leaves home now—but, avidly reading illustrated magazines, he has identified, with his usual acute eye for novelty, the essence of the new aesthetic.

The cinema is a great success. While Maroni acts as projectionist, d'Annunzio watches films in rapt silence. (In public cinemas, films are shown with live musical accompaniment.) He enjoys westerns. His favourite star is Greta Garbo. He likes Fritz Lang's *Metropolis*, *The Mask of Zorro*, Chaplin's *The Gold Rush*. He shakes with laughter at the antics of Harold Lloyd.

Mussolini enjoys comic films too. It is after watching Laurel and Hardy that he decides to leave off wearing his bowler hat. He hadn't previously realised that his favourite headgear might be considered funny.

SEPTEMBER 1931. D'Annunzio writes about diaphanous blouses, a new fashion of which he heartily approves, and about silk stockings, about the way their colour is only visible at their seams, as the colour of a fine Murano glass is perceptible only in its rim. Memories of Nike have set him off on this train of thought. Now they become more explicit. Menstrual blood on his fingers, the silvery skin on her breasts, his "indefatigable poignard" thrusting away. Sex as a stimulus to writing: writing as a means to sexual stimulation. D'Annunzio's libido has always been his most helpful muse.

Eating watermelon, he seeks for similes with which to express his pleasure in its glassy pinks and greens. Sometimes he eats nothing for days on end—his appetite killed by cocaine—but he takes lascivious pleasure in the eventual satisfying of his hunger. He is a connoisseur of spring water. He abominates coffee now—especially coffee with milk, *"Puah!'*

He says that the three wonders of the terrestrial world are lobster, the pubic hair of a blonde woman, and the "clean, clean, clean" flavour of oranges. He enjoys delivering dicta of this kind. He also says that "a greyhound or a thoroughbred race horse, Ida Rubinstein's legs, the body of an *Ardito* fording the Piave, the form and structure of my highly polished cranium—these are the most beautiful phenomena in the world."

He is still taking sleeping pills, which control the pain in his useless eye and relieve him of his exhausting hallucinations. He has vivid dreams from which he awakens as though from a trance. Immured in his gorgeous refuge, he likens himself to Napoleon on St. Helena, to a werewolf, to Bluebeard in his castle, to Nero the artist-tyrant, or to an ancient king, entombed with his treasure "according to ancient rites."

He has another gramophone. The futurist painter Carlo Carra calls him "the gramophone-prophet." This one is in the little ante-room called the Room of the Mask, with its art deco bronze horse and its Murano glass chandelier which is supposed to represent a cluster of cornucopiae, but looks more like a bunch of ice-cream cones. He listens to jazz, foxtrots, spirituals, rumba. He has a record of Josephine Baker's *J'ai deux amours*, and plays it until it is all but worn out.

12 DECEMBER 1931. The ceremonies and liturgy of fascism are becoming ever more elaborate, its choreography more ambitious. Mussolini tells a journalist: "Every revolution creates new forms, new myths and new rites." It is decreed that every official meeting will begin, as d'Annunzio's did in Fiume, with a ritual "Salute to the *Duce*."

An article in the journal *Critica Fascista* urges Italians to imitate Mussolini (as Christians are enjoined to imitate Christ). A priest declares that Mussolini is St. Francis of Assisi reborn. Pilgrims arrive in his hometown in lorries decorated with flowers. They visit the house in which he was born, reverently kissing the walls, the furniture, the floor. Schoolchildren are being taught a new creed: "I believe in the high *Duce*—maker of the blackshirts . . . He came down to Rome; on the third day he re-established the state. He ascended into high office . . . ." D'Annunzio has been making this kind of political use of sacred rhetoric since before the war, but age hasn't rendered him devout. Jotting down some thoughts on the contrast between the ethereal "spark" of consciousness and the two "bestialities" of eating and sex, he writes: "God is a tyrant and a buffoon, with a fake crown and cap with bells on . . . I abominate him!"

APRIL 1932. D'Annunzio is sixty-nine years old and he is thinking, as he does almost constantly now, about mortality. Life, he writes, is "putrid," but it has a kind of lovely fuzz like that which gilds the legs of beautiful women. "I run my lips along each of them [life and women]." The pleasure is marvellous, but his lips can sense the imminent rot, the skeleton beneath the luminous flesh. He hears that an old friend has died. He asks his musicians to play him Beethoven's late string quartets, and he stays up until dawn listening. "Every profound piece of music weeps for the loss of something good."

6 JULY 1932. D'Annunzio is in a misanthropic mood. His relatives are milking him of money, he complains, until he feels like a Swiss cow, or like the many-breasted Diana of the Ephesians. His sister and niece come to visit him. He refuses to receive them.

JULY 1932. Mussolini's contribution to the national encyclopaedia is published. Written with the assistance of the philosopher Giovanni Gentile, it is on the "Doctrine of Fascism." Among the tenets are the following: individual freedom is a delusion; the only real virtue is dedication to the state; war bestows moral grandeur; Italy must continue to expand; man is ennobled by struggle; the nineteenth century was the century of the individual, the twentieth is a "collective" century, *"a fascist century."*

In an appendix to Mussolini's essay, the historian Giacchino Volpe laments the fascist heroes killed in fighting with "communists or deserters" during the turmoil of 1919. They were exemplary men, writes Volpe, and he sketches out a typical curriculum vitae. They were interventionists, they volunteered to fight and, best of all, they were legionaries at Fiume. D'Annunzio has still pointedly omitted to ask his followers to become fascists, but willy-nilly, the fascists are claiming them for their own.

OCTOBER 1932. The tenth anniversary of the March on Rome. The "Avenue of the Empires" has been cut through ancient Rome, slicing between the Colosseum and the Capitol. Eleven streets of what Mussolini scornfully calls "filthy picturesque" mediaeval buildings have been demolished to allow him to parade his military might in the heart of the city.

Four million people visit the "Exhibition of the Fascist Revolution" in the Palace of Exhibitions. The palace's neo-classical façade has been masked with a new frontage, all black and red and silver, with a colonnade of four gigantic fasces faced with riveted aluminium. The exhibition's most striking rooms are those framed as symbolic tableaux: the

Gallery of *Fasci*, a hall where pilasters rear upwards out of the wall as though in the fascist salute towards a ceiling inscribed with the word *"DUCE"*; the Hall of Mussolini, a mock-up of the leader's office; the Shrine of the Martyrs, a dark, domed room whose walls are covered with thousands of metal plaques, each representing a dead soldier. The art in which d'Annunzio has been experimenting in his seclusion—installation-art-cum-interior-décor—is now being practised on a massive scale by the regime.

In November, Mussolini visits d'Annunzio. He still needs to show his respect to the older man, who describes himself as the "Giver of cities and of coastlines, the precursor of all that is good about fascism."

30 JANUARY 1933. Adolf Hitler becomes Chancellor of Germany. Hitler has a great admiration for the "incomparable Mussolini," whom he considers a "brilliant statesman." There is much dividing the two leaders and their regimes—not least Nazi racial theory. Italians are not Aryan, they are not even Indo-European. They are "Mediterranean," third-best of the European blood groups. Then there is the fact that Italy betrayed Germany, siding with the Allies in the Great War, and there is the ongoing dispute over the South Tyrol/Trento. On the other side there is Italians' centuries-old hostility to their Austro-German oppressors.

Despite all this the two leaders are warmly disposed towards each other. Hitler keeps a life-size bust of Mussolini in his party headquarters in Munich and in 1922, a couple of weeks after his March on Rome, Mussolini was gratified to be informed by one of his agents that the Nazis' political programme "to restore the authority of the state; to abolish strikes . . . in a word to restore order," was "in great part taken from the Italian *Fascio*."

FEBRUARY 1933. Italo Balbo leads a flight of twenty-four seaplanes across the Atlantic, flying from Orbetello to Chicago and back in tight formation, an exploit as magnificent as d'Annunzio's once-projected flight to Tokyo would have been. During his stopover in the United States, Balbo is inducted into the Sioux tribe as Chief Flying Eagle, and enjoys himself at the coconut shies of Luna Park.

JULY 1933. After years of complaining about it, d'Annunzio succeeds in having the "filthy tavern" by the Vittoriale's entrance gate closed down and demolished. The drunkards there have been frightening off his lady friends, he tells his lawyer. In the newly cleared space, Maroni starts work on plans for the Square of the Fallen—a piazza-cum-war memorial. Stone arches frame an inscription describing the Vittoriale as a "religious book" composed of "living stones."

MUSSOLINI APPOINTS HIMSELF MINISTER OF CORPORATIONS. Fascist philosopher Ugo Spirito publishes a definition of "corporatism." It is opposed both to the "levelling state" (socialism) and the "anarchic individual" (liberalism). Its essence is unanimity. "Wills unite to form a single will: multiple goals coalesce to form a single goal." This monolithic state has at its apex the great leader. It is now conventional to use capitals when writing about Mussolini, as in writing about God. "The Revolution is Him. He is the Revolution." "He is the GENIUS who brings good fortune to the Italic people."

All citizens, workers or employers alike, must belong to one or other of the corporations, within which they will operate on equal terms "with full dedication to the cause of the nation and fascism." The constitution elaborated in Fiume by d'Annunzio and de Ambris has finally been realised.

FEBRUARY 1934. D'Annunzio has a new lover whom he calls Lachne, a twenty-five-year-old prostitute from Milan whom Aélis has found for him. Lachne has tuberculosis: she will die in four years' time. He loves her long hands, her pallor and the violet shadows around her eyes. She lodges above a trattoria, Lo Sport, down by the lake. He titillates himself with thinking of her in a narrow bed, in squalid surroundings. He writes verse in a mediaeval metre in celebration of her pubic hair. He sends his big shiny car to fetch her. He feeds her on his favourite risotto. He gives her a fur coat. He takes it off her, and strips her naked and then dresses her again, now in a golden tunic, now in a swathe of fine muslin he has painted himself. He writes her marvellous letters, describing their love-making, as he has done to so many women before her. When her period begins he dismisses her brusquely, and tells her to amuse herself at the cinema with another prostitute and leave him to his true love, Melancholy. After one of their extended trysts he overdoses himself with cocaine, collapses on the bed and passes out.

Mussolini decrees that Italians must be taught to love their country and its past. Displays of traditional costume, performances of folk dance and folk music, re-enactments of rustic ceremonies—both Christian and otherwise—like those d'Annunzio and Michetti used to track down in the 1880s, are encouraged in order to arouse "that national spirit without which nothing great has ever been achieved in this world."

JUNE 1934. D'Annunzio has written to Mussolini urging him to keep his distance from Hitler, "that ignoble face spattered with whitewash and glue." Mussolini, ignoring his advice, now meets Hitler for the first time, in Venice. It is not a happy visit. Hitler is revolted by the rooms full of degenerate modernist art on show at the Biennale. Mussolini thinks he looks like "a plumber in a mackintosh" and is bored by his diatribes. On returning to Germany, Hitler orders the murders of the Night of the Long Knives. The following month President von Hindenburg dies and Hitler assumes absolute power, proclaiming himself Führer. Nazis murder the Austrian chancellor Engelbert Dollfuss, with whom Mussolini has been friendly. Dollfuss's wife and children are staying with the Mussolini family at the time of his death.

Mussolini visits the Vittoriale again. Three days later, back in Rome, he and the King attend the opening of a production of *Jorio's Daughter*, directed by Pirandello and with sets designed by de Chirico. D'Annunzio and his work are still in favour.

D'Annunzio has a new playmate, a blonde young woman in her early twenties from the Alto Adige region, named Emy Huefler (opposite, on left). Sometimes he shuts himself into his private apartments with her for two or three days on end. Huefler will remain at the Vittoriale until d'Annunzio's death.

29 OCTOBER 1934. On the twelfth anniversary of the March on Rome, thirty-seven fascist "martyrs" are reburied in Santa Croce, the church in Florence where Michelangelo, Machiavelli and Galileo all lie. The coffins are carried through the streets in solemn procession—as those of d'Annunzio's Fiuman "martyrs" were—each one preceded by a banner bearing the dead man's name. The ceremony is at once sacred and secular. A newspaper comments on the "civil liturgy of fascism," and on the assembled crowd's "great faith," not in God, but in Mussolini.

8 NOVEMBER 1934. D'Annunzio is ill and depressed. He writes to sculptor Renato Brozzi. For three days, he says, his only companions have been Brozzi's bronze eagles, cats, ducks, gazelle, dogs and pigs. He identifies

with the last-named. He, the man who tripped around Fiume showing off a waist which looked, and perhaps was, corseted, has grown flabby. Food is a growing preoccupation. He writes to his cook telling her he has a "mad desire" for cutlets beaten to the thinness of a banana skin. To Brozzi he describes himself as an "angelic winged pig."

DECEMBER 1934. The Brescia Combatants' Association gives d'Annunzio a copy of the first-century statue of Victory which played a part in *Maybe Yes, Maybe No*. Maroni builds a temple in which to house it, within the tremendous honey-stuccoed loggias which now encircle d'Annunzio's house and link it with the towers of the Archives and Library. More such gifts follow. The commune of Milan present a newly commissioned *Victory of the Piave*, another woman in bondage, inspired by d'Annunzio's line: "On that shore of death we held Victory our immortal prisoner." Maroni places it atop a high pillar and surrounds it with a colonnade of broken arches.

JUNE 1935. A new Ministry of Popular Culture is inaugurated. Half a century earlier d'Annunzio had insisted that journalism had a greater influence than literature. Now fascists agree. To think that a political idea can spread via books and high culture, "with lots of homework," is a delusion. A leading fascist reflects that "the advent of the masses into political life" has made it necessary to advertise an ideology, just as one advertises a bank or a business. A leader's face, his tone, his words, must be repeated "over and over again through photography, film and photography once more . . . Just as in commercial advertising." Another d'Annunzian lesson learnt.

SEPTEMBER 1935. Publication of d'Annunzio's autobiography, *The Hundred and Hundred and Hundred Pages of the Secret Book by Gabriele d'Annunzio Tempted to Die. The Secret Book* is a discontinuous work: autobiography with fictional interjections, narrative repeatedly interrupted by musings. Most of it is based on material from d'Annunzio's notebooks, much of which has already been reworked and published in the *Faville*, or in *Notturno*. But though the matter is old, the form is modern, modernist in fact.

"These fragments I have shored against my ruins," wrote T. S. Eliot in 1922, the year d'Annunzio began work on what would become *The Secret Book*. D'Annunzio, converting his life into a literary mosaic of reminiscence and introspective thought and stored-up fragments of the by now enormous library of texts with which his mind is furnished, is once more displaying his gift for scenting the zeitgeist.

2 OCTOBER 1935. Mussolini, from the balcony of the Palazzo Venezia, declares war on Ethiopia. His speech is broadcast all over the country, booming out from loudspeakers in every piazza. Two weeks later the League of Nations condemns the invasion, and imposes sanctions against Italy. The British, many of whom have so far admired Mussolini, have second thoughts. Anthony Eden calls him a "complete gangster" and the "anti-Christ." But in Italy even those liberals who have been most critical of the regime, d'Annunzio's friend and editor Luigi Albertini among them, declare their support for Mussolini's attempt to win for Italians a "little place in the sun" and to expunge the shame of the defeat at Adua four decades earlier.

D'Annunzio writes to tell Mussolini he is moved "to my very depths—as by a kind of supernatural revelation." He offers Mussolini a sword bearing a solid gold model of the city of Fiume on its hilt. He writes a diatribe against the League of Nations and sends it, bound in crimson silk with gold clasps and tassels, to the French President Albert Lebrun. The President does not acknowledge it.

JANUARY 1936. Antongini visits d'Annunzio, having not seen him for a year. He is kept waiting for several days before he is granted an appointment and, when he is finally summoned to d'Annunzio's rooms, he is shocked by how much his former employer has aged. His body seems shrivelled. The slope of his left shoulder is more pronounced. His face is ravaged. He is still loquacious. For hours on end he delivers fantastically elaborate sentences ornamented with extravagant images—but his conversation is disjointed and repetitive: its main topic is sex. The cafés along the lake's shore, notes Antongini, "buzz with stories of the recent loves of Gabriele d'Annunzio."

5 MAY 1936. Marshall Badoglio, having overcome the Ethiopian army with the illegal help of mustard gas and arsine, enters Addis Ababa. In Rome, 400,000 people cram into the streets around the Palazzo Venezia to hear Mussolini's victory speech, calling him out onto the balcony ten times to acknowledge their cheering, while a choir of 10,000 children, disposed on the steps of the Victor Emmanuel monument, sing an anthem. D'Annunzio fires twenty-seven shots from the *Puglia* in celebration and writes the *Duce* a congratulatory letter: "You have subjugated all the uncertainties of fate and defeated every human hesitation."

17 JULY 1936. A group of Spanish generals headed by Francisco Franco rise up against Spain's democratic government, initiating a three-year civil war. Mussolini, who has said of the Spanish Republic, "to found a parliamentary republic today means using an oil lamp in the era of electric lights," supports the rebels.

26 AUGUST 1937. Ugo Ojetti visits the Vittoriale for the last time. D'Annunzio is sweet and affectionate, he reports, but physically he is a wreck. He is toothless, his face at once wrinkled and puffy. He who was once so meticulously clean is now slovenly. His shoes are decrepit, their laces mis-tied. His jacket and trousers are "lamentable."

28 SEPTEMBER 1937. Mussolini is visiting Germany. Hermann Göring demonstrates his toy train-set for his visitor's entertainment. In Berlin, Mussolini addresses a crowd of nearly a million people, pointing out how much Fascist Italy and Nazi Germany have in common. They emerged as unified nations at about the same time. In each of their cul-

tures youth and energy are exalted and the human will is seen as being the force driving history.

On his return journey his train passes through Verona. This is the occasion of his last meeting with d'Annunzio.

1 MARCH 1938. D'Annunzio, aged seventy-four, dies of a brain haemorrhage while sitting at his desk. The telephonist who transmits the news of his death to Mussolini's headquarters hears someone at the other end exclaim, "At last!"

Emy Huefler, d'Annunzio's blonde girlfriend, leaves the Vittoriale immediately. Shortly afterwards she is in Berlin working for Foreign Minister von Ribbentrop. She is a Nazi agent who has been planted in d'Annunzio's household to spy on him. It has been suggested that she has killed him with an overdose of cocaine, but given his history of drug abuse and venereal infections, and his well-documented physical decline, it's unlikely that she needed to.

Mussolini, accompanied by most of the highest-ranking fascists, arrives at the Vittoriale the next day to claim the role of chief mourner and to ensure that, however evasive the poet has been in life, in death he will be securely claimed for the fascist cause. D'Annunzio's body lies in state on the *Puglia*, while an honour guard of soldiers keeps vigil by torchlight. All day and all night mourners file past the coffin.

His funeral takes place in the church at his gates, to whose priests he once offered a large bribe in an attempt to stop them disturbing his peace with their bell-ringing. The banner that Olga Levi made for him, the banner which he draped over Randaccio's coffin, and which he so often employed as a prop thereafter, is hung over his own catafalque. Mussolini and the King's representative lead the mourners, followed by d'Annunzio's wife, who has been, of late, a frequent visitor, and his children (none of whom he has seen for years). There is no mention of Luisa Baccara or of Aélis in accounts of the ceremony—nor of the prostitute whom d'Annunzio called Titti and who was his favourite sexual partner during his last months.

His body is lodged, pending the construction of the mausoleum he and Maroni have been planning, in the "little temple of the holocaust," in the forecourt of the Vittoriale.

1 SEPTEMBER 1938. *The Ship* is performed al fresco on the Venetian island of Sant'Elena. The stage is enormous and so is the cast. The set is

as elaborate as d'Annunzio always wanted it to be. A half-constructed basilica, a ship and a massive rampart-and-moat set-up complete with gun emplacements, are all simultaneously on stage, all plausibly close to actual size. Audiences of 4,000 people attend night after night. The Minister for Culture, who has funded the production, fixes a marble plaque to the Casetta Rossa and announces: "By the will of the Regime, Gabriele d'Annunzio is truly commemorated."

D'ANNUNZIO IS DEAD, but Maroni, who is now director of the Foundation of the Vittoriale, is still working for him. Architect and client communicate by means of séances. D'Annunzio's spirit, speaking through a medium, insists that the planned amphitheatre and mausoleum be completed. Maroni passes d'Annunzio's posthumous messages on to Mussolini, with requests for yet more money. Mussolini complies.

The mausoleum caps the hill which d'Annunzio called the Keep or the Holy Mount. White, slabby and portentous, it looms, a brutalist shrine, above the muddled yellow stucco and terracotta of the Vittoriale. Three concentric circular platforms of stone, the "Rings of the Victory of the Humble, of the Artificers and of the Heroes," polished stone stairways, a portico with tall, smooth arches: everything massive and imposing. On the Ring of the Heroes there are ten sarcophagi dedicated to (and in some cases containing the remains of) d'Annunzio's disciples, including Guido Keller and Luigi Siverio, the first legionary to die at Fiume. In the centre, raised above his fellows by another round platform and four blocky pillars of unadorned stone, is d'Annunzio's sarcophagus.

The mausoleum is an incongruous memorial for one who liked to soften the walls and even the ceilings of his rooms with damask, who planted 10,000 rose bushes in his garden and draped his statues in necklaces and painted silk. We have Maroni's word for it that d'Annunzio, speaking from beyond the grave, approved of it, but we may be permitted to doubt it. Throughout the last years of his life d'Annunzio hid himself away while "young imitators, infatuated with usurpation" made use of his ideas, his words, his fame, for purposes he refused to endorse. Dead, he was finally obliged to "line up." His mausoleum is a quintessentially fascist monument.

NOTES

In most cases the sources of quotations are made clear in the text. With the help of the bibliography interested readers will be able to trace them without undue trouble. The following notes are intended to help where sources are not self-evident, and to indicate where I have found further information. In reusing a quotation cited by other Anglophone authors I have used their translations: all other translations are my own. Readers wanting precise page references are welcome to contact me via the Fourth Estate website, www.4thestate.co.uk.

ABBREVIATIONS
For collections of d'Annunzio's works:

AT—*Altri Taccuini*
PDRi—*Prose di Ricerca di Lotta di Commando*
PDRo—*Prose di Romanzi*
SG—*Scritti Giornalistici*
T—*Taccuini*
TN—*Tutte le Novelle*

For d'Annunzio's individual works:

Autobiographical writings:
DG—*Diari di Guerra*
DM—*Di Me a Me Stesso*
FM—*Faville del Maglio*
LdA—*Lettere d'Amore*
LL—*La Licenza*
LS—*Cento e Cento e Cento Pagine del Libro Segreto di Gabriele d'Annunzio Tentato di Morir*
N—*Notturno*
PV—*La Penultima Ventura*
SAS—*Solus ad Solam*

Novels:
F—*Il Fuoco*
FSFN—*Forse che sí, Forse che no*
I—*L'Innocente*
P—*Il Piacere*
TdM—*Il Trionfo della Morte*
VdR—*Le Virgine delle Rocche*

PART I: ECCE HOMO

THE PIKE (PAGES 3–16)

For Fiume see Comisso, Berghaus, Kochnitzky and Ledeen. For syndicalism and nationalism see Angelo Olivetti in Alatri. For fascist "blueprint" see Nardelli. For Boylesve see Jullian. For Vansittart see Chadwick. For Sarfatti see Schnapp. D'Annunzio's description of bundled corpses is in LL.

SIGHTINGS (PAGES 17–38)

For Scarfoglio and Westerhout see Andreoli (2001—all references to Andreoli are to this book). For Hérelle see Alatri (1983—all references to Alatri are to this book). For Gide see Andreoli and Kochnitzky. For the anonymous lady see Antongini. For Saba see Andreoli. For Kafka see Wohl. For French impressions see Jullian. For Ida Rubinstein see DM. For Reims see Ojetti, Tosi and DG. For the Capitol see PDRi and N. For Hemingway see Allan Massie, *Telegraph* (28 Feb. 1998). Letter to Venturina in Andreoli. For the return to Venice see Antongini.

SIX MONTHS (PAGES 39–65)

The main sources for this chapter, from which all otherwise unattributed quotations are taken, are d'Annunzio's own notebooks, published in DG. For Paquin see Giannantoni. For the "Amazon" and d'Annunzio's other lovers in Paris see Chiara. For the details of his departure see Tosi. For Carducci, and for the professor in Genoa, see Rhodes. "Rapt in his . . . ," cited in Thompson. For d'Annunzio's appearance at Quarto see *Corriere della Sera* (16 May 1915), and www.cronologia.leonardo.it. Text of this and subsequent speeches in PDRi. For Trier and other hostile caricatures see Chiara. Rolland cited in Woodhouse. Ojetti cited in Chiara. Deputy's question in Andreoli. Support for Giolitti—see Roger Griffin. Hugh Dalton cited in Woodhouse. Mussolini cited in Chiara. Carrère in Antongini. "The light gleaming . . . ," see Muñoz. Mann and Kosztolanyi are in Strachan. Martini in Tosi. For the Queen Mother see Antongini. For the constitutional crisis of May 1915 see Alatri and Thompson. Turati in Thompson. D'Annunzio's account of his speech on the Capitol and the crowd's response is in N. His description of a sculptor casting bronze is in FSFN. Nietszche in Hollingdale. "With ever before . . . ," from P. Mario d'Annunzio on the Argentinian lady in Rhodes. "I have a horror . . . ," letter to Albertini in Ledda. "It is certain death . . . ," letter to Fraternali in Woodhouse. Martini in Alatri. Albertini's letter in Andreoli. Letter to Salandra in Ledda. Martini in Alatri. "A pyrrhic dance . . . ," see Damerini. "The thought of returning . . . ," see LL. Lloyd George is in Parker. "... than all my odes . . . ," in Damerini. "All the past . . . ," see N. "All my life . . . ," letter to Albertini in Ledda.

PART II: STREAMS

For my account of d'Annunzio's life I have drawn on a number of biographies as well as on primary sources. All those I have found useful are listed in the bibliography. I am particularly indebted to books by Annamaria Andreoli and Paolo Alatri, both for their comprehensive narratives and for their copious quotation from d'Annunzio's contemporaries. Those by Piero Chiara, Giordano Bruno Guerri and (in English) John Woodhouse have also been especially helpful.

WORSHIP (PAGES 69–78)

"The Angel . . . ," see Winwar. "A painted cart . . . ," and "in profile . . . ," see N. "A wind of fanaticism . . . ," see TDM. "I come . . . ," see LS. "He never . . . ," and "Her glances . . . ," and "a rare beast," see LS. "Do you remember?" letter to Francesco Paolo d'Annunzio in Ledda. "Life scared me . . . ," see N. Visit to the Abbess, see LS. For magic see LS and "The Virgin Orsola" in TN and TdM. D'Annunzio's recollections of songs and rituals are in TdM. Bird's nest and balcony incident, see LS. School reports in Chiara and Guerri.

GLORY (PAGES 79–89)

Shellfish and knife incident in FM. "The troops scattered . . . ," see TN. For the King's visit see Alatri. For d'Annunzio's recollections of his schooldays see FM. His letters to his parents are in Ledda. "He is entirely dedicated . . . ," cited in Guerri. For life at the Cicognini see Fracassini in Chiara. Letters to Carducci, Nencioni, Fontana and Chiarini are in Ledda. For d'Annunzio's fake death see Chiara.

LIEBESTOD (PAGES 90–99)

There are selections of d'Annunzio's letters to Giselda Zucconi in Ledda and in LdA, with useful extra information in each. For rape of peasant girl see "Il Grappolo del Pudore" in FM. Letters to Tito Zucconi and Chiarini are in Alatri. "What vaporous floating . . . ," from "Aternum" in SG. For Magnico see Chiara. For trip to Sardinia see Scarfoglio's and d'Annunzio's accounts in SG, and Winwar. On d'Annunzio's inability to say no, see Antongini. "He would be off . . . ," Scarfoglio cited in Guerri. For Elda's wish to sell d'Annunzio's letters see Woodhouse.

HOMELAND (PAGES 100–106)

For Michetti and his *cenacolo* see Andreoli; and d'Annunzio's "Ricordi Francavillesi" in SG; and his letters to Giselda Zucconi cited in Andreoli. Toscanini in Antongini. Easter ceremony commemorated on a plaque outside the Convent. "Found among the common . . . ," see Zipes. "Suddenly there burst . . . ," see 1921 interview cited in Andreoli. For the pilgrims at Miglianico see d'Annunzio's "Il Voto" in SG, and TdM. "Mass of lice . . . ," see TdM. "I carry . . . ," see LS.

YOUTH (PAGES 107–110)

All d'Annunzio's pieces quoted in this and the next ten sections are published in SG. Letters to Giselda Zucconi in Ledda. Scarfoglio in Guerri. "Chestnut locks . . . ," see Antongini. For d'Annunzio's early social life in Rome see Andreoli, Ojetti, Antongini and d'Annunzio in SG.

NOBILITY (PAGES 111–121)

Visit to Poggio a Caiano described in d'Annunzio's letter to his mother, in Ledda. "Some of them knelt," see LS. "He would fire up," cited in Guerri. "Superior beings . . . ," see VdR. Andreoli on Elena Muti seen from behind—introduction to SG. D'Annunzio's social and fashion notes in "La Cronachetta delle Pellicce," "In Casa Huffer" and "Alla Vigilia di Carnevale" in SG. Scarfoglio in Rhodes and in SG. Crispi and Hare cited in Duggan. D'Annunzio on the desecration of the villas in introduction to SG. "Your hand can brush . . . ," from "Christmas" in SG. Maria di Gallese in "Venere Capitolina Favente" in SG. "A graceful creature . . . ," cited in Guerri. Descriptions of Primoli in Andreoli. D'Annunzio's "Casa Primoli" in SG. "A young poet . . . ," Primoli cited in Andreoli.

BEAUTY (PAGES 122–128)

"Bric-à-bracomania" in SG. The Beretta sisters' shop in "Toung-Hoa-Lou, Ossia Cronica del Fiore dell'Oriente" in SG. "I went round . . . ," and "It yelled . . . ," letters to Nencioni in Ledda. Brass bands in Andreoli. Letters to Scarfoglio in Ledda. D'Annunzio's dream from "Balli e Serate" in SG. "Light and gay . . . ," cited in Chiara. Hotelier and cheque in Antongini. Letter to Prince Maffeo Colonna in Andreoli. Carducci in Duggan.

ELITISM (PAGES 129–131)

For the political background see Mack Smith and Duggan: all quotations in this section are cited in Duggan. "Make much of yourself . . . ," letter to Vittorio Pepe in Alatri.

MARTYRDOM (PAGES 132–137)

"When I married . . . ," cited in Guerri. For Olga Ossani see "Il Ballo della Stampa" in SG, and letters to her in Ledda, Andreoli and LdA. For Henry James, see http://www.romeartlover .it/James.html#Medici. For d'Annunzio as St. Sebastian see DM and letter to Olga cited in Andreoli. For St. Sebastian iconography see Boccardo. "We smiled . . . ," from "Il Compagno dagli Occhi senza Cigli" in FM. Letter to Fontana in Ledda. Pietà fantasy in Andreoli.

SICKNESS (PAGES 138–143)

Letters to Elvira Fraternali in Ledda and LdA. "Neither the strength . . . ," d'Annunzio cited in Guerri. "The most beautiful eyes . . . ," Gatti cited in Woodhouse.

THE SEA (PAGES 144–148)

"Marine nativity" letter to Hérelle cited in Andreoli. "My body completely naked . . . ," see LS. "Playful sketch" is "I Progetti" in SG. For picnics on beaches see Morello in Damerini. "Mere poet . . . ," cited in Alatri. *L'Armata Italiana* in PDRi.

DECADENCE (PAGES 149–154)

"Garden parties . . . ," from "La Vita Ovunque—Piccolo Corriere" in SG. "The only women . . . ," see LS. "I write all day . . . ," letter cited in Alatri. For d'Annunzio's ideas on fiction, and on writing P, see his introduction to TdM. For Mallarmé and de Montesquiou see Baldick. D'Annunzio acknowledges similarity of P and *À Rebours* in G. Gatti. Letter to Treves in Alatri.

BLOOD (PAGES 155–157)

For Italian patriotism and eagerness for war see Mack Smith and Duggan. All quotations cited in this chapter in Duggan, except for Verdi cited in Gilmour.

FAME (PAGES 158–160)

For Liszt and Heine see Walker, and "Franz Liszt" in SG. "Who knows how to *launch* . . . ," cited in Guerri. "We'll print . . . ," letter to Sartorio in Andreoli. "I like this quick communication . . . ," in introduction to SG. "Thousands of young men . . . ," cited in Alatri.

SUPERMAN (PAGES 161–179)

For the wet night see letter to Fraternali in Andreoli. For d'Annunzio's wretchedness at being separated from Fraternali see LS. "My worst enemy . . . ," letter to Fraternali in LdA. "Blood, so much blood . . . ," letter to Fraternali in Andreoli. For Maria di Gallese and her father see G. Gatti. For Maria and "Rastignac" see Chiara. For German suicides see de Waal. For inventory see Andreoli. "I departed ill . . . ," cited in Alatri. Fanfulla review in introduction to Oscar edition of *L'Innocente*. "Dreary procession . . . ," in Guerri. Letters to Fraternali in LdA. Crispi cited in Sassoon. "Putrefaction," see d'Annunzio's speech cited in Antona-Traversi. For Nietzsche see Safranski and Hollingdale: quotations all cited in Safranski. "Am I of the same . . . ," in DG. "I can barely see . . . ," in Alatri. "I would throw myself . . . ," in Guerri. "It has begun . . . ," in Woodhouse. "For a whole hour . . . ," in Andreoli. Correspondence with Hérelle in Ledda. Scarfoglio in Andreoli.

VIRILITY (PAGES 180–186)

For d'Annunzio's letters about Maria Gravina's madness see Andreoli and Chiara. Hérelle on Venetian interlude, cited in Andreoli. "Musical book," and "mystery with thought," from d'Annunzio's introduction to TdM. "I feel as though . . . ," notebook entry cited in Andreoli.

ELOQUENCE (PAGES 187–192)

For Duse's early life see Weaver and Winwar. "The strange Japanese . . . ," from "Carnevale" in SG. "Rather die," in Winwar. "When the theatre . . . ," in F. Duse's letters cited in Winwar. D'Annunzio's recollections in DG and LS. Descriptions of d'Annunzio's voice in Damerini. For his training his own voice see LS, FM and introduction to TdM. "Colourless," and "monotonous," see Rolland and Marinetti. "An ancient savage game . . . ," and "In the communion . . . ," from F.

CRUELTY (PAGES 193–200)

"Like an underwater flower" see LS. D'Annunzio's recollections in LS. Duse's letters cited in Winwar unless stated otherwise. "Wounded Pierrot . . . ," in Guerri. "Torch of passion . . . ," in Rolland. "More poetic . . . more sincere," in Rolland. "I would like to unmake myself," Duse cited in Andreoli. Duse/Ossani interview in Andreoli. "Not an intelligent woman . . . ," in Antongini. "Slaughtering flowers," cited in Andreoli. "Exhausted, stupefied," in Rolland. "An absolute right . . . ," in Andreoli. "Mad about her," in Guerri. For the maze see F, for d'Annunzio's account, and Winwar for Duse's.

LIFE (PAGES 201–207)

For d'Annunzio on parliament see Antongini, VdR and letter to Treves in Ledda. "I am beyond . . . ," letter to Lodi in Alatri. For Nietzsche and Heine see Safranski. For d'Annunzio on the campanile see Guerri. D'Annunzio's pieces for the Convito are in PDRi. For Vitalism see Alatri and Thompson. For electioneering see letters to Treves in Ledda, and Marinetti cited in SG. For political background see Alatri, Duggan and Woodhouse. "With the agility of a goat," see Palmerio. D'Annunzio on "life" and Heraclitus' bow in LS. Nitti quoted in Alatri. "The hedge," see Palmerio.

DRAMA (PAGES 208–210)

For d'Annunzio on Wagner see "Il Caso Wagner" in SG and F. For literacy rates see Riall. Duse and the Roman marchese in Winwar. D'Annunzio on drama in PDRi. On Orange in Andreoli.

SCENES FROM A LIFE (PAGES 211–240)

For descriptions of the Capponcina, and for d'Annunzio's style of life there see Palmerio. For d'Annunzio's immediate impressions see his notebooks in T and AT, letters to Treves and Tenneroni and others in Ledda. For his recollections of the period see FM and the Proemio to his Vita di Cola di Rienzo. Visit to Assisi—"Scrivi che Quivi è Perfecta Letitia" in FM. "Better decorator," see Antongini. Pizzetti in Andreoli. For d'Annunzio in Paris see his letters cited in Andreoli, Hérelle, Scarfoglio cited in Andreoli, and Marinetti (1906). For his obsessive cleanliness see Antongini and Palmerio. For visit to Egypt see Andreoli. For Duse's jealousy in Corfu see Weaver. For *Gloria* in Naples see Chiara. Speech at Orsanmichele in PDRi. "From the muddy sea . . . ," in Alatri. "I know the novel . . . ," Duse in Palmerio. "The faint lines . . . ," quoted in Antongini. For d'Annunzio in Vienna see LS. For Gabriellino's visit see Andreoli. For dog kennel see Palmerio. For de Pougy see Souhami. De Amicis cited in Andreoli. For d'Annunzio's gym see LS. For ping-pong see Rolland. For fortieth birthday see "Esequie della Giovinezza" in FM. For conversation overheard in Lucerne, and for trials of celebrity, see LS. "I *phonographed* . . . ," cited in Ledda. Duse's statements in introduction to *La Figlia di Jorio*. "An episode . . . ," from LS. Della Robbia in Jullian.

SPEED (PAGES 241–271)

"Mingy little scribblers," see DM. For hunting see Antongini and LS. Alessandra's letters cited in Woodhouse and Winwar. D'Annunzio on her operations in Palmerio and Antongini. Berenson in Andreoli. For Casati see Jullian and Ryerson. On reception of *Più che l'Amore* see Alatri. For relationship with Giuseppina Mancini see letters to her in Ledda and LdA, and SAS. "Most bitter Adriatic . . . ," and political context see Alatri. For banquet in Venice see Damerini. "In the carriages . . . ," in Andreoli. Giuseppina's breakdown from SAS. For Puccini see Andreoli. "The sterile carnal work," see SAS. For Nathalie see d'Annunzio's notebooks and his letters to her in Ledda and LdA. For Marinetti and Futurism see Ottinger, Berghaus and Marinetti (1972). For the Marchesa di Toledo see Andreoli. For flight see Wohl. For d'Annunzio on flight see FSFN. Gabriellino in Chiara. Barzini in Andreoli. H. G. Wells in Wohl.

KALEIDOSCOPE (PAGES 272–298)

Règnier and Boylesve in Alatri. Mascagni's daughter in Guerri. De Montesquiou in Jullian. De Castellane in DM and Alatri. For Rubinstein see Alatri, Antongini, Jullian, Winwar. D'Annunzio on Maeterlinck in Jullian. Barrès in Jullian. For Romaine Brooks see Souhami, Jullian and Woodhouse. For the house at Arcachon see Antongini. For Hahn see LS. "The old French beauty," in Carr. Proust and Règnier in Jullian. Vierne in LS. Mussolini in Stonor Saunders. For Giolitti see Gentile and Thompson. Von Hofmannsthal in Guerri. Croce in Chiara. For the drowned man see PDRi. D'Annunzio on film-making in Alatri and Guerri. Barney "all the rage," in Jullian. Visit to England in LS. Prezzolini and Donato in Berghaus. D'Annunzio's depression in LL. Letter to Paléologue in Tosi.

THE DOGS OF WAR (PAGES 299–313)

Tosi is the main source for this chapter. Quotations from d'Annunzio are from LL or DG. Mann and Rilke in Strachan. Hitler in Sassoon. Barjansky in Ryerson. Giolitti in Thompson. Prezzolini in Alatri. For the Huards' house see Ojetti. Federzoni in Bosworth (1983). Corradini in Duggan. *La Voce* in Alatri. Mussolini in Sassoon. Marinetti in Berghaus.

PART III: WAR AND PEACE

WAR (PAGES 317–378)

D'Annunzio's accounts of his personal experiences are taken from LL, DG, N and LS, and from letters in Ledda and LdA. His speeches, with useful supporting material, are in PV and PDRi. For wartime Venice see Damerini. For a narrative of the war on the Italian front see Mark Thompson's superb and comprehensive account: nearly all facts and figures relating to the fighting, and many eye-witness impressions, are from his book. Malipiero in Damerini. Marinetti, Piazza and Lawrence in Wohl. Emperor Karl in Bello. "Ordinary soldiers," see Bosworth (2006). "It looked . . . ," see Thompson. Mazzini in Riall. Respect accorded the blind in Roshwald. "Swift as the wing," trans. Thompson. For "war bread," America and Barrès, see Alatri. For the fighting by the Timavo see Thompson. Evandro the bittern in Antongini. Diaz in Alatri. Gatti in Thompson. "An officer," Rodd and Gatti in Thompson. Giarda in Damerini. For Caporetto see Thompson and Duggan. Malaparte in Duggan. Diaz in Thompson. Martini in Alatri. Wells in Wohl. Musil in Thompson.

PEACE (PAGES 379–408)

For Mussolini see Griffin, Duggan, Bosworth and Berghaus. For D'Annunzio's depression see Ojetti and Antongini. For the peace talks see Macmillan and Thompson. "He wholeheartedly," in Woodhouse. "By divine right," in Giuriati. Albertini in Andreoli. British officer in Macmillan. "With a violent magnificence," in Damerini. "Discontent began," Santoro. Balbo in Duggan. Mannarese in Alatri. For the *Arditi* see Berghaus, Bosworth 2002, Duggan and Ledeen. Carli in Berghaus. "We have no direction . . . ," in Ledeen. Caviglia in Ledeen. Mussolini in Berghaus. "The true Italy," in Woodhouse. Bissolati's proposal in Thompson. "The administration, the law . . . ," see Schnapp. For the raid on *Avanti!* see Ledeen and Bosworth (2002). For Orlando in Paris see Macmillan. Hankey in Duggan. British ambassador and Clemenceau in Macmillan. Hardinge in Sassoon. First Sea Lord in Thompson. "Very white . . . ," in Macmillan. "The Rubicon . . . ," see Rhodes. "A young poet," Comisso. Orlando and Lloyd George in Macmillan. Mussolini in Duggan. "He is thought . . . ," in Sassoon. For Fiume's history, demography and economy see Žic (1998). For the war's end in Fiume see Žic (1998) and Macdonald. For events in Fiume, Nov. 1918–Aug. 1919, see Macdonald, Comisso, Giuriati, Powell, de Felice 1974, Ledeen, and Lyttleton. "The public life . . . ," see Powell. House in Macmillan. "Await me . . . ," in Ledeen. "Tell the faithful . . . ," see Macdonald. "Believe me . . . ," in Powell. Badoglio in Andreoli. "In barely educated . . . ," in de Felice. "I no longer speak," in Macdonald. "Tell our brothers," in Giuriati. "We have sworn," in Ledeen.

THE CITY OF THE HOLOCAUST (PAGES 409–441)

Letter to Mussolini in Ledda. For the march on Fiume see Susmel, Santoro, Macdonald and de Felice (1974). For d'Annunzio's speeches in Fiume see PV with commentary by de Felice, and PDRi. "Sealing their ears . . . ," see Comisso. Countess di Robilant in Ledeen. "Supremely beautiful," and "Who? Me?" in Comisso. "Gaits, cries, songs . . . ," see Kochnitzky. "Sceptical observer," see Nitti. "Everyone enjoys," in Ledeen. "Each soldier . . . ," in Comisso. For d'Annunzio's intentions see Žic (1998), Rhodes, Ledeen, de Felice and Chiara. Letter to Mussolini in Andreoli. Nitti and Badoglio in Andreoli. Marinetti in Ledeen and Berghaus. Vice-consul in Ledeen. The "American observer," in Powell. "The people stormed," see LS. "Colloquies," see Macdonald and Sitwell (1925). "All the members . . . ," in Ledeen. "Chorus Girls and Champagne," in Sitwell (1925). "A Bordello . . . ," in Ledeen. "It is a known fact . . . ," in Woodhouse. For the "Black Band," see Nardelli and Kochnitzky. "The words of the poet . . . ," Maranini in Ledeen. For hostility to Croats see Macdonald, Ledeen, and Žic. "Rabble stuffed . . . ," in Woodhouse. "The money-changer . . . ," in Ledeen. For the *Modus Vivendi* see Giuriati.

THE FIFTH SEASON (PAGES 442–480)

Caviglia in de Felice. For the feast of St. Sebastian see Žic (1998) and Ledeen. "The art of command . . . ," in Comisso. For Fiume's intellectual life see Berghaus and Comisso. For Keller see Comisso. "Madame, in future . . . ," in Antongini. The Bishop in Alatri. Italian communist in Ledeen. "Virtually empty . . . ," in Ledeen. For *La Disperata*, the theft of Keller's eagle and his planned Festa see Comisso. The text of the Carta di Carnaro is in PV and PDRi, with commentaries. "It was a period . . . ," in Ledeen. "Look at my soldiers . . . ," in Comisso. "Traitors . . . robust blood," in Ledeen. Caviglia in Ledeen. For cults and sects see Comisso and Berghaus. Festa Yoga in Berghaus. Zanella in Macdonald. De Ambris in Ledeen. "A kind of king," in Jullian. Boulanger in Antongini. "Treacherous government . . . ," in Comisso. Gramsci in de Felice (1974). "He never went near . . . ," in Alatri. "Help me . . . ," in Alatri. "This one Italy . . . ," in Rhodes. "You haven't seen," in Comisso.

CLAUSURA (PAGES 481–544)

For my account of Italy's inter-war political and economic history and the rise of fascism I have drawn on the works of Bosworth (from whom Mussolini's words and the majority of other quotations are taken), Duggan (another important source for quotations), Mack Smith, Lyttleton, Sassoon, Gentile, de Felice, Schnapp. For d'Annunzio's life at the Vittoriale the prime sources are his own DM and LS, and numerous letters collected in Ledda and LdA or cited in Andreoli. Ojetti, Antongini, Jullian, Nardelli, Damerini, Winwar, Chiara, Andreoli and Guerri have all provided anecdotes. Beerbohm in Woodhouse. "One can imagine . . . ," in Ojetti. Sarfatti in Schnapps. Tasca in Lyttleton. Cabruna in Winwar. Marinetti in Griffin. Strachey in Stonor Saunders. Ward Price in Foot. Pirandello in Duggan. Carra in Andreoli.

SELECT BIBLIOGRAPHY

D'Annunzio's works are available in Mondadori's excellent Meridiani editions under the following titles:

Altri Taccuini (1976)
Prose de Romanzi (two volumes, 1988 and 1989)
Prose di Ricerca di Lotta di Commando (two volumes, 2005)
Scritti Giornalistici (two volumes, 1996 and 2003)
Taccuini (1965)
Teatro: Tragedie, Sogni e Misteri (two volumes, 1939 and 1940)
Tutte le Novelle (1992)
Versi d'Amore e di Gloria (two volumes, 1982 and 1984)

Each volume is copiously annotated, with introductions, chronology and bibliography.

The introductions are by various hands. The original series editor was E. Bianchetti. He has been succeeded by the great d'Annunzio scholar, Annamaria Andreoli.

Individual works are also available in Mondadori's Oscar paperback editions, with scholarly notes and introductions. Particularly useful are: *Le Faville del Maglio* (ed. Andreoli, 1995); *Diari di Guerrra* (ed. Andreoli, 2002); *Lettere d'Amore* (ed. Andreoli, 2000).

Adamson, Walter L., "The Impact of World War I on Italian Political Culture," in Aviel Roshwald and Richard Stites (Cambridge, 2002)
Alatri, Paolo, *Gabriele d'Annunzio* (Turin, 1983)
———(ed.), *Scritti Politici di Gabriele d'Annunzio* (Milan, 1980)
———*Nitti, d'Annunzio e la Questione Adriatica* (Milan, 1959)
Albertini, Luigi, *Origins of the War of 1914–18* (London, 2005)
Andreoli, Annamaria, *Il Vivere Inimitabile: Vita di Gabriele d'Annunzio* (Milan, 2001)
———*D'Annunzio* (Bologna, 2004)
———*Il Vittoriale degli Italiani* (Milan, 2004)
Antona-Traversi, Camillo, *Vita di Gabriele d'Annunzio* (Florence, 1933)
Antongini, Tom, *D'Annunzio* (London, 1938)
Baldick, Robert, *The Life of J. K. Huysmans* (Cambridge, 2006)
Barjansky, Catherine, *Portraits with Backgrounds* (New York, 1947)
Bello, Piero, *La Notte di Ronchi* (Milan, 1920)
Berghaus, Günter, *Futurism and Politics* (Oxford, 1996)
Boccardo, Piero, and Xavier F. Salomon, *The Agony and the Ecstasy—Guido Reni's St. Sebastians* (Dulwich/Milan, 2007)
Boccioni, Umberto, *Gli Scritti Editi e Inediti* (Milan, 1971)
Bosworth, R. J., *Italy and the Approach of the First World War* (London, 1983)

————*Mussolini* (London, 2002)

————*Mussolini's Italy* (London, 2006)

Bourke, Joanna, *An Intimate History of Killing* (London, 1999)

Brendon, Piers, *The Dark Valley* (London, 2000)

Bultrini, Nicola, and Maurizio Casarola, *Gli Ultimi* (Chiari, 2005)

Cadorna, Luigi, *La Guerra alla Fronte Italiano* (Milan, 1921)

Carli, Mario, *Con d'Annunzio a Fiume* (Milan, 1920)

Carlyle, Thomas, *On Heroes, Hero-worship and the Heroic in History* (London, 1993)

Carr, Helen, *The Verse Revolutionaries* (London, 2009)

Caviglia, Enrico, *Il Conflitto di Fiume* (Milan, 1948)

Chadwick, Owen, *Britain and the Vatican during the Second World War* (Cambridge, 1987)

Chiara, Piero, *Vita di Gabriele d'Annunzio* (Milan, 1978)

Clark, Martin, *Modern Italy* (London, 1996)

Clarke, I. F., *Voices Prophesying War* (Oxford, 1966)

Comisso, Giovanni, *Opere* (Milan, 2002)

Croce, Benedetto, *A History of Italy* (Oxford, 1929)

D'Annunzio, Mario, *Con Mio Padre sulla Nave del Ricordo* (Milan, 1950)

Damerini, Gino, *D'Annunzio e Venezia, Postfazione di Giannantonio Paladini* (Venice, 1992)

De Felice, Renzo, *Sindicalismo Revoluzionario e Fiumanesimo nel Carteggio de Ambris/d'Annunzio* (Milan, 1973)

————*D'Annunzio Politico* (Milan, 1979)

————(ed.), *Carteggio d'Annunzio-Mussolini* (Milan, 1971)

————*La Penultima Ventura—Scritti e Discorsi Fiumani a cura di Renzo de Felice* (Milan, 1974)

De Waal, Edmund, *The Hare with Amber Eyes* (London, 2010)

Dos Passos, John, *The Fourteenth Chronicle* (London, 1974)

Duggan, Christopher, *The Force of Destiny: A History of Italy since 1796* (London, 2007)

Farrell, Joseph, *A History of Italian Theatre* (Cambridge, 2006)

Flaubert, Gustave, *Salammbô*, trans. A. J. Krailsheimer (Harmondsworth, 1977)

Foot, Michael, *The Trial of Mussolini by "Cassius'* (London, 1943)

Gadda, Carlo Emilio, *Giornale di Guerra e di Prigionia* (Milan, 1999)

Gatti, Angelo, *Caporetto: diario di guerra* (Bologna, 1997)

Gatti, Guglielmo, *Vita di Gabriele d'Annunzio* (Firenze, 1956)

Gentile, Emilio, *Storia del Partito Fascista* (Bari, 1989)

————*The Sacralisation of Politics in Fascist Italy*, trans. Keith Botsford (Harvard, 1996)

Germain, André, *La Vie amoureuse de Gabriele d'Annunzio* (Paris, 1925)

Gerra, Ferdinando, *L'Impresa di Fiume* (Milan, 1974)

Giannantoni, Mario, *La Vita di Gabriele d'Annunzio* (Mondadori, 1933)

Gilmour, David, *The Pursuit of Italy* (London, 2011)

Giuriati, Giovanni, *Con d'Annunzio e Millo in Difesa dell'Adriatico* (Rome, 1953)

Glenny, Misha, *The Balkans* (London, 1999)

Griffin, Gerald, *Gabriele d'Annunzio: The Warrior Bard* (London, 1935)

Griffin, Roger, *The Nature of Fascism* (London, 1991)

————(ed.), *Fascism* (Oxford, 1995)

Guerri, Giordano Bruno, *D'Annunzio: l'Amante Guerriero* (Milan, 2008)

Hemingway, Ernest, *Across the River and into the Trees* (London, 1966)

————*A Farewell to Arms* (London, 2005)

Hérelle, Georges, *Notolette dannunziane* (Pescara, 1984)

Hollingdale, R. J. (ed.), *A Nietzsche Reader* (Harmondsworth, 1978)

Huysmans, Joris Karl, *Against Nature*, trans. Robert Baldick (London, 2003)

James, Henry, *Selected Literary Criticism*, ed. Morris Shapira (Cambridge, 1981)

Jullian, Philippe, *D'Annunzio* (Paris, 1971)

Kochnitzky, Leone, *La Quinta Stagione o i Centauri de Fiume* (Bologna, 1922)

Ledda, Elena (ed.), *Il Fiore delle Lettere—Epistolario* (Alessandria, 2004)

Ledeen, Michael A., *The First Duce: d'Annunzio at Fiume* (London, 1977)

Lussu, Emilio, *Sardinian Brigade* (London, 2000)

Lyttleton, Adrian, *The Seizure of Power* (Princeton 1987; revised edition 2004)

Macbeth, George, *The Lion of Pescara* (London, 1984)

Macdonald, J. N., *A Political Escapade: The Story of Fiume and d'Annunzio* (London, 1921)

Mack Smith, Denis, *Modern Italy: A Political History* (London, 1997)

——*Mussolini* (London, 1981)

MacMillan, Margaret, *Peacemakers* (London, 2003)

Marinetti, Filippo Tomaso, *Les Dieux s'en vont: d'Annunzio reste* (Paris, 1906)

——*Selected Writings*, ed. R. W. Flint (London, 1972)

Martini, Ferdinando, *Diario 1914–18* (Milan, 1966)

Melograni, Piero, *Storia Politica della Grande Guerra, 1915–18* (Bari, 1977)

Moretti, Vito, *D'Annunzio Pubblico e Privato* (Venice, 2001)

Muñoz, Antonio (ed.), *Ricordi Romani di Gabriele d'Annunzio* (Rome, 1938)

Mussolini, Benito, *My Autobiography* (New York, 1928)

Nardelli, Federico and Livingston, Arthur, *D'Annunzio: a Portrait* (London, 1931)

Nicolson, Harold, *Some People* (London, 1926)

Nietzsche, Friedrich, *A travers l'oeuvre de F. Nietzsche; extraits de tous ses ouvrages*, ed. Lauter-
   bach and Wagnon (Paris, 1893)

Nitti, Francesco Saverio, *Rivelazioni* (Naples, 1948)

Ojetti, Ugo, *As They Seemed To Me*, trans. Henry Furst (London, 1928)

Ottinger, Didier (ed.), *Futurism* (London, 2009)

Paléologue, Maurice, *My Secret Diary of the Dreyfus Case, 1894–99*, trans. Erich Mosbacher
   (London, 1957)

Palmerio, Benigno, *Con d'Annunzio alla Capponcina* (Florence, 1938)

Panzini, Alfredo, *La Guerra del '15* (Bologna, 1995)

Parker, Peter, *The Old Lie* (London, 1987)

Pasquaris, G. M., *Gabriele d'Annunzio—Gli Uomini del Giorno* (Milan, 1923)

Pater, Walter, *The Renaissance: Studies in Art and Poetry* (London, 1902)

——*Marius the Epicurean* (London, 2008)

Paxton, R. O., *The Anatomy of Fascism* (London, 2004)

Powell, Edward Alexander, *The New Frontiers of Freedom from the Alps to the Aegean* (www.
   gutenberg.org/files/17292/17292-h/17292-h.htm)

Praz, Mario, *The Romantic Agony* (Oxford, 1970)

Procacci, Giovanna, *Soldati e Prigionieri nella Grande Guerra* (Turin, 2000)

Rhodes, Anthony, *The Poet as Superman: A Life of Gabriele d'Annunzio* (London, 1959)

Riall, Lucy, *Garibaldi: Invention of a Hero* (London, 2007)

Ridley, Jasper, *Mussolini* (London, 1997)

Roberts, David, *Syndicalist Tradition and Italian Fascism* (Manchester, 1979)

Rodd, Sir J. Rennell, *Social and Diplomatic Memories* (http://net.lib.byu.edu/~rdh7/wwi/
   memoir/Rodd/Rodd10.htm)

Rolland, Romain, *Gabriele d'Annunzio et la Duse: Souvenirs* (Paris, 1947)

Roshwald, Aviel, and Richard Stites (eds), *European Culture in the Great War* (Cambridge, 2002)

Ryerson, Scot D., and Michael Yaccarino, *Infinite Variety, the Life and Legend of the Marchesa
   Casati* (Minnesota, 2004)

Safranski, Rüdiger, *Nietzsche: a Philosophical Biography* (London, 2002)

Santoro, Antonio, *L'Ultimo dei Fiumani: Un Cavaliere di Vittorio Veneto Racconta* (Salerno, 1994)

Sassoon, Donald, *Mussolini and the Rise of Fascism* (London, 2007)

Schiavo, Alberto (ed.), *Futurismo e Fascismo* (Rome, 1981)

Schnapp, Jeffrey T. (ed.), *A Primer of Italian Fascism* (Lincoln, Nebraska, 2000)

Sforza, Carlo, *L'Italia dalla 1914 al 1944 quale io la vidi* (Rome, 1944)

Sitwell, Osbert, *Discursions on Travel, Art and Life* (London, 1925)

——*Noble Essences* (London, 1950)

Soffici, Ardengo, *I diari della Grande Guerra* (Florence, 1986)

Sontag, Susan, "Fascinating Fascism," in *A Susan Sontag Reader* (Harmondsworth, 1983)

Souhami, Diana, *Wild Girls* (London, 2004)

Stanford, Derek (ed.), *Writing of the Nineties: from Wilde to Beerbohm* (London, 1971)

Starkie, Walter, *The Waveless Plain: An Italian Autobiography* (London, 1938)

Stonor Saunders, Frances, *The Woman who Shot Mussolini* (London, 2010)

Susmel, E., *La Città di Passione; Fiume negli Anni 1914–20* (Milan, 1921)

Tasca, Angelo, *The Rise of Italian Fascism 1918–22* (London, 1938)

Thompson, Mark, *The White War* (London, 2008)

Toseva-Karpowicz, Ljubinka, *D'Annunzio u Rijeci* (Rijeka, 2007)

Tosi, Guy, *La Vie et le rôle de d'Annunzio en France au début de la Grande Guerre, 1914–15* (Paris, 1961)

Trevelyan, G. M., *Scenes from Italy's War* (London, 1919)

Turr, Stefania, *Alle Trincee d'Italia* (Milan, 1918)

Valeri, Nino, *d'Annunzio davanti al Fascismo* (Florence, 1963)

Vecchi, Ferruccio, *Arditismo Civile* (Milan, 1920)

Walker, Alan, *Liszt, the Virtuoso Years* (Cornell, 1988)

Weaver, William, *Duse* (London, 1984)

Wickham Steed, Henry, *Through Thirty Years: 1892–1922* (London, 1924)

Winwar, Frances, *Wingless Victory* (New York, 1956)

Wohl, Robert, *A Passion for Wings: Aviation and the Western Imagination* (London, 1994)

Woodhouse, John, *Gabriele d'Annunzio: Defiant Archangel* (Oxford, 1998)

Woodward, Christopher, *In Ruins* (London, 2001)

Žic, Igor, *Kratka Povijest grada Rijeke* (Rijeka, 1998)

——*Riječki Orao, Venecijanski Lav i Rimska Vučica* (Rijeka, 2003)

Zipes, Jack (ed.), *The Complete Fairytales of the Brothers Grimm* (New York, 1987)

ACKNOWLEDGEMENTS

Thanks to Jonathan Keates, David Jenkins, Rupert Christiansen and—most especially—my brother James Hughes-Hallett, for reading and commenting on early drafts of this book. Thanks to the numerous people with whom I've talked about d'Annunzio and related topics over the past eight years: those conversations helped to focus my ideas and set me off on new lines of enquiry. I'm especially grateful to Mladen Urem, whose help in the archives made my visit to Rijeka so fruitful and who introduced me to Igor Zič. The two of them made it possible for me to be the first of d'Annunzio's biographers to write an account of d'Annunzio's Fiume which includes the Croatian view of that episode. Thanks to the London Library for entrusting their beautiful early editions of d'Annunzio's works to me.

Thanks to everyone involved in the book's publication: my agent Felicity Rubinstein; my publisher Nicholas Pearson and everyone else at Fourth Estate; Andrew Miller and his colleagues at Knopf.

Thanks as well to Jayne Hanks, without whose remarkable kindness and devotion to my family this book could never have been written.

Thanks to Mary and Lettice for the immense pleasure of their company. Thanks and much love to Dan.

ILLUSTRATION CREDITS

The great majority of the illustrations are reproduced by kind permission of the Fondazione il Vittoriale degli Italiani. I am grateful to the archivist Alessandro Tonacci for his helpfulness in finding and supplying them. The exceptions are as follow:

The photograph of d'Annunzio on the beach (p. 146) is reproduced by permission of the Alinari Archive-Michetti Archive, Florence. The photograph of Luisa Casati by Adolphe Meyer (p. 247) is reproduced by permission of The Casati Archives. The cartoon by Sem (p. 273) is reproduced by permission of the Bridgeman Art Library. The photograph of Ida Rubinstein (p. 283) is reproduced by permission of the Mary Evans Picture Library. In a few cases I regret that I have been unable to trace the copyright-holder of an image. Copyright-holders in images that are not credited here are asked to contact the publisher so that this can be rectified for all future editions.

INDEX

Duse, Eleonora: d'Annunzio's relations with, 7, 14, 20–1, 188–90, 193–9, 216, 223, 236–7, 238–40; affair with d'Annunzio ends, 22, 198, 239; d'Annunzio pawns and redeems emeralds from, 42, 326; in Tuscany with d'Annunzio, 70, 227; gives emeralds to d'Annunzio, 76; supposed bisexuality, 136; in Venice circle, 182; d'Annunzio meets, 187–8; background and career, 188–9; literary style, 189; manner, 189; beautiful hands, 193–4, 199–200; physical frailty, 194, 235; d'Annunzio writes plays for, 196–7, 198; helps d'Annunzio financially, 197; Settignano house, 196, 212; and d'Annunzio's infidelities, 197, 217, 238–9; in Egypt with d'Annunzio, 199–200, 204, 217; plans national theatre, 208, 209–10, 486; visits Assisi with d'Annunzio, 211; d'Annunzio accompanies on tours, 219, 224, 232; at Capponcina, 219, 220; portrayed in *Fire*, 219, 222; confides in Madame Rolland, 221; reads d'Annunzio's manuscripts, 220; plays Francesca da Rimini, 230; gifts to d'Annunzio, 232; isolation, 233; praises *Jorio's Daughter*, 234; as model for character in *Maybe Yes, Maybe No*, 267; resumes acting tours, 491, 499; reunion with d'Annunzio (1922), 499–501; death, 514–15; daughter destroys letters from d'Annunzio, 515
Duse, Enrichetta, 515

Eden, Anthony (*later* 1st Earl of Avon), 540
Egypt: d'Annunzio and Duse visit, 199–200, 204, 217

Elettra (Gd'A; poetry), 222
Eliot, T.S., 540
England: d'Annunzio visits, 294–5
Eroica, L' (journal), 312
Ethiopia (Abyssinia): Italian expedition to (1887), 155, 157, 248; Adua defeat (1896), 236; Mussolini wages war on (1935–6), 201
Evandro (pet bittern), 362
Ezekiel, Moïse, 109

Facta, Luigi, 505–6
Fanfulla della Domenica (journal), 88, 107, 169
Farinacci, Roberto, 490, 500, 517, 519
Fasci di Combattimento, 389
Fascist Grand Council: created, 510
fascists and fascism: d'Annunzian nature, 5–6; symbol (*fascio*), 16; spread in post-war Italy, 387–8, 390, 437–8; hostility to socialists, 390, 488–9, 491, 499, 500; march on Rome (1922), 421–3, 504–7; failure in 1919 election, 437; revival, 461; activist squads, 481–2, 488, 493, 500, 505, 517; membership increase, 482; public life under, 488; Mussolini controls, 492; control trade unions and press, 496; rallies and demonstrations, 497, 498; dominance, 503, 505, 510; repressive acts, 510, 518, 519; election victory (1924), 513; opponents declare government unconstitutional, 516; calendar, 528; ceremonies and rituals, 534, 538; Mussolini writes on doctrine of, 535; influence on Nazism, 536; and corporatism, 537; advertising, 540
Faville del Maglio (*Sparks from the Anvil*; Gd'A; autobiographical fragments), 285, 498, 540

A NOTE ABOUT THE AUTHOR

Lucy Hughes-Hallett is the author of the award-winning *Cleopatra: Histories, Dreams, and Distortions* and *Heroes: Saviors, Traitors, and Supermen*. She is a highly respected critic, who has reviewed for all the major British newspapers, and fellow of the Royal Society of Literature. She lives in London.

A NOTE ON THE TYPE

This book was set in Monotype Dante, a typeface designed by Giovanni Mardersteig (1892–1977). Its first use was in an edition of Boccacio's *Trattatello in laude di Dante* that appeared in 1954. Although modeled on the Aldine type used for Pietro Cardinal Bembo's treatise *De Aetna* in 1495, Dante is a thoroughly modern interpretation of the venerable face.

Composed by North Market Street Graphics, Lancaster, Pennsylvania

Printed and bound by Berryville Graphics, Berryville, Virginia

Designed by Maggie Hinders